COLLECTED

POEMS

1 9 2 0 - 1 9 5 4

EUGENIO MONTALE

Collected Poems

1920–1954

OSSI DI SEPPIA / CUTTLEFISH BONES

LE OCCASIONI / THE OCCASIONS

LA BUFERA E ALTRO / THE STORM, ETC.

TRANSLATED AND ANNOTATED

BY *Jonathan Galassi*

FARRAR, STRAUS AND GIROUX

NEW YORK

Farrar, Straus and Giroux
19 Union Square West, New York 10003

Translation, notes, and "Reading Montale" copyright © 1998 by Jonathan Galassi
Italian poems copyrighted © 1948, 1949, 1957, and 1984
by Arnoldo Mondadori Editore, Milano
All rights reserved
Distributed in Canada by Douglas & McIntyre Ltd.
Printed in the United States of America
Designed by Cynthia Krupat
First edition, 1998

Library of Congress Cataloging-in-Publication Data
Montale, Eugenio, 1896–
   [Selections. English & Italian. 1997]
   Collected poems 1920–1954 / Eugenio Montale ; translated from the
Italian and annotated by Jonathan Galassi.
     p.   cm.
   Includes bibliographical references and index.
   ISBN 0-374-12554-6 (alk. paper)
   1. Montale, Eugenio, 1896– —Translations into English.
I. Galassi, Jonathan. II. Title.
PQ4829.0565A244   1997
851'.912—dc21   97-16641

*Grateful acknowledgment is made for permission to reprint the following: Excerpts
from* The Occasions, *by Eugenio Montale. Translated, with preface and commentary,
by William Arrowsmith. Translation copyright © 1987 by William Arrowsmith.
Reprinted by permission of the Estate of William Arrowsmith. Excerpts from*
Eugenio Montale's Poetry: A Dream in Reason's Presence, *by Glauco Cambon.
Copyright © 1982 by Princeton University Press. Reprinted by permission of
Princeton University Press. Excerpts from* Three Modern Italian Poets: Saba,
Montale, Ungaretti, *by Joseph Cary. Copyright © 1969, 1993 by Joseph Cary.
Reprinted by permission of Joseph Cary. Excerpts from* The Second Life of Art:
Selected Essays of Eugenio Montale, *by Eugenio Montale. Edited and translated by
Jonathan Galassi. Translation copyright © 1977, 1978, 1979, 1980, 1981, 1982 by
Jonathan Galassi. Reprinted by permission of The Ecco Press.*

Some of these translations have appeared, some in different form, in The Harvard
Review, The New York Review of Books, The Paris Review, Ploughshares, Poetry, *and* Scripsi.

FOR MY PARENTS

— J.G.

Contents

OSSI DI SEPPIA / CUTTLEFISH BONES

In limine / On the Threshold 4

MOVIMENTI / MOVEMENTS 6

OSSI DI SEPPIA / CUTTLEFISH BONES 36

MEDITERRANEO / MEDITERRANEAN 64

MERIGGI E OMBRE / NOONS AND SHADOWS 80

RIVIERE / SEACOASTS 140

LE OCCASIONI / THE OCCASIONS

Il balcone / The Balcony 148

I. 150

II. MOTTETTI / MOTETS 190

III. 212

IV. 220

LA BUFERA E ALTRO / THE STORM, ETC.

I. FINISTERRE 266

II. DOPO / AFTERWARDS 298

III. INTERMEZZO 308

IV. 'FLASHES' E DEDICHE /
FLASHES AND INSCRIPTIONS 320

V. SILVAE 352

VI. MADRIGALI PRIVATI / PRIVATE MADRIGALS 386

VII. CONCLUSIONI PROVVISORIE /
PROVISIONAL CONCLUSIONS 404

READING MONTALE   413

CHRONOLOGY   431

NOTES   439
Works Cited   439
Ossi di seppia / Cuttlefish Bones   443
Le occasioni / The Occasions   483
La bufera e altro / The Storm, Etc.   536

ACKNOWLEDGMENTS   611

INDEX OF TITLES AND FIRST LINES   613

COLLECTED

POEMS

1920 - 1954

_____

OSSI

DI SEPPIA

1920-1927

CUTTLEFISH

BONES

1920 - 1927

In limine

Godi se il vento ch'entra nel pomario
vi rimena l'ondata della vita:
qui dove affonda un morto
viluppo di memorie,
orto non era, ma reliquiario.

Il frullo che tu senti non è un volo,
ma il commuoversi dell'eterno grembo;
vedi che si trasforma questo lembo
di terra solitario in un crogiuolo.

Un rovello è di qua dall'erto muro.
Se procedi t'imbatti
tu forse nel fantasma che ti salva:
si compongono qui le storie, gli atti
scancellati pel giuoco del futuro.

Cerca una maglia rotta nella rete
che ci stringe, tu balza fuori, fuggi!
Va, per te l'ho pregato,—ora la sete
mi sarà lieve, meno acre la ruggine . . .

On the Threshold

Be happy if the wind inside the orchard
carries back the tidal surge of life:
here, where a dead web
of memories sinks under,
was no garden, but a reliquary.

The whir you're hearing isn't flight,
but the stirring of the eternal womb;
watch this solitary strip of land
transform into a crucible.

There's fury over the sheer wall.
If you move forward you may come upon
the phantom who will save you:
histories are shaped here, deeds
the endgame of the future will dismantle.

Look for a flaw in the net that binds us
tight, burst through, break free!
Go, I've prayed for this for you—now my thirst
will be easy, my rancor less bitter . . .

MOVIMENTI

MOVEMENTS

I limoni

Ascoltami, i poeti laureati
si muovono soltanto fra le piante
dai nomi poco usati: bossi ligustri o acanti.
Io, per me, amo le strade che riescono agli erbosi
fossi dove in pozzanghere
mezzo seccate agguantano i ragazzi
qualche sparuta anguilla:
le viuzze che seguono i ciglioni,
discendono tra i ciuffi delle canne
e mettono negli orti, tra gli alberi dei limoni.

Meglio se le gazzarre degli uccelli
si spengono inghiottite dall'azzurro:
più chiaro si ascolta il susurro
dei rami amici nell'aria che quasi non si muove,
e i sensi di quest'odore
che non sa staccarsi da terra
e piove in petto una dolcezza inquieta.
Qui delle divertite passioni
per miracolo tace la guerra,
qui tocca anche a noi poveri la nostra parte di ricchezza
ed è l'odore dei limoni.

Vedi, in questi silenzi in cui le cose
s'abbandonano e sembrano vicine
a tradire il loro ultimo segreto,
talora ci si aspetta
di scoprire uno sbaglio di Natura,
il punto morto del mondo, l'anello che non tiene,
il filo da disbrogliare che finalmente ci metta
nel mezzo di una verità.
Lo sguardo fruga d'intorno,
la mente indaga accorda disunisce
nel profumo che dilaga
quando il giorno più languisce.
Sono i silenzi in cui si vede

The Lemons

Listen to me, the poets laureate
walk only among plants
with rare names: boxwood, privet and acanthus.
But I like roads that lead to grassy
ditches where boys
scoop up a few starved
eels out of half-dry puddles:
paths that run along the banks,
come down among the tufted canes
and end in orchards, among the lemon trees.

Better if the hubbub of the birds
dies out, swallowed by the blue:
we can hear more of the whispering
of friendly branches in not-quite-quiet air,
and the sensations of this smell
that can't divorce itself from earth
and rains a restless sweetness on the heart.
Here, by some miracle, the war
of troubled passions calls a truce;
here we poor, too, receive our share of riches,
which is the fragrance of the lemons.

See, in these silences where things
give over and seem on the verge of betraying
their final secret,
sometimes we feel we're about
to uncover an error in Nature,
the still point of the world, the link that won't hold,
the thread to untangle that will finally lead
to the heart of a truth.
The eye scans its surroundings,
the mind inquires aligns divides
in the perfume that gets diffused
at the day's most languid.
It's in these silences you see

in ogni ombra umana che si allontana
qualche disturbata Divinità.

Ma l'illusione manca e ci riporta il tempo
nelle città rumorose dove l'azzurro si mostra
soltanto a pezzi, in alto, tra le cimase.
La pioggia stanca la terra, di poi; s'affolta
il tedio dell'inverno sulle case,
la luce si fa avara—amara l'anima.
Quando un giorno da un malchiuso portone
tra gli alberi di una corte
ci si mostrano i gialli dei limoni;
e il gelo del cuore si sfa,
e in petto ci scrosciano
le loro canzoni
le trombe d'oro della solarità.

in every fleeting human
shadow some disturbed Divinity.

But the illusion fails, and time returns us
to noisy cities where the blue
is seen in patches, up between the roofs.
The rain exhausts the earth then;
winter's tedium weighs the houses down,
the light turns miserly—the soul bitter.
Till one day through a half-shut gate
in a courtyard, there among the trees,
we can see the yellow of the lemons;
and the chill in the heart
melts, and deep in us
the golden horns of sunlight
pelt their songs.

Corno inglese

Il vento che stasera suona attento
—ricorda un forte scotere di lame—
gli strumenti dei fitti alberi e spazza
l'orizzonte di rame
dove strisce di luce si protendono
come aquiloni al cielo che rimbomba
(Nuvole in viaggio, chiari
reami di lassù! D'alti Eldoradi
malchiuse porte!)
e il mare che scaglia a scaglia,
livido, muta colore,
lancia a terra una tromba
di schiume intorte;
il vento che nasce e muore
nell'ora che lenta s'annera
suonasse te pure stasera
scordato strumento,
cuore.

English Horn

The intent wind that plays tonight
—recalling a sharp clash of metal sheets—
the instruments of the thick trees and sweeps
the copper horizon
where streaks of light are trailing,
kites in the sky that roars
(traveling clouds, bright
kingdoms up above,
High Eldorados' half-shut doors!)
and the livid sea
which, scale by scale,
turns color, hurls
a horn of contorted spume ashore;
the wind that's born and dies
in the hour that slowly goes dark—
if only it could play you, too, tonight,
discordant instrument,
heart.

Falsetto

Esterina, i vent'anni ti minacciano,
grigiorosea nube
che a poco a poco in sé ti chiude.
Ciò intendi e non paventi.
Sommersa ti vedremo
nella fumea che il vento
lacera o addensa, violento.
Poi dal fiotto di cenere uscirai
adusta più che mai,
proteso a un'avventura più lontana
l'intento viso che assembra
l'arciera Diana.
Salgono i venti autunni,
t'avviluppano andate primavere;
ecco per te rintocca
un presagio nell'elisie sfere.
Un suono non ti renda
qual d'incrinata brocca
percossa!; io prego sia
per te concerto ineffabile
di sonagliere.

La dubbia dimane non t'impaura.
Leggiadra ti distendi
sullo scoglio lucente di sale
e al sole bruci le membra.
Ricordi la lucertola
ferma sul masso brullo;
te insidia giovinezza,
quella il lacciòlo d'erba del fanciullo.
L'acqua è la forza che ti tempra,
nell'acqua ti ritrovi e ti rinnovi:
noi ti pensiamo come un'alga, un ciottolo,
come un'equorea creatura
che la salsedine non intacca
ma torna al lito più pura.

Falsetto

Esterina, twenty's out for you,
rose-gray cloud that's slowly
closing in on you.
You know, but you're fearless all the same.
We'll see you swallowed by the haze
the wind breaks through
or whips up, wild.
Then you'll emerge from the ashen wave
browner than ever,
face like Diana
the archer's intent
on a farther adventure.
Your twenty falls are rising,
past springs fold you in;
now an omen tolls for you
in the Elysian spheres.
May no sound leave
you thunderstruck,
like a cracked jug;
let it be for you an ineffable
concert of collarbells.

Unknowable tomorrow doesn't faze you.
Lying lithe
on the rock that shimmers
with salt, you bake in the sun.
You make me think of the lizard,
stock-still on naked rock;
youth is waiting
like the boy's grass snare.
Water is the power that tempers you,
you find yourself, renew yourself in her:
to us you're seaweed or a stone,
a water creature
salt can't corrode
that shows up all the purer on the shore.

Hai ben ragione tu! Non turbare
di ubbie il sorridente presente.
La tua gaiezza impegna già il futuro
ed un crollar di spalle
dirocca i fortilizî
del tuo domani oscuro.
T'alzi e t'avanzi sul ponticello
esiguo, sopra il gorgo che stride:
il tuo profilo s'incide
contro uno sfondo di perla.
Esiti a sommo del tremulo asse,
poi ridi, e come spiccata da un vento
t'abbatti fra le braccia
del tuo divino amico che t'afferra.

Ti guardiamo noi, della razza
di chi rimane a terra.

How right you are! Don't muddy
the happy present with worry.
Your gaiety already
has mortgaged the future,
and a shrug demolishes
the tall walls of your clouded tomorrow.
You rise and head for the platform
over the hissing deep,
profile etched against a pearl background.
At the end of the quivering board
you hesitate, then smile,
and, as if snared by a wind,
hurl yourself into the arms of the godlike
friend who pulls you down.

We watch you, we of the race
who are earthbound.

Minstrels

da C. Debussy

Ritornello, rimbalzi
tra le vetrate d'afa dell'estate.

Acre groppo di note soffocate,
riso che non esplode
ma trapunge le ore vuote
e lo suonano tre avanzi di baccanale
vestiti di ritagli di giornali,
con istrumenti mai veduti,
simili a strani imbuti
che si gonfiano a volte e poi s'afflosciano.

Musica senza rumore
che nasce dalle strade,
s'innalza a stento e ricade,
e si colora di tinte
ora scarlatte ora biade,
e inumidisce gli occhi, così che il mondo
si vede come socchiudendo gli occhi
nuotar nel biondo.

Scatta ripiomba sfuma,
poi riappare
soffocata e lontana: si consuma.
Non s'ode quasi, si respira.
      Bruci
tu pure tra le lastre dell'estate,
cuore che ti smarrisci! Ed ora incauto
provi le ignote note sul tuo flauto.

Minstrels

after C. Debussy

Refrain, echoing
through summer's hazy windowpanes.

Acid knot of suffocated notes,
laugh that won't explode
but cuts across the empty hours,
played by three stragglers from a bacchanal
dressed in newsprint, carrying
instruments never seen before,
strange funnels that swell up
and then fall flat.

Noiseless music
born in the streets,
that rises haltingly, then falls,
and takes on colors,
scarlet then sky blue,
bringing tears, until the world
is seen as though through half-closed eyes,
swimming in blond.

It breaks out sinks evaporates,
then reappears,
muffled, far off: and fades,
almost more breathed than heard.
                   You, too, burn
in summer's windows, troubled
heart! And reckless now try out
the new notes on your flute.

Poesie per Camillo Sbarbaro

I. Caffè a Rapallo

Natale nel tepidario
lustrante, truccato dai fumi
che svolgono tazze, velato
tremore di lumi oltre i chiusi
cristalli, profili di femmine
nel grigio, tra lampi di gemme
e screzi di sete . . .
        Son giunte
a queste native tue spiagge,
le nuove Sirene!; e qui manchi
Camillo, amico, tu storico
di cupidige e di brividi.

S'ode grande frastuono nella via.

È passata di fuori
l'indicibile musica
delle trombe di lama
e dei piattini arguti dei fanciulli:
è passata la musica innocente.

Un mondo gnomo ne andava
con strepere di muletti e di carriole,
tra un lagno di montoni
di cartapesta e un bagliare
di sciabole fasciate di stagnole.
Passarono i Generali
con le feluche di cartone
e impugnavano aste di torroni;
poi furono i gregari
con moccoli e lampioni,
e le tinnanti scatole
ch'ànno il suono più trito,
tenue rivo che incanta

Poems for Camillo Sbarbaro

I. Café at Rapallo

Christmas in the gleaming
tepidarium, decked
with smoke the coffeecups exhale,
veiled shimmering of lights behind
shut windows, women's profiles in the dusk,
jewel-flash,
silk sheen . . .
                    They're here,
the new Sirens, on your native
shores! And you're missed,
Camillo, chronicler
of lusts and excitations.

There's an enormous uproar in the street.

The indescribable
music of children's
tin horns and clashing cymbals
passed outside:
the innocent music passed by.

With it went a gnomelike world,
rumbling baby carts and mules,
bleating papier-mâché
rams, and flashing sabers
sheathed in foil.
The Generals passed
in their cardboard hats
brandishing nougat spears,
and then the troops
with candles, lamps,
and the jangling tops that make
the tritest sound,
faint rivulet that enchants

l'animo dubitoso:
(meraviglioso udivo).

L'orda passò col rumore
d'una zampante greggia
che il tuono recente impaura.
L'accolse la pastura
che per noi più non verdeggia.

II. Epigramma

Sbarbaro, estroso fanciullo, piega versicolori
carte e ne trae navicelle che affida alla fanghiglia
mobile d'un rigagno; vedile andarsene fuori.
Sii preveggente per lui, tu galantuomo che passi:
col tuo bastone raggiungi la delicata flottiglia,
che non si perda; guidala a un porticello di sassi.

the doubting soul
(I listened in amazement).

The horde went by with the roar
of a stampeding herd
frightened by recent thunder.
And were welcomed by the field
that for us is green no longer.

II. Epigram

Sbarbaro, whimsical boy, folds multicolored
papers and builds boats he consigns
to the flowing ooze of a gutter; see them float away.
Be watchful for him, gentle passerby:
catch the fragile flotilla with your cane, before it's gone;
guide it to a little port of stones.

Quasi una fantasia

Raggiorna, lo presento
da un albore di frusto
argento alle pareti:
lista un barlume le finestre chiuse.
Torna l'avvenimento
del sole e le diffuse
voci, i consueti strepiti non porta.

Perché? Penso ad un giorno d'incantesimo
e delle giostre d'ore troppo uguali
mi ripago. Traboccherà la forza
che mi turgeva, incosciente mago,
da grande tempo. Ora m'affaccerò,
subisserò alte case, spogli viali.

Avrò di contro un paese d'intatte nevi
ma lievi come viste in un arazzo.
Scivolerà dal cielo bioccoso un tardo raggio.
Gremite d'invisibile luce selve e colline
mi diranno l'elogio degl'ilari ritorni.

Lieto leggerò i neri
segni dei rami sul bianco
come un essenziale alfabeto.
Tutto il passato in un punto
dinanzi mi sarà comparso.
Non turberà suono alcuno
quest'allegrezza solitaria.
Filerà nell'aria
o scenderà s'un paletto
qualche galletto di marzo.

Like a Fantasia

Day is dawning, I can tell
by the old-silver shimmer
on the walls:
a gleam edges the shut windows.
The coming of the sun returns again,
without the scattered voices
and old noises.

Why? I fantasize a magic day
to counteract the hours' game
of sameness. The power pent up
in this unconscious magus for so long
will overflow. Now I'll show myself
and subjugate high houses, empty avenues.

I'll look out on a land of untouched snows
but insubstantial, as if seen on a screen.
A slow ray will slide down from the cottony sky.
Woods and hills alive with invisible light
will sing to me their joyful reoccurrence.

Happily, I'll read the black
signs of branches on the white
like an essential alphabet.
All the past will gather
in one point in front of me.
No sound will spoil
my solitary joy.
A hoopoe or two,
March cockerels, will sail
the air or light on a pole.

Sarcofaghi

Dove se ne vanno le ricciute donzelle
che recano le colme anfore su le spalle
ed hanno il fermo passo sì leggero;
e in fondo uno sbocco di valle
invano attende le belle
cui adombra una pergola di vigna
e i grappoli ne pendono oscillando.
Il sole che va in alto,
le intraviste pendici
non han tinte: nel blando
minuto la natura fulminata
atteggia le felici
sue creature, madre non matrigna,
in levità di forme.
Mondo che dorme o mondo che si gloria
d'immutata esistenza, chi può dire?,
uomo che passi, e tu dagli
il meglio ramicello del tuo orto.
Poi segui: in questa valle
non è vicenda di buio e di luce.
Lungi di qui la tua via ti conduce,
non c'è asilo per te, sei troppo morto:
seguita il giro delle tue stelle.
E dunque addio, infanti ricciutelle,
portate le colme anfore su le spalle.

❀

Ora sia il tuo passo
più cauto: a un tiro di sasso
di qui ti si prepara
una più rara scena.
La porta corrosa d'un tempietto
è rinchiusa per sempre.
Una grande luce è diffusa

Sarcophagi

Where are they going, the girls with little curls,
bearing the brimming wine jars on their shoulders
with such a light, sure step;
and beyond, an open valley
waits in vain for the lovely ones
shaded by a pergola of vines
where grapes hang down and sway.
The climbing sun,
the just-glimpsed mountain peaks,
are colorless: in the mild moment
nature, thunderstruck,
harboring not harsh,
invests her happy creatures
with lightness of form.
A sleeping world or one that thrives
on changeless being—who can say?
But give it, passerby,
the best branch from your garden.
Then onward: in this valley
there's no alternating dark and light.
Your path leads you afar,
no haven for you here, you are too dead:
follow your wheeling stars.
So farewell, little curly-headed girls,
carry your brimming wine jars on your shoulders.

❋

Now step
more carefully:
at a stone's throw
a rarer scene is being set for you.
A little temple's rusty door
has shut forever.
A high light pours

sull'erbosa soglia.
E qui dove peste umane
non suoneranno, o fittizia doglia,
vigila steso al suolo un magro cane.
Mai più si muoverà
in quest'ora che s'indovina afosa.
Sopra il tetto s'affaccia
una nuvola grandiosa.

✻

Il fuoco che scoppietta
nel caminetto verdeggia
e un'aria oscura grava
sopra un mondo indeciso. Un vecchio stanco
dorme accanto a un alare
il sonno dell'abbandonato.
In questa luce abissale
che finge il bronzo, non ti svegliare
addormentato! E tu camminante
procedi piano; ma prima
un ramo aggiungi alla fiamma
del focolare e una pigna
matura alla cesta gettata
nel canto: ne cadono a terra
le provvigioni serbate
pel viaggio finale.

✻

Ma dove cercare la tomba
dell'amico fedele e dell'amante;
quella del mendicante e del fanciullo;
dove trovare un asilo
per codesti che accolgono la brace
dell'originale fiammata;
oh da un segnale di pace lieve come un trastullo
l'urna ne sia effigiata!

across a grassy threshold.
And here, where human feet
or unreal grief will not be heard,
a scrawny watchdog stands his ground.
He will never stir again
in this moment that's becoming haze.
Over the roof a grandiose
cloud is showing its face.

        ✻

The fire that spits
on the hearth turns green,
and a dark air weighs
on an unsure world. A tired old man
sleeps the sleep of the abandoned
next to an andiron.
In this deep light
simulating bronze,
sleeper, don't wake. And you who walk,
go quietly; but first
add a branch to the home fire
and a ripe pine nut
to the hamper in the corner:
from it the provisions
set aside for the final
journey fall to ground.

        ✻

But where to find the tomb
of the faithful friend and the lover;
of the beggar and the boy;
where to discover a haven
for those who take up the torch
that carries the primal fire;
oh, may their urn be etched
with a sign of peace as simple as a toy!

Lascia la taciturna folla di pietra
per le derelitte lastre
ch'ànno talora inciso
il simbolo che più turba
poiché il pianto ed il riso
parimenti ne sgorgano, gemelli.
Lo guarda il triste artiere che al lavoro si reca
e già gli batte ai polsi una volontà cieca.
Tra quelle cerca un fregio primordiale
che sappia pel ricordo che ne avanza
trarre l'anima rude
per vie di dolci esigli:
un nulla, un girasole che si schiude
ed intorno una danza di conigli . . .

Leave the silent crowd of stone
for those abandoned slabs
incised once with
the most moving symbol,
for tears and laughter
flow from it equally, as twins.
The sad sculptor sees it on his way to work
and already a blind will beats in his veins.
Find among them a primordial frieze
which, through the memory that lives,
will have the power to lead the unlettered
soul on trails of sweet exile:
a trifle, an unfurling sunflower
circled by a ring of dancing hares . . .

Altri versi

Vento e bandiere

La folata che alzò l'amaro aroma
del mare alle spirali delle valli,
e t'investì, ti scompigliò la chioma,
groviglio breve contro il cielo pallido;

la raffica che t'incollò la veste
e ti modulò rapida a sua imagine,
com'è tornata, te lontana, a queste
pietre che sporge il monte alla voragine;

e come spenta la furia briaca
ritrova ora il giardino il sommesso alito
che ti cullò, riversa sull'amaca,
tra gli alberi, ne' tuoi voli senz'ali.

Ahimè, non mai due volte configura
il tempo in egual modo i grani! E scampo
n'è: ché, se accada, insieme alla natura
la nostra fiaba brucerà in un lampo.

Sgorgo che non s'addoppia,—ed or fa vivo
un gruppo di abitati che distesi
allo sguardo sul fianco d'un declivo
si parano di gale e di palvesi.

Il mondo esiste . . . Uno stupore arresta
il cuore che ai vaganti incubi cede,
messaggeri del vespero: e non crede
che gli uomini affamati hanno una festa.

Other Lines

Wind and Flags

The gust that lifted the bitter scent
of the sea to the valley's twists and turns
and struck you, ruffled your hair,
brief tangle on the pale sky;

the squall that glued your dress to you
and shaped you swiftly in its image,
now you're gone it's returned to the rocks
the mountain shoulders over the abyss;

and, now the drunken rage is spent,
it's come back to the garden, the gentle breeze
that lulled you in your hammock in the trees,
on your flights without wings.

Alas, time never spills its sand
the same way twice. And there's hope in this:
for, if it happens, not nature alone
but our story, too, will burn in a flash.

Outflow that doesn't quicken—
and now brings to life a group of dwellings
exposed to the eye on the flank of a hill
and festooned with pennants and flowers.

The world exists . . . Amazement halts
the heart that surrenders to straying ghosts,
heralds of evening: and won't believe
starved men are celebrating.

Fuscello teso dal muro . . .

Fuscello teso dal muro
sì come l'indice d'una
meridiana che scande la carriera
del sole e la mia, breve;
in una additi i crepuscoli
e alleghi sul tonaco
che imbeve la luce d'accesi
riflessi—e t'attedia la ruota
che in ombra sul piano dispieghi,
t'è noja infinita la volta
che stacca da te una smarrita
sembianza come di fumo
e grava con l'infittita
sua cupola mai dissolta.

Ma tu non adombri stamane
più il tuo sostegno ed un velo
che nella notte hai strappato
a un'orda invisibile pende
dalla tua cima e risplende
ai primi raggi. Laggiù,
dove la piana si scopre
del mare, un trealberi carico
di ciurma e di preda reclina
il bordo a uno spiro, e via scivola.
Chi è in alto e s'affaccia s'avvede
che brilla la tolda e il timone
nell'acqua non scava una traccia.

Twig that juts from the wall . . .

Twig that juts from the wall
like the needle of a sundial
scanning the sun's career
and my brief one;
you describe the twilights
while you root in plaster
the light imbues with fired
reflections—and you're tired
of the wheel your shadow leaves
on the wall, unendingly bored
with the dome that lifts a pale
resemblance from you like smoke
and bears down with its heavy
aura that never dissolves.

But this morning you don't shadow
what holds you anymore
and a veil you stole last night
from an unseen horde hangs at your tip,
glistening in new light.
Down below where the plain
of the sea is revealed,
a three-master ballasted
with crew and booty lists
at a breath and slips away.
Those above who look out
will see the deck gleams and the rudder
leaves no wake in the water.

OSSI DI SEPPIA

CUTTLEFISH BONES

Non chiederci la parola che squadri da ogni lato
l'animo nostro informe, e a lettere di fuoco
lo dichiari e risplenda come un croco
perduto in mezzo a un polveroso prato.

Ah l'uomo che se ne va sicuro,
agli altri ed a se stesso amico,
e l'ombra sua non cura che la canicola
stampa sopra uno scalcinato muro!

Non domandarci la formula che mondi possa aprirti,
sì qualche storta sillaba e secca come un ramo.
Codesto solo oggi possiamo dirti,
ciò che *non* siamo, ciò che *non* vogliamo.

Don't ask us for the word to frame
our shapeless spirit on all sides,
and proclaim it in letters of fire to shine
like a lone crocus in a dusty field.

Ah, the man who walks secure,
a friend to others and himself,
indifferent that high summer prints
his shadow on a peeling wall!

Don't ask us for the phrase that can open worlds,
just a few gnarled syllables, dry like a branch.
This, today, is all that we can tell you:
what we are *not*, what we do *not* want.

Meriggiare pallido e assorto
presso un rovente muro d'orto,
ascoltare tra i pruni e gli sterpi
schiocchi di merli, frusci di serpi.

Nelle crepe del suolo o su la veccia
spiar le file di rosse formiche
ch'ora si rompono ed ora s'intrecciano
a sommo di minuscole biche.

Osservare tra frondi il palpitare
lontano di scaglie di mare
mentre si levano tremuli scricchi
di cicale dai calvi picchi.

E andando nel sole che abbaglia
sentire con triste meraviglia
com'è tutta la vita e il suo travaglio
in questo seguitare una muraglia
che ha in cima cocci aguzzi di bottiglia.

Sit the noon out, pale and lost in thought
beside a blistering garden wall,
hear, among the thorns and brambles,
snakes rustle, blackbirds catcall.

In the cracked earth or on the vetch,
watch the red ants' files
now breaking up, now meeting
on top of little piles.

Observe between branches the far-off
throb of sea scales,
while cicadas' wavering screaks
rise from the bald peaks.

And walking in the dazzling sun,
feel with sad amazement
that all life and its torment
consists in following along a wall
with broken bottle shards imbedded in the top.

Non rifugiarti nell'ombra
di quel fólto di verzura
come il falchetto che strapiomba
fulmineo nella caldura.

È ora di lasciare il canneto
stento che pare s'addorma
e di guardare le forme
della vita che si sgretola.

Ci muoviamo in un pulviscolo
madreperlaceo che vibra,
in un barbaglio che invischia
gli occhi e un poco ci sfibra.

Pure, lo senti, nel gioco d'aride onde
che impigra in quest'ora di disagio
non buttiamo già in un gorgo senza fondo
le nostre vite randage.

Come quella chiostra di rupi
che sembra sfilaccicarsi
in ragnatele di nubi;
tali i nostri animi arsi

in cui l'illusione brucia
un fuoco pieno di cenere
si perdono nel sereno
di una certezza: la luce.

Don't escape into the shade
of that green thicket
the way the kestrel sinks like lead,
lightning in the summer heat.

It's time to leave the stunted cane
that seems to be dozing off
and observe the forms life takes
as it disintegrates.

We move in a wavering
mother-of-pearl haze,
in a glare that snares the eyes,
and weakens us a little.

Still, you feel, in the play of dry waves
slowing in this uneasy hour
let's not toss our vagrant lives
into a bottomless abyss.

Like that choir of cliffs
that seems to dissipate
in spiderwebs of clouds,
so our scorched spirits

in which illusion
sets a fire of ashes
dissolve in the bright sky
of one certainty: the light.

a K.

Ripenso il tuo sorriso, ed è per me un'acqua limpida
scorta per avventura tra le petraie d'un greto,
esiguo specchio in cui guardi un'ellera i suoi corimbi;
e su tutto l'abbraccio d'un bianco cielo quieto.

Codesto è il mio ricordo; non saprei dire, o lontano,
se dal tuo volto s'esprime libera un'anima ingenua,
o vero tu sei dei raminghi che il male del mondo estenua
e recano il loro soffrire con sé come un talismano.

Ma questo posso dirti, che la tua pensata effigie
sommerge i crucci estrosi in un'ondata di calma,
e che il tuo aspetto s'insinua nella mia memoria grigia
schietto come la cima d'una giovinetta palma . . .

Mia vita, a te non chiedo lineamenti
fissi, volti plausibili o possessi.
Nel tuo giro inquieto ormai lo stesso
sapore han miele e assenzio.

Il cuore che ogni moto tiene a vile
raro è squassato da trasalimenti.
Così suona talvolta nel silenzio
della campagna un colpo di fucile.

to K.

I think back on your smile, and for me it's a clear pool
found by chance among the rocks of a riverbed,
little mirror where the ivy can watch her corymbs,
embraced by a quiet white sky overhead.

This I remember; I can't say, distant one,
whether your look gives voice to a simple spirit,
or if you're one of those wanderers the world's evil harms
who carry their suffering with them like a charm.

But I can say this: that your contemplated image
drowns extravagant fears in a wave of calm,
and that your look finds its way into my gray memory
sharp like the crest of a young palm . . .

My life, I ask of you no stable
contours, plausible faces, property.
Now in your restless circling, wormwood and honey
have the same savor.

The heart that disdains all motion
occasionally is convulsed by a jolt.
As sometimes the stillness of the country
sounds with a rifle shot.

Portami il girasole ch'io lo trapianti
nel mio terreno bruciato dal salino,
e mostri tutto il giorno agli azzurri specchianti
del cielo l'ansietà del suo volto giallino.

Tendono alla chiarità le cose oscure,
si esauriscono i corpi in un fluire
di tinte: queste in musiche. Svanire
è dunque la ventura delle venture.

Portami tu la pianta che conduce
dove sorgono bionde trasparenze
e vapora la vita quale essenza;
portami il girasole impazzito di luce.

Spesso il male di vivere ho incontrato:
era il rivo strozzato che gorgoglia,
era l'incartocciarsi della foglia
riarsa, era il cavallo stramazzato.

Bene non seppi, fuori del prodigio
che schiude la divina Indifferenza:
era la statua nella sonnolenza
del meriggio, e la nuvola, e il falco alto levato.

Bring me the sunflower, let me plant it
in my field parched by the salt sea wind,
and let it show the blue reflecting sky
the yearning of its yellow face all day.

Dark things tend to brightness,
bodies fade out in a flood of colors,
colors in music. So disappearing is
the destiny of destinies.

Bring me the plant that leads the way
to where blond transparencies
rise, and life as essence turns to haze;
bring me the sunflower crazed with light.

Often I've encountered evil:
it was the stream that chokes and roars,
the shriveling of the scorched leaf,
the fallen horse.

I knew no good, beyond the prodigy
that reveals divine Indifference:
it was the statue in the drowsiness
of noon, and the cloud, and the hawk that soars.

Ciò che di me sapeste
non fu che la scialbatura,
la tonaca che riveste
la nostra umana ventura.

Ed era forse oltre il telo
l'azzurro tranquillo;
vietava il limpido cielo
solo un sigillo.

O vero c'era il falòtico
mutarsi della mia vita,
lo schiudersi d'un'ignita
zolla che mai vedrò.

Restò così questa scorza
la vera mia sostanza;
il fuoco che non si smorza
per me si chiamò: l'ignoranza.

Se un'ombra scorgete, non è
un'ombra—ma quella io sono.
Potessi spiccarla da me,
offrirvela in dono.

What you knew of me
was only a coat of paint,
the veil that clothes
our human fate.

And maybe behind the canvas
was the still blue;
only a seal kept out
the limpid sky.

Or else it was the fiery
change in me,
revealing a burning ember
I'll never see.

So that this husk became
my true substance;
the fire that isn't quenched
for me was called: ignorance.

If you see a shadow
it's no shadow—it's me.
If only I could tear it off
and offer it to you.

Là fuoresce il Tritone
dai flutti che lambiscono
le soglie d'un cristiano
tempio, ed ogni ora prossima
è antica. Ogni dubbiezza
si conduce per mano
come una fanciulletta amica.

Là non è chi si guardi
o stia di sé in ascolto.
Quivi sei alle origini
e decidere è stolto:
ripartirai più tardi
per assumere un volto.

So l'ora in cui la faccia più impassibile
è traversata da una cruda smorfia:
s'è svelata per poco una pena invisibile.
Ciò non vede la gente nell'affollato corso.

Voi, mie parole, tradite invano il morso
secreto, il vento che nel cuore soffia.
La più vera ragione è di chi tace.
Il canto che singhiozza è un canto di pace.

Portovenere

There the Tritone surges
into the breakers lapping
a Christian temple's floor,
and every coming hour
is ancient. Every doubt
is taken by the hand
like a little friend.

No one ever eyes himself
or listens for his own voice there.
There you're at the origin
and it's foolish to decide:
later you will leave again
to find a face to wear.

I know the moment when a raw grimace
crosses the most impassive face:
for an instant an invisible pain is revealed.
The people in the crowded street don't see it.

You, my words, betray in vain the secret
sting, the gale in the heart that howls.
The deeper truth is that of the man who is silent.
The song that sobs is a song of peace.

Gloria del disteso mezzogiorno
quand'ombra non rendono gli alberi,
e più e più si mostrano d'attorno
per troppa luce, le parvenze, falbe.

Il sole, in alto,—e un secco greto.
Il mio giorno non è dunque passato:
l'ora più bella è di là dal muretto
che rinchiude in un occaso scialbato.

L'arsura, in giro; un martin pescatore
volteggia s'una reliquia di vita.
La buona pioggia è di là dallo squallore,
ma in attendere è gioia più compita.

Felicità raggiunta, si cammina
per te su fil di lama.
Agli occhi sei barlume che vacilla,
al piede, teso ghiaccio che s'incrina;
e dunque non ti tocchi chi più t'ama.

Se giungi sulle anime invase
di tristezza e le schiari, il tuo mattino
è dolce e turbatore come i nidi delle cimase.
Ma nulla paga il pianto del bambino
a cui fugge il pallone tra le case.

Glory of expanded noon
when the trees give up no shade,
and more and more the look of things
is turning bronze, from excess light.

Above, the sun—and a dry shore;
so my day is not yet done:
over the low wall is the finest hour,
ending in a pale setting sun.

Drought all around: kingfisher hovers
over something life has left.
The good rain is beyond the barrenness,
but there's greater joy in waiting.

Happiness achieved, for you
we walk on a knife-edge.
You're an uncertain glimmer to the eyes,
underfoot taut, cracking ice;
so he who loves you best must never touch you.

If you encounter souls assailed
by sadness and delight them,
your morning's sweet and aflutter, like nests in the eaves.
But nothing comforts the child who grieves
for the balloon that's gone between the houses.

Il canneto rispunta i suoi cimelli
nella serenità che non si ragna:
l'orto assetato sporge irti ramelli
oltre i chiusi ripari, all'afa stagna.

Sale un'ora d'attesa in cielo, vacua,
dal mare che s'ingrigia.
Un albero di nuvole sull'acqua
cresce, poi crolla come di cinigia.

Assente, come manchi in questa plaga
che ti presente e senza te consuma:
sei lontana e però tutto divaga
dal suo solco, dirupa, spare in bruma.

Forse un mattino andando in un'aria di vetro,
arida, rivolgendomi, vedrò compirsi il miracolo:
il nulla alle mie spalle, il vuoto dietro
di me, con un terrore di ubriaco.

Poi come s'uno schermo, s'accamperanno di gitto
alberi case colli per l'inganno consueto.
Ma sarà troppo tardi; ed io me n'andrò zitto
tra gli uomini che non si voltano, col mio segreto.

The canebrake sends its little shoots
into the brightness that doesn't fret with clouds:
the thirsty orchard puts out bristling sprigs
beyond the shut gates, in the stagnant heat.

An hour of waiting climbs the sky,
empty, from the sea that's turning gray.
A cloud tree grows on the water,
then crumbles like ashes.

Absent one, how I miss you on this shore
that conjures you and fades if you're away:
you're gone, so each thing strays
from its furrow, topples, vanishes in haze.

Maybe one morning, walking in dry, glassy air,
I'll turn, and see the miracle occur:
nothing at my back, the void
behind me, with a drunkard's terror.

Then, as if on a screen, trees houses hills
will suddenly collect for the usual illusion.
But it will be too late: and I'll walk on silent
among the men who don't look back, with my secret.

Valmorbia, discorrevano il tuo fondo
fioriti nuvoli di piante agli àsoli.
Nasceva in noi, volti dal cieco caso,
oblio del mondo.

Tacevano gli spari, nel grembo solitario
non dava suono che il Leno roco.
Sbocciava un razzo su lo stelo, fioco
lacrimava nell'aria.

Le notti chiare erano tutte un'alba
e portavano volpi alla mia grotta.
Valmorbia, un nome—e ora nella scialba
memoria, terra dove non annotta.

Tentava la vostra mano la tastiera,
i vostri occhi leggevano sul foglio
gl'impossibili segni; e franto era
ogni accordo come una voce di cordoglio.

Compresi che tutto, intorno, s'inteneriva
in vedervi inceppata inerme ignara
del linguaggio più vostro: ne bruiva
oltre i vetri socchiusi la marina chiara.

Passò nel riquadro azzurro una fugace danza
di farfalle; una fronda si scrollò nel sole.
Nessuna cosa prossima trovava le sue parole,
ed era mia, era *nostra*, la vostra dolce ignoranza.

Valmorbia, flowering clouds of plants
crossed over your deeps on puffs of wind.
In us, whirled by blind chance,
oblivion of the world was born.

The shooting stopped; in the lonely womb
the only sound was the Leno's roar.
A rocket blossomed on its stem,
wept faintly in the air.

The bright nights were all a dawn
and brought foxes to my den.
Valmorbia, a name—and now in my wan memory,
land where night never comes.

Your hand was trying the keyboard,
your eyes were following the impossible
signs on the sheet: and every chord
was breaking, like a voice in grief.

I noticed everything nearby turn tender,
seeing you helpless stalled unsure
of the language that was most your own:
beyond the half-shut windows the bright sea hummed it.

In the blue square butterflies
danced fleetingly: a branch shook in the sun.
Not one thing near us found its words
and your sweet ignorance was mine, was *ours*.

La farandola dei fanciulli sul greto
era la vita che scoppia dall'arsura.
Cresceva tra rare canne e uno sterpeto
il cespo umano nell'aria pura.

Il passante sentiva come un supplizio
il suo distacco dalle antiche radici.
Nell'età d'oro florida sulle sponde felici
anche un nome, una veste, erano un vizio.

Debole sistro al vento
d'una persa cicala,
toccato appena e spento
nel torpore ch'esala.

Dirama dal profondo
in noi la vena
segreta: il nostro mondo
si regge appena.

Se tu l'accenni, all'aria
bigia treman corrotte
le vestigia
che il vuoto non ringhiotte.

Il gesto indi s'annulla,
tace ogni voce,
discende alla sua foce
la vita brulla.

The line of dancing children on the shore
was life exploding from the drought.
Among thin reeds and branches the human plant
grew in pure air.

The passerby felt his separateness
from the old roots as an agony.
In that golden age in flower on the happy sand
even a name, and clothes, were a sin.

Feeble sistrum in the wind
of a lost cicada,
no sooner touched than done for
in the exhaling torpor.

The secret vein
branches out of the deep
in us: our world
barely holds up.

If you point they tremble
in the gray air,
corrupted leavings
the void won't devour.

So the gesture fades,
the voices die
and barren life
flows down and out.

Cigola la carrucola del pozzo,
l'acqua sale alla luce e vi si fonde.
Trema un ricordo nel ricolmo secchio,
nel puro cerchio un'immagine ride.
Accosto il volto a evanescenti labbri:
si deforma il passato, si fa vecchio,
appartiene ad un altro . . .
                              Ah che già stride
la ruota, ti ridona all'atro fondo,
visione, una distanza ci divide.

Arremba su la strinata proda
le navi di cartone, e dormi,
fanciulletto padrone: che non oda
tu i malevoli spiriti che veleggiano a stormi.

Nel chiuso dell'ortino svolacchia il gufo
e i fumacchi dei tetti sono pesi.
L'attimo che rovina l'opera lenta di mesi
giunge: ora incrina segreto, ora divelge in un buffo.

Viene lo spacco; forse senza strepito.
Chi ha edificato sente la sua condanna.
È l'ora che si salva solo la barca in panna.
Amarra la tua flotta tra le siepi.

The well's pulley creaks,
the water rises to the light, dissolving.
A memory trembles in the brimming pail,
an image smiles inside the perfect circle.
I bring my face to evanescent lips:
the past disintegrates, turns old, belongs
to someone else . . .
                              Ah, and already
the wheel shrieks, gives you back to the black deep,
vision, a distance keeps us separate.

Haul your paper ships on the seared
shore, little captain,
and sleep, so you won't hear
the evil spirits setting sail in swarms.

In the kitchen garden the owl darts
and the smoke hangs heavy on the roofs.
The moment that overwhelms the slow work of months
is here: now it cracks in secret, now it bursts with a gust.

The break is coming: maybe with no sound.
The builder knows his day of reckoning.
Only the grounded boat is safe for now.
Tie up your flotilla in the canes.

Upupa, ilare uccello calunniato
dai poeti, che roti la tua cresta
sopra l'aereo stollo del pollaio
e come un finto gallo giri al vento;
nunzio primaverile, upupa, come
per te il tempo s'arresta,
non muore più il Febbraio,
come tutto di fuori si protende
al muover del tuo capo,
aligero folletto, e tu lo ignori.

Sul muro grafito
che adombra i sedili rari
l'arco del cielo appare
finito.

Chi si ricorda più del fuoco ch'arse
impetuoso
nelle vene del mondo;—in un riposo
freddo le forme, opache, sono sparse.

Rivedrò domani le banchine
e la muraglia e l'usata strada.
Nel futuro che s'apre le mattine
sono ancorate come barche in rada.

Hoopoe, happy bird maligned
by poets, you rotate your crest
atop the henhouse aerial and spin
like a weathercock in the wind;
hoopoe, ambassador of spring,
time stands still for you just so,
February never dies,
and everything beyond bends down
going where your head is going,
crazy winged thing, and you don't know it.

Above the scribbled wall
that shades a seat
or two, the arc of the sky
appears complete.

Who remembers the fire that ran
impetuous in the world's veins;
—opaque, the shapes are scattered
in a cold repose.

Tomorrow I'll see the wharves again,
and the wall and the usual road.
In the future opening ahead
the mornings are moored like boats.

MEDITERRANEO

MEDITERRANEAN

A vortice s'abbatte
sul mio capo reclinato
un suono d'agri lazzi.
Scotta la terra percorsa
da sghembe ombre di pinastri,
e al mare là in fondo fa velo
più che i rami, allo sguardo, l'afa che a tratti erompe
dal suolo che si avvena.
Quando più sordo o meno il ribollio dell'acque
che s'ingorgano
accanto a lunghe secche mi raggiunge:
o è un bombo talvolta ed un ripiovere
di schiume sulle rocce.
Come rialzo il viso, ecco cessare
i ragli sul mio capo; e via scoccare
verso le strepeanti acque,
frecciate biancazzurre, due ghiandaie.

*

Antico, sono ubriacato dalla voce
ch'esce dalle tue bocche quando si schiudono
come verdi campane e si ributtano
indietro e si disciolgono.
La casa delle mie estati lontane
t'era accanto, lo sai,
là nel paese dove il sole cuoce
e annuvolano l'aria le zanzare.
Come allora oggi in tua presenza impietro,
mare, ma non più degno
mi credo del solenne ammonimento
del tuo respiro. Tu m'hai detto primo
che il piccino fermento
del mio cuore non era che un momento
del tuo; che mi era in fondo

Racketing catcalls spiral down
on my bent head.
The earth burns
swept by slanting shadows
of cluster pines, and, more than branches,
haze, escaping now and then
from the cracking earth, obscures the sight
of the sea in the distance.
When the boiling
of waters that choke on long shoals
reaches me more or less muffled:
or sometimes it's thunder
and foam raining back on the rocks . . .
I raise my eyes, the braying overhead
ceases: and bluewhite arrows,
two jays,
shoot by toward the roaring waters.

*

Ancient one, I'm drunk with the voice
that comes out of your mouths
when they open like green bells,
then implode and dissolve.
You know the house of my long-gone
summers stood by you,
there in the land where the sun bakes
and mosquitoes cloud the air.
Today as then I turn to stone
in your presence, sea,
but no longer feel worthy
of the solemn admonition of your breathing.
It was you who first told me
the petty ferment of my heart was no more
than a moment of yours; that deep in me

la tua legge rischiosa: esser vasto e diverso
e insieme fisso:
e svuotarmi così d'ogni lordura
come tu fai che sbatti sulle sponde
tra sugheri alghe asterie
le inutili macerie del tuo abisso.

✻

Scendendo qualche volta
gli aridi greppi ormai
divisi dall'umoroso
Autunno che li gonfiava,
non m'era più in cuore la ruota
delle stagioni e il gocciare
del tempo inesorabile;
ma bene il presentimento
di te m'empiva l'anima,
sorpreso nell'ansimare
dell'aria, prima immota,
sulle rocce che orlavano il cammino.
Or, m'avvisavo, la pietra
voleva strapparsi, protesa
a un invisibile abbraccio;
la dura materia sentiva
il prossimo gorgo, e pulsava;
e i ciuffi delle avide canne
dicevano all'acque nascoste,
scrollando, un assentimento.
Tu vastità riscattavi
anche il patire dei sassi:
pel tuo tripudio era giusta
l'immobilità dei finiti.
Chinavo tra le petraie,
giungevano buffi salmastri
al cuore; era la tesa
del mare un giuoco di anella.
Con questa gioia precipita

was your hazardous law: to be vast
and various yet fixed:
and so empty myself of all uncleanliness
like you who toss on the beaches
among cork and seaweed and starfish
the useless rubble of your abyss.

✻

Sometimes, coming down
the dry cliffs, distant now
from the many-humored
Autumn that swelled them,
the wheel of the seasons
and the dripping of inexorable
time were gone from my heart;
yet the sense of you
still filled my soul,
surprised in the gasping air
that was still before
on the rocks that edged the road.
Now, I saw, the stone
wanted to escape, was reaching
for an invisible embrace;
the hard matter sensed
the eddy there, and throbbed;
and the shaking tufts of thirsty cane
nodded an assent
to the hidden waters.
Vastness, you redeemed
the suffering of the stones as well:
your exultation justified
the fixedness of finite things.
I slid down among the rubble,
briny gusts rose to my heart;
the line of the sea
was a game of rings.
With this joy the lost

dal chiuso vallotto alla spiaggia
la spersa pavoncella.

❋

Ho sostato talvolta nelle grotte
che t'assecondano, vaste
o anguste, ombrose e amare.
Guardati dal fondo gli sbocchi
segnavano architetture
possenti campite di cielo.
Sorgevano dal tuo petto
rombante aerei templi,
guglie scoccanti luci:
una città di vetro dentro l'azzurro netto
via via si discopriva da ogni caduco velo
e il suo rombo non era che un susurro.
Nasceva dal fiotto la patria sognata.
Dal subbuglio emergeva l'evidenza.
L'esiliato rientrava nel paese incorrotto.
Così, padre, dal tuo disfrenamento
si afferma, chi ti guardi, una legge severa.
Ed è vano sfuggirla: mi condanna
s'io lo tento anche un ciottolo
róso sul mio cammino,
impietrato soffrire senza nome,
o l'informe rottame
che gittò fuor del corso la fiumara
del vivere in un fitto di ramure e di strame.
Nel destino che si prepara
c'è forse per me sosta,
niun'altra mai minaccia.
Questo ripete il flutto in sua furia incomposta,
e questo ridice il filo della bonaccia.

lapwing swoops
out of the hidden valley to the shore.

❉

I've paused at times in the caves
beside you, vast
or narrow, shadowy and bitter.
Seen from within, their mouths
etched mighty architecture
on the sky's backdrop.
Thundering airy temples
rose from your breast,
spires shooting lights:
a city of glass inside the pure azure
slowly shrugged off each ephemeral veil
and its roar was no more than a whisper.
The dreamed-of homeland rose from the flood.
Out of the uproar came the evidence.
The exile returned to his uncorrupted country.
So, Father, your unleashing
affirms a hard rule for him who watches you.
And it's pointless to evade it: if I try
even an eroded pebble on my way
condemns me,
hardened nameless sufferance,
or the shapeless wreckage
the flood of life tossed by the wayside
in a tangle of branches and grass.
In the destiny being prepared
there may be respite for me,
an end to threats forever.
The sea repeats this in its restless fury,
and the trickle of calm air says it again.

Giunge a volte, repente,
un'ora che il tuo cuore disumano
ci spaura e dal nostro si divide.
Dalla mia la tua musica sconcorda,
allora, ed è nemico ogni tuo moto.
In me ripiego, vuoto
di forze, la tua voce pare sorda.
M'affisso nel pietrisco
che verso te digrada
fino alla ripa acclive che ti sovrasta,
franosa, gialla, solcata
da strosce d'acqua piovana.
Mia vita è questo secco pendio,
mezzo non fine, strada aperta a sbocchi
di rigagnoli, lento franamento.
È dessa, ancora, questa pianta
che nasce dalla devastazione
e in faccia ha i colpi del mare ed è sospesa
fra erratiche forze di venti.
Questo pezzo di suolo non erbato
s'è spaccato perché nascesse una margherita.
In lei tìtubo al mare che mi offende,
manca ancora il silenzio nella mia vita.
Guardo la terra che scintilla,
l'aria è tanto serena che s'oscura.
E questa che in me cresce
è forse la rancura
che ogni figliuolo, mare, ha per il padre.

✿

Noi non sappiamo quale sortiremo
domani, oscuro o lieto;
forse il nostro cammino
a non tócche radure ci addurrà

Now and then, suddenly,
there comes a time when your inhuman heart
terrifies us, separates from ours.
Your music then discords with mine
and all your movements are inimical.
I fold inside myself, devoid of forces,
your voice sounds stifled.
I stand amid the rubble
that scales down to you, down
to the steep bank above you,
prone to landslides, yellow, etched
by rivers of rainwater.
My life is this dry slope,
a means not an end, a way
open to runoff from gutters and slow erosion.
And it's this, too: this plant
born out of devastation
that takes the sea's lashing in the face,
hanging in the wind's erratic gales.
This piece of grassless earth
broke open so a daisy could be born.
In her I nod toward the sea that offends me,
silence is still missing from my life.
I watch the glistening earth,
the air so blue it goes dark.
And what rises in me, sea,
may be the rancor
that each son feels for his father.

❉

We don't know how we'll turn up
tomorrow, hard-pressed or happy:
perhaps our path
will lead to virgin clearings

dove mormori eterna l'acqua di giovinezza;
o sarà forse un discendere
fino al vallo estremo,
nel buio, perso il ricordo del mattino.
Ancora terre straniere
forse ci accoglieranno: smarriremo
la memoria del sole, dalla mente
ci cadrà il tintinnare delle rime.
Oh la favola onde s'esprime
la nostra vita, repente
si cangerà nella cupa storia che non si racconta!
Pur di una cosa ci affidi,
padre, e questa è: che un poco del tuo dono
sia passato per sempre nelle sillabe
che rechiamo con noi, api ronzanti.
Lontani andremo e serberemo un'eco
della tua voce, come si ricorda
del sole l'erba grigia
nelle corti scurite, tra le case.
E un giorno queste parole senza rumore
che teco educammo nutrite
di stanchezze e di silenzi,
parranno a un fraterno cuore
sapide di sale greco.

      ✿

Avrei voluto sentirmi scabro ed essenziale
siccome i ciottoli che tu volvi,
mangiati dalla salsedine;
scheggia fuori del tempo, testimone
di una volontà fredda che non passa.
Altro fui: uomo intento che riguarda
in sé, in altrui, il bollore
della vita fugace—uomo che tarda
all'atto, che nessuno, poi, distrugge.
Volli cercare il male
che tarla il mondo, la piccola stortura
d'una leva che arresta

where youth's water murmurs eternal;
or maybe come down
to the last valley in the dark,
the memory of morning gone.
Foreign lands
may welcome us again; we'll lose
the memory of the sun, the chime
of rhymes will abandon the mind.
Oh the fable that explains our life
will suddenly become
the murky tale that can't be told!
Still, Father, you assure us of one thing:
that a little of your gift
has gone for good into the syllables
we carry with us, humming bees.
We'll travel far yet keep
an echo of your voice,
as gray grass recalls the sun
in dark courtyards, between houses.
And one day these noiseless words
we raised beside you, nourished
on fatigue and silence,
will taste of Greek salt
to a brother heart.

❖

I would have liked to feel harsh and essential
like the pebbles you tumble,
gnawed by the sea brine;
a splinter out of time in evidence
of a cold, constant will.
I was different: a brooding man
who sees the turbulence of fleeting life
in himself, in others—who's slow to take
the action no one later can undo.
I wanted to find out the evil
that bores at the world, the littlest
jilt of a lever that stalls

l'ordegno universale; e tutti vidi
gli eventi del minuto
come pronti a disgiungersi in un crollo.
Seguìto il solco d'un sentiero m'ebbi
l'opposto in cuore, col suo invito; e forse
m'occorreva il coltello che recide,
la mente che decide e si determina.
Altri libri occorrevano
a me, non la tua pagina rombante.
Ma nulla so rimpiangere: tu sciogli
ancora i groppi interni col tuo canto.
Il tuo delirio sale agli astri ormai.

*

Potessi almeno costringere
in questo mio ritmo stento
qualche poco del tuo vaneggiamento;
dato mi fosse accordare
alle tue voci il mio balbo parlare:—
io che sognava rapirti
le salmastre parole
in cui natura ed arte si confondono,
per gridar meglio la mia malinconia
di fanciullo invecchiato che non doveva pensare.
Ed invece non ho che le lettere fruste
dei dizionari, e l'oscura
voce che amore detta s'affioca,
si fa lamentosa letteratura.
Non ho che queste parole
che come donne pubblicate
s'offrono a chi le richiede;
non ho che queste frasi stancate
che potranno rubarmi anche domani
gli studenti canaglie in versi veri.
Ed il tuo rombo cresce, e si dilata
azzurra l'ombra nuova.
M'abbandonano a prova i miei pensieri.
Sensi non ho; né senso. Non ho limite.

the universal contraption;
and I saw all the doings
of the minute as ready to crumble.
I followed one path but kept
the other in mind, and its lure;
and maybe I needed the knife that severs,
the mind that decides
and determines. I needed other books
than your roaring page.
Yet I can't regret a thing: you still
dissolve internal tangles with your song.
And now your frenzy rises to the stars.

      ✿

If at least I could force
some small part of your raving
into this halting rhythm;
if I could harmonize
my stammer with your voices:—
I who dreamed of stealing
your briny words
where art and nature fuse,
the better to shout out the sadness
of an aging boy who shouldn't have been thinking.
But all I have are threadbare
dictionary letters
and the dark voice love dictates
goes hoarse, becomes whining writing.
All I have are these words
which prostitute themselves
to anyone who asks;
only these tired phrases
the student rabble can steal tomorrow
to make real poetry.
And your roaring rises,
the new shadow waxes blue.
My ideas desert me at the test.
I have no senses and no sense. No limit.

＊

Dissipa tu se lo vuoi
questa debole vita che si lagna,
come la spugna il frego
effimero di una lavagna.
M'attendo di ritornare nel tuo circolo,
s'adempia lo sbandato mio passare.
La mia venuta era testimonianza
di un ordine che in viaggio mi scordai,
giurano fede queste mie parole
a un evento impossibile, e lo ignorano.
Ma sempre che traudii
la tua dolce risacca su le prode
sbigottimento mi prese
quale d'uno scemato di memoria
quando si risovviene del suo paese.
Presa la mia lezione
più che dalla tua gloria
aperta, dall'ansare
che quasi non dà suono
di qualche tuo meriggio desolato,
a te mi rendo in umiltà. Non sono
che favilla d'un tirso. Bene lo so: bruciare,
questo, non altro, è il mio significato.

✿

Dissolve if you will this frail
lamenting life,
the way the eraser wipes the ephemeral
scrawl off a slate.
I'm waiting to return inside your circle,
my straggler's wandering is done.
My coming was in witness
to an order I forgot in traveling,
these words of mine pledge faith
in an impossible event, and don't know it.
But always when I overheard
your sweet backwash along the shore
I was dumbfounded
like a man deprived of memory
whose country comes back to him.
I learned my lesson
not so much from your open glory
as from the almost-
silent heaving
of some of your deserted noons;
I offer myself in humility. I am only
the spark from a beacon. And I know for certain
burning, nothing else, is what I mean.

MERIGGI E OMBRE

NOONS AND SHADOWS

Fine dell'infanzia

Rombando s'ingolfava
dentro l'arcuata ripa
un mare pulsante, sbarrato da solchi,
cresputo e fioccoso di spume.
Di contro alla foce
d'un torrente che straboccava
il flutto ingialliva.
Giravano al largo i grovigli dell'alighe
e tronchi d'alberi alla deriva.

Nella conca ospitale
della spiaggia
non erano che poche case
di annosi mattoni, scarlatte,
e scarse capellature
di tamerici pallide
più d'ora in ora; stente creature
perdute in un orrore di visioni.
Non era lieve guardarle
per chi leggeva in quelle
apparenze malfide
la musica dell'anima inquieta
che non si decide.

Pure colline chiudevano d'intorno
marina e case; ulivi le vestivano
qua e là disseminati come greggi,
o tenui come il fumo di un casale
che veleggi
la faccia candente del cielo.
Tra macchie di vigneti e di pinete,
petraie si scorgevano

End of Childhood

Thundering, a throbbing sea
hatched by furrows
wrinkled and flocked with foam
was engulfed in the curved shore.
The tide
turned yellow where it met the mouth
of a flooding stream.
Offshore, tangled seaweed
and drifting tree trunks rolled.

In the inviting
arc of the beach
were just a few scarlet houses
built of ancient brick
and the thin hair
of tamarisks, paler every hour;
stunted creatures
lost in a horror of visions.
There was no joy in seeing them
for one who read in those
unsteady apparitions
the music of a restless,
undecided soul.

Yet hills surrounded
shore and houses; olives dressed them,
scattered here
and there like herds or wispy,
smoke from a village sailing
the shining face of the sky.
Among daubs of vines and pine groves,
one saw outcropping rocks,

calve e gibbosi dorsi
di collinette: un uomo
che là passasse ritto s'un muletto
nell'azzurro lavato era stampato
per sempre—e nel ricordo.

Poco s'andava oltre i crinali prossimi
di quei monti; varcarli pur non osa
la memoria stancata.
So che strade correvano su fossi
incassati, tra garbugli di spini;
mettevano a radure, poi tra botri,
e ancora dilungavano
verso recessi madidi di muffe,
d'ombre coperti e di silenzi.
Uno ne penso ancora con meraviglia
dove ogni umano impulso
appare seppellito
in aura millenaria.
Rara diroccia qualche bava d'aria
sino a quell'orlo di mondo che ne strabilia.

Ma dalle vie del monte si tornava.
Riuscivano queste a un'instabile
vicenda d'ignoti aspetti
ma il ritmo che li governa ci sfuggiva.
Ogni attimo bruciava
negl'istanti futuri senza tracce.
Vivere era ventura troppo nuova
ora per ora, e ne batteva il cuore.
Norma non v'era,
solco fisso, confronto,
a sceverare gioia da tristezza.
Ma riaddotti dai viottoli
alla casa sul mare, al chiuso asilo
della nostra stupita fanciullezza,
rapido rispondeva
a ogni moto dell'anima un consenso
esterno, si vestivano di nomi
le cose, il nostro mondo aveva un centro.

the bald, hunched backs
of hillocks: a man who passed there
sitting on a mule
was stamped on the washed blue
—and in the mind—forever.

We seldom crossed the nearest
ridge of hills;
nor does exhausted memory dare to now.
I know trails
ran along steep embankments
through bramble thickets;
they led to clearings,
past ravines,
and on to alcoves dank with mold,
dark shadows, silences.
I'm still amazed, recalling one
where every human impulse
seems shrouded in a millennial haze.
Every now and then a wisp of breeze
falls on that ledge of world, astounding it.

But we turned back from the mountain paths,
ever-changing,
ever-unfamiliar,
for the rhythm that governs them eluded us.
Every instant burned
into the future moment without ash.
Life was too new a venture every hour,
and our hearts were racing:
no norm, no fixed groove,
no comparison
to sever joy from sadness.
But led back by the trails
to the house by the sea,
the safe harbor of our astounded childhood,
we found an outward correspondence
quickly met each motion of the soul,
things were dressed in names,
our world had a center.

Eravamo nell'età verginale
in cui le nubi non sono cifre o sigle
ma le belle sorelle che si guardano viaggiare.
D'altra semenza uscita
d'altra linfa nutrita
che non la nostra, debole, pareva la natura.
In lei l'asilo, in lei
l'estatico affisare; ella il portento
cui non sognava, o a pena, di raggiungere
l'anima nostra confusa.
Eravamo nell'età illusa.

Volarono anni corti come giorni,
sommerse ogni certezza un mare florido
e vorace che dava ormai l'aspetto
dubbioso dei tremanti tamarischi.
Un'alba dové sorgere che un rigo
di luce su la soglia
forbita ci annunziava come un'acqua;
e noi certo corremmo
ad aprire la porta
stridula sulla ghiaia del giardino.
L'inganno ci fu palese.
Pesanti nubi sul torbato mare
che ci bolliva in faccia, tosto apparvero.
Era in aria l'attesa
di un procelloso evento.
Strania anch'essa la plaga
dell'infanzia che esplora
un segnato cortile come un mondo!
Giungeva anche per noi l'ora che indaga.
La fanciullezza era morta in un giro a tondo.

Ah il giuoco dei cannibali nel canneto,
i mustacchi di palma, la raccolta
deliziosa dei bossoli sparati!
Volava la bella età come i barchetti sul filo
del mare a vele colme.

That was the virgin time
when clouds aren't numbers or signs
but beautiful sisters one watches travel.
Nature seemed
the fruit of another sowing
fed by another sap than our thin kind.
She was our shelter, our ecstatic
attachment; the portent
our soul in its confusion didn't dream
—or only barely—of attaining.
It was the time of illusion.

Years as short as days flew by,
an exuberant, voracious sea
that drowned all certainty took on
the dubious look of the shivering tamarisks.
A dawn had to come, announced
like a downpour by a line of light
on the scrubbed threshold,
and of course we ran
to open the door, which grumbled
on the garden gravel.
The game was up.
Soon heavy clouds hung over the anxious
sea that boiled in our faces.
The air was full of waiting
for a stormy occurrence.
Which also distances
the zone of childhood that explores
a raked courtyard like a world.
The hour of questioning arrived for us, too.
Our childhood died in a ring around the rose.

Ah, the game of cannibals in the cane,
the palm-leaf mustaches, the wondrous
harvesting of empty cartridges!
The golden age flew by like boats
in full sail on the horizon.

Certo guardammo muti nell'attesa
del minuto violento;
poi nella finta calma
sopra l'acque scavate
dové mettersi un vento.

Yes, we watched and waited silently
for the violent moment;
finally, in the false
calm over carved waters
a wind had to come.

L'agave su lo scoglio

Scirocco

❶ rabido ventare di scirocco
che l'arsiccio terreno gialloverde
bruci;
e su nel cielo pieno
di smorte luci
trapassa qualche biocco
di nuvola, e si perde.
Ore perplesse, brividi
d'una vita che fugge
come acqua tra le dita;
inafferrati eventi,
luci-ombre, commovimenti
delle cose malferme della terra;
oh alide ali dell'aria
ora son io
l'agave che s'abbarbica al crepaccio
dello scoglio
e sfugge al mare da le braccia d'alghe
che spalanca ampie gole e abbranca rocce;
e nel fermento
d'ogni essenza, coi miei racchiusi bocci
che non sanno più esplodere oggi sento
la mia immobilità come un tormento.

The Agave on the Reef

Sirocco

❶ rabid sirocco
gale that burns
the parched land's yellowgreen;
and in the sky alive
with pale lights
a few cloud columns pass
and are lost.
Worried hours, vibrations
of a life that flees
like water through the fingers;
unsnared events,
light-shadows, shakings
of the wobbling things of earth;
oh arid wings of air
today I am
the agave that takes root
in the crevice of the rock
and in the algae's arms escapes the sea
that opens its huge jaws and mouths the boulders;
and in the ferment of every
essence, with my furled-up buds
that no longer explode, today I feel
my rootedness as torment.

Tramontana

Ed ora sono spariti i circoli d'ansia
che discorrevano il lago del cuore
e quel friggere vasto della materia
che discolora e muore.
Oggi una volontà di ferro spazza l'aria,
divelle gli arbusti, strapazza i palmizi
e nel mare compresso scava
grandi solchi crestati di bava.
Ogni forma si squassa nel subbuglio
degli elementi; è un urlo solo, un muglio
di scerpate esistenze: tutto schianta
l'ora che passa: viaggiano la cupola del cielo
non sai se foglie o uccelli—e non son più.
E tu che tutta ti scrolli fra i tonfi
dei venti disfrenati
e stringi a te i bracci gonfi
di fiori non ancora nati;
come senti nemici
gli spiriti che la convulsa terra
sorvolano a sciami,
mia vita sottile, e come ami
oggi le tue radici.

Tramontana

And now the ripples of anxiety
that troubled the heart's lake have disappeared
and the vast seething of matter
that turns colorless and dies.
Today a will of iron sweeps the air,
uproots the bushes, tears the palms
and etches on the compressed sea
high furrows topped with foam.
Each shape shakes in the elemental clamor;
it's all one howl, an uproar
of uprooted beings:
the passing hour shears everything away:
leaves or birds, who knows,
cross the sky's dome—are gone.
And you, all buffeted by gales
of unleashed wind, who wrap your arms around you,
heavy with flowers yet unborn;
how inimical
the spirits seem that swarm
the ravaged earth,
my slender life, and how
you love your roots today.

Maestrale

S'è rifatta la calma
nell'aria: tra gli scogli parlotta la maretta.
Sulla costa quietata, nei broli, qualche palma
a pena svetta.

Una carezza disfiora
la linea del mare e la scompiglia
un attimo, soffio lieve che vi s'infrange e ancora
il cammino ripiglia.

Lameggia nella chiaria
la vasta distesa, s'increspa, indi si spiana beata
e specchia nel suo cuore vasto codesta povera mia
vita turbata.

O mio tronco che additi,
in questa ebrietudine tarda,
ogni rinato aspetto coi germogli fioriti
sulle tue mani, guarda:

sotto l'azzurro fitto
del cielo qualche uccello di mare se ne va;
né sosta mai: perché tutte le immagini portano scritto:
'più in là!'.

Mistral

Calm has returned
to the air: the choppy sea talks in the rocks.
On the quieted coast, in the gardens,
a few palms barely stir.

A caress skims
the line of the sea and dishevels it a moment,
wispy puff that breaks up and takes
to the road again.

The vast stretch
shines like a knife in the brightness, ripples,
goes happily flat, and in its vast heart mirrors
my poor, unsettled life.

O trunk of mine
that illustrates pure rebirth in the blooming
buds on your hands in this late
drunkenness, look up:

under the sky's dense azure
a few seabirds are flying;
they never stop: for all the images keep saying:
Higher, higher!

Vasca

Passò sul tremulo vetro
un riso di belladonna fiorita,
di tra le rame urgevano le nuvole,
dal fondo ne riassommava
la vista fioccosa e sbiadita.
Alcuno di noi tirò un ciottolo
che ruppe la tesa lucente:
le molli parvenze s'infransero.

Ma ecco, c'è altro che striscia
a fior della spera rifatta liscia:
di erompere non ha virtù,
vuol vivere e non sa come;
se lo guardi si stacca, torna in giù:
è nato e morto, e non ha avuto un nome.

Pool

A blooming belladonna smile
passed on the trembling glass,
clouds pressed between the branches,
their cottony pale billows
rose from below.
One of us skipped a stone
that broke the shining surface:
the soft appearances shattered.

But look, there's more than a streak
on the mirror that's newly sleek:
no way for it to break through,
it wants to live and doesn't know how;
watch and it drops, falls back where it came from:
it lived and died and never had a name.

Egloga

Perdersi nel bigio ondoso
dei miei ulivi era buono
nel tempo andato—loquaci
di riottanti uccelli
e di cantanti rivi.
Come affondava il tallone
nel suolo screpolato,
tra le lamelle d'argento
dell'esili foglie. Sconnessi
nascevano in mente i pensieri
nell'aria di troppa quiete.

Ora è finito il cerulo marezzo.
Si getta il pino domestico
a romper la grigiura;
brucia una toppa di cielo
in alto, un ragnatelo
si squarcia al passo: si svincola
d'attorno un'ora fallita.
È uscito un rombo di treno,
non lunge, ingrossa. Uno sparo
si schiaccia nell'etra vetrino.
Strepita un volo come un acquazzone,
venta e vanisce bruciata
una bracciata di amara
tua scorza, istante: discosta
esplode furibonda una canea.

Tosto potrà rinascere l'idillio.
S'è ricomposta la fase che pende
dal cielo, riescono bende
leggere fuori . . . ;
                            il fitto dei fagiuoli
n'è scancellato e involto.
Non serve più rapid'ale,

Eclogue

It was good getting lost
in the undulant gray of my olives—
talkative with bickering
birds and singing
brooks—in the old days.
The way the heel
sank in the cracked earth
among the silver
blades of tender leaves. Ideas
came to mind unorganized
in the all-too-quiet air.

Now the blue marbling is gone.
The local pine has grown
to breach the grayness;
a patch of sky burns overhead,
a spider's web
tears at my step: a failed
hour unlinks its chain around me.
Nearby, the rumble of a train
detunnels, swells. A shot
crazes the glassy air. A flight
pelts like a downpour;
instant, an armful of your bitter rind,
surges, goes down burned:
a pack of unleashed hounds
explodes in fury.

Soon the idyll will be born again.
The phase that hangs in the sky
gets recomposed, light streamers
slowly unfurl . . . ;
                    the thicket of beans
vanishes, shrouded in them.
Swift wings are no help now,

né giova proposito baldo;
non durano che le solenni cicale
in questi saturnali del caldo.
Va e viene un istante in un folto
una parvenza di donna.
È disparsa, non era una Baccante.

Sul tardi corneggia la luna.
Ritornavamo dai nostri
vagabondari infruttuosi.
Non si leggeva più in faccia
al mondo la traccia
della frenesia durata
il pomeriggio. Turbati
discendevamo tra i vepri.
Nei miei paesi a quell'ora
cominciano a fischiare le lepri.

nor bald proposals;
only the solemn cicadas
survive the saturnalia of the heat.
The image of a woman comes and goes
for an instant in a crowd.
She disappears; she wasn't a Bacchante.

Later, a crescent moon.
Backtracking
from our pointless wanderings
we could no longer read on the world's face
the trace of the frenzy
that lasted the afternoon.
Uneasily, we scrambled down
among the brambles.
In my country this is when
the hares begin to hiss.

Flussi

I fanciulli con gli archetti
spaventano gli scriccioli nei buchi.
Cola il pigro sereno nel riale
che l'accidia sorrade,
pausa che gli astri donano ai malvivi
camminatori delle bianche strade.
Alte tremano guglie di sambuchi
e sovrastano al poggio
cui domina una statua dell'Estate
fatta camusa da lapidazioni;
e su lei cresce un roggio
di rampicanti ed un ronzio di fuchi.
Ma la dea mutilata non s'affaccia
e ogni cosa si tende alla flottiglia
di carta che discende lenta il vallo.
Brilla in aria una freccia,
si configge s'un palo, oscilla tremula.
La vita è questo scialo
di triti fatti, vano
più che crudele.
       Tornano
le tribù dei fanciulli con le fionde
se è scorsa una stagione od un minuto,
e i morti aspetti scoprono immutati
se pur tutto è diruto
e più dalla sua rama non dipende
il frutto conosciuto.
—Ritornano i fanciulli . . . ; così un giorno
il giro che governa
la nostra vita ci addurrà il passato
lontano, franto e vivido, stampato
sopra immobili tende
da un'ignota lanterna.—
E ancora si distende
un dòmo celestino ed appannato
sul fitto bulicame del fossato:

Flux

The boys with snares
scare the wrens in their nests.
The slow sky leaks into the stream
nibbled by indolence, a pause
the stars allow the dazed
sleepwalkers in the dusty streets.
The high points of the elders shiver
on the hilltop crowned
by a statue of Summer,
who's lost her nose to stones;
a tuft of vines grows around her,
and a humming of drones.
But the faceless goddess won't appear
and everything joins the paper fleet
bobbing slowly down the ditch.
An arrow shimmers in the air,
pierces a stake and quivers there.
Life is this wearing-down
of threadbare facts,
more vain than cruel.
                    The tribes of boys
come back with slings
if a season or a minute passes,
to find the dead appearances unchanged,
though everything's
run down and the usual fruit
no longer hangs on the bough.
—The boys come back . . . ; the way the wheel
that rules our life
will bring the past someday,
long-gone, shattered, vivid,
printed on still curtains
by an unknown light.—
And a sky-blue, hazy dome
still covers the thick
bubbling in the trench:

e soltanto la statua
sa che il tempo precipita e s'infrasca
vie più nell'accesa edera.
E tutto scorre nella gran discesa
e fiotta il fosso impetuoso tal che
s'increspano i suoi specchi:
fanno naufragio i piccoli sciabecchi
nei gorghi dell'acquiccia insaponata.
Addio!—fischiano pietre tra le fronde,
la rapace fortuna è già lontana,
cala un'ora, i suoi volti riconfonde,—
e la vita è crudele più che vana.

and only the statue knows
time rushes, burrows deeper
in the blazing ivy.
Everything hurtles in the great descent,
the headlong stream is burbling
so wildly its pools corrugate:
the little schooners shipwreck
in whorls of soapy slime.
Farewell!—pebbles whistle in the leaves,
rapacious Lady Luck's long gone,
a moment ends, reshapes its faces,—
and life is much more cruel than vain.

Clivo

Viene un suono di buccine
dal greppo che scoscende,
discende verso il mare
che tremola e si fende per accoglierlo.
Cala nella ventosa gola
con l'ombre la parola
che la terra dissolve sui frangenti;
si dismemora il mondo e può rinascere.
Con le barche dell'alba
spiega la luce le sue grandi vele
e trova stanza in cuore la speranza.
Ma ora lungi è il mattino,
sfugge il chiarore e s'aduna
sovra eminenze e frondi,
e tutto è più raccolto e più vicino
come visto a traverso di una cruna;
ora è certa la fine,
e s'anche il vento tace
senti la lima che sega
assidua la catena che ci lega.

Come una musicale frana
divalla il suono, s'allontana.
Con questo si disperdono le accolte
voci dalle volute
aride dei crepacci;
il gemito delle pendìe,
là tra le viti che i lacci
delle radici stringono.
Il clivo non ha più vie,
le mani s'afferrano ai rami
dei pini nani; poi trema
e scema il bagliore del giorno;
e un ordine discende che districa
dai confini
le cose che non chiedono

Slope

A sound of trumpets comes
from the cliff as it sheers away,
sinks to the sea that shudders
and shatters to take it in.
Into the windy gorge
with its shadows falls the word
the land dissolves on the breakers;
the world shrugs memory off, to live again.
Along with the boats of dawn
the light spreads its wide sails
and hope finds room in the heart.
But now that morning's gone
the brightness flees to regroup
on heights and leaves
and everything's more gathered-in and nearer
as if seen through a needle's eye;
now the end is sure,
and when the wind too dies
you hear the file that saws away
at the chain that binds us.

An avalanche of music,
the sound cascades, moves on.
With it go voices gathered
from the dry
corkscrews of the cliffs;
the moaning of the shelves,
there among the vines
clutched by their knotted roots.
The slope's paths have disappeared,
the hands grab at the branches
of dwarf pines; until
the day's dazzle quakes, abates;
and an order descends that frees
from their limits
the things that ask

ormai che di durare, di persistere
contente dell'infinita fatica;
un crollo di pietrame che dal cielo
s'inabissa alle prode . . .

Nella sera distesa appena, s'ode
un ululo di corni, uno sfacelo.

only to last, to persist now,
content with their endless task;
a crumbling of rock that hurtles
out of the sky to the shore . . .

One hears, in the evening unfolding,
a wailing of horns, a fading.

Arsenio

I turbini sollevano la polvere
sui tetti, a mulinelli, e sugli spiazzi
deserti, ove i cavalli incappucciati
annusano la terra, fermi innanzi
ai vetri luccicanti degli alberghi.
Sul corso, in faccia al mare, tu discendi
in questo giorno
or piovorno ora acceso, in cui par scatti
a sconvolgerne l'ore
uguali, strette in trama, un ritornello
di castagnette.

È il segno d'un'altra orbita: tu seguilo.
Discendi all'orizzonte che sovrasta
una tromba di piombo, alta sui gorghi,
più d'essi vagabonda: salso nembo
vorticante, soffiato dal ribelle
elemento alle nubi; fa che il passo
su la ghiaia ti scricchioli e t'inciampi
il viluppo dell'alghe: quell'istante
è forse, molto atteso, che ti scampi
dal finire il tuo viaggio, anello d'una
catena, immoto andare, oh troppo noto
delirio, Arsenio, d'immobilità . . .

Ascolta tra i palmizi il getto tremulo
dei violini, spento quando rotola
il tuono con un fremer di lamiera
percossa; la tempesta è dolce quando
sgorga bianca la stella di Canicola
nel cielo azzurro e lunge par la sera
ch'è prossima: se il fulmine la incide

Arsenio

Whirligigs of wind stir up the dust
in eddies over the roofs and empty places
where horses wearing paper hats
tethered in front of gleaming hotel
windows nose the ground.
Down the avenue that fronts the sea
you come this day, now rainswept
now on fire, in which it seems
a refrain of castanets explodes
to contradict the repetitious,
interwoven hours.

Sign of another orbit: follow it.
Descend to the horizon, overhung
by a lead stormcloud high above the riptide
and still more erratic: a salty, roiling
maelstrom, blown
from the rebellious element up to the clouds;
let your step rasp on the gravel
and the tangled seaweed trip you:
this may be the long-awaited hour when you escape
from finishing your journey, link in a chain,
stalled motion, oh too familiar
frenzy, Arsenio, of immobility . . .

Hear among the palms the wavering
stream of violins, which ends when thunder
rolls with a struck-metal clang;
the storm is sweet
when the white Dog Star spurts in the blue sky
and the imminent evening's still far:
if lightning cuts across

dirama come un albero prezioso
entro la luce che s'arrosa: e il timpano
degli tzigani è il rombo silenzioso.

Discendi in mezzo al buio che precipita
e muta il mezzogiorno in una notte
di globi accesi, dondolanti a riva,—
e fuori, dove un'ombra sola tiene
mare e cielo, dai gozzi sparsi palpita
l'acetilene—
        finché goccia trepido
il cielo, fuma il suolo che s'abbevera,
tutto d'accanto ti sciaborda, sbattono
le tende molli, un frùscio immenso rade
la terra, giù s'afflosciano stridendo
le lanterne di carta sulle strade.

Così sperso tra i vimini e le stuoie
grondanti, giunco tu che le radici
con sé trascina, viscide, non mai
svelte, tremi di vita e ti protendi
a un vuoto risonante di lamenti
soffocati, la tesa ti ringhiotte
dell'onda antica che ti volge; e ancora
tutto che ti riprende, strada portico
mura specchi ti figge in una sola
ghiacciata moltitudine di morti,
e se un gesto ti sfiora, una parola
ti cade accanto, quello è forse, Arsenio,
nell'ora che si scioglie, il cenno d'una
vita strozzata per te sorta, e il vento
la porta con la cenere degli astri.

it branches like a heavenly tree
in the light that's turning pink: and the gypsies'
tambour is its silent roar.

Go down into the falling dark
that makes the noon into a night
of lit globes, swaying by the shore—
and out there, where a single shadow
covers sea and sky, acetylene
torches throb on the scattered dories—

                              till the apprehensive sky
starts spattering, the earth smokes as it drinks,
everything around you overflows,
drenched awnings flap, an enormous rustling
grazes the earth, the shrieking paper lanterns
go soggy in the streets.

Lost thus among wicker and waterlogged
matting, reed that drags your roots behind you,
slimy, never sleek, you shake with life
and reach out to an emptiness
that echoes muffled cries, the crest
of the old wave that rolls you
swallows you again; and everything
that locks you in: street colonnade
walls mirrors freezes you
in one gelid gathering of the dead;
and if a movement grazes you,
a word falls close to you, Arsenio,
it may be the sign, in the hour that fails,
of a strangled life arisen for you, and the wind
carries it off with the ashes of the stars.

Crisalide

L'albero verdecupo
si stria di giallo tenero e s'ingromma.
Vibra nell'aria una pietà per l'avide
radici, per le tumide cortecce.
Son vostre queste piante
scarse che si rinnovano
all'alito d'Aprile, umide e liete.
Per me che vi contemplo da quest'ombra,
altro cespo riverdica, e voi siete.

Ogni attimo vi porta nuove fronde
e il suo sbigottimento avanza ogni altra
gioia fugace; viene a impetuose onde
la vita a questo estremo angolo d'orto.
Lo sguardo ora vi cade su le zolle;
una risacca di memorie giunge
al vostro cuore e quasi lo sommerge.
Lunge risuona un grido: ecco precipita
il tempo, spare con risucchi rapidi
tra i sassi, ogni ricordo è spento; ed io
dall'oscuro mio canto mi protendo
a codesto solare avvenimento.

Voi non pensate ciò che vi rapiva
come oggi, allora, il tacito compagno
che un meriggio lontano vi portava.
Siete voi la mia preda, che m'offrite
un'ora breve di tremore umano.
Perderne non vorrei neppure un attimo:
è questa la mia parte, ogni altra è vana.
La mia ricchezza è questo sbattimento
che vi trapassa e il viso

Chrysalis

The deep-green tree
gets streaked with tender yellow and crusts over.
The air quivers with pity
for the greedy roots, the swollen bark.
They're yours, these meager plants
that come alive again with the breath of April,
drenched and elated.
For me, who contemplate you from this shade,
another shoot turns green again: you are.

Every moment brings new leaves to you,
amazement overwhelming every other
fleeting joy: life arrives on headlong waves
in this far garden corner.
Now you stare down at the soil;
an undertow of memories
reaches your heart and almost overwhelms it.
A shout in the distance: see, time plummets,
disappears in hurried eddies
among the stones, all memory gone; and I
from my dark lookout reach
for this sunlit occurrence.

You don't know what, then as now,
stole the mute companion
that a long-gone noon once brought you.
You are my prey, who offer me
one brief hour of human fervor.
I don't want to waste an instant:
this is my share, and nothing else has meaning.
My wealth is this beating
that moves in you and lifts

in alto vi rivolge; questo lento
giro d'occhi che ormai sanno vedere.

Così va la certezza d'un momento
con uno sventolio di tende e di alberi
tra le case; ma l'ombra non dissolve
che vi reclama, opaca. M'apparite
allora, come me, nel limbo squallido
delle monche esistenze; e anche la vostra
rinascita è uno sterile segreto,
un prodigio fallito come tutti
quelli che ci fioriscono d'accanto.

E il flutto che si scopre oltre le sbarre
come ci parla a volte di salvezza;
come può sorgere agile
l'illusione, e sciogliere i suoi fumi.
Vanno a spire sul mare, ora si fondono
sull'orizzonte in foggia di golette.
Spicca una d'esse un volo senza rombo,
l'acque di piombo come alcione profugo
rade. Il sole s'immerge nelle nubi,
l'ora di febbre, trepida, si chiude.
Un glorioso affanno senza strepiti
ci batte in gola: nel meriggio afoso
spunta la barca di salvezza, è giunta:
vedila che sciaborda tra le secche,
esprime un suo burchiello che si volge
al docile frangente—e là ci attende.

Ah crisalide, com'è amara questa
tortura senza nome che ci volve
e ci porta lontani—e poi non restano
neppure le nostre orme sulla polvere;
e noi andremo innanzi senza smuovere
un sasso solo della gran muraglia;
e forse tutto è fisso, tutto è scritto,
e non vedremo sorgere per via
la libertà, il miracolo,
il fatto che non era necessario!

your face to the sky; this slow
staring around of eyes that now can see.

So the sureness of a moment passes
in a fluttering of curtains and trees
among the houses; but the opaque
shadow that reclaims you won't dissolve.
Then you seem, like me, to live
in the bleak limbo of maimed existences;
and even your rebirth is a barren secret,
a failed prodigy like all the others
flowering around us.

And the wave we see through the bars—
sometimes it speaks of salvation;
how nimbly illusion can arise
and release its mists.
They spiral out over the sea,
then gather on the horizon, shaped like schooners.
One of them takes off silently,
skimming the leaden waters like a gull
in flight. The sun hides in the clouds;
the shaky hour of fever ends.
A showy, soundless breathlessness
rises in our throats: in the hazy afternoon
the bark of salvation appears, is here:
see it awash among the shoals,
letting down a longboat
which makes for the gentle breakers—and awaits us there.

Ah chrysalis, how bitter
is this nameless torture that envelops us
and spirits us away—
till not even our footprints last in the dust;
and we'll go on, not having moved
a single stone in the great wall;
and maybe everything is fixed, is written,
and we'll never see it come our way:
freedom, the miracle, the act
that wasn't sheer necessity!

Nell'onda e nell'azzurro non è scia.
Sono mutati i segni della proda
dianzi raccolta come un dolce grembo.
Il silenzio ci chiude nel suo lembo
e le labbra non s'aprono per dire
il patto ch'io vorrei
stringere col destino: di scontare
la vostra gioia con la mia condanna.
È il voto che mi nasce ancora in petto,
poi finirà ogni moto. Penso allora
alle tacite offerte che sostengono
le case dei viventi; al cuore che abdica
perché rida un fanciullo inconsapevole;
al taglio netto che recide, al rogo
morente che s'avviva
d'un arido paletto, e ferve trepido.

No wake on the waves or in the sky.
The signs on the shore
that gathered in a gentle lap before
have altered. Silence wraps us in her shroud
and my lips won't open to speak
the pact I want to make
with destiny: to redeem
your joy through my condemning.
This is the hope that still lives in my heart;
after which all motion ceases.
And I think of the unspoken offerings that prop up
the houses of the living; of the heart that abdicates
so an unsuspecting child may laugh;
of the stroke that severs,
the dying fire that flares
on a dry stalk and, trembling, blazes.

Marezzo

Aggotti, e già la barca si sbilancia
e il cristallo dell'acque si smeriglia.
S'è usciti da una grotta a questa rancia
marina che uno zefiro scompiglia.

Non ci turba, come anzi, nell'oscuro,
lo sciame che il crepuscolo sparpaglia,
dei pipistrelli; e il remo che scandaglia
l'ombra non urta più il roccioso muro.

Fuori è il sole: s'arresta
nel suo giro e fiammeggia.
Il cavo cielo se ne illustra ed estua,
vetro che non si scheggia.

Un pescatore da un canotto fila
la sua lenza nella corrente.
Guarda il mondo del fondo che si profila
come sformato da una lente.

Nel guscio esiguo che sciaborda,
abbandonati i remi agli scalmi,
fa che ricordo non ti rimorda
che torbi questi meriggi calmi.

Ci chiudono d'attorno sciami e svoli,
è l'aria un'ala morbida.
Dispaiono: la troppa luce intorbida.
Si struggono i pensieri troppo soli.

Tutto fra poco si farà più ruvido,
fiorirà l'onda di più cupe strisce.
Ora resta così, sotto il diluvio
del sole che finisce.

Moiré

You bail, already the boat lists
and the water's crystal clouds.
We've come out of a grotto on
this copper water riffled by a breeze.

The swarm of bats that sunset scatters
doesn't worry us in the dark the way it did;
and the oar that sounds the shadow
no longer strikes the rocky wall.

Outside, the sun: it stands stock-still
and bursts into flames in its track.
The empty sky is lit by it and flares,
pane of glass that won't crack.

From a skiff a fisherman
lets down his line in the current.
He sees the world below defined
as if a lens deformed it.

In this frail shell the water laps,
oars abandoned in their locks,
let no memory eat at you
or cloud this tranquil afternoon.

Swarms and swoopings circle us,
the air is one soft wing.
They're gone: the excess of light stuns.
Too-lonely thoughts are fading.

Soon everything will turn more rough,
the waves making darker stripes.
Stay this way for now, in the rain
of the dying sun.

Un ondulamento sovverte
forme confini resi astratti:
ogni forza decisa già diverte
dal cammino. La vita cresce a scatti.

È come un falò senza fuoco
che si preparava per chiari segni:
in questo lume il nostro si fa fioco,
in questa vampa ardono volti e impegni.

Disciogli il cuore gonfio
nell'aprirsi dell'onda;
come una pietra di zavorra affonda
il tuo nome nell'acque con un tonfo!

Un astrale delirio si disfrena,
un male calmo e lucente.
Forse vedremo l'ora che rasserena
venirci incontro sulla spera ardente.

Digradano su noi pendici
di basse vigne, a piane.
Quivi stornellano spigolatrici
con voci disumane.

Oh la vendemmia estiva,
la stortura nel corso
delle stelle!—e da queste in noi deriva
uno stupore tinto di rimorso.

Parli e non riconosci i tuoi accenti.
La memoria ti appare dilavata.
Sei passata e pur senti
la tua vita consumata.

Ora, che avviene?, tu riprovi il peso
di te, improvvise gravano
sui cardini le cose che oscillavano,
e l'incanto è sospeso.

An undulation disassembles shapes,
edges go abstract:
every firm force has been derailed.
Life grows by fits and starts.

It's like a bonfire with no flame
that was built to make clear signs:
in this light our own goes dim,
this fire burns faces, plans.

Drop your swollen heart into
the wave that takes it in;
sink your name in water
with a splash, like a ballast-stone!

A delirium of stars breaks out,
a calm and gleaming evil.
Maybe we'll see the clearing hour
confront us on the burning mirror.

The tendrils of the low vines hang
down on us from the terraces.
There the gleaners sing their songs
with inhuman voices.

Oh, the summer harvesting,
the swerve in the stars' course—
and from them comes down to us
a stupor colored with remorse.

You speak but don't know your own voice.
Your memory seems washed away.
You were here and yet you feel
your life has been consumed.

And now? You feel your weight again,
and things that used to spin
suddenly sit on their pinions,
the spell's broken.

Ah qui restiamo, non siamo diversi.
Immobili così. Nessuno ascolta
la nostra voce più. Così sommersi
in un gorgo d'azzurro che s'infolta.

Ah, let's stay here, we're unchanged.
Still this way. No one hears us anymore,
drowned as we are
in an eddy of deepening blue.

Casa sul mare

Il viaggio finisce qui:
nelle cure meschine che dividono
l'anima che non sa più dare un grido.
Ora i minuti sono eguali e fissi
come i giri di ruota della pompa.
Un giro: un salir d'acqua che rimbomba.
Un altro, altr'acqua, a tratti un cigolio.

Il viaggio finisce a questa spiaggia
che tentano gli assidui e lenti flussi.
Nulla disvela se non pigri fumi
la marina che tramano di conche
i soffi leni: ed è raro che appaia
nella bonaccia muta
tra l'isole dell'aria migrabonde
la Corsica dorsuta o la Capraia.

Tu chiedi se così tutto vanisce
in questa poca nebbia di memorie;
se nell'ora che torpe o nel sospiro
del frangente si compie ogni destino.
Vorrei dirti che no, che ti s'appressa
l'ora che passerai di là dal tempo;
forse solo chi vuole s'infinita,
e questo tu potrai, chissà, non io.
Penso che per i più non sia salvezza,
ma taluno sovverta ogni disegno,
passi il varco, qual volle si ritrovi.
Vorrei prima di cedere segnarti
codesta via di fuga
labile come nei sommossi campi
del mare spuma o ruga.
Ti dono anche l'avara mia speranza.
A' nuovi giorni, stanco, non so crescerla:
l'offro in pegno al tuo fato, che ti scampi.

House by the Sea

The journey ends here:
in the petty worries that split
the heart that can't cry out anymore.
The minutes now are regular and fixed
like the revolutions of the pump.
One turn: water surfaces, resounds.
Another turn: more water, and some creaking.

The journey ends here, on this beach
worked by these assiduous, slow waves.
All the shoreline shows are sluggish mists
which the light breezes
weave into spirals:
and rarely in the still calm do you see
among the migrant islands of the air
spiny Corsica or Capraia.

You ask if everything dissolves like this
in a thin haze of memories,
if every destiny's fulfilled in this torpid hour
or the sigh of the breaker.
I'd like to say no, that the moment
when you'll pass out of time is rushing toward you;
maybe only those who want to become infinite,
and, who knows, you can do it; I cannot.
I think for most of us there's no salvation,
but there's someone who foils every plan,
crosses over, finds he's what he hoped for.
Before I abdicate I'd like
to show you this way out,
unstable as foam or a trough
in the troubled fields of the sea.
And I'm leaving you my miser's hope.
I'm too tired to grow it for the future;
I pledge it against your fate, so you'll escape.

Il cammino finisce a queste prode
che rode la marea col moto alterno.
Il tuo cuore vicino che non m'ode
salpa già forse per l'eterno.

The road ends on this shore
the tide gnaws with its come-and-go.
Maybe your nearby heart that doesn't hear me
already has set sail for the eternal.

I morti

Il mare che si frange sull'opposta
riva vi leva un nembo che spumeggia
finché la piana lo riassorbe. Quivi
gettammo un dì su la ferrigna costa,
ansante più del pelago la nostra
speranza!—e il gorgo sterile verdeggia
come ai dì che ci videro fra i vivi.

Or che aquilone spiana il groppo torbido
delle salse correnti e le rivolge
d'onde trassero, attorno alcuno appende
ai rami cedui reti dilunganti
sul viale che discende
oltre lo sguardo;
reti stinte che asciuga il tocco tardo
e freddo della luce; e sopra queste
denso il cristallo dell'azzurro palpebra
e precipita a un arco d'orizzonte
flagellato.
                    Più d'alga che trascini
il ribollio che a noi si scopre, muove
tale sosta la nostra vita: turbina
quanto in noi rassegnato a' suoi confini
risté un giorno; tra i fili che congiungono
un ramo all'altro si dibatte il cuore
come la gallinella
di mare che s'insacca tra le maglie;
e immobili e vaganti ci ritiene
una fissità gelida.
                    Così
forse anche ai morti è tolto ogni riposo
nelle zolle: una forza indi li tragge
spietata più del vivere, ed attorno,
larve rimorse dai ricordi umani,
li volge fino a queste spiagge, fiati
senza materia o voce

The Dead

The sea that founders on the other shore
sends up a cloud that foams until
the flats reabsorb it. There one day
onto the iron coast we heaved
our hope, more frantic than the ocean
—and the barren abyss turns green as in the days
that saw us among the living.

Now the north wind has calmed the muddied knot
of brackish currents and rerouted them
to where they started, someone hangs out nets
on the pruned branches—
faded nets that trail
onto the path that sinks from sight
and dry in the late, cold
touch of the light; and over them
the dense blue crystal blinks
and plunges to a curve of flayed
horizon.
      More than seaweed sucked
into the seething being revealed to us, our life
is rousing from such torpor;
the part of us that stalled one day,
resigned to limits, rages; the heart flails
in the lines binding one branch
to another, like the water hen
bagged in the meshes;
and a cold deadlock holds us
static and drifting.
      So, too, perhaps
the dead are denied all rest in the soil:
a power more ruthless than life itself
pulls them away and, all around,
drives them to these beaches,
shades gnawed by human memory,
breaths without body or voice

traditi dalla tenebra; ed i mozzi
loro voli ci sfiorano pur ora
da noi divisi appena e nel crivello
del mare si sommergono . . .

expelled from the dark;
and their broken flights,
still barely shorn from us, graze us
and in the sieve of the sea they drown . . .

Delta

La vita che si rompe nei travasi
secreti a te ho legata:
quella che si dibatte in sé e par quasi
non ti sappia, presenza soffocata.

Quando il tempo s'ingorga alle sue dighe
la tua vicenda accordi alla sua immensa,
ed affiori, memoria, più palese
dall'oscura regione ove scendevi,
come ora, al dopopioggia, si riaddensa
il verde ai rami, ai muri il cinabrese.

Tutto ignoro di te fuor del messaggio
muto che mi sostenta sulla via:
se forma esisti o ubbia nella fumea
d'un sogno t'alimenta
la riviera che infebbra, torba, e scroscia
incontro alla marea.

Nulla di te nel vacillar dell'ore
bige o squarciate da un vampo di solfo
fuori che il fischio del rimorchiatore
che dalle brume approda al golfo.

Delta

The life that breaks apart
in secret streams I've linked with you:
that argues with itself and almost
seems not to know you, suffocated presence.

When time overflows its dikes
you rhyme your fate with her immensity,
and surface, memory, more manifest
out of the darkness you descended to,
as now, after rain, green comes back strong
on branches and the cinnabar reddens the walls.

I know nothing of you but the wordless
message that sustains me on my way:
if you exist as form or a mirage
in the haze of a dream
fed by the shore as it rages, eddies, roars
against the tide.

Nothing of you in the flux of hours,
gray or rent by a sulphur flash,
other than the whistle of the tugboat
leaving the mist and making for the gulf.

Incontro

Tu non m'abbandonare mia tristezza
sulla strada
che urta il vento forano
co' suoi vortici caldi, e spare; cara
tristezza al soffio che si estenua: e a questo,
sospinta sulla rada
dove l'ultime voci il giorno esala
viaggia una nebbia, alta si flette un'ala
di cormorano.

La foce è allato del torrente, sterile
d'acque, vivo di pietre e di calcine;
ma più foce di umani atti consunti,
d'impallidite vite tramontanti
oltre il confine
che a cerchio ci rinchiude: visi emunti,
mani scarne, cavalli in fila, ruote
stridule: vite no: vegetazioni
dell'altro mare che sovrasta il flutto.

Si va sulla carraia di rappresa
mota senza uno scarto,
simili ad incappati di corteo,
sotto la volta infranta ch'è discesa
quasi a specchio delle vetrine,
in un'aura che avvolge i nostri passi
fitta e uguaglia i sargassi
umani fluttuanti alle cortine
dei bambù mormoranti.

Se mi lasci anche tu, tristezza, solo
presagio vivo in questo nembo, sembra
che attorno mi si effonda
un ronzio qual di sfere quando un'ora
sta per scoccare;
e cado inerte nell'attesa spenta

Encounter

My sadness, don't desert me
on this street
lashed by the offshore wind's
hot eddies till it dies; beloved
sadness in the gust that fades: and wafted
toward it over the moorings
where day exhales its last voices
a mist sails, a cormorant's
wing beats above.

Beside us is the rivermouth,
waterless, but alive with rocks and lime;
but more a mouth of withered human acts,
of wan lives setting over the horizon
that locks us in a circle:
ravaged faces, raw hands, files
of horses, screaming wheels:
not lives: vegetation
of the other sea that rides the waves.

We travel on a roadway of dried
mud, no deviation,
like hooded figures in a cortege,
under the shattered vault that fell
to mirror the windows,
in a dense fog that shrouds our steps
and makes the swaying human
seaweed seem
like curtains of murmuring bamboo.

If you too leave me, sadness,
my one live omen in this haze,
a whirring spreads around me,
like clockworks when the hour's
about to strike;
and I go lifeless, waiting listlessly,

di chi non sa temere
su questa proda che ha sorpresa l'onda
lenta, che non appare.

Forse riavrò un aspetto: nella luce
radente un moto mi conduce accanto
a una misera fronda che in un vaso
s'alleva s'una porta di osteria.
A lei tendo la mano, e farsi mia
un'altra vita sento, ingombro d'una
forma che mi fu tolta; e quasi anelli
alle dita non foglie mi si attorcono
ma capelli.

Poi più nulla. Oh sommersa!: tu dispari
qual sei venuta, e nulla so di te.
La tua vita è ancor tua: tra i guizzi rari
dal giorno sparsa già. Prega per me
allora ch'io discenda altro cammino
che una via di città,
nell'aria persa, innanzi al brulichio
dei vivi; ch'io ti senta accanto; ch'io
scenda senza viltà.

for the one incapable of fear
on this shore surprised
by the slow tide, who won't appear.

Maybe I'll find a face again:
in the glancing light a movement leads me
to a sad bough craning from a jar
by a tavern door.
I reach for it, and feel
another life becoming mine, encumbered
with a form that was taken from me;
and it's hair, not leaves, that winds
round my fingers like rings.

Then nothing more. Drowned one, you disappear
the way you came and I know nothing of you.
Your life is still your own: already scattered
amid the day's few glimmers. Pray for me now
that I may come down by another route
than a city street
in the brown air, ahead of the press
of the living; and may I feel you with me, may I
come without cowardice.

RIVIERE

SEACOASTS

Riviere,
bastano pochi stocchi d'erbaspada
penduli da un ciglione
sul delirio del mare;
o due camelie pallide
nei giardini deserti,
e un eucalipto biondo che si tuffi
tra sfrusci e pazzi voli
nella luce;
ed ecco che in un attimo
invisibili fili a me si asserpano,
farfalla in una ragna
di fremiti d'olivi, di sguardi di girasoli.

Dolce cattività, oggi, riviere
di chi s'arrende per poco
come a rivivere un antico giuoco
non mai dimenticato.
Rammento l'acre filtro che porgeste
allo smarrito adolescente, o rive:
nelle chiare mattine si fondevano
dorsi di colli e cielo; sulla rena
dei lidi era un risucchio ampio, un eguale
fremer di vite,
una febbre del mondo; ed ogni cosa
in se stessa pareva consumarsi.

Oh allora sballottati
come l'osso di seppia dalle ondate
svanire a poco a poco;
diventare
un albero rugoso od una pietra
levigata dal mare; nei colori
fondersi dei tramonti; sparir carne
per spicciare sorgente ebbra di sole,
dal sole divorata . . .

Seacoasts,
a few blades of sword grass are enough,
clinging to a cliff
above the frenzied sea;
or a pair of pale camellias
in the empty gardens,
and a blond eucalyptus that dips
amid rustlings and wild flights
into the light;
and suddenly
invisible lines snake round me,
butterfly in a net
of shuddering olive trees and staring sunflowers.

Seacoasts, sweet captivity today
for the man who almost surrenders
as if reliving an old
but unforgotten game.
I remember the bitter dose you offered
to a lost adolescent, coasts:
the hills in the bright mornings
melted into the sky; a heavy
undertow sucked at the beaches
and a like tremor of lives,
a fever of the world; and every thing
seemed consumed by itself.

Oh, tumbled then
like the cuttlefish bone by the waves,
to vanish bit by bit;
to become
a gnarled tree or a stone
smoothed by the sea; to blend
with the sunset's colors; deliquesce as flesh
and re-emerge a spring drunk with the sun,
drunk by the sun . . .

        Erano questi,
riviere, i voti del fanciullo antico
che accanto ad una rósa balaustrata
lentamente moriva sorridendo.

Quanto, marine, queste fredde luci
parlano a chi straziato vi fuggiva.
Lame d'acqua scoprentisi tra varchi
di labili ramure; rocce brune
tra spumeggi; frecciare di rondoni
vagabondi . . .
            Ah, potevo
credervi un giorno o terre,
bellezze funerarie, auree cornici
all'agonia d'ogni essere.
                Oggi torno
a voi più forte, o è inganno, ben che il cuore
par sciogliersi in ricordi lieti—e atroci.
Triste anima passata
e tu volontà nuova che mi chiami,
tempo è forse d'unirvi
in un porto sereno di saggezza.
Ed un giorno sarà ancora l'invito
di voci d'oro, di lusinghe audaci,
anima mia non più divisa. Pensa:
cangiare in inno l'elegia; rifarsi;
non mancar più.
            Potere
simili a questi rami
ieri scarniti e nudi ed oggi pieni
di fremiti e di linfe,
sentire
noi pur domani tra i profumi e i venti
un riaffluir di sogni, un urger folle
di voci verso un esito; e nel sole
che v'investe, riviere,
rifiorire!

These, coasts,
were the hopes of the age-old boy
who stood at a rusted balustrade
and, smiling, slowly died.

Shores, how much these cold lights say
to the tormented one who fled from you.
Blades of water glimpsed between the arcs
of shifting branches; rocks brown in the foam;
arrows of roving
swifts . . .
O lands,
if I could trust in you one day,
funeral trappings, gilded frames
for the agony of every being.
Now I return to you
stronger (or deluded) though the heart
seems to dissolve in glad—and savage—memories.
Sad spirit of the past
and you, new will that calls me,
perhaps it's time to unite you
in a calm harbor of wisdom.
And one day we'll hear the call again
of golden voices, bold enticements,
no more divided soul. Think:
to make the elegy a hymn; to be reborn;
to want no more.
To be able
like these branches,
yesterday rude and bare, alive today
with quivering and sap,
for us too to feel
among tomorrow's fragrances and winds
a rising tide of dreams, a frenzied rush
of voices toward an outcome; and in the sun
that swathes you, coasts,
to flower again!

LE OCCASIONI

1928 – 1939

a I.B.

THE OCCASIONS

(1 9 2 8 – 1 9 3 9)

to I.B.

Il balcone

Pareva facile giuoco
mutare in nulla lo spazio
che m'era aperto, in un tedio
malcerto il certo tuo fuoco.

Ora a quel vuoto ho congiunto
ogni mio tardo motivo,
sull'arduo nulla si spunta
l'ansia di attenderti vivo.

La vita che dà barlumi
è quella che sola tu scorgi.
A lei ti sporgi da questa
finestra che non s'illumina.

The Balcony

It seemed simple to make nothing from
the space that had opened for me,
to forge uncertain tedium
from your sure fire.

Now to that emptiness I bring
my every belated motive.
The sheer void stirs with the anguish
of awaiting you while I live.

The life that glimmers is
the one only you see.
You lean toward it
from this unlighted window.

PARTE I

PART I

Vecchi versi

Ricordo la farfalla ch'era entrata
dai vetri schiusi nella sera fumida
su la costa raccolta, dilavata
dal trascorrere iroso delle spume.
Muoveva tutta l'aria del crepuscolo a un fioco
occiduo palpebrare della traccia
che divide acqua e terra; ed il punto atono
del faro che baluginava sulla
roccia del Tino, cerula, tre volte
si dilatò e si spense in un altro oro.

Mia madre stava accanto a me seduta
presso il tavolo ingombro dalle carte
da giuoco alzate a due per volta come
attendamenti nani pei soldati
dei nipoti sbandati già dal sonno.
Si schiodava dall'alto impetuoso
un nembo d'aria diaccia, diluviava
sul nido di Corniglia rugginoso.
Poi fu l'oscurità piena, e dal mare
un rombo basso e assiduo come un lungo
regolato concerto, ed il gonfiare
d'un pallore ondulante oltre la siepe
cimata dei pitòsfori. Nel breve
vano della mia stanza, ove la lampada
tremava dentro una ragnata fucsia,
penetrò la farfalla, al paralume
giunse e le conterie che l'avvolgevano
segnando i muri di riflessi ombrati
eguali come fregi si sconvolsero
e sullo scialbo corse alle pareti
un fascio semovente di fili esili.

Era un insetto orribile dal becco
aguzzo, gli occhi avvolti come d'una
rossastra fotosfera, al dosso il teschio

Old Lines

I remember the moth that flew in
through the open window in the haze of evening
on that lost coast, eroded by
the mad washboarding of the foam.
All the twilit air was moving
in a dark westward pulsing of the line
dividing land and water;
and the faint beacon of the lighthouse
that blinked on the cerulean rock of Tino
swelled three times, to die in another gold.

My mother sat beside me at the table
cluttered with cards
propped up in pairs as tents
for the tin soldiers of her grandsons
already cashiered by sleep.
A cloud of freezing air unhooked itself
from the impetuous mountaintop
and rained down on Corniglia's rusty nest.
Then total darkness,
and from the sea a low, unending roar
like a long, cautious concert
while a wavering paleness swelled
beyond the hedge topped by pittosporums.
The moth entered the small space
of my bedroom where the bulb
shimmered under a fuchsia
net; it hit the lampshade
fringed with beads,
etching shadows on the room like friezes,
and self-propelling bursts of little lines
flew across the wanness to the walls.

It was a hideous bug with a sharp
beak, eyes ringed as if by reddish
photospheres, and a man's skull on its back;

umano; e attorno dava se una mano
tentava di ghermirlo un acre sibilo
che agghiacciava.

Batté più volte sordo sulla tavola,
sui vetri ribatté chiusi dal vento,
e da sé ritrovò la via dell'aria,
si perse nelle tenebre. Dal porto
di Vernazza le luci erano a tratti
scancellate dal crescere dell'onde
invisibili al fondo della notte.

Poi tornò la farfalla dentro il nicchio
che chiudeva la lampada, discese
sui giornali del tavolo, scrollò
pazza aliando le carte—
                              e fu per sempre
con le cose che chiudono in un giro
sicuro come il giorno, e la memoria
in sé le cresce, sole vive d'una
vita che disparì sotterra: insieme
coi volti familiari che oggi sperde
non più il sonno ma un'altra noia; accanto
ai muri antichi, ai lidi, alla tartana
che imbarcava
tronchi di pino a riva ad ogni mese,
al segno del torrente che discende
ancora al mare e la sua via si scava.

and if you tried to grab it,
it made an acrid,
petrifying hiss.

It hit the table dully several times,
struck the windows that the wind had shut,
then found the airway by itself
and was lost to the dark.
At times the lights from Vernazza's port
were erased by invisible waves that rose up
deep in the night.

Then the moth was back
under the lamp's skullcap;
it landed on the papers on the table,
shook insanely, knocking down the cards—

                                      and became
one of those things immured forever
in a closed circle like the day,
and they're magnified in memory,
for they only live a life
gone underground: along with the familiar faces
that not sleep but another boredom
scatters today; with the old walls, the beaches,
the tartan that took on pine logs
at the landing every month,
and the sign of the stream that still carves its way
as it falls to the sea.

Buffalo

Un dolce inferno a raffiche addensava
nell'ansa risonante di megafoni
turbe d'ogni colore. Si vuotavano
a fiotti nella sera gli autocarri.
Vaporava fumosa una calura
sul golfo brulicante; in basso un arco
lucido figurava una corrente
e la folla era pronta al varco. Un negro
sonnecchiava in un fascio luminoso
che tagliava la tenebra; da un palco
attendevano donne ilari e molli
l'approdo d'una zattera. Mi dissi:
Buffalo!—e il nome agì.
                             Precipitavo
nel limbo dove assordano le voci
del sangue e i guizzi incendiano la vista
come lampi di specchi.
Udii gli schianti secchi, vidi attorno
curve schiene striate mulinanti
nella pista.

Buffalo

A sweet inferno, gusting, funneled
crowds of every color in the oval
echoing with megaphones. The buses
emptied out in waves into the evening.
The heat evaporated into smoke
above the seething gulf: a shining
arc inscribed a current down below
and the crowd was ready at the crossing.
A black man dozed inside a beam of light
that sliced the shadows: in a box
breezy, easy women waited
for a ferry to arrive. I whispered:
Buffalo! —and the name took.
                              I plummeted
into the limbo where the voices of the blood
are deafening and gleaming burns the sight
like mirror flashes.
I heard the dry whip crack and everywhere
saw striped backs, bent and churning
on the track.

Keepsake

Fanfan ritorna vincitore; Molly
si vende all'asta: frigge un riflettore.
Surcouf percorre a grandi passi il cassero,
Gaspard conta denari nel suo buco.
Nel pomeriggio limpido è discesa
la neve, la Cicala torna al nido.
Fatinitza agonizza in una piega
di memoria, di Tonio resta un grido.
Falsi spagnoli giocano al castello
i Briganti; ma squilla in una tasca
la sveglia spaventosa.
Il Marchese del Grillo è rispedito
nella strada; infelice Zeffirino
torna commesso; s'alza lo Speziale
e i fulminanti sparano sull'impiantito.
I Moschettieri lasciano il convento,
Van Schlisch corre in arcioni, Takimini
si sventola, la Bambola è caricata.
(Imary torna nel suo appartamento).
Larivaudière magnetico, Pitou
giacciono di traverso. Venerdì
sogna l'isole verdi e non danza più.

Keepsake

Fanfan returns the victor; Molly's sold
at auction: a reflector fries.
Surcouf strides the quarterdeck,
Gaspard counts his money in his hole.
Snow fell in the limpid afternoon,
the Cicada flies back to his nest.
Fatinitza agonizes in a lapse of memory,
a shout is all that's left of Tonio.
False Spaniards play *The Brigands*
at the castle; but the bloodcurdling
alarm squeals in a pocket.
The Marchese del Grillo's sent
into the street again; unhappy Zeffirino
returns a clerk; the Druggist stands,
and the matches strike on the floor.
The Musketeers desert the convent,
Van Schlisch hurries to his horse,
Takimini fans herself, the Doll gets wound.
(Imary goes back to his apartment.)
Thrilling La Rivaudière and Pitou
lie askance. Friday dreams
of his green islands and won't dance.

Lindau

La rondine vi porta
fili d'erba, non vuole che la vita passi.
Ma tra gli argini, a notte, l'acqua morta
logora i sassi.
Sotto le torce fumicose sbanda
sempre qualche ombra sulle prode vuote.
Nel cerchio della piazza una sarabanda
s'agita al mugghio dei battelli a ruote.

Lindau

The swallow brings back blades of grass,
not wanting life to go.
But at night, between the banks, the stagnant
water wears down the stones.
Under the smoking torches a few shadows
still float off across the empty sand.
In the open square, a saraband
churns to the lowing of the paddleboats.

Bagni di Lucca

Fra il tonfo dei marroni
e il gemito del torrente
che uniscono i loro suoni
èsita il cuore.

Precoce inverno che borea
abbrividisce. M'affaccio
sul ciglio che scioglie l'albore
del giorno nel ghiaccio.

Marmi, rameggi—
               e ad uno scrollo giù
foglie a èlice, a freccia,
nel fossato.

Passa l'ultima greggia nella nebbia
del suo fiato.

Bagni di Lucca

Amid the blending
sounds of chestnuts thudding
and the stream that moans
the heart hesitates.

Early winter the north wind
sets shivering. I look out
over the edge dissolving
the dawn white in ice.

Marble, branches—
                  with a shake
leaves eddy, arrow down
into the ditch.

The last herd passes
in the mist of its breath.

Cave d'autunno

su cui discende la primavera lunare
e nimba di candore ogni frastaglio,
schianti di pigne, abbaglio
di reti stese e schegge,

ritornerà ritornerà sul gelo
la bontà d'una mano,
varcherà il cielo lontano
la ciurma luminosa che ci saccheggia.

Autumn Quarries

where the moonlit spring descends,
haloing every notch and knob with brightness:
dropping pinecones, dazzle
of hung nets and shards;

the kindness of a hand will come
again, come over the chill,
into the distant sky the shining swarm
will pass that plunders us.

Altro effetto di luna

La trama del carrubo che si profila
nuda contro l'azzurro sonnolento,
il suono delle voci, la trafila
delle dita d'argento sulle soglie,

la piuma che s'invischia, un trepestìo
sul molo che si scioglie
e la feluca già ripiega il volo
con le vele dimesse come spoglie.

Another Moon Effect

The carob's mare's-nest that stands stark
against the drowsy blue,
voices, silver fingers
tracing the sills,

the snagged feather, a stampede
on the pier that falls away,
and the felucca comes about,
sails puffed like shedding skins.

Verso Vienna

Il convento barocco
di schiuma e di biscotto
adombrava uno scorcio d'acque lente
e tavole imbandite, qua e là sparse
di foglie e zenzero.

Emerse un nuotatore, sgrondò sotto
una nube di moscerini,
chiese del nostro viaggio,
parlò a lungo del suo d'oltre confine.

Additò il ponte in faccia che si passa
(informò) con un soldo di pedaggio.
Salutò con la mano, sprofondò,
fu la corrente stessa . . .
                Ed al suo posto,
battistrada balzò da una rimessa
un bassotto festoso che latrava,

fraterna unica voce dentro l'afa.

Near Vienna

The baroque convent
foam and biscuit
shaded a brief moment of slow water
and set tables, scattered here and there
with leaves and ginger.

A swimmer emerged, dripping
under a cloud of gnats, inquired
about our journey, going on
about his own across the border.

He pointed to the bridge in front of us
that costs (he said) a penny to cross over.
He waved, dove in again, became
the river . . .
       And, in his stead
a happy dachshund, our pacesetter,
bounded barking out of a garage,

the one fraternal voice inside the heat.

Carnevale di Gerti

Se la ruota s'impiglia nel groviglio
delle stelle filanti ed il cavallo
s'impenna tra la calca, se ti nevica
sui capelli e le mani un lungo brivido
d'iridi trascorrenti o alzano i bimbi
le flebili ocarine che salutano
il tuo viaggio ed i lievi echi si sfaldano
giù dal ponte sul fiume,
se si sfolla la strada e ti conduce
in un mondo soffiato entro una tremula
bolla d'aria e di luce dove il sole
saluta la tua grazia—hai ritrovato
forse la strada che tentò un istante
il piombo fuso a mezzanotte quando
finì l'anno tranquillo senza spari.

Ed ora vuoi sostare dove un filtro
fa spogli i suoni
e ne deriva i sorridenti ed acri
fumi che ti compongono il domani:
ora chiedi il paese dove gli onagri
mordano quadri di zucchero alle tue mani
e i tozzi alberi spuntino germogli
miracolosi al becco dei pavoni.

(Oh il tuo Carnevale sarà più triste
stanotte anche del mio, chiusa fra i doni
tu per gli assenti: carri dalle tinte
di rosolio, fantocci ed archibugi,
palle di gomma, arnesi da cucina
lillipuziani: l'urna li segnava
a ognuno dei lontani amici l'ora
che il Gennaio si schiuse e nel silenzio
si compì il sortilegio. È Carnevale
o il Dicembre s'indugia ancora? Penso
che se tu muovi la lancetta al piccolo

Gerti's Carnival

If your wheel gets snared in tangled
shooting stars and the stallion
rears in the crowd, if a long
shiver of pale confetti falls like snow
on your hair and hands, or children raise
their plaintive ocarinas to salute
your passing, and faint echoes
scale down from the bridge onto the river;
if the street empties, leading you
to a world blown inside a trembling bubble
of air and light where the sun salutes your grace—
it may be you've found the way,
the avenue a piece of melted lead
suggested for a moment on that midnight
when a calm year ended without gunfire.

And now you want to stay on
where a filter muffles the noise,
distilling the bright and bitter mists
that make up your tomorrow;
now you want the land where onagers
nuzzle sugar cubes in your hand
and stunted trees sport magic seeds
that sprout in the peacocks' beaks.

(Oh tonight your Carnival will be
sadder still than mine, shut in as you are
with your gifts for the missing:
rosolio-colored wagons, puppets,
harquebuses, rubber balls,
Lilliputian kitchen tools:
the urn assigned one to each absent friend
the moment January was unmasked
and the prophecy silently fulfilled.
Is it Carnival, or still December?
If you move the hands on the little watch

orologio che rechi al polso, tutto
arretrerà dentro un disfatto prisma
babelico di forme e di colori . . .).

E il Natale verrà e il giorno dell'Anno
che sfolla le caserme e ti riporta
gli amici spersi, e questo Carnevale
pur esso tornerà che ora ci sfugge
tra i muri che si fendono già. Chiedi
tu di fermare il tempo sul paese
che attorno si dilata? Le grandi ali
screziate ti sfiorano, le logge
sospingono all'aperto esili bambole
bionde, vive, le pale dei mulini
rotano fisse sulle pozze garrule.
Chiedi di trattenere le campane
d'argento sopra il borgo e il suono rauco
delle colombe? Chiedi tu i mattini
trepidi delle tue prode lontane?

Come tutto si fa strano e difficile,
come tutto è impossibile, tu dici.
La tua vita è quaggiù dove rimbombano
le ruote dei carriaggi senza posa
e nulla torna se non forse in questi
disguidi del possibile. Ritorna
là fra i morti balocchi ove è negato
pur morire; e col tempo che ti batte
al polso e all'esistenza ti ridona,
tra le mura pesanti che non s'aprono
al gorgo degli umani affaticato,
torna alla via dove con te intristisco,
quella che additò un piombo raggelato
alle mie, alle tue sere:
torna alle primavere che non fioriscono.

you wear, I think that everything
will run backwards, in a dissolving Babel-
like prism of shapes and colors . . .).

And Christmas will come, and New Year's Day
that empties the barracks and brings you
your scattered friends, even this Carnival
escaping now through these already cracking walls
will come back, too.
Do you want to call a halt to time
over the landscape that unfolds around you?
Its great mottled wings are grazing you,
the porches dangle living dolls—slender, blond—
in the open air; the millwheel paddles
churn on in the babbling ponds.
Do you want to still the silver bells
over the village, and the raucous
cooing of the doves? Do you want
the anxious mornings of your distant shores?

How everything turns strange and difficult,
everything's impossible, you say.
Your life is here below, where carriage wheels
rumble ceaselessly and nothing
adds up except, perhaps, in these
derangings of what's possible. Return
among the dead toys where death itself is denied;
and with the time that beats at your wrist
and gives you back to being, inside the heavy
walls that won't open to the exhausted
gorgon of humanity, come again
to the street where I lament with you,
the one a hardened piece of lead
predicted for your evenings, and mine;
come back to the springs that aren't flowering.

Verso Capua

. . . rotto il colmo sull'ansa, con un salto,
il Volturno calò, giallo, la sua
piena tra gli scopeti, la disperse
nelle crete. Laggiù si profilava
mobile sulle siepi un postiglione,
e apparì su cavalli,
in una scia di polvere e sonagli.
Si arrestò pochi istanti, l'equipaggio
dava scosse, d'attorno volitavano
farfalle minutissime. Un furtivo
raggio incendiò di colpo il sughereto
scotennato, a fatica ripartiva
la vettura: e tu in fondo che agitavi
lungamente una sciarpa, la bandiera
stellata!, e il fiume ingordo s'insabbiava.

Near Capua

. . . its yellow floodtide cresting at the bend,
the Volturno plunged and dropped
into the heath, dissolving in the clay.
Down below, in profile, a postilion
cantered above the hedgerows,
then he appeared with horses,
trailing harness bells and dust.
He halted for a bit, the equipage
shook, aswarm with tiny butterflies.
Then a sudden surreptitious ray
lit the flayed cork forest,
the carriage groaned and started up again:
and inside, you kept waving
your scarf, your spangled banner!
while the gorging river sank in sand.

A Liuba che parte

Non il grillo ma il gatto
del focolare
or ti consiglia, splendido
lare della dispersa tua famiglia.
La casa che tu rechi
con te ravvolta, gabbia o cappelliera?,
sovrasta i ciechi tempi come il flutto
arca leggera—e basta al tuo riscatto.

To Liuba, Leaving

Not the cricket but the cat
at hearthside, many-splendored
lar of your scattered clan,
counsels you now.
The house you carry, cage or hat-
box?, rides these blind days
the way a buoyant ark
rides out the flood—and is enough to save you.

Bibe a Ponte all'Asse

Bibe, ospite lieve, la bruna tua reginetta di Saba
mesce sorrisi e Rùfina di quattordici gradi.

Si vede in basso rilucere la terra fra gli àceri radi
e un bimbo curva la canna sul gomito della Greve.

Bibe a Ponte all'Asse

Bibe, easy host, your brown-haired little Queen of Sheba
serves up smiles and high-test Rufina.

Below, one sees the earth shine through the slender maples
and a youngster bends his pole above the Greve's elbow.

Dora Markus

I

Fu dove il ponte di legno
mette a Porto Corsini sul mare alto
e rari uomini, quasi immoti, affondano
o salpano le reti. Con un segno
della mano additavi all'altra sponda
invisibile la tua patria vera.
Poi seguimmo il canale fino alla darsena
della città, lucida di fuliggine,
nella bassura dove s'affondava
una primavera inerte, senza memoria.

E qui dove un'antica vita
si screzia in una dolce
ansietà d'Oriente,
le tue parole iridavano come le scaglie
della triglia moribonda.

La tua irrequietudine mi fa pensare
agli uccelli di passo che urtano ai fari
nelle sere tempestose:
è una tempesta anche la tua dolcezza,
turbina e non appare,
e i suoi riposi sono anche più rari.
Non so come stremata tu resisti
in questo lago
d'indifferenza ch'è il tuo cuore; forse
ti salva un amuleto che tu tieni
vicino alla matita delle labbra,
al piumino, alla lima: un topo bianco,
d'avorio; e così esisti!

Dora Markus

I

It was where the wooden bridge
spans the high tide at Porto Corsini
and a few men, almost motionless,
sink or haul in their nets.
With the flourish of a hand you signaled
your true country on the other, invisible shore.
Then we followed the canal
to the city dock, slick with soot,
in the lowland where a listless spring,
devoid of memory, was sinking.

And here, where an ancient life
diffracts in a gentle
Oriental anxiousness,
your words were iridescent like the scales
of a dying mullet.

Your restlessness reminds me
of those migrant birds that hurl themselves
at lighthouse beams on stormy nights:
your sweetness is a storm as well,
that clouds up and won't show itself;
its periods of rest are rarer still.
I don't know how
you hold on, spent,
in the lake of indifference your heart is:
maybe what saves you is an amulet
you keep with your lipstick, powder, file:
a white ivory
mouse; and so you live!

II

Ormai nella tua Carinzia
di mirti fioriti e di stagni,
china sul bordo sorvegli
la carpa che timida abbocca
o segui sui tigli, tra gl'irti
pinnacoli le accensioni
del vespro e nell'acque un avvampo
di tende da scali e pensioni.

La sera che si protende
sull'umida conca non porta
col palpito dei motori
che gemiti d'oche e un interno
di nivee maioliche dice
allo specchio annerito che ti vide
diversa una storia di errori
imperturbati e la incide
dove la spugna non giunge.

La tua leggenda, Dora!
Ma è scritta già in quegli sguardi
di uomini che hanno fedine
altere e deboli in grandi
ritratti d'oro e ritorna
ad ogni accordo che esprime
l'armonica guasta nell'ora
che abbuia, sempre più tardi.

È scritta là. Il sempreverde
alloro per la cucina
resiste, la voce non muta,
Ravenna è lontana, distilla
veleno una fede feroce.
Che vuole da te? Non si cede
voce, leggenda o destino . . .
Ma è tardi, sempre più tardi.

II

Now in your Carinthia
of flowering myrtle and ponds,
you lean at the rim and watch
the timid carp gasp, or follow
over the lime trees and steep
eaves dusk lighting up,
and on the water a flaring
of curtains from pensions and docks.

The evening that stretches out
on the wet bay only brings
the wail of geese with the motors' throb
and a snow-white majolica
interior tells the darkening
mirror that sees you different
a tale of unperturbed
wandering, etching it
where the eraser can't reach.

Your legend, Dora!
but it's written already
in the stares of men with proud,
thin whiskers in heavy gold frames,
and echoes in every
chord the broken
spinet emits as night falls,
later every evening.

It's written there. The evergreen
laurel for the kitchen lasts,
the voice won't change, Ravenna's far,
a savage faith distills its venom.
What does it want from you?
Voice, legend, destiny—
nothing's surrendered . . .
But it's late, always later.

Alla maniera di Filippo De Pisis
nell'inviargli questo libro

. . . *l'Arno balsamo fino*
—LAPO GIANNI

Una botta di stocco nel zig zag
del beccaccino—
e si librano piume su uno scrìmolo.

(Poi discendono là, fra sgorbiature
di rami, al freddo balsamo del fiume).

In the Style of Filippo De Pisis, on Sending Him This Book

. . . l'Arno balsamo fino
—LAPO GIANNI

A sharp shot at the zig-
zag snipe—
and feathers teeter on a brink.

(Then they descend, amid sketched
branches, to the cold balm of the stream.)

Nel Parco di Caserta

Dove il cigno crudele
si liscia e si contorce,
sul pelo dello stagno, tra il fogliame,
si risveglia una sfera, dieci sfere,
una torcia dal fondo, dieci torce,

—e un sole si bilancia
a stento nella prim'aria,
su domi verdicupi e globi a sghembo
d'araucaria,

che scioglie come liane
braccia di pietra, allaccia
senza tregua chi passa
e ne sfila dal punto più remoto
radici e stame.

Le nòcche delle Madri s'inaspriscono,
cercano il vuoto.

In the Park at Caserta

Where the cruel swan
preens and bends
on the surface of the pond,
among the leaves a sphere revives, ten spheres,
a torch out of the water, then ten torches

—and a sun wobbles,
unsure in new air,
over deep green domes and slanting globes
of monkey-puzzle trees,

shattering arms
of stone like creeper vines,
clutching whoever passes with no mercy,
ripping out roots and stamens
all the way down.

The Mothers' knuckles roughen,
tapping for the void.

Accelerato

Fu così, com'è il brivido
pungente che trascorre
i sobborghi e solleva
alle aste delle torri
la cenere del giorno,
com'è il soffio
piovorno che ripete
tra le sbarre l'assalto
ai salici reclini—
fu così e fu tumulto nella dura
oscurità che rompe
qualche foro d'azzurro finché lenta
appaia la ninfale
Entella che sommessa
rifluisce dai cieli dell'infanzia
oltre il futuro—
poi vennero altri liti, mutò il vento,
crebbe il bucato ai fili, uomini ancora
uscirono all'aperto, nuovi nidi
turbarono le gronde—
fu così,
rispondi?

Local Train

It was like this, like the biting
shudder that ruffles the suburbs
and lifts the day's ash up
to the flags on the towers,
like the rain-drenched
wind through the bars
that has at the prostrate
willows over and over—
it was like this, an uproar
in the hard dark
cut by a few
blue slits
till gently the nymph
Entella appears,
meekly flowing back from childhood's
skies beyond the future—
then came other shores,
another wind,
wash grew on lines,
men ventured out again,
new nests tormented the eaves—
like this, you say?

PARTE II

MOTTETTI

Sobre el volcán la flor.
— G. A. BÉCQUER

PART II

MOTETS

Sobre el volcán la flor.
— G. A. BÉCQUER

Lo sai: debbo riperderti e non posso.
Come un tiro aggiustato mi sommuove
ogni opera, ogni grido e anche lo spiro
salino che straripa
dai moli e fa l'oscura primavera
di Sottoripa.

Paese di ferrame e alberature
a selva nella polvere del vespro.
Un ronzìo lungo viene dall'aperto,
strazia com'unghia ai vetri. Cerco il segno
smarrito, il pegno solo ch'ebbi in grazia
da te.
        E l'inferno è certo.

Molti anni, e uno più duro sopra il lago
straniero su cui ardono i tramonti.
Poi scendesti dai monti a riportarmi
San Giorgio e il Drago.

Imprimerli potessi sul palvese
che s'agita alla frusta del grecale
in cuore . . . E per te scendere in un gorgo
di fedeltà, immortale.

You know: I'm going to lose you again
and I can't. Each action, every shout
jars me like a perfect shot,
even the salt breeze that floods the wharves,
and breeds the lightless spring
of Sottoripa.

Land of ironwork and mast-
forests in the evening dust.
A long drone enters from outside,
torments like a fingernail on glass.
I'm after the lost sign, the single
pledge I had from you.
                              And hell is certain.

Many years, and one still harder
above the foreign lake the sunsets burn on.
Then you came down from the mountains to bring me
Saint George and the Dragon.

If only I could print them on the banner
that dances to the whiplash of the heart's
east wind . . . And for you descend
in a maelstrom of undying faithfulness.

Brina sui vetri; uniti
sempre e sempre in disparte
gl'infermi; e sopra i tavoli
i lunghi soliloqui sulle carte.

Fu il tuo esilio. Ripenso
anche al mio, alla mattina
quando udii tra gli scogli crepitare
la bomba ballerina.

E durarono a lungo i notturni giuochi
di Bengala: come in una festa.

È scorsa un'ala rude, t'ha sfiorato le mani,
ma invano: la tua carta non è questa.

Lontano, ero con te quando tuo padre
entrò nell'ombra e ti lasciò il suo addio.
Che seppi fino allora? Il logorìo
di *prima* mi salvò solo per questo:

che t'ignoravo e non dovevo: ai colpi
d'oggi lo so, se di laggiù s'inflette
un'ora e mi riporta Cumerlotti
o Anghébeni—tra scoppi di spolette
e i lamenti e l'accorrer delle squadre.

Frost on the windowpanes; the sick
forever together, and apart;
and at the tables the endless
soliloquies over the cards.

That was your exile. I remember
mine, the morning that I heard
the ballerina bomb ricochet
on the rocks.

And the nightly fireworks went on
and on, as at a party.

A harsh wing passed, and grazed your hands,
to no avail: it's not your card.

Distant, I was with you when your father
went into shadow, leaving his farewell.
What did I know till then? The wearing-down
of *earlier* saved me for this alone:

that I didn't know you but had to;
by today's blows I do, if an hour
from down there bends back, bringing me
Cumerlotti or Anghébeni—to exploding mines
and moans and the advancing of the squadrons.

Addii, fischi nel buio, cenni, tosse
e sportelli abbassati. È l'ora. Forse
gli automi hanno ragione. Come appaiono
dai corridoi, murati!

. . . .

—Presti anche tu alla fioca
litania del tuo rapido quest'orrida
e fedele cadenza di carioca?—

La speranza di pure rivederti
m'abbandonava;

e mi chiesi se questo che mi chiude
ogni senso di te, schermo d'immagini,
ha i segni della morte o dal passato
è in esso, ma distorto e fatto labile,
un *tuo* barbaglio:

(a Modena, tra i portici,
un servo gallonato trascinava
due sciacalli al guinzaglio).

Farewells, whistling in the dark, waves, coughs,
and lowered windows. It's time.
Maybe the robots have it right. See how they look
from the corridors, walled in!

. . . .

—Do you too lend your train's
faint hymn
this awful, faithful carioca rhythm?

The hope of even seeing you again
was leaving me;

and I asked myself if this which closes off
all sense of you from me, this screen of images,
is marked by death, or if, out of the past,
but deformed and diminished, it entails
some flash *of yours*:

(under the arcades, at Modena,
a servant in gold braid dragged
two jackals on a leash).

Il saliscendi bianco e nero dei
balestrucci dal palo
del telegrafo al mare
non conforta i tuoi crucci su lo scalo
né ti riporta dove più non sei.

Già profuma il sambuco fitto su
lo sterrato; il piovasco si dilegua.
Se il chiarore è una tregua,
la tua cara minaccia la consuma.

Ecco il segno; s'innerva
sul muro che s'indora:
un frastaglio di palma
bruciato dai barbagli dell'aurora.

Il passo che proviene
dalla serra sì lieve,
non è felpato dalla neve, è ancora
tua vita, sangue tuo nelle mie vene.

The white-and-black sine
wave of the martins from the telegraph
pole to the sea
won't soothe your agitation on the platform
or bring you back where you no longer are.

Already the elder sends its thick perfume
across the pit; the squall fans out.
If the brightness is a truce,
your sweet threat consumes it.

See the sign; it flares
on the wall that turns to gold:
a palm-leaf crenellation
burnt by the dazzle of dawn.

The step that arrives
from the greenhouse so faint
isn't felted with snow: it's still
your life, your blood in my veins.

Il ramarro, se scocca
sotto la grande fersa
dalle stoppie—

la vela, quando fiotta
e s'inabissa al salto
della rocca—

il cannone di mezzodì
più fioco del tuo cuore
e il cronometro se
scatta senza rumore—

. . . .

e poi? Luce di lampo
invano può mutarvi in alcunché
di ricco e strano. Altro era il tuo stampo.

Perché tardi? Nel pino lo scoiattolo
batte la coda a torcia sulla scorza.
La mezzaluna scende col suo picco
nel sole che la smorza. È giorno fatto.

A un soffio il pigro fumo trasalisce,
si difende nel punto che ti chiude.
Nulla finisce, o tutto, se tu fólgore
lasci la nube.

The green lizard, if it darts
out of the stubble
under the great heat—

the sail, when it luffs
and dives at the jolt
from the reef—

the noon cannon
fainter than your heart
and the stopwatch if it sounds
without a sound—

.   .   .   .

and then? Lightning in vain
can change you into something
rich and strange. Your stamp was different.

Why wait? The squirrel beats his torch-tail
on the pine tree's bark.
The half-moon with its peak sinks down
into the sun that snuffs it out. It's day.

The sluggish mist is startled by a breeze,
but holds firm at the point that covers you.
Nothing ends, or everything,
if, thunderbolt, you leave your cloud.

L'anima che dispensa
furlana e rigodone ad ogni nuova
stagione della strada, s'alimenta
della chiusa passione, la ritrova
a ogni angolo più intensa.

La tua voce è quest'anima diffusa.
Su fili, su ali, al vento, a caso, col
favore della musa o d'un ordegno,
ritorna lieta o triste. Parlo d'altro,
ad altri che t'ignora e il suo disegno
è là che insiste *do re la sol sol* . . .

Ti libero la fronte dai ghiaccioli
che raccogliesti traversando l'alte
nebulose; hai le penne lacerate
dai cicloni, ti desti a soprassalti.

Mezzodì: allunga nel riquadro il nespolo
l'ombra nera, s'ostina in cielo un sole
freddoloso; e l'altre ombre che scantonano
nel vicolo non sanno che sei qui.

The spirit that dispenses
forlana and rigadoon at each new
season of the street
feeds on secret passion, finds it
more intense at every turn.

Your voice is this irradiated essence.
By wire, by wing, by wind or chance,
favored by muse or instrument, it echoes,
happy or sad. I speak of something else
to one who doesn't know you, but its theme
is there insisting, *do re la sol sol . . .*

I free your forehead of the ice
you gathered as you crossed the cloudy
heights; your wings were shorn
by cyclones; you startle awake.

Noon: in the square the medlar's black
shade lengthens, a chilled sun hangs on
in the sky: and the other shadows turning
into the alley aren't aware you're here.

La gondola che scivola in un forte
bagliore di catrame e di papaveri,
la subdola canzone che s'alzava
da masse di cordame, l'alte porte
rinchiuse su di te e risa di maschere
che fuggivano a frotte—

una sera tra mille e la mia notte
è più profonda! S'agita laggiù
uno smorto groviglio che m'avviva
a stratti e mi fa eguale a quell'assorto
pescatore d'anguille dalla riva.

Infuria sale o grandine? Fa strage
di campanule, svelle la cedrina.
Un rintocco subacqueo s'avvicina,
quale tu lo destavi, e s'allontana.

La pianola degl'inferi da sé
accelera i registri, sale nelle
sfere del gelo . . . —brilla come te
quando fingevi col tuo trillo d'aria
Lakmé nell'Aria delle Campanelle.

The gondola that glides
in a harsh tar-and-poppy glare,
the deceiving song that rose
from piles of rope, the high doors
shut on you, and merriment
of masks disappearing in droves—

one evening in a thousand, and my night
is deeper! Down below
a blurred knot writhes arousing me
by fits and starts and makes me kin
to the intent eel-fisher on the shore.

Is it salt that strafes or hail? It slays
the bellflowers, uproots the verbena.
An underwater tolling nears,
as if aroused by you, and moves away.

Hell's player piano speeds
up on its own, and rises
to the icy spheres—to shine like you
when you were Lakmé,
trilling the Bell Song.

Al primo chiaro, quando
subitaneo un rumore
di ferrovia mi parla
di chiusi uomini in corsa
nel traforo del sasso
illuminato a tagli
da cieli ed acque misti;

al primo buio, quando
il bulino che tarla
la scrivanìa rafforza
il suo fervore e il passo
del guardiano s'accosta:
al chiaro e al buio, soste ancora umane
se tu a intrecciarle col tuo refe insisti.

Il fiore che ripete
dall'orlo del burrato
non scordarti di me,
non ha tinte più liete né più chiare
dello spazio gettato tra me e te.

Un cigolìo si sferra, ci discosta,
l'azzurro pervicace non ricompare.
Nell'afa quasi visibile mi riporta all'opposta
tappa, già buia, la funicolare.

At first light, when
a sudden railroad
rumble speaks to me
of men in transit
locked in rock caves
lit by shafts of mottled
sky and water:

at first dark, when
the chisel etching at
the desk accelerates
its fervor and the watchman's
step draws near:
light and dark, still human intervals
as long as you will stitch them with your thread.

The flower that repeats
forget me not
from the rim of the ravine
has no colors happier or purer
than the space forced between me and you.

A creaking lets loose, pulling us apart,
the overweaning blue won't reappear.
In haze you almost see, the cable car
takes me across, where it's already dark.

La rana, prima a ritentar la corda
dallo stagno che affossa
giunchi e nubi, stormire dei carrubi
conserti dove spenge le sue fiaccole
un sole senza caldo, tardo ai fiori
ronzìo di coleotteri che suggono
ancora linfe, ultimi suoni, avara
vita della campagna. Con un soffio
l'ora s'estingue: un cielo di lavagna
si prepara a un irrompere di scarni
cavalli, alle scintille degli zoccoli.

Non recidere, forbice, quel volto,
solo nella memoria che si sfolla,
non far del grande suo viso in ascolto
la mia nebbia di sempre.

Un freddo cala . . . Duro il colpo svetta.
E l'acacia ferita da sé scrolla
il guscio di cicala
nella prima belletta di Novembre.

The frog, first to strike his chord
out of the pond that clogs
with clouds and rushes,
the laced carobs' rustle
where a heatless sun puts out its torches,
late buzz of coleoptera in the flowers
still sucking lymph, last noises, avaricious
country life. The hour goes in a gust:
a blackboard sky prepares
for starved horses to stampede,
for sparks from their hooves.

Shears, don't cut away that face
alone in my emptying memory,
don't make her great listening look
into my everyday haze.

A chill descends . . . The sharp blow strikes.
And by itself the hurt acacia
shakes off the cicada's husk
into the first November mud.

La canna che dispiuma
mollemente il suo rosso
flabello a primavera;
la rèdola nel fosso, su la nera
correntìa sorvolata di libellule;
e il cane trafelato che rincasa
col suo fardello in bocca,

oggi qui non mi tocca riconoscere;
ma là dove il riverbero più cuoce
e il nuvolo s'abbassa, oltre le sue
pupille ormai remote, solo due
fasci di luce in croce.
E il tempo passa.

. . . ma così sia. Un suono di cornetta
dialoga con gli sciami del querceto.
Nella valva che il vespero riflette
un vulcano dipinto fuma lieto.

La moneta incassata nella lava
brilla anch'essa sul tavolo e trattiene
pochi fogli. La vita che sembrava
vasta è più breve del tuo fazzoletto.

The reed that softly
molts its red
flabellum in spring;
the path down in the ditch, along the black
rivulet alive with dragonflies;
and the panting dog that trudges home,
his trophy in his mouth, here and today

it's not for me to recognize;
but there where the reflection bakes
hottest and the cloud hangs low,
beyond her distant pupils, now
two simple light beams crossing.
                              And time passes.

. . . so be it. Blare of a cornet
argues with the bee swarms in the oaks.
In the seashell mirroring the sunset
a painted volcano brightly smokes.

The coin locked in the lava paperweight
shines on the table also, holding down
a few brief pages. Life, which seemed
immense, is smaller than your handkerchief.

PARTE III

PART III

Tempi di Bellosguardo

Oh come là nella corusca
distesa che s'inarca verso i colli,
il brusìo della sera s'assottiglia
e gli alberi discorrono col trito
mormorio della rena; come limpida
s'inalvea là in decoro
di colonne e di salci ai lati e grandi salti
di lupi nei giardini, tra le vasche ricolme
che traboccano,
questa vita di tutti non più posseduta
del nostro respiro;
e come si ricrea una luce di zàffiro
per gli uomini
che vivono laggiù: è troppo triste
che tanta pace illumini a spiragli
e tutto ruoti poi con rari guizzi
su l'anse vaporanti, con incroci
di camini, con grida dai giardini
pensili, con sgomenti e lunghe risa
sui tetti ritagliati, tra le quinte
dei frondami ammassati ed una coda
fulgida che trascorra in cielo prima
che il desiderio trovi le parole!

*

Derelitte sul poggio
fronde della magnolia
verdibrune se il vento
porta dai frigidari
dei pianterreni un travolto
concitamento d'accordi
ed ogni foglia che oscilla

Times at Bellosguardo

Oh how there in the glittering
stretch that bends toward the hills
the hum of evening lessens
and the trees chat with the hackneyed
murmur of the sand; and how this common life
no more our own than our breath
gets channeled there, crystalline,
into orders of columns
and willows at the edges
and great moats in the gardens
by the overbrimming pools,
and how a sapphire light returns
for the men who live down there: it is too sad
such peace should enlighten in glimmers
and everything then roll on, with infrequent
flashes over the steaming riverbends,
with intersecting chimneys
and shouts from the hanging gardens
and consternation and long laughter
over patched roofs, among the arrases
of massed branches and a brilliant tail
that trails across the sky before
desire can find the words!

❁

Forlorn on the hill
browngreen magnolia boughs,
when the wind arouses a troubled
agitation of chords
from the frigidaria
of the ground floors
and every leaf that sways

o rilampeggia nel folto
in ogni fibra s'imbeve
di quel saluto, e più ancora
derelitte le fronde
dei vivi che si smarriscono
nel prisma del minuto,
le membra di febbre votate
al moto che si ripete
in circolo breve: sudore
che pulsa, sudore di morte,
atti minuti specchiati,
sempre gli stessi, rifranti
echi del batter che in alto
sfaccetta il sole e la pioggia,
fugace altalena tra vita
che passa e vita che sta,
quassù non c'è scampo: si muore
sapendo o si sceglie la vita
che muta ed ignora: altra morte.
E scende la cuna tra logge
ed erme: l'accordo commuove
le lapidi che hanno veduto
le immagini grandi, l'onore,
l'amore inflessibile, il giuoco,
la fedeltà che non muta.
E il gesto rimane: misura
il vuoto, ne sonda il confine:
il gesto ignoto che esprime
se stesso e non altro: passione
di sempre in un sangue e un cervello
irripetuti; e fors'entra
nel chiuso e lo forza con l'esile
sua punta di grimaldello.

❉

Il rumore degli émbrici distrutti
dalla bufera
nell'aria dilatata che non s'incrina,

or flares back in the thicket
drinks that greeting in
in every fiber;
and more forlorn, the limbs
of the living that get lost
in the prism of the minute,
fevered limbs devoted
to motion that goes on
and on in its small round:
sweat that throbs, sweat of death,
mirrored acts and minutes
that never change, refracting
echoes of the beating up above
that facets sun and rain,
swift swaying between life
that goes and life that stays,
no escape up here:
we die knowing or else choose
chameleon, heedless life: another death.
And the road descends
among loggias and herms: the chord
stirs the stones that have seen
the great images, honor,
unbending love, the test,
unchanging faithfulness.
Yet the gesture remains: it measures
the emptiness, sounds its limits:
the unknown gesture that describes
itself and nothing else: eternal
passion in a blood and brain
that won't return: and maybe
it enters the close and breaks
the lock with its fine pick.

＊

The clatter of the rooftiles, shattered by
the storm
in the expanded air that doesn't crack,

l'inclinarsi del pioppo
del Canadà, tricuspide, che vibra
nel giardino a ogni strappo—
e il segno di una vita che assecondi
il marmo a ogni scalino come l'edera
diffida dello slancio solitario
dei ponti che discopro da quest'altura;
d'una clessidra che non sabbia ma opere
misuri e volti umani, piante umane;
d'acque composte sotto padiglioni
e non più irose a ritentar fondali
di pomice, è sparito? Un suono lungo
dànno le terrecotte, i pali appena
difendono le ellissi dei convolvoli,
e le locuste arrancano piovute
sui libri dalle pergole; dura opera,
tessitrici celesti, ch'è interrotta
sul telaio degli uomini. E domani . . .

the bending of the three-point Canada
poplar that shivers
in the garden at every gust, and the sign—
of a life that accords with the marble
at each step, the way that ivy
shrinks from the solitary thrust
of bridges I can make out from this height;
of an hourglass measuring not sand
but works and human faces, human plants;
of water calm under follies,
no longer raging to explore the pumice
grottoes—is it gone?
A long sound comes from the tiles, the stakes
barely hold up the morning glories' coils,
and the locusts that rained
from the arbors onto the books limp off;
hard labor, heavenly weavers, interrupted
on the loom of men. And tomorrow . . .

PARTE IV

Sap check'd with frost, and lusty leaves quite gone,
Beauty o'ersnow'd and bareness every where.
— SHAKESPEARE, *Sonnets*, V

PART IV

Sap check'd with frost, and lusty leaves quite gone,
Beauty o'ersnow'd and bareness every where.
— SHAKESPEARE, *Sonnets*, V

La casa dei doganieri

Tu non ricordi la casa dei doganieri
sul rialzo a strapiombo sulla scogliera:
desolata t'attende dalla sera
in cui v'entrò lo sciame dei tuoi pensieri
e vi sostò irrequieto.

Libeccio sferza da anni le vecchie mura
e il suono del tuo riso non è più lieto:
la bussola va impazzita all'avventura
e il calcolo dei dadi più non torna.
Tu non ricordi; altro tempo frastorna
la tua memoria; un filo s'addipana.

Ne tengo ancora un capo; ma s'allontana
la casa e in cima al tetto la banderuola
affumicata gira senza pietà.
Ne tengo un capo; ma tu resti sola
né qui respiri nell'oscurità.

Oh l'orizzonte in fuga, dove s'accende
rara la luce della petroliera!
Il varco è qui? (Ripullula il frangente
ancora sulla balza che scoscende . . .).
Tu non ricordi la casa di questa
mia sera. Ed io non so chi va e chi resta.

The House of the Customs Men

You won't recall the house of the customs men
on the bluff that overhangs the reef:
it's been waiting, empty, since the evening
your thoughts swarmed in
and hung there, nervously.

Sou'westers have lashed the old walls for years
and your laugh's not careless anymore:
the compass needle wanders crazily
and the dice no longer tell the score.
You don't remember: other times
assail your memory; a thread gets wound.

I hold one end still; but the house recedes
and the smoke-stained weathervane
spins pitiless up on the roof.
I hold on to an end; but you're alone,
not here, not breathing in the dark.

Oh the vanishing horizon line,
where the tanker's lights flash now and then!
Is the channel here? (The breakers
still seethe against the cliff that drops away . . .)
You don't recall the house of this, my evening.
And I don't know who's going or who'll stay.

Bassa marea

Sere di gridi, quando l'altalena
oscilla nella pergola d'allora
e un oscuro vapore vela appena
la fissità del mare.

Non più quel tempo. Varcano ora il muro
rapidi voli obliqui, la discesa
di tutto non s'arresta e si confonde
sulla proda scoscesa anche lo scoglio
che ti portò primo sull'onde.

Viene col soffio della primavera
un lugubre risucchio
d'assorbite esistenze; e nella sera,
negro vilucchio, solo il tuo ricordo
s'attorce e si difende.

S'alza sulle spallette, sul tunnel più lunge
dove il treno lentissimo s'imbuca.
Una mandria lunare sopraggiunge
poi sui colli, invisibile, e li bruca.

Low Tide

Clamorous evenings, when the swing
sways in the pergola of then
and a thick mist barely veils
the fixedness of the sea.

That time is over. Now swift, slanting flights
arc across the wall, the coming-down
of everything is endless, and even the reef
that first brought you to the waves
gets lost on the steep coast.

A gloomy tide of swallowed-up
existences arrives with the breath of spring;
and in the evening,
only your memory, black bindweed,
writhes and resists.

It rises over the breakers and the tunnel beyond
where the train enters at a snail's pace.
Later, a lunar flock, invisible,
arrives on the hills to graze.

Stanze

Ricerco invano il punto onde si mosse
il sangue che ti nutre, interminato
respingersi di cerchi oltre lo spazio
breve dei giorni umani,
che ti rese presente in uno strazio
d'agonie che non sai, viva in un putre
padule d'astro inabissato; ed ora
è linfa che disegna le tue mani,
ti batte ai polsi inavvertita e il volto
t'infiamma o discolora.

Pur la rete minuta dei tuoi nervi
rammenta un poco questo suo viaggio
e se gli occhi ti scopro li consuma
un fervore coperto da un passaggio
turbinoso di spuma ch'or s'infitta
ora si frange, e tu lo senti ai rombi
delle tempie vanir nella tua vita
come si rompe a volte nel silenzio
d'una piazza assopita
un volo strepitoso di colombi.

In te converge, ignara, una raggèra
di fili; e certo alcuno d'essi apparve
ad altri: e fu chi abbrividì la sera
percosso da una candida ala in fuga,
e fu chi vide vagabonde larve
dove altri scorse fanciullette a sciami,
o scoperse, qual lampo che dirami,
nel sereno una ruga e l'urto delle
leve del mondo apparse da uno strappo
dell'azzurro l'avvolse, lamentoso.

In te m'appare un'ultima corolla
di cenere leggera che non dura
ma sfioccata precipita. Voluta,

Stanzas

I'm searching vainly for the point the blood
that nourishes you began from, endless
rippling out beyond the narrow
space of human days, that put you here
in a lacerating agony
you have no knowledge of,
alive in a stinking swamp of foundered star;
and it's lymph now that sketches your hands,
that beats unseen at your wrists,
and inflames or discolors your face.

Yet the intricate net of your nerves
remembers its journey a little
and when I uncover your eyes, they're being consumed
by a fever under a wave of seething foam
that concentrates, then breaks apart,
and the roar at your temples tells you
it's vanishing into your life
the way a deafening
storm of doves erupts
into the silence of a sleepy square.

In you, unknowing, a crown of rays converges,
and some of them, no doubt, appeared to others:
one man shivered in the evening,
struck by a white wing in flight;
one was visited by wandering ghosts
where someone else saw little girls in swarms,
or made out, like forked lightning,
a crease in the clear sky
and the scream of the world's gears escaped
from a tear in the blue and enveloped him, wailing.

In you I see a last light crown of ashes
that won't stay, but disintegrates and falls.
Such is your nature, coiling and uncoiling.

disvoluta è così la tua natura.
Tocchi il segno, travàlichi. Oh il ronzìo
dell'arco ch'è scoccato, il solco che ara
il flutto e si rinchiude! Ed ora sale
l'ultima bolla in su. La dannazione
è forse questa vaneggiante amara
oscurità che scende su chi resta.

You strike the mark, cross over. Oh,
the hum of the shot arc, the groove
that carves the wave and closes!
And now the last bubble rises.
It may be damnation is the bitter
raving darkness that descends
on those who remain.

Sotto la pioggia

Un murmure; e la tua casa s'appanna
come nella bruma del ricordo—
e lacrima la palma ora che sordo
preme il disfacimento che ritiene
nell'afa delle serre anche le nude
speranze ed il pensiero che rimorde.

'Por amor de la fiebre' . . . mi conduce
un vortice con te. Raggia vermiglia
una tenda, una finestra si rinchiude.
Sulla rampa materna ora cammina,
guscio d'uovo che va tra la fanghiglia,
poca vita tra sbatter d'ombra e luce.

Strideva Adiós muchachos, compañeros
de mi vida, il tuo disco dalla corte:
e m'è cara la maschera se ancora
di là dal mulinello della sorte
mi rimane il sobbalzo che riporta
al tuo sentiero.

Seguo i lucidi strosci e in fondo, a nembi,
il fumo strascicato d'una nave.
Si punteggia uno squarcio . . .
                   Per te intendo
ciò che osa la cicogna quando alzato
il volo dalla cuspide nebbiosa
rèmiga verso la Città del Capo.

In the Rain

A murmur; and your house gets blurred
as in the mists of memory—
and the palm weeps, now that dull
disintegration weighs us down,
trapping our naked hopes and the thought that stings
in the haze of the greenhouses.

"Por amor de la fiebre" . . . a maelstrom
whirls me with you. A curtain gleams vermilion,
a window shuts. On your mother's stairs
a bit of life, an eggshell on the slime,
totters now in and out
of light and shadow.

Your record screamed, "Adiós muchachos,
compañeros de mi vida," from the courtyard:
and I'll gladly play the part
if beyond the hurricane of fate
the jump will still be there that lands me
back on your path.

I follow the bright squalls and down below,
the puffing smoke-trail of a ship.
A hole pricks open . . .
                         Thanks to you I know
the risk the stork takes when it lifts
from its cloudy pinnacle
and rows for Cape Town.

Punta del Mesco

Nel cielo della cava rigato
all'alba dal volo dritto delle pernici
il fumo delle mine s'inteneriva,
saliva lento le pendici a piombo.
Dal rostro del palabotto si capovolsero
le ondine trombettiere silenziose
e affondarono rapide tra le spume
che il tuo passo sfiorava.

Vedo il sentiero che percorsi un giorno
come un cane inquieto; lambe il fiotto,
s'inerpica tra i massi e rado strame
a tratti lo scancella. E tutto è uguale.
Nella ghiaia bagnata s'arrovella
un'eco degli scrosci. Umido brilla
il sole sulle membra affaticate
dei curvi spaccapietre che martellano.

Polene che risalgono e mi portano
qualche cosa di te. Un tràpano incide
il cuore sulla roccia—schianta attorno
più forte un rombo. Brancolo nel fumo,
ma rivedo: ritornano i tuoi rari
gesti e il viso che aggiorna al davanzale,—
mi torna la tua infanzia dilaniata
dagli spari!

Punta del Mesco

In the sky above the quarry, scored at dawn
by the plumb-line flight of partridges,
smoke from the mines was slowly thinning,
climbing the sheer cliffs.
Silent bugling naiads dove
from the stern of the pilot boat
and drowned in the foam
your footsteps used to trace.

I see the path I ran along one day
like a nervous dog; it laps the stream,
rises among the rocks where wisps of straw
keep hiding it. And nothing's changed.
The washed gravel rumbles,
echoing the roar. The sun shines wet
on the tired stonecutters' backs
hunkered over their hammers.

Figureheads that resurface and bring me
something of you. A drill etches
the heart on rock—a louder blast
explodes around. I grope in smoke,
but see again: your few gestures come alive
and the face that dawns at the windowsill—
your childhood shattered by gunfire
lives again!

Costa San Giorgio

Un fuoco fatuo impolvera la strada.
Il gasista si cala giù e pedala
rapido con la scala su la spalla.
Risponde un'altra luce e l'ombra attorno
sfarfalla, poi ricade.

Lo so, non s'apre il cerchio
e tutto scende o rapido s'inerpica
tra gli archi. I lunghi mesi
son fuggiti così: ci resta un gelo
fosforico d'insetto nei cunicoli
e un velo scialbo sulla luna.
                            Un dì
brillava sui cammini del prodigio
El Dorado, e fu lutto fra i tuoi padri.
Ora l'Idolo è qui, sbarrato. Tende
le sue braccia fra i càrpini: l'oscuro
ne scancella lo sguardo. Senza voce,
disfatto dall'arsura, quasi esanime,
l'Idolo è in croce.

La sua presenza si diffonde grave.
Nulla ritorna, tutto non veduto
si riforma nel magico falò.
Non c'è respiro; nulla vale: più
non distacca per noi dall'architrave
della stalla il suo lume, Maritornes.

Tutto è uguale; non ridere: lo so,
lo stridere degli anni fin dal primo,
lamentoso, sui cardini, il mattino
un limbo sulla stupida discesa—
e in fondo il torchio del nemico muto
che preme . . .
                    Se una pendola rintocca
dal chiuso porta il tonfo del fantoccio
ch'è abbattuto.

Costa San Giorgio

A will-o'-the-wisp dusts the street with powder.
The gas man jumps down, races off,
pedaling fast, with his ladder on his shoulder.
Another light-burst answers
and the dark around it flares, to fall again.

I know, the circle's closed, and everything
slips or rises steeply on its sides.
The long months flew this way:
what's left for us
is a phosphorescent insect chill in the tunnels
and a wan veil across the moon.
                              One day
it shone on the prodigious *El Dorado*'s wanderings,
and there was mourning among your forebears.
Now the Idol's present, barred from us.
He stretches out his arms among the hornbeams;
the dark obscures his gaze. Undone by thirst,
voiceless, nearly lifeless,
the Idol's crucified.

His presence fans out heavily around.
Nothing adds up, everything unseen
takes shape again inside the magic fire.
Nothing holds; there is no air:
no more for us does Maritornes
unhook her lantern from the stable crossbeam.

It's all the same; don't laugh; I know,
the screaming of the years since the beginning,
their moaning on their hinges, morning
a limbo on the stupid downward slide—
and below, the press of the mute
enemy, crushing . . .
                    If a bell
tolls in the courtyard it echoes the thud
of a fallen puppet.

L'estate

L'ombra crociata del gheppio pare ignota
ai giovinetti arbusti quando rade fugace.
E la nube che vede? Ha tante facce
la polla schiusa.

Forse nel guizzo argenteo della trota
controcorrente
torni anche tu al mio piede fanciulla morta
Aretusa.

Ecco l'òmero acceso, la pepita
travolta al sole,
la cavolaia folle, il filo teso
del ragno su la spuma che ribolle—

e qualcosa che va e tropp'altro che
non passerà la cruna . . .

Occorrono troppe vite per farne una.

Summer

The crossed shadow of the kestrel seems unknown
to the young bushes that it barely grazes.
And the cloud sees what? The welling spring
has countless faces.

Maybe in the silvery upstream
flash of the trout
you, too, dead girlchild Arethusa
return at my feet.

Here's the burning shoulder, the gold nugget
upturned in the sun,
the cabbage moth gone wild, the spider's line
strung over boiling foam—

and some things pass, but too much else
won't wriggle through the needle's eye . . .

Too many lives go into making one.

Eastbourne

'Dio salvi il Re' intonano le trombe
da un padiglione erto su palafitte
che aprono il varco al mare quando sale
a distruggere peste
umide di cavalli nella sabbia
del litorale.

Freddo un vento m'investe
ma un guizzo accende i vetri
e il candore di mica delle rupi
ne risplende.

Bank Holiday . . . Riporta l'onda lunga
della mia vita
a striscio, troppo dolce sulla china.
Si fa tardi. I fragori si distendono,
si chiudono in sordina.

Vanno su sedie a ruote i mutilati,
li accompagnano cani dagli orecchi
lunghi, bimbi in silenzio o vecchi. (Forse
domani tutto parrà un sogno).
       E vieni
tu pure voce prigioniera, sciolta
anima ch'è smarrita,
voce di sangue, persa e restituita
alla mia sera.

Come lucente muove sui suoi spicchi
la porta di un albergo
—risponde un'altra e le rivolge un raggio—
m'agita un carosello che travolge
tutto dentro il suo giro; ed io in ascolto
('mia patria!') riconosco il tuo respiro,
anch'io mi levo e il giorno è troppo folto.

Eastbourne

The trumpets blare "God Save the King"
from a bandstand built on stilts
that let the rising tide flow in
to eat the wet
prints of the horses'
hooves on the sand of the shore.

A cold wind flails me
but a glint ignites the windows
and the mica-whiteness of the cliffs
shines with it.

Bank Holiday . . . The long, slow
tide of my life is shambling in,
too easy on the backward slide.
It's getting late. The breaker's crash
takes longer, fades away.

The wounded pass in wheelchairs,
with long-eared dogs, grim children,
or the old. (Maybe tomorrow
it will all have been a dream.)
                              And you
come, too, imprisoned voice, freed
spirit gone astray,
voice of blood, lost and restored
to my evening.

The way a gleaming hotel door
spins on its axis, each glass panel
reflecting back the glare of the one before,
a carousel is whirling me,
sucking everything along with it;
and listening ("my country!") I can hear you breathe,
I rise too and the day's too full.

Tutto apparirà vano: anche la forza
che nella sua tenace ganga aggrega
i vivi e i morti, gli alberi e gli scogli
e si svolge da te, per te. La festa
non ha pietà. Rimanda
il suo scroscio la banda, si dispiega
nel primo buio una bontà senz'armi.

Vince il male . . . La ruota non s'arresta.

Anche tu lo sapevi, luce-in-tenebra.

Nella plaga che brucia, dove sei
scomparsa al primo tocco delle campane, solo
rimane l'acre tizzo che già fu
Bank Holiday.

It will all seem hopeless: even the might
that holds in its tenacious grip
the living and the dead, the trees and rocks,
and comes from you, for you. The merrymaking's
merciless. The band sends back its roar.
A powerless benevolence
unfurls in the early dark.

Evil is winning . . . The wheel won't stop.

And you knew it, light-in-shadow.

What's left on the burning shore, where you disappeared
at the first clash of bells,
is the bitter ember that was once
Bank Holiday.

Corrispondenze

Or che in fondo un miraggio
di vapori vacilla e si disperde,
altro annunzia, tra gli alberi, la squilla
del picchio verde.

La mano che raggiunge il sottobosco
e trapunge la trama
del cuore con le punte dello strame,
è quella che matura incubi d'oro
a specchio delle gore
quando il carro sonoro
di Bassareo riporta folli mùgoli
di arieti sulle toppe arse dei colli.

Torni anche tu, pastora senza greggi,
e siedi sul mio sasso?
Ti riconosco; ma non so che leggi
oltre i voli che svariano sul passo.
Lo chiedo invano al piano dove una bruma
èsita tra baleni e spari su sparsi tetti,
alla febbre nascosta dei diretti
nella costa che fuma.

Correspondences

Now that in the distance a mirage
of vapors shifts, dispels,
the green woodpecker's shrilling in the trees
announces something else.

The hand that fumbles in the underbrush
to break through the heart's woof
with bits of straw
is the same hand feeding golden dreams
mirrored in the canals
when Bassareus' groaning chariot
brings back the crazy bleating of the rams
to the burned stubble of the hills.

Do you come back, too, shepherdess
without a flock, and sit down on my stone?
I know you: but I don't know what you read
beyond the flights that swerve above your path.
In vain I ask the plains, where a mist
stalls between lightning and shots over scattered roofs,
I ask the hidden fever of the trains
that ply the steaming coast.

Barche sulla Marna

Felicità del sùghero abbandonato
alla corrente
che stempra attorno i ponti rovesciati
e il plenilunio pallido nel sole:
barche sul fiume, agili nell'estate
e un murmure stagnante di città.
Segui coi remi il prato se il cacciatore
di farfalle vi giunge con la sua rete,
l'alberaia sul muro dove il sangue
del drago si ripete nel cinabro.

Voci sul fiume, scoppi dalle rive,
o ritmico scandire di piroghe
nel vespero che cola
tra le chiome dei noci, ma dov'è
la lenta processione di stagioni
che fu un'alba infinita e senza strade,
dov'è la lunga attesa e qual è il nome
del vuoto che ci invade.

Il sogno è questo: un vasto,
interminato giorno che rifonde
tra gli argini, quasi immobile, il suo bagliore
e ad ogni svolta il buon lavoro dell'uomo,
il domani velato che non fa orrore.
E altro ancora era il sogno, ma il suo riflesso
fermo sull'acqua in fuga, sotto il nido
del pendolino, aereo e inaccessibile,
era silenzio altissimo nel grido
concorde del meriggio ed un mattino
più lungo era la sera, il gran fermento
era grande riposo.
                    Qui . . . il colore
che resiste è del topo che ha saltato
tra i giunchi o col suo spruzzo di metallo
velenoso, lo storno che sparisce

Boats on the Marne

Bliss of the cork abandoned to the current
that melts around
the upside-down bridges
and the full moon, pale in the sun:
boats on the river, nimble in summer,
and a stagnant city hum.
Row by the meadow when the butterfly
hunter comes with his net,
along the stand of trees beside the wall
where dragon's blood repeats as cinnabar.

Voices on the river, shouts from the shore,
oh rhythmic scansion of canoes
in the evening sifting through
the tresses of the walnut trees, but where
is the slow parade of seasons
that was an endless, roadless dawn,
where is the long wait, and what do we call
this emptiness invading us.

Here is the dream: one vast, unending day
replenishing its splendor,
nearly motionless between the banks,
and man's good works at every turn,
the unseen future that won't terrify.
The dream was more, too, but its mirror-image
firm on the fleeting water, under the oriole's
nest, high up and inaccessible,
was final silence in the harmonized
shout of noon and evening
was a longer morning, the great ferment
was great repose.
          But here . . .
the color that lasts is the color of the mouse
that leapt into the rushes,
or the starling with his poison metal splash,

tra i fumi della riva.

     Un altro giorno,
ripeti—o che ripeti? E dove porta
questa bocca che brùlica in un getto
solo?

  La sera è questa. Ora possiamo
scendere fino a che s'accenda l'Orsa.

(Barche sulla Marna, domenicali, in corsa
nel dì della tua festa).

dissolved in the mists of the shore.
                              Another day,
you say—or what are you saying?
And where does it lead, this mouth that seethes
in a single stream?
                  Here is the evening:
now we can float until the Dipper rises.

(Boats on the Marne, Sunday races
on your feast day.)

Elegia di Pico Farnese

Le pellegrine in sosta che hanno durato
tutta la notte la loro litania
s'aggiustano gli zendadi sulla testa,
spengono i fuochi, risalgono sui carri.
Nell'alba triste s'affacciano dai loro
sportelli tagliati negli usci i molli soriani
e un cane lionato s'allunga nell'umido orto
tra i frutti caduti all'ombra del melangolo.
Ieri tutto pareva un macero ma stamane
pietre di spugna ritornano alla vita
e il cupo sonno si desta nella cucina,
dal grande camino giungono lieti rumori.
Torna la salmodia appena in volute più lievi,
vento e distanza ne rompono le voci, le ricompongono.

    'Isole del santuario,
    viaggi di vascelli sospesi,
    alza il sudario,
    numera i giorni e i mesi
    che restano per finire'.

Strade e scale che salgono a piramide, fitte
d'intagli, ragnateli di sasso dove s'aprono
oscurità animate dagli occhi confidenti
dei maiali, archivolti tinti di verderame,
si svolge a stento il canto dalle ombrelle dei pini,
e indugia affievolito nell'indaco che stilla
su anfratti, tagli, spicchi di muraglie.

    'Grotte dove scalfito
    luccica il Pesce, chi sa
    quale altro segno si perde,
    perché non tutta la vita
    è in questo sepolcro verde'.

Pico Farnese Elegy

The pilgrims stopping over who have kept
their litany alive all night
adjust the wimples on their heads,
put out their fires, get back into the carts.
In the sad dawn the soft tabbies stare
out of windows cut into the doors,
and a tawny dog lies in the sodden garden
among the fruit in the shade of the bitter orange.
Everything was a steeping yesterday,
but now the spongy stones come back to life,
the kitchen shakes off its dark sleepiness
and happy noises come from the great hearth. The psalms
keep echoing in fainter spirals, wind and distance
break the voices up, then piece them back together:

> "Islands of the sanctuary,
> ships asail in midair,
> lift the veil,
> number the days
> and months to fulfill."

Streets and stairways pyramiding skyward
thick with carvings, spiderwebs of stone,
caverns animated by the trusting stares
of swine, vaults stained with verdigris;
the on-and-off song of the umbrella pines
begins and lingers, weakened in the indigo
that drips on gorges, clearings, broken walls.

> "Grottoes where the etched Fish
> glitters, who can say
> what other sign is doomed,
> for not all of life
> is in this green tomb."

Oh la pigra illusione. Perché attardarsi qui
a questo amore di donne barbute, a un vano farnetico
che il ferraio picano quando batte l'incudine
curvo sul calor bianco da sé scaccia? Ben altro
è l'Amore—e fra gli alberi balena col tuo cruccio
e la tua frangia d'ali, messaggera accigliata!
Se urgi fino al midollo i diòsperi e nell'acque
specchi il piumaggio della tua fronte senza errore
o distruggi le nere cantafavole e vegli
al trapasso dei pochi tra orde d'uomini-capre,

    ('*collane di nocciuole,*
    zucchero filato a mano
    sullo spacco del masso
    miracolato che porta
    le preci in basso, parole
    di cera che stilla, parole
    che il seme del girasole
    se brilla disperde')

il tuo splendore è aperto. Ma più discreto allora
che dall'androne gelido, il teatro dell'infanzia
da anni abbandonato, dalla soffitta tetra
di vetri e di astrolabi, dopo una lunga attesa
ai balconi dell'edera, un segno ci conduce
alla radura brulla dove per noi qualcuno
tenta una festa di spari. E qui, se appare inudibile
il tuo soccorso, nell'aria prilla il piattello, si rompe
ai nostri colpi! Il giorno non chiede più di una chiave.
È mite il tempo. Il lampo delle tue vesti è sciolto
entro l'umore dell'occhio che rifrange nel suo
cristallo altri colori. Dietro di noi, calmo, ignaro
del mutamento, da lemure ormai rifatto celeste,
il fanciulletto Anacleto ricarica i fucili.

Lazy illusion! Why wait here
for this love of bearded women, for an empty raving
which the Pico blacksmith scatters by himself,
beating his anvil, bent to its white heat?
Love is something else—and it flashes in the trees
with your sorrow and your fringe of wings, sullen messenger!
If you force the persimmons to their core
and mirror your forehead's faultless plumage in the water
or destroy the dark wives' tales when you stand vigil
at the passing of the few among hordes of goat-men,

> ("necklaces of hazelnut,
> sugar spun by hand
> over the crack
> in the miraculous healed rock
> that carries our prayers down,
> words of dripping wax,
> words the sunflower
> seed sows when it gleams")

your splendor is clear. But more explicit now
that from the frigid vestibule, the childhood
theater deserted for years, the gloomy
attic of glass and astrolabes, after
a long wait on ivied balconies, a sign directs us
to the bleak barrenness where someone
has staged a shoot for us. And here, though it seems
your help cannot be heard, the skeet
whirls in the air and shatters at our shots!
The day asks only one key. The weather's mild.
The glow of your robes dissolves in the eye's temper,
refracting other colors in its crystal. Behind us, calm,
blind to his change from lemur to celestial,
young Anacleto loads the guns again.

Nuove stanze

Poi che gli ultimi fili di tabacco
al tuo gesto si spengono nel piatto
di cristallo, al soffitto lenta sale
la spirale del fumo
che gli alfieri e i cavalli degli scacchi
guardano stupefatti; e nuovi anelli
la seguono, più mobili di quelli
delle tue dita.

La morgana che in cielo liberava
torri e ponti è sparita
al primo soffio; s'apre la finestra
non vista e il fumo s'agita. Là in fondo,
altro stormo si muove: una tregenda
d'uomini che non sa questo tuo incenso,
nella scacchiera di cui puoi tu sola
comporre il senso.

Il mio dubbio d'un tempo era se forse
tu stessa ignori il giuoco che si svolge
sul quadrato e ora è nembo alle tue porte:
follìa di morte non si placa a poco
prezzo, se poco è il lampo del tuo sguardo,
ma domanda altri fuochi, oltre le fitte
cortine che per te fomenta il dio
del caso, quando assiste.

Oggi so ciò che vuoi; batte il suo fioco
tocco la Martinella ed impaura
le sagome d'avorio in una luce
spettrale di nevaio. Ma resiste
e vince il premio della solitaria
veglia chi può con te allo specchio ustorio
che accieca le pedine opporre i tuoi
occhi d'acciaio.

New Stanzas

Now that with a flourish you've stubbed out
the last shreds of tobacco
in the crystal ashtray, a slow spiral
rises to the ceiling.
The knights and bishops of the chess set stare
amazed; and new rings follow,
more alive
than those you wear.

The phantom that set towers and bridges free
in the sky has disappeared
with the first breeze; an unseen window opens,
the smoke stirs. Below, another swarm
is on the move: a pandemonium
of men that doesn't recognize
your incense, on the board whose meaning
only you can organize.

There was a time I doubted you yourself
knew the game unfolding on the squares
that's now become a storm outside your door:
mad death is bought off at no little price,
if the lightning of your look is little,
but calls for other fires, beyond the heavy
curtains that the god of chance
hangs for you when he's in residence.

Today I know what you want: the Martinella
tolls its dull note and terrifies
the ivory shapes in a spectral, snowy light.
But the man who lives to win
the boon of his solitary vigil
is he who, standing by you, will
counter the burning mirror that blinds the pawns
with your eyes of steel.

Il ritorno

Bocca di Magra

Ecco bruma e libeccio sulle dune
sabbiose che lingueggiano
e là celato dall'incerto lembo
o alzato dal va-e-vieni delle spume
il barcaiolo Duilio che traversa
in lotta sui suoi remi; ecco il pimento
dei pini che più terso
si dilata tra pioppi e saliceti,
e pompe a vento battere le pale
e il viottolo che segue l'onde dentro
la fiumana terrosa
funghire velenoso d'ovuli; ecco
ancora quelle scale
a chiocciola, slabbrate, che s'avvitano
fin oltre la veranda
in un gelo policromo d'ogive,
eccole che t'ascoltano, le nostre vecchie scale,
e vibrano al ronzìo
allora che dal cofano tu ridésti leggera
voce di sarabanda
o quando Erinni fredde ventano angui
d'inferno e sulle rive una bufera
di strida s'allontana; ed ecco il sole
che chiude la sua corsa, che s'offusca
ai margini del canto—ecco il tuo morso
oscuro di tarantola: son pronto.

The Return

Bocca di Magra

Here's mist and wild wind on the sandy,
flickering dunes, and there,
hidden by the foam's fudged edge
or lifted on its rise and fall,
Duilio the boatman makes the crossing
battling his oars;
here's the sharper turpentine of the pines
rising through poplar and willow,
and windmills flailing their arms
and the path that follows
the waves into the muddy stream
mushrooming poison ovula;
and here are the worn spiral stairs again
that climb to the veranda
in a multicolored
ice of arches;
here they are listening, our old stairs,
ahum with the buzz,
now you've revived the saraband's soft voice
out of your treasure chest or when cold Furies
vent their hell-snakes and a storm of screams
moves off along the shore;
and here's the sun
ending his run and dying out
at the song's edges—here's your black
tarantula bite: I'm ready.

Palio

La tua fuga non s'è dunque perduta
in un giro di trottola
al margine della strada:
la corsa che dirada
le sue spire fin qui,
nella purpurea buca
dove un tumulto d'anime saluta
le insegne di Liocorno e di Tartuca.

Il lancio dei vessilli non ti muta
nel volto; troppa vampa ha consumati
gl'indizi che scorgesti; ultimi annunzi
quest'odore di ragia e di tempesta
imminente e quel tiepido stillare
delle nubi strappate,
tardo saluto in gloria di una sorte
che sfugge anche al destino. Dalla torre
cade un suono di bronzo: la sfilata
prosegue fra tamburi che ribattono
a gloria di contrade.
              È strano: tu
che guardi la sommossa vastità,
i mattoni incupiti, la malcerta
mongolfiera di carta che si spicca
dai fantasmi animati sul quadrante
dell'immenso orologio, l'arpeggiante
volteggio degli sciami e lo stupore
che invade la conchiglia
del Campo, tu ritieni
tra le dita il sigillo imperioso
ch'io credevo smarrito
e la luce di prima si diffonde
sulle teste e le sbianca dei suoi gigli.

Palio

Your flight, then, didn't fade out
in the spinning of a top
by the side of the road:
the course that spirals
down to here,
the purple pit
where a riot of souls salutes the flags
of Unicorn and Tortoise.

The hurling of the standards doesn't change
your look; too much fire
has consumed the signs you recognized;
last forewarnings are this scent
of turpentine and coming storm,
and this tepid dripping from the broken clouds—
final salute to glorify a fate
evading destiny itself. A sound of bronze
falls from the tower: the parade moves on
to drums tattooing
the *contrade*'s glory.
                    It's strange: you
who watch the whipped-up vastness,
the rain-dark tiles, the shaky
paper balloon rising
from the animated
phantoms on the immense clock's face,
the zigzagging arpeggios of swarms
and the stupor that invades the Campo's shell—
you hold in your fingers the imperious
seal I thought was lost,
and the light of before
falls on the heads
and blanches them lily-white.

Torna un'eco di là: 'c'era una volta . . .'
(rammenta la preghiera che dal buio
ti giunse una mattina)

   'non un reame, ma l'esile
   traccia di filigrana
   che senza lasciarvi segno
   i nostri passi sfioravano.

   Sotto la volta diaccia
   grava ora un sonno di sasso,
   la voce dalla cantina
   nessuno ascolta, o sei te.

   La sbarra in croce non scande
   la luce per chi s'è smarrito,
   la morte non ha altra voce
   di quella che spande la vita',

ma un'altra voce qui fuga l'orrore
del prigione e per lei quel ritornello
non vale il ghirigoro d'aste avvolte
(Oca e Giraffa) che s'incrociano alte
e ricadono in fiamme. Geme il palco
al passaggio dei brocchi salutati
da un urlo solo. È un volo! E tu dimentica!
Dimentica la morte
toto coelo raggiunta e l'ergotante
balbuzie dei dannati! C'era *il* giorno
dei viventi, lo vedi, e pare immobile
nell'acqua del rubino che si popola
di immagini. Il presente s'allontana
ed il traguardo è là: fuor della selva
dei gonfaloni, su lo scampanìo
del cielo irrefrenato, oltre lo sguardo
dell'uomo—e tu lo fissi. Così alzati,
finché spunti la trottola il suo perno
ma il solco resti inciso. Poi, nient'altro.

An echo from there: "Once upon a time . . ."
(it brings back the prayer you heard
one morning in the dark)

> *"not a kingdom, but the grace-*
> *ful bit of filigree*
> *our footsteps sketched*
> *and left no trace.*
>
> *Under the frozen vault*
> *a sleep of stone now weighs.*
> *No one hears the voice*
> *from the cellar, or it's you.*
>
> *The bar of the cross won't scan*
> *the light for the man who's lost.*
> *Death has no other voice*
> *than the one life sows,"*

but another voice here flees
the prisoner's terror
and for it the refrain can't match
the flourish of rolled banners (Goose and Giraffe)
that clash above and fall in flames. The grandstand
groans as the nags pass, hailed by a single roar.
It's a flight! And you, forget!
Forget death
arrived at *toto coelo* and the caviling
babble of the damned! There was *the* day
of the living, you see it,
still in the ruby's water
peopling with images. The present fades
and the finish line is there: beyond the pennant-
forest, over the pealing
in the unleashed air, out of the sight
of man—and you fix on it. So rise,
until the top's point blunts
but the groove gets etched. Then nothing more.

Notizie dall'Amiata

Il fuoco d'artifizio del maltempo
sarà murmure d'arnie a tarda sera.
La stanza ha travature
tarlate ed un sentore di meloni
penetra dall'assito. Le fumate
morbide che risalgono una valle
d'elfi e di funghi fino al cono diafano
della cima m'intorbidano i vetri,
e ti scrivo di qui, da questo tavolo
remoto, dalla cellula di miele
di una sfera lanciata nello spazio—
e le gabbie coperte, il focolare
dove i marroni esplodono, le vene
di salnitro e di muffa sono il quadro
dove tra poco romperai. La vita
che t'affàbula è ancora troppo breve
se ti contiene! Schiude la tua icona
il fondo luminoso. Fuori piove.

⁕

E tu seguissi le fragili architetture
annerite dal tempo e dal carbone,
i cortili quadrati che hanno nel mezzo
il pozzo profondissimo; tu seguissi
il volo infagottato degli uccelli
notturni e in fondo al borro l'alluccioliò
della Galassia, la fascia d'ogni tormento.
Ma il passo che risuona a lungo nell'oscuro
è di chi va solitario e altro non vede
che questo cadere di archi, di ombre e di pieghe.
Le stelle hanno trapunti troppo sottili,
l'occhio del campanile è fermo sulle due ore,
i rampicanti anch'essi sono un'ascesa
di tenebre ed il loro profumo duole amaro.

News from Mount Amiata

The stormy weather's fireworks
will be a murmur of beehives by late evening.
The room's beams
are worm-eaten and a smell of melons
rises through the floorboards. Wisps of mist
climb an elf-and-mushroom valley
to the mountain's alabaster cone,
clouding my window as I write from here,
this far-off table,
this honey-cell of a sphere launched into space—
and the covered cages, the chestnuts
popping on the hearth,
the veins of saltpeter and mold,
are the frame in which you'll soon erupt.
The life that makes myth of you is still
too brief if it contains you!
Your icon shows the radiant
interior. Outside it's raining.

                ✿

If you were following
the fragile structures black with time and soot,
the foursquare courtyards with the deep,
deep wells in the middle; following
the twig-laden journeys of night birds
and the winking of the Galaxy,
shroud of every torment, in the bottom of the ditch.
But the step that keeps on echoing in the dark
belongs to the man who walks alone
and sees only these falling arches, shadows, edges.
The stars' embroidery is too minute,
the tower's eye is fixed on two o'clock,
even the climbing vines are an ascent
of shadows and their bitter fragrance hurts.

Ritorna domani più freddo, vento del nord,
spezza le antiche mani dell'arenaria,
sconvolgi i libri d'ore nei solai,
e tutto sia lente tranquilla, dominio, prigione
del senso che non dispera! Ritorna più forte
vento di settentrione che rendi care
le catene e suggelli le spore del possibile!
Son troppo strette le strade, gli asini neri
che zoccolano in fila dànno scintille,
dal picco nascosto rispondono vampate di magnesio.
Oh il gocciolìo che scende a rilento
dalle casipole buie, il tempo fatto acqua,
il lungo colloquio coi poveri morti, la cenere, il vento,
il vento che tarda, la morte, la morte che vive!

*

Questa rissa cristiana che non ha
se non parole d'ombra e di lamento
che ti porta di me? Meno di quanto
t'ha rapito la gora che s'interra
dolce nella sua chiusa di cemento.
Una ruota di mola, un vecchio tronco,
confini ultimi al mondo. Si disfà
un cumulo di strame: e tardi usciti
a unire la mia veglia al tuo profondo
sonno che li riceve, i porcospini
s'abbeverano a un filo di pietà.

Come again colder tomorrow, wind from the north,
shatter the ancient sandstone hands,
upset the books of hours in the attic,
let all be quiet pendulum, dominion, prison
for the sense that won't despair!
Come again bolder, north wind that makes us love our chains
and seals the spores of possibility!
The alleys are too narrow, the black mules
clip-clopping single file are striking sparks,
magnesium tongues talk back from the hidden peak.
Oh the slow dripping-down from the dark hovels,
time made water, the long talks
with the poor dead, ashes, wind,
the wind that lingers, death, the death that lives!

      ❋

This Christian wrangle that knows only
words of shadow and lament—
what does it bring you of me?
Less than what the millrace softly silting
in its cement basin stole from you.
A millwheel, an old tree trunk,
last ends of the earth. A pile of straw
dissolves: and emerging late
to make my vigil one with your deep sleep
that takes them in, the porcupines
will slake their thirst at a trickle of pity.

LA BUFERA

E ALTRO

1940-1954

—————

THE STORM,

ETC.

1940-1954

PARTE I

FINISTERRE

PART I

FINISTERRE

La bufera

Les princes n'ont point d'yeux pour voir ces grand's merveilles,
Leurs mains ne servent plus qu'à nous persécuter . . .
—AGRIPPA D'AUBIGNÉ, À *Dieu*

La bufera che sgronda sulle foglie
dure della magnolia i lunghi tuoni
marzolini e la grandine,

(i suoni di cristallo nel tuo nido
notturno ti sorprendono, dell'oro
che s'è spento sui mogani, sul taglio
dei libri rilegati, brucia ancora
una grana di zucchero nel guscio
delle tue palpebre)

il lampo che candisce
alberi e muri e li sorprende in quella
eternità d'istante—marmo manna
e distruzione—ch'entro te scolpita
porti per tua condanna e che ti lega
più che l'amore a me, strana sorella,—

e poi lo schianto rude, i sistri, il fremere
dei tamburelli sulla fossa fuia,
lo scalpicciare del fandango, e sopra
qualche gesto che annaspa . . .
                                    Come quando
ti rivolgesti e con la mano, sgombra
la fronte dalla nube dei capelli,

mi salutasti—per entrar nel buio.

The Storm

Les princes n'ont point d'yeux pour voir ces grand's merveilles,
Leurs mains ne servent plus qu'à nous persécuter . . .
—AGRIPPA D'AUBIGNÉ, À *Dieu*

The storm that drums the hard
magnolia leaves with long March
thunder and hail,

(the sounds of crystal in your nighttime
nest surprise you; a grain of sugar
of the gold now gone
from the mahogany
and the tooled backs of the leather books
burns still in your eyelids' shell)

the flash that candies
trees and walls, surprising them
in that eternal instant—marble
manna and destruction—which you carry
carved in you as your sentence and which binds you to me
closer than love, strange sister—

and then the awful crack, the timbrels,
tambour-rasp above the ditch of thieves,
stomp of the fandango, and a few
groping motions above . . .
                              As when
you turned and, forehead clear
of its cloud of hair,

waved to me—and went into the dark.

Lungomare

Il soffio cresce, il buio è rotto a squarci,
e l'ombra che tu mandi sulla fragile
palizzata s'arriccia. Troppo tardi

se vuoi esser te stessa! Dalla palma
tonfa il sorcio, il baleno è sulla miccia,
sui lunghissimi cigli del tuo sguardo.

Promenade

The wind picks up, the dark is torn to shreds,
the shadow that you send out on the fragile
balustrade is curling. Too late, if

you want to be yourself! The mouse
drops from the palm, the lightning's on the fuse,
on the long, long lashes of your look.

Su una lettera non scritta

Per un formicolìo d'albe, per pochi
fili su cui s'impigli
il fiocco della vita e s'incollani
in ore e in anni, oggi i delfini a coppie
capriolano coi figli? Oh ch'io non oda
nulla di te, ch'io fugga dal bagliore
dei tuoi cigli. Ben altro è sulla terra.

Sparir non so né riaffacciarmi; tarda
la fucina vermiglia
della notte, la sera si fa lunga,
la preghiera è supplizio e non ancora
tra le rocce che sorgono t'è giunta
la bottiglia dal mare. L'onda, vuota,
si rompe sulla punta, a Finisterre.

On an Unwritten Letter

Is it for a swarm of dawns, for a few
strands on which the fleece of life
might snag and entwine into hours and years,
that today these pairs of dolphins
caper with their young? Oh let me
hear nothing of you, flee the flash
of your lashes. There's far more on earth.

I can no more disappear
than show myself again; the night's vermilion
forge is stalling, evening drags on,
prayer is torment and the bottle
has yet to reach you among the rocks
that climb out of the sea. The empty wave
breaks on the point, at Finisterre.

Nel sonno

Il canto delle strigi, quando un'iride
con intermessi palpiti si stinge,
i gemiti e i sospiri
di gioventù, l'errore che recinge
le tempie e il vago orror dei cedri smossi
dall'urto della notte—tutto questo
può ritornarmi, traboccar dai fossi,
rompere dai condotti, farmi desto
alla tua voce. Punge il suono d'una
giga crudele, l'avversario chiude
la celata sul viso. Entra la luna
d'amaranto nei chiusi occhi, è una nube
che gonfia; e quando il sonno la trasporta
più in fondo, è ancora sangue oltre la morte.

In Sleep

The song of the screech owls, when a rainbow
pulses intermittently, then fades,
the moans and sighs of youth, the fault
that binds the temples,
the faint horror of the cedars
stirred by the thrust of night—all this
can come back to me, overflow the ditches,
pour from the culverts, wake me
at your voice. The music of a cruel jig
stings, the enemy lowers his visor
over his face. The amaranth moon
streams into my shut eyes, a swelling cloud;
and when sleep takes it even deeper,
it's still blood beyond death.

Serenata indiana

È pur nostro il disfarsi delle sere.
E per noi è la stria che dal mare
sale al parco e ferisce gli aloè.

Puoi condurmi per mano, se tu fingi
di crederti con me, se ho la follia
di seguirti lontano e ciò che stringi,

ciò che dici, m'appare in tuo potere.

. . .

Fosse tua vita quella che mi tiene
sulle soglie—e potrei prestarti un volto,
vaneggiarti figura. Ma non è,

non è così. Il polipo che insinua
tentacoli d'inchiostro tra gli scogli
può servirsi di te. Tu gli appartieni

e non lo sai. Sei lui, ti credi te.

Indian Serenade

The raveling of the evenings is ours, too,
and the stripe of light out of the sea
that rises to the park and strikes the aloes.

You can take my hand, if you pretend
to think you're with me, if I'm fool enough
to follow you for long and what you're holding,

what you're saying, seems within your power.

    .   .   .

Were it your life that stalls me at the threshold—
and I could lend a face to you,
imagine you a form. But no,

it's not that way. The octopus that works
inky tentacles among the shoals
knows how to use you. You belong to him

unwittingly. You're him; you think you're you.

Gli orecchini

Non serba ombra di voli il nerofumo
della spera. (E del tuo non è più traccia).
È passata la spugna che i barlumi
indifesi dal cerchio d'oro scaccia.
Le tue pietre, i coralli, il forte imperio
che ti rapisce vi cercavo; fuggo
l'iddia che non s'incarna, i desiderî
porto fin che al tuo lampo non si struggono.
Ronzano èlitre fuori, ronza il folle
mortorio e sa che due vite non contano.
Nella cornice tornano le molli
meduse della sera. La tua impronta
verrà di giù: dove ai tuoi lobi squallide
mani, travolte, fermano i coralli.

The Earrings

The lampblack of the mirror shows
no shadow of flight. (And of yours no trace remains.)
The sponge has passed across the golden circle,
given the defenseless glimmers chase.
I looked there for your stones, the corals,
the strong power taking you;
I flee the goddess who won't be flesh,
bear my desires till they're burned in your flash.
Elytra drone outside, the insane
funeral drones on and knows two lives don't count.
Evening's soft medusas reappear
inside the frame. Your stamp will come
from below: where pale, contorted
hands affix the corals to your ears.

La frangia dei capelli . . .

La frangia dei capelli che ti vela
la fronte puerile, tu distrarla
con la mano non devi. Anch'essa parla
di te, sulla mia strada è tutto il cielo,
la sola luce con le giade ch'ài
accerchiate sul polso, nel tumulto
del sonno la cortina che gl'indulti
tuoi distendono, l'ala onde tu vai,
trasmigratrice Artemide ed illesa,
tra le guerre dei nati-morti; e s'ora
d'aeree lanugini s'infiora
quel fondo, a marezzarlo sei tu, scesa
d'un balzo, e irrequieta la tua fronte
si confonde con l'alba, la nasconde.

The bangs . . .

The bangs that hide your childlike forehead—
don't disturb them with your hand.
They too speak of you, along my way
they're all the sky, the only light
beyond the jades you wear around your wrist,
the curtain your condoning hangs
across the roar of sleep,
the wing on which you fly,
transmigratory Artemis, unscathed
among the wars of the stillborn; and if now
those depths get flocked with airy down
it's you who've marbled them, come down
in one fell swoop, and your unquiet brow
gets melded with the dawn, eclipses it.

Finestra fiesolana

Qui dove il grillo insidioso buca
i vestiti di seta vegetale
e l'odor della canfora non fuga
le tarme che sfarinano nei libri,
l'uccellino s'arrampica a spirale
su per l'olmo ed il sole tra le frappe
cupo invischia. Altra luce che non colma,
altre vampe, o mie edere scarlatte.

Fiesole Window

Here where the insidious cricket
bores into clothes of vegetable silk
and the smell of camphor doesn't rout
the moths that turn to powder in the books,
the little bird whirls up the elm
and the snared sun fails among the leaves.
Another light that doesn't overflow,
other fires, O my scarlet ivies.

Il giglio rosso

Il giglio rosso, se un dì
mise radici nel tuo cuor di vent'anni
(brillava la pescaia tra gli stacci
dei renaioli, a tuffo s'inforravano
lucide talpe nelle canne, torri,
gonfaloni vincevano la pioggia,
e il trapianto felice al nuovo sole,
te inconscia si compì);

il giglio rosso già sacrificato
sulle lontane crode
ai vischi che la sciarpa ti tempestano
d'un gelo incorruttibile e le mani,—
fiore di fosso che ti s'aprirà
sugli argini solenni ove il brusìo
del tempo più non affatica . . . : a scuotere
l'arpa celeste, a far la morte amica.

The Red Lily

The red lily, if one day
it took root in your twenty-year-old heart
(the weir was sparkling
under the sand-diggers' sieves,
sleek moles dove and burrowed in the rushes,
towers, flags withstood the rain,
and the happy graft in the new sun
knit without your knowing);

the red lily, long since sacrificed
on far-off crags to mistletoe
that scintillates your scarf and hands
with an incorruptible chill—
ditchflower that will unfurl for you
on those solemn banks where the hum of time
no longer wearies us . . . : to strike
the harp of heaven, make death a friend.

Il ventaglio

Ut pictura . . . Le labbra che confondono,
gli sguardi, i segni, i giorni ormai caduti
provo a figgerli là come in un tondo
di cannocchiale arrovesciato, muti
e immoti, ma più vivi. Era una giostra
d'uomini e ordegni in fuga tra quel fumo
ch'Euro batteva, e già l'alba l'inostra
con un sussulto e rompe quelle brume.
Luce la madreperla, la calanca
vertiginosa inghiotte ancora vittime,
ma le tue piume sulle guance sbiancano
e il giorno è forse salvo. O colpi fitti,
quando ti schiudi, o crudi lampi, o scrosci
sull'orde! (Muore chi ti riconosce?).

The Fan

Ut pictura . . . The confounding lips,
the looks, sighs, days now long since gone:
I try to fix them there as in
the wrong end of a telescope,
silent and motionless, but more alive.
It was a joust of men and armaments, a rout
in smoke that Eurus raised, but now the dawn
has turned it purple and breaks through those mists.
The mother-of-pearl gleams, the dizzying
precipice still swallows victims, but
the feathers on your cheeks are whitening
and maybe the day is saved. O raining blows
when you reveal yourself, sharp flashes, downpour
over the hordes! (Must he who sees you die?)

Personae separatae

Come la scaglia d'oro che si spicca
dal fondo oscuro e liquefatta cola
nel corridoio dei carrubi ormai
ischeletriti, così pure noi
persone separate per lo sguardo
d'un altro? È poca cosa la parola,
poca cosa lo spazio in questi crudi
noviluni annebbiati: ciò che manca,
e che ci torce il cuore e qui m'attarda
tra gli alberi, ad attenderti, è un perduto
senso, o il fuoco, se vuoi, che a terra stampi,
figure parallele, ombre concordi,
aste di un sol quadrante i nuovi tronchi
delle radure e colmi anche le cave
ceppaie, nido alle formiche. Troppo
straziato è il bosco umano, troppo sorda
quella voce perenne, troppo ansioso
lo squarcio che si sbiocca sui nevati
gioghi di Lunigiana. La tua forma
passò di qui, si riposò sul riano
tra le nasse atterrate, poi si sciolse
come un sospiro, intorno—e ivi non era
l'orror che fiotta, in te la luce ancora
trovava luce, oggi non più che al giorno
primo già annotta.

Personae Separatae

Like the scale of gold that lifts off from
the black backdrop and liquefied runs down
the corridor of carobs turned to bones,
are we too separate persons
in another's eyes? The word's
a little thing, space is little
in these raw, misted
new moons: what's missing,
what torments our hearts and holds me here
waiting for you in the trees, is a lost sense,
or, if you will, the fire that brands the earth,
parallel figures, shadows in agreement,
shafts of a sun
that frames trunks in the clearings
and even fills the hollow stumps, ant-nests.
The human forest is too flayed,
that voice of always is too deaf,
the gash that melts above the Lunigiana's
snowy passes is too anxious.
Your form came this way,
stayed by the ditch among the grounded eel-pots,
then faded like a sigh, around—
and there was no gushing horror here; in you
the light could still find light, but no longer:
now at daybreak it's already night.

L'arca

La tempesta di primavera ha sconvolto
l'ombrello del salice,
al turbine d'aprile
s'è impigliato nell'orto il vello d'oro
che nasconde i miei morti,
i miei cani fidati, le mie vecchie
serve—quanti da allora
(quando il salce era biondo e io ne stroncavo
le anella con la fionda) son calati,
vivi, nel trabocchetto. La tempesta
certo li riunirà sotto quel tetto
di prima, ma lontano, più lontano
di questa terra folgorata dove
bollono calce e sangue nell'impronta
del piede umano. Fuma il ramaiolo
in cucina, un suo tondo di riflessi
accentra i volti ossuti, i musi aguzzi
e li protegge in fondo la magnolia
se un soffio ve la getta. La tempesta
primaverile scuote d'un latrato
di fedeltà la mia arca, o perduti.

The Ark

The spring storm has upended
the willow's umbrella,
the April gale in the garden has caught
the golden fleece that hides my dead,
my trusty dogs, my ancient
nurses—how many since then
(when the willow was yellow
and I clipped its curls with my sling)
have fallen into the snare alive.
Surely the storm will gather them
under that same roof again,
but far away, much farther than
this thunderstruck earth where blood and lime
ferment in a human footprint. The ladle
steams in the kitchen, its bowl distills
the bony faces and keen snouts
it mirrors, and the magnolia
shelters them at the bottom, if a gust
should land them there. The storm of spring
batters my ark with baying
loyalty, O lost.

Giorno e notte

Anche una piuma che vola può disegnare
la tua figura, o il raggio che gioca a rimpiattino
tra i mobili, il rimando dello specchio
di un bambino, dai tetti. Sul giro delle mura
strascichi di vapore prolungano le guglie
dei pioppi e giù sul trespolo s'arruffa il pappagallo
dell'arrotino. Poi la notte afosa
sulla piazzola, e i passi, e sempre questa dura
fatica di affondare per risorgere eguali
da secoli, o da istanti, d'incubi che non possono
ritrovare la luce dei tuoi occhi nell'antro
incandescente—e ancora le stesse grida e i lunghi
pianti sulla veranda
se rimbomba improvviso il colpo che t'arrossa
la gola e schianta l'ali, o perigliosa
annunziatrice dell'alba,
e si destano i chiostri e gli ospedali
a un lacerìo di trombe . . .

Day and Night

A floating feather, too, can sketch your image
or the sunbeam playing hide-and-seek
in the furniture, rebounding off
a baby's mirror or the roofs. Above the walls
wisps of steam draw out the poplars' spires
and the knifegrinder's parrot down below
fans his feathers on his perch. And then the hazy night
in the little square, and footsteps, and always
this painful effort to sink under
to re-emerge the same for centuries, or seconds,
by ghosts who can't win back the light of your eyes
inside the incandescent cave—and still
the same shouts and long wailing on the veranda
if suddenly the shot rings out
that reddens your throat and shears
your wings, O perilous harbinger of dawn,
and the cloisters and the hospitals awake
to a rending chorus of horns . . .

Il tuo volo

Se appari al fuoco (pendono
sul tuo ciuffo e ti stellano
gli amuleti)
due luci ti contendono
al borro ch'entra sotto
la volta degli spini.

La veste è in brani, i frùtici
calpesti rifavillano
e la gonfia peschiera dei girini
umani s'apre ai solchi della notte.

Oh non turbar l'immondo
vivagno, lascia intorno
le cataste brucianti, il fumo forte
sui superstiti!

Se rompi il fuoco (biondo
cinerei i capelli
sulla ruga che tenera
ha abbandonato il cielo)
come potrà la mano delle sete
e delle gemme ritrovar tra i morti
il suo fedele?

Your Flight

If you appear in the fire
(amulets droop from your forelock
so you shine)
two lights contend for you
in the ditch running under
the vault of thorns.

Your dress is shreds, the trampled
bushes twinkle back
and the fishpond crammed with human tadpoles
opens to the furrows of the night.

Oh don't disturb the filthy
selvage, leave the burning piles
around, the bitter smoke
above the survivors!

If you break into the fire
(blond, ash-blond your hair
on the tender
ridge that deserted the sky)
how will the hand of silk and jewels
retrieve its true believer
from the dead?

A mia madre

Ora che il coro delle coturnici
ti blandisce nel sonno eterno, rotta
felice schiera in fuga verso i clivi
vendemmiati del Mesco, or che la lotta
dei viventi più infuria, se tu cedi
come un'ombra la spoglia
                              (e non è un'ombra,
o gentile, non è ciò che tu credi)

chi ti proteggerà? La strada sgombra
non è una via, solo due mani, un volto,
quelle mani, *quel* volto, il gesto d'una
vita che non è un'altra ma se stessa,
solo questo ti pone nell'eliso
folto d'anime e voci in cui tu vivi;

e la domanda che tu lasci è anch'essa
un gesto tuo, all'ombra delle croci.

To My Mother

Now that the choir of rock partridges
lulls you in eternal sleep, uneven
glad formation making for the harvested
cliffs of the Mesco, now the struggle of
the living rages wilder, if you shrug
your spoils off like a shadow

                          (but they're not a shadow,
gentle one, they're not what you believe),

who will watch over you? The emptied street
is not a way, only two hands, a face,
those hands, *that* face, the gesture of
a life that's nothing but itself,
only this settles you in that Elysium
crowded with souls and voices where you live;

and the question that you leave
is a gesture of yours, too, in the shadow of the crosses.

PARTE II

DOPO

PART II

AFTERWARDS

Madrigali fiorentini

I

11 settembre 1943

Suggella, Herma, con nastri e ceralacca
la speranza che vana
si svela, appena schiusa ai tuoi mattini.
Sul muro dove si leggeva MORTE
A BAFFO BUCO passano una mano
di biacca. Un vagabondo di lassù
scioglie manifestini sulla corte
annuvolata. E il rombo s'allontana.

II

11 agosto 1944

Un Bedlington s'affaccia, pecorella
azzurra, al tremolio di quei tronconi
—*Trinity Bridge*—nell'acqua. Se s'infognano
come topi di chiavica i padroni
d'ieri (di sempre?), i colpi che martellano
le tue tempie fin lì, nella corsia
del paradiso, sono il gong che ancora
ti rivuole fra noi, sorella mia.

Florentine Madrigals

I

11 September 1943

Herma, seal with wax and string
the hope that's understood as vain
the moment it's revealed to your mornings.
Someone's slapping whitewash on
the wall that once read DEATH
TO BAFFO BUCO. Up above,
a vagabond spills leaflets on the clouding
courtyard. And the rumble fades.

II

11 August 1944

A Bedlington, blue lamb, pokes out
above the shimmer of those stumps
—*Trinity Bridge*—in the water.
If the lords of yesterday (of always?)
are sunk like sewer rats, the blows
that pound your temples even there,
in the corridor that leads to heaven, are
the gong that calls you back among us, sister.

Da una torre

Ho visto il merlo acquaiolo
spiccarsi dal parafulmine:
al volo orgoglioso, a un gruppetto
di flauto l'ho conosciuto.

Ho visto il festoso e orecchiuto
Piquillo scattar dalla tomba
e a stratti, da un'umida tromba
di scale, raggiungere il tetto.

Ho visto nei vetri a colori
filtrare un paese di scheletri
da fiori di bifore—e un labbro
di sangue farsi più muto.

From a Tower

I've seen the waterdipper
rise from the lightning rod:
I knew him by his pride in flight,
by his flutelike trill.

I've seen long-eared Piquillo leap
elated out of the tomb
and bound up the wet shell
of steps to reclaim the roof.

I've seen a town of skeletons
filter through stained-glass mullion
flowers—and a blood-red lip
go stiller still.

Ballata scritta in una clinica

Nel solco dell'emergenza:

quando si sciolse oltremonte
la folle cometa agostana
nell'aria ancora serena

—ma buio, per noi, e terrore
e crolli di altane e di ponti
su noi come Giona sepolti
nel ventre della balena—

ed io mi volsi e lo specchio
di me più non era lo stesso
perché la gola ed il petto
t'avevano chiuso di colpo
in un manichino di gesso.

Nel cavo delle tue orbite
brillavano lenti di lacrime
più spesse di questi tuoi grossi
occhiali di tartaruga
che a notte ti tolgo e avvicino
alle fiale della morfina.

L'iddio taurino non era
il nostro, ma il Dio che colora
di fuoco i gigli del fosso:
Ariete invocai e la fuga
del mostro cornuto travolse
con l'ultimo orgoglio anche il cuore
schiantato dalla tua tosse.

Attendo un cenno, se è prossima
l'ora del ratto finale:
son pronto e la penitenza
s'inizia fin d'ora nel cupo

Ballad Written in a Hospital

In the trough of the emergency:

when over the hills the insane
August comet let go
in air that was still blue

—but dark, for us, and terror
and porches and bridges that fell
down on us buried like Jonah
in the belly of the whale—

and I turned and my mirror-image
wasn't what it had been
for your throat and chest
had just been encased
in a plaster manikin.

In the hollows of your sockets
your tears like lenses shone,
thicker than the great big
tortoiseshell glasses
I take off you and set down
at night, by the phials of morphine.

The bull-god wasn't ours
but the God who paints fire on
the lilies in the ditch:
I called on Aries and
the horned monster's flight undid
the heart your cough had shattered
along with the last of my pride.

I wait for a sign that the hour
of the final rapture is near:
I'm ready, and remorse is
rising now in the gloomy

singulto di valli e dirupi
dell'*altra* Emergenza.

Hai messo sul comodino
il bulldog di legno, la sveglia
col fosforo sulle lancette
che spande un tenue lucore
sul tuo dormiveglia,

il nulla che basta a chi vuole
forzare la porta stretta;
e fuori, rossa, s'inasta,
si spiega sul bianco una croce.

Con te anch'io m'affaccio alla voce
che irrompe nell'alba, all'enorme
presenza dei morti; e poi l'ululo

del cane di legno è il mio, muto.

sobbing of valleys and gorges
of the *other* Emergency.

You've set the wooden bulldog
on the nightstand by the clock
whose phosphorescent sweep
scatters a faint brightness
over your half-sleep,

the nothing that does for him who wants
to force the narrow gate;
and outside rises and opens
a red cross on a field of white.

With you I look out toward the voice
that is breaking into the dawn,
toward the enormous presence of the dead;

and the bulldog's howl, unuttered, is my own.

PARTE III

INTERMEZZO

PART III

INTERMEZZO

Due nel crepuscolo

Fluisce fra te e me sul belvedere
un chiarore subacqueo che deforma
col profilo dei colli anche il tuo viso.
Sta in un fondo sfuggevole, reciso
da te ogni gesto tuo; entra senz'orma,
e sparisce, nel mezzo che ricolma
ogni solco e si chiude sul tuo passo:
con me tu qui, dentro quest'aria scesa
a sigillare
il torpore dei massi.

           Ed io riverso
nel potere che grava attorno, cedo
al sortilegio di non riconoscere
di me più nulla fuor di me: s'io levo
appena il braccio, mi si fa diverso
l'atto, si spezza su un cristallo, ignota
e impallidita sua memoria, e il gesto
già più non m'appartiene;
se parlo, ascolto quella voce attonito,
scendere alla sua gamma più remota
o spenta all'aria che non la sostiene.

Tale nel punto che resiste all'ultima
consunzione del giorno
dura lo smarrimento; poi un soffio
risolleva le valli in un frenetico
moto e deriva dalle fronde un tinnulo
suono che si disperde
tra rapide fumate e i primi lumi
disegnano gli scali.

           . . . le parole
tra noi leggere cadono. Ti guardo
in un molle riverbero. Non so
se ti conosco; so che mai diviso
fui da te come accade in questo tardo

Two in Twilight

An underwater brightness flows
between us on the belvedere, distorting
your profile with the outline of the hills.
The background wavers, every motion
carved away from you—arriving out of nowhere
then gone, into the medium
that fills each furrow, swallowing your steps:
you here with me, inside this air
come down to seal
the torpor of the boulders.

                              And lying back
inside the power that weighs down around,
I yield to the sorcery of not knowing
anything of me beyond myself:
if I barely raise my arm, the act
shears off from me, shatters on a crystal,
its memory unknown and pale,
already now the movement isn't mine;
if I speak I hear that amazed voice
fall to the bottom of its range
or die out in the air that won't sustain it.

So bewilderment lives on
in the moment that resists the day's
last dying; then a breeze
rouses the valleys in a frantic
turbulence and takes
a tinny sound from the leaves that gets lost
in the smoke's fast Morse code
and the first lights outline the docks.

                                    . . . words
fall lightly between us. I watch you
in a watery wavering. I don't know
if I know you; I'm certain
I was never as estranged from you

ritorno. Pochi istanti hanno bruciato
tutto di noi: fuorché due volti, due
maschere che s'incidono, sforzate,
di un sorriso.

as here, in this late return. A few seconds
have burned us all away: all but two faces,
two masks forcibly etched
with smiles.

Dov'era il tennis . . .

Dov'era una volta il tennis, nel piccolo rettangolo difeso dalla massicciata su cui dominano i pini selvatici, cresce ora la gramigna e raspano i conigli nelle ore di libera uscita.

Qui vennero un giorno a giocare due sorelle, due bianche farfalle, nelle prime ore del pomeriggio. Verso levante la vista era (è ancora) libera e le umide rocce del Corone maturano sempre l'uva forte per lo 'sciacchetrà'. È curioso pensare che ognuno di noi ha un paese come questo, e sia pur diversissimo, che dovrà restare il *suo* paesaggio, immutabile; è curioso che l'ordine fisico sia così lento a filtrare in noi e poi così impossibile a scancellarsi. Ma quanto al resto? A conti fatti, chiedersi il come e il perché della partita interrotta è come chiederselo della nubecola di vapore che esce dal cargo arrembato, laggiù sulla linea della Palmaria. Fra poco s'accenderanno nel golfo le prime lampare.

Intorno, a distesa d'occhio, l'iniquità degli oggetti persiste intangibile. La grotta incrostata di conchiglie dev'essere rimasta la stessa nel giardino delle piante grasse, sotto il tennis; ma il parente maniaco non verrà più a fotografare al lampo di magnesio il fiore unico, irripetibile, sorto su un cacto spinoso e destinato a una vita di pochi istanti. Anche le ville dei sudamericani sembrano chiuse. Non sempre ci furono eredi pronti a dilapidare la lussuosa paccottiglia messa insieme a suon di pesos o di milreis. O forse la sarabanda dei nuovi giunti segna il passo in altre contrade: qui siamo perfettamente defilati, fuori tiro. Si direbbe che la vita non possa accendervisi che a lampi e si pasca solo di quanto s'accumula inerte e va in cancrena in queste zone abbandonate.

'Del salón en el ángulo oscuro—silenciosa y cubierta de polvo— veíase el arpa . . .'. Eh sì, il museo sarebbe impressionante se si potesse scoperchiare l'ex-paradiso del Liberty. Sul conchiglione-terrazzo sostenuto da un Nettuno gigante, ora scrostato, nessuno apparve più dopo la sconfitta elettorale e il decesso del Leone del Callao; ma là, sull'esorbitante bovino affrescato di peri meli e serpenti da paradiso terrestre, pensò invano la signora Paquita buonanima di produrre la sua serena vecchiaia confortata di truffatissimi agi e del sorriso della posterità. Vennero un giorno i mariti delle

Where the Tennis Court Was . . .

Where the tennis court once was, in the little rectangle hidden by the railway embankment and watched over by wild pines, weeds grow now and rabbits scratch in their hours in the open.

One day two sisters, two white butterflies, came here to play in the early afternoon. The view to the east was open (and still is) and the wet rocks of the Corone still ripen the strong grapes used in making *sciacchetrà*. It's curious to think that each of us has a place like this, however different, which is bound to remain *his* landscape, immutable; it's curious that the order of things is so slow to seep into us and so impossible to eradicate later. And then? In the end, asking the why and wherefore of the game that got interrupted is like asking the reason for the little puff of smoke coming from the docked freighter down there on the Palmaria line. Soon the first night trawlers will light their lamps in the gulf.

All around, as far as the eye can see, the recalcitrance of things continues insensibly. The grotto encrusted with seashells must still be just the way it was in the succulent garden, below the tennis court; but our maniacal relation will no longer come with his magnesium flash to photograph the unique, unrepeatable flower that blossomed on a spiny cactus and was destined to live a few seconds. The villas of the South Americans look closed up, too. There weren't always heirs ready to scatter the luxurious bric-a-brac amassed to the sound of pesos and milreis. Or perhaps the saraband of the new arrivals marks time elsewhere: here we're entirely out of step, out of range. One might say that life can catch fire only from lightning and feeds solely on what accumulates inertly and goes to gangrene in these desert places.

"*Del salón en el ángulo oscuro—silenciosa y cubierto de polvo— veíase el arpa . . .*" Ah yes, what an impressive museum we'd uncover if we could lift the lid off that old Liberty paradise. No one appeared again on the shell-shaped balcony supported by a huge, now-peeling Neptune after the electoral defeat and demission of the Lion of Callao; but there, in the extravagant bow window frescoed with pears, apples, and serpents from an earthly paradise, the good-hearted Signora Paquita thought in vain to live out a serene old age eased by the cunningest of comforts and the benevolence of her

figlie, i generi brazileiri e gettata la maschera fecero man bassa su quel ben di Dio. Della dueña e degli altri non si seppe più nulla. Uno dei discendenti rispuntò poi fuori in una delle ultime guerre e fece miracoli. Ma allora si era giunti sì e no ai tempi dell'inno tripolino. Questi oggetti, queste case, erano ancora nel circolo vitale, fin ch'esso durò. Pochi sentirono dapprima che il freddo stava per giungere; e tra questi forse mio padre che anche nel più caldo giorno d'agosto, finita la cena all'aperto, piena di falene e d'altri insetti, dopo essersi buttato sulle spalle uno scialle di lana, ripetendo sempre in francese, chissà perché, «*il fait bien froid, bien froid*», si ritirava subito in camera per finir di fumarsi a letto il suo Cavour da sette centesimi.

progeny. One day her daughters' husbands, her Brazilian sons-in-law, arrived, unmasked themselves, and laid evil hands on that heavenly bounty. We heard no more about the *dueña* and the others. A descendant later resurfaced abroad in one of the recent wars and performed miracles. But by then we had more or less reached the era of the Tripoli hymn. These things, these houses, stayed in the vital circle while it lasted. Few sensed ahead of time that the cold was coming; but one of them may have been my father, who even on the hottest August day, after dinner in the open air thick with moths and other insects, would throw a woolen shawl over his shoulders, saying, always in French for some reason, *"Il fait bien froid, bien froid,"* then quickly retire to his room to finish smoking his seven-centime Cavour in bed.

Visita a Fadin

Passata la Madonna dell'Orto e seguìti per pochi passi i portici del centro svoltai poi su per la rampa che conduce all'ospedale e giunsi in breve dove il malato non si attendeva di vedermi: sulla balconata degli incurabili, stesi al sole. Mi scorse subito e non parve sorpreso. Aveva sempre i capelli cortissimi, rasi da poco, il viso più scavato e rosso agli zigomi, gli occhi bellissimi, come prima, ma dissolti in un alone più profondo. Giungevo senza preavviso, e in giorno indebito: neppure la sua Carlina, 'l'angelo musicante', poteva esser là.

Il mare, in basso, era vuoto, e sulla costa apparivano sparse le architetture di marzapane degli arricchiti.

Ultima sosta del viaggio: alcuni dei tuoi compagni occasionali (operai, commessi, parrucchieri) ti avevano già preceduto alla chetichella, sparendo dai loro lettucci. T'eri portato alcuni pacchi di libri, li avevi messi al posto del tuo zaino d'un tempo: vecchi libri fuor di moda, a eccezione di un volumetto di poesie che presi e che ora resterà con me, come indovinammo tutti e due senza dirlo.

Del colloquio non ricordo più nulla. Certo non aveva bisogno di richiamarsi alle questioni supreme, agli universali, chi era sempre vissuto in modo umano, cioè semplice e silenzioso. Exit Fadin. E ora dire che non ci sei più è dire solo che sei entrato in un ordine diverso, per quanto quello in cui ci muoviamo noi ritardatari, così pazzesco com'è, sembri alla nostra ragione l'unico in cui la divinità può svolgere i propri attributi, riconoscersi e saggiarsi nei limiti di un assunto di cui ignoriamo il significato. (Anch'essa, dunque, avrebbe bisogno di noi? Se è una bestemmia, ahimè, non è neppure la nostra peggiore).

Essere sempre tra i primi e *sapere*, ecco ciò che conta, anche se il perché della rappresentazione ci sfugge. Chi ha avuto da te quest'alta lezione di *decenza quotidiana* (la più difficile delle virtù) può attendere senza fretta il libro delle tue reliquie. La tua parola non era forse di quelle che si scrivono.

Visit to Fadin

Past Madonna dell'Orto, a few feet along the arcades of the center, and I turned up the steps that lead to the hospital where I soon found the patient who wasn't expecting me: on the balcony where the terminal cases were set in the sun. He saw me immediately and showed no surprise. He had very short hair still, recently cut, a more ravaged face, red at the cheekbones, beautiful eyes as before, but dissolved in a deeper halo. I came without warning and on the wrong day: not even his Carlina, his "musical angel," could be there.

The sea below was empty, and on the coast one could see the scattered marzipan confections of the newly rich.

Last stop on the journey: a few of your recent companions (workers, clerks, hairdressers) had stolen silently ahead of you, disappearing from their cots. You'd brought with you a few stacks of books, which you set where you'd once put your knapsack: old, unfashionable books, except for a small volume of poems which I took and which will now remain with me, as we both understood without saying.

I remember nothing more of our conversation. Surely a man who had always lived humanely, that is, simply and silently, had no need to refer to ultimate, universal questions. Exit Fadin. And now to say you're no longer here is simply to say you've entered another order, given that the one we move in, we stragglers, insane as it is, appears to our reason the only place where divinity can reveal its attributes, be recognized and assayed as an enterprise whose significance we don't understand. (Might it, in turn, have need of us, then? If this is blasphemy, alas, it's by no means our worst.)

Always to be among the first, and *know*: this is what counts, even if the why of the performance escapes us. He who has learned from you this great lesson of *daily decency* (the most difficult of the virtues) can wait patiently for the book of your remains. It may be your word was not among those that get written.

PARTE IV

'FLASHES' E

DEDICHE

PART IV

FLASHES AND

INSCRIPTIONS

Verso Siena

Ohimè che la memoria sulla vetta
non ha chi la trattenga!

(La fuga dei porcelli sull'Ambretta
notturna al sobbalzare della macchina
che guada, il carillon di San Gusmè
e una luna maggenga, tutta macchie . . .).

La scatola a sorpresa ha fatto scatto
sul punto in cui il mio Dio gittò la maschera
e fulminò il ribelle.

Near Siena

Alas, that memory at its height
has no one to contain it!

(The piglets' night flight over the Ambretta
to the bucking car, the carillon
of San Gusmè
and a May moon, all stains . . .)

The jack-in-the-box broke open when
my God unmasked himself and hurled
forked lightning at his rebel.

Sulla Greve

Ora non ceno solo con lo sguardo
come quando al mio fischio ti sporgevi
e ti vedevo appena. Un masso, un solco
a imbuto, il volo nero d'una rondine,
un coperchio sul mondo . . .

E m'è pane quel boccio di velluto
che s'apre su un glissato di mandolino,
acqua il frùscio scorrente, il tuo profondo
respiro vino.

On the Greve

Now I feast not just my eyes
as when I whistled, you leaned out,
and I barely could see you. A rock, a narrowing
furrow, the black flight of a swallow,
a cover over the world . . .

And it's bread to me, this bud of velvet
unfurling to a trill of mandolin,
its fluent whispering is water,
your deep breathing wine.

La trota nera

Reading

Curvi sull'acqua serale
graduati in Economia,
Dottori in Divinità,
la trota annusa e va via,
il suo balenio di carbonchio
è un ricciolo tuo che si sfa
nel bagno, un sospiro che sale
dagli ipogei del tuo ufficio.

The Black Trout

Reading

Graduates in Economics,
Doctors in Divinity
bent to the evening river,
the trout breaks water, disappears,
its carbuncle glare
is a ringlet of yours
uncurling in your bath, a sigh
that rises from your office catacomb.

Di un natale metropolitano

Londra

Un vischio, fin dall'infanzia sospeso grappolo
di fede e di pruina sul tuo lavandino
e sullo specchio ovale ch'ora adombrano
i tuoi ricci bergère fra santini e ritratti
di ragazzi infilati un po' alla svelta
nella cornice, una caraffa vuota,
bicchierini di cenere e di bucce,
le luci di Mayfair, poi a un crocicchio
le anime, le bottiglie che non seppero aprirsi,
non più guerra né pace, il tardo frullo
di un piccione incapace di seguirti
sui gradini automatici che ti slittano in giù . . .

A Metropolitan Christmas

London

Cluster of faith and frost, the mistletoe
hanging since childhood over your sink,
and in the oval mirror, shadowed now
by your bergère curls, with holy cards
and pictures of boys
jammed into its frame,
an empty carafe, glasses full
of ash and orange peel, the lights of Mayfair,
then an intersection: souls,
bottles that wouldn't open, no more war or peace,
late whir of a pigeon who can't follow
on the moving stairs that take you down . . .

Lasciando un 'Dove'

Cattedrale di Ely

Una colomba bianca m'ha disceso
fra stele, sotto cuspidi dove il cielo s'annida.
Albe e luci, sospese; ho amato il sole,
il colore del miele, or chiedo il bruno,
chiedo il fuoco che cova, questa tomba
che non vola, il tuo sguardo che la sfida.

Leaving a Dove

Ely Cathedral

A white dove has landed me
among headstones, under spires where the sky nests.
Dawns and lights in air; I've loved the sun,
color of honey, now I crave the dark,
I want the smoldering fire, this tomb
that doesn't soar, your stare that dares it to.

Argyll Tour

Glasgow

I bimbi sotto il cedro, funghi o muffe
vivi dopo l'acquata,
il puledrino in gabbia
con la scritta 'mordace',
nafta a nubi, sospese
sui canali murati,
fumate di gabbiani, odor di sego
e di datteri, il mugghio del barcone,
catene che s'allentano
—ma le tue le ignoravo—,
                              sulla scia
salti di tonni, sonno, lunghe strida
di sorci, oscene risa, anzi che tu
apparissi al tuo schiavo . . .

Argyll Tour

Glasgow

Toddlers under the cedar, mushrooms
or must sprouting after the squall,
the colt in a cage
with the label "Bites,"
clouds of gas fumes
over walled canals,
clouds of gulls, odor of tallow and clams,
the lowing barge,
chains loosening—
but I didn't know yours—
                              the tuna
leaping in our wake,
sleep, long-shrieking mice and obscene laughter,
till you appeared to your slave . . .

Vento sulla Mezzaluna

Edimburgo

Il grande ponte non portava a te.
T'avrei raggiunta anche navigando
nelle chiaviche, a un tuo comando. Ma
già le forze, col sole sui cristalli
delle verande, andavano stremandosi.

L'uomo che predicava sul Crescente
mi chiese «Sai dov'è Dio?». Lo sapevo
e glielo dissi. Scosse il capo. Sparve
nel turbine che prese uomini e case
e li sollevò in alto, sulla pece.

Wind on the Crescent

Edinburgh

The great bridge didn't lead to you.
I would have found you trailing through
the sewers, even, at a single word.
But my powers, like the sun on the porch windows,
were already failing.

The man preaching on the Crescent asked,
"Do you know where God is?"
I knew, and said. He shook his head,
then vanished in the whirlwind that raised men
and houses over the pitch.

Sulla colonna più alta

Moschea di Damasco

Dovrà posarsi lassù
il Cristo giustiziere
per dire la sua parola.
Tra il pietrisco dei sette greti, insieme
s'umilieranno corvi e capinere,
ortiche e girasoli.

Ma in quel crepuscolo eri tu sul vertice:
scura, l'ali ingrommate, stronche dai
geli dell'Antilibano; e ancora
il tuo lampo mutava in vischio i neri
diademi degli sterpi, la Colonna
sillabava la Legge per te sola.

On the Highest Column

Damascus Mosque

Christ the Judge, supposedly,
will stand up there
to pronounce his word.
In the rubble of the seven rivers,
crows and blackcaps, nettles and sunflowers,
all will make obeisance together.

But in that twilight it was you on high:
dark, your wings encrusted, broken by
the ice of the Anti-Lebanon; and your flash
turned the black crowns of thorn
to mistletoe again;
the Column spoke the Law through you alone.

Verso Finistère

Col bramire dei cervi nella piova
d'Armor l'arco del tuo ciglio s'è spento
al primo buio per filtrare poi
sull'intonaco albale dove prillano
ruote di cicli, fusi, razzi, frange
d'alberi scossi. Forse non ho altra prova
che Dio mi vede e che le tue pupille
d'acquamarina guardano per lui.

Near Finistère

The arc of your eyebrow ended
at Armor with the bellowing of the stags
in rain in the early dark, to infiltrate
the dawn whitewash where bike wheels, spindles,
rockets, whiplashed branches whirl.
Maybe I have no other proof
God sees me and your sea-green pupils
see through him.

Sul Llobregat

Dal verde immarcescibile della canfora
due note, un intervallo di terza maggiore.
Il cucco, non la civetta, ti dissi; ma intanto, di scatto,
tu avevi spinto l'acceleratore.

On the Llobregat

Out of the incorruptible green of the camphor tree
two notes, their interval a major third.
A cuckoo, not an owl, I said;
but you'd stepped on the pedal suddenly.

Dal treno

Le tortore colore solferino
sono a Sesto Calende per la prima
volta a memoria d'uomo. Così annunziano
i giornali. Affacciato al finestrino,
invano le ho cercate. Un tuo collare,
ma d'altra tinta, sì, piegava in vetta
un giunco e si sgranava. Per me solo
balenò, cadde in uno stagno. E il suo
volo di fuoco m'accecò sull'altro.

From the Train

The blood-red turtledoves
are at Sesto Calende for the first time
in human memory. So the papers say.
I've hung out the window, hunting them in vain.
One of your necklaces, another color, true,
bent down a reed and unbeaded.
It flashed for me alone, then fell in a pond.
And its flight of fire
left me blind to the other.

Siria

Dicevano gli antichi che la poesia
è scala a Dio. Forse non è così
se mi leggi. Ma il giorno io lo seppi
che ritrovai per te la voce, sciolto
in un gregge di nuvoli e di capre
dirompenti da un greppo a brucar bave
di pruno e di falasco, e i volti scarni
della luna e del sole si fondevano,
il motore era guasto ed una freccia
di sangue su un macigno segnalava
la via di Aleppo.

Syria

The ancients said that poetry
is a stairway to God. Maybe not
when you read me. But I knew it was true
the day I found my voice again through you,
freed among a herd of clouds and goats
stampeding from a ravine to browse
the spume of thorns and marsh grass,
and the gaunt faces of the sun and moon
were one, the car broke down
and an arrow of blood on a boulder pointed
the way to Aleppo.

Luce d'inverno

Quando scesi dal cielo di Palmira
su palme nane e propilei canditi
e un'unghiata alla gola m'avvertì
che mi avresti rapito,

quando scesi dal cielo dell'Acropoli
e incontrai, a chilometri, cavagni
di polpi e di murene
(la sega di quei denti
sul cuore rattrappito!),

quando lasciai le cime delle aurore
disumane pel gelido museo
di mummie e scarabei (tu stavi male,
unica vita) e confrontai la pomice
e il diaspro, la sabbia e il sole, il fango
e l'argilla divina—
                alla scintilla
che si levò fui nuovo e incenerito.

Winter Light

When I came down from the sky above Palmyra
over palmettos and ruined gates
and a scratch at my throat warned me
you were going to have me;

when I came out of the sky above the Acropolis
and, for miles, found
hampers of octopus and eel
(the sawmarks of those teeth
on the stunned heart!);

when I left those high inhuman
dawns for the chill
museum of mummies and scarabs (you were ill,
my only life) and I compared
pumice and jasper, sand and sun,
mud and the heavenly clay—
                                        in the spark that flared
I was new, and ashes.

Per un 'Omaggio a Rimbaud'

Tardi uscita dal bozzolo, mirabile
farfalla che disfiori da una cattedra
l'esule di Charleville,
oh non seguirlo nel suo rapinoso
volo di starna, non lasciar cadere
piume stroncate, foglie di gardenia
sul nero ghiaccio dell'asfalto! Il volo
tuo sarà più terribile se alzato
da quest'ali di polline e di seta
nell'alone scarlatto in cui tu credi,
figlia del sole, serva del suo primo
pensiero e ormai padrona sua lassù . . .

For an "Homage to Rimbaud"

Late from your cocoon, miraculous
butterfly who from your lectern
grazes the Charleville exile,
oh don't follow him on his rapacious
partridge flight, don't let
shattered feathers fall, gardenia leaves
on the black asphalt ice! Your flight
will be more terrible if lifted
on these silk and pollen wings
into the scarlet halo you believe in,
daughter of the sun, handmaiden of
his first idea, and now its queen above . . .

Incantesimo

Oh resta chiusa e libera nell'isole
del tuo pensiero e del mio,
nella fiamma leggera che t'avvolge
e che non seppi prima
d'incontrare Diotima,
colei che tanto ti rassomigliava!
In lei vibra più forte l'amorosa cicala
sul ciliegio del tuo giardino.
Intorno il mondo stinge; incandescente,
nella lava che porta in Galilea
il tuo amore profano, attendi l'ora
di scoprire quel velo che t'ha un giorno
fidanzata al tuo Dio.

Incantation

Oh stay locked and free
in the islands of your thought and mine,
in the gentle flame that folds you in,
the one I didn't know until
I met Diotima,
so much like you!
In her, the amorous cicada
chirrs louder in your garden cherry tree.
The world beyond fades out;
incandescent in the lava that transports
your profane love to Galilee,
you await the hour to raise
the veil that once betrothed you to your God.

PARTE V

SILVAE

PART V

SILVAE

Iride

Quando di colpo San Martino smotta
le sue braci e le attizza in fondo al cupo
fornello dell'Ontario,
schiocchi di pigne verdi fra la cenere
o il fumo d'un infuso di papaveri
e il Volto insanguinato sul sudario
che mi divide da te;

questo e poco altro (se poco
è un tuo segno, un ammicco, nella lotta
che me sospinge in un ossario, spalle
al muro, dove zàffiri celesti
e palmizi e cicogne su una zampa non chiudono
l'atroce vista al povero
Nestoriano smarrito);

è quanto di te giunge dal naufragio
delle mie genti, delle tue, or che un fuoco
di gelo porta alla memoria il suolo
ch'è tuo e che non vedesti; e altro rosario
fra le dita non ho, non altra vampa
se non questa, di resina e di bacche,
t'ha investito.

       • • •

Cuore d'altri non è simile al tuo,
la lince non somiglia al bel soriano
che apposta l'uccello mosca sull'alloro;
ma li credi tu eguali se t'avventuri
fuor dell'ombra del sicomoro
o è forse quella maschera sul drappo bianco,
quell'effigie di porpora che t'ha guidata?

Perché l'opera tua (che della Sua
è una forma) fiorisse in altre luci
Iri del Canaan ti dileguasti

Iris

When suddenly Saint Martin shunts his embers
down his sluiceway, stirring them
deep in Lake Ontario's dark furnace,
the popping of green pinecones in the ashes,
or the steam from a fume of poppies
and the bloodied Face on the shroud
that keeps me from you;

this and little else (if a sign,
a wink from you is little, in the war
that shoves me in a charnelhouse, back to the wall,
where sky-blue sapphires, palms
and storks aloft on one leg
can't hide the atrocious view
from the poor dismayed Nestorian);

this is all of you that reaches me
from the shipwreck of my people,
and yours, now an icy fire
evokes the land of yours you didn't see;
and I hold no other rosary in my hand,
no other flame than this of resin and berries
has given you form.

        · · ·

Another's heart is not your heart,
the lynx is nothing like the lovely tabby
stalking the hummingbird up in the laurel,
but they're the same to you, if you step out
beyond the shadow of the sycamore,
or can it be that mask on the white cloth,
the purple effigy that guided you?

So that your work (which is a form
of His) might flourish in other lights,
Iris of Canaan, you deliquesced

in quel nimbo di vischi e pugnitopi
che il tuo cuore conduce
nella notte del mondo, oltre il miraggio
dei fiori del deserto, tuoi germani.

Se appari, qui mi riporti, sotto la pergola
di viti spoglie, accanto all'imbarcadero
del nostro fiume—e il burchio non torna indietro,
il sole di San Martino si stempera, nero.
Ma se ritorni non sei tu, è mutata
la tua storia terrena, non attendi
al traghetto la prua,

non hai sguardi, né ieri né domani;

perché l'opera Sua (che nella tua
si trasforma) *dev'esser continuata.*

into that halo of mistletoe and holly
which bears your heart into the night
of the world, beyond the mirage
of the desert flowers, your kin.

If you appear, you bring me here again,
under the pergola of barren vines
by the landing on our river—and the ferry's not returning,
the Indian summer sun dissolves, goes black.
But if you come back, you're not you,
your earthly history is changed,
you don't wait for the prow at the pier,

you watch for nothing: yesterday or tomorrow;

for His work (which is transforming
into yours) *has to continue.*

Nella serra

S'empì d'uno zampettìo
di talpe la limonaia,
brillò in un rosario di caute
gocce la falce fienaia.

S'accese sui pomi cotogni,
un punto, una cocciniglia,
si udì inalberarsi alla striglia
il poney—e poi vinse il sogno.

Rapito e leggero ero intriso
di te, la tua forma era il mio
respiro nascosto, il tuo viso
nel mio si fondeva, e l'oscuro

pensiero di Dio discendeva
sui pochi viventi, tra suoni
celesti e infantili tamburi
e globi sospesi di fulmini

su me, su te, sui limoni . . .

In the Greenhouse

The lemon-house was being over-
ridden by the moles' stampedes.
The scythe shone in a rosary
of wary waterbeads.

A spot among the quinces blazed,
a bug—cochineal.
We heard the pony rear up at
the comb—then sleep was all.

Rapt, weightless, I was drenched with you,
my hidden breathing was your form,
your face was merging into mine,
and the dark idea of God

descended on the living few
to celestial tones
and children's drums
and globes of lightning strung above

the lemons, and me, and you . . .

Nel parco

Nell'ombra della magnolia
che sempre più si restringe,
a un soffio di cerbottana
la freccia mi sfiora e si perde.

Pareva una foglia caduta
dal pioppo che a un colpo di vento
si stinge—e fors'era una mano
scorrente da lungi tra il verde.

Un riso che non m'appartiene
trapassa da fronde canute
fino al mio petto, lo scuote
un trillo che punge le vene,

e rido con te sulla ruota
deforme dell'ombra, mi allungo
disfatto di me sulle ossute
radici che sporgono e pungo

con fili di paglia il tuo viso . . .

In the Park

In the magnolia's
ever-shrinking shade,
a puff on a pipe and the arrow
grazes me, melts away.

It felt like a leaf from the poplar
that fades in a gust of wind—
and maybe a hand
riffling down in the glade.

A laugh that didn't come from me
penetrates old foliage
right to my chest, hits home
with a trill that stings the veins,

and I laugh with you
on the shade's warped wheel,
free of myself I sprawl on the bony
roots that protrude, and I needle

your face with bits of straw . . .

L'orto

Io non so, messaggera
che scendi, prediletta
del mio Dio (del tuo forse), se nel chiuso
dei meli lazzeruoli ove si lagnano
i luì nidaci, estenuanti a sera,
io non so se nell'orto
dove le ghiande piovono e oltre il muro
si sfioccano, aerine, le ghirlande
dei carpini che accennano
lo spumoso confine dei marosi, una vela
tra corone di scogli
sommersi e nerocupi o più lucenti
della prima stella che trapela—

io non so se il tuo piede
attutito, il cieco incubo onde cresco
alla morte dal giorno che ti vidi,
io non so se il tuo passo che fa pulsar le vene
se s'avvicina in questo intrico,
è quello che mi colse un'altra estate
prima che una folata
radente contro il picco irto del Mesco
infrangesse il mio specchio,—
io non so se la mano che mi sfiora la spalla
è la stessa che un tempo
sulla celesta rispondeva a gemiti
d'altri nidi, da un fólto ormai bruciato.

L'ora della tortura e dei lamenti
che s'abbatté sul mondo,
l'ora che tu leggevi chiara come in un libro
figgendo il duro sguardo di cristallo
bene in fondo, là dove acri tendìne
di fuliggine alzandosi su lampi
di officine celavano alla vista
l'opera di Vulcano,

The Garden

Messenger descending,
favorite of
my God (and maybe yours),
I don't know if in the medlar orchard
where the nestling warblers complain,
exhausted by evening,
I don't know if in the kitchen garden
where acorns rain and hornbeam catkins
fraying in the air across the wall
nod to the foaming crest of waves,
a sail between rock crowns
sunk and pitch-black or brighter
than the first star leaking light—

I don't know if your muffled step,
the blind nightmare in which I've moved
toward death since the day I saw you—
I don't know if your step that makes
my veins throb when it nears me in this tangle
is the one I felt another summer,
before a gust that sheared
the Mesco's shaggy summit
broke my mirror—
I don't know if the hand grazing my shoulder
is the same hand that once at the celesta
answered cries from other nests
in a thicket long since burned.

The hour of torture and lament
that rang down on the world,
the hour you read as clear as in a book,
fixing your sheer crystal gaze
deep down where acrid sheets
of grime rose up in lightning
flashes from the foundry,
hiding the work of Vulcan from our sight,

il dì dell'Ira che più volte il gallo
annunciò agli spergiuri,
non ti divise, anima indivisa,
dal supplizio inumano, non ti fuse
nella caldana, cuore d'ametista.

O labbri muti, aridi dal lungo
viaggio per il sentiero fatto d'aria
che vi sostenne, o membra che distinguo
a stento dalle mie, o diti che smorzano
la sete dei morenti e i vivi infocano,
o intento che hai creato fuor della tua misura
le sfere del quadrante e che ti espandi
in tempo d'uomo, in spazio d'uomo, in furie
di dèmoni incarnati, in fronti d'angiole
precipitate a volo . . . Se la forza
che guida il disco *di già inciso* fosse
un'altra, certo il tuo destino al mio
congiunto mostrerebbe un solco solo.

the *dies irae* that the cock
announced repeatedly to the forsworn,
didn't divide you, undivided soul,
from the inhuman suffering, didn't render you
in its crucible, heart of amethyst.

O still lips, parched from your long flight
on the path of air that held you up,
O limbs that I can barely tell from mine,
O fingers that assuage the thirst of the dying
and inflame the living,
O purpose who created the clock's hands
beyond your measure and expand
into human time and human space,
into furious incarnate demons,
into brows of angels swooping down . . . If the power
that drives the disk *already etched* were another
surely your destiny conjoined with mine
would show a single groove.

Proda di Versilia

I miei morti che prego perché preghino
per me, per i miei vivi com'io invoco
per essi non resurrezione ma
il compiersi di quella vita ch'ebbero
inesplicata e inesplicabile, oggi
più di rado discendono dagli orizzonti aperti
quando una mischia d'acque e cielo schiude
finestre ai raggi della sera,—sempre
più raro, astore celestiale, un cutter
bianco-alato li posa sulla rena.

Broli di zinnie tinte ad artificio
(nonne dal duro sòggolo le annaffiano,
chiuse lo sguardo a chi di fuorivia
non cede alle impietose loro mani
il suo male), cortili di sterpaglie
incanutite dove se entra un gatto
color frate gli vietano i rifiuti
voci irose; macerie e piatte altane
su case basse lungo un ondulato
declinare di dune e ombrelle aperte
al sole grigio, sabbia che non nutre
gli alberi sacri alla mia infanzia, il pino
selvatico, il fico e l'eucalipto.

A quell'ombre i primi anni erano folti,
gravi di miele, pur se abbandonati;
a quel rezzo anche se disteso sotto
due brandelli di crespo punteggiati
di zanzare dormivo nella stanza
d'angolo, accanto alla cucina, ancora
nottetempo o nel cuore d'una siesta
di cicale, abbagliante nel mio sonno,
travedevo oltre il muro, al lavandino,
care ombre massaggiare le murene
per respingerne in coda, e poi reciderle,

Shore of Versilia

My dead, to whom I pray so they may pray
for me, and for the living, as for them
I invoke not resurrection
but the fulfillment of the life they lived
unexplained and inexplicable—
today they descend less often out of the wide
horizon, when a squall of sky and water
opens windows to the rays of evening;
less and less often now a white-winged cutter,
celestial goshawk, leaves them on the shore.

Gardens of neon zinnias
(sisters in hard wimples water them,
with stony looks for the stranger who won't
deliver his troubles into their pitiless hands);
courtyards of sun-bleached weeds
where, if a monk-gray cat should venture,
angry voices warn him from the garbage;
rubble; terraces on flat-topped houses
strung along a wave of sloping dunes;
umbrellas open under the gray sun;
sand that doesn't feed the trees
sacred to my childhood: the wild pine,
fig and eucalyptus.

My first years were verdant in their shade,
heavy with honey, if solitary;
when I slept they kept watch over me,
sprawled under two scraps of netting
dotted with mosquitoes in the corner
bedroom by the kitchen—
whether at night or deep in a siesta
of cicadas, dazzling in my dream,
through the wall I saw loved shadows
stand at the sink and massage the moray eels
to force their spines into their tails,

le spine; a quel perenne alto stormire
altri perduti con rastrelli e forbici
lasciavano il vivaio
dei fusti nani per i sempreverdi
bruciati e le cavane avide d'acqua.

Anni di scogli e di orizzonti stretti
a custodire vite ancora umane
e gesti conoscibili, respiro
o anelito finale di sommersi
simili all'uomo o a lui vicini pure
nel nome: il pesce prete, il pesce rondine,
l'àstice—il lupo della nassa—che
dimentica le pinze quando Alice
gli si avvicina . . . e il volo da trapezio
dei topi familiari da una palma
all'altra; tempo che fu misurabile
fino a che non s'aperse questo mare
infinito, di creta e di mondiglia.

then hack them off; in that high, enduring hum
other lost ones with rakes and shears
left the seedbed of dwarf trees
for the sunbaked evergreens
and the ditches, desperate for water.

Years of cliffs and horizons shaped
to shelter lives still human,
knowable gestures,
breath or last gasp of submerged creatures
similar to man, if in name only:
the "priest fish" and the "swallow fish,"
the lobster—wolf of the trap—
who forgets his claws when Alice approaches . . .
and the trapeze act
of the family mice from one palm to another;
time that one could measure
until it opened out, this boundless
sea of muck and refuse.

'Ezekiel saw the Wheel . . .'

Ghermito m'hai dall'intrico
dell'edera, mano straniera?
M'ero appoggiato alla vasca
viscida, l'aria era nera,
solo una vena d'onice tremava
nel fondo, quale stelo alla burrasca.
Ma la mano non si distolse,
nel buio si fece più diaccia
e la pioggia che si disciolse
sui miei capelli, sui tuoi
d'allora, troppo tenui, troppo lisci,
frugava tenace la traccia
in me seppellita da un cumulo,
da un monte di sabbia che avevo
in cuore ammassato per giungere
a soffocar la tua voce,
a spingerla in giù, dentro il breve
cerchio che tutto trasforma,
raspava, portava all'aperto
con l'orma delle pianelle
sul fango indurito, la scheggia,
la fibra della tua croce
in polpa marcita di vecchie
putrelle schiantate, il sorriso
di teschio che a noi si frappose
quando la Ruota minacciosa apparve
tra riflessi d'aurora, e fatti sangue
i petali del pesco su me scesero
e con essi
il tuo artiglio, come ora.

"Ezekiel saw the Wheel . . ."

Snatched me from the ivy's tangle,
did you, stranger hand?
I was leaning over the slimy
pool, the air was black;
only a vein of onyx waved
in the depths, like a stem in a storm.
But the hand wouldn't let go,
got icier in the dark
and the rain that fell
on my hair and yours of then,
too thin, too fine,
kept groping for a trace
buried in me by a pile,
a mountain of sand
I'd stored in my heart
to try to stifle your voice,
force it down into the small
circle that changes all;
it kept digging, bringing things to light:
your slipper print on hardened mud,
the splinter, fiber of your cross,
made from rotten bits of shattered beams,
the grinning skull
that rose before us
when the threatening Wheel
appeared in the shimmering
dawn and the peach tree's
petals, blood, rained down on me
and with them your claw,
as now.

La primavera hitleriana

Né quella ch'a veder lo sol si gira . . .
—Dante (?) a Giovanni Quirini

Folta la nuvola bianca delle falene impazzite
turbina intorno agli scialbi fanali e sulle spallette,
stende a terra una coltre su cui scricchia
come su zucchero il piede; l'estate imminente sprigiona
ora il gelo notturno che capiva
nelle cave segrete della stagione morta,
negli orti che da Maiano scavalcano a questi renai.

Da poco sul corso è passato a volo un messo infernale
tra un alalà di scherani, un golfo mistico acceso
e pavesato di croci a uncino l'ha preso e inghiottito,
si sono chiuse le vetrine, povere
e inoffensive benché armate anch'esse
di cannoni e giocattoli di guerra,
ha sprangato il beccaio che infiorava
di bacche il muso dei capretti uccisi,
la sagra dei miti carnefici che ancora ignorano il sangue
s'è tramutata in un sozzo trescone d'ali schiantate,
di larve sulle golene, e l'acqua séguita a rodere
le sponde e più nessuno è incolpevole.

Tutto per nulla, dunque?—e le candele
romane, a San Giovanni, che sbiancavano lente
l'orizzonte, ed i pegni e i lunghi addii
forti come un battesimo nella lugubre attesa
dell'orda (ma una gemma rigò l'aria stillando
sui ghiacci e le riviere dei tuoi lidi
gli angeli di Tobia, i sette, la semina
dell'avvenire) e gli eliotropi nati
dalle tue mani—tutto arso e succhiato
da un polline che stride come il fuoco
e ha punte di sinibbio . . .
                              Oh la piagata
primavera è pur festa se raggela

The Hitler Spring

Né quella ch'a veder lo sol si gira . . .
—Dante (?) to Giovanni Quirini

The thick white cloud of mad moths whirls
around the pale lights and the parapets,
spreading a blanket on the earth that snaps
like sugar underfoot; the coming summer
frees the night frost locked in the dead season's
secret cellars and the gardens
that scale down from Maiano to these sands.

An infernal messenger flew just now along the avenue,
to a chant of thugs; an orchestra pit,
firelit and arrayed with swastikas,
seized and devoured him, the windows,
shabby and inoffensive, though adorned
with cannons and war toys, are shuttered up,
the butcher who laid berries on the snouts
of his slaughtered goats has closed; the feast
of the mild murderers still innocent of blood
has turned into a foul Virginia reel of shattered wings,
larvae on the sandbars, and the water rushes in
to eat the shore and no one's blameless anymore.

All for nothing then?—and the Roman
candles at San Giovanni, slowly whitening
the horizon, and the vows and long farewells
definitive as baptism in the dismal
vigil of the horde (but a jewel scored the air,
sowing the icy edges of your beaches
with the angels of Tobias, the seven,
seed of the future) and the sunflowers born
of your hands—all burned, sucked dry
by pollen that hisses like fire
and stings like hail . . .

                        Oh the wounded spring
is still a festival if it will chill

in morte questa morte! Guarda ancora
in alto, Clizia, è la tua sorte, tu
che il non mutato amor mutata serbi,
fino a che il cieco sole che in te porti
si abbàcini nell'Altro e si distrugga
in Lui, per tutti. Forse le sirene, i rintocchi
che salutano i mostri nella sera
della loro tregenda, si confondono già
col suono che slegato dal cielo, scende, vince—
col respiro di un'alba che domani per tutti
si riaffacci, bianca ma senz'ali
di raccapriccio, ai greti arsi del sud . . .

this death to death!
Clizia, it's your fate: look up again,
changed one harboring your changeless love,
until the sightless sun you bear within you
is blinded in the Other and consumed
in Him, for all. Perhaps the sirens and the tolling
that hail the monsters on the eve
of their pandemonium already blend
with the sound released from the sky that descends victorious—
with the breath of a dawn that may break tomorrow for all,
white, but without wings of terror,
over the scorched rockbeds of the south . . .

Voce giunta con le folaghe

Poiché la via percorsa, se mi volgo, è più lunga
del sentiero da capre che mi porta
dove ci scioglieremo come cera,
ed i giunchi fioriti non leniscono il cuore
ma le vermene, il sangue dei cimiteri,
eccoti fuor dal buio
che ti teneva, padre, erto ai barbagli,
senza scialle e berretto, al sordo fremito
che annunciava nell'alba
chiatte di minatori dal gran carico
semisommerse, nere sull'onde alte.

L'ombra che mi accompagna
alla tua tomba, vigile,
e posa sopra un'erma ed ha uno scarto
altero della fronte che le schiara
gli occhi ardenti ed i duri sopraccigli
da un suo biocco infantile,
l'ombra non ha più peso della tua
da tanto seppellita, i primi raggi
del giorno la trafiggono, farfalle
vivaci l'attraversano, la sfiora
la sensitiva e non si rattrappisce.

L'ombra fidata e il muto che risorge,
quella che scorporò l'interno fuoco
e colui che lunghi anni d'oltretempo
(anni per me pesante) disincarnano,
si scambiano parole che interito
sul margine io non odo; l'una forse
ritroverà la forma in cui bruciava
amor di Chi la mosse e non di sé,
ma l'altro sbigottisce e teme che
la larva di memoria in cui si scalda
ai suoi figli si spenga al nuovo balzo.

Voice That Came with the Coots

Since the road traveled, if I look back, is longer
than the goat-path bringing me
to where we'll melt like wax,
and not the flowering rushes but verbena,
the blood of cemeteries, soothes the heart,
here you are, Father, out of the dark that held you,
upright in the glare,
no shawl or beret,
in the dull dawn rumble that announced
the miner's barges, half sunk with their cargo,
black on the high waves.

The shade that comes with me
and stands watch at your grave,
who sits on a herm and haughtily
tosses her childish bangs
freeing her burning eyes and severe brow—
this shade weighs no more than yours
interred so long;
the day's first rays transfix her,
lively butterflies dance through her,
and the sensitive mimosa
touches her and won't recoil.

The loyal shadow and the mute one
upright again; she whom an inner fire
unbodied and the one long years out of time
(years for me in my heaviness) have unfleshed,
exchange words that I can't hear,
stiff at the sidelines; perhaps the first
will recover the form that burned with love
for Him who moved her, not self-love;
but the other quails, afraid that the ghost
of memory in which he is warm for his children
will be lost in this new leap.

—Ho pensato per te, ho ricordato
per tutti. Ora ritorni al cielo libero
che ti tramuta. Ancora questa rupe
ti tenta? Sì, la bàttima è la stessa
di sempre, il mare che ti univa ai miei
lidi da prima che io avessi l'ali,
non si dissolve. Io le rammento quelle
mie prode e pur son giunta con le folaghe
a distaccarti dalle tue. Memoria
non è peccato fin che giova. Dopo
è letargo di talpe, abiezione

che funghisce su sé . . . —
                            Il vento del giorno
confonde l'ombra viva e l'altra ancora
riluttante in un mezzo che respinge
le mie mani, e il respiro mi si rompe
nel punto dilatato, nella fossa
che circonda lo scatto del ricordo.
Così si svela prima di legarsi
a immagini, a parole, oscuro senso
reminiscente, il vuoto inabitato
che occupammo e che attende fin ch'è tempo
di colmarsi di noi, di ritrovarci . . .

"I've thought for you, I've remembered
for all. Now you return to the open
sky that transmutes you. Does the cliff
still tempt you? Yes, the high-water mark
is the same as ever, the sea
that linked you with my beaches before I had wings
hasn't dissolved. I remember them,
my shores, yet I've come with the coots
to take you from yours.
Memory is no sin while it avails.
After, it's molelike torpor, misery

that mushrooms on itself . . ."
                       The wind of day
melds the living shadow
and the other, still reluctant one
in an amalgam that repels my hands,
and the breath breaks out of me at the swelling point,
in the moat that surrounds the release of memory.
So it reveals itself before attaching
to images, or words, dark reminiscent
sense, the unlived-in void we occupied
that waits for us until the time has come
to fill itself with us, to find us again . . .

L'ombra della magnolia . . .

L'ombra della magnolia giapponese
si sfoltisce or che i bocci paonazzi
sono caduti. Vibra intermittente
in vetta una cicala. Non è più
il tempo dell'unìsono vocale,
Clizia, il tempo del nume illimitato
che divora e rinsangua i suoi fedeli.
Spendersi era più facile, morire
al primo batter d'ale, al primo incontro
col nemico, un trastullo. Comincia ora
la via più dura: ma non te consunta
dal sole e radicata, e pure morbida
cesena che sorvoli alta le fredde
banchine del tuo fiume,—non te fragile
fuggitiva cui zenit nadir cancro
capricorno rimasero indistinti
perché la guerra fosse in te e in chi adora
su te le stimme del tuo Sposo, flette
il brivido del gelo . . . Gli altri arretrano
e piegano. La lima che sottile
incide tacerà, la vuota scorza
di chi cantava sarà presto polvere
di vetro sotto i piedi, l'ombra è livida,—
è l'autunno, è l'inverno, è l'oltrecielo
che ti conduce e in cui mi getto, cèfalo
saltato in secco al novilunio.
                    Addio.

The Magnolia's Shadow

The shadow of the Japanese magnolia
is thinning now that its royal-blue
buds have fallen. At the top a lone cicada
chirrs off and on. The time of voices joined
in unison, Clizia, of the boundless power
devouring and replenishing his faithful,
is over. Spending oneself was easier,
dying at the first rush of wings, the first
encounter with the enemy, was a game.
Now the harder way begins: but not you
consumed by the sun and rooted,
yet gentle fieldfare soaring high above
the cold banks of your river—not you does
the shuddering cold bow low,
fragile fugitive for whom
zenith nadir Cancer Capricorn
stayed indistinct so that the war
might be in you and in him who loves
the Stigmata of your Spouse upon you . . .
The rest fall back and fold. The file
that etches finely will be still,
the empty husk of him who sang will soon
be powdered glass underfoot, the shadow's pale—
it's fall, it's winter, it's the great beyond
that draws you and I hurl myself in it,
mullet beached under the new moon.
                                        Farewell.

Il gallo cedrone

Dove t'abbatti dopo il breve sparo
(la tua voce ribolle, rossonero
salmì di cielo e terra a lento fuoco)
anch'io riparo, brucio anch'io nel fosso.

Chiede aiuto il singulto. Era più dolce
vivere che affondare in questo magma,
più facile disfarsi al vento che
qui nel limo, incrostati sulla fiamma.

Sento nel petto la tua piaga, sotto
un grumo d'ala; il mio pesante volo
tenta un muro e di noi solo rimane
qualche piuma sull'ilice brinata.

Zuffe di rostri, amori, nidi d'uova
marmorate, divine! Ora la gemma
delle piante perenni, come il bruco,
luccica al buio, Giove è sotterrato.

The Capercaillie

Where you fall after the sharp shot
(your voice boils up, red-black ragout
of sky and earth at a low heat)
I too lie low, burn in the ditch with you.

Your sob's a cry for help. Living
was sweeter than sinking into this mire,
easier to come undone in the wind
than here in the mud, crusted over the fire.

I feel your wound in my own breast,
under a clot of wing; I try
to lumber over a wall and all that lasts
of us are feathers on the frosted holly.

Scuffling beaks, couplings, nests for eggs
marbled, unearthly! Now the jewel-buds
of the perennials glow like the grub
in the gloom. Jove is underground.

L'anguilla

L'anguilla, la sirena
dei mari freddi che lascia il Baltico
per giungere ai nostri mari,
ai nostri estuarî, ai fiumi
che risale in profondo, sotto la piena avversa,
di ramo in ramo e poi
di capello in capello, assottigliati,
sempre più addentro, sempre più nel cuore
del macigno, filtrando
tra gorielli di melma finché un giorno
una luce scoccata dai castagni
ne accende il guizzo in pozze d'acquamorta,
nei fossi che declinano
dai balzi d'Appennino alla Romagna;
l'anguilla, torcia, frusta,
freccia d'Amore in terra
che solo i nostri botri o i disseccati
ruscelli pirenaici riconducono
a paradisi di fecondazione;
l'anima verde che cerca
vita là dove solo
morde l'arsura e la desolazione,
la scintilla che dice
tutto comincia quando tutto pare
incarbonirsi, bronco seppellito;
l'iride breve, gemella
di quella che incastonano i tuoi cigli
e fai brillare intatta in mezzo ai figli
dell'uomo, immersi nel tuo fango, puoi tu
non crederla sorella?

The Eel

The eel, siren
of cold seas, who leaves
the Baltic for our seas,
our estuaries, rivers, rising
deep beneath the downstream flood
from branch to branch, from twig to smaller twig,
ever more inward,
bent on the heart of rock,
infiltrating muddy
rills until one day
light glancing off the chestnuts
fires her flash
in stagnant pools,
in the ravines cascading down
the Apennine escarpments to Romagna;
eel, torch, whiplash,
arrow of Love on earth,
whom only our gullies
or dessicated Pyrenean brooks lead back
to Edens of generation;
green spirit seeking life
where only drought and desolation sting;
spark that says that everything begins
when everything seems charcoal,
buried stump;
brief rainbow, iris,
twin to the one your lashes frame
and you set shining virginal among
the sons of men, sunk in your mire—
can you fail to see her as a sister?

PARTE VI

MADRIGALI PRIVATI

PART VI

PRIVATE MADRIGALS

So che un raggio di sole (di Dio?) ancora
può incarnarsi se ai piedi della statua
di Lucrezia (una sera ella si scosse,
palpebrò) getti il volto contro il mio.

Qui nell'androne come sui trifogli;
qui sulle scale come là nel palco;
sempre nell'ombra: perché se tu sciogli
quel buio la mia rondine sia il falco.

I know a ray of sun (of God?) can still
be flesh if down below Lucretia's statue
(one night she shuddered, blinked) you
press your face to mine.

Here in the aisle as in the clover;
here on the stairs as up there in the box;
always in shadow: for if you dissolve
that darkness, let my swallow be a hawk.

Hai dato il mio nome a un albero? Non è poco;
pure non mi rassegno a restar ombra, o tronco,
di un abbandono nel suburbio. Io il tuo
l'ho dato a un fiume, a un lungo incendio, al crudo
gioco della mia sorte, alla fiducia
sovrumana con cui parlasti al rospo
uscito dalla fogna, senza orrore o pietà
o tripudio, al respiro di quel forte
e morbido tuo labbro che riesce,
nominando, a creare; rospo fiore erba scoglio—
quercia pronta a spiegarsi su di noi
quando la pioggia spollina i carnosi
petali del trifoglio e il fuoco cresce.

You've named a tree for me? It isn't nothing;
still I'm not resigned to being trunk or shadow,
abandoned in a suburb. I've named a river
after you, a lasting fire,
the cruel game of my fate, the superhuman
trustingness with which you spoke to the toad
that came from the sewer, no horror,
pity or exaltation; and the exhalation
of that strong, soft lip of yours that manages
in naming to create; toad flower
grass shoal—oak about to spread above us
when rain rinses the pollen from the clover's
fleshy petals and the fire flares.

Se t'hanno assomigliato . . .

Se t'hanno assomigliato
alla volpe sarà per la falcata
prodigiosa, pel volo del tuo passo
che unisce e che divide, che sconvolge
e rinfranca il selciato (il tuo terrazzo,
le strade presso il Cottolengo, il prato,
l'albero che ha il mio nome ne vibravano
felici, umidi e vinti)—o forse solo
per l'onda luminosa che diffondi
dalle mandorle tenere degli occhi,
per l'astuzia dei tuoi pronti stupori,
per lo strazio
di piume lacerate che può dare
la tua mano d'infante in una stretta;
se t'hanno assomigliato
a un carnivoro biondo, al genio perfido
delle fratte (e perché non all'immondo
pesce che dà la scossa, alla torpedine?)
è forse perché i ciechi non ti videro
sulle scapole gracili le ali,
perché i ciechi non videro il presagio
della tua fronte incandescente, il solco
che vi ho graffiato a sangue, croce cresima
incantesimo jattura voto vale
perdizione e salvezza; se non seppero
crederti più che donnola o che donna,
con chi dividerò la mia scoperta,
dove seppellirò l'oro che porto,
dove la brace che in me stride se,
lasciandomi, ti volgi dalle scale?

If they've compared you . . .

If they've compared you
to the vixen, it will be for your prodigious
lope, your darting step
that joins and dissevers, that scatters
and freshens the gravel (your terrace,
the streets by the Cottolengo, the meadow,
the tree named after me all quiver with it,
happy, wet and won)—or maybe simply
for the gleaming wave you broadcast
from the tender almonds of your eyes,
for the shrewdness of your easy stupors,
for the havoc
of shredded feathers your baby's
hand can wreak with a tug;
if they've compared you
to a blond carnivore, the faithless
genius of the thicket (and why not the foul
fish that shocks, the stingray?) it may be
because the blind had failed to see
the wings behind your slender shoulder blades,
because the blind had failed to see
the omen of your incandescent forehead,
the line I've etched in blood there, cross and chrism
charm calamity vow farewell
perdition and salvation; if they failed
to see you as more than weasel or woman,
whom will I share my discovery with,
where will I bury the gold I carry,
the ember hissing deep in me,
if leaving me you turn away from the stairs?

Le processioni del 1949

Lampi d'afa sul punto del distacco,
livida ora annebbiata,
poi un alone anche peggiore, un bombito
di ruote e di querele dalle prime
rampe della collina,
un rigurgito, un tanfo acre che infetta
le zolle a noi devote,

            . . . se non fosse
per quel tuo scarto *in vitro*, sulla gora,
entro una bolla di sapone e insetti.

Chi mente più, chi geme? Fu il tuo istante
di sempre, dacché appari.
La tua virtù furiosamente angelica
ha scacciato col guanto i madonnari
pellegrini, Cibele e i Coribanti.

The Parades of 1949

Heat-lightning at the outset,
livid hazy hour,
then an aura even worse,
grumbling wheels and quarrels
from the first rise of the hill,
reflux, harsh stench that infects
the soil apportioned to us,
                              . . . were it not
for that swerve of yours *in vitro*, on the canal,
between a soap bubble and gnats.

Who's still lying, wailing? It was your usual
moment, where you appear.
Your furiously angelic power
and glove dispelled the holy-mother pilgrims,
Cybele and her Corybants.

Nubi color magenta . . .

Nubi color magenta s'addensavano
sulla grotta di Fingal d'oltrecosta
quando dissi «pedala,
angelo mio!» e con un salto
il tandem si staccò dal fango, sciolse
il volo tra le bacche del rialto.

Nubi color di rame si piegavano
a ponte sulle spire dell'Agliena,
sulle biancane rugginose quando
ti dissi «resta!», e la tua ala d'ebano
occupò l'orizzonte
col suo fremito lungo, insostenibile.

Come Pafnuzio nel deserto, troppo
volli vincerti, io vinto.
Volo con te, resto con te; morire,
vivere è un punto solo, un groppo tinto
del tuo colore, caldo del respiro
della caverna, fondo, appena udibile.

Magenta-colored clouds . . .

Magenta-colored clouds were gathering
over the Fingal's Cave on the far shore
when I shouted, "Pedal, angel,"
and with a lurch the tandem tore
free from the mud, took flight among
the berries on the bank.

Copper-colored clouds were making bridges
over the Agliena's coils and rusty
shoals when I cried out, "Enough!"
and your ebony wing
filled up the horizon
with its long shudder, unsustainable.

Conquered, like Paphnutius in the desert,
I was too intent on conquest.
Fly with you, stay with you: dying,
living is one moment, a knot that's dyed your color,
warm with the breath in the cave,
deep, barely audible.

Per album

Ho cominciato anzi giorno
a buttar l'amo per te (lo chiamavo 'il lamo').
Ma nessun guizzo di coda
scorgevo nei pozzi limosi,
nessun vento veniva col tuo indizio
dai colli monferrini.
Ho continuato il mio giorno
sempre spiando te, larva girino
frangia di rampicante francolino
gazzella zebù ocàpi
nuvola nera grandine
prima della vendemmia, ho spigolato
tra i filari inzuppati senza trovarti.
Ho proseguito fino a tardi
senza sapere che tre cassettine
—SABBIA SODA SAPONE, la piccionaia
da cui partì il tuo volo: da una cucina—
si sarebbero aperte per me solo.
Così sparisti nell'orizzonte incerto.
Non c'è pensiero che imprigioni il fulmine
ma chi ha veduto la luce non se ne priva.
Mi stesi al piede del tuo ciliegio, ero
già troppo ricco per contenerti viva.

For an Album

Long before daybreak I started
casting my lure for you (I called it "allure").
But I saw no tail-flash
in the slimy pools,
no wind arrived with your sign
from the Monferrato hills.
I spent my whole day
on the lookout for you, larva
tadpole fringe of creeper partridge
gazelle zebu okapi
black cloud hail before harvest,
I went gleaning
in the soaked vines without finding you.
I kept on until late
not knowing that three canisters
—SAND, SODA, SOAP, the dovecote
you took flight from: in a kitchen—
would open only for me.
And so you vanished into the vague horizon.
There's no idea locks the lightning in,
but he who's seen the light can't do without it.
I set myself at the foot of your cherry tree,
already far too rich to contain you alive.

Da un lago svizzero

Mia volpe, un giorno fui anch'io il 'poeta
assassinato': là nel noccioleto
raso, dove fa grotta, da un falò;
in quella tana un tondo di zecchino
accendeva il tuo viso, poi calava
lento per la sua via fino a toccare
un nimbo, ove stemprarsi; ed io ansioso
invocavo la fine su quel fondo
segno della tua vita aperta, amara,
atrocemente fragile e pur forte.

Sei tu che brilli al buio? Entro quel solco
pulsante, in una pista arroventata,
àlacre sulla traccia del tuo lieve
zampetto di predace (un'orma quasi
invisibile, a stella) io, straniero,
ancora piombo; e a volo alzata un'anitra
nera, dal fondolago, fino al nuovo
incendio mi fa strada, per bruciarsi.

From a Swiss Lake

My vixen, I myself was once the *"poète*
Assassiné": there where the hazel grove,
Razored by a bonfire, makes a cave;
In that den
A sequined halo
Lit your face, then slowly fell
Until it touched a cloud, dissolved; and anxiously
I called for the end above that deep
Sign of your open, bitter life,
Abominably delicate, yet strong.

Shining in the darkness, is it you?
Pacing that throbbing furrow, on
A blazing path, in hot pursuit of your
Zombie predator pawprint (nearly
Invisible star-like trace),
A stranger, I still sink; and a black duck
Now rising from the bottom of the lake
Invites me to the new fire that will singe her.

Anniversario

Dal tempo della tua nascita
sono in ginocchio, mia volpe.
È da quel giorno che sento
vinto il male, espiate le mie colpe.

Arse a lungo una vampa; sul tuo tetto,
sul mio, vidi l'orrore traboccare.
Giovane stelo tu crescevi; e io al rezzo
delle tregue spiavo il tuo piumare.

Resto in ginocchio: il dono che sognavo
non per me ma per tutti
appartiene a me solo, Dio diviso
dagli uomini, dal sangue raggrumato
sui rami alti, sui frutti.

Anniversary

From the moment you were born,
my vixen, I've been on my knees.
Ever since that day I've felt
evil was overcome, my sins appeased.

A flame kept burning; on your roof,
and mine, I saw the horror overflowing.
New shoot, you rose; and from the shade
of truce I spied your plumage growing.

I'm still on my knees; the gift I dreamed
not mine but everyone's belongs
to me alone, God separate
from mankind, from the clotted blood
on the high branches, on the fruit.

PARTE VII

CONCLUSIONI

PROVVISORIE

PART VII

PROVISIONAL

CONCLUSIONS

Piccolo testamento

Questo che a notte balugina
nella calotta del mio pensiero,
traccia madreperlacea di lumaca
o smeriglio di vetro calpestato,
non è lume di chiesa o d'officina
che alimenti
chierico rosso, o nero.
Solo quest'iride posso
lasciarti a testimonianza
d'una fede che fu combattuta,
d'una speranza che bruciò più lenta
di un duro ceppo nel focolare.
Conservane la cipria nello specchietto
quando spenta ogni lampada
la sardana si farà infernale
e un ombroso Lucifero scenderà su una prora
del Tamigi, del Hudson, della Senna
scuotendo l'ali di bitume semi-
mozze dalla fatica, a dirti: è l'ora.
Non è un'eredità, un portafortuna
che può reggere all'urto dei monsoni
sul fil di ragno della memoria,
ma una storia non dura che nella cenere
e persistenza è solo l'estinzione.
Giusto era il segno: chi l'ha ravvisato
non può fallire nel ritrovarti.
Ognuno riconosce i suoi: l'orgoglio
non era fuga, l'umiltà non era
vile, il tenue bagliore strofinato
laggiù non era quello di un fiammifero.

Little Testament

This, which flickers at night
in the skullcap of my thought,
mother-of-pearl snail's trace
or mica of crushed glass,
isn't church or factory light
to feed
red cleric or black.
All I can leave you is
this rainbow in evidence
of a faith that was contested,
a hope that burned more slowly
than hardwood on the hearth.
Keep its powder in your compact
till every light is out,
the sardana becomes infernal,
and a shadowy Lucifer sweeps down on a prow
on the Thames, the Hudson, the Seine,
flailing his pitch-black wings half-
severed from effort to tell you: it's time.
It's no inheritance, no talisman
to survive the monsoons' railing
on the spider's thread of memory,
but a history lasts only as ashes
and persistence is pure extinction.
The sign was right: he who saw it
can't fail to find you again.
Everyone makes out his own: pride
wasn't flight, humility wasn't craven,
the thin glimmer striking down there
wasn't that of a match.

Il sogno del prigioniero

Albe e notti qui variano per pochi segni.

Il zigzag degli storni sui battifredi
nei giorni di battaglia, mie sole ali,
un filo d'aria polare,
l'occhio del capoguardia dallo spioncino,
crac di noci schiacciate, un oleoso
sfrigolìo dalle cave, girarrosti
veri o supposti—ma la paglia è oro,
la lanterna vinosa è focolare
se dormendo mi credo ai tuoi piedi.

La purga dura da sempre, senza un perché.
Dicono che chi abiura e sottoscrive
può salvarsi da questo sterminio d'oche;
che chi obiurga se stesso, ma tradisce
e vende carne d'altri, afferra il mestolo
anzi che terminare nel *pâté*
destinato agl'Iddii pestilenziali.

Tardo di mente, piagato
dal pungente giaciglio mi sono fuso
col volo della tarma che la mia suola
sfarina sull'impiantito,
coi kimoni cangianti delle luci
sciorinate all'aurora dai torrioni,
ho annusato nel vento il bruciaticcio
dei buccellati dai forni,
mi son guardato attorno, ho suscitato
iridi su orizzonti di ragnateli
e petali sui tralicci delle inferriate,
mi sono alzato, sono ricaduto
nel fondo dove il secolo è il minuto—

The Prisoner's Dream

Here few signs distinguish dawns from nights.

The zigzag of the starlings over the watchtowers
on battle days, my only wings,
a thread of polar air,
the head guard's eye at the peephole,
nuts cracking, fatty crackling
in the basements, roastings
real or imagined—but the straw is gold,
the wine-red lantern is hearth light,
if sleeping I can dream I'm at your feet.

The purge goes on as before, no reason given.
They say that he who recants and enlists
can survive this slaughtering of geese;
that he who upbraids himself, but betrays and sells
his fellow's hide grabs the ladle by the handle
instead of ending up in the pâté
destined for the pestilential Gods.

Slow-witted, sore
from my sharp pallet, I've become
the flight of the moth my sole
is turning into powder on the floor,
become the light's chameleon kimonos
hung out from the towers at dawn.
I've smelled the scent of burning on the wind
from the cakes in the ovens,
I've looked around, I've conjured rainbows
shimmering on fields of spiderwebs
and petals on the trellises of bars,
I've stood, and fallen back
into the pit where a century's a minute—

e i colpi si ripetono ed i passi,
e ancora ignoro se sarò al festino
farcitore o farcito. L'attesa è lunga,
il mio sogno di te non è finito.

and the blows keep coming, and the footsteps,
and I still don't know if at the feast
I'll be stuffer or stuffing. The wait is long,
my dream of you isn't over.

READING MONTALE

The story begins in an enclosed garden, an orchard to be precise. The wind enters, bringing the sound of the sea, which arouses dead memories. Suddenly the garden is not a garden but a graveyard, a mortuary, and the solitary strip of coastline where it lies has become a crucible, where history itself is forged. The story is being told to someone else, a "you" who, unlike the storyteller, may be able to take flight out of the constricting enclosure with the assistance of an intervening apparition, a creature out of a dream. The one hope of salvation imaginable to the anxious, disaffected storyteller is that his own existence may somehow be justified in helping his interlocutor escape the surroundings he finds so inimical.

The story continues, rippling out from here, gathering density, specificity, and color, growing in complexity and resonance. The elemental coastline is vividly evoked: churning sea; impenetrable, azure sky; blinding, hallucinatory sun; unforgiving cliffs and shoals —outward manifestations of the narrator's interior landscape. We get to know him in other ways as well. He is melancholy, solitary, obsessed with death and his past, preoccupied with limitations, both his and his world's, and he shoulders the burden of an overriding sense of universal wrong. He is an old young man, desperate for a counterpart, a companion who will recognize him and thus rescue him from the prison of himself, who will belie his conviction that he is extraneous to life.

Gradually, this other, too, emerges out of the haze of the shore; but she is more absent than present, a phantom herself. Later her nature will be clarified, but by then she has more or less left the narrator behind. Yet his one possession is his anxiously posited faith in her reality, and her capacity not to be saved herself now, but to redeem him. This character so doubtful of his own existence has come to stake his life on the conviction that she is the only real being in an alien and insubstantial world; outside her—and himself—is no one and nothing.

The storyteller ventures into the wider world. It is crowded with things—props, toys, keepsakes, exotic animals: the detritus of life past and present—but these become invested with significance only when they function as signs, somehow, of *her* existence. The loved one appears in several guises before she takes shape as a definitive figure, but each of her manifestations reveals her essential nature as the storyteller's mirror and inspiration. Yet her relationship to her faithful servant is difficult and troubled; she is often harshly judgmental, quasi-parental, for she is patently superior to him, partaking as she does of divinity. Still, she is with him, even when she is not physically present; she becomes a part of him, endowing him with the courage and strength to combat an enemy—one especially dangerous for her—who has begun to intervene threateningly in the world and to menace the storyteller and his beloved. Eventually, her battle with the enemy takes her far from him, and as she withdraws he sees their private drama projected against a background of universal conflict: she has become an actor not only in his story but in the history of the cosmos itself, her angelic mission now not simply to save him but to protect mankind from self-destruction.

Eventually, the enemy is defeated; but the angel has been fatally wounded in the struggle and dies, or is translated into another reality, imitating in her own way the trajectory of the Savior who was her precursor and model. The storyteller now is left with only the memory of her splendor and his anguish and resentment at being abandoned to an existence that is even more unpalatable than before—corrupt, decaying, profane, like himself. He is visited by idealized images of the closed coastal world of his childhood, which had once felt alien and cruel but which now, in memory, appears nurturing and humane. And now that his experience of divinely inspired love has ended, he consoles himself with a new, earthly love who competes with the fierce angel who inhabits his memory for ownership of his soul. This new figure, his Dark Lady, also appears in various guises before her character is definitively revealed. She is the angel's alter ego: dark, sensual, carnal—and ever-present. With her, he knows the profane ecstasy of physical passion, but the experience remains an intensely private one; the dream of universal salvation aroused by the angel's struggle with the enemy—which is also the storyteller's dream of liberation from solipsism—remains a dream. In his mind, his new love starts to resemble the angel, and they begin to meld into one life-giving figure, for each represents an episode in the ongoing attempt to escape himself that is the storyteller's fundamental drama. The illusion fails; finally, it cannot defeat the overpowering, innate conviction of his apartness that a lifetime of experience has confirmed. Nevertheless, the dream of faith in a saving other endures as the essential meaning of the narrator's story: his one talisman to ward off desolate reality.

If Montale's poetry can be construed as a novel, and there are many indications that he himself regarded it in these terms, this would be its plot. An existential drama, one that has much in common with the itineraries of his fellow European modernists, but with its own highly specific coloration and character; for Montale's story is also written as a version of the *canzoniere* or songbook, the collection of poems indited to a beloved woman that has been the determining form of Italian lyric poetry since Petrarch. More deeply, more comprehensively than any other modernist poet, Montale draws on the tradition that formed him, appropriating its essential story and reshaping it to serve his contemporary purposes.

This book is not a translation of all of Montale's poetry. In 1971, after a hiatus of more than fifteen years, he published a fourth collection, *Satura*, which was to be followed in the next decade by three more books that equal the output of his first thirty years of writing. But Montale's later poetry, written in his sixties, seventies, and eighties, is largely an ironic commentary on what came before, the *retrobottega,* or back of the shop, as he called it, a second and secondary body of work. As more than one critic has observed, it constitutes a progressive unmasking, a demystification and parody of the erotic-religious myth that reaches its apogee in *La bufera e altro* and constitutes Montale's major achievement. Our sense of the totality of Montale's contribution would be incomplete without his dryly prosaic, diaristic "second manner"—as it would be without his stories, his pointed criticism of literature, music, and the culture of his times, and even his painting. Nevertheless, the work that begins with *Ossi di seppia* and ends with *La bufera* describes a complete arc, one of the greatest in modern literature.

What do Italian readers hear in Montale? I'm going to offer a response, informed by my reading in his critics, though of course no one not born into a language can truly know how poetry sounds to those for whom it was written. First, I believe they hear a nervous, astringent music, one that asserts its individuality in sharp contradistinction to the prevailing norms of its era. Instead of orotund mellifluousness they encounter harshness and abruptness, enclosed in predominantly short forms tending to the paratactic, which are often in themselves self-conscious ironic reprises of traditional stanzas. They encounter a large, often arcane vocabulary which, in its restless search for expressive authenticity, employs rare words from sources ranging from the highly artificial and archaic to local dialect, frequently deployed in surprising conjunctions calculated to "strike sparks." They find, as a rule, compressed expression and thematic reiteration to the point of obsession, along with prodigious inventiveness in handling the inevitable, even oppressive riches of Italian rhyme, and great variation in the use of the Italian version of iambic pentameter—the hendecasyllable—which Montale alternates freely with *settenari, ottonari*, and *novenari*, or seven-, eight-, and nine-syllable lines in his search for constant rhythmic variety, occasionally resorting to longer forms as he experiments with his own kind of Hopkinsesque "sprung rhythm." In sum, Italian readers of Montale experience a restless will to reinvent, to renew the time-honored materials of their poetry by submitting them to arduous contemporary challenges.

They also hear constant echoes of an entire tradition. Italian lyric poetry can be seen as constituting a remarkably concise and unified line, starting with the thirteenth-century *stilnovisti* and their exemplar, Dante, the defining presence in Italian literature and the first to move the language out of the shadows of the classical past which in some respects endure to this day. The major figures—Petrarch, Foscolo, Manzoni, Leopardi—are relatively few, and all of them echo in Montale's work. The poetic novel that ends with *La bufera*, then, can be read as a résumé, a summation, perhaps a farewell to the Italian lyric enterprise, that love story tinged with an aura of the religious which begins with Dante and his inspiration, Beatrice.

In *Ossi di seppia* the Italian reader hears echoes, too, of Montale's immediate forebears, the *crepuscolari*, the post-symbolist "twilight" poets of his native Liguria, and behind them the sweet, sentimental, inventive voice of their major precursor, Giovanni Pascoli. This domestic, naturalistic strain alternates with the overstuffed turn-of-the-century rhetorical grandeur, tilted toward grandiosity, of Gabriele D'Annunzio, the Victor Hugo of Italian letters, who did everything that could be done with the language of his time—and via whom Montale makes his first approaches to the style and vocabulary of Dante. *Ossi di seppia* has been seen as a rewriting of D'Annunzio's *Alcyone*, an attempt at wringing the neck of its overweening eloquence—though Montale cannot help but resort at times to the very excesses he is fighting to liberate himself from. The book is a series of experiments—many of them French-influenced, post-symbolist, impressionistic, synesthetic—in creating a voice, which he achieves, definitively, in the *ossi brevi*, the brief lyrics at the heart of the book which express an unconsoled pessimism in terse, paradoxical formulations.

Montale's stylistic maturity emerges in *Le occasioni*, written in the late twenties and thirties, after he had left Genoa and the Cinque Terre behind. In Florence, where he was eventually acknowledged as a major figure of his generation, he made contact with the wider universe of Italian letters and with European modernism, and perfected the method of compression and figuration, the "poetry of the object," that was to define his mature style. But, as Montale himself acknowledged, his wider experience and experimenting finally only confirm and deepen his Italianness. He exchanges his poetic fathers, Pascoli and D'Annunzio, for his primary forebears, Dante and Foscolo, who, perhaps not coincidentally, happen to be Tuscan (the other great classic, Leopardi, was with him from the beginning, a characterological model of solitary melancholy—perhaps the ultimate literary source for Montale's attitudes in that Leopardi offered literary confirmation of the young poet's native temperament). Dante's influence intensifies as Montale's narrative coalesces as an amorous and later a religious allegory, taking on the methods as well as the coloration of Florentine *stilnovismo*. The book against which Montale can be said to work in his middle years is the *Vita nuova*, the allegorical "novel" in which Dante's beloved Beatrice leads him to revelation. Indeed, allegory can be seen as the determining method for the metaphysical "dream in the presence of reason" that Montale's entire poetry becomes, and it is increasingly haunted by the *Commedia* in *La bufera* as the poet comes to read the apocalyptic history of his own era more and more within the framework of the greatest model in Italian.

There are countless other echoes, too: of Shakespeare and the Anglo-American Romantic tradition, including Shelley, Keats, Browning (whose commingling of the prosaic and the domestic Montale admired and absorbed); of Dickinson and Hopkins; of Baudelaire, Rimbaud, and Mallarmé, whose symbolist poetics he tests to the point of overload; of Italian, French, Spanish, and English near-contemporaries, the most important being Valéry and Eliot—with whom Montale clearly felt an affinity and from whom he felt the need to differentiate himself, striving to establish that his own poetry of the object was arrived at independently of Eliot's objective correlative. As Gianfranco Contini has observed, Montale's work is written at the point of "veritable cultural saturation"; it is so heavily layered with allusion and quotation, particularly self-quotation, that at times it seems to approximate the echo chamber of Walter Benjamin's ideal work, the collage of borrowings. Yet Montale's weft of references and echoes performs a function in his poetry similar to that of his famously difficult vocabulary, his odd, seemingly reluctant rhyming, and his shifting metric: all are evidence of his determination to use every tool at his disposal in the attempt to unburden himself of something that nevertheless remains virtually impossible to convey.

Montale's critics talk about the "non-poetry" that is mixed in with the "poetry" of his first book, by which they mean the philosophical assertions out of which the lyric effusions spring. Much has been made of his indebtedness to contingentist philosophy, yet as he him-self has said, what he was essentially doing was obeying "a need for musical expression," his voluminous reading providing ex post facto verification for ideas he had already sensed or felt. As his work ma-tured, he learned, as he said, "to go deeper," "to express the object and conceal the occasion-spur," the engendering event or perception that are his poems' "occasions." Objects dominate the poems, and the style, of *Le occasioni*: verbs are subordinated to nouns, which characteristically pile up in lists or catalogues—one of the notable features of mature Montalean rhetoric. And as they develop, the catalogues become ever more extravagant and surprising, a sinuous, constantly transforming series of metaphors spiraling around an elu-sive central core, until in "L'anguilla," which many consider the apex of Montale's poetry and of the modern Italian lyric, the eel is named as "siren," "torch," "whiplash," "arrow," "spirit," "spark," "rainbow," and "sister"—all in one polymorphous thirty-line sentence. Monta-le's metaphorical restlessness, like his constant resorting to allusion, gives voice to his essential insecurity about his ability to fix his mean-ing, to pin it down for good. The subordination of verbs to nouns (actions are often locked within noun forms) also tends to confirm the sense, fundamental to his work, of confinement in an immutable status quo.

As a young man, Montale referred to his poetry as "a waiting for the miracle," the contingent miracle of flight which would release his beloved female figures from the imprisonment his poetics embodies with such dynamism but which is unavailable to the poet himself, whose groundedness and heavy corporality are frequently emphasized. This obsessive sense of stasis is reflected in his tendency to resort over and over to similar forms. The short lyrics of the *ossi brevi*, typically two or three stanzas of four or five lines, usually balanced in various inventive ways (metrically, in rhyme, and in imagery), become a basic unit of his poetry, repeated in the central MOTTETTI of *Le occasioni*, and in the 'FLASHES' E DEDICHE and certain of the MADRIGALI PRIVATI of *La bufera*. In each book, these alternate with longer pieces, and Montale's comments make it clear that the structure of the later collections was meant to replicate that of the first ("Tempi di Bellosguardo" in *Le occasioni*, for example, was originally intended as a "pendant" equal in length to MEDITERRANEO in *Ossi di seppia*).

Likewise with Montale's images, which he once said exist within the poems like knots in wood, integral to their meaning, or, rather, constitutive of it. It is remarkable how consistent his figurative vocabulary is, how the same images occur in poem after poem, accruing significance and value through use and across time. Almost all of them can first be found in *Ossi di seppia*: the wall; wind and clouds; flight (with its associated imagery: birds, wings); light and its sources and effects (sun, moon, heat, dawn, noon, sunset, shadow, lightning, night, sunflower); storm (rain, thunder); haze, fog, mist; mountain, rock, beach, shoreline; the sea and other water imagery (especially river, pool, whirlpool, eddy or vortex, and related images of entropy), as well as their opposites: dryness, parchedness; the mirror (or well or pool), locus of self-recognition; the circle or wheel, representative of constricting, inexorable fate; plants and vegetation, almost always symbolic of human beings; eyes; hair; jewelry; blood; the hunt; the ditch—these things, virtually all of them drawn from the elemental early world that is the substrate of Montale's first poetry, are constantly returned to, as if they had not yet "betray[ed] their final secret," as the poet attempts again and again to restate the fundamental problem of his work in ever more complexly enriched, not to say overdetermined, ways.

I want to take a brief look here at one minor Montalean image, the cicada, to demonstrate the cumulative, pearllike layering process by which meaning intensifies in his poetry. Others, like the sunflower

—which becomes a sign of Clizia, the prime mover of Montale's songbook/novel—or the mirror, the ditch, or the wounded bird, are more centrally significant; nevertheless, the process by which a Montalean image gathers connotative resonance is always fundamentally the same.

The cicada appears in Montale's first canonical poem, the *osso breve* "Meriggiare pallido e assorto," written before he was twenty. The insects' "wavering screaks / rise from the bald peaks," a seemingly pure descriptive component of the scene—though in Montale the landscape is always, as he made clear, *his*, i.e., it is always invoked to express an interior state. The insects appear twice more in *Ossi di seppia*. In "Egloga" ("only the solemn cicadas / survive the saturnalia of the heat") they are ceremonial, even priestly—already other than, set apart from, the general folly. And in the gloomy *osso* "Debole sistro al vento" ("Feeble sistrum in the wind / of a lost cicada, / no sooner touched than done for / in the exhaling torpor"), the figure has moved beyond naturalistic description, for the cicada, or rather its husk, the "corrupted leavings / the void won't devour," is represented as a kind of musical instrument, albeit a stilled one.

The figure appears twice in *Le occasioni*. In "Keepsake," Montale's catalogue of moments from the operettas he loved as a boy, the Cicada, a character from Edmond Audran's *La Cigale et la Fourmie*, "flies back to his nest," encapsulating an entirely private meaning, while in the motet "Non recidere, forbice, quel volto," as the cycle of love songs is nearing its despairing end, the theme reappears: "the hurt acacia / shakes off the cicada's husk / into the first November mud," and we begin to see that the cicada has become a figure for the poet[1]—one which tends to emphasize his transience, mortality, and ineffectuality. The husk is a kind of inverse image of the "creature of flight" apotheosized in an early version of "Crisalide," about a metaphorical insect which will eventually leave behind a similar shell of its own.

The identification intensifies in the late poems of *La bufera*—not so much in the seemingly purely descriptive "siesta / of cicadas,

---

[1] *scorza*, a synonym for *guscio* [shell or husk], occurs several times in the poetry before "L'ombra della magnolia . . . ," notably in the *osso breve* "Ciò che di me sapeste," where it is equated with the poet's "actual substance."

dazzling in my dream" of "Proda di Versilia," a nostalgic reprise of the scene painting of *Ossi di seppia*, as in the ecstatic symbolic drama of "Incantesimo," where "the amorous cicada chirrs" in his beloved's cherry tree, and most tellingly in "L'ombra della magnolia . . . ," where "a lone cicada / chirrs off and on" (as in "Meriggiare . . .")—but not for long, for, as we learn a few lines later, "the empty husk of him who sang will soon / be powdered glass underfoot." Here, the poet has at last stepped forth and openly declared his identification with the singing but soon-to-be-silenced insect.

The cicada, in fact, is an age-old symbol for the poet, going back at least as far as Plato's *Phaedrus*, where Socrates narrates the legend of the cicada who sings unendingly from birth to death without sustenance of any kind. No doubt this philosophical heritage informs the poet's use of the image in his later poetry, particularly in "Incantesimo," which is influenced by the Neoplatonism of Hölderlin. But, as always, Montale "begins with the real": the sound of the cicadas evokes a vivid memory out of childhood—and is thus an "occasion" for his poetry. The image of the insect becomes internalized and self-identified, after which additional connotations, even external, cultural ones, are gradually accrued, until the cicada becomes synonymous not only with the speaker of "L'ombra della magnolia . . ." but with the entire figure of the poet, sole inheritor and continuer of a threatened, perhaps even mortally wounded, tradition.

Similar principles apply in the construction of the poetry's dominant personae, Clizia and Volpe. Clizia's major biographical inspiration was the American Italianist Irma Brandeis, whom Montale met in Florence in the early thirties and who returned to America in 1938. *Le occasioni*, in which Clizia achieves definitive form and where she dominates the action (though she remains unnamed until *La bufera*), is dedicated to "I.B.," and the identification with Brandeis has long been accepted: Clizia's character and characteristics— her Jewishness, her style of dress, her forehead and bangs—are all Brandeis's. It has also become clear, however, that the late poems of *Ossi di seppia* and the early ones of *Le occasioni* were, in fact, inspired by others, most important the "Arletta" to whom much of the early poetry is addressed and who re-emerges in Montale's last work as the Ur-beloved, his first and most enduring amorous object. Clizia, then, as her evolving nature in the poems suggests, is a figure who metamorphoses as she is developed and revealed, and she is clearly derived from literary as well as experiential sources, inspired in different degrees not only by Irma Brandeis, Anna degli Uberti, and Paola Nicoli but by Marianna and Giuseppina Montale, by Gerti Frankl, Liuba Blumenthal, and Dora Markus, as well as by Dante's Beatrice, Cavalcanti's Mandetta, the Delia of Tibullus, Foscolo's *amica risanata* Antonietta Fagnani, Leopardi's Silvia and Nerina, Plato's (and Hölderlin's) Diotima, and others. She is a constantly elaborating symbol as much as she is a character, and the same is true for the anti-Clizian Volpe of *La bufera*.

Indeed, it has been asserted that nothing in Montale's amorous story is real, that his loves are mere literary conventions around which he constructs his work; it has been argued that the *tu*, or "you," to whom his love poems are addressed is really his own poetry, and that the anguish they express is simply a representation of the anxiety of artistic creation. These are extreme views, inspired by theoretical enthusiasm; but it is also true that, at least until the late poems for Volpe, Montale's work is "amorous but not erotic." Clizia, as some of Montale's most searching critics have noted, descends from the realm of the superego, more and more so as the amorous-religious heights of *La bufera* are reached; subliminally, she is associated with the family circle, ultimate seat of religious values, and especially with the figure of the poet's mother, though he is careful to conceal the connection.

It has been argued that Montale's poetry should be read allegorically, i.e., that its surface meaning always conceals another "essential and even existential significance in the ultimate and higher sense," as the writer himself put it.[2] The "metaphysical" poetry of *Le occasioni* and *La bufera* is clearly cast within Dante's allegorical frame, and there is no question that "higher meanings" are involved in the figuration of Clizia and Volpe. But, as we have also seen, Montale's images and figures tend to acquire existential significance from the very beginning of *Ossi di seppia*, where the landscape is not itself alone but also figures forth the poet's own psychic reality. The *trobar clus*, or encrypted song, of the *dolce stil nuovo* that gives voice to the

[2] "Augurio" (1944), translated as "A Wish" in *The Second Life of Art: Selected Essays*, ed. and tr. by Jonathan Galassi (New York: Ecco Press, 1982), 10.

allegory of the *Vita nuova* and the *Commedia*, then, is embraced not only for its chivalric associations and the expediency of its trope of concealment but more fundamentally because it confirms the poet's own symbolizing predisposition.

Allegory, as a means of endowing the world of appearances with evidence of things unseen, is, historically and essentially, an instrument of faith. Montale's existential quest, his search for liberation from the confining self, is at heart a spiritual drama, and though the poet struggles terribly against "the splendor of Catholicism," the faith of his tradition defeats him in the end: Clizia is ultimately "consumed by her God"; her absorption by Christian altruism takes her from him, abandoning him to his earthly, corruptible body, an unbeliever defeated by belief. The poet remains divorced from the uppercase God, limited to the lesser ecstasy of sublunary love with Volpe. Montale's novel, then, becomes the story of the failure of allegory, of the inability of the two levels of figuration to converge, except in the distanced figure of Clizia; as it has been from the beginning, an "ultimate and higher sense" beyond the world of appearances is unreachable for the storyteller, who remains "on the ground," haunted by his tragic ability to imagine an unattainable existence, while the irresistible thrust of his poetry continually directs both him and his reader toward an unavoidable if unreachable transcendence.

This sense of religious failure is consonant with the social pessimism that colors the end of the "novel" and predicts the ironic detachment of Montale's second manner. Montale's politics were defined in the liberal pre–World War I "Italietta" of Giovanni Giolitti in which the poet came to maturity; the upheaval of Fascism, not to mention the devastation it wrought, was deeply inimical to him, as was the rapid escalation of hard-line social divisions in a postwar society attempting to reform and renew itself. Yet the undifferentiated mass of others was alien to Montale from the outset; only the sentient few, those able to perceive the inauthenticity of their surroundings and to resist it in the core of their being, ever truly existed for him. This sense of fundamental apartness left him open to accusations of overweening superiority: Giuseppe Tomasi di Lampedusa, the Sicilian prince who was the author of *The Leopard*, has, for instance, left a memorable portrait of Montale and Emilio Cecchi at a literary prize ceremony, carrying themselves with the self-importance of "marshals of France."[3] Certainly, Montale was castigated on the left for his pessimistic, proud withdrawal from the polemical debates of the postwar years, an attack epitomized most vividly by his bitter exchange with the poet, filmmaker, and cultural agitator Pier Paolo Pasolini, who inspired the blistering "Lettera a Malvolio" in *Diario del '71*. Montale's "respectable keeping of distances," his rejection of the "permanent oxymoron" of the left/right polarization of Italian society, are prefigured in the later poems of *La bufera*, where the false social cohesion cobbled together in the fight against Fascism yields to a "harder way," as the poet attempts to steer a course between "red" and "black"—Communist and Christian Democrat—clerisies, retiring disillusioned into a private vision of interpersonal communion, his hopes for true social harmony, "the gift / I dreamed not mine but everyone's," bitterly disappointed. The political dream, which is a reflection in another key of the existential and religious one, has, predictably, failed as well.

Why has the incandescent poetry that narrates this anguished itinerary not only set the course of twentieth-century Italian verse but also had an increasingly resonant influence on our own? One reason, perhaps, is that Montale's work epitomizes modernity's confrontation not only with the terrors and failings of the present but with the great ruin of the past, revealing its insufficiencies and lacunae with unequaled splendor. What is remarkable in Montale is his determination not to break with what has come before him, as, for example, his near contemporaries the Futurists did, but to remain connected and engaged with tradition without being consumed by it, as he struggles to transform it into something of his own. This is the fundamental source of Montale's greatness—his idiosyncratic musicality, his lyric decisiveness, his striking originality and sheer memorability. He is so successful in his enterprise that, far from being overcome by the past, he ends up devouring it himself, like the greatest of his fellow modernists, turning it inside out in his rage to deliver his own intractable message.

It is helpful, in thinking about Montale's relationship to the literature that gave him birth, to return to his 1925 manifesto, "Stile

---

[3] See David Gilmour, *The Last Leopard: A Life of Giuseppe di Lampedusa* (New York: Pantheon, 1988), 125–27.

e tradizione,"[4] published a few months before *Ossi di seppia*, which remains a valid guide to his aims and concerns throughout his career. In it he discusses "the problem of tradition," "the problem common to all of us," which he conceives "not as a dead weight of forms, of extrinsic rules and habits, but as an inner spirit, a genius of the race, a consonance with the most enduring spirits that our country has produced" (the essay makes it clear that the figures he has in mind are Leopardi, Manzoni, and Foscolo); and he goes on to say that "tradition is continued not by those who want to, but by those who can."

It is in this light that Montale's poetic experience asks to be viewed. He is the last major Italian poet to see his spirit as fundamentally consonant with those of his predecessors, to conceive of his own project as a full-scale coming to terms with the engendering past. His approach is necessarily suspicious, off-center, often parodic, and ironically enough his appropriation of his heritage ends in its exhaustion, which is the theme of his disillusioned late work. The failure of the mythos of the Italian lyric for Montale is tantamount to the end of the world as he knew it. Yet, in spite of reason, conviction, and experience, a small minimum of faith—in his dream, in himself, in the essential power of poetry—survives in him; and his work ends up incarnating new life for the very myth that deserted him—the latest, hardest chapter in an ongoing story which has no way of dying. Almost in spite of himself, Montale's high ambition was ultimately achieved: Italian poetry has embraced its difficult offspring as the last—or latest—of the classics, and now waits patiently for the man or woman who can bring it to life again.

[4] Translated as "Style and Tradition" in *The Second Life of Art*, 3–8.

Chronology

Notes

Acknowledgments

Index of Titles and First Lines

———————

Chronology

This chronology is largely based on similar documents in a number of books, in particular Giorgio Zampa's edition of Montale's collected poetry, *Tutte le poesie*. The dating of the poems is derived from manuscripts, from Montale's letters, notes, and statements (which sometimes need to be taken with a grain or two of salt), and from records of first publication, supplied in Rosanna Bettarini and Gianfranco Contini's edition of *L'opera in versi*. Titles at time of first publication, if divergent from final titles, are given in brackets.

1896 Eugenio Montale is born at Corso Dogali, 5, Genoa, at 11:00 p.m. on Columbus Day, October 12, the sixth and last child of Domenico, called Domingo, Montale (1855–1931) and Giuseppina Ricci Montale (1862–1942). His siblings are Salvatore (1885–1972); Ugo (1887–1963); Ernesto (1889, who died as a baby); Alberto (1890–1978); and Marianna (1894–1938), who will play an important role in his upbringing and education. The family is comfortably off; Domingo Montale, from a family of notaries established in the Cinque Terre since 1633, is co-owner with two cousins of a firm that imports marine paints.

1900 Montale's father and partner cousins undertake the construction of a villa at Fegina, near Monterosso, native village of the Montales, then reachable only by train or boat, on the rocky Ligurian coastline west of La Spezia. Here Montale will spend long summer holidays until he is nearly thirty, and absorb the elemental landscape—hallucinatory sun, agitated sea, barren cliffs and shoals—that is the primary material of his first poetry.

1902 Enrolls at a boys' elementary school, which he will attend through the fourth grade.

1908 Student with the Barnabite Fathers in the Istituto Vittorino da Feltre. Baptized on May 21.

1911 May 5: First Communion. Receives his "licenza tecnica" on the second try; enrolls in the Istituto Tecnico Vittorio Emmanuele.

1915 Begins singing lessons with the baritone Ernesto Sivori; reads in the city library. Obtains his diploma as "ragioniere" in June and works briefly for his father's firm.

1916 Writes his first article, a review of Leoncavallo's *Goffredo Mameli*, for the *Piccolo* of Genoa (it is signed by the paper's critic, Vittorio Guerriero); also, "Meriggiare pallido e assorto" (revised 1922).

1917 Keeps the journal published in 1983 as the *Quaderno genovese*, which reflects his intense reading, particularly in French literature, and the influence of his sister, Marianna, then a philosophy student at the University of Genoa, who introduces him to the contingentism of Boutroux, Schopenhauer, and others. At a concert in March, hears Debussy's "Les collines d'Anacapri" and "Minstrels." August: Enlists in the 23rd infantry regiment stationed at Novara. November: Attends an accelerated officers' course at Parma, where he meets Sergio Solmi, destined to be a lifelong friend.

1918 January: Assigned as a junior officer to the 158th infantry regiment, Liguria Brigade. Volunteers for assignment to the front in Vallarsa in the Trentino, where he commands an outpost near the village of Valmorbia, later immortalized in *Ossi di seppia*. At the end of the war, is eventually transferred to Genoa.

1920 Befriends writers Angelo Barile and Adriano Grande, sculptor Francesco Messina, painter and poet Filippo De Pisis. Considers becoming a banker. March: Writes RIVIERE. In May, is discharged from the army with the rank of lieutenant. Meets the family of Reserve Admiral Guglielmo degli Uberti, who are renting the adjacent villa of his cousin Lorenzo in Monterosso; among them is sixteen-year-old Anna, whom Montale will call "Arletta" and who will serve as the primary inspiration of his early poetry. November 10: Reviews Sbarbaro's *Trucioli* in *L'Azione*.

1921 Complains in a letter to Solmi of serious insomnia, which is to remain an enduring affliction, as well as "exhausted nerves, weak constitution, and a psychology very ill-suited to everyday life." Returns to the study of singing with Ernesto Sivori.

1922 June: Publishes "Accordi" (later he asserts they were written "much earlier" than RIVIERE) and, in August–September, "L'agave su lo scoglio." November: Writes "I limoni."

1923 Writes: "Non rifugiarti nell'ombra," "Minstrels"; February–June: "Lettera levantina"; March(?): "Ripenso il tuo sorriso . . ."; June: "Portami il girasole . . ."; July: "Forse un mattino andando . . ." and "Non chiederci la parola. . . ." Death of Ernesto Sivori; Montale ends his study of singing. Anna degli Uberti, who lives in Rome, spends her last summer in Monterosso. September: Writes "Egloga"; October: "Vasca." In the fall, Montale makes his first visit to the capital. At year's end, writes "Sarcofaghi." In the winter, meets the Triestine Roberto Bazlen, who will introduce him to the "new world" of Mitteleuropa, including the work of Kafka, Musil, and Svevo.

1924 February: Writes "Falsetto"; spring–summer: "Crisalide." May 31: Publishes five of the *ossi di seppia* under that title in *Il Convegno*, among them "Mia vita, a te non chiedo lineamenti." June: Writes "Tentava la vostra mano la tastiera"; August: "Arremba su la strinata proda" and "Flussi." September: Publishes "Fine dell'infanzia," "Gloria del disteso mezzogiorno" ["Meriggio"], "Vasca." Tries unsuccessfully to obtain a post in the library of the Istituto Internazionale di Agricoltura in Rome and as a journalist in Milan. Also from 1924: "Godi se il vento ch'entra nel pomario" (later titled "In limine"), and MEDITERRANEO.

1925 January: The essay "Stile e tradizione" appears in *Il Baretti*. February–March: Publishes "Marezzo," "Casa sul mare." June: Piero Gobetti, the anti-Fascist editor of *Il Baretti*, publishes *Ossi di seppia*. November–December: Publishes his critical article "Omaggio a Italo Svevo," which will prove instrumental in establishing the Triestine novelist's Italian reputation.

1926 The search for work continues; finally, is offered a position with the publishing house of Bemporad in Florence, to begin in November. August: "Incontro" ["Arletta"]. September: "Due nel crepuscolo" (revised 1943), "Dora Markus I." November–December: Publishes "I morti," "Delta," "Vento e bandiere" ["La folata che alzò l'amara aroma"], "Fuscello teso dal muro," "Vecchi versi."

1927 In February, moves at last to Florence and begins work. June: Publishes "Arsenio." Contributes to numerous periodicals, including *L'Ambrosiano*, *La Fiera Letteraria* (where he has a regular column reviewing poetry), *Il Convegno*. Becomes a regular, and central, figure in the group of writers—including Alessandro Bonsanti, Alberto Carrocci, Carlo Emilio Gadda, Arturo Loria, Elio Vittorini—who together found the review *Solaria* and who gather, often several times a day, at Le Giubbe Rosse, a café in the Piazza Vittoria (now Piazza della Repubblica). Other friends in this period include Gianfranco Contini, Tommaso Landolfi, Carlo Levi, Aldo Palazzeschi, Enrico Pea, Renato Poggioli, Mario Praz, Salvatore Quasimodo, Ottone Rosai, Umberto Saba.

1928 January: Ribet, in Turin, publishes a second edition of *Ossi di seppia*, with six new poems and an introduction by Alfredo Gargiulo. June: Montale publishes "Carnevale di Gerti." Spends the summer at Monterosso, returning to Bemporad in the fall.

1929 March: Assumes the post of director of the Gabinetto G.P. Vieusseux, a private library in the Palazzo di Parte Guelfa. Becomes a paying guest in the home of Matteo and Drusilla Tanzi Marangoni, via Benedetto Varchi, 6. Begins reviewing for *Pegaso*. September: First trip to Paris. November: Publishes "Buffalo," "Keepsake," "Stanze" (begun 1927).

1930 Continues to review for *Pegaso*. September: Publishes "La casa dei doganieri."

1931 February: Carabba, in Lanciano, issues a third edition of *Ossi di seppia*. June: Death of Domingo Montale. To Solmi (July 22): "I can't manage to read—and consequently can't manage to review a single book. . . . I find myself in conditions one would have to experience to understand. In a certain sense I am living the most difficult years of my life. If only I could enrich my mind with some serious travel and a bit of urgent reading (so many blanks in the brain!) I could recover." Publishes six articles; writes "Cave d'autunno."

1932 Writes "Lindau," "Bagni di Lucca," "Altro effetto di luna," "Bassa marea." June: A chapbook of five poems, *La casa dei doganieri e altri versi* (Firenze: Vallecchi), is published for Montale as winner of the Premio del Antico Fattore. August: Visits London. Also travels to Nuremberg and Vienna. Publishes six articles, including "Omaggio a T. S. Eliot."

1933 April: A young American Italianist, Irma Brandeis, visits Montale at the Vieusseux. July: Publishes "Sotto la pioggia." August: Holiday in Eastbourne, Sussex, with stops in Paris and London; writes "Eastbourne" (revised 1935). November: Publishes "Punta del Mesco." Also from 1933: "Il balcone," "Verso Vienna" (revised 1938), "Costa San Giorgio" (revised 1938), "Barche sulla Marna" (revised 1937).

1934 August: Irma Brandeis returns to Florence. September: Montale visits Naples. December: Publishes three of the MOTTETTI: "Lo sai: debbo riperderti e non posso," "Molti anni, e uno più duro sopra il lago," "Brina sui vetri; uniti."

1935 July: Publishes "L'estate." October 12 postcard to Solmi: "In fact today I am 39, alone like a dog and with no desire to live longer. . . . If I almost never write you it's continually due to my state of mind which could not be more depressed and bankrupt. It wasn't wise to focus everything on a bit of literature and renounce life, which after all is the one thing we have. Nor was it even courageous. But it's useless to recriminate now."

1936 To Solmi, February 26: "I don't write, because I'm worse than before and don't want to annoy my friends. The times we are living through, and which I sense spasmodically, play their part as well." Writes "Corrispondenze," publishes one review.

1937 November: Writes "Non recidere, forbice, quel volto." Also from 1937: "Bibe a Ponte all'Asse," "Nel parco di Caserta," "La speranza di pure rivederti," "Il ramarro, se scocca," "Il fiore che ripete," ". . . ma così sia. Un suono di cornetta."

1938 October: Montale's sister, Marianna Montale Vignolo, dies, age 44. Montale publishes "Il saliscendi bianco e nero dei." November: Writes "Perché tardi? Nel pino lo scoiattolo." December: Is dismissed from his post at the Gabinetto Vieusseux because he is not a Fascist Party member. Considers following Irma Brandeis, who has returned to the United States, to take up a teaching position there. Also from 1938: "Verso Capua," "A Liuba che parte," "Accelerato," "Ecco il segno; s'innerva," "L'anima che dispensa," "La gondola che scivola in un forte," "Infuria sale o grandine? Fa strage," "La rana, prima a ritentar la corda," "La canna che dispiuma," "Notizie dall'Amiata."

1939 Begins to work as a translator, primarily of English and American fiction, often with the silent collaboration of his friend Lucia Rodocanachi. April: Moves with Drusilla Marangoni, called Mosca, to an apartment at viale Duca di Genova 38/A (now viale Amendola). April–June: "Elegia di Pico Farnese." May: "Dora Markus II," "Nuove stanze." May–June: "Palio." Also from 1939: "Lontano, ero con te quando tuo padre," "Addii, fischi nel buio, cenni, tosse," "Al primo chiaro, quando," "Tempi di Bellosguardo," "La primavera hitleriana" (revised 1946). June 18, to Bobi Bazlen: "I've sent the ms. [of *Le occasioni*] to Einaudi. There are 50 poems of which 40 are short and 17 unpublished. 1131 lines compared to 1600 in the *Ossi*. 2731 lines altogether; Leopardi wrote 3996 (not counting the Batracomiomachia). I'm behind by 1654 lines, but hope to die ahead. Now the fountain has truly been shut off for a long time. I've started translating Timon of Athens, then I'll move on to The Winter's Tale." End of October: *Le occasioni* is published in Turin by Einaudi.

1940 January: Writes "Ti libero la fronte dai ghiaccioli" and publishes "Il ritorno." February: Publishes "Alla maniera di Filippo De Pisis nell'inviargli questo libro." August: Publishes "Su una lettera non scritta," "Nel sonno." November: Writes "Serenata indiana." December: Publishes "Gli orecchini." Also in 1940: *Le occasioni*, 2nd edition (Turin: Einaudi), with four new poems; translation of Steinbeck's *The Battle*.

1941 Publishes "La bufera" (February) and "La frangia dei capelli . . ." (April) and translations of Cervantes, Bécquer, Gomez de la Serna, Marlowe (*Dr. Faustus*), Dorothy Parker. Writes "Lungomare," "Finestra fiesolana."

1942 Spring: Writes "Il giglio rosso." May: "Il ventaglio." November: "Personae separatae." Also "A mia madre." To Giulio Einaudi (November): "My house in Genoa including my books has been completely destroyed; my mother (though not in connection with this event) is dead. If she had been in Genoa we would all have died with her. Now I've turned to translation to discharge old obligations, but you can imagine in what state of mind." Publishes translations of stories by Hawthorne, Melville (including *Billy Budd*), Twain, Bret Harte, Evelyn Scott, Fitzgerald, Kay Boyle, Faulkner.

1943 February: Writes "Il tuo volo," publishes "L'arca." March–April: Publishes "Visita a Fadin" ["Passata la Madonna dell'Orto"], middle stanza of "Verso Siena" ["La fuga dei porcelli sull'Ambretta"], "Dov'era il tennis . . ." ["Dov'era una volta il tennis"]. Also "Giorno e notte" (spring). The chapbook FINISTERRE, smuggled into Switzerland by Gianfranco Contini, is published in Lugano by the Collana di Lugano on June 24, "a month before the fall of the House of Usher," i.e., before the demission of Mussolini on July 25. Writes "Il gallo cedrone." Also from 1943–44: "Iride." In the winter of 1943–44, shelters Umberto Saba, Carlo Levi, and other friends forced into hiding.

1944 During the battle for Florence (August), hides with Mosca in an apartment at via Cavour, 81. In September, Mosca suffers an acute attack of spondylitis, spending several weeks in a hospital. October: Montale publishes "Madrigali fiorentini."

1945 Made a member of the Committee for Culture and Art named by the Committee for National Liberation. Joins the liberal Partito d'Azione, shares the editorship of the daily

L'Italia Libera with Leo Valiani. Writes theater reviews for Florence's *La Nazione del Popolo*. Barbèra, in Florence, issues a second edition of FINISTERRE. In April, helps found the biweekly *Il Mondo*. In May, vacationing at Vittoria Apuana, begins to paint, first with oils, later with pastels and tempera. Publishes "Ballata scritta in una clinica" (August), "Da una torre" (November); writes "Nella serra."

1946 Begins to write (mainly stories) for the Milanese *Il Corriere della Sera*, Italy's leading newspaper, and its sister paper, *Il Corriere d'Informazione*, and for *La Lettura*. Publishes "Nel parco" and "L'orto" (April), "Proda di Versilia," " 'Ezekiel saw the Wheel . . .' " (December); also "Intenzioni: Intervista immaginaria" (Intentions: Imaginary Interview). Summer in Forte dei Marmi.

1947 Writes 21 articles for *Il Corriere della Sera* and *Il Corriere d'Informazione*. Publishes "Voce giunta con le folaghe" ["Una voce è giunta con le folaghe"] (June), "L'ombra della magnolia . . ." (November–December).

1948 January: Hired as an editor at *Il Corriere della Sera*. Moves to Milan, where he lives at the Albergo Ambasciatori. March 5–17: Travels to London with Alberto Moravia and Elsa Morante as guests of the British Council, speaking at Oxford, Cambridge, and Edinburgh. Visits T. S. Eliot at Faber & Faber. Sees G.B.H., a young woman working for a travel agency, whom he had met in Florence in 1945. Returns to London in June. July: Publishes "L'anguilla." September: *Quaderno di traduzioni* published by Edizioni della Meridiana, in Milan. December: Reports on the third UNESCO conference in Beirut; articles from Beirut, Palmyra, Tripoli. Also visits Damascus, Ba'abda. Writes "La trota nera," "Di un natale metropolitano," "Lasciando un 'Dove,' " "Argyll Tour," "Vento sulla Mezzaluna," "Sulla colonna più alta."

1949 January: Meets Maria Luisa Spaziani at the University of Turin. May: Publishes "Il gallo cedrone." Writes "Le processioni del 1949" ["Oltrepò"] (June), "Da un lago svizzero" (September). September: In Geneva for the Rencontres Internationaux. Publishes his 1943 translation of *Hamlet*. December: Attends the European Conference on Culture in Lausanne; publishes the MADRIGALI PRIVATI "So che un raggio di sole (di Dio?) ancora," "Hai dato il mio nome a un albero? Non è poco," "Se t'hanno assomigliato. . . ."

1950 April: Publishes "Nubi color magenta. . . ." June: Writes "Per un 'Omaggio a Rimbaud.' " July: Travels to New York for 48 hours for the inauguration of Alitalia's Rome–New York air route. August: Reports on the sessions of the Council of Europe in Strasbourg. September: Visits Brittany; awarded the San Marino poetry prize. October: Publishes "Verso Siena," "Sulla Greve."

1951 Moves to via Bigli, 11. Writes 87 newspaper articles.

1952 January: Publishes "Dal treno," "Siria," "Luce d'inverno." June: Delivers address, "La solitudine dell'artista" (The Artist's Solitude), at the International Congress for Cultural Freedom in Paris. Writes 108 articles.

1953 April: Attends the opening of Beckett's *En attendant Godot* in Paris; interviews Braque, Brancusi; meets Camus. May: Writes "Piccolo testamento" ["Congedo provvisorio"]. Summer in Forte dei Marmi. Writes "Per album" ["Da un album ritrovato"].

1954 March: Interviews Hemingway in Venice. June: Visits Provence, Spain, Portugal. Writes "Sul Llobregat." September: Begins writing music criticism for *Il Corriere d'Informazione*, an assignment he will continue until 1967. October: Publishes "Il sogno del prigioniero."

1955 Publishes 104 articles. August: In Normandy.

1956 June: Neri Pozza in Venice issues an edition of 1,000 copies of *La bufera e altro*. September: Montale is awarded the Premio Marzotto for poetry. December: Neri Pozza prints a private edition of *Farfalla di Dinard*, stories. Montale writes 119 articles.

1957 *La bufera e altro* published by Arnoldo Mondadori Editore, in Milan. 110 articles. August: Again at Forte dei Marmi.

1958 101 articles. August: At Forte dei Marmi.

1959 April 29: Anna degli Uberti dies in Rome. August: At Forte dei Marmi. November: Is made a member of the French Legion of Honor. 103 articles.

1960 Mondadori publishes an expanded edition of *Farfalla di Dinard*. 81 articles.

1961 Honorary doctor of letters from the University of Milan.

1962 *Satura* published in a private edition by the Oficina Bodoni, in Verona. Scheiwiller, in Milan, publishes *Accordi & Pastelli*. May: In Greece as guest of the Italian Cultural Institute. July 23: Religious marriage to Drusilla Tanzi in Fiesole.

1963 April 30: Civil marriage to Drusilla Tanzi in Florence. In August, she breaks her leg in a fall and dies in Milan on October 20.

1964 January: Reports on Pope Paul VI's pilgrimage to Jerusalem.

1965 April: Reads his lecture "Dante ieri e oggi" (Dante Yesterday and Today) in Florence at the International Congress of Dante Studies marking the 500th anniversary of the poet's death. July 27: Death of Bobi Bazlen. October: In Paris for the celebration of Dante's centenary.

1966 Private edition (50 copies) of XENIA, poems in memory of Mosca. *Auto da fé: Cronache in due tempi*, cultural criticism, published in Milan by Il Saggiatore. De Donato, in Bari, publishes Montale's correspondence with Svevo (along with his writings on the Triestine author). Gallimard, in Paris, publishes Patrice Angelini's translations of *Ossi di seppia*, *Le occasioni*, and *La bufera e altro*.

1967 June: Honorary degree from Cambridge University; named senator for life by President Giuseppe Saragat. August: Again in Forte dei Marmi. September: Moves from via Bigli #11 to #15, his final residence.

1968 Publishes additional *xenia*.

1969 Mondadori issues *Fuori di casa*, travel writings.

1971 January: Mondadori publishes *Satura (1962–1970)*. February: Scheiwiller publishes *La poesia non esiste*, prose. December: Private edition (100 copies) of *Diario del '71* (Scheiwiller).

1973 March: *Diario del '71 e del '72* (Mondadori). Giorgio Lucini, in Milan, publishes *Trentadue variazioni* (250 copies). November: Retires from *Il Corriere della Sera*.

1974 Honorary degree from the University of Rome.

1975 Mondadori issues an expanded edition of *Quaderno di traduzioni*. October 23: Awarded the Nobel Prize in Literature, which he receives in Stockholm on December 10.

1976 Mondadori publishes *Sulla poesia*, collected writings on poetry, in honor of the poet's eightieth birthday.

1977 Named an honorary citizen of the city of Florence. Mondadori publishes *Quaderno di quattro anni* and *Tutte le poesie*.

1978 Elected a foreign member of the American Academy of Arts and Letters.

1980 Summer in Forte dei Marmi. December: Publication of the Bettarini-Contini edition of *L'opera in versi* (Einaudi).

1981 May: Mondadori issues *Altri versi e poesie disperse* (previously published in *L'opera in versi*). September 12: Montale dies in the Clinica San Pio X in Milan. September 14: State funeral in the Duomo of Milan. The following day, the poet is buried next to his wife in the cemetery of San Felice a Ema, Florence. *Prime alla Scala*, music criticism, ed. Gianfranca Lavezzi (Mondadori). *Lettere a Quasimodo*, ed. Sebastiano Grasso (Bompiani).

1983 *Quaderno genovese*, ed. Laura Barile (Mondadori).

1984 *Tutte le poesie*, ed. Giorgio Zampa (Mondadori).

1991 *Diario postumo: Prima parte: 30 poesie*, ed. Annalisa Cima (Mondadori).

1994 *Ventidue prose elvetiche*, ed. Fabio Soldini (Scheiwiller).

1995 *Lettere e poesie a Bianca e Francesco Messina*, ed. Laura Barile (Scheiwiller); *Prose e racconti*, ed. Marco Forti (Mondadori).

1996 *Diario postumo: 66 poesie e altre*, ed. Annalisa Cima (Mondadori). For the centenary of Montale's birth, Mondadori completes its Meridiani edition of all his published writings, issuing *Il secondo mestiere: Arte, musica, società* and *Il secondo mestiere: Prose 1920–1979* (in two volumes), ed. Giorgio Zampa.

Notes

These notes are drawn from reading in the enormous body of Montale criticism that exists in Italian (and, to a growing extent, in English), much of it illuminating and suggestive in spite of Montale's famously sardonic views of his critics. My aim has been to stay close to the text of the poems themselves, offering the non-Italian reader information that can be helpful in elucidating idiosyncrasies in the author's vocabulary, pointing out significant stylistic traits, analyzing images and themes, and giving some sense of the intricate net of relationships that makes Montale's among the most internally coherent bodies of work in modern poetry. I have also tried—through what can be only a partial, intermittent sounding—to do some kind of justice to the enormous multiplicity of echoes and allusions at play in his verse.

I have not been interested here in advancing any one theoretical hypothesis about Montale. I have borrowed from numerous approaches, citing contradictory views when I feel they can be helpful in considering the text. The aim is to provide the English reader with a degree of awareness of how much is going on in Montale's work, of the specific nature of his complicated engagement with literature, history, and philosophy and their role in the creation of his art. As he himself wrote, "True culture isn't notional, it's what remains in a man when he's forgotten everything he has learned" (*Auto da fé*, 313). The scholar's task is to try to uncover what the poet learned and then did—or didn't—forget, and to show it at work in his art.

The notes to individual poems begin as a rule with the poet's own statements about the relevant text. Published works of Montale are abbreviated as follows, and critical works are cited by author (and number, if more than one).

WORKS CITED

WORKS OF EUGENIO MONTALE

Alt *Altri versi e poesie disperse*. Milan: Arnoldo Mondadori Editore, 1981. [Included in *Tutte*; most but not all poems in *Op*]

Auto *Auto da fé: Cronache in due tempi*. 2nd ed. Milan: Il Saggiatore, 1972. [in *SM/A*]

D71/2 *Diario del '71 e del '72*. Milan: Arnoldo Mondadori Editore, 1973. [In *Tutte, Op*]

Eus *Eusebio e Trabucco: Carteggio di Eugenio Montale e Gianfranco Contini*. Ed. Dante Isella. Milan: Adelphi Edizioni, 1997.

Farf *Farfalla di Dinard*. Milan: Arnoldo Mondadori Editore, 1960; expanded ed., 1973. [In *Pro*]

FdiC *Fuori di casa*. Milan: Arnoldo Mondadori Editore, 1975. [In *Pro*]

Op *L'opera in versi*. Ed. Rosanna Bettarini and Gianfranco Contini. Milan: Giulio Einaudi Editore, 1980. [The authoritative text]

Oth *Otherwise: Last and First Poems*. Tr. Jonathan Galassi. New York: Random House, 1984. [Translation of *Alt*]

Pro *Prose e racconti*. Ed. and with an introduction by Marco Forti. Textual notes and variants ed. Luisa Previtera. Milan: Arnoldo Mondadori Editore, 1996.

QuaG *Quaderno genovese.* Ed. Laura Barile with an essay by Sergio Solmi. Milan: Arnoldo
Mondadori Editore, 1983. [In *SM/A*]

QuaQ *Quaderno di quattro anni.* Milan: Arnoldo Mondadori Editore, 1977. [In *Tutte, Op*]

QuaT *Quaderno di traduzioni.* Milan: Edizioni della Meridiana, 1948; Arnoldo Mondadori
Editore, 1975. [In *Tutte, Op*]

Sat *Satura.* Milan: Arnoldo Mondadori Editore, 1971. [In *Tutte, Op*]

Sec *The Second Life of Art: Selected Essays.* Ed. and tr. Jonathan Galassi. New York: The
Ecco Press, 1982.

SM/A *Il secondo mestiere: Arte, musica e società.* Ed. Giorgio Zampa. Milan: Arnoldo Mon-
dadori Editore, 1996.

SM/P *Il secondo mestiere: Prose 1920–1979.* Ed. Giorgio Zampa. 2 vols. Milan: Arnoldo
Mondadori Editore, 1996.

Su *Sulla poesia.* Ed. Giorgio Zampa. Milan: Arnoldo Mondadori Editore, 1976. [In *SM/P*]

Tutte *Tutte le poesie.* Ed. Giorgio Zampa. 2nd ed. Milan: Arnoldo Mondadori Editore, 1991.
[The most comprehensive edition of Montale's poems]

OTHER WORKS

Almansi, Guido. Review of A. Valentini, *Lettura di Montale: 'Le occasioni'* (1975). In *Modern
Language Review* 72, no. 1 (January 1977), 218–19.

Almansi, Guido, and Bruce Merry. *Eugenio Montale: The Private Language of Poetry.* Edin-
burgh: Edinburgh University Press, 1977.

Angelini, Patrice Dyerval, ed. (1). *Poésies, I: Os de seiche, Ossi di seppia (1920–1927),* by
Eugenio Montale. Bilingual ed. Tr. and with a preface by Patrice Angelini with the col-
laboration of Louise Herlin and Georges Brazzola. Paris: Editions Gallimard, 1966.

———, ed. (2). *Poésies, II: Les occasions, Le occasioni (1928–1939),* by Eugenio Montale.
Tr. Patrice Angelini with the collaboration of Louise Herlin, Georges Brazzola, and Phi-
lippe Jacottet. Paris: Editions Gallimard, 1966.

———, ed. (3). *Poésies, III: La tourmente et autres poèmes, La bufera e altro (1940–1957),*
by Eugenio Montale. Tr. Patrice Angelini with the collaboration of Louise Herlin, Gennie
Luccioni, and Arnaud Robin. Paris: Editions Gallimard, 1966.

——— (4). "Tradurre Montale in francese: Problemi e documenti." In *La poesia di Eugenio
Montale: Atti del convegno internazionale tenuto a Genova dal 25 al 28 novembre, 1982.*
Ed. Sergio Campanilla and Cesare Federico Goffis. Florence: Le Monnier, 1984. 357–
401.

Arrowsmith, William, ed. (1). *Cuttlefish Bones (1920–1927),* by Eugenio Montale. Tr., with
preface and commentary, by William Arrowsmith (additional commentary by Rosanna
Warren and Claire Huffman). New York: W. W. Norton & Company, 1993.

———, ed. (2). *The Occasions,* by Eugenio Montale. Tr., with preface and commentary, by
William Arrowsmith. New York: W. W. Norton & Company, 1987.

———, ed. (3). *The Storm and Other Things,* by Eugenio Montale. Tr., with preface and
commentary, by William Arrowsmith. New York: W. W. Norton & Company, 1985.

Avalle, D'Arco Silvio. *Tre saggi su Montale.* Turin: Giulio Einaudi Editore, 1970 and 1972.

Baldissone, Giusi. *Il male di scrivere: L'inconscio e Montale.* Turin: Giulio Einaudi Editore,
1973.

Bàrberi Squarotti, Giorgio. *Gli inferi e il labirinto: Da Pascoli a Montale.* Bologna: Cappelli,
1974.

Barile, Laura (1). *Bibliografia montaliana*. Milan: Arnoldo Mondadori Editore, 1977.

———— (2). *Adorate mie larve: Montale e la poesia anglosassone*. Bologna: Il Mulino, 1990.

———— (3). "Per qualche variante del gallo cedrone." In *Montale tradotto dai poeti: Atti del convegno internazionale di Firenze [1996]*. Ed. Antonella Francini. Monographic issue of *Semicerchio*, XVI–XVII. Florence: Le Lettere, 1997. 52–57.

Becker, Jared. *Eugenio Montale*. Boston: Twayne Publishers, 1986.

Bettarini, Rosanna (1). "Appunti sul 'Taccuino' di 1926 di Eugenio Montale." *Studi di Filologia Italiana*, XXXVI (1978), 457–512.

———— (2). "Un altro lapillo." In *La poesia di Eugenio Montale: Atti del Convegno internazionale, Milano, 12/13/14 settembre, Genova 15 settembre 1982*. Milan: Librex, 1983. 219–25.

Biasin, Gian-Paolo. *Montale, Debussy, and Modernism* [Translation of *Il vento di Debussy*]. Princeton: Princeton University Press, 1989.

Bonfiglioli, Piero (1). "Pascoli e Montale." In *Studi per il centenario della nascita di Giovanni Pascoli pubblicati nel cinquantenario della morte*. Bologna: Commissione per i Testi di Lingua, I, 1962. 219–43.

———— (2). "Dante Pascoli Montale." In *Materiali critici per Giovanni Pascoli*. Ed. Mario Petrucciani, Marta Bruscia, and Gianfranco Mariani. Rome: Edizioni dell'Ateneo, 1971. 72–90. [Originally in *Nuovi studi pascoliani*. Bolzano-Cesena: Centro di Cultura dell'Alto Adige—Società di Studi Romagnoli, 1963. 36–62]

Bonora, Ettore (1). *Lettura di Montale. 1. Ossi di seppia*. Turin: Tirrenia-Stampatori, 1980.

———— (2). *Le metafore del vero: Saggi sulle "Occasioni" di Eugenio Montale*. Rome: Bonacci Editore, 1981.

Cambon, Glauco. *Eugenio Montale's Poetry: A Dream in Reason's Presence*. Princeton: Princeton University Press, 1982.

Carpi, Umberto. *Il poeta e la politica: Belli, Leopardi, Montale*. Naples: Liguori Editore, 1978.

Cary, Joseph. *Three Modern Italian Poets: Saba, Ungaretti, Montale*. 2nd ed. Chicago: University of Chicago Press, 1993.

Cima, Annalisa, and Cesare Segre, eds. *Profilo di un autore: Eugenio Montale*. Milan: Biblioteca Universale Rizzoli, 1997.

Contini, Gianfranco (1). *Una lunga fedeltà: Scritti su Eugenio Montale*. 2nd ed. Turin: Giulio Einaudi Editore, 1974.

———— (2). "Istantanee montaliane." Introduction to *Eugenio Montale: Immagini di una vita*. Ed. Franco Contorbia. Milan: Librex, 1985. v–xii.

Ferraris, Angiola. *Se il vento: Lettura degli "Ossi di seppia" di Eugenio Montale*. Rome: Donzelli Editore, 1995.

Forti, Marco (1). *Eugenio Montale: La poesia, la prosa di fantasia e d'invenzione*. 2nd ed. Milan: Mursia, 1983.

———— (2). *Il nome di Clizia: Eugenio Montale: Vita, opera, ispiratrici*. Milan: All'Insegna del Pesce d'Oro, 1985.

Fortini, Franco. "I latrati di fedeltà." In *Letture montaliane*. Genoa: Bozzi, 1977. 377–85.

Giachery, Emerico. *Metamorfosi dell'orto e altri scritti montaliani*. Rome: Bonacci Editore, 1985.

Greco, Lorenzo. *Montale commenta Montale*. Parma: Practiche Editrice, 1980. [Contains Silvio Guarnieri's correspondence with Montale about his work (see Macrì 2, 381–85, for correction and amplification of Greco's transcription of Guarnieri's questionnaire)]

Grignani, Maria Antonietta. *Prologhi ed epiloghi: Sulla poesia di Eugenio Montale; con una prosa inedita*. Ravenna: Longo Editore, 1987.

Huffman, Claire de C. L. *Montale and the Occasions of Poetry*. Princeton: Princeton University Press, 1983.

Isella, Dante, ed. (1). *Mottetti*, by Eugenio Montale. [3rd ed.] Milan: Adelphi Edizioni, 1988. [Now in Isella 2]

———, ed. (2). *Le occasioni*, by Eugenio Montale. Turin: Giulio Einaudi Editore, 1996.

——— (3). "La fontana delle ultime 'Occasioni.'" *Strumenti Critici*, New series III, 2, no. 57 (May 1988), 179–208.

Jacomuzzi, Angelo (1). *La poesia di Montale: Dagli Ossi ai Diari*. Turin: Giuliano Einaudi Editore, 1978.

——— (2). "'Incontro': Per una costante della poesia montaliana." In *La poesia di Eugenio Montale: Atti del Convegno internazionale, Milano, 12/13/14 settembre, Genova 15 settembre 1982*. Milan: Librex, 1983. 149–60.

Lavezzi, Gianfranca. "Occasioni variantistiche per la metrica delle prime tre raccolte montaliane." In *Metrica* II (1981), 159–72.

Lonardi, Gilberto. *Il vecchio e il giovane e altri studi su Montale*. Bologna: Zanichelli, 1980.

Luperini, Romano (1). *Storia di Montale*. Rome: Editori Laterza, 1986.

——— (2). *Montale o l'identità negata*. Naples: Liguori Editore, 1984.

Macchia, Giovanni. "Il romanzo di Clizia." In *Saggi italiani*. Milan: Arnoldo Mondadori Editore, 1982. 302–16.

Macrì, Oreste (1). "Esegesi del terzo libro di Montale." In *Realtà del simbolo*. Florence: Vallechi, 1968. 75–146.

——— (2). *La vita della parola: Studi montaliani*. Florence: Casa Editrice Le Lettere, 1996. [Includes Macrì 1]

Marcenaro, Giuseppe, and Piero Boragina. *Una dolcezza inquieta: L'universo poetico di Eugenio Montale* [Catalogue of an exhibition at the Palazzo del Banco di Chiavari e della Riviera Ligure, Genoa, February 14–April 20, 1996; and at Palazzo Besana, Milan, May 16–June 30, 1996]. Milan: Electa, 1996.

Marchese, Angelo, ed. (1). *Poesie*, by Eugenio Montale. Milan: Arnoldo Mondadori Scuola, 1991.

——— (2). *Visiting Angel: Interpretazione semiologica della poesia di Montale*. Turin: Società Editrice Internazionale, 1977.

——— (3). "Le ispiratrici dei Mottetti." In *Strategie di Montale: Atti del seminario internazionale di Barcellona su "La costruzione del testo in italiano" (8–9 e 15–16 marzo 1996)*. Ed. María de Las Nieves Muñiz Muñiz and Francisco Amella Vela. Barcelona: Universitat de Barcelona, 119–41.

Martelli, Mario. *Il rovescio della poesia: Interpretazioni montaliane*. Milan: Longanesi, 1977.

Mengaldo, Pier Vincenzo. *La tradizione del novecento*. 2nd ed. Milan: Feltrinelli Editore, 1980.

Nascimbeni, Giulio. *Montale*. Milan: Longanesi & C., 1975.

Orelli, Giorgio. *Accertamenti montaliani*. Bologna: Il Mulino, 1984.

Pipa, Arshi. *Montale and Dante*. Minneapolis: University of Minnesota Press, 1968.

Ramat, Silvio. *L'acacia ferita e latri saggi su Montale*. Venice: Marsilio Editori, 1986.

Rebay, Luciano (1). "I diaspori di Montale." *Italica* 46, no. 1 (1969), 33–53.

——— (2). "Sull' 'autobiografismo' di Montale." In *Innovazioni tematiche espressive e lin-*

guistiche della letteratura italiana del novecento: Atti dell'VIII Congresso dell'Associazione Internazionale per gli Studi di Lingua e Letteratura Italiana, New York, 25–28 aprile, 1973. Florence: Leo S. Olschki Editore, 1976. 73–83.

—— (3). "Montale, Clizia e l'America." *Forum Italicum* 16, no. 3 (1982), 171–202.

—— (4). "Un cestello di Montale: Le gambe di Dora Markus e una lettera di Roberto Bazlen." *Italica* 61, no. 2 (1984), 160–69.

Sanguineti, Edoardo. "Da Gozzano a Montale." In *Tra Liberty e crepuscolarismo*. Milan: Mursia, 1970. 17–39.

Savoca, Giuseppe. "Sul petrarchismo di Montale." In *Per la lingua di Montale: Atti dell'incontro di studio (Firenze, 26 novembre 1987)*. Ed. Giuseppe Savoca. Florence: Leo S. Olschki Editore, 1989. 53–70.

Segre, Cesare. "Invito alla Farfalla di Dinard." In *I segni e la critica*. Turin: Giulio Einaudi Editore, 1969. 135–51.

Spaziani, Maria Luisa. "Un carteggio inedito di Montale." In *La poesia di Eugenio Montale: Atti del convegno internazionale tenuto a Genova 25–28 novembre 1982*. Ed. Sergio Campanilla and Cesare Federico Goffis. Florence: Felice Le Monnier, 1984. 321–24.

Talbot, George. *Montale's* Mestiere Vile: *The Elective Translations from English of the 1930s and 1940s*. Dublin: Irish Academic Press, 1995.

Valentini, Alvaro. *Lettura di Montale: Ossi di seppia*. Rome: Bulzoni, 1971.

West, Rebecca J. *Eugenio Montale: Poet on the Edge*. Cambridge: Harvard University Press, 1981.

Zambon, Francesco. *L'iride nel fango: L'anguilla di Eugenio Montale*. Parma: Nuova Pratiche Editrice, 1994.

OSSI DI SEPPIA / CUTTLEFISH BONES

First published by Piero Gobetti in Turin in 1925; republished by Ribet (Turin) in 1928, with additions ("Vento e bandiere," "Fuscello teso dal muro," "Arsenio," "I morti," "Delta," "Incontro") and an introduction by Alfredo Gargiulo; third edition published by Carabba (Lanciano) in 1931; republished by Einaudi (Turin) in 1942 and by Mondadori (Milan) in 1948.

Originally dedicated "To my friend Adriano Grande"; this, as well as the dedications to many of the individual poems, was suppressed after the third edition.

Montale's first book draws its primary inspiration from the landscape of the Tuscan coast, and in particular the Cinque Terre, a group of villages on the Riviera di Levante north of La Spezia, cut off from the mainland by high mountain ridges and until after World War II accessible only by boat or train. Here, near Monterosso al Mare, Montale spent long summer holidays well into his adult years at his family's house at Fegina, a locale on the low slopes of the Punta del Mesco. Arrowsmith quotes Montale as saying that his years in this secluded environment led "to introversion, to an imprisonment in the cosmos" (1, xvi). The dry, rocky coastline facing the Tyrrhenian Sea and the gardens and surroundings of the Montale house provide the setting for many of the poems of *Ossi di seppia* (and, later, in a more deeply elegiac key, of *La bufera e altro*). They generally evoke the summer season, especially the blazing, almost blinding light of midday. Their themes, as Montale himself described them, are "landscape, love, and evasion" (Valentini, 11).

Barile (*QuaG*, 183–84) quotes a description of the Montale villa written by the poet's sister, Marianna, which gives many clues to the topography and *topoi* of his poems:

You enter through the gate and immediately there are a bench and two palms; some hydrangeas, some dahlias: imagine, when I walk among the beds, I'm invisible, they're so tall. They're as high as I am. On the other side there's a rustic railing covered with cassia; then you walk up a long avenue of pittosporums and arrive at the balustrade where two staircases rise, one to the right and one to the left, and you're in front of the house; there are masses of flowers, patterned beds with flowers in them, too, and patterned borders. Four tall palms, pittosporums, firs and poplars, and a splendid view of the sea as far as the little island of Tino; you see some little villages grouped on the cliffs, hanging over the sea. There's a lovely pool with a jet of water and goldfish, surrounded by ivy and honeysuckle. Behind the house are more flowers and the swing. Then you climb a small flight of stairs and you're in the little (artificial) woods, I say artificial because it wasn't there originally, little trees were planted there—now they've grown up. There are maples, horse-chestnuts, little oaks, chestnuts, etc., and paths that intersect; then you climb another small flight and go into the vines and on up as high as you wish. On either side of the avenue of pittosporums when you enter there are vines, an orchard, the farmer's house, the farmer's garden, ditches. When you're on the piazza, in front of the house, you go to the right and there you enter a large garden, where there's the greenhouse, another pool, a grotto grown over with ivy where we put all the pretty shells we find (the ceiling is entirely shells), where there are cyclamens and maidenhair ferns; then there's a marble statue representing summer with a crown of ears of corn and a scythe. There are magnolias, eucalyptus, pittosporums, a gigantic cedar of Lebanon, and other trees and lots of flowers and many succulents in small pots, more curiosities than anything else. There's a grouping of tall pittosporums which is empty inside, since the pittosporums come together up top, so it's like a little room of leaves that has chairs and a little table. Nearby is another house which belongs to my cousin [Lorenzo Montale, the collector of succulents of "Le piante grasse" in *Alt*]. You climb a staircase and you're in another garden with a pergola of very sweet grapes and a boccie court and then another bit of land with pear trees; then you climb a last staircase and you're in the very shady pine grove with a wandering walk, and benches at every turn; and wisteria and ranunculus. You go up the path and come to the top of the pine grove where there is a tower which serves no purpose; we go there sometimes for amusement, but it's lovely, with crenellations and windows with circular glass panes and it's built out of big rusticated stones. There's a fence that begins at the tower and a wall that descends and encircles the villa. I forgot to tell you that below the pine grove there's another gate. Right in front is the road and then the beach.

Some critics have seen *Ossi di seppia* as a kind of response—often a hostile or critical one—to Gabriele D'Annunzio's *Alcyone* (1903), a diary in verse which celebrates in panegyric, often Dionysian terms a summer spent on the Tuscan coast just south of Montale's native ground. Montale's summer landscape by comparison is closed, turbulent, harsh, the elements corresponding to troubled interior states, "the inverse," as Alessandro Parronchi put it, "of the intolerable hedonism and paganism of D'Annunzio" (quoted in Bonora 1, 74). As Montale himself wrote in 1970, "The Ligurian riviera was never halcyon or Panic in the torrential sense of the word. It was rather, in its natural forms, anthropomorphic and exquisitely human, if lowercase" (*SM/A*, 1459).

Montale wrote in "Intentions: Imaginary Interview," paraphrasing Verlaine, that as a young man he wanted to "wring the neck of our old aulic language, even at the risk of a counter-eloquence" (*Sec*, 300). The poems in *Ossi di seppia* are experiments in that counter-eloquence, a search for a language that is not overwhelmed by its predecessors, "a reply that a new and original poetry makes to the poetry that has preceded it, not negating it reflexively but concretely counterposing other values" (Bonora 1, 74). Yet Montale also fully recognized the depth of his stylistic debts to D'Annunzio, as is clear from this 1956 statement: "D'Annunzio in the recent Italian tradition is a little bit like Hugo in his French descendants, from Baudelaire on: he is present in everyone because he tested and touched on all the linguistic and prosodic possibilities of our time. In this sense, to have learned nothing from him would be a bad sign indeed" (*Su*, 68).

Montale also grew up under the immediate influence of the *crepuscolari*, the Ligurian counterpart of Yeats's Celtic Twilight. "Poets of aftermath," professional amateurs and *poètes maudits*, they rejected classicizing formality and big ideas in favor of plain, prosaic speaking about intimate details. They included Sergio Corazzini, Ceccardo Roccatagliata Ceccardi, Giovanni Boine, Camillo Sbarbaro, and, most notably, Guido Gozzano, who added a dose of irony borrowed, like Eliot's, from Jules Laforgue. Behind them stands the major figure of Giovanni Pascoli (1855–1912), whose mixture of tones, domestic preoccupations, concentration on particulars, and inventive musicality contrasted with the rhetorical grandeurs of D'Annunzio. (See Cary, chapter 1, for an excellent discussion of Montale's precursors. Bonfiglioli [1] provides a discriminating study of Pascoli's lexical influence on Montale, but demonstrates [2, 89] that "Montale's Pascolism is . . . dialectically and practically an anti-Pascolism.")

D'Annunzio and Pascoli are, in effect, the poetic "fathers" whose necks Montale had to wring, and his "rancor" toward them is a determining factor in the forging of his own style. Still further back are his "grandfathers," above all Dante, but also Giacomo Leopardi and Ugo Foscolo, who will exert a deeper influence on Montale's mature work. But to begin with he has to write against the rich and multivalent language of D'Annunzio and the domestic ingenuousness of Pascoli in creating his own much more restrictive and symbolic poetry. What he said of Gozzano was true, mutatis mutandis, of himself: he "managed (as was necessary and probably remained so after him, too) to pass through D'Annunzio to arrive at a territory of his own, just as, on a larger scale, Baudelaire had passed through Hugo to establish the bases for a new poetry" (*Su*, 62).

In limine / On the Threshold (1924)

Original title, "La libertà" (Liberty). In form and function, one of the short lyrics, or *ossi brevi*, of the section OSSI DI SEPPIA, which lends its name to the entire collection, and one of the last poems included in the first edition of the book; Montale: "It was supposed to be the summa or the send-off for all the rest" (*Op*, 862).

Montale to Paola Nicoli (August 24, 1924) (*Op*, 862): "It's a little difficult for me to manage to work at the moment; my kind is all *a waiting for the miracle*, and miracles in these times without religion are rather rarely seen. When the book is finished—and it can almost be called such—I'll either shift viewpoint, changing genres, or *silentium*. I have no desire to vivisect myself further. But yes, 'Godi se il vento' ["In limine"] exists—and the 'top of the tree' was seen with deep feeling. Now I'm left with the parts of a certain 'chrysalis' [see "Crisalide"] which will emerge one day or another."

Many of Montale's major themes make their first appearance here: the static, memory-haunted garden enclosure as the site for a visitation from a world beyond; the wind as a sign of that life; flight as a means of escape or an agency of salvation; the phantom or apparition that may bring that salvation; the "oblatory gesture" (Marchese 1, 17), the act of renunciation in favor of another (cf. "Crisalide" and "Casa sul mare"), which will later fall to Clizia, on behalf of all mankind, in the major poems of *La bufera*. Most significant of all, the poem is addressed to an (unidentified) interlocutor, the beneficiary of the poet's renunciatory act, "one of the lexical and psychic constants of Montale's poetry" (West, 13). Montale wrote to Pietro Pancrazi (March 22, 1934): "The companion of 'In limine' was a woman, the same one who can be found in 'Incontro,' 'Stanze,' and 'Casa sul mare' " (Marchese 1, 16). (See note on "Incontro," where she is identified as "Arletta," the Montalean figure inspired by Anna degli Uberti.) For Bettarini (2, 221), the second (Ribet) edition of *Ossi di seppia* is "a totally Arlettian" book, and "In limine" is its "conclusion," its "farewell and viaticum," rather than its introduction.

Almansi and Merry, Montale's most radically deconstructive critics, suggest (7) that the *tu* is the reader himself; but, as always in Montale, there is also an objective reality that gives rise to the poem. As he himself famously put it (see p. 550), "I always begin with the real, I'm incapable of inventing anything."

pomario, crogiuolo: Neoclassic language. Contini (1, 28–29): Desperate "Parnassian gelidity," contrasting with the "stirring" engendered by the wind, itself reminiscent of Shelley's "Ode to the West Wind."

orto: For Montale's late explanation of the significance of this term, see note to "L'orto."

reliquiario: Giachery (21) notes the affinity with Valéry's "Le cimetière marin." In the 1948 story "Reliquie" (*Farf*, 156–60), the box where the character keeps "clippings, old letters tied up with a ribbon, and some little saints he didn't dare destroy" is referred to derisively as "your private reliquary," i.e., the storehouse for obsessive, perhaps useless memories.

di qua dall'erto muro: Cf. "di là dell'erto muro," from "Il pesco" in Pascoli's *Myricae*. The wall of sheer necessity, an enduring image of harsh reality, countered only by an occasional contingent event or apparition.

gli atti / scancellati . . . : According to Isella (2, 149), for Montale " 'the game of the future' is nothing but the recombination of the 'canceled acts' of the past."

pel giuoco del futuro: *Pel* is an old-fashioned literary contraction of *per il*. Note also the hypermetric rhyme *fuggi/ruggine*, a frequent Montalean device in the style of Pascoli and Gozzano (but also used by D'Annunzio) (Mengaldo, 65–66), in which, for the purposes of rhyme, the last, unstressed syllable of the *sdrucciolo*, or dactyl (*rúggi/ne*), is considered dropped.

una maglia rotta . . . : For a discussion of Montale's notions of contingency, see note to "Avrei voluto sentirmi . . ." in MEDITERRANEO.

MOVIMENTI / MOVEMENTS

The title of this section, perhaps derived from Debussy's "Mouvements," one of the *Images* for piano (Biasin, 8), underlines Montale's early modernist experiments in relating poetry and music. Apart from "Corno inglese," "Falsetto," "Minstrels," and "Quasi una fantasia," below, a number of early poems not originally incorporated in Montale's canon—"Musica silenziosa," "Suonatina di pianoforte," and the suite of "Accordi" (eventually published in *Alt* and translated into English in *Oth*; see note to "Corno inglese," below)—attempt to imitate the aesthetic values Montale admired in the music of Debussy (and Ravel and Stravinsky): the rejection of late Romantic grandiosity and a desire to move beyond symbolism to find new formal means—including dissonance—of expressing inner experience. As Debussy himself wrote in 1889: "Music begins where the word is impotent to express: music is written for the inexpressible. . . . I dream of poems that do not condemn me to drag long, heavy actions . . . poems where the characters do not discuss but suffer life and destiny" (Biasin, 12). The work of Montale's twenties and thirties similarly experiments with alternatives to symbolist representation, which will result in the objective, nominalist poetics of *Le occasioni*.

I limoni / The Lemons (November 1922)

Ms. dedicated to Paola Nicoli (see notes to the first motet) "with fraternal wishes" (*Op*, 862).

Like "In limine," a poem about poetics. It bears comparison with Montale's celebrated 1925 manifesto "Stile e tradizione" ("Style and Tradition" in *Sec*, 3–8), in which he argues in favor of a "superior dilettantism": "The problem of style understood as something organic and absolute, as the supreme moment of literary creation, still remains at the point where Manzoni and Leopardi left it; . . . since then there has seemingly been only debasement, compromise, dialect, and falsetto. . . . Style perhaps will come to us from the sensible and shrewd disenchanted, who are conscious of the limits of their art and prefer loving it in humility to reforming humanity." "I limoni" is the poem of Montale's that is closest to the poetics of the *crepuscolari*. It promulgates direct, non-aulic language, nature over "civilization," and the miracle of sunlight—an early instance of one of his most salient images.

bossi ligustri . . . : Ironic reference to D'Annunzio, Pascoli, and Virgil. The "poeti laureati" must also necessarily include Petrarch, the creator of Laura.

qualche sparuta anguilla: First appearance of the image of the eel, which will reach its culmination in "L'anguilla" (see note to this poem for discussion of the recurrence of this and connected images throughout Montale's work); Zambon (21) finds in "I limoni" "a whole constellation of elements ['grassy ditches," "half-dry puddles," and sunlight] which will recompose, now projected in a mythical and soteriological dimension, around 'L'anguilla' in *La bufera*."

divertite: Latinism derived from Manzoni and Pascoli.

qui . . . ricchezza: Bettarini (1, 463) notes that in the ms. version, this line ended with the apostrophe "Sbarbaro" (see "Poesie per Camillo Sbarbaro").

uno sbaglio di Natura . . . : Cf. the "maglia rotta" of "In limine."

disturbata Divinità: The human shade prefigures the absent/present companion/angel of the later poetry. Cf. also the "parvenza di donna" of "Egloga." Arrowsmith (1, 180) notes the correspondence (and rhyming) of *Divinità* and *solarità*.

Corno inglese / English Horn (1916–20)

First published in 1922 in the group "Accordi (Sensi e fantasmi di una adolescente)" (Chords [Feelings and Fantasies of an Adolescent Girl], in *Oth*), of which it was the sixth component (originally titled "Corni inglesi" [Mengaldo, 303]). The other sections were "Violini," "Violoncelli," "Contrabasso," "Flauti-fagotto," "Oboe," and "Ottoni."

Montale to Giacinto Spagnoletti (August 27, 1960) (*Op*, 865): "I couldn't give a date to ['Accordi'] with absolute precision; they certainly postdate the first real and proper *osso* ('Meriggiare' of 1916) but are much earlier than RIVIERE (March 1920). . . . The 'Corno inglese' was the only one that could be lifted out of the series: whose general sense, along with the general pretense of imitating musical instruments (not to mention the bit of starch that can be found here and there), displeased me, and still does. I must therefore conclude that in my youthful *château d'eaux* (as Lorenzo Montano called my poetry) alongside a more troubled vein, or even *within* that vein, the thinner but more limpid trace of the *Ossi* was making its way for a long while. The entire opening section of the *Ossi* (except for 'In limine' . . .) thus belongs to the proto-Montale: and in this group—though even within this context I later rejected them—go the poems of 'Accordi' " (*Op*, 865).

Biasin (18): "The 'Accordi' suite is a true orchestral rehearsal of themes and motives that will be found again throughout Montale's poetic oeuvre, from the expectation of a miracle to the greyness of daily life, from sadness to a fragile joy or rare happiness, from perplexity or existential bewilderment to the invention of the female *tu* interlocutor." And "Corno inglese" itself is "a small concentrate, a self-sufficient microcosm of Montale's themes, images and techniques, in a circular structure which closes upon itself at the phonic, lexical and syntatic levels" (29). The poem is one sentence, albeit a complex one, as are a number of Montale's most concentrated poems; the collocation of appositive nouns of which it is composed antic-ipates the famous catalogues of the poet's mature style.

Almansi and Merry (15) cite Emily Dickinson's "There came a wind like a bugle," later translated by Montale as "La tempesta" (in *QuaT*), as a probable source, while Mengaldo (303–13 and 37) notes numerous D'Annunzian borrowings (notably from "La sera fiesolana" in *Alcyone*) and correspondences with his rhythmic techniques.

vento: Cf. the wind of "In limine" and "Falsetto," the enlivening force that brings change into the poet's affectless world. Note the rhyme with *attento* and *strumento*.

lame: Ligurian dialect for *lamiere*, metal sheets. Ferraris (10) notes that the *lame/rame* rhyme can be found in Valéry's "La jeune Parque"—though also (*rame/Lame*) in "Le madri" in *Alcyone*.

s'annera: Bonora (1, 50) notes that this is a poeticism (for *annerire*), with precedents in Dante, Leopardi, and D'Annunzio.

scordato: Forgotten as well as discordant.

Falsetto (February 11, 1924)

Dedicated in early editions "to Esterina" (Rossi), a teenage friend of the sculptor Francesco Messina; Montale had observed her at the beach of Genova Quarto.

Angelini (1, 216): "A bit of a parody . . . of a certain neoclassic taste dominant at the time—with [Vincenzo] Cardarelli, author of an 'Adolescent' of a similar inspiration, and his review *La Ronda*," which promoted a narrow renewal of *italianità*. For Marchese (1, 2), the poem "shines with the irony of Foscolo's ode, 'All'amica risanata.' " Cary (246) and others note the use of Latinate archaisms (*paventi, fumea, assembra, impaura*, the Leopardian *equo-rea creatura, lito*) and baroque metaphors (*ponticello esiguo, tremulo asse*) within the context of its primarily colloquial language and "descriptive realism" (Bonora 1, 61). For Mengaldo (45) the "largely crepuscular-Gozzanian background of the situation and 'character' neverthe-less easily permits the addition of D'Annunzian elements"—a combination found elsewhere in Montale—from certain characteristics of the feminine figures of *Maia* to linguistic bor-rowings.

The title is, for Cary (245), an ironic reference to the speaker's "(self-)consciousness" confronted with the stunning reality of the wholly natural Esterina; cf. Montale's use of the term in his critique of the style of his predecessors (see note to "I limoni"). Avalle (40) and others note that "Falsetto" (like "In limine") constitutes an embryonic presentation of the fundamental situation of many Montale poems: a woman—who is capable of action, and indeed of flight, facilitated by the vivid wind of "In limine" and elsewhere—observed by an earthbound man. Esterina thus is one of the early precursors of the active, potentially saving feminine figure who finds her ultimate incarnations in Clizia and Volpe. Almansi and Merry (26), despite the reference to Diana, see her as a Persephone, with her alternating seasons and "her youth which draws on her the desire of the God of the Underworld."

grigiorosea: Cf. the "mare grigio-roseo" in Sbarbaro's *Trucioli*. Mengaldo (63–64) discusses Montale's affection for the "impressionistic," synesthetic combination of two colors in one adjective (*biancazzure, verdibrune, bianco e nero*, etc.), ultimately derived from D'Annunzio but in common usage among Montale's immediate predecessors.

l'arciera Diana: "The 'intangible,' 'the goddess of distances' " (Walter Otto, *Gli dei della Grecia*, cited by Lonardi [191]). The construction with *assembra* is D'Annunzian (Mengaldo, 34).

le braccia / . . . che t'afferra: Ferraris (11) notes the affinity with Pound's description of Helen in Canto II: "And by the beach-run, Tyro / Twisted arms of the sea-god, / Lithe sinews of water, gripping her, cross-hold." Cf. also "il forte imperio / che ti rapisce" in "Gli orecchini."

Minstrels (1923)

Originally titled "Musica sognata" (Dreamed Music). Dropped from Ribet; included again in Mondadori's 1977 *Tutte le poesie*. "Minstrels" is the title of the twelfth piece in Debussy's first book of *Préludes*.

Montale in "Intentions" (*Sec*, 297): "When I began to write the first poems of *Ossi di seppia* I certainly had an idea of the new music and the new painting. I had heard the 'Minstrels' of Debussy, and in the first edition of the book there was a little something that tried to imitate it: 'Musica sognata.' " Montale heard the piece at a concert in Genoa in March 1917, and in an early diary wrote that it "is, or is taken to be, ironic music. . . . Why didn't I study music, too? I have been asking myself for a long time. Who knows whether pure music wouldn't be my life! How many ideas flash in my mind, which might mislead the public!" (*QuaG*, 33–34).

For Biasin (23), "the musical subject is the very form of the poem," which in its evocation of the harlequin theme, widely treated in modernist art and literature as representing the alienated, anti-heroic artist, foreshadows "Arsenio."

Bruci: First instance of the theme of burning, which will be an enduring presence in Montale's work; the note of sexual frustration is evident.

Poesie per Camillo Sbarbaro / Poems for Camillo Sbarbaro

Sbarbaro (who was born and died in Santa Margherita Ligure, 1886–1967) was, along with Roccatagliata Ceccardi and Boine, one of the Ligurian *crepuscolari*, an important early influence on Montale, and a close friend. Among his works are *Pianissimo* and *Trucioli* (Shavings), and his insistence, as his titles suggest, on the minor key was an influential counter to the grandiosity of the D'Annunzian tradition. Montale wrote in an obituary reminiscence: "Sbarbaro's art consisted of brief flashes, and the drug that brought him to these happy moments was life; life sensed as something inexplicable but nonetheless worthy of being accepted. To write for him was to wait for the moment when the dictation—whose dictation?—was fully matured. . . . After leaving Genoa, then a city of slight intellectual interchange, he immediately sequestered himself in Spotorno, facing the sea, which rarely appears in his poems and prose. He was a man of *terra firma* and of few but faithful friendships" ("Recollections of Sbarbaro," in *Sec*, 277–80).

I. *Caffè a Rapallo* / *I. Café at Rapallo* (undated)

tepidario: Precious neoclassicism parodying the Rondisti (see note to "Falsetto"). Bonora (1, 57) quotes Emerico Giachery's suggestion that the word may derive from D'Annunzio's novel *Il piacere*, which would be in keeping with "the voluptuous, inauthentic mundanity of the Ligurian cafés." For Bettarini (1, 463), the setting "reproduces a typical Sbarbaro *tea-room* interior," and the vocabulary (e.g., *femmine, sete*) is drawn from his poetry.

Avalle (45) cites the first appearance of jewelry as a feminine motif, later strongly linked to Clizia (see "Nuove stanze" and "Gli orecchini," etc.), and notes that an earlier version (in the first two editions) was more "in the style of Toulouse-Lautrec."

II. *Epigramma* / *II. Epigram* (undated)

Arrowsmith (1, 187) sees this as a "fondly critical tribute" in Sbarbaro's own vein to Montale's mentor and friend, the "man of terra firma"; Montale, though likewise one of those who "remain aground," is powerfully engaged by the sea. The paper boats recur in the *osso* "Arremba su la strinata proda" and in "Flussi."

Quasi una fantasia / *Like a Fantasia* (undated)

The title possibly refers to a musical composition (Bonora 1, 121–22); Beethoven used the term to denote the two sonatas in Opus 27 (Lonardi, 79). Lonardi (74) points out affinities with "Barche sulla Marna" in *Le occasioni* and "Il sogno del prigioniero" in *La bufera*, poems in which Montale uncharacteristically resorts to the dream to create—within a negatively construed present—a vision of salvation. Lonardi (75–79) sees the poem (like "Caffè a Rapallo," above) as descending from the tradition of the Provençal *plazer*—in which the poet evokes the things that are pleasing to him—by way of Dante's sonnet to Cavalcanti, "Guido, i'vorrei che tu e Lapo e io," with its expressed desire for escape; he also discerns borrowings from D'Annunzio and Leopardi. But "Quasi una fantasia" is uncomfortable in its relation to the regular, lighthearted tradition of the *plazer* because "it arises from the depths, both recognized and acknowledged, of tedium, and attempts, more like the Leopardian idyll, to escape the assault of the void."

ore troppo uguali: A recurrent image of stasis, immobility; cf. "Incontro," "Casa sul mare," "Arsenio."

galletto di marzo: Ligurian term for the hoopoe, a favored denizen of Montale's aviary (see "Upupa, ilare uccello . . .").

Sarcofaghi / *Sarcophagi* (1923)

Montale to Francesco Messina (September 27, 1924) (*Op*, 868): "Piero Gobetti has half agreed to publish my book: it will include 'Sarcofaghi,' dedicated to you [Messina was a sculptor, n.b.], which ends with a vision of Life-Death which relates the three preceding bas-reliefs, a bit objective, to the rest of my things."

The classicizing experiments of Montale's early poetry reach their apogee here, in this depiction of ancient tombs (quite possibly suggested by Keats's "Ode on a Grecian Urn," not to mention Foscolo's *Sepolcri*) which contrasts pagan and Christian attitudes toward life and death; after the elegant bronzes of the first three sections, the poet looks for "the primal fire" in a more humble urn (cf. the theme of humility in "I limoni") "etched / with a sign of peace as simple as a toy!" The "most moving symbol" is (Bonora 1, 56) the Christian Alpha and Omega, source of both tears and laughter.

madre non matrigna: Literally, "mother, not stepmother."

s'affaccia / una nuvola grandiosa: Neoclassical preciosity.

Ma dove cercare la tomba: The ms. of this part began with these (Leopardian) lines:

> Sono codeste l'arche e le figure
> per chi nel mondo è trascorso
> con passo di dominatore
> e ancora sono gli emblemi che si guardavano
> senza tremore.

(These are the arches and figures / for him who passed through the world / with a dominator's step / and are still the emblems that were looked on / without terror.)

il triste artiere: Angelini (1, 217) notes the Leopardian pessimism of this line (*artiere* is literary and archaic), adding that the hares recall Leopardi's "La vita solitaria" (they reappear at the end of "Egloga").

un girasole: First appearance of this image, which will be developed in "Portami il girasole . . ." and expanded in the Ovid-inspired figure of Clizia. It is worth noting that even here the image has a religious subtext. It prefigures the notion of the minimal saving sign that is the animating emblem of all Montale's poetry. Cf. "il nulla che basta a chi vuole / forzare la porta stretta" in "Ballata scritta in una clinica."

Altri versi / Other Lines
Added to the Ribet edition of 1928.

Vento e bandiere / Wind and Flags (1925?)
Montale wrote to Sergio Solmi (probably September 1927) (*Tutte*, xxxii–xxxiii): "I've put it with the juvenilia, because I saw that in the last group [MERIGGI E OMBRE] it felt somewhat *mièvre* [finical]."

In this poem, which has affinities with "Casa sul mare," published in 1925 (and with "La casa dei doganieri" of 1930), Montale arrives at what may be called the classic situation of his poetry, already announced in "In limine": a lament addressed to an absent woman (identified by Zampa [*Tutte*, xxviii] as the Arletta of "Incontro" and several other poems), whose apparition—often accompanied by meteorological disturbances (which will reach their metaphorical apotheosis in the poems of *La bufera*) and described in terms of flight (though at this point only "flights without wings")—offers a fleeting image of escape from the poet's barren, static situation. Note the hypermetric rhymes (*valli/pallido* and *alito/ali*) and the unconventional rhyme of *veste* with the definite article *queste*; rhyming with minor parts of speech will become a frequent emphatic device.

La folata che alzò: This phrase and "la raffica che t'incollò la veste," below, demonstrate

Montale's tendency in his mature style to favor nouns over verbs and to enclose actions in noun clauses, features of the "poetics of the object" that dominates *Le occasioni*. Similar openings in the late poems of *Ossi di seppia* are "Il mare che s'infrange" ("I morti") and "La vita che si rompe" ("Delta").

i grani: Bonora (1, 181) sees these as the beads of a rosary slowly being said; the image of sand in an hourglass, however, seems more convincing, particularly in relation to the "Sgorgo che non s'addoppia" in the next stanza.

Fuscello teso dal muro . . . / Twig that juts from the wall . . . (1926?)
Some critics have called this one of Montale's most obscure poems. Arrowsmith (1, 192) sees the twig as "the poet's totemic *semblable*, or persona," an interpretation supported by its "boredom" and fixedness. Bonora (1, 182) sees the *velo* as a spiderweb, which drapes the twig, thus altering its shape.

alleghi: Montale (*Eus*, 103) cites the "Genoese sense of *allignare*" (to take root).

un trealberi: Cf. the ironic (and thus cruel) "barca di salvezza" of "Crisalide."

il timone / . . . non scava una traccia: The image of tracelessness recurs in "Crisalide." Cf. by contrast the all-important "sign" carved by the stream in "Vecchi versi," which will metamorphose into the "solco" etched by the spinning top in "Palio," and the groove in the record of "L'orto."

OSSI DI SEPPIA / CUTTLEFISH BONES

A March 1923 ms. grouping of three poems ("Meriggiare, pallido e assorto," "Non rifugiarti nell'ombra," and "Ripenso il tuo sorriso, ed è per me un'acqua limpida") bore the title ROTTAMI (REFUSE), perhaps too close to Sbarbaro's *Trucioli* (Shavings); in July, three additional poems ("Portami il girasole . . . ," "Forse un mattino . . . ," and "Non chiederci la parola . . .") were added, and the new title, OSSI DI SEPPIA, made its appearance.

The group, which Montale called "my rondels" (see below), is the first of his series of short songlike lyrics, which will be more closely interrelated in the great MOTTETTI (another collection of minstrel song-poems) and the XENIA (in *Satura*), but which also bear comparison with the unnamed first section of *Le occasioni* and with the 'FLASHES' E DEDICHE and MA- DRIGALI PRIVATI of *La bufera*. The *osso di seppia*, derived from D'Annunzio, occurs as an image of the sea's rubble prey to elemental forces in RIVIERE.

Ferraris (32): "In the world of the *Ossi di seppia* the poet finds no presence that seems like a mirror of himself. The language available to him in fact announces his detachment from the 'ancient roots,' speaks to him from the point of view of the wall, the uncrossable boundary that suggests the presence of the other side but precludes access to it. It is the icon of poetry in its ungraspable essence, which both gives and removes itself at the same time, in the motion of the wind.

"The poet, too, then, is present in the labile, fleeting form of a shadow, of which he can say nothing, because it comes to him detached from its source, which remains *elsewhere*, unknown in its law, which it transcends, and because it offers itself to him only in the ironic, elusive apparition of the 'still blue,' or rather of the fire of an inspiration whose muse is ignorance. . . . The poet's gift, too, has the fragility of a shadow, of something that dissolves, removes itself, in the very act of offering itself."

Non chiederci la parola che squadri da ogni lato / *Don't ask us for the word to frame* (July 10, 1923)

Montale to Angelo Barile (August 12, 1924) (*Op*, 874): "You're right, 'Non chiederci la parola . . .' is a bit the keystone of my 'rondels'; and in fact will end them, conclusion and commentary . . .'" (Montale is speaking of the group of six poems described above).

Apart from the famous self-definition by negation—what Almansi and Merry (27) call "the poetics of near-silence" in "the true manifesto of the volume" (as opposed to "I limoni" or "In limine")—it is notable that this is one of the relatively few instances (along with the "Noi non sappiamo quale sortiremo" section of MEDITERRANEO) in which Montale makes forceful use in a generic manner of the first person plural and is willing, however recalcitrantly, to speak broadly for his generation.

squadri: Savoca (63–64) shows the Petrarchan ascendancy of the term, quoting Leopardi's note glossing the term as "square off, order, refine, polish. And it means make capable of expressing his [Petrarch's] amorous feelings with sweetness and grace."

Meriggiare pallido e assorto / *Sit the noon out, pale and lost in thought* (1916; revised 1922) The earliest poem in *Ossi di seppia*, and Montale's most widely known composition. Here the sun-baked, blinding, and transfixing noon scene that becomes a characteristic Montalean locus and metaphor is already fully developed. Montale (in "Intentions," *Sec*, 298): "By 1916 I had already written my first fragment *tout entier à sa proie attaché*: 'Meriggiare pallido e assorto,' of which I later revised the last stanza. The prey was, it's understood, *my* landscape."

Zampa (*Tutte*, xvii) notes the influence of Giovanni Boine's prose poem "Conclusioni di ottobre," published in the review *Riviera Ligure* in March 1916 and "thematically and formally very close to Montale's lyric." Boine (1887–1917) was a leading poet of the Ligurian school, the author of *Frantumi* and *Plausi e botte*, and a contributor to *La Voce* and to *Riviera Ligure*. Bonfiglioli (2, 82ff.), citing the poem's "openly Pascolian" terminology, "minimalist perceptions, . . . natural analogies, and alliteration," calls "Meriggiare" "perhaps the one example of continuous Pascolism in Montale," though even here Montale has already superimposed antinaturalistic Dantesque pessimism on Pascoli's naturalism. Indeed, Bonfiglioli (2, 84) notes the relation of the poem's language "(*pruni*, the rhyme *sterpi/serpi*, the rhyme *formiche/biche*, *spiar* and numerous other elements) to that of the Dantesque canto of the suicides" (*Inferno* XIII), and calls it "a first image of that inferno . . . , the underworld of the 'bosco umano' and its vegetative existences (an uncertain area between the squalid forest of failed hopes and the purgatorial limbo of suspended hopes)." See note to "Arsenio" for a discussion of the importance of the imagery of the "human plant" in Montale.

Meriggiare: Mengaldo (50) cites sources for this striking term in D'Annunzio, Pascoli, and Boine, and finds (43) that D'Annunzio, Boine, and Sbarbaro all make similar use of series of infinitives. Bonora (1, 37) points out the Dantean lineage of the rhymes *sterpi/serpi* and *scricchi/picchi*. The "phonetic clashes" (Almansi and Merry, 32) characteristic of this early poem will become an important feature of Montale's mature style. The irregularity of the metrics, especially the elongated last line, is also notable and characteristic.

spiar le file di rosse formiche: Almansi and Merry (33) show that the image is derived from Dante's description of the sodomites in *Purgatorio* XXVI, 34–36.

frondi: Mengaldo (49) describes this as a typically D'Annunzian archaism.

scricchi: According to Bonfiglioli (2, 82), a verbal noun of Montalean invention.

Non rifugiarti nell'ombra / Don't escape into the shade (1922)

Bonora (1, 160) speculates that this may be one of the earlier of the *ossi brevi* because of a certain abstractness of method and lack of concision in the poem, which touches on many of their themes. He also (159) notes the frequent resorting to "aulic" D'Annunzian rhetoric: *caldura* for *calura, s'addorma* for *s'addormenti, impigra* for *impigrisce, sfilaccicarsi* for *sfilacciarsi* in conjunction with the use of violent verbs like *sgretolarsi*. See Mengaldo (35) for sources of D'Annunzian borrowings.

È ora di lasciare . . . : Mengaldo (82–85) emphasizes how one of the major tasks of the early Montale is to dissociate himself from a D'Annunzian Panic identification with nature as whole, and with poetry as similarly naturalistic (cf. "your briny words / where art and nature fuse" in the "Potessi almeno costringere" section of MEDITERRANEO): "A first formulation of Montale's mature poetics, as the necessity of taking a disenchanted look at fragmentary and disintegrated reality, immediately requires, even within *Ossi di seppia*, the preliminary refutation of an acritical immersion in nature as a refuge, or as a justification for atony." The only aspect of D'Annunzio's naturalism that survives in Montale, then, is the "negative" aspect of inert, sick, decomposed physical reality; "the vital fullness of nature dies continually into deafness, indifference, and menacing decay, and the 'Gloria del disteso mezzogiorno' quickly, necessarily becomes *arsura* and *squallore*." Similarly with D'Annunzio's language: Montale's "admiration for its splendid sensual quality" is matched by the need to translate it immediately into lines that express Montale's peculiar "sensuality," described by himself (in *La Fiera Letteraria*, May 6, 1928) as "dryness, nervousness, sense of the essential" (cf. the desire to be "scabro ed essenziale," "harsh and essential," in MEDITERRANEO).

canneto/sgretola: Hypermetric rhyme.

impigra: Mengaldo (58) describes Montale's tendency to form similar parasynthetic verbs as partaking of the poet's "Dantism"; "but the nearest and most significant concurrent model remains D'Annunzio, who is the modern poet in whom the elaboration of the Dantesque exemplar is richest and freest." (See Mengaldo, 59ff., for similar examples with the prefixes *dis-* and *ad-* and suffixes *-ura* and *-mento* [mainly in *Ossi di seppia*—and illustrative of Montale's tendency wherever possible to embed actions in noun forms].)

ragnatele di nubi: Cf. "nella serenità che non si ragna" in "Il canneto rispunta i suoi cimelli." The off-rhymes *rupi/nubi* and *cenere/sereno*, below, are typical Montalean semirhyme, with a D'Annunzian ascendancy (Mengaldo, 66). Mengaldo emphasizes Montale's "various and broad-based use of assonance to differentiate or contrast with other coexisting rhyme schemes, both perfect and imperfect," adding that Montale, "if he attacks and overturns the comfortable traditional schemes on all sides, also systematically attempts to avoid the simple opposition of more or less canonical regular rhymes and simple assonance, consonance, etc., inventing or developing a series of intermediate types of quasi rhymes with rich if not 'perfect' phonic resonances" (see also for examples of other Montalean metric invention).

la luce: Cf. the conclusion of "Portami il girasole. . . ." Light—but not "too much light" (see "Due sciacalli al guinzaglio," quoted in note to the motet "La speranza di pure rivederti")—is an ultimate value in Montale's "contradictory solar mythology" (Almansi and Merry, 34).

Ripenso il tuo sorriso, ed è per me un'acqua limpida / I think back on your smile, and for me it's a clear pool (1923)

Zampa (*Tutte*, 1070) identifies the dedicatee as "the Russian dancer Boris Knasieff, whom

Montale met in Francesco Messina's studio after having admired him at the Teatro Verdi when he was working in the Maria Yureva Company."

Bonora (1, 169) draws the connection between Montale's portrait of "K." ("without indulgence, however, in facile descriptive elements") and the similar depictions of later characters like Dora Markus, Liuba, and Fadin, victims buffeted by "the world's evil" in much more concrete ways, whose only defense—or, indeed, defining feature—is the "charm," the talisman, of their suffering, and their courage in absorbing their troubles. K.'s smile, in an almost surreal fashion, becomes an autonomous object detached from a context, an example of the figural method that will achieve full development in *Le occasioni.*

ellera . . . corimbi: Mengaldo (35) discusses the D'Annunzian derivation of this baroque trope.

dei raminghi . . . . : The *crepuscolaro* theme of the "wanderer" appears also in "Flussi" (see note) and elsewhere.

mia memoria grigia: Cf. the "scialba/memoria" of "Valmorbia, discorrevano il tuo fondo."

schietto come la cima d'una giovinetta palma: A recurrent image associated with events or individuals who break through the grayness, the enclosure, of existence as experienced by the poet. Savoca (60–61) demonstrates that it originates in Petrarch (CCCXXIII, 26): "lauro giovinetto e schietto." Cf. also the "giovinetti arbusti" in "L'estate."

Mia vita, a te non chiedo lineamenti / My life, I ask of you no stable (published 1924)
The bipartite structure anticipates that of certain of the MOTTETTI (e.g., "Il ramarro, se scocca"). Cary (256) says "vocational senility" is the theme of this *osso*, which echoes the vows of renunciation in "In limine" and elsewhere. *Senilità* is the title of a novel by the Triestine writer Italo Svevo, with whom Montale felt a deep affinity, and whose reputation he helped to establish near the end of the older man's life. Montale defines Svevian senility as "not due to time but . . . the state of being of whoever feels he has already lived for himself and others, suffered and lived for all" (Cary, 256)—which is not far from Montale's representation of the fate of his heroine Clizia (see note to "Iride") and, by extension, of himself. (For an extensive Montalean analysis of Svevo, see "Italo Svevo in the Centenary of His Birth," *Sec*, 92–117.) In Montale, however, renunciation is not total, as in Leopardi; "rare" contingent interventions offer the promise of transformation.

volti plausibili: See notes to "Là fuoresce il Tritone" and "Incontro" for discussion of the theme of the face as a projection of the self.

miele e assenzio: The coupling derives from Petrarch, CCXV, 14.

Il cuore che ogni moto . . . . : Cf. Leopardi, "A se stesso."

un colpo di fucile: Cf. Leopardi, "Il passero solitario," 30. The image of violent emergence recurs in the "volo strepitoso di colombi" of "Stanze" and in the shot that is the *occasione* of "Elegia di Pico Farnese."

Portami il girasole ch'io lo trapianti / Bring me the sunflower, let me plant it (June 1923)
The sunflower, already introduced in "Sarcofaghi," written in the same year, will become a central image in Montale's later work, via the figure of Clizia, the protagonist especially of much of the major poetry of *La bufera* (see note to "La primavera hitleriana"). There the sunflower's attribute of staring at the sun has religious connotations; here, the flower seems to be aspiring to Panic self-extinction.

salino: Ligurian dialect for the wind inpregnated with sea salt (Marchese 1, 34).

un fluire / di tinte: Cf. the synesthetic changing colors of "Corno inglese" and "Minstrels."

Spesso il male di vivere ho incontrato / Often I've encountered evil (undated)

Leopardian pessimism, Epicurean indifference objectified in stark, essential imagery. The objects named "are not symbols . . . : they are creatures who enjoy the prodigious and sole happiness allowed to living beings and gods alike. . . . The objects by merely being named reveal their entire psychic life" (Bonora 1, 150). Here, as in "Ripenso il tuo sorriso . . . ," we can see the origins of the essentialism of *Le occasioni*.

l'incartocciarsi della foglia: Cf. Pascoli, *Canti di Castelvecchio*, "Diario autunnale": "Ora ogni foglia stride e s'accartoccia."

che schiude la divina Indifferenza: The phrase is ambiguous; "la divina Indifferenza" may be either the subject or the object of "schiude"; most commentators, however, read it as object.

la statua: Cf. the faceless, inexpressive statue of Summer in the Montale garden at Monterosso which appears in "Flussi."

Ciò che di me sapeste / What you knew of me (undated)

A lyric in the form of a madrigal, probably dedicated to Paola Nicoli (Bonora 1, 169), on the theme of the poet's unknowability. For Marchese (1, 8), this has its roots in a "fragmentation of the ego" and in "the impossibility of recognizing oneself and thus of giving oneself to others except as 'wash of paint,' 'veil,' 'shell,' and finally 'shadow.' "

falòtico: Neologism, from French *falot*.

ignita: Latinate adjective derived from D'Annunzio.

questa scorza: The image is Petrarchan ("la scorza / di me," CLXXX, 1–2), as is that of the poet as shadow below ("i' per me sono un'ombra," CXIX, 99) (Savoca, 61).

l'ignoranza: Cf. the conclusion of "Tentava la vostra mano la tastiera." Ignorance in the *ossi* is a positive condition, a form of spiritual virginity.

Potessi . . . : The renunciation and the "oblatory gesture" recall "In limine" and "Casa sul mare."

Là fuoresce il Tritone / There the Tritone surges (undated)

Titled "Portovenere" in the first two editions. The Tritone (named for the demi-god with the head of a man and a fish's tail) is a stream near the village of Portovenere (Portus Veneris, Port of Venus) on the Ligurian coast not far from the Cinque Terre. Arrowsmith (1, 209) says it was here that Saint Peter supposedly first entered Italy. An evocation of "spiritual virginity" before one has "decided" between pagan and Christian, before one has assumed the face, the mask, of an identity (cf. the treatment of this theme in "Incontro").

So l'ora in cui la faccia più impassibile / I know the moment when a raw grimace (undated)

For further treatment of the theme of mistrust of language and "lamentosa letteratura," see "Potessi almeno costringere" in MEDITERRANEO. The virtue of silence is also a theme in "Forse un mattino andando in un'aria di vetro."

Gloria del disteso mezzogiorno / Glory of expanded noon (published 1924)
Montale to Angelo Barile (August 12, 1924) (*Op*, 874): "Beyond the twenty *ossi di seppia* the book will contain more than fifteen lyrics, not all of them brief—on the contrary!—and very different; some of them are more 'singing' and consoled, from the period of RIVIERE; the image of me that will emerge from the book will perhaps seem to you less coherent but broader and more complex; and the undersigned will come to light more like a 'troubadour' than a sophist or a laboratory poet. . . . The 1st of September [*Le*] *Opere e i Giorni* will publish . . . : a 'Vasca,' which will seem new and perhaps not unwelcome; an *osso*—the best to me, in fact the only one that truly pleases me: 'Gloria del disteso mezzogiorno,' which I've provisionally baptized 'Meriggio' [Midday]; and 'Fine dell'infanzia,' in which I have glimpsed —with the help of memory—the first arising of doubt in children's souls: I don't know with what results."

The opening echoes Ceccardo Roccatagliata Ceccardi's "Chiara felicità della riviera," which Montale cites for its musicality in "Intentions" (*Sec*, 297).

falbe: Adjective used by D'Annunzio and Pascoli.

gioia più compita: Stilnovistic phraseology, derived from Guinizelli. See Montale's August 24, 1924, letter to Paola Nicoli quoted in note to "In limine," in which he describes his "kind" as "all *a waiting for the miracle.*"

Felicità raggiunta, si cammina / Happiness achieved, for you (undated)
Contini (in *Esercizi di lettura* [Firenze, 1947], 80, quoted in Mengaldo, 40) notes that Montale's depiction of Happiness is derived from the portrayal of Felicità in D'Annunzio's *Maia*, 353–56.

Il canneto rispunta i suoi cimelli / The canebrake sends its little shoots (undated)
Again, an invocation to a beloved but absent figure. Zampa (*Tutte*, xxviii) identifies this as one of the poems dedicated to Arletta, the addressee of "Vento e bandiere," "Delta," "Incontro," and "I morti."

Remarkable, especially in the first quatrain, is "language which forces its expressivity by conjoining words that are distant in origin and usage" (Bonora 1, 157). For Mengaldo (51), the poem is "wholly woven together by the alternation and interweaving of materials" derived from Pascoli and D'Annunzio.

cimelli: Ligurian dialect. The image recalls the "cima d'una giovinetta palma" of "Ripenso il tuo sorriso. . . ."

nella serenità che non si ragna: Literary trope, in which the sky is "fretted" with clouds like a spiderweb or a net (cf. Pascoli, *Nuovi poemetti*, "Gli emigranti nella Luna," *Canto primo*, III, 18: "come la nuvola che batte / nella luna, e si ragna e si deforma"). Cf. also "ragnatele di nubi" in "Non rifugiarti nell'ombra." Mengaldo (20) notes that it is "a typically Montalean order" to have an abstract noun followed by a concrete verbal metaphor.

ramelli: Archaic (used by Guittone d'Arezzo). Note Montale's rhyming of dialect and precious words. The juxtaposition of diverse vocabularies was most likely absorbed from Gozzano. Montale (in his 1951 essay "Gozzano, dopo trent'anni" [*Su*, 52–62]) called him "the first to strike sparks butting the aulic up against the prosaic."

cinigia: D'Annunzian archaism.

consuma: Unusual, intensified intransitive usage without reflexive.

dirupa: Violent Dantean verb.

Forse un mattino andando in un'aria di vetro / Maybe one morning, walking in dry, glassy air (July 12, 1923)

The "miracle" achieved here is, as Italo Calvino describes it in his notable analysis (in *Letture montaliane in occasione del 80° compleanno del poeta* [Genoa: Bozzi Editore, 1977], 38–40, translated in full in Arrowsmith 1, 214–20), that of breaking out of the prison of subjectivity to experience "the *other* truth . . . beyond the continuing wall of the world. . . . The protagonist of Montale's poem succeeds through a combination of factors both objective (air of dry glass) and subjective (receptivity to an epistemological miracle) in turning around so quickly that he manages, let's say, to look at a space still unoccupied by his own visual field. And what he sees is nothingness, the void."

Lonardi (45) agrees with Sanguineti (in the same *Letture montaliane*, 38–40) that the poem derives from "a precise Tolstoyan recollection," and quotes the following passage from the Russian writer's "Boyhood" (in *Childhood, Boyhood, Youth*, tr. Rosemary Edmonds [London: Penguin Books, 1964], 158–59): "I fancied that besides myself nobody and nothing existed in the universe, that objects were not real at all but images which appeared when I directed my attention to them, and that so soon as I stopped thinking of them these images immediately vanished. In short, I came to the same conclusion as Schelling, that objects do not exist but only my relation to them exists. There were moments when I became so deranged by this *idée fixe* that I would glance sharply round in some opposite direction, hoping to catch unawares the void (the *néant*), where I was not." The quotation also evokes aspects of "Due nel crepuscolo."

Ferraris (36) reads the poem in the context of the myth of Orpheus: "It is the look of him who turns, like Orpheus, to bring Eurydice near that causes her to be irrevocably lost: this is the paradox of poetic language, which only *touches* things in order to evoke the silence that envelops their essence, rendering them ungraspable. Thus the 'usual deceit' of the world as representation is revealed."

aria di vetro: Montale in "Intentions" (*Sec*, 300): "I seemed to be living under a bell jar, and yet I felt I was close to something essential. A subtle veil, a thread, barely separated me from the definitive *quid*. Absolute expression would have meant breaking that veil, that thread: an explosion, the end of the illusion of the world as representation."

miracolo/ubriaco: Hypermetric rhyme.

il nulla . . . il vuoto: Cf. the same conjunction in "Il balcone." "Il vuoto" is a major, constantly elaborating Montalean motif; see also "Debole sistro al vento," "Il balcone," "Nel Parco di Caserta," and "Voce giunta con le folaghe."

s'uno schermo: Calvino, who says that Montale's poem antedates the automobile rearview mirror, claims this is the first time an Italian poet refers to a screen in the sense of "a surface on which images are projected." Related images occur in "Quasi una fantasia" ("viste in un arazzo") and "Flussi" ("immobili tende").

zitto: Cf. "the deeper truth is that of the man who is silent" in "So l'ora. . . ."

Valmorbia, discorrevano il tuo fondo / Valmorbia, flowering clouds of plants (undated)

One of Montale's few references to his experiences as a soldier in World War I (cf. also the motets "Brina sui vetri . . ." and "Lontano, ero con te quando tuo padre," which like this poem make talismanic use of place-names). In 1918, Montale commanded a forward post above the river Leno near the village of Valmorbia in the Vallarsa region of the Trentino. The poem offers an almost perversely gentle picture of war, intensified, as Almansi and Merry

(37–38) note, by the connotations (*morbido* = soft; *lene* = mild) of the place-names (which is perhaps the point, that the names themselves are all that give meaning to the evoked "memory"). Montale has yet to arrive at the non-connotative (or connotation-suppressed) *flatus vocis* of "Keepsake," but the magic power inherent in a name that is evoked in "Buffalo" finds a precedent here.

fioriti nùvoli *di piante agli* àsoli: The image recurs in "Vasca." Mengaldo (65) cites the line with the double *sdrucciolo*, or dactyl, as a characteristic Montalean metric device derived from D'Annunzio (e.g., the motet "La gòndola che scìvola . . .").

scialba / memoria: Recalls the "memoria grigia" of "Ripenso il tuo sorriso . . ."; an early indication of what Lonardi (49–56) calls Montale's "Proustian" sense of the "intermittencies" of memory. See also "Cigola la carrucola del pozzo."

Tentava la vostra mano la tastiera / Your hand was trying the keyboard (June 18, 1924)
Dedicated to P[aola Nicoli]. The rare (in Montale), old-fashioned second-person plural *vostra* suggests the formality of the relationship evoked in this lyric (see note to the related "Crisalide"). The woman's difficulty at the keyboard is another instance of the "sweet ignorance" of "Ciò che di me sapeste," probably also a poem for Nicoli. The world's inability to "find its words" resonates with the poet's own lament of inarticulateness in "Potessi almeno costringere . . ." in MEDITERRANEO.

La farandola dei fanciulli sul greto / The line of dancing children on the shore (undated)
farandola: A Provençal dance to the accompaniment of flute and tambourine, in which the dancers, holding hands, snake in and out.

la vita che scoppia dall'arsura: See note to "L'anguilla" for the recurrence of this centrally significant Montalean imagery at the climax of *La bufera*.

il cespo umano: For discussion of the Dantean image of the "human plant," which occurs frequently in Montale, see note to "Arsenio."

antiche radici: Arrowsmith (1, 224) sees a reference to Dante's Earthly Paradise (*Purgatorio* XXVIII, 142), where the "umana radice" was innocent.

un nome: Cf. the end of "Vasca," where, however, a "name" is posited as desirable. *Nome* here is consonant with the *volto* of "Là fuoresce il Tritone."

Debole sistro al vento / Feeble sistrum in the wind (undated)
This, "one of the bleakest poems Montale ever wrote" (Arrowsmith 1, 224), can be read as a lament for the inability of life (or poetry—see *una persa cicala*, below) to defeat "the void."

sistro: One of the instruments that accompanies the infernal fandango of "La bufera."

una persa cicala: Foreshadows the image of the poet in "L'ombra della magnolia. . . ." For a discussion of Montale's development of this image, see "Reading Montale."

il vuoto: See note to "Forse un mattino andando. . . ."

alla sua foce: A recurrent point of convergence between animate and inanimate realms in *Ossi di seppia*. "La foce" was an earlier title for "Incontro."

Cigola la carrucola del pozzo / The well's pulley creaks (undated)
The image of a beloved face rising in the well water—some say it is that of Arletta, the protagonist of "Incontro"—is related to the *riso* of "Vasca" and the smile of "Ripenso il tuo sorriso . . ." and prefigures the ghostly apparitions in the mirror of "Gli orecchini." Avalle, in

his exhaustive analysis of that poem (esp. 21–33), shows that, as Calvino puts it in his essay on "Forse un mattino andando . . . ," "in Montale's mirrors . . . the images are not reflected, but emerge ('from below'), rising to meet the observer."

Marchese (1, 22–25) performs a thorough structural dissection of "Cigola la carrucola . . . ," pointing out: "The central verse ["Accosto . . . labbri"] verifies the unreality and impossibility of approach of subject to object. . . . This reconfirms again the 'law' of the Montalean semiotic system, according to which the subject is alienated, submits to an action" (as in "Ciò che di me sapeste"). Bàrberi Squarotti (211) sees the well as "a chthonian image which connects the living with the dead, where the rescuing operation of Eurydice is vainly attempted by the Orphic poet."

Note the onomatopoeia of line 1 (reinforced by *stride* in line 7), and the rhythmic repetition of the *sdruccioli cigola* and *carrucola*. Mengaldo (41) finds a possible source in D'Annunzio's "Notturno"—"Odo stridere la carrucola del pozzo. Il passato mi piomba addosso col rombo delle valanghe; mi curva, mi calca"—but notes that Montale inverts D'Annunzio's conventional treatment of the well as archetypal evoker of the past, turning it instead into the "very Montalean theme of the schism between the present and the experience of an earlier, different self, the impossibility of recapturing the past in the *gray, washed-out, tired* memory, except in rare glimmers."

ridona, atro: Literary language.

Arremba su la strinata proda / *Haul your paper ships on the seared* (August 23, 1924)
Arremba: Genoese.

fanciulletto padrone: Montale to Gianfranco Contini (October 31, 1945) (*Op*, 877), who was working on a French translation: "By *padrone* I meant the man who can operate a small coastal vessel without being a certified captain; so if you find something like 'my little sea wolf, my two-bit commander' you're more on target. Still, *padrone* is a legally recognized title." The *fanciulletto* and the paper boats recall the "Epigramma" for Sbarbaro. This represents a rare instance of a poem addressed to a child; is it perhaps directed to the poet himself?

Upupa, ilare uccello calunniato / *Hoopoe, happy bird maligned* (undated)
Upupa: The hoopoe is the "galletto di marzo" of "Quasi una fantasia," and the poem shares in its (uncharacteristic) sanguine outlook. Arrowsmith (1, 226): "The common European hoopoe (*Upupa epops*—derived onomatopoetically from its call, 'a low, far-carrying *poo-poo-poo*') is a thrush-sized bird with barred black-and-white wings and tail. Its most conspicuous feature is its great semicircular erectile crest, bordered with white and tipped with black. . . . The crest is normally depressed but, when erect, opens and shuts like a fan, repeatedly. . . . The hoopoe was first 'slandered' (that is, represented as an avine clown) [as is common in popular tradition; see Bonora 1, 175] in Aristophanes' *Birds* . . . ; but Montale is probably referring to Parini, Boito, and Foscolo, in whose writings the hoopoe appears in an ominous, even sinister light."

aereo stollo: Quotation from Pascoli, which Bonfiglioli (1, 225) claims "has an ironic, antinaturalistic, and clearly anti-Pascolian flavor." The hoopoe "is represented ironically by poetic and literary elements: 'aereo stollo,' 'nunzio primaverile,' 'aligero folletto.' . . . This literary dress, which perhaps recalls youthful exercises and games, is meant to reduce the bird to a happy sign or announcement: an inadvertent and automatic Ariel."

Sul muro grafito / Above the scribbled wall (undated)

The final poem of the group recapitulates, with the affectless calm of a postmortem, many of the themes of the *ossi brevi*. The tone of resignation is reminiscent of "In limine" (itself an *osso*), but without the anguish—and hope—excited by the presence of an interlocutor.

muro grafito: The "erto muro" of "In limine," the "scalcinato muro" of "Non chiederci la parola . . . ," the "rovente muro d'orto" of "Meriggiare pallido e assorto" (with the synonymous *muraglia* repeated from the last of these—see note to "Crisalide" on the philosophical sources of the image); but this time "scribbled" over—perhaps with the *ossi brevi* themselves (cf. the "few brief pages" in the last motet)?

l'arco del cielo: Arrowsmith (1, 227): "A literary locution whose purpose is to evoke the grand celestial architecture, Ptolemaic and Dantesque, which it once designated . . . but [which] is now 'finished,' 'gone,' 'done for.' " Cf. the "arco d'orizzonte / flagellato" of "I morti" and related images in "Incontro" and "Arsenio." Marchese (1, 47) sees a negation (*finito*) of Leopardi's "L'infinito."

fuoco: The "fuoco che non si smorza" of "Ciò che di me sapeste" and the "originale fiammata" of "Sarcofaghi"; also the "bruciare" of the concluding lines of MEDITERRANEO and the "vita che scoppia dall'arsura" of "La farandola dei fanciulli. . . ." Fire and burning are associated with vitality—and, by extension, with the "luce" (light) of "Non rifugiarti nell'ombra" and "Portami il girasole . . ."—which is also potentially injurious to the poet's self.

un riposo / freddo: Recalls "la taciturna folla di pietra" of "Sarcofaghi."

Rivedrò . . . : A recapitulation of the "inganno consueto" of "Forse un mattino andando . . ."; "le banchine / e la muraglia e l'usata strada" are equivalent to the "alberi case colli" of that poem.

MEDITERRANEO / MEDITERRANEAN (1924)

Originally dedicated to Roberto Bazlen. A *poemetto*, or short long poem—Montale's longest composition—in nine sections, which may have been partly inspired by Debussy's *La Mer* (Biasin, 9), and which numerous critics have read—like the whole of *Ossi di seppia*—as a response to D'Annunzio's *Alcyone*. To Cary (264), D'Annunzio's "mood *passim* is ecstatic and dithyrambic . . . the rhythms are ebullient and skillfully hammered to create an exultant and somewhat hypnotic effect. Stress is all on the sphere of physical sensation and the brake or 'inhibition' of intellect or *coscienza* is utterly absent. . . . The point . . . is elemental—he loses his name, his historical and psychological identity, and becomes his environment." In Montale, however, this ecstatic fusion is more often sought after than achieved, defeated by an almost paralyzing self-consciousness. Cary (265): "Even Montale's rhythms . . .—a kind of Italian 'blank verse' grounded on an approximate hendecasyllable that can be expanded or contracted to fit the tempo of thought—suggest meditation and a highly speculative mind rather than any sort of dithyrambic release."

For Mengaldo (82), MEDITERRANEO and the related poems of *Ossi di seppia* "clearly reveal Montale's tendency to utilize D'Annunzio's Panic and vitalistic themes in retrospective, elegiac projections. . . . The mythical dimension, the justification of existence sought in the total immersion in the movement of nature, of the 'fermenting sea,' are pushed largely into the past, before being definitively removed. . . . Of course, attempts at recovery . . . , at retransferring the mythical-vitalist into the present, are not absent: but more often the recovery of such a possibility, which is linked with a prior existence, is presented in forms that are not assertive but, as has been noted, problematic (optative, future) [cf. the last lines of RIVIERE].

MEDITERRANEO is the locus tipicus of this crisis, and of these often-unresolved contradictions." It is also, as Jacomuzzi (1, 122) notes, "the most easily individualizable, and individualized, area of declarations of poetics in Montale's poetry."

Marchese (1, 56): "MEDITERRANEO has been the object of numerous, somewhat differing critical readings. . . . In particular, the meaning assigned to the central symbol of the sea differs greatly: 'symbol of indifference, order or law of variation-fixity . . . which becomes hostile precisely as an encouragement to indecision,' according to Contini [1, 24]; paternal image, moralistic superego, model of fidelity to existential law and destiny, for E. Gioanola ["MEDITERRANEO," in *Letture montaliane in occasione del 80° compleanno del poeta* (Genoa: Bozzi Editore, 1977), 55ff.]; . . . complex and ambivalent emblem, maternal and paternal at the same time, for Luperini ["Il 'significato' di MEDITERRANEO," *L'Ombra d'Argo*, I (1–2), 1983; expanded in Luperini (2, 65)], who sees in the first aspect the tendency to variety and vastness, in the second the values of fixity, order, and rigor: 'The symbol of the sea functions two directions: on the one hand, it is the point of comparison through which [man's] distance from his origins and the limits of the human condition become clear; on the other, it is a paradigm which functions in this condition as a tendency toward self-determination: man separates from the sea but will continue to carry within him its echo and its lesson.'"

Biasin (70–71) quotes Luperini's emphasis (in "Il 'significato' di MEDITERRANEO," 25 and 47) on the "decidedly narrative rather than musical slant" of MEDITERRANEO, which he calls a "fundamental chapter" in that "true novel of identity which is *Ossi di seppia*," citing the "links connecting the various movements"; "an existential balance sheet which presupposes a development, a temporal arc"; "a subject posing himself as a character . . . (almost an *n*th portrait of the artist as a young man)"; and a final "meaning as a conclusion of his search for truth, for a sense of his life."

A vortice s'abbatte / Racketing catcalls spiral down

sghembe ombre di pinastri: Derived (Mengaldo, 17) from "tonde ombre di pini" (Pascoli, "Gog e Magog," V, 5, in *Poemi conviviali*). The word *pinastri* appears in Pascoli as well; but Montale superimposes "expressionist" elements (*sghembe*) on Pascoli's realism.

avvena: Neologism, from *avvenato*.

strepeanti: Latinism, derived from Roccatagliata Ceccardi (Bonora 1, 89).

Antico, sono ubriacato dalla voce / Ancient one, I'm drunk with the voice

La casa . . . : Note the anti-idyllic description of the locale, which is reversed in "Fine dell'infanzia."

impietro: Cf. *Inferno* XXXIII, 49.

Scendendo qualche volta / Sometimes, coming down

The same landscape is portrayed, in a different mood, in "Clivo."

il gocciare / del tempo: Mengaldo (16) cites a source in Pascoli's *Myricae*, "Il nunzio," 8–10: "E cadono / l'ore, giù, giù, con un lento / gocciare"—"but one notes immediately in Montale the absence of all the elements of realistic reduction of the metaphor," such as Pascoli's verb, adverb, and adjective. The figure, typically, is further compressed and objectified in "Notizie dall'Amiata": "Oh il gocciolìo che scende a rilento / . . . il tempo fatto acqua."

Chinavo: Genoese.

Ho sostato talvolta nelle grotte / I've paused at times in the caves

architetture / . . . campite di cielo: Bonora (1, 95): "*Campire* is to paint on a surface, without shading, to create a background, especially for a fresco. The mighty structures against the sky's backdrop are the reflection and the indication of more hidden structures which the sea conceals in its depths, of the city that is 'the dreamed-of homeland.'" Bonora sees the "city of glass" as related to Debussy's "La cathédrale engloutie" (*Préludes*, I, 10), which Montale offers as a source for the motet "Infuria sale o grandine?"

Nasceva dal fiotto . . .: This and the next two lines are remarkable for their prosaicness and rhythmic formlessness (Mengaldo, 70); cf. the similar "In lei titubo al mare che mi offende, / manca ancora il silenzio nella mia vita" in "Giunge a volte, repente."

fiumara: For *fiumana*, probably used for assonance with *ramure, strame*, etc.

Giunge a volte, repente / Now and then, suddenly

spaura: Bonora (1, 98): A verb from the 1300s, used by Leopardi in "L'infinito." *Ripa* and *acclive* are also literary; *strosce* is Tuscan idiom (Mengaldo, 55).

questa pianta . . .: Cf. "L'agave su lo scoglio."

Questo pezzo di suolo . . .: The act of self-sacrifice of "In limine," "Crisalide," and "Casa sul mare." Cf. the "croco / perduto" of "Non chiederci la parola . . ." (in ms. originally "un croco / di margherita"). Bonora (1, 99) also mentions the epigraph to the MOTTETTI, "Sobre el volcán la flor," of Gustavo Adolfo Bécquer.

Guardo la terra . . .: Bonora (1, 99): "Stupendous note of scene-painting, which in its sensual perception of the light recalls D'Annunzio at his greatest . . . and demonstrates with what sense of measure Montale made use of D'Annunzio's best lesson."

rancura: Literary, for *rancore*; see *Purgatorio* X, 133; also used by D'Annunzio. Montale's father appears in "Dov'era il tennis . . ." and, with greater psychological impact, in "Voce giunta con le folaghe."

Noi non sappiamo quale sortiremo / We don't know how we'll turn up

un discendere . . .: Suggests the infernal descent at the conclusion of "Incontro," which is, as Lonardi notes, a typical movement of *Ossi di seppia* (cf., e.g., "Arsenio" and the end of "Incontro").

api ronzanti: Mengaldo (15) derives the line from D'Annunzio's translation of an ode of Horace (IV, 2) in *Primo Vere*, "Io come una ronzante / ape matina," adding that the adjective is the translator's amplification. The citation suggests that Montale means *api* to be in apposition with *noi* and not *sillabe*. Mengaldo sees the poem as influenced by similar D'Annunzian coloration on the one hand and, on the other, "by the various connotations of the [poem's] theme of poetic activity," making use of a language that is characteristically "aulic-professional" (*il tintinnare delle rime, educammo, sapide di sale greco*).

l'erba grigia . . .: Cf. the winter scenery of "I limoni."

Avrei voluto sentirmi scabro ed essenziale / I would have liked to feel harsh and essential

Volli cercare il male . . . .: "Synthetic résumé of Montale's reading of 'contingentist' philosophy" (Marchese 1, 53). Cf. "l'anello che non tiene" of "I limoni" and "la libertà, il miracolo, / il fatto che non era necessario" of "Crisalide"; here, however, Montale's attitude is more doubting and negative.

Montale ("Intentions," *Sec*, 299–300): "Perhaps in the years in which I wrote *Ossi di seppia* (between 1920 and 1925) the French philosophers of contingency influenced me, especially Boutroux, whom I knew better than Bergson. For me, the miracle was evident, like necessity. Immanence and transcendence aren't separable, and to make a state of mind out of the perpetual mediation of the two terms, as modern historicism proposes, doesn't resolve the problem, or resolves it with a defensive optimism. One needs to live his own contradiction without loopholes, but also without enjoying it too much. Without making it into polite gossip."

Étienne-Émile-Marie Boutroux (1845–1921), professor of the history of modern philosophy at the Sorbonne, formulated the idealist, anti-positivist philosophy of contingency, which emphasized the non-absolutism of natural cause and effect and by extension argued against necessity and in favor of free will.

Marchese (1, 21–24) argues that the emphasis of Boutroux's religious and optimistic philosophy is effectively undermined in *Ossi di seppia*. The "miracle" that Boutroux posits is, for Montale, something waited for but not found: "Montale's gnoseology is from the outset alien from every form of optimistic idealism and absolute historicism: one notes, in fact, in contrast with the too-facile affirmations of freedom in the realm of nature, typical of Boutroux, a feeling, remotely Leopardian at heart, that denies every illusionary appearance of goodness, beauty, and Rousseauistic positivity in things, seeing behind them a deception, a trick of our 'representation.' . . . Montale reverses the optimism of Boutroux, emphasizing the precariousness and, finally, the failure of a 'miracle' that is as evident as 'necessity' but aleatory like an unattainable mirage. Contingentism, in sum, only contemplates the improbable probability of the miracle."

Marchese sees Schopenhauer, "for whom the phenomenal world is always a precarious and painful illusion covered by the 'veil of Maya,'" as more in key with Montale's outlook, and it is in the context of this Leopardian-Schopenhauerian pessimism that Montale's reading of Shestov (see note to "Crisalide") and, through him, of Dostoyevsky takes place. Marchese also quotes B. Rosada ("Il contingentismo di Montale," in *Studi Novecenteschi*, X, 1983), who asserts that Montale was much more indebted to Bergson than he admitted, and cites Bergson's notions of the self, of the insufficiencies of language and the unmeasurability of time, and in particular the image of the "chain," reflecting "a blocked and inexorable temporality."

Seguìto il solco . . . : Montale ("Intentions," *Sec*, 296): "I thought early on, and I still think, that art is the form of life of the man who truly doesn't live: a compensation or a surrogate." Bonora (1, 100) sees this passage as indicative of Montale's temperamental affinity with the work of Svevo—and above all with the character of Emilio Brentani, protagonist of *Senilità*.

Il tuo delirio . . . : Cf. "Arsenio" ("delirio . . . d'immobilità" and the concluding "cenere degli astri").

Potessi almeno costringere / If at least I could force

fanciullo invecchiato . . . : Cf. the "fanciullo antico" of RIVIERE. Ferraris (42–43) sees a reference to Pascoli's "fanciullino," the boy Eros who dictates to the poet (cf. "l'oscura / voce che amore detta s'affioca," below), and who is in turn derived from Dante's celebrated self-description (*Purgatorio* XXIV, 52–54): "E io a lui: 'I' mi son un che, quando / Amor mi spira, noto, e a quel modo / ch'e' ditta dentro vo significando" (And I to him: "I am one who, when / Love inspires me, note it, and in that vein / which he dictates within go expressing it").

More important, however, the notion of the old young man, according to Lonardi (106ff.), reflects Montale's "native congeniality" with Leopardi, "a continuous presence" in Montale and a vital inspiration for the Arsenio/Eusebio character who represents the poet's alter ego: "Leopardi is the leading type of the Italian *desdichado*"; he represents the old young man who hasn't needed experience to have a pessimistic understanding of evil and the void; he is "the figure par excellence in which lonely youth encounters the knowing solitude of the Old Man"—reflected in both the early and late phases of Montale's poetry (while engagement with the other occupies the middle phase, through *La bufera*).

lamentosa letteratura: Cf. Mallarmé, "Brise marine": "La chair est triste, hélas, et j'ai lu tous les livres."

studenti canaglie: The "ridiculous" (Cary, 263) outbreak of Dantesque invective antici-pates the harsh judgments of the later Montale (e.g., "questo sterminio d'oche" in "Il sogno del prigioniero").

Dissipa tu se lo vuoi / Dissolve if you will this frail

circolo: Usually an image of fixity, enclosure, helplessness in Montale. Cf. "la ruota" of "Cigola la carrucola del pozzo," which is the agent of the vision's return to the depths; or the closed circle of anomie in "Costa San Giorgio." The submission to the sea's (father's) order recalls the desire to "vanish" of "Portami il girasole . . . ," and the already cited renunciatory acts of "In limine," etc.

favilla d'un tirso: Cary (263), who says, "Primarily *tirso* is a literary noun [meaning] 'thyrsus,' the ivy wreathed and phallic staff carried by Dionysus and his followers," sees this as a possible reference in response to the ecstatic mood of *Alcyone*. Bonora (1, 104), however, emphasizes another meaning: in Cary's words, a " 'beacon' . . . , a seaside structure emitting warning signs by means of flags and lights" (265). Related images occur elsewhere, e.g., in the "acetilene" of "Arsenio," in the intermittent port lights of Vernazza in "Vecchi versi," and, by extension, throughout Montale's work, where the "spark" or "flash" or other brief illumi-nation functions as the liberating, informing, saving sign (cf. the "tenue bagliore" of "Piccolo testamento"). For Isella (2, 181), *tirso* "stands, incorrectly, for *tizzo*," a smoking coal; cf. the "spark" of "L'anguilla." Cary (265): "[The speaker's] staying, his burning, constitutes in itself a sort of witness: he becomes a sign and warning for others. And in this sense a commitment and relation *is* established—not with 'nature' but with other men. . . . This climactic *bruciare* [see note on fire imagery in "Sul muro grafito"] that is the speaker's significance might, given the intention, be understood *not only* as hellish suffering but as vocation, as a service offered up to others who move 'outward' towards some inconceivable *varco*."

MERIGGI E OMBRE / NOONS AND SHADOWS

Simply MERIGGI in the Gobetti edition. Montale (note to first Einaudi edition, 1942) (*Op*, 879): "The series MERIGGI E OMBRE belongs to the period 1922–24, except the poems added to the 1928 edition ('Vento e bandiere,' 'Fuscello teso dal muro' [these two in fact are in MOVIMENTI], 'Arsenio,' 'I morti,' 'Delta,' and 'Incontro'), which were written in '26 and '27."

Fine dell'infanzia / End of Childhood (published 1924)

For Montale's 1924 comments on this poem, see note to "Gloria del disteso mezzogiorno."

The longest single poem in *Ossi di seppia*. Contini (1, 11): "We encounter a 'descriptive' phase, a thicket, an engorgement of objects: a good part of this world could be cut away." Angelini (1, 219) finds the tone is reminiscent of Leopardi's "Le ricordanze" (cf. "Quei monti azzurri . . . che varcare un giorno io mi pensava"). The same scene is redrawn, in a more elegiac key, in "Proda di Versilia" (1946).

The poem recapitulates numerous themes and topoi of *Ossi di seppia* ("la foce"; "l'anima inquieta / che non si decide"; sun, sky, and sea; the enclosing hills; clouds and ships as symbolic actors; and, not least, the wind as precipitator of change), and seems almost Wordsworthian in its evocation of the child's prelapsarian participation in the natural world (as in "La farandola dei fanciulli . . .").

alighe: For *alghe*; D'Annunzian.

memoria stancata: "A' nuovi giorni, stanco, non so crescerla" ("Casa sul mare"). The central Montalean theme of exhausted and thus unreliable memory derives from Leopardi (cf. "Il sogno": "Oggi nel dubitar si stanca / la mente mia" [Today my mind / is exhausted by doubt] [Lonardi, 91–92]), and perhaps also from Proust.

diroccia: Cf. *Inferno* XIV, 115.

un mare florido / e vorace: Mengaldo (38) notes that the application of the adjective *vorace* to the sea is a typical borrowing from D'Annunzio, adding that it is characteristic of Montale to link two adjectives in a pair which, rather than reinforcing each other, offer a surprising oxymoronic disharmony and tension (e.g., "quest'*orrida* / e *fedele* cadenza di carioca" in the motet "Addii, fischi nel buio . . ."). But there are numerous examples involving nouns as well—as in "Di un natale metropolitano": "sospeso grappolo / di *fede* e di *pruina*" —the coupling usually involving a metaphor and a conventionally descriptive noun.

L'agave su lo scoglio / The Agave on the Reef (1922)

In a ms. version, the terms "Scirocco," "Maestrale," and "Tramontana" appear in the left margin as subtitles or melodic rubrics.

Bonora (1, 79): " 'L'agave sul lo scoglio' is born in the wake of symbolism, both in the significance attributed to the agave and the [various] winds . . .—all transparent emblems of the human condition—and, even more, in the musical nature of the three fragments."

Scirocco/Sirocco: Hot, humid, unceasing wind from Africa. Bonora (1, 82): "The metrical structure of 'Scirocco' and 'Maestrale' confirm [Montale's] debts to D'Annunzio, debts which derive from their symbolism, from the particular anthropomorphism of the two fragments, and . . . (Mengaldo, 34) from the 'acute sensual, almost tactile, perception of the events that occur in the marine world.' "

alide ali dell'aria: Cf. D'Annunzio, *Maia* 150: "le fibre / alide dell'alidore / celeste." Mengaldo (34) points out that the echoing effect (*alide ali de-*) and the rhythmic uniformity of the line (all three accents fall on the letter *a*) produce "hyper-D'Annunzian" results.

(See Mengaldo, 34–55 passim, for an exhaustive catalogue of Montalean borrowings from D'Annunzio, Pascoli, Gozzano, and other modern poets; only a few representative examples can be recorded in these notes.)

Tramontana: Strong, cold northern wind which Arrowsmith (1, 237) sees as an antecedent of the storm-wind of *La bufera*.

discorrevano il lago del cuore: Mengaldo (16) finds that the aulic, Dantesque metaphor "the heart's lake" (*Inferno* I, 20) typically attracts the rare verb, while simultaneously being balanced and rationalized by the nearby, semantically similar but more "technical" metaphor "the ripples of anxiety." Cf. "questo lago / d'indifferenza ch'è il tuo cuore" in "Dora Markus I."

Maestrale/Mistral: Arrowsmith (1, 237): "Strong, cold, dry wind from the north—milder in Liguria than in the Rhone valley—always accompanied by brilliant sunlight and cloudless skies." Bonora (1, 85): "By its very theme, which involves recovered harmony among things and almost an abandonment to the enticing rhythm of nature returned to calm, closer to the D'Annunzian model" (cf. RIVIERE). "It is here that the D'Annunzianism of *Ossi di seppia* attains its greatest complexity and gives the most appreciable results" (79). The language— *svetta, disfiora, lameggia, chiaria, ebrietudine*—is also D'Annunzian, as are the verse forms —though Bonora (1, 221) points out that *maretta* is out of Pascoli by way of Sbarbaro. "Montale, even when he adopted, a little cerebrally, a closed metric scheme, dissolved it internally, . . . and this is perhaps the truest sign of the lesson learned from D'Annunzio" (80).

The Dantean image of the human plant (as in "La farandola dei fanciulli . . .") is developed in "Vasca" (and see note to "Arsenio").

Vasca / Pool (August 1923)
The following third stanza appeared in the first three editions of *Ossi di seppia*; it was cut from the first Einaudi edition:

> Ancora nell'ingannevole anello
> trapassano le carovane dell'aria,
> e meglio vi si stemprano allora quando snello
> il fugace zampillo in alto svaria.
> Vanno e non lasciano segno
> in codesto concluso mondo
> anche le nostre giornate
> di fronte a un altro regno;
> ché dove s'apre un tondo
> d'acque, comeché angusto,
> tutte le vagheggiate
> fantasime nel tuo profondo
> s'umiliano;—tale l'arbusto
> procace sotto il vento—e l'ore ambigue
> ti crescono nel petto, e minacciate.

(In the deceiving ring / the caravans of the air pass again, / and dissolve there better now / when the fleeting jet wavers above. / Our days pass too / without a trace / in this closed world, / which borders another realm; / and where a circle of waters / opens, however narrow, / all the dreamed-of / phantoms in the deep / bend low;—like the bush / bowed down by the wind—and the hours, / ambiguous—and menaced—/ grow in your breast.)

(The "caravans of the air" are the "Nuvole in viaggio" of "Corno inglese," as well as the "isole dell'aria migrabonde" of "Casa sul mare" and the "belle sorelle" of "Fine dell'infanzia.")

riso di belladonna fiorita: Arrowsmith (1, 238–39) sees this as a reference to Dante's Earthly Paradise (*Purgatorio* XXVIII) and "the springlike apparition of Matelda, her arms full of freshly gathered flowers."

That the *riso* is that of a *bella donna* is suggested by Montale's dedication of the ms. to "the father of 'the Virgin,' " presumably Francesco Messina (*Op*, 882). Angelini (1, 220), however, reads the image as a "fleeting laugh, a betraying promise like the look of belladonna, a poisonous plant containing atropine, all adorned in the summer with its beautiful reddish-brown flowers as the Italian women of the Renaissance were with the cosmetic derived from its leaves (hence the etymology)."

The pregnant figure of an image swimming to a mirrorlike surface occurs also in the *osso* "Cigola la carrucola del pozzo." Here, too, there is an abortive encounter with a stillborn identity that has not managed to find expression, "a name"; the notion is often linked in Montale with the finding of a "volto" or "aspetto," a public face. Bettarini (1, 478) cites the tradition, "from Pseudo-Dionysus on down, that to name [an individual] is to certify his existence."

The poet's niece, Marianna Montale, in her essay "La Liguria di Montale" (Marcenaro and Boragina, 17–23) mentions the "waterlily pool" in the Montale family garden "into which as a baby Eugenio fell headfirst and nearly drowned"—an incident which reinforces the impression that for Montale, seeing oneself reflected in water or a mirror (as in "Cigola la carrucola del pozzo" or "Gli orecchini") is linked with death. (See also "Ribaltamento" [Head over Heels] in *QuaQ*, where the aged poet relives this childhood experience.)

Egloga / Eclogue (September 19, 1923)

pino domestico: Montale (Angelini 1, 220): "There is a Mediterranean pine (*pinus italica*) with a large parasol (the pine of Rome) and also a wild pine which here I call familiar [local] because it is the only one found in Liguria."

rombo di treno: In Montale's youth, Monterosso and the other villages of the Cinque Terre could be reached only by boat or by the trains which passed through the tunnels cut in the rocky hills of the coast. (The image recurs in the motet "Al primo chiaro, quando" and in "Bassa marea.")

etra vetrino: The "aria di vetro" of "Forse un mattino andando. . . ." Mengaldo (94) gives this as an example of how in the evolution, i.e., the condensation, of the metaphor—part of the development of Montale's "objective" poetics—the "preciously technical adjective" (in this case also alliterative with the substantive) contributes both to objectifying the image and to rendering it more technical. This is a typical process of exchange, in which everyday or specialized language takes on "preciousness" by association with poetic vocabulary at the same time that "poetic" terms "become concrete and almost technical."

esplode furibonda una canea: Recalls the violent emergence embodied in the "colpo di fucile" of "Mia vita. . . ." See note to "Il gallo cedrone," concerning the significance of hunting imagery in Montale.

saturnali . . . Baccante: Ironic, perhaps anti-D'Annunzian classicizing references, reminiscent of "Sarcofaghi," which serve to underline the nonheroic domestic character of Montale's *paesi*. The *lepri*, too, recall the conclusion of that poem, with its homemade (Christian) symbol of the sunflower surrounded by dancing hares.

Flussi / Flux (August 9, 1924)

The bipartite, but also circular, structure of the poem recalls "Corno inglese," and reinforces the recurrent image of "the wheel that rules our life," as in "Costa San Giorgio" and elsewhere. Details of the setting recall Montale's sister's description of the family garden at Fegina (see introductory note to *Ossi di seppia*); see also "La casa delle due palme" in *Farf*; for discussion of the imagery of the ditch see note to "Il gallo cedrone."

Cola, riale, sorrade, diruto: Literary language; *rama* is Tuscan dialect.

malvivi / camminatori: The "uomini che non si voltano" of "Forse un mattino andando . . . ," with which this poem shares other affinities, especially the cinematic image of the "unknown light" projecting the past onto "still curtains." The hobolike figure of the solitary man walking along dusty roads is prominent in the poetry of Roccatagliata Ceccardi (see his *Viandante* [Wayfarer], 1904) and Dino Campana. Cf. also "those wanderers the world's evil harms" in "Ripenso il tuo sorriso. . . ."

una statua dell'Estate: The statue in the Montale garden; cf. the statue in "Spesso il male di vivere. . . ." Arrowsmith (1, 242) sees a reference to "Le Stagioni camuse," the noseless seasons, in Gozzano's "Signorina Felicità."

il giro che governa / la nostra vita: Cf. the frequent image of the wheel as the instrument of relentless fate in "Costa San Giorgio," "Eastbourne," and elsewhere. See note to "La casa dei doganieri."

accesa edera: The image recurs in "Finestra fiesolana."

gran discesa: The Heraclitean notion of *panta rhei*, entropy or flux.

sciabecchi: Angelini (1, 220): "*Chébecs* . . . very delicate Mediterranean constructions with sails and oars, carrying three masts equipped with Latin sails and sometimes armed with a ram, much used in the eighteenth century in the too-violent backwaters created by *panta rhei*, the fleeing of time." See also Bonora (1, 120): "I suppose . . . an ironic intention in [these] lines because currently, especially in Liguria, *sciabecco* is a term for a badly constructed or badly maintained ship."

acquiccia: Mengaldo (94) notes Montale's predilection, in *Ossi di seppia*, for rare, often diminutive suffixes for common terms, e.g., *fumea, fumacchi, fanghiglia, ortino, vallotto, fiumara, pietrisco*.

i suoi volti riconfonde: The theme of the face as a mask, an assumed identity (see the "morti aspetti"—originally "vecchi volti" [old faces]—of line 24), is broached in "Là fuoresce il Tritone," "Incontro," and elsewhere.

Clivo / Slope (1924–26?)

In MEDITERRANEO, Montale wrote, "My life is this dry slope"; here he offers a portrait of "[his] landscape" as a vision of defeat and dissolution. "The chain that binds us" is mortality; "the end is certain" (cf. "l'inferno è certo," which closes the first motet, "Lo sai: debbo riperderti e non posso"). Bonora (1, 126): "Perhaps nowhere before 'Arsenio' has Montale expressed as intensely as in 'Clivo' the drama of existence, the struggle between the inexpressible suffering that is the destiny of every creature, and the desperate will to live."

trova stanza in cuore la speranza: Mengaldo (301) cites a passage from the aria "Chi son? Sono un poeta" in the first scene of Puccini's *La Bohème*—"v'ha preso stanza / la speranza"—as the source for this line.

la lima: Arrowsmith (1, 244) takes this to be the voice of the cicada, which in *La bufera* will come to stand for the poet himself (cf. "L'ombra della magnolia . . .").

divalla: Cf. *Inferno* XVI, 98.

pendìe: Tuscan.

cielo/sfacelo: Arrowsmith (1, 244): "The word *cielo* (sky, heaven), as Cambon [15] has without exaggeration observed, 'touches off the *Götterdammerung* of *sfacelo* [undoing, ruin].' . . . Accented on the antepenult, it pointedly refuses closure and . . . the poem, like the cliff it describes, crumbles away."

I I

Arsenio (published June 1927)

A brilliant though "difficult and obscure" (Almansi and Merry, 49) summation of the poet's preoccupations in *Ossi di seppia*, here given a form or mask in the autobiographical character of Arsenio. (Montale [*Su*, 580]: "Arsenio and the Nestorian [see "Iride"] are projections of myself.") Bonora (1, 193–94) shows how the language of the poem evokes the themes of the entire book: "Places and figures in his landscape are so profoundly rooted in Montale's memory that they return almost like harassing phantoms in *Ossi di seppia*. But the singularly thick texture composed in 'Arsenio' by the reprise of themes and phrases already assayed confirms the significance one must attribute to this poem, which, last in order of [composition], is the conclusion, albeit provisional, of the book."

Marcenaro and Boragina (141) quote Montale's assertion (in Domenico Porzio, *Conversazioni con Montale*, 1977) that he wrote the poem "in an afternoon." Various sources for the name have been adduced, but it is clear that it draws its inspiration at least in part from the poet's well-known nickname Eusebio, given him by Bobi Bazlen and often used by the poet himself. Giachery (65) reports that Bazlen asked Montale to write a poem about Eusebius, "the name given by Robert Schumann to the gentle, dreamy, contemplative, and 'poetic' side of his 'split' personality" (Cary, 278). Montale never wrote the poem, and Bazlen began calling him by the name. Almansi and Merry (52) derive *Arsenio* from the same root as *arsenic*, which they say means "white, bleached," thus lending the poem's character "the desolate purity of cuttle-fish bones." Arrowsmith (1, 249) connects the name with *arso*, past participle of *ardere* (to burn), which, as we have seen, is a motif throughout *Ossi di seppia*, from "Minstrels" on, while Bettarini (2, 222) wonders if it might be "a little bit arsenic and a little bit Arsène Lupin?," the scoundrel hero of Maurice Leblanc's popular detective novels of the period; but she adds that the first syllable of the name derives primarily from the pseudonym for the interlocutor of Montale's first love poems, Arletta (see note to "Incontro"), the assonant names creating a kind of ironic modern commedia dell'arte pair reminiscent of, say, Papageno and Papagena in *The Magic Flute*.

Arsenio is a "Chaplinesque, improbable bourgeois clown" (Biasin, 103) who, in his indecision, has much in common with "the 'devitalized' characters in Svevo's novels" (Almansi and Merry [49], citing Claudio Scarpati, *Invito all lettura di Montale* [Milan: Mursia, 1973]). He is described as on the verge of a "long-awaited hour" which will free him from his perpetual condition as a "link in a chain," from the "too familiar frenzy, / . . . of immobility." The "miracle" is announced, as so often in Montale, by a violent change of weather, a "sign of another orbit": not the cosmic storm of *La bufera* but the "maltempo" of, e.g., "Notizie dall'Amiata." The longed-for escape doesn't eventuate, however, and Arsenio finds himself swallowed again by "the old wave." The "sign . . . of a strangled life" is all he receives, and that, too, is carried off by "the wind." "Arsenio," then, is a poem about an existence imagined but not achieved. West (30) quotes Forti (1, 108): " 'The poem itself leads . . . the character to the threshold of a fully meaningful, creative and liberating gesture'; and it is on that threshold that he remains." She continues: "If, then, we identify Arsenio with the poetic consciousness that brings the poem into being (and not simplistically with the man Montale), the poem itself, like its marginal protagonist, remains on the threshold, and its primary message is that of its own emergence into form."

un ritornello / di castagnette: Some critics suggest the musical references throughout the poem (cf. also the "getto tremulo / dei violini" and the "timpano / degli tzigani") are meant to anthropomorphize the sounds of the storm; to others they indicate the actual presence of a dance orchestra. The castanets will reappear in "La bufera."

Discendi . . . : Descent is the primary trope of movement in the late poems of *Ossi di seppia*.

anello d'una / catena: Cf. the "anello che non tiene" of "I limoni," and Montale's implicit notion of contingency (see note to "Avrei voluto sentirmi scabro ed essenziale," in MEDITERRANEO).

delirio . . . d'immobilità: Almansi and Merry (52) link the phrase with the "astri" of the last line and with the "astrale delirio" of "Marezzo" and "Il tuo delirio sale agli astri ormai" in "Avrei voluto sentirmi scabro ed essenziale," noting "the emphatic and one could even say euphoric [orgasmic?] combination in Montale."

sgorga: D'Annunzian verb; to Marchese (1, 59), the entire scene has a D'Annunzian flavor.

gozzi: Genoese.

sciaborda: Nautical terminology.

un frùscio immenso: Cf. the "frullo" of "In limine."

giunco: The Dantesque image of the enfeebled human plant (see the wood of the suicides in *Inferno* XIII—derived in turn from Virgil, *Aeneid* II, 41, and Ovid, *Metamorphoses* II, 358–66—where the suicides' unnatural rupture of the "link that binds man to himself is translated into the spectacle of a deformed nature antithetical to the data of daily experience" [Dante Alighieri, *La divina commedia*, ed. Natalino Sapegno, vol. I: *Inferno* (Firenze: "La Nuova Italia" Editrice, 2nd ed., 1968), 143–44]). Montale borrows the figure frequently in *Ossi di seppia* (cf. "La farandola dei fanciulli . . . ," "L'agave su lo scoglio," "Vasca," and especially "Incontro") and elsewhere; see the "Troppo / straziato . . . bosco umano" of "Personae separatae." There is an echo here, also, of Pascal's *roseau pensant*. Cary (268): "Generally Montale's usage involves the sense of a potential unable to express or extrapolate itself." ˙

strada portico / mura specchi: The paratactic list recalls the "usual deceit" of "alberi case colli" in "Forse un mattino andando . . . ," and prefigures the elaborate catalogues of *La bufera*.

ghiacciata moltitudine di morti: Cf. the vision of Cocytus in *Inferno* XXXII.

vita strozzata: Marchese (1, 60) sees this as a tacit reference to Arletta, the "drowned one" to whom "Incontro" and "La casa dei doganieri" are addressed, "the woman whom Montale considers as having died young, the Silvia or Nerina of a secret amorous *canzoniere*." The saving sign that is efficacious elsewhere in Montale, however, is abortive here; though he may have received it, it vanishes, like the vision in the well of "Cigola la carrucola del pozzo."

la cenere degli astri: Jacomuzzi (1, 74) reads this as a quotation from Mallarmé's *Igitur* V: "les cendres des astres, celles indivises de la famille," linking the image—and Arsenio—to the "moltitudine dei morti," above. Giachery (48ff.), however, notes that *Igitur* appeared only in 1925 in a limited edition, and that it is unlikely Montale could have read it before writing "Arsenio." The image of ashes does nevertheless seem to be linked with the name of the poem's protagonist.

I I I

Crisalide / Chrysalis (Spring–Summer 1924)
One of Montale's most complex and searching and formally least resolved poems, which, like many of the compositions of *Ossi di seppia*, reiterates several of the preoccupations of the work as a whole, but which also incorporates important thematic developments, notably the identification of an object, "the poet's beloved for whose salvation he wishes" (West, 30), though her emergence here remains partial and inconclusive; the "creature del volo" of an earlier ms. version quoted below (which clarifies the movement of the poem in several respects) will not be fully elaborated until the later poems of *Le occasioni*.

Zampa (*Tutte*, xxviii) identifies the addressee of the poem as Paola Nicoli, to whom "In limine," "Marezzo," and "Casa sul mare" (as well as "Tentava la vostra mano la tastiera") are directed (see also note to the first motet, "Lo sai: debbo riperderti e non posso").

A ms. draft (*Op*, 885–88) differs significantly from the published text. The most important variations are as follows, starting with the beginning of stanza 2:

> Mia pianta voi, che invano
> strinò scirocco e declinò garbino,
> bell'albero proteso
> al crescer della luce,
> germoglio che ci dà testimonianza
> d'un lontano mattino che non vedremo.
> Ogni attimo vi porta nuove fronde. . . .

(You are my plant, in vain / sirocco scorched you and sou'wester bent you down, / beautiful tree stretched / toward the growing light, / sowing that brings us evidence / of a distant morning we won't see. / Every moment brings new leaves to you. . . .)

End of stanza 3:

> . . . giro d'occhi ch'ormai hanno veduto.
> E nessuno farà che non sia nato
> un gergo d'iniziati tra le nostre
> deboli vite: l'una che ricerca,
> l'altra, la mia, che addita e si ritrae.
>
> Forse non vincerete l'ombra oscura
> che da ogni parte tenta di rinchiudervi;
> forse non sorgerà dalla crisalide
> la creatura del volo. M'apparite
> come me condannata al limbo squallido
> delle monche esistenze. . . .

(. . . staring around of eyes that now have seen. / And no one will allow there not to be / a language of initiates / between our feeble lives: one that seeks, / the other, mine, that points and withdraws. // Maybe you won't defeat the dark shadow / that tries to close over you on every side; / maybe the creature of flight / won't emerge from the chrysalis. You seem to me / to be condemned like me to the bleak limbo / of maimed existences. . . .)

Last stanza:

> Che posso dirvi? Torcersi le dita
> per fatti inesorabili d'altrui
> è mio destino: al mondo
> ci ha luogo per chi sperpera e per quegli
> che raccatta i rottami abbandonati.
> Il silenzio ci lega col suo filo
> e le labbra non s'aprono per dire
> l'estremo patto che vorrei fermare
> col torbido destino: di scontare
> la vostra gioia con la mia condanna.
> È il voto che mi fruga ancora il petto
> —poi finirà ogni moto—:
> nel rogo della vostra
> vita foss'io il paletto
> che si getta sul fuoco e cresce l'ilare
> fiamma d'attorno!
>
> E forse non m'è dato.

(What can I tell you? To wring my hands / for the inexorable fate of another / is my destiny: the world / has room for him who squanders / and for him who gathers abandoned rubble. / Silence binds us with her thread / and my lips won't open to utter / the extreme pact I'd like to forge / with muddy destiny: to redeem / your joy through my condemnation. / This is the will that still ransacks my heart /—after which all motion will cease—: / on the pyre of your / life might I be the stalk / that is thrown on the fire and the joyous / flame grows around! / And maybe this isn't granted me.)

"The 'you' is not the customary *tu*, but *voi*, a plurality" (Cary, 269), as in the related poem "Tentava la vostra mano la tastiera." This "sweet nineteenth-twentieth century *voi*" (Maria Corti, quoted in Bonora [1, 136], who notes that this reflects "an earlier moment" in the speaker's relationship with his addressee, "when confidence needed to be corrected by a note of gallantry") "seems to refer here to the myriad aspects of a burgeoning natural life within the garden, a kind of Aprilic composite or coalition fermenting around the staring shade" (Cary, 269). Similarly (Cary, 272), "the 'I' . . . is not presented as a more or less stable entity upon which other entities press or impinge but as a consciousness in continuous flux and process. . . . 'Crisalide' is the dramatization of the fortunes of a consciousness moving from an obsessional and lacerating sense of its own impotence to a commitment, *nevertheless*, to the well-being of another; a dramatic aria—if one wishes—of an evolving *coscienza* [consciousness/conscience]."

rapiva: Anticipates "il forte imperio / che ti rapisce" of "Gli orecchini" and the related "Ghermito" of " 'Ezekiel saw the Wheel. . . .' " The watcher/voyeur of "Crisalide" also foreshadows the "spy" of "Anniversario."

Siete voi la mia preda: Cary (269): "His contemplation . . . has its succubic or vampirical side—the speaker 'preys' upon the life-energies about him." (Likewise Giovanni Macchia [quoted in *Tutte*, 1098], writing about Montale's fetishistic focus on Clizia's attributes, such as her bangs, in *La bufera*, refers to them as "precious visual obsession, a form of gentle spiritual vampirism.")

della gran muraglia: Lonardi (43) sees this as a reference to the "wall of evidence and strict causality" in Dostoyevsky's *Notes from Underground*, as discussed in the existentialist Lev Shestov's *Revelations of Death* (1921): "The world . . . , since it has ceased to offer itself freely, . . . is *that* wall," which is opposed by imponderable, unpredictable liberty.

la libertà, il miracolo . . . : See notes to "In limine," the original title of which was "La libertà," and MEDITERRANEO for discussion of the philosophical notion of contingency expressed here. Lonardi (44): "Naturally, the 'fatto che non era necessario' of 'Crisalide' will descend from the recollection of Raskolnikov in *Crime and Punishment*."

un arido paletto: Cf. the "tirso" at the end of MEDITERRANEO, with the attendant connotations. The ms. draft makes it clear that the "arido paletto" is a figure for the poet, consumed by fire (as in "Minstrels," etc.).

Marezzo / Moiré (published February 1925)

One of Montale's least-discussed poems, about a mutually experienced loss of identity which transpires in a boat becalmed in a harbor on a blazing afternoon. Like the expected epiphany of "Arsenio," the visionary moment doesn't hold, leaving the speaker and his companion "no different" (though transformed by the experience). Arrowsmith (1, 253) notes parallels to the *ossi brevi* "Non rifugiarti nell'ombra" and "Gloria del disteso mezzogiorno." An early poem, "Nel vuoto," of 1924 (tr. in *Oth*, 113) is a kind of precursor; the setting and conclusion also prefigure aspects of "Barche sulla Marna."

Zampa (*Tutte*, xviii) identifies the addressee of the poem once again as Paola Nicoli (though she is addressed in the second person singular here).

The poem is structured in quatrains, albeit of a "studied irregularity" (Bonora 1, 114–15), with rhyme scheme and rhythm varying according to Montale's goals, as will be the case in several of the late additions to *Ossi di seppia*. The vocabulary, too, is a remarkable hybrid of the aulic, the technical, and the everyday. Arrowsmith (1, 257) quotes Mengaldo's (92–94) analysis of the style in the first two stanzas: "Colloquial and/or prosaic terms are joined to poetic and/or literarily elegant ones [a technique Montale learned from Gozzano, as we have seen], and, by combining what they least share—on the one hand, precise and exact meaning; on the other, objective particularization of individual phenomena—they reciprocally define and specify, with a brilliance and clarity often bordering on hallucination and visual distortion."

Il cavo cielo se ne illustra *ed* estua: D'Annunzian vocabulary—as is Montale's use of the root meaning of *illustra* (Mengaldo, 36).

affonda / il tuo nome: Cf. the losing or assumption of a name (as in "Vasca")—or a face, as in "Là fuoresce il Tritone," "Incontro," and elsewhere. The speaker urges his companion to "jettison that individuality that for Montale is conveyed by the possession of a face and a name . . . [cf. the related statement "this fire burns faces, plans," below, which recalls "Là fuoresce il Tritone"]. The undifferentiated self vanishes, melting into the Undifferentiated, the world of pure, sheeted Being represented by the absolute *meriggio* of this and other poems" (Arrowsmith 1, 254).

Un astrale delirio: See note to "Arsenio." Arrowsmith (1, 254) argues that *astrale* should be taken in the Dantesque sense, i.e., as referring to "*the* star, the sun," and that the phrase thus means "passion for the sun" or "solar frenzy," recalling the sunflower of "Portami il girasole . . . ," which is "crazed with light," and the "scorched spirits" of "Non rifugiarti nell'ombra," who "dissolve in the bright sky / of one certainty: the light."

un gorgo d'azzurro: Mengaldo (37) notes that the phrase occurs in both Roccatagliata Ceccardi and Boine.

Casa sul mare / House by the Sea (published February 1925)

Almansi and Merry (56) note that this poem "is usually seen as standing at the dividing-point between the different seasons of *Ossi di seppia* and *Le occasioni*."

The Montalean lyric has achieved nearly definitive form: an address, composed without any "concession to the descriptive" (Bonora 1, 131) and with great rhythmic variation, to a female companion (still Paola Nicoli, according to Zampa [*Tutte*, xviii]) who is either physically absent or, as here, spiritually remote, having, as the speaker guesses, access to a world of "the miracle" from which he is excluded. The preoccupation with salvation is the constant anxiety that drives the poet's quest for communion with the woman, who will later be perceived as the only agent who can close the gap between the poet's tormented earthly existence and "the beyond"; here, however, the speaker is still "leaving you my miser's hope," in the oblatory gesture of "In limine."

Almansi and Merry (56) note that the title recalls a line of Sbarbaro's, "la casa sul mare di Loano."

Il viaggio finisce qui: Cf. the "viaggio" which Arsenio is hoping to finish; *finisce* rhymes with *vanisce* (vanish), at the beginning of the third stanza.

minuti . . . eguali e fissi: A recurrent image in *Ossi di seppia*, expressing the poet's sense of stasis, boredom, anomie. Cf. the "ore / uguali" of "Arsenio" and the "ore troppo uguali" of "Quasi una fantasia." The image of the pump recurs from "Cigola la carrucola del pozzo."

isole dell'aria migrabonde: The (D'Annunzian) clouds of "Corno inglese," "Vasca," and other poems.

la Corsica dorsuta . . . : Arrowsmith (1, 260) quotes the *Guida all'Italia legendaria* (Milan, 1971, 311): "According to legend, the promontory of Portofino is thought to be the farthest frontier of the living, from which can be seen, floating in the distance of the sea, the Island of the Blessed. This may be a rationalized reference to Corsica, which on very clear days can be seen rising from the sea." Bonora (1, 133–34), who notes that the line recalls a celebrated passage in Dante (*Inferno* XXXIII, 82ff.), says that *dorsuta* as well as *migrabonde* and *s'infinita* are Montalean inventions.

questa poca nebbia di memorie: Cf. "la mia nebbia di sempre" in the motet "Non recidere, forbice . . . ," both derived, according to Lonardi (90–91), from "tanta nebbia di tedio" in Leopardi's "Ad Angelo Mai."

s'infinita: Dantesque neologism, comparable to *transumanar* (*Paradiso* I, 70).

codesta: Marchese (1, 63) notes the literary, "Tuscan" use of the demonstrative adjective to denote something that is close to the addressee but not to the speaker.

ruga: Cf. "the rudder" that "leaves no wake in the water" in "Fuscello teso dal muro. . . ."

Ti dono . . . : As already noted, the donation (*dono* is more formal than *do*) of the speaker's hope is the characteristic gesture in *Ossi di seppia* of the poet's persona, who cannot himself live, being "too tired" (see "the exhausted memory" of "Fine dell'infanzia"). Cf. the fifth section of MEDITERRANEO, where the "piece of grassless earth / broke open so a daisy could be born," and the close of "Crisalide": "the unspoken offerings that prop up / the houses of the living; . . . the heart that abdicates / so an unsuspecting child may laugh."

Il tuo cuore vicino che non m'ode: Prefigures the distant, focused-elsewhere quality ("non hai sguardi") ascribed to Clizia in "Iride" and other poems of *La bufera*. Already here the poet's interlocutor seems to be embarking on a journey into transcendence that will leave him behind.

I morti / The Dead (published November 1926)

One of the compositions added to the 1928 edition. A powerful carving-out of Montale's personal theology, unusual in its displacement of subjectivity; the personal references are seemingly overwhelmed by the intensity of imagining the still-earthbound, purgatorial existences of the dead (with whom the speaker links himself and his interlocutor—specified by Zampa [*Tutte*, xxviii] as the "Arletta" of "Incontro"). These are the "gelid gathering" of "Arsenio," here "gnawed by human memory," i.e., tormented by their continued life in the minds of those who survive them rather than released into the salvation posited throughout *Ossi di seppia* but unavailable "for most" ("Casa sul mare").

Montale's dead reappear in *La bufera*, in the "Madrigali fiorentini," "L'arca," and "Proda di Versilia," which echoes "I morti," and in the poems about his parents, "A mia madre" and "Voce giunta con le folaghe," where Clizia tries to relieve the poet—and his father—of the burden of memory. It is the women, however, his mother and sister (in the "Madrigali fiorentini"), who are pictured in Paradise—albeit one of their own contriving which the poet can neither assent to nor conceive of for himself. For Talbot (47), the theme of "the return of the dead in memory" derives from Joyce's story "The Dead" in *Dubliners*, which Montale reviewed in 1926.

ferrigna: Cf. *Inferno* XVIII, 1–2. The language of the poem is Dantesque throughout.

il gorgo sterile . . . : The *gorgo* (also *vortice, mulinello*, etc.) is a recurrent image of inexorable fate in *Ossi di seppia* and elsewhere (cf. the "mulinello della sorte" in "Sotto la pioggia"); *verdeggia* is cousin to *riverdica* in "Crisalide" and *riaddensa / il verde* in "Delta." The death-life chiasmus is typically Montalean.

una forza . . . spietata . . . : Cf. Foscolo, *Dei sepolcri*: "involve / tutte cose l'oblio nella sua notte; e una forza operosa affatica / di moto in moto." Mengaldo (77) notes that Foscolo's strong thematic (as opposed to merely semantic) influence here is an indication that Montale is beginning to move beyond the influence of his more recent predecessors in favor of classical writers.

i mozzi / loro voli: The haunted, unsuccessful flight of unliberated souls contrasts vividly with the nearly constant use of the image to indicate the desired passage (*varco*) toward otherworldly liberation. The "broken" flights of the dead are a poor, parodic imitation of the soaring suggested in "In limine" and elsewhere, which will reach its apogee in Clizia's angelic imagery (though after her sacrifice, her wings, too, will be shattered).

Delta (published November 1926)

Added to the Ribet edition. Stylistically the most concentrated poem in the collection; Montale has already succeeded in his aim, after the first edition of *Ossi di seppia*, to "express the object and conceal the occasion-spur" ("Intentions," *Sec*, 302), i.e., he has moved from the "descriptive" to the "assertive" (Contini 1, 11) stage of his work, which focuses on a highly condensed, even obscure declaration of faith, what Contini calls the "harsh affirmation of possession: insisting on the *presence*, the *essence* of objects. . . . The subtext of all Montale's poetry is the poet's dramatic struggle with the object [here the absent 'suffocated presence']: to find, almost, a justification for *seeing*."

Arrowsmith (1, 265) quotes Valentini (195): "That ['Delta'] anticipates *Le occasioni* is undeniable, but we need to understand in what way. . . . To my mind the interesting point is that, in the fatalistic round of existence, in the prison of the hours, alongside the wall that cannot be crossed, perhaps no longer hoping to find *varco*, a break in the meshes of the net, or salvation in another orbit, the poet accepts the message that sustains him in life. Accepts it with a religious feeling, perhaps with the certainty that, by so doing, he lives in the soul of another: the woman he loves. The interpretation is strengthened if we bring to it one of Montale's later observations in *Le occasioni*: 'Too many lives go into making one' [in "L'estate"]—a statement clearly intended not in a purely physical sense . . . but in the more obvious psychological sense of a man who needs to see himself reflected in eyes that reassure him."

Most important of all, "Delta" marks the decisive point in the formation of Montale's myth of the other, for it is here that the "oblatory gesture" that has been operative from "In limine" to "Casa sul mare" is superseded by the "messaggio / muto" which the poet is now able to derive from his interlocutor; that is, instead of positing giving as a form of renunciation, a "compensation or a surrogate" for living, the speaker now finds himself acting, in motion *sulla via*, and deriving essential sustenance from the other's "gift," which is her "message." Still, the speaker is only able to "live" in the "presence" of the message of the absent beloved; as "Marezzo" suggests, a mutual epiphany cannot last.

The theme is further developed in "Incontro," where the drowned one, the "sommersa," is actively urged to "pray" for the speaker. From here on out, it is the loved woman, not the poet, who is expected to perform the oblatory gesture and, eventually in *La bufera*, to be sacrificed—ideally "for all" (see "La primavera hitleriana"), but, primarily and in actuality, only for the poet himself (see "Anniversario"). Here at the end of *Ossi di seppia*, in the all-important pre-*Occasioni* phase of Montale's work, the poet can be seen as passing out of the anteroom of (post-adolescent) pre-engagement into the arena of mature relations with others; he has found a way of assuming the adult, masculine role (*volto* or *nome*) which he avoided or rejected throughout *Ossi di seppia*; his earlier acts of renunciation can be interpreted as not-fully-convinced efforts to identify with the sacrificial "giving" which he perceives as the highest form of (Christian) existence, the means of escape from the prison of everyday life and which he consistently associates with femininity. The earthbound male, from "Falsetto" to "Il gallo cedrone," cannot join the female in flight; in the early poetry, this means that the poet/speaker cannot truly live, because although he feels an empathetic identification with feminine figures (see Lonardi [64] for discussion of the dominant—but suppressed—influence of the maternal sphere in Montale), the female nevertheless remains "other." It is only when, in "Delta," he takes the decisive action of "linking," of fully investing his female interlocutor with "The life that erupts in secret / streams," frontally recognizing and confronting her otherness, that he is able to derive encouragement and succor from that very separateness (though, significantly, this is only achieved in her absence). Thus the blockade of *Ossi di seppia* is broken and the longed-for *varco* opens up.

Translations of "Delta" and "Ripenso il tuo sorriso . . ." by Samuel Beckett and Samuel Putnam were published in *This Quarter* 2 (April-May-June 1930).

La vita che si rompe: "si rompe" is both "breaks up" and "breaks out"; the image of violent emergence occurs throughout Montale; cf., e.g., the "rifle shot" analogy in "Mia vita, a te non chiedo. . . ."

a te ho legata: The speaker has made a definitive, preemptive, perhaps obsessional intervention, bringing the object into the world of his memory on his own terms, an independent existential act not preordained by external conditions, and without external confirmation.

presenza soffocata: Zampa (*Tutte*, xxviii) identifies the addressee as the "Arletta" of "Incontro" and "I morti," a character who is presented as dead, or at least permanently absent, "suffocated," able to "surface" only in the poet's memory, on his terms.

messaggio / muto . . .: First metaphorical embodiment of the saving "signs" that give rise to the "occasions" of *Le occasioni*. The sign here is "the whistle of the tug," the one external descriptive element in the poem, but which implies the approaching successful completion of a journey, arrival at a desired destination. As suggested above, the meaning assigned to it is entirely of the poet's own devising. His doubts about it, and about his interlocutor, are evoked in "se forma esisti . . . ," which Lonardi (115) sees as a less Platonic echo of Leopardi's "Alla sua donna" ("se dell'eterne idee / l'una sei tu . . .").

Incontro / Encounter (August 14–16, 1926)

One of the six poems added to the Ribet edition. Titled "La foce" in ms. (as we will see below, the mouth is that of the river Bisagno in Genoa) and "Arletta" in *Il Convegno* (VII, 11–12, [November 25–December 25,] 1926), where it was first published.

"Incontro" is aptly titled, for it describes the confrontation of Montale's poetic persona with the saving figure who will provide him with the way out of the closed system of the "garden" of *Ossi di seppia* (see note to "Delta"). The encounter, however, is with a "drowned," that is, absent, figure, synonymous with his own "sadness," available to him only in barely readable "glimmers" which he prays may make her presence felt on his journey, so that she may be, as Marchese (1, 67) puts it, "the unknowing Beatrice of the purgatorial and salvific journey of the poet," here envisioned as a Dantesque traveling through a purgatorial life-in-death. As in "Arsenio" and many of the later pieces in *Ossi di seppia*, the poem cumulatively recapitulates numerous topoi delineated in the course of the entire collection.

sulla strada: Bettarini (1, 463) cites Martelli (159), according to whom the poem's "suburban 'voyage'" (Lonardi, 34) follows the descent of via Montaldo in Genoa, which runs alongside the Bisagno as it flows down to the sea, as described by Sbarbaro, who lived there, in his *Trucioli*, 201–4; figuratively, it is the Dantesque way of the speaker's journey, of his life.

viaggia una nebbia: Cf. the traveling clouds throughout *Ossi di seppia*; Pascolian description according to Marchese (1, 64).

La foce . . . : The image, representative of the encounter of life and death, appears throughout *Ossi di seppia*. The poem becomes specific about its allegorical significance two lines later. Rebay (2, 79) notes that in a ms. version, there was a comma after *allato*, making it clear that the word is intended as adverbial here, not prepositional.

a cerchio: See note to "La casa dei doganieri" on the circle as an image of "existential constriction" (M. J. Meynaud, quoted in Marchese 1, 65).

vegetazioni: See note to "Arsenio" regarding the theme of the "pianta umana," which receives its most expanded treatment here.

dell'altro mare: Arrowsmith (1, 268) notes that most commentators read this as a reference to Dante's "gran mar dell'essere" (*Paradiso* I, 113); Arrowsmith, however, sees the "flood" as an image of time.

Si va sulla carraia . . . : This stanza and the next seem to revisit imagery from "Arsenio" —the hooded horses, "the shattered vault" that "mirrors the windows," the reedlike bamboo, the sounds that announce an hour about to strike, but which does not. Marchese (1, 65): "Montale, recalling Dante and (perhaps) Eliot, has created a suggestive urban inferno, in which life regresses to a vegetal level"; the seaweed recalls the line of hooded hypocrites (cf. also the "cowardice" of the final line of the poem) in *Inferno* XXIII, 58–63.

presagio vivo: Bettarini (1, 459) notes that this was "presenza viva" (cf. the "presenza soffocata" of "Delta") in the version printed in *Il Convegno*.

chi non sa temere: The Christ-like savior, who will lead the dead out of Purgatory.

Forse riavrò un aspetto: Cf. the many references elsewhere to the issue of a "face" or "name" (see note to "Delta"); Bonfiglioli (in V. Boarini and P. Bonfiglioli, *Avanguardia e restaurazione* [Bologna: Zanichelli, 1976], 319; quoted in Marchese 1, 65) reads this, "Perhaps I shall reassume *the form that was taken from me* [see line 43], my lost individuality"; Marchese, by contrast (1, 66), notes that "aspetto" in Montale is always used to denote the face, and sees this as a reference to Arletta. The face, however, especially when it is termed a "volto" as in "Là fuoresce il Tritone" (cf. the similarity of the setting, at the mouth of a river, to that of "Incontro"), is precisely a metaphor for the poet's own character or individuality, which has been taken from him yet may, perhaps, be restored.

una misera fronda: Allusion, as we learn ex post facto, to the myth of Daphne. As Marchese (1, 66) relates it, once Daphne was changed into a laurel tree, Apollo continued to love her, feeling her heartbeat under her bark (is there perhaps a glancing reference here to the "swollen bark" of "Crisalide"?); Marchese notes that the myth here has undergone a "realistic de-sublimation"; "misera" is perhaps related to the "tristezza" of line 1.

una / forma che mi fu tolta: The "form" is the incarnated spiritual reality of a being, an essential term in Montale; see "Non rifugiarti nell'ombra," "Sul muro grafito," and "Delta," and, later, "Personae separatae" and "Nella serra" in *La bufera*, etc. It has been wrested from the speaker by death. The phrase is derived from "la persona [i.e., body] che mi fu tolta," *Inferno* V, 102, where Francesca da Rimini is mourning her physical identity, of which she was deprived when she and her lover, Paolo Malatesta, were murdered by her jealous husband.

e quasi anelli . . . : Marchese (1, 66) again quotes Bonfiglioli (in Boarini and Bonfiglioli, op. cit., 320): "The metamorphosis of Daphne into laurel, at least in D'Annunzio's version in 'L'oleandro' [in *Alcyone*] recalled here by several verbal elements, is the literary pretext which Montale overturns by grafting onto it the Dantesque theme of the reconversion of the plant into a human figure. The branch that turns into hair, twisting around the fingers of a beloved hand, certainly represents an amorous *encounter*. But Eros here, as in other lyrics of the *Ossi*, is sacrificial religion, oblation: the woman, recognizing herself in the man as the man sees himself in her, grants him her own life both to allow him to live and to live in him herself, or rather she restores him to himself, and disappears." (See also note to "Delta.")

sommersa: Drowned, like the dead of "I morti" and "Proda di Versilia" in *La bufera*. Bettarini (1, 464) notes that in the first printed version, the word was "Arletta."

nulla so di te: Cf. "Delta": "Nulla di te. . . ."

La tua vita è ancor tua: The possession of the other (cf. the kind of spiritual absorption described in "Crisalide") is an illusion which fails like the illusion in "I limoni," or in "Marezzo." The other remains locked in her otherness.

altro cammino: Marchese (1, 67) identifies the "route" as that of death; or rather, it is an Orphic descent, as in "Arsenio" and elsewhere in *Ossi di seppia*, into the underworld that is the life which the "living" don't see: the perilous journey that had previously been left to others but which the speaker is now himself undertaking. Lonardi (105): "Little *catabases* ("Casa sul mare," "Incontro," "Arsenio"), they are par excellence journeys without a female mediator, voyages of the solitary ego toward the entirely symbolic hell of a beach or a sea."

nell'aria persa: Cf. the "aere perso" of *Inferno* V, 89, which Arrowsmith (1, 268) notes is derived from the reddish-brown or purplish-black or blue-gray color of Persian cloth; Dante (*Convivio* IV, xx, 2): "Persian [*lo perso*] is a color mixed of purple, and black, but black dominates." As Bettarini (1, 465) points out, however, the association with the past participle of *perdere* (to lose) is inevitable.

"Arletta" is identified by Zampa (*Tutte*, xxviii and xxxvi) as the "occulted" addressee of "Vento e bandiere," "I morti," "Delta," and "Incontro" in *Ossi di seppia*; and of "Il balcone," "La casa dei doganieri," "Bassa marea," and "Punta del Mesco," and, according to Grignani (24–25), as the "nymph Entella" in "Accelerato" in *Le occasioni*; she also probably appears as the "dead girlchild Arethusa" of "L'estate." As Zampa puts it (*Tutte*, xxviii), she is "presented as a ghost [cf. the "fantasma che ti salva" of "In limine"] and as a ghost is destined to traverse [Montale's] entire *canzoniere*." Her engendering inspiration was a young woman named Anna degli Uberti (1904–59), whom Montale knew at Monterosso during the summers of 1919–23, when her father, Reserve Admiral Guglielmo degli Uberti, rented Lorenzo Montale's villa. Bettarini (2, 222) suggests that Montale's pseudonym for her may have been derived from the highly popular 1917 Ivor Novello operetta *Arlette*. Montale calls her "Annetta" and "La capinera," the blackcap, in his late poetry, where she is an increasingly dominant presence; eventually, all his feminine figures are subsumed in her. In 1977, the poet told Annalisa Cima (195), "The most real character [in my poetry] and the one who lasts through time (we meet her the first time in 'La casa dei doganieri' [*sic*] and later in *Diario del '71*) is Annetta. She will continue to live in a new poem, 'La capinera [non fu uccisa]' [in *QuaQ*]."

Annetta, in fact, is a character in several late poems: in "Una visita," which has the epigraph "Roma 1922," and in the brief "Postilla a 'Una visita'" (both translated in *Oth*, 75–77), which describe and muse on a typical awkward end to a youthful infatuation, and, more significantly, in "Annetta," a 1972 poem in *D71/2*, where Montale writes:

> Perdona, Annetta, sei dove tu sei
> (non certo tra di noi, i sedicenti
> vivi) poco ti giunge il mio ricordo.
> Le tue apparizioni furono per molti anni
> rare e impreviste, non certo da te volute.
> Anche i luoghi (la rupe dei doganieri,
> la foce del Bisagno dove ti trasformasti in Dafne)
> non avevano senso senza di te. . . .

(Pardon, Annetta, if where you are / [certainly not among us, the self-styled / living] my memory seldom reaches you. / For many years your apparitions were / rare and unforeseen, certainly unwished by you. / Even their locales [the cliff of the customs men, / the mouth of the Bisagno where you turned into Daphne] / had no meaning without you. . . .)

The poem concludes:

> Ma ero pazzo
> e non di te, pazzo di gioventù,
> pazzo della stagione più ridicola
> della vita. Ora sto
> a chiedermi che posto tu hai avuto
> in quella mia stagione. Certo un senso
> allora inesprimibile, più tardi
> non l'oblio ma una punta che feriva
> quasi a sangue. Ma allora eri già morta
> e non ho mai saputo dove e come.
> Oggi penso che tu sei stata un genio
> di pura inesistenza, un agnizione
> reale perché assurda. Lo stupore
> quando s'incarna è lampo che ti abbaglia
> e si spenge. Durare potrebbe essere
> l'effetto di un droga nel creato,
> in un medium di cui non si ebbe mai
> alcuna prova.

(But I was insane / and not with you, insane with youth, / insane with the most ridiculous season / of life. Now I want / to ask myself what place you had / in that season of mine. Clearly a meaning / inexpressible then, later / not oblivion but a wound that hurt / till it almost bled. But then you were already dead / and I never knew where and how. / Today I think you were a genius / of pure inexistence, a recognition / real because absurd. Amazement / when it becomes flesh is a flash that dazzles / and is spent. Its survival could be / the effect of a drug in the created, / in a medium of which there was never / any proof.)

Barile (2, 134–35): "Annetta . . . is the first [and, as Lonardi (107–11) has made clear, the primary] object in Montale's poetry, the template on which all the others are modeled: she is the experience through which the poet, using the language of love stilnovistically, expresses an intellectual experience; the first experience that is simultaneously amorous and mystical, intellectual, metaphysical, and rational all at once. An experience linked to his encounter with the poetry of Browning . . . in which love is the signifier of the Beyond. . . . Annetta-Arletta is at once first love and philosophical theme."

Zampa (*Tutte*, xxviii) tells us that Anna degli Uberti lived with her family in Rome, that Montale visited her there in 1924, and that she died there, unmarried, in 1959. "In all the poems for which she is the inspiration," however, and in all of Montale's comments about her (see note to "La casa dei doganieri"), "Arletta is a creature who no longer belongs to the world of the living. . . . The doubt whether this life of ours or that beyond the tomb is the real life has long made him have Arletta appear in a kind of limbo" (Bonora 2, 36). Zampa questions whether Montale could be being deliberately misleading, something of which he was certainly capable, and asks: "Did Montale consider Arletta 'dead,' that is, removed from his life, when in 1924 she stopped going to Monterosso?" (He notes further that Montale remained in touch with the degli Uberti family until at least 1931.) But Lonardi (99) associates this "eros almost without individuation, of which in fact Annetta is the genius, a genius 'of pure inexistence,' returning again and again in the late Montale," with Leopardi's first love, "Annetta-Silvia-Nerina," and argues convincingly (113–14) that Montale's Arletta-Annetta becomes conflated in his statements about her with the heroine of Leopardi's "A Silvia," Teresa Fattorini, who died young. Montale has said, "I always begin with the real, I'm incapable of inventing anything"; but he is capable of investing his own myth with an aura borrowed from the poetry of the great predecessors who inspired his work.

Zampa has nevertheless identified a fundamental aspect of Montale's portrayal of the female protagonists of his "novel": that once they are no longer present actors in Montale's drama, they effectively cease to exist. This is the fate of Clizia in *La bufera*; in "Due destini" (in *QuaQ*) she is described as having been "consumed by her God." After they have abandoned him, Montale's heroines are removed from the scene; but, in the eternal return of the repressed, they continue to haunt—and inspire—him, "absent," "suffocated," but still unshakable presences (see, e.g., " 'Ezekiel saw the Wheel . . .' ").

RIVIERE / SEACOASTS (March 1922)
One of Montale's earliest poems, later nearly repudiated in response to the critical consensus that its tone was out of keeping with the later work in *Ossi di seppia*, particularly after the additions of 1928. Montale (quoted in Cima, 193): "RIVIERE, which is the favorite poem of the incompetents, is the epilogue to a poetic phase that never existed." And in "Intentions" (*Sec*, 300–1): "Actually [*Ossi di seppia*] was a book that was hard to place. It contained poems that were unrelated to the intentions I've described, and lyrics (like RIVIERE) which constituted too premature a synthesis and cure and were followed by a successive relapse or disintegration (MEDITERRANEO [which revisits the same setting in another mood])."

Preparing the Ribet edition, Montale at one point planned to put RIVIERE among the "juvenile" poems and end the book with "Arsenio" (which he also considered excluding from the new edition). He wrote Sergio Solmi about his concerns about adding the new poems ("I morti," "Delta," and "Incontro") to the end of MERIGGI E OMBRE since "they show up RIVIERE even more in its juvenile bombast, with those pale camellias, those golden voices, etc.!!" (*Tutte*, xxxi).

Mengaldo (42): "The most complex example of [Montale's] linguistic-thematic affinity with D'Annunzio"—especially in the third stanza, where the "osso di seppia" appears. Mengaldo calls attention to the series of infinitives, both descriptive (as in "Meriggiare pallido e assorto") and optative, and notes that what is deeply D'Annunzian is "the desire to dissolve his own human nature into trees, nature, stone, sunset, etc."

Even more than the D'Annunzianisms, however, Bonora (1, 77) points out the originality of the Montalean "impasto" of elements of diverse lexical provenance: "neologisms derived from dialect or from other languages, the use of words in meanings willfully removed from the current one, boldly invented words, literary archaisms," e.g.: *stocchi*, horticultural terminology; *erbaspada*, Italianization of *erba spà*, Ligurian term for the American aloe; *asserpare*, Montalean invention, from *serpe*, snake; *spicciare*, ancient, Dantesque verb; *ramure*, derived from French, instead of *ramature*.

girasoli: Note this early use of an image that will become central in Montale's solar/religious mythology. Cf. also the "spring drunk with the sun," which evokes "Portami il girasole . . . ," and the praise of the sun in the last lines.

dorsi di colli . . . : Cf. the landscape of "Fine dell'infanzia," and of the book as a whole.

Oh allora sballottati . . . : Mengaldo (42–43) sees the linked chain of infinitives here as deriving from D'Annunzio's *Maia*, 103–4 (the trope is picked up in the last stanza and brings the poem—and the entire book—to its conclusion).

l'osso di seppia: Cf. D'Annunzio, *Alcyone*, "Ditirambo III," 28: "l'osso della seppia" (Mengaldo, 38).

un esito: The hoped-for *varco* glimpsed in "Delta."

LE OCCASIONI / THE OCCASIONS

First published by Einaudi, in Turin, in October 1939. Four poems (the motets "Lontano, ero con te quando tuo padre" and "Ti libero la fronte dai ghiaccioli," "Alla maniera di Filippo De Pisis nell'inviargli questo libro," and "Il ritorno") were added to the second Einaudi edition in 1940, which was republished by Mondadori (Milan) in 1949. (A chapbook, *La casa dei doganieri e altri versi*, comprising "La casa dei doganieri," "Cave d'autunno," "Vecchi versi," "Stanze," and "Carnevale di Gerti," had been published by Vallecchi [Florence] in 1932, after Montale won the Premio dell'Antico Fattore.)

Montale (in a note to the second Einaudi edition [*Op*, 894]): "The present volume contains almost all the poems written by me since 1928, the year that the second, augmented edition of *Ossi di seppia* appeared (the third edition of '31 had no additions); and the brackets 1928–1939 should be understood in this sense. In fact, two poems from *Le occasioni* go back to 1926 ["Vecchi versi" and "Dora Markus I"]; and two of the four poems added to this second edition belong to the first days of 1940.

"In the notes that follow, beyond offering the common reader a few indications of place and fact, I have taken care to clarify a few occasional passages where an excessive confidence in my material may have led me to lesser clarity."

Lonardi (120) quotes Montale's friend Sergio Solmi ("La poesia di Montale," in *Scrittori negl'anni: Saggi e note sulla letteratura del '900* [Milan: Il Saggiatore, 1963], 295) on the movement from *Ossi di seppia* to *Le occasioni*, from a "universalistic" poetry of youth, in which "the individual who as yet lacks an appreciable history, his roots still tangled in the magma of 'others,' starts to speak, posing a first identification of himself with everyone, the situations of his autobiography as exemplary, general situations," to "poetry of maturity now that it describes, in Rilke's words, the 'uniqueness' of a personal story."

For Contini (1, 70), "This book, wholly consecrated, as Montale once wrote me, using the phrase of Shakespeare, to an 'Only Begetter,' is in sum a long poem of absence and separation, not simply physical absence and separation from a beloved woman, but an Absence and Separation which, being dominant and exclusive, become metaphysical." If *Ossi di seppia* was dominated largely by "transcendent landscape, prejudged nature, not-feeling, and the ceased probability of feeling" (Contini 1, 54), expressed in certain prosaic qualities of its style (what Contini calls its *non-poesia*, not-poetry), the controlling emotion in *Le occasioni* is anguish, "infinite waiting . . . for the instant of improbable and gratuitous [i.e., contingent] liberation" (28). Again Contini (1, 86): "The distance from the absent one, which . . . seemed bearable when one foresaw that it was being buried in the usual indolence and tedium, can only be tolerated in a precise process of re-evocation. *Le occasioni* consists of this conversion from nothingness-inertia to the motive of waiting: no longer a book, so to speak, without content, but a collection of love songs."

The dedicatee of these songs and the dominant female presence in Montale's poetry is the fierce, proud, angelic figure whose name, Clizia, will be revealed only in *La bufera*, but who develops an identity and attributes and becomes invested with the characteristics of the waited-for other in *Le occasioni*. Her primary inspiration was Irma Brandeis (1905–90), an American scholar of Italian literature whom Montale met in Florence in 1933 and with whom he was closely involved before she returned to America on the eve of the promulgation of the Fascist racial laws in 1938 (like other characters in the book, Liuba and Dora Markus, she was Jewish). An alumna of Barnard College who attended Columbia University Graduate School, Brandeis taught Italian at Bard College from 1944 to 1969.

Le occasioni, which Montale dedicated to "I.B." beginning with its first Mondadori edition, is fundamentally a Florentine book, as profoundly influenced by its place and time of composition (Montale had moved to Florence in 1927) as was *Ossi di seppia*, not only in the actual settings of the poems—there are many references to Tuscan locales—but more profoundly in the early-Renaissance air that pervades its style and its poetics. Montale's appropriation (influenced to a degree by the investigations of Eliot and Pound) of the hermetic *trobar clus* (closed or secret song) of the Florentine *stilnovisti*, and of the chivalric imagery of the early Renaissance, which is strongly felt in the atmosphere of the city itself, reaches its apogee in the MOTTETTI. The discretion, the mask and artifice, of the poet's self-portrayal as a "cavaliere servente" suited Montale for a complex of personal and political as well as poetic reasons (*Le occasioni*, written in the increasingly ominous years of Fascism, first appeared a month after the Nazi invasion of Poland and the British and French declaration of war against Germany). His own "new style" imitated that of his illustrious early precursors in its indirection, difficulty, and occasional obscurity; hence the so-called hermeticism for which he was later criticized. (Dante and the *stilnovisti*, however, are not the only Florentine poets who influenced Montale; Foscolo echoes here, too, particularly in the classicizing pages of "Tempi di Bellosguardo.")

For Jacomuzzi (1, 5–6), "*Le occasioni* seems like Montale's truly experimental collection, his emergence from the line of the *crepuscolari* and the symbolist experience, both on the linguistic plane and on that of his attitude to things. Here is attempted, and, in the most successful results, achieved, an objective animation of reality that breaks the egocentric autonomy of the subject, rejects 'the illusion of the world as representation.' Testimony is entrusted to objects, and the 'negative' character of that testimony . . . has the cathartic function of purifying things from their acquired lyric suggestions, unchaining them from the semantic system of the late romantic and early-twentieth-century literary tradition.

"In *Le occasioni* the process tends to regress from discourse to the object, in the search for a 'more adherent' music and 'absolute expression,' [to quote the poet himself]. The object and the event close in on themselves: 'and became / one of those things immured forever / in a closed circle like the day' ('Vecchi versi'), close themselves off to developments in the very body of the language. The dependence on the verb and verbal attribution becomes slighter and tends to disappear in elliptical enumeration." (See examples and discussion of this highly characteristic device in "Altro effetto di luna," and the motets "Il ramarro, se scocca," "La gondola che scivola in un forte," and "La rana, prima a ritentar la corda.")

To Macrì (2, 15), "the contingency of *Le occasioni* as liberation from the determinism of nature and matrix of poem fractions expressed itself in the genres of the *motet, flash, madrigal* . . . , in a growing, neurotic, infinite diaristic-momentary fragmentation."

The "objective" poetics of the new period, which crystallize the Goethean "occasions" of contingent illumination that provide the book with its first principle of organization, are described by Montale in "Intentions" (*Sec*, 302): "I didn't think of pure lyric in the sense it later had in Italy, too, of a game of sound-suggestions; but rather of a result which would contain its motives without revealing them, or better without blabbing them. Granted that there exists a balance in art between the external and the internal, between the occasion and the work or object, it was necessary to express the object and conceal the occasion-spur. A new means, not Parnassian, of immersing the reader *in medias res*, a total absorption of one's intentions in objective results.

"Here, too, I was moved by instinct, not by a theory (Eliot's theory of the 'objective correlative' did not yet exist, I believe, in 1928, when [Mario Praz's translation of] my 'Arsenio' was published in [Eliot's review,] *The Criterion*). In substance, I don't feel the new book contradicted the achievements of the first: it eliminated some of the impurities and tried to attack the barrier between external and internal which seemed insubstantial to me even from the gnoseological point of view. Everything is internal *and* external for contemporary man: not that the so-called world is necessarily our representation. We live with an altered sense of time and space. In *Ossi di seppia* everything was attracted and absorbed by the fermenting sea, later I saw that the sea was everywhere, for me, and that even the classic architecture of the Tuscan hills was also in itself movement and flight. And in the new book I also continued my struggle to unearth another dimension in our weighty polysyllabic language, which seemed to reject an experience such as mine. I repeat that the struggle wasn't programmatic. Perhaps the unwelcome translating I was forced to do helped me. I've often cursed our language, but in it and through it I came to realize I am incurably Italian; and without regret."

Il balcone / The Balcony (1933)

Montale (*Op*, 895): "Part of the MOTTETTI [just as "In limine" was one of the *ossi brevi*]. It's printed at the beginning for its value as a dedication."

The poem's title is drawn from Baudelaire, perhaps ironically, since the relationship evoked by Montale is far more hesitant and remote than Baudelaire's richly sensual recollection. The dedicatee of the poem is "Arletta," i.e., Anna degli Uberti (see note to "Incontro"), as Montale told Rebay (2, 76).

mutare in nulla lo spazio / che m'era aperto: Guarnieri (Greco, 89) asked Montale if this meant "to annul the small possibility of life that had been offered me"; Montale struck out the word "small" and wrote "Sì." For Isella (2, 4), "nulla" is "tedium, programmatic indifference (typical of *Ossi di seppia*)." Marchese (1, 73) notes that "nulla" recalls "il nulla," "the negative miracle" of "Forse un mattino andando . . ."; "lo spazio / che m'era aperto" is a refiguring of the "varco," the way out, intimated in "Casa sul mare" and other poems at the end of *Ossi di seppia*.

il certo tuo fuoco: The dedicatee of the poem, as Montale "insisted" to Rebay (2, 76), "cannot yet be the Clizia of the last seventeen motets—more decisive, stronger, sure of herself and her mission, energetically alive; rather, she is a 'donna "crepuscolare," ' a woman marked by death. In reality, she was a person who died very young of an incurable disease" (but see note to "Incontro").

The fire imagery prefigures the angelic fire-and-ice of Clizia; the image recurs in the "luce-in-tenebra" of "Eastbourne."

quel vuoto . . . nulla: Cf. the same conjunction, "il nulla alle mie spalle, il vuoto dietro / di me," in "Forse un mattino andando. . . ." The situation of the poem is comparable to that of the motet "Il fiore che ripete," with its "spazio gettato tra me e te."

ogni mio tardo motivo: Montale (Greco, 27): "Every remaining reason for living."

l'ansia di attenderti vivo: Montale (ibid.): "The anxiety of continuing to live without you." Idiom of the "cavalier servente": *attendere* signifies not only waiting but waiting on, serving. Isella (2, 4) notes that the first edition had "estro" (sting) for "ansia," which links more closely with "si spunta"; cf. the "ansietà" of "Portami il girasole. . . ."

La vita che dà barlumi: Montale (ibid.): "The interior life, which appears and disappears off and on." In a poem of May 24, 1977, "Se al più si oppone il meno" (*QuaQ*), the "Capinera," i.e., Annetta-Arletta, says, "Anche il faro, lo vedi, è intermittente" (The lighthouse beam, too, you see, is intermittent); Bettarini (1, 510) sees the lighthouse (on the rock of Tino facing the Montale house at Monterosso) as the ultimate engendering source for "La vita che dà barlumi" and hence for the whole complex imagery of intermittent illumination that is, in effect, the primary metaphor in Montale's poetry. In one of his last poems, "I pressepapiers" (*QuaQ*), he writes: "lampi che s'accendono / e si spengono. È tutto il mio bagaglio" (light beams that are lit / and extinguished. They're all my baggage). For Lonardi (111), "the image of the extinguishing-lighting of the beams also leads to the first years; it is the recuperation of a mythic stamp latent since the most remote childhood in Montale's memory, that of the intermittent beam of a lighthouse, the old lighthouse that also carries us back, among other things, to 'La casa dei doganieri,' the house of the beacon, and to Annetta, 'quella del faro' [she of the beacon, title of another poem in *QuaQ*]."

quella che sola tu scorgi: The line can be read "the one only you see" or "the only one you see." Montale (Greco, 28) indicates the former.

ti sporgi: Montale (ibid.): "In my memory and imagination."

finestra che non s'illumina: Montale (ibid.): "It's 'also' a real window." Isella (2, 25) sees this as a critical response to Ungaretti's famous Nietzschean lines in "Mattino": "M'illuminò / d'immenso" (I was lit up / by immensity).

I .

Vecchi versi / Old Lines (1926)
Published in *Il Giornale di Genova* (December 23, 1931) under the title "Ricordo delle Cinque Terre" (Recollection of the Cinque Terre).

Angelini (2, 165): "Old lines, in effect, and not only because of their date. The omnipresence of the sea, of the marine landscape of Liguria familiar to the poet of *Ossi di seppia* (Vernazza, Corniglia, the rock of Tino, seen from the family house at Monterosso on the Riviera di Levante), the theme of childhood, down to the pessimism of the final stanza—all recall the first collection. Yet note the differences: the shrewdly calculated [hendecasyllabic] rhythm, of a slightly monotonous classicism, a certain external quality in the details—more encyclopedic than is properly consistent with lyric thought—a tenderness toward family memories unknown to the poet of *Ossi di seppia* (first appearance of the mother) which prefigures the poems of *La bufera*: 'A mia madre,' 'L'arca,' 'Voce giunta con le folaghe,' 'Dov'era il tennis . . . ,' a tenderness which diminishes into pessimism at the end—all of which demonstrates that for the poet of *Le occasioni* the present of *Ossi di seppia* has become the past."

Contini (1, 37–38) discerns a "double register" of memory at work in the poem: the "excess of chorography" (Tino, Corniglia, Vernazza), in key with the loose hendecasyllable "with its possibilities of indefinite prolongation" in piling up an "exhaustive, . . . quantitative and not qualitative" wealth of evocative detail, when in fact it is the "subterranean objects, grown in the memory, which evoke the ending, correcting the poet's error and distinguishing between the two sets of recollections." In the later *occasioni*—see "Buffalo," below—the poet will "conceal the occasion-spur" and simply "express the object."

la farfalla: Contini (1, 68) calls it "the moth of death."

la costa raccolta: Literally enclosed, protected. The landscape is so described in "Crisalide," "Fine dell'infanzia," and elsewhere.

pitòsfori: Angelini (2, 166): "Term invented by the poet. The real word is *pittospori*, . . . which denotes bushes with many branches, with evergreen leaves. . . . The undulating pittosporum evoked by the poem is cultivated in gardens; its white flowers, which open in profusion in springtime, spread an odor of jasmine when pressed."

Poi tornò . . . : Bettarini (1, 462) notes that the moth reappears transfigured as a bat in the story "Il pipistrello" in *FdiC*.

le cose che chiudono in un giro / sicuro: Cf. the constricting "cerchio" of "Incontro," "Costa San Giorgio," and elsewhere. Isella (2, 14): "Minimal fragments which . . . emerge out of [an amorphous reality], only to disappear into the abyss: endowed with an autonomous objectivity of their own, closed in themselves like the sun in its orbit and . . . indelibly preserved and magnified in memory." The sudden, improvisatory moment of perception is an "occasion" typical of the poems of this period, which foreshadow the later "flashes" and snapshots of *La bufera*.

una / vita che disparì sotterra: Cf. the "sommersa" of "Incontro"—perhaps an allusion to Arletta. Lonardi (54) points out Foscolo's *Dei sepolcri* as the source for "sotterra," which also occurs in "I morti."

coi volti familiari: Cf. "L'arca."

alla tartana: A single-masted Mediterranean coasting vessel with one lateen sail.

al segno del torrente: Isella (2, 15): "Objective correlative of that which, in a living-death, has the power to leave an authentic, vital sign." Cf. the groove etched by the spinning top in "Palio."

Buffalo (1929)

Montale (Angelini 2, 166): "Parisian velodrome, situated in the suburbs, at Montrouge [and named for the city on Lake Erie (Isella 2, 17)]. We're at a race of 'stayers' [i.e., a long-distance event, a *nocturne*]—cyclists preceded by motorcycles who break the resistance of the air for them. They run for 100/200 km and can achieve considerable speeds."

Cary (286) describes this as a characteristic *occasione* because of "its nervous and sinewy speed, its immediacy, its effect of private life revealed, its dramatic thrust. . . . Clearly a real risk of obscurity is run. The problem . . . is simply a paucity of information, plus the poem's own self-confident speed, plus, above all, the novice reader's fear of trusting his own guesses which, after all, are directed and influenced by the poem itself." As Becker (53) puts it, "This technique . . . basically means cutting away those 'metaphysical' statements that are so often paired with the physical illustration of *Ossi di seppia*."

Cary (285–86) himself supplies the following explanatory details: "*Le Six-day* [bicycle race] . . . ranked high in the period as the last word in fashionable imports from the U.S.A.

(hence the exotic name of the arena). It had its obligatory jazz band, its loudspeakers and limelights, flask parties and film stars, cacophony of hot music, cheers, imprecations, and the roar of motorcycles preceding the bicyclists. . . . The first twelve lines are an impersonal inventory of the inferno of this *dolce vita* [Montale (Greco, 29) refers to it as a "landscape of Acheron"], the milling mobs, the shouts, the violent alteration of light and shadow, smoke arising from the 'burning gulf,' the bright blond wood of the track, which I take to be the gleaming arc or arch, suggesting an Acheron at the side of which the giggling and hysterical damned line up."

It is worth noting that the infernal scene here near the outset of *Le occasioni* resonates with the hellish storm of "La bufera" at the beginning of *La bufera*; in both poems a sign or gesture of some sort, in this case an exotic name, lifts the poet out of his fugue state into another reality. For a discussion of the importance of names in Montale (as in the poem that follows), see Grignani, 38–46.

Keepsake (1929)

Montale (*Op*, 896): "Reduced to their pure nominal essence, *flatus vocis*, the characters from the following operettas return here: *Fanfan la Tulipe* [Louis Varney, 1882], *The Geisha* [Sidney Jones, 1896; with Miss Molly, Takimini, and Imary], *Surcouf* [Robert Planquette, 1887], *Les Cloches de Corneville* [Planquette, 1877; featuring Gaspard], *La Cigale et la Fourmie* [Edmond Audran, 1886], *Fatinitza* [Franz von Suppé, 1876], *La Mascotte* [Audran, 1880; Pippo is called Tonio in the Italian version], *Les Brigands* [book by Meilhac and Halévy, music by Offenbach, 1869], *Il Marchese del Grillo* [Giovanni Mascetti, 1889], *Frühlings Luft* (in Italian *Primavera scapigliata*) [Ernst Reiterer, adapting music of Josef Strauss, 1903; with Zeffirino], *Il Campanello dello speziale* [Donizetti, 1836], *Les Mousquetaires au Couvent* [Varney, 1880], *Die Dollarprinzessen* [Leo Fall, 1907; with Van Schlick (*sic*)], *La Fille de Madame Angot* [Charles Lecocq, 1872; with Larivaudière and Pitou], *Robinson Crusoe* [Offenbach, 1887]."

Montale to Giorgio Zampa, 1975 (*Su*, 603): "Reread 'Keepsake'; it's half my life. But according to Gargiulo, it lacks feeling. Imagine!"

Angelini (2, 167), who identified the composers and their characters (the Doll who becomes a clock is from Offenbach's *Les Contes d'Hoffmann*, 1881), sees the poem as full of ironic references to the poet's beloved "enfances musicales" and related to the "innocent music" of the "Poesie per Camillo Sbarbaro," "Carnevale di Gerti," and others.

For Cary (284), " 'Keepsake' is just that: a catalogue of *moments musicaux* made into hendecasyllables and kept 'for luck,' a fairly private and slight 'charm' whose odd vivacity endows it with a geniality which, at least, is public. It stands by itself, a *cul de sac* or extreme, in the *opera* of Montale." Yet this keepsake also bears a resemblance to the "amulet," the "white ivory mouse" of "Dora Markus" and the "rainbow" or "ash" of "Piccolo testamento": meaningless things in themselves, yet essential for the maintenance of the self; and its inconsequential list prefigures the catalogues of *Le occasioni* and *La bufera*.

Lindau (1932)

Lindau is a resort on Lake Constance in Bavaria. Isella (2, 25): "The first of a series of 'premotets,' written in the absence of the loved one." The saraband is one of the many exotic dances ("sardana," "farandola," "trescone," etc.) which in Montale indicate strife, especially in the political realm; Bonora (2, 112) asserts it is to be construed not as the stately court dance of the seventeenth and eighteenth centuries but rather as the "rapid, unrestrained movement" of its Spanish incarnation. (It is also evoked in "Il ritorno" and "Dov'era il tennis. . . .") Isella (2, 26) notes that the term is used by extension to denote "great confusion, a collocation of disparate movements." Given its date, setting, and imagery ("smoking torches," "open square"), the poem may refer in a muted way to the rise of Fascism (cf. also "Verso Vienna").

Bagni di Lucca (1932)
A noted resort with hot springs twenty-three kilometers from Lucca.

In a version of the poem published in 1933 (*Op*, 896), the third stanza read: "Marmi, rameggi, e tu / gioventù a capofitto / nel fossato" (Marble, branches, and you / youth headlong / into the ditch). "The last herd" in the penultimate line was "The last man."

This example shows how Montale's revisions tend to work to conceal the theme of the poem (anxiety about aging, mortality—as in "Eastbourne," 1933), leaving "objective correlatives" in the depiction of autumn.

il tonfo dei marroni: Cf. "il tonfar delle castagne" in "La bellezza cangiante," Montale's translation of Hopkins's "Pied Beauty" (*QuaT*).

borea: Note hypermetric rhyme with *cuore*.

Cave d'autunno / Autumn Quarries (1931)
Montale (Angelini 2, 168): "The shining swarm constitutes 'another moon effect' [see poem below]; a lunar flock appears again in 'Bassa marea': images of light which pass and *graze*."

Montale (Greco, 30): "The swarm of shadows-lights of the moon's effects will cross the distant sky, will move on after having pillaged us."

Isella (2, 30): "Moon effects, precisely illusory images . . . Connoted by a *surplus* of baroque artifice (in the style of seventeenth-century English metaphysical poetry), . . . lucid objective correlatives of a double state of mind: of an entirely fictitious life, a life that is not-life, and of a firm resistance against the assault of fate. The cold that buries the heart will thaw in the heat of feeling; the malevolent celestial influences will disappear."

la bontà d'una mano: To Becker (56) this and the image of water wearing out the stones in "Lindau" are "intimations . . . of the Manichean struggle between good and evil, light and darkness, that will be elaborated in subsequent poems with much greater directness." Cf. the "mano straniera" of " 'Ezekiel saw the Wheel. . . .' "

la ciurma luminosa: Isella (2, 31) finds the source of the image in a Latin poem by the English metaphysical poet Richard Crashaw translated by Montale's friend Mario Praz: "Hic grex velleris aurei / Grex pellucidus aetheris, / Qui noctis nigra pascua / Puris morsibus atterit" (Here is the flock of the golden fleece, / the shining flock of heaven; / which browses the black pasture of night / with pure bites). Isella notes the recurrence of the image in diffracted form in the "mandria lunare" of "Bassa marea" and in "Corrispondenze"; cf. also the "orda invisibile" of "Fuscello teso dal muro."

Altro effetto di luna / Another Moon Effect (1932)
Isella (2, 32): Each image in the second stanza here alludes to "an impetus, an initiative, a daring that has failed." In the two poems that make up the pair, "Cave d'autunno" was dominated by actions, but here, more typically, verbs are all but absent: an early example of a Montalean catalogue.

feluca: A narrow, fast Mediterranean sailing vessel propelled by oars and lateen sails.

Verso Vienna / Near Vienna (1933)

Montale (Greco, 30): "Tables of an outdoor restaurant, at Linz on the Danube."

The first anticipation of Clizia in Montale's work, in what Rebay (3, 186) calls a "discreet allusion to her European roots." The poem describes a trip to Austria, homeland of Irma Brandeis's forebears (though it seems to have been made before Montale met her). Marcenaro and Boragina (135) quote Montale's October 10, 1932, letter to Lucia Rodocanachi: "I wrote no one on my trip. Nuremberg is very tiresome but Vienna is lovely and German women seem less ugly to me than expected."

Becker (55) notes the relationship of the dachshund here to the symbolic jackals of the motet "La speranza di pure rivederti"; dogs are constant familial symbols throughout Montale (see "L'arca," "Da una torre"). The figure of the swimmer appears in the story "Sul limite" in *Farf*.

Carnevale di Gerti / Gerti's Carnival (1928)

Montale (letter to Angelo Barile, July 6, 1932 [*Op*, 898]): "Gerti [Gertruden Frankl, 1902–89] was and is a lady from Graz. Her husband [Carlo Tolazzi, an engineer from Trieste] was a soldier (reference to the barracks) and she saw him only on furlough. On New Year's Day we had cast lots for a few presents for our friends in Trieste and for them we'd also made a kind of prediction that is fairly popular in the north. Throw a spoonful of melted lead for each person into a cup of cold water and guess his fate based on the strange shapes the lead takes when it solidifies. The rest (regression in time, etc.) is clear. This poem ought to have remained 'private'; this explains its diffuseness and its relative obscurity, unusual in me. Still, I was told it was moving even to the uninitiated and so was induced to publish it."

Montale (Greco, 34): " 'Your distant shores' may also be the shores of Trieste, where Gerti lived, but Gerti was from Graz, Austria. It is she who occupies part II of 'Dora Markus.' "

Isella (2, 37) tells us that Gerti, after studying piano in Vienna, danced with Mary Wigman in Dresden, worked for Fritz Lang on the making of *Masquerade*, and, above all, followed her passion for photography.

An early fragment in French on the same theme, later dated 1928 and carrying the dedication "Pour Mme. Gerti T[olazzi]. F[rankl]. / 1er fragment," was published in *Alt* (tr. in *Oth*, 116). Marcenaro and Boragina (103): "Gerti, in Montale's poetic imagination, must have seemed to him like a *cobold*, a mysterious little woman capable of revealing, through witchcraft, the meaning of the times."

iridi trascorrenti: Montale indicated to Contini (*Op*, 898) that the "iridi" here are confetti. The word will acquire powerful connotations in *La bufera*.

dal ponte . . . : Montale (Greco, 30): The detail indicates that the poem is set in Florence. The setting is reminiscent of those of the Florentine "Tempi di Bellosguardo" and "La primavera hitleriana."

una tremula / bolla d'aria: Isella (2, 41): "Gerti, the 'white sorceress' [Cambon's term, in Cima, 55], seems suspended, in accordance with her immature creature's desires, in a 'quivering bubble of air and light' which exalts and defends her grace." The image of a fragile reality held within a bubble goes back to the early "Elegia" (tr. in *Oth*, 83), and the image can be found elsewhere, e.g., in "Le processioni del 1949."

(Oh il tuo Carnevale . . .): Cf. Rimbaud, "Les étrennes des orphelins": "Oh! que le jour de l'an sera triste pour eux!" Montale's poem, as Bettarini (1, 481–82) demonstrates, shares

other characteristics with Rimbaud's, including the old-fashioned "giorno dell'Anno" in line 38.

Verso Capua / Near Capua (1938)

A companion piece to "Verso Vienna," this time directly addressing Clizia. The scene is on the bank of the Volturno River near Capua in Campania, not far from Caserta (see "Nel Parco di Caserta").

la bandiera / stellata: Clizia's scarf, with its small white circles on a blue ground (see notes to "Il giglio rosso"), here becomes the American star-spangled banner, symbol of her nationality, and of freedom. Brandeis, whom Becker (55) calls Montale's "Jewish Beatrice," left Italy in 1938, the year of the promulgation of the Fascists' racial laws. She thus enters the book dedicated to her in the act of departing (Rebay 3, 186).

A Liuba che parte / To Liuba, Leaving (1938 [*Op*], but Isella [2, 49] says the poem dates from May 1939)

Montale (*Op*, 899): "Ending of an unwritten poem. Antecedent *ad libitum*. It will be useful to know that Liuba—like Dora Markus—was Jewish."

The powerful contrast of Roman (lar, protective divinity of the home) and Jewish (ark, home of the homeless) themes is noted by Becker (69); the conjunction of classical and Biblical imagery, usually associated with the Jewish-Christian figure of Clizia, will intensify in *La bufera*.

The contradictory "information" circulated about the origins of the poem is typical of Montale's mischievous attitude toward critics. Rebay (1, 33ff.) demonstrates that Liuba Blumenthal was a friend of Bobi Bazlen's and known to Montale (Isella [2, 49] says her maiden name was Flesch, and that she was a Carpathian Jew who was an intimate of Bazlen's and that in her youth in Vienna she acted with Max Reinhardt); Montale, however, told his biographer (Nascimbeni, 115) that Liuba was a Jewish woman he encountered at the Florence train station, leaving for England because of the imminent persecution of her coreligionists, while to Avalle (95), he wrote: "Liuba is an invention. I believe she was already a British subject and living in London at the time of the persecutions. I didn't see her leave, I know nothing of her possible baggage. Thus what I told Guarnieri—'[The cage] contained personal effects, but it recalls the feast of the cricket, which is bought in a cage' [Greco, 31]—means nothing. It's possible that the idea of the cricket is a memory of that holiday in Florence, when crickets are sold in cages. But everything goes into the soup in poetry."

Lonardi (129) shows that certain of the rhymes (*focolare/lare, cappelliera/leggera*) recreate rhymes in Foscolo's "All'amica risanata"—signs of a like-minded imitation of "neo-classical madrigalism"—while Avalle, taking note of the copious internal rhyming in this brief lyric (*consiglia/famiglia; lare/focolare; ciechi/rechi; leggera/cappelliera*), has with great ingenuity reset the poem into ten lines which constitute a *ballata*, a popular sung verse form with a refrain. According to Avalle's formulation, the refrain would be the first line, "Non il grillo ma il gatto," with the following rhyme scheme: X-ABAB-CDCD-X:

> Non il grillo ma il gatto
> del focolare
> or ti consiglia,
> splendido lare

della dispersa tua famiglia.
La casa che tu rechi
con te ravvolta, gabbia o cappeliera?,
sovrasta i ciechi
tempi come il flutto arca leggera—
e basta al tuo riscatto.

Avalle (98) goes on to say, "one may ask whether this retrieval is the result of a calculated decision, whether the poet, in sum, set out to truly 'parody' the genre of the *ballata*, later shuffling the cards (a hypothesis he has explicitly denied), or whether it is a case of a form which reflowered unconsciously in the poet's memory during the act of composition of the poem"—a solution which Avalle prefers, and which is consistent with Montale's own musical orientation. Whether or not Avalle's highly imaginative conjecture is correct, it underscores the importance of internal rhyme in Montale's poems, and the sense of contrapuntal composition such rhymes suggest, particularly in brief lyrics like the MOTTETTI. (See note to "La casa dei doganieri" for a similar case of "contrapuntal" structure.)

il grillo: The cricket on Pinocchio's hearth, "voice of wise prudence who speaks as the protective deity of the family" (Isella 2, 50).

arca leggera: Cf. "L'arca." Montale to Giacomo Debenedetti (1926) (Grignani, 60): "In Milan I'm thought to be Jewish, because of the Svevo 'case.' If it were possible to be Jewish without knowing it, this would be my 'case'; such is my capacity for suffering, and my sense of the ark, more than 'home,' made of a few affections and memories that could follow me everywhere, unobscured." Montale's identification with the Jews as oppressed victims and as preservers of a tradition intensifies in the pages of *Le occasioni* and especially in *La bufera*; the theme is touched on in the note to "Iride."

Bibe a Ponte all'Asse (1937)

Trattoria on the Greve River (possibly also the setting for "Sulla Greve" in *La bufera*) on the southern outskirts of Florence, near the monastery of Galluzzo. Montale (Angelini 2, 168): "*Bibe*, Latin imperative = drink. It was both the name of the host and his sign"—a typically Montalean *senhal* (signal; see note to MOTTETTI), and no doubt the occasion for the poem.

lieve: Isella (2, 51), who notes the Horatian elegance—and the Carduccian style and rhythm—of the epigram, derives the adjective from the Latin and translates the word as *discreto*, i.e., moderate, good-natured.

Rùfina: Village in the Val di Sieve, twenty kilometers northeast of Florence, where an excellent Chianti is produced.

Dora Markus

Montale (*Op*, 901): "The first part survives in a fragmentary state. It was published without my knowledge in '37. Thirteen years later (and it shows) I gave it a conclusion, if not a center."

Montale (Greco, 34): "[Gerti (see "Carnevale di Gerti")] occupies the second part of Dora M. I never knew Dora; I made that first bit of a poem at the invitation of Bobi Bazlen, who sent me a snapshot of her legs." Rebay (1, 48) quotes a September 25, 1928, letter from Bazlen to Montale about "a friend of Gerti, with *marvelous legs. Make her a poem.* She's called Dora Markus"; Marcenaro and Boragina (103) indicate that the photo was in fact by Gerti.

Teresa Serrao, writing in *La Repubblica*, October 9, 1997, 41, indicates that the real-life Dora Markus was born into a prosperous family in Hungary in 1904, and was sent to Vienna to study, where, presumably, she met Gerti.

Rebay (4, 162) argues convincingly that Gerti is actually the "undeclared model" for Dora, whom he also associates with Irma Brandeis, the primary inspiration for Clizia. Grignani (20–21) points out that a later poem published in *QuaQ* (1977) and called, significantly, "Dall'altra sponda" (From the Other Shore), refers explicitly to Gerti within Dora's context, adding, "As always, the late Montale deprives the critic of the pleasure of the adventurous hypothesis."

(Bettarini [1, 491] suggests that Dora's name evokes that of Teodora, the Byzantine empress portrayed in the mosaics of Ravenna.)

I. (Montale claimed 1926, but 1928 is plausible)

Porto Corsini: The port of Ravenna.

la tua patria vera: Carinthia, the Austrian province, not far beyond the shores of Istria across the Adriatic from Ravenna. Or, perhaps, as Arrowsmith suggests (2, 140), her "true homeland," as a Jew, is Palestine, in which case "Oriental anxiousness" has a double meaning. "But the combination of 'invisible shore' with 'your true fatherland' suggests at least a hint of later Montalean transcendence." Cf. the "prode lontane" of "Carnevale di Gerti."

una dolce / ansietà d'Oriente: Reference to the Byzantine mosaics of Ravenna's churches, the figures of which display a characteristic anxious expression.

La tua irrequietudine: Macrì (1, 103) observes that Dora's traits here prefigure those of Clizia the stormy petrel/angel of annunciation: "The sweetness-tempest of Dora smolders for years and becomes fire and blood in the 'flight' ["volo"] of *La bufera*."

lago / d'indifferenza: The Dantean trope ("il lago del cor," *Inferno* I, 20) appeared earlier in the "Tramontana" section of "L'agave su lo scoglio."

II. (1939)

Montale to Bazlen (May 7, 1939; quoted in Rebay 4, 163): "After 13 [*sic*] years I've given a coda to 'Dora Markus' and I'm sending it to you; it ought to make a diptych, but with the explanatory dates. . . . I find that the poem isn't terrible in itself and that it's rescued from the accusation of neo-post-crepuscularism by the post-Anschluss flavor that is lightly diffused throughout [the German annexation of Austria occurred in March 1938]. . . . In any case, it's certain that the value of the diptych (as such) would be, rather than diminished, enhanced by the difference in style. In reality, it has the flavor of the past.

"I'm sending you the first part, too, to check the effect of the *pendant*. Does Carinthia have lakes? And the lady is a mixture of almost Gerti with Brandeis-type ancestors; the reference to Ravenna makes for comparison with the first part."

un interno / di nivee maioliche: Lonardi (142 and passim in chapter) discusses the bourgeois interior, derived from Baudelaire, as "the locus of ornament and of the feminine gaze," and hence of epiphany in Montale; see "Vecchi versi," "Nuove stanze," "Gli orecchini," and elsewhere.

errori / imperturbati: Latinate; a reference to the historical wandering of the Jews.

grandi / ritratti d'oro: Marchese (1, 87): "A touching recollection . . . of the Hapsburg *felix Austria* destroyed by World War I." The "fedine" were long whiskers worn as a mark of fidelity to the Hapsburg dynasty (Isella 2, 61).

Il sempreverde / alloro: Marchese (1, 87): "The laurel is the classical symbol of poetry, here reduced to the prosaic and domestic herb, to indicate nevertheless the resistance [*resiste* in Italian means both "endures" and "resists"] of tradition [to oppression]."

la voce: Isella (2, 61): "The so-called voice of the blood, which cannot lie."

una fede feroce: Montale to Bazlen (May 11, 1939) (Isella 3, 190): "Not only the faith of the *Gauleiter* [representative of Nazi Germany in post-Anschluss Austria] but every sort of coherence and logic destined to *froisser* [wound] Dora, woman of the moment."

Montale (Greco, 34): "The savage faith coincides with Gerti's retiring into an imaginary Carinthia. There's not a condemnation of all faith, but the recognition that for her everything is over and she must resign herself to her destiny. Still, there remains a hiatus between the unexploded life of Dora and Gerti's already lived life. The fusion of the two figures isn't perfect; something happened in midcourse which isn't expressed and which I don't understand."

Alla maniera di Filippo De Pisis nell'inviargli questo libro / In the Style of Filippo De Pisis, on Sending Him This Book (1940)
De Pisis (1896–1956) was a brilliant painter (and a poet), originally a disciple of his fellow Ferrarese Giorgio De Chirico, who later became a kind of latter-day post-impressionist. Marchese (1, 88): "His brushstroke, rapid and nervous (hence the 'sgorbiature' alluded to in Montale's poem), aims to render the emotion of a fragment of reality caught with vivid immediacy." Montale clearly saw affinities between De Pisis's method and his own style of description in *Le occasioni*. Lonardi (169–70) quotes an article by Montale (" 'Poesie' di Filippo De Pisis," 1943 [*Sm/P*, 600–3]) in which he praises De Pisis's "strong positive obstacle of an external subject matter to dominate" and "that prodigious pictorial stenography . . . like a hen's foot, which is his form, and his syntax." (See also a 1954 article by Montale, "Letture," a review of De Pisis's *Poesie* and Ottiero Ottieri's *Memorie dell'incoscienza* [*SM/P*, 1701–2].)

The "style of . . . De Pisis" that Montale is honoring here is "his nervous, contrasting fauvism, his whiplash pictorial style, his 'exaggerated' mark" (Lonardi, 170). When Montale became a painter in the postwar years, both his subject matter and his style, though rougher, less elegant, and less energetic, owed more than a little to De Pisis. Montale owned a 1940 still life by the artist, called *Il beccaccino*, which was given to the poet in exchange for this poem (Isella 2, 65).

l'Arno balsamo fino: Lapo Gianni was a Florentine *stilnovo* poet, a friend of Dante active between 1298 and 1328 (he figures in Dante's famous *plazer* to Cavalcanti, "Guido, i' vorrei . . ."). Montale's epigraph is drawn from Lapo's *plazer*-like *canzone*, "Amor, eo chero mia donna in domino." Marchese (1, 88): " 'l'Arno balsamo fino' expresses a fantastic desire, for in reality the water of the river is muddy and polluted. Montale makes use of the lines in a far different sense, not perhaps without irony." (See note to "Quasi una fantasia" concerning Montale's debt to the stilnovistic tradition of the *plazer*.) Isella (2, 63–64) sees the poem as an encrypted motet for Clizia (*rami* is an anagram of Irma, and the imagery of the poem— cold, river, feathers, etc.—figures in other poems dedicated to her).

Una botta di stocco: Literally, a rapier thrust.

piume: Cf. the feathers of "Il gallo cedrone" and of other Clizian texts.

scrìmolo: D'Annunzian, derived from an analogous situation in *Alcyone*, "Ditirambo IV" (Mengaldo, 39).

sgorbiature: Marks made with a gouge or woodworking tool.

Nel Parco di Caserta / In the Park at Caserta (1937)

Montale (*Op*, 903): "Re: the Mothers, see the (somewhat insufficient) explanations of Goethe."

    Caserta: Angelini (2, 169): "The Versailles of the kings of Naples, started in 1752 by Vanvitelli by order of Charles III"—near the setting of "Verso Capua." The park is decorated with groups of classical statuary.

    e un sole: The image of the sun as ultimate solvent in this "illusory scene raised over the void" (Sergio Solmi, quoted by Isella [2, 66]) is frequent in Montale, particularly in *Ossi di seppia* (see "Marezzo" and, in a different sense, "Portami il girasole . . ."), but moonlight can also achieve a similar effect (as in "Altro effetto di luna").

    chi passa: Isella (2, 68) notes the kinship with "il passante" in "La farandola dei fanciulli . . . ," another "human plant" likewise severed from "old roots."

    delle Madri: Arrowsmith (2, 141): "Montale is alluding to the famous sequence in *Faust* II, Act i (lines 6173ff.), in which Faust and Mephistopheles descend to the realm of the 'Mothers,' Goethe's *matrices*"—"haughty goddesses who, beyond space or time, guard the eternal essences in which, in the incessant universal metamorphosis, everything has its origin and demise" (Isella 2, 66). Theirs is (Arrowsmith 2, 141 again) "the realm of Chaos, that pullulating void from which the Mothers (not unlike Platonic Ideas) produce forms or copies for the phenomenal world. Depending on one's viewpoint, Faust *descends* (into Chaos) or *ascends* (into the heavenly void of Being). 'Can you conceive of total Void?' Mephistopheles asks Faust, to which Faust replies that this void has the smell of 'witch's kitchen' about it: 'Did I not learn and teach vacuity?' But Mephistopheles darkly dismisses this response. The void of the Mothers is of a different order. But 'in the distant eternal void [there is] *Nothing*! Your footstep falls without a sound. And there is no solid ground wherever you stop.' [And later (lines 6283–88): "A flaming tripod will finally tell you that you have reached the lowest depth of the abyss. In its light you will see the Mothers. Some are seated, some stand and move as the case requires. Formation, transformation, eternal game of the eternal womb."] The Goethe sequence is, as Montale acknowledges, insufficient but probably deliberately so. 'The Mothers,' like the Chaos from which, in the classical mind, all forms of being spring, or the (chaotic) modern void of the Copernican universe, are a mystery toward which the mind—whether rooted in the matrix of the 'unraveling' monkey-puzzle tree or the quotidian world of real mothers with real kitchen-roughened knuckles—can only grope with transcendental striving."

    According to Isella (2, 68), Montale here has associated the classical Fates with Goethe's Mothers. Montale used the same image of knocking on a wall to discover empty spaces within in a 1923 article about Emilio Cecchi's criticism of Pascoli: "His knuckles have tapped justly on the empty spaces in the wall" (*SM/P*, 11).

Accelerato / Local Train (1938)

The *accelerato* is the maddeningly misnamed local train of the Italian railway system. The poem describes a journey from Genoa to Monterosso, hence a return, metaphorically, to the past. Like "L'anguilla" and some other poems ("Corno inglese," the motet "Al primo chiaro . . ."), it is composed of a single complex sentence.

    la cenere del giorno: Cf. "la cenere degli astri" of "Arsenio."

    qualche foro d'azzurro: Slits in the railway tunnel running along the steep Ligurian coastline, to let in light and air. The image recurs in the motet "Al primo chiaro . . ."; the tunnel can be found in "Bassa marea."

la ninfale / Entella: The river Entella flows into the bay of Genoa near the town of Lavagna, between Sestri Levante and Chiavari. It is mentioned in *Purgatorio* XIX, 100–2. Arrowsmith (2, 141): "The allusion here is characteristic of Italian baroque personifications of pastoral landscapes, and . . . suggests a return to a lost paradise."

Grignani (24–25) sees the "nymph Entella" as a hidden reference to Arletta (see note to "Incontro") and in general notes that in *Le occasioni* "an insistence on Ligurian place-names (which almost never figured in *Ossi di seppia*, even though that landscape is its institutional frame) corresponds to the burying of the Name [of Arletta] and almost substitutes for it. It's likely she is the interlocutor addressed in the poem."

II. MOTTETTI / MOTETS

Montale, writing to Bazlen (May 31, 1939) (Isella 1, 14), referred to the MOTTETTI as an "autobiographical novelette," calling them "the most decent group of love lyrics to appear in Ausonia [i.e., Italy] in a number of years"; but he criticized as a "psychological" defect the lack, after the third motet, "of all pretext of quasi-narrative development," all the rest continuing "in the same key on the same theme." What Montale is getting at is that the poetics of the "snapshot" that *Le occasioni* represents have strict limitations; the MOTTETTI, which gather a string of such moments sequentially, represent an attempt, but only a partially successful one, at overcoming these limits.

The early-Renaissance flavor of the MOTTETTI is implied in the very name of the sequence, since motets were "vocal music of [thirteenth-century] liturgic origins which was later secularized and appropriated for the amorous song of the troubadours" (Cary, 304). The vocabulary and angle of approach of many of the poems, and the theme of devotion to a distant loved one, are derived from stilnovistic practice (itself a version of the courtly love tradition), the great type of which is Dante's dedication to the impossibly remote Beatrice. (Another source is D'Annunzio's "Madrigali dell'estate" [Summer Madrigals] in *Alcyone*, also an influence on the *ossi brevi*, as we have seen.) *Amor de lonh*, love from afar, is the defining convention of stilnovistic poetry (see Cary, 304): since the beloved is often married or otherwise unavailable, the use of occult symbols, symbolic names, and other covering devices (*trobar clus*) becomes standard practice. The "sign" to which Montale makes reference several times in the sequence corresponds to the *senhal*, or signal, from the beloved that the suitor's attentions are welcome.

It is worth noting that in the late thirties, when most of the MOTTETTI were composed, Montale's friend Gianfranco Contini was preparing a new edition of Dante's *Rime* (it appeared in 1939), and it is likely that Montale's interest in the *stilnovisti* and their practices was intensified by his friend's research; hence the reference to Lapo Gianni in the poem for De Pisis and, more important, the citations and even the methodology of the MOTTETTI; Montale's "hermeticism" starts here, in the continuation and re-elaboration of a long-standing tradition.

Sobre el volcán la flor: "Above the volcano the flower." The quotation, which recalls the Leopardian daisy of MEDITERRANEO ("Questo pezzo di suolo non erbato / s'è spaccato perche nascesse una margherita"), is from the *Rimas* of the Spanish poet Gustavo Adolfo Bécquer (1836–70; also quoted in "Dov'era il tennis . . ."):

> Come vive esa rosa que has prendido
> junto a tu corazón?

Nunca hasta ahora contemplé en la tierra
sobre el volcán la flor.

(How does this rose you picked live / next to your heart? / Never till now have I seen on earth / the flower above the volcano.)

Montale admired the *Rimas* for their musicality (they also employ alternating hendecasyllables and *settenari*, like the MOTTETTI and much of the rest of Montale's poetry) and "for the strongly suggestive fusion . . . of the world of reality and the world of the dream" (Isella 1, 16).

Lo sai: debbo riperderti e non posso / You know: I'm going to lose you again (1934)
The addressee of the first three motets, all of them from 1934, was not the Arletta who is the inspiration for "Il balcone" but, according to Montale (Greco, 33), "a Peruvian who was, however, of Genoese origin and lived in Genoa," whom Montale met in Florence in 1929–30 (Rebay 2, 75). Forti (2, 56) identifies her as Paola Nicoli, to whom a number of poems in *Ossi di seppia* ("In limine," "Ciò che di me sapeste," "Tentava la vostra mano la tastiera," "Crisalide," "Marezzo," and "Casa sul mare") as well as "Sotto la pioggia" in *Le occasioni* are dedicated. In Nascimbeni (74) Montale calls her "a splendid woman: she had been an actress and everyone who got near her fell in love with her. She was married to a weak, defenseless man: they went to South America. I heard no more of her after that."

riperderti: The intensive *ri* is extremely common, even obsessive, in Montale. Actions are very frequently presented as repetitions, reiterations, replays of constant, unchanging situations.

Sottoripa: Montale (*Op*, 904): "The arcades of [Piazza Caricamento] in Genoa, by the sea."

il segno / smarrito: See note on the method of stilnovistic *trobar clus* above.

Molti anni, e uno più duro sopra il lago / Many years, and one still harder (1934)
uno più duro: Because spent in a hospital (see "Brina sui vetri . . ."). The theme of the bedridden loved one is recurrent in Montale (cf. "Ballata scritta in una clinica," "Luce d'inverno").

San Giorgio e il Drago: Symbol of the struggle against evil (and emblem of the city of Genoa). Isella (1, 32): "*Riportarmi* means 'restore to me' or 'reawaken in me' (the necessary strength)."

grecale: Wind from the northeast.

per te: Both "for you" and "because of you, through you," the latter usage frequent in Montale, particularly in *La bufera*.

scendere: Cf. the theme of descent in "Incontro" and other late poems of *Ossi di seppia*; the movement (into the underworld) has Orphic undertones, here and elsewhere.

Brina sui vetri; uniti / Frost on the windowpanes; the sick (1934)
Montale (*Op*, 904): "Life in a sanatorium and life at war contrasted. The 'ballerina' bomb was used by our infantry in 1915 and perhaps later as well." Montale (Greco, 33): "The 'rocks' weren't far. The 'harsh wing' is perhaps the moment of choice, decision. But we decided nothing, my luck and hers."

Montale was sent to the front at Vallarsa in the Trentino, a cadet in the 158th infantry regiment of the Liguria Brigade, in the months following the Italian army's defeat at Caporetto in late 1917.

The poem evokes the separate lives of the lovers before their encounter.

un'ala rude: Cf. Baudelaire, "Un fantôme" IV, "Le portrait": "Et que le Temps, injurieux vieillard, / Chaque jour frotte avec son aile rude." Also, the "grandi ali / screziate" of "Carnevale di Gerti," and, later, the otherworldly wing-imagery, both Clizia's and Volpe's, of *La bufera*.

Lontano, ero con te quando tuo padre / *Distant, I was with you when your father* (date uncertain, probably 1939)

The first of the motets written for Clizia, and one of the last to be added to the sequence, in June 1939, just prior to publication of *Le occasioni* (*Op*, 905).

Montale (*Op*, 904): "Cumerlotti and Anghébeni, villages in Vallarsa."

Il logorìo: Mengaldo (55–56) shows how Montale borrows this "frequentative" noun form from Pascoli—and D'Annunzio—(evidence of Montale's objectifying tendency, which favors substantives over verbs), but instead of using it "impressionistically," like Pascoli, employs it idiosyncratically, i.e., expressionistically, emphasizing "violent novelty." His long list of examples includes *sventolìo* ("Crisalide"); *trepestìo* ("Altro effetto di luna"); *alluciolìo*, a Montalean neologism ("Notizie dall'Amiata"); *scampanìo* ("Palio"); *zampettìo* ("Nella serra").

per questo: "For this," but also "because of this"; cf. "per te" in "Molti anni. . . ."

lo so: Isella (1, 41): "The dazzling awareness acquired under the harsh blows of the present is translated in this affirmative formula, typical of Montale's minimal certainties" (cf., e.g., "Bene lo so: bruciare" in MEDITERRANEO).

spolette: Literally, fuses.

Addii, fischi nel buio, cenni, tosse / *Farewells, whistles in the dark, waves, coughs* (1939; included in the second edition of *Le occasioni*, 1940)

Addii . . . : Reprise, in an ironic modern key, of a famous similarly constructed line of Petrarch: "Fior', frondi, erbe, ombre, antri, onde, aure soavi."

The poem, particularly in an earlier version where it was not divided in two by the line of periods, echoes a famous Carduccian *barbara*, or Italian poem written in classical quantitative meter, "Alla stazione in una mattino d'autunno."

gli automi: Montale (Greco, 34): "Men walled in their compartments, men understood as mass (and ignorance)." (Also perhaps a critique of the "barbarity" of Futurism.)

Montale's disdain for "the men who don't look back" ("Forse un mattino andando . . .") or for the "other shadows" of "Ti libero la fronte" intensifies through his career (cf., e.g., the goat-men of "Elegia di Pico Farnese"). Humanity is divided into two categories: the small circle of those who feel (and suffer) and the rest, who are not truly alive.

litania . . . orrida: Isella (1, 44) calls this a "Montale-brand hendecasyllable," where the *sdrucciolo*, or proparoxytone accent (on the antepenult), of *rapido* is duplicated by the rhythmically similar *orrida*. Isella cites numerous other examples, cf. "ronzìo di *coleotteri* che *suggono*" in the motet "La rana, prima a ritentar la corda"; here, the repetitive rhythm suggests the motion of the train. Mengaldo (90) points out that the two *sdruccioli* are also "alliterative," and that the second repeats the vowels of the first, in reverse.

carioca: Another of the exotic dances which appear throughout Montale's work, "always striking a woeful note" (Macrì 2, 245). The Brazilian carioca was popular in Italy and elsewhere in the thirties.

Mengaldo's sensitive analysis (89–91) shows how the poem's largely prosaic vocabulary is activated and "neutralized" by its elaborate rhythmic and phonic structure, playing a fundamental role in its dynamic dialectic: "Here as often . . . [Montale's] wide openness to antitraditional, stale, 'unpoetic' linguistic materials is absorbed by a marked tendency to stylistic unification on a 'high' level, resulting in an unexceptionably coherent formal organization of an exquisitely poetic character."

La speranza di pure rivederti / The hope of even seeing you again (1937)
Montale (Greco, 34): "The jackals were seen by me in Modena and were interpreted as a *senhal* from her, because when I saw them I thought of her. Very realistic poem."

La speranza . . . : Recalls the opening of Dante's *canzone*: "La dispietata mente, che pur mira / di retro al tempo che se n'è andato." *Pure* here means "yet" or "still."

schermo d'immagini: The screen of external reality which obscures truth (cf. the screen in "Forse un mattino andando . . .").

ha i segni della morte: In an early draft, "è / il segno della morte"; see note to "Lo sai: debbo riperderti. . . ."

(a Modena . . . / guinzaglio): Note the similar closure in parentheses in "Barche sulla Marna," also written in 1937.

In 1950, Montale published a typically ironic, disarmingly informal article in *Il Corriere della Sera*, "Due sciacalli al guinzaglio," about the writing of the MOTTETTI and their critical reception, which is greatly revealing about his general motives and attitudes. It is reprinted here from *Sec* (305–9):

Many years ago, Mirco, a noted poet who has now changed professions, wrote in his head, transcribed onto pieces of paper that he kept balled-up in his jacket pockets, and finally published a series of short poems dedicated, or rather sent by air mail (but only on the wings of the imagination), to a certain Clizia who was living about three thousand miles away. Clizia's real name wasn't Clizia at all; her model can be found in a sonnet of uncertain authorship which Dante, or someone else, sent to Giovanni Quirini; and Mirco's name isn't Mirco either; but my necessary discretion doesn't detract from the import of this note. Let it suffice to identify the typical situation of that poet, and I should say of almost every lyric poet who lives besieged by the absence/presence of a distant woman, in this case a Clizia, who had the name of the woman in the myth who was changed into a sunflower.

Mirco's little poems, which later became a series, an entirely unmysterious little autobiographical novel, were born day by day. Clizia knew nothing about them and may not even have read them until many years later; but every now and then the news of her that reached Mirco provided the impetus for a motet; and thus new epigrams were born and shot off like arrows across the seas, though the interested lady hadn't offered the pretext for them, even involuntarily. Two very different cases, of which I'll give examples. Here is the first:

One day Mirco learned that Clizia's father had died. He felt her loss, and regretted even more deeply the three thousand miles which kept him distant, too distant, from her grief. And it seemed to him that all the anxieties and risks of his life up to that point had converged on a Clizia who was then unknown to him, and on a meeting which would have to wait for many years. Perhaps, he said to himself, the war saved me precisely for this: for without Clizia my life would have had no meaning, no direction. He dredged up his past, saw himself again in certain contested villages in Vallarsa, at Cumerlotti, Anghébeni, under Monte Corvo; he found himself in mortal danger again, but already aided even then, unawares, by Clizia's star, by the umbrella of her sunflower.

That day Mirco sat in a café and wrote these lines on the margin of a newspaper, then cast them to the wind, which carried them to their destination:

> Lontano, ero con te quando tuo padre
> entrò nell'ombra e ti lasciò il suo addio.
> Che seppi fino allora? Il logorìo
> di prima mi salvò solo per questo:
>
> che t'ignoravo e non dovevo: ai colpi
> d'oggi lo so, se di laggiù s'inflette
> un'ora e mi riporta Cumerlotti
> o Anghébeni—tra scoppi di spolette
> e i lamenti e l'accorer delle squadre.

Second and final example: One summer afternoon Mirco found himself at Modena walking under the arcades. Anxious as he was, and still absorbed in his "dominating idea," it astonished him that life could present him with so many distractions, as if painted or reflected on a screen. It was too gay a day for a man who wasn't gay. And then an old man in gold-braided livery appeared to Mirco, dragging two reluctant champagne-colored puppies on a leash, two little dogs who at first glance seemed to be neither wolfhounds nor dachshunds nor Pomeranians. Mirco approached the old man and asked him, "What kind of dogs are these?" And the old man, dry and proud, answered, "They're not dogs, they're jackals." (He spoke like a true, uneducated Southerner, then turned the corner with his pair.) Clizia loved droll animals. How amused she would have been to see them! thought Mirco. And from that day on he never read the name Modena without associating the city with his idea of Clizia and the two jackals. A strange, persistent idea. Could the two beasts have been sent by her, like an emanation? Were they an emblem, an occult signature, a *senhal*? Or were they only an hallucination, the premonitory signs of her fall, her end?

Similar things often happened; there were no more jackals, but other strange products from the grab-bag of life: poodles, monkeys, owls on a trestle, minstrels . . . And always, a healing balm entered the heart of the wound. One evening Mirco heard some lines in his head, took a pencil and a tram ticket (the only paper in his pocket) and wrote:

> La speranza di pure rivederti
> m'abbandonava;
>
> e mi chiesi se questo che mi chiude
> ogni senso di te, schermo d'immagini
> ha i segni della morte o dal passato

> *è in esso, ma distorto e fatto labile,*
> *un tuo barbaglio.*

He stopped, erased the period, and substituted a colon because he sensed the need for an example that would also be a conclusion. And he ended:

> *(a Modena, fra i portici,*
> *un servo gallonato trascinava*
> *due sciacalli al guinzaglio).*

The parentheses were intended to isolate the example and suggest a different tone of voice, the jolt of an intimate and distant memory.

When the poems were published with others that were related and easier to understand and that ought to have explained even their two least limpid sisters, great was the bafflement of the critics. And the objections of the detractors were totally out of line with the nature of the case. If the poet had perhaps abandoned himself too freely to his antecedent, his "situation," the critics demonstrated a very different, and more serious, mental torpor.

The first investigations concerned Cumerlotti and Anghébeni, which were mistaken for two characters essential to the understanding of the text. Anghébeni, Carneade, who was he? asked one critic, now a doctor, who we hope brings a better clinical eye to his new profession. And who, asked others, was "Cumerlotti's girl"? Were the jackals hers? And what did Modena have to do with it? Why Modena and not Parma or Voghera? And the man with the jackals? Was he a servant? A publicist? And the father? How did he die and where and why?

I have touched on one aspect (and only one) of the obscurity or apparent obscurity of certain contemporary art: that which is born of an intense concentration and of a confidence, perhaps excessive, in the material being treated. Faced with this, the critics act like the visitor at an art exhibition who looks at two pictures, a still life of mushrooms, for example, or a landscape with a man walking with an open umbrella, and asks himself: What do these mushrooms cost per pound? Were they picked by the artist or bought at the market? Where is that man going? What's his name? And is that umbrella real silk or synthetic? The obscurity of the classics, not only of Dante and Petrarch but also of Foscolo and Leopardi, has been partly unraveled by the commentary of whole generations of scholars: and I don't doubt that those great writers would be flabbergasted by the exegeses of certain of their interpreters. And the obscurity of certain of the moderns will finally give way too, if there are still critics tomorrow. Then we shall all pass from darkness into light, too much light: the light the so-called aesthetic commentators cast on the mystery of poetry. There is a middle road between understanding nothing and understanding too much, a *juste milieu* which poets instinctively respect more than their critics; but on this side or that of the border there is no safety for either poetry or criticism. There is only a wasteland, too dark or too bright, where two poor jackals cannot live or venture forth without being hunted down, seized, and shut behind the bars of a zoo.

Il saliscendi bianco e nero dei / The white-and-black sine wave (1938)

dei: Note the unusual rhyme of the preposition with *sei*, "a happy rhythmic rendering" (Isella 1, 53) of the motion of the birds. In general, Montale's rhyming in the motets is daring (see the "composed" rhyme [fit]*to su* in line 6, which rhymes—almost—with *consu*[ma] in line 9), and numerous lines end in prepositions. Montale himself criticized this in a letter to Bazlen (May 31, 1939) (Isella 1, 53): "Too many unusual enjambments (*col, nelle, dei, su,* and rhymes in *me, te*), which if there were more normal poems with them would go less observed, but instead are too apparent." Yet the quasi-independent character of the syllables (as things, almost, more than parts of speech) enhances the sense of the compositions as music, over and above their existence as verbal structures.

balestrucci: Arrowsmith (2, 147): "The house martin is the only European swallow with a pure white rump and underparts but elsewhere black . . . Montale [is] always precise in his ornithology." But Pascoli has "uno scoppietto veloce / di balestrucci" in his "Primi poemetti," and D'Annunzio had referred to "neribianchi stormi" (black-and-white flocks) of these birds in *Alcyone*. Mengaldo (51–53) cites multiple sources for *balestrucci* in Pascoli and D'Annunzio, and sees it as part of "a poetic vocabulary that belongs equally to both" which is the basis for "a broad Pascolian-D'Annunzian *koiné*" fundamental in the establishment of a twentieth-century Italian literary language. Montale had also already used the rhyme *crucci/balestrucci* in the early "Accordi" (1916–20; tr. in *Oth*, 93–101). A natural detail, then, with symbolic resonance *and* a literary heritage, a typical Montalean overdetermination.

Ecco il segno; s'innerva / See the sign; it flares (1938)

Montale (Greco, 34): "*il passo* . . . signs of a purely illusory waiting. She is almost never present or is so magically (Ti libero la fronte)."

The lost sign of the first motet is now dazzlingly present: in an intimation from nature. The use of bodily imagery ("s'innerva," "sangue," "vene") suggests how fundamentally the reality of Clizia has invested the poet's senses.

un frastaglio di palma: "The Orient sun and the palm tree have to do with Clizia's . . . Palestinian ancestry" (Cambon, 71).

Il passo . . . : Cf. "il tuo passo che fa pulsar le vene" in "L'orto." Note the intricate interplay of *ve* sounds (*neve* is an anagram of *vene*), combined with soft *l*'s throughout the second stanza, "in calculated contrast with the harsh phonosymbolic series of the first quatrain" (Isella 1, 58).

Il ramarro, se scocca / The green lizard, if it darts (1937)

Montale (Greco, 34): "The lizard disappears over the side of the steep rock."

A series of allusive "snapshots," *d'après nature*, but also cultural" (Isella 1, 59), as is almost always the case with Montale. The poem's catalogue, delivered with "hammered energy" of language, "Dantesque in tone" (Isella 1, 60), "presents some (probably not fortuitous) similarity to the Negative Way of the mystics who strove to express the ineffability of God by successively discarding every created aspect of beauty or power that could seem to approach Him: God is not this, nor that, nor even that. Like Dante in *Purgatorio*, Montale is here a poet exploring the limits of his own art and humbly declaring it (along with Nature) unable to capture the transcendent" (Cambon, 75).

It should be mentioned that Irma Brandeis was a student of medieval mysticism; a late poem, "Clizia nel '34" (1980), speaks of her reading "lives of half-unheard-of saints" (*Oth*, 65); her study of Dante, *The Ladder of Vision: A Study of Dante's Comedy* (New York: Doubleday & Co., 1961), is cited by Montale in his 1965 lecture on Dante (tr. in *Sec*, 134–54) as "the most suggestive study I have read on the theme of the stairway which leads to

God, and which for good reason is entrusted to the patronage of Saint Bonaventure" (mystic, contemplative, author of the *Itinerarium mentis in Deum*).

Il ramarro: "Come'l ramarro sotto la gran fersa / dei dì canicular, cangiando sepe, / folgore par se la via attraversa" (As the lizard under the great scythe / of the dog days, darting from hedge to hedge, / seems like lightning if it crosses the way) (*Inferno* XXV, 79–81). *Scocca*, too, is Dantesque, while *rocca* here is Ligurian for *scoglio*, reef.

Luce di lampo: The quotation from Ariel's song in *The Tempest* (I, ii, 398–99) perhaps indicates an Eliotic influence.

il tuo stampo: Cf. "La tua impronta" in "Gli orecchini" and the "sigillo imperioso" of "Palio," as well as "la tua carta" in the motet "Brina sui vetri. . . ."

Perché tardi? Nel pino lo scoiattolo / Why wait? The squirrel beats his torch-tail (1938–39)
Montale (Greco, 34): "The peak is one of the horns of the half-moon. The you is addressed to the woman-thunderbolt."

Montale to Bobi Bazlen (May 10, 1939) (*Op*, 930): "It happens *often* to me (and often *voluntarily*) that I'm ambiguous in this way. For example, in the motet of the woman who's about to leave her cloud:

> A un soffio il pigro fumo . . . (?)
> *si difende nel punto che ti chiude*

it's clear that *nel punto* can have two meanings: at the *moment when* and in the *place where*, both of them legitimate. For Landolfi this uncertainty is horrendous, for me it's a richness."

lo scoiattolo: The image was first used in "Lettera levantina" (1923), unpublished until *Op* (tr. in *Oth*).

Nulla . . . tutto: The *Nada* and *Todo* of the mystics; see note to "Il ramarro, se scocca."

fólgore: Citation from Manzoni's "La risurrezione," 66: "Era folgore l'aspetto" (His look was lightning) (but see also the quotation from Dante in reference to the preceding motet), which Montale mentions in his memorable 1949 essay on the survival of art across time, translated as "The Second Life of Art" in *Sec* (20–24): "I cannot meet certain persons— Clizia or Angela or . . . *omissis omissis* without seeing once again the mysterious faces of Piero and Mantegna or having a line of Manzoni ('era folgore l'aspetto') flash in my memory." And since it is the Angel of the Resurrection that is described in Manzoni (Avalle, 114), "here already we find the identification of the beloved with 'the visiting Angel' and she is endowed with one of her essential attributes: her manifestation in the guise of lightning" (Isella 1, 69). One of the first steps, then, in the construction of the myth and symbology of Clizia.

L'anima che dispensa / The spirit that dispenses (1938)
Mengaldo (299): "The citation-recollection of a musical theme (and above all, given the preferences of the author, an operatic one) lends itself excellently to the operation of gathering or fixing in memory the experience around a privileged, magic event or object, which has a fundamental role in Montale's poetry, particularly at the height of *Le occasioni*." See similar moments in "Sotto la pioggia" and "Il ritorno." In "Donna Juanita," in *Farf* (20), the narrator says: "A woman: *donna Juanita*. The music she had brusquely dismissed was her: or rather the symphony of the comic opera by Suppé that bears this title. But for me it actually brought her back in the flesh."

furlana . . . : A highly animated dance originating in Friuli; "the exact origin of the *rigodon* or *rigaudon* is unknown . . . ; it was a dance widespread in the South, especially in the seventeenth and eighteenth centuries, which appears in numerous operas as well" (Angelini 2, 171).

ordegno: Literary variant for *ordigno*.

do re la sol sol: Rebay (3, 199) reveals these as the notes of a song popular in the prewar period ("Amore amor portami tante rose"). Isella (1, 74) points out that *do re* is a "composite rhyme" with *favore*.

Ti libero la fronte dai ghiaccioli / I free your forehead of the ice (1940?; published in the second (1940) edition of *Le occasioni*)

Montale (Greco, 34): "Visitation from the beyond. . . . The other men are those who *don't know*, who are ignorant of the possibility of such occurrences."

First flight of Clizia as Visiting Angel; introduction of some of her most salient stilnovistic attributes (forehead, icicles, lacerated wings), which will reappear elsewhere, particularly in *La bufera*, and of the theme of her sacrificial-salvific nature.

cicloni: Cf. the storm of *La bufera*. The cyclones are versions of the agitated weather (external and internal) characteristic of the poet's world. Marchese (1, 96): "Clizia had returned to America in 1938: here the poet imagines her coming back to him in the figure of an angel crossing the three thousand miles that separate her from Italy in an exhausting stratospheric flight."

un sole / freddoloso: The oxymoron marks an early instance of the juxtaposition of heat (fire) and cold (ice) that is fundamental to the elaboration of Clizia's myth (see note to "La primavera hitleriana," written about the same time). These are "the elements with which symbolically she is identified and within which mythically she is concealed . . . ; and they are at the same time the 'signs' which reveal her to be spiritually present and render her recognizable to the poet, also through the effect of a game of semantic references which one suspects are linked to her name, analogous to those which permitted Petrarch to 'recognize' Laura in 'l'aura' [the breeze] and the 'lauro' [laurel]" (Rebay 1, 44–45). The semantic references are the German *Brand* (fire) and *Eis* (ice), which together form the surname of Irma Brandeis, the fundamental inspiration for Clizia (see "Iride").

l'altre ombre: Like the "automi" of the motet "Addii, fischi nel buio . . ." and the "altri che t'ignora" in "L'anima che dispensa," a further elaboration of the theme of ignorance-exclusion vs. awareness-initiation that opposes the multitude of the blind to the "few" who see. The notion of initiation is fundamental to the private style of stilnovistic poetry; in Montale's hands, the theme has social and political as well as amorous significance. Lonardi (160–61) notes that the first word (*Ti*) and last (*qui*) are rhyming monosyllables, and that they set up a system of "rhythmic-tonal" relationships within the entire poem: *Ti/ti/Mezzodì/s'ostina/vicolo/qui*. A similar structure can be found in the motet "Infuria sale o grandine? . . ." (*sé/te/Lakmé*, extended to a whole syllabic network within the poem: *accelera/nelle/sfere/gelo/fingevi/Campanelle*).

La gondola che scivola in un forte / The gondola that glides (1938)

Published in *Corrente* in 1939 under the title "La Venezia di Hoffmann—e la mia" (Hoffmann's Venice—and Mine). Montale (in author's note): "The deceiving song could be the 'canzone of Dappertutto,' in the second act [Isella (1, 82) says it is actually Act III, scene iv] of Offenbach's *Tales of Hoffmann*; but the theme of the poem isn't mannered. Unfortunately, I'm never able to carve out anything from pure invention."

Montale (Greco, 34): "Piles of rope on some bank. The doors *were* high. Certainly, they separated from her. But all is separation in the MOTTETTI and elsewhere."

Isella (1, 79) sees, beyond the "ambiguous Carnival Venice, à la Hoffmann . . . , a sort of Hades where a 'deceiving song' imperils the journey of Orpheus in search of his Beloved."

uno smorto groviglio: Cf. the "morto / viluppo di memorie" of "In limine."

Infuria sale o grandine? Fa strage / Is it salt that strafes or hail? It slays (1938)
Once again, music is invoked, as often in these poems with a musical title, this time in order both to describe a natural phenomenon, a storm, and to evoke the memory of the beloved.

Montale (*Op*, 913): "The 'underwater tolling': very probably [Debussy's] 'La cathédrale engloutie.' "

Montale (Greco, 34): "*quale tu lo destavi.* Certainly, she played. The *pianola degl' inferi* maintains the poem in a hellish climate that's also mechanical. The aria from [Delibes's] *Lakmé* was actually sung and is a *hail* of vocal sounds." Montale (Cima, 195): "I wanted to suggest an airy voice . . . , trilling. The 'Bell Song' is in fact a typical piece for *soprano leggero*, full of trills and embellishments."

Stefano Verdino (Marcenaro and Boragina, 216–17): "I believe Clizia's voice for Montale could only ideally be the voice of a light and vibrant soprano. . . . In the angel-woman there is all the excess typical of the role of the operatic high soprano, vocally always dominating the other roles and essentially inaccessible in her vocal verticality. Basically, the soprano voice, according to Montale's taste, was a voice located beyond, in an oxymoronic setting near those borders of the metaphysical which he eyed furtively."

Fa strage / di campanule . . . : Cf. "Tramontana": "divelle gli arbusti, strapazza i palmizi. . . ."

Al primo chiaro, quando / At first light, when (Date unknown, but added to the ms. just before publication; 1939 is thus likely, as with the fourth motet, "Lontano, ero con te . . .")
Isella (1, 90–91) points out how the two parts of the poem, devoted respectively to morning and evening, make up one sentence (as in "Corno inglese," "Accelerato," and "L'anguilla"), its halves "stitched together" by Montale's masterfully intricate rhyming; each verse of the first stanza (lines 1–7) rhymes with a line in the second (8–14), "like a thread that truly joins day and night in the insistent thought of the beloved." To wit: 1:*quando*/ 8:*quando* (identical rhyme); 2:*rumore*/ 11:*fervore*; 2:*subitaneo*/ 12:*guardiano* and 13:*umane* (quasi rhyme); 3:*parla*/ 9:*tarla*; 3:*ferrovia*/ 10:*scrivanìa*; 4:*corsa*/ 10:*rafforza* (imperfect rhyme); 5:*sasso*/ 11:*passo*; 6:*tagli* is also assonant-consonant with 9:*tarla*, and 7:*misti* relates to 14:*insisti*. Furthermore, 12:*accosta* is a quasi rhyme with 13:*soste* as is 5:*traforo* with 13:*ancora*.

chiusi uomini: For the image, cf. "Accelerato"; also the "automi" of "Addii, fischi nel buio. . . ."

Il fiore che ripete / The flower that repeats (1937)
Il fiore: Cf. Bécquer's epigraph to the entire sequence.
burrato: Dantesque. See *Inferno* XII, 10, and XVI, 14: "lo gittò in quel alto burrato" (he threw him into that deep pit).

non scordarti . . . : In Italian the flower is called *nontiscordardimé*.

gettato: Isella (1, 97): "Like a bridge."

Un cigolìo: Cf. "Cigola la carrucola del pozzo," which also deals with the theme of separation, and the intervention of a mechanical device that both unites and separates lover and beloved. The funicular is, presumably, the one in Genoa.

La rana, prima a ritentar la corda / The frog, first to strike his chord (1938)
The only motet from which Clizia is in all ways absent, and the only one not divided into two or more stanzas (indeed, the characteristic bipartite division of most of the lyrics is striking). "More than a country landscape . . . a spectacle coming to a close, a stage going dark. The recourse to artificially literary metaphors . . . , like the frog who strikes the chord of his instrument and the sun that 'puts out its torches,' contributes to this effect" (Isella 1, 98). The apocalyptic presentiment of war was even clearer in the version included up to the eighth (1956) edition, in which the last lines read:

> l'ora s'estingue; un cielo di lavagna
> si prepara all'irrompere dei tre
> cavalieri! Salutali con me.

(the hour goes out; a blackboard sky / prepares for the eruption of the three / horsemen! Salute them with me.)

(In this version, note that Clizia *is* present, as the addressee of the final command.)

un sole senza caldo: Cf. Baudelaire, "De profundis clamavo," 10: "Un soleil sans chaleur"; and the similarly oxymoronic "sole freddoloso" of the twelfth motet, "Ti libero la fronte. . . ."

tardo ai fiori / ronzìo: The artificial word order contributes to the "literary" aura of the composition.

scarni / cavalli: Recalls "Incontro": "mani scarne, cavalli in fila," with its pre-apocalyptic air.

Non recidere, forbice, quel volto / Shears, don't cut away that face (1937)
See Huffman (87–106) for a detailed analysis of the poem.

quel volto: "The face that the shears of the autumn gardener cut away along with the branches of the acacia" (Contini 1, 69). The gardener is Atropos, or Time, who "va dintorno con le force" (goes abroad with his scissors) (*Paradiso* XVI, 9).

non far . . . : Montale to Renzo Laurano (November 22, 1937) (*Op*, 915): "Don't make, O shears, in the act of cutting, haze of that face, i.e., 'don't destroy it.' "

nebbia: Cf. the "poca nebbia di memorie" of "Casa sul mare" (see note on the theme of the insufficiency of memory in Montale); also the "bruma" of "Il canneto rispunta i suoi cimelli."

Duro il colpo svetta: In an early version, the phrase was "il guizzo par d'accetta" (the gleam seems like a hatchet's). Montale to Laurano: "I vote for the second version. The significant ambiguity of *svettare* (among other things it also means: cut off the top), though untranslatable, came to me spontaneously, not dragged by the hair, and it's valuable at that point. And also in the first version you had thought that the *guizzo* referred to the cold that is falling, while for me it was the gleam of the shears-hatchet that deals the blow; so the first version was more equivocal."

Macrì (1, 140) sees a link here and in the next motet—by way of the theme of memory —with the familial world of "Vecchi versi" and "La casa dei doganieri," "the archetypal sphere *mother-house-memory*" and thus with the (largely suppressed) figure of the poet's mother (see note to "A mia madre"). For Marchese (3, 137–38), the last three motets are Arlettian.

l'acacia ferita: Marchese (1, 98): "The adjective implies a human subject, victim of painful aggression; the acacia is an evident *transfert* of the self, wounded by the shears of time."

scrolla / il guscio: Cf. "uno scrollo giù" in "Bagni di Lucca," and the similar action of "Alla maniera di Filippo De Pisis. . . ."

cicala: Marchese (1, 98): "The close relationship between the acacia and the cicada is emphasized by the grammatical structure. The cicada removed from the plant . . . corresponds, obviously, to the woman's face cut away by the cruel shears of time and sent into the haze of oblivion." See "Reading Montale" on the cicada as an emblem of the poet, which Marchese does not consider as relevant here; yet the woman as object of the poet's desire is identified with, incorporated into his own self; the connection seems fundamental.

belletta: Dantesque. See *Inferno* VII, 124: "belletta negra"; but also D'Annunzio: "La belletta," in the "Madrigali d'estate" in *Alcyone*.

La canna che dispiuma / The reed that softly (1938)

Montale (Greco, 34): "The path runs along the ditch, the cross is a symbol of suffering— elsewhere it will be Ezekiel's wheel."

Isella (1, 108): "A kind of programmatic declaration of the new development in Montale's poetry" in the movement from the "infinite waiting" of *Le occasioni* to the central "demiurgic role of Clizia" in *La bufera*. "The hope of salvation can no longer be entrusted . . . to the enumeration of absurdly privileged fantasies, aleatory references to the beloved Object (of which lines 1–7 offer yet one last precious specimen); it is necessary, now, to read her impenetrable signs 'out of the sight of man' ('Palio'), where Clizia's 'distant pupils' direct, among blinding reflections, the eyes of her faithful one."

dispiuma: "Very precious" (Mengaldo, 60) literary form of *spiuma*.

rèdola . . . : D'Annunzian; also used by Boine. For discussion of the ditch as a primordial familial locus in Montale, see note to "Il gallo cedrone."

riconoscere: Isella (1, 112): "*Conoscere* [to know], in the Montalean world, is always a *riconoscere* [recognition] . . . , a recollection" (cf., e.g., "Corrispondenze": "Ti riconosco"; "Il ventaglio": "Muore chi ti riconosce?").

là dove . . . : Recalls lines from "Antico, sono ubriacato . . . ," in MEDITERRANEO: "là nel paese dove il sole cuoce / e annuvolano l'aria le zanzare"; the "là" here represents the same location as the "traguardo" (finish line) of "Palio": "out of the sight of man."

s'abbassa, oltre: The elision of the two vowels in the seventh syllable of this line (*sa-ol*) (a similar elision occurs in "Palio") is, according to Lavezzi (162–65), the classic Montalean rhythmic marker of a key syntagm.

pupille ormai remote . . . : Cf. *Paradiso* I, 63–65. The image of the cross recurs in "A mia madre" (1942), and the coincidence reinforces Macrì's intuition (1, 140) that the eighteenth and nineteenth motets are tinged with maternal associations: "the whole motet is a *cipher* of the poet's familial intimacy, through which Iride [see "Iride"] is colored for us with the same *maternal* 'light,' like all the feminine phantoms of the soteriological Dantean-Petrarchan demonology of the West."

. . . ma così sia. Un suono di cornetta / . . . so be it. Blare of a cornet (1937)

Isella (1, 113): "The motet closes the cycle on a note of resigned acceptance of his own destiny . . . as a man, above all, forced to recognize that the yearning for wide horizons, proper to youth, has come down to the small space of dailiness; but, in particular, as a man of letters, who, looking back, can only offer in comparison with the true life of the man of action his 'sheaf of pages,' in which he has succeeded not in living but in representing his own life." Cf. Montale in "Intentions" (*Sec*, 296): "I too acquired a smattering of psychoanalysis in its time, but even without recourse to its lights I thought early, and I still think, that art is the form of life of the man who truly doesn't live: a compensation or a surrogate."

Cambon (88): "The epiphany afforded by this last motet is of the phenomenal, the limited reality—not of the noumenal, as was formerly the case." In this, it prefigures the trajectory of Montale's poetry as a whole.

così sia: The Italian "Amen" (Cambon, 87).

dialoga: Montale to Isella (1, 116): "It's a 'synchrony': the two sounds come from different points and almost blend" (as in "Bagni di Lucca"); it's also "a picture, a still life in movement." Cf. "Potessi almeno costringere" in MEDITERRANEO: "your briny words / where art and nature fuse."

Nella valva: The painted seashell depicting Vesuvius ("a keepsake": Montale [Greco, 34]) and the lava paperweight containing an ancient coin are typical Neapolitan souvenirs. Cambon (88): "A painted volcano on the seashell, a hardened piece of lava on the desk remind him that his own life no longer seethes with the ardors of youth" (cf. "Eastbourne," also from 1937, and "Sul muro grafito," which "appears to foreshadow the present motet in more than one respect" [Cambon, 88]). The art/life "dialogue" of cornet with bees is further elaborated by the contrasting souvenirs.

tuo fazzoletto: Hers, but just as easily the poet's.

III.

Tempi di Bellosguardo / Times at Bellosguardo (1939?)

Inserted in the ms. of *Le occasioni* at the last minute, along with the motets "Lontano, ero con te quando tuo padre" and "Al primo chiaro, quando." Contini and Bettarini, the editors of *Op*, write (916): "Montale says that the composition of 'Tempi . . . ,' like that of the two motets, is not far from the date of submission [of the ms.], adding that the series, now of three elements, was meant to be longer, in analogy with MEDITERRANEO in *Ossi di seppia*."

Montale (Greco, 35): "I was rarely at Bellosguardo. The poem 'Tempi . . .' was supposed to be the pendant to MEDITERRANEO, a storm at sea, but this time 'humanistic.' Movement surprised as secret immobility."

Bellosguardo is a hill west of the Porta Romana in the Oltrarno sector of Florence. The large villas that occupy it have extensive views of the city and the hills beyond. This opening onto landscape is the occasion for one of Montale's most philosophically meditated poems, which evokes European civilization on the brink of possible destruction. The neoclassical form (and the locale itself) calls to mind Foscolo's *Grazie*, and links the series with the "Sarcofaghi" of *Ossi di seppia*; "Tempi" is intended in the double sense of time and musical tempo.

———

For Mengaldo (302), the first section recalls one of D'Annunzio's *Elegie romane*, "Sera sui colli d'Alba."

nella corusca / distesa: Cf. the *osso* "Gloria del disteso mezzogiorno," where time likewise halts in a moment of contemplation.

trito / mormorio della rena: Cf. the "triti fatti" of "Flussi," which this poem evokes in its contemplation of the cyclical nature of time. Montale (Greco, 35): "The sand is the hour-glass of time"; the image, which Montale first used in "Vento e bandiere," is elaborated in part 3.

salti / di lupi: Bonora (2, 42) says that Montale is here translating the French term *saut-de-loup*, which describes "a wide ditch, so called because a wolf would have difficulty jumping across it"—not unlike the English ha-ha; while Isella (2, 131) says the term refers to the different levels of the terraces in an Italian garden, as in the Boboli Gardens below Bello-sguardo. Angelini, however (4, 391), asserts that Montale indicated he meant the term literally.

spiragli: Cf. the "barlumi" of "Il balcone" and elsewhere. Bonora (2, 43) refers to them as "intermittences of the psychic life."

tutto ruoti: The image of the wheel of time recurs in part 2 and frequently elsewhere, e.g., in "Costa San Giorgio."

The poem moves in the second section from irregular hendecasyllables to more sober *settenari*, seven-beat lines, later interspersed with eight- and nine-beat *ottonari* and *novenari*.

Derelitte: In normal usage, a word only applied to humans. Anticipation of the metaphoric "fronde / dei vivi" below, which recalls the "giunco" of "Arsenio," the "vegetazioni" of "In-contro," with which this second section has numerous affinities; the Dantesque image of the human plant recurs throughout Montale (see note to "Arsenio"). The magnolia will become a "symbol of civilization itself" (Isella 2, 129) in *La bufera*.

frigidari: Bonora (2, 45–46) points out that this is a Montalean neologism (congruent with the use of "tepidario" in "Caffè a Rapallo"). In the Roman bathhouse, the *frigidarium* was the room for cold baths; Montale is referring here to kitchens.

un travolto / concitamento d'accordi: Cf. "La pianola degl'inferi" in the motet "Infuria sale o grandine? . . ."; Montale (Macrì 2, 384) indicates the image refers to a piano being played inside. "Travolto" recurs notably in "Gli orecchini."

le membra . . . votate: Isella (2, 134) notes Montale's relentless insistence "on the frenzy of an animal life reduced to an absurd biological agitation."

E scende la cuna . . . : The "cuna" (more commonly "cunetta") is the old sunken roadway that descends from Bellosguardo (Montale [Greco, 36] says the term refers to "l'avvallamento," the sinking of the ground); but it can also be a cradle (fr. Latin *culla*). Bonora (2, 48): "If the cradle that descends among loggias and herms is a figure for the journey of life, it can also be, given what precedes its fall toward death [the catalogue of images evoking "the absolute inutility of existence"], that the idea of the cradle implies that of the grave: *Le berceau touche à la tombe!* And the array of loggias and statues only constitutes the decor of the brief journey; the chord, which is to be read as a reprise of the 'travolto / concitamento d'accordi' which comes from the cool rooms of the ground floors, probably signifies the lucidity with which one can stoically live one's life knowing that the cradle is almost the prefiguration of the grave."

le lapidi: Montale (Greco, 36): "There may be some gravestones, or not." More than an actual topographical reference, Isella (2, 135) sees Montale as invoking a literary *topos*, as epitomized in Foscolo's *Sepolcri*: "manly disenchantment and intrepid moral power, stoic acceptance of death and passion for great-hearted virtues, of which the tombs . . . are testimony and encouragement." Cf. the "derelitte lastre" of "Sarcofaghi," with its similar evocation of "those who take up / the torch that carries the primal fire."

le immagini grandi: Isella (2, 129): "The magnanimous illusions of Foscolo's poetry to which 'Tempi di Bellosguardo' renders homage from its title on. Not real values, only images; 'eternal/ passion,' out of an era remote from today, yet in concrete individual experience, an adventure that is different each time. What counts is the attempt to be truly alive, the gesture in and of itself."

l'amore inflessibile . . . : Cf. Clizia's "non mutato amor" in "La primavera hitleriana."

il giuoco: Cf. the "giuoco del futuro" of "In limine" and the "facile giuoco" of "Il balcone," as well the "giuoco" on the chessboard of "Nuove stanze."

il gesto: Cf. the "segno" of the motets and of part 3 below, in opposition to the "moto" above. For Macrì (2, 139) the poem "is based on the sexual 'gesto' of generation and on the generations who alternate in the cemeterylike neoclassical Foscolian villa between humble kitchens . . . and the salons above . . . , between the cradle and the grave . . . , between life and death . . ."; the same oppositions are operative in "Elegia di Pico Farnese."

esprime / se stesso e non altro: Cf. "A mia madre": "a life that's nothing but itself."

entra / nel chiuso: Montale (Greco, 36): "Enters into the intimate world of the poet."

grimaldello: Cf. Montale's comment on this word in note to "Elegia di Pico Farnese." Bonora (2, 49): "Alludes to an act of persuasion achieved without any prevarication or violence."

Bonora (2, 49–50) hypothesizes that the parts of the "Tempi" were written at different times, and that part 3 belongs to the period of the last great lyrics of *Le occasioni*, i.e., just before the Nazi invasion of Poland in 1939. The reference to "la bufera" and the sense of impending violence throughout support this view.

pioppo / del Canadà: A veiled allusion to Clizia (cf. the "Ontario" of "Iride"), who is now in North America.

il segno: The saving sign, sought in vain, of "a certainty, which can no longer be recognized in the serenity of the landscape of the first movement, nor in the firm stoicism of the gesture witnessed by 'the stones that have seen / the great images' " (Bonora 2, 51). Bonora compares the end of the "Tempi" with that of "Notizie dall'Amiata," with the exception that the signs there, albeit minimal, are apparent.

una vita che assecondi . . . : Bonora (2, 51): "An ascent without risks and without flights, like that offered by the steps of a marble staircase, whose rising movement is similar to that of the ivy, which climbs slowly, bending as it rises in contrast with the thrusting arches of the bridges that span the Arno."

piante umane: The "derelitte frondi" of part 1.

le locuste . . . : Montale (quoted in Isella 2, 137): The Biblical locusts "are an image of the destruction that endlessly brings the work of man . . . to a new beginning, in which everything has to be done again." Montale (Greco, 36): "Flight of grasshoppers, precariousness that enters this place, humanistic and almost fixed in an eternal perfection." Montale (Angelini

2, 172): "The grasshoppers, like man, are part of this rupture, this fracture of the order of all things; it is very doubtful that they themselves are heavenly weavers: but it is certain that they come from on high, where the destiny of man is sewn." Cary (296): "Surely the locusts are black-shirted."

sui libri: According to Angelini (4, 391), who cites "a botanical interpretation of [G.] Zazzaretta," not books but rather the liber, or bast (i.e., phloem)—or, by extension, the bark of vines or trees.

tessitrici celesti: The Fates. Isella (2, 138): "It's possible that the image . . . derives from the third hymn of [Foscolo's] *Grazie*, where the Hours and the Fates, with the assistance of Iris, Flora, Psyche, Thalia, Terpsichore, Erato, Aurora, and finally Hebe, weave the invisible and elaborate 'eternal veil,' symbol of human life, which the Graces put on, before they descend 'to bring joy to earth.' On the veil are splendidly represented, in needlepoint, youth, conjugal love, hospitality, filial piety, and maternal tenderness."

E domani . . . : Rhymes with *umani* (and *umane*) in line 12. Bonora (2, 53): "Resounds like a dolorous interrogative on the destiny of civilization and culture. . . . The 'Tempi' remained unfinished: the movement of the storm was to be next."

I V .

La casa dei doganieri / The House of the Customs Men (1930)
Montale (Nascimbeni, 116): "I wrote it for a young vacationer who died very young. In the short time she lived, it may be she was never even aware I existed" (but see note to "Incontro").

Montale to Alfonso Leone, June 19, 1971 (*Op*, 917): "The house of the customs men was destroyed when I was six. The girl in question never could have seen it; she went on . . . to die, but I only learned this many years later. I stayed and still remain. It's unclear who made a better choice. But in all likelihood there was no choice."

A photograph reproduced in Franco Contorbia, *Eugenio Montale: Immagini di una vita* (Milan: Librex, 1985), 141, shows the building in question, a shedlike structure with a door and small square window on one side, on the reef below the tower mentioned in Marianna Montale's description of the Montale property at Fegina (see introductory note to *Ossi di seppia*).

As Contini and Bettarini note, this poem develops the "Arletta theme," which emerges in "Incontro." Lonardi (119–20) demonstrates that the poem's four stanzas can be read contrapuntally as five quatrains with the rhyme scheme ABBA, CDCD, EEFF, GHGH, IBII, finished with a concluding couplet, JJ—a kind of exploded version of an Elizabethan sonnet.

Libeccio: The southwest wind; borrowed, as Bonora (2, 221) notes, from Pascoli, though the harshness ("sferza") attributed to it by Montale is Dantesque.

la bussola: Arrowsmith (2, 154): "The geometrical image of the circle—whether as spinning compass, turning wheel [cf. the pump in "Casa sul mare"], whirling weathervane, revolving doors, mill wheels, whirlpool—is present in Montale's poetry from the very beginning ["a kind of existential descendant of the old wall" (Cary, 297)], but here takes on mostly negative aspects: meaningless repetitions, recurrent despair and *noia*, an almost Nietzschean sense of *nausée*, all linked to life grimly perceived as out of control, a fatalistic mechanism, a web or trap from which one cannot break."

un filo . . . : Lonardi (116) demonstrates that the image, ultimately derived from the myth of Theseus and Ariadne, comes from Browning's "Two in the Campagna," also the inspiration for another poem of the period, "Due nel crepuscolo" (in *La bufera*), while the theme of the absent loved one has affinities with Browning's "Love in a Life."

la luce della petroliera: Cf. "Vecchi versi" (1926) and especially "Casa sul mare" (1925), of which one might say this is nearly a rewritten version, except that the poet's companion is now permanently absent, in another realm, and the renunciatory tone of the early poem is superseded by an anguished and frustrated desire for communion. Also cf. "Delta," "the first lyric of an explicit, fully characterized Montale," in which "a privileged phantom as the absolute presence of the unknown" appears (Contini 1, 33).

Il varco: Cf. "taluno . . . passi il varco, qual volle si ritrovi" in "Casa sul mare." Montale (Greco, 36) indicated that the "varco" was located "on the horizon."

Bassa marea / Low Tide (1932)

Also an "Arlettian" poem, and a virtual anthology of reprises of motifs from other poems in her cycle and elsewhere. The setting and atmosphere are those of "Casa sul mare" and "Delta"; "La casa dei doganieri," "Bassa marea," and "Punta del Mesco" involve a return to the landscape of *Ossi di seppia*, which is virtually absent from the first parts of *Le occasioni*. The poem, as Sergio Solmi says (quoted in Isella 2, 147), evokes the central theme of Montale's mature poetry: "the supreme longing for an absent reality, saturated by lacerating nostalgia," which has its "most elementary formula" here, where "a present sensation, the 'sign,' liberates a second plane of memory, suddenly tearing the veil over a living underground of feeling, of which current reality ends up configuring itself as a sort of colored and hallucinated materialization."

Mengaldo (18–19) points out Montale's characteristic chiastic, mirroring stanza structure (4-5-5-4 lines) and the tendency, also habitual, to regularize metric and rhyming schemes in the final stanza. He notes that the poem, down to the final rhyme, is full of Pascolian usages, but that the borrowings are put to polemical, subversive use; eventually, "the movement of reaction against tradition, and most often obviously against the 'fathers,' shifts from declarations of poetics to the actual deploying of linguistic material" in "complex and ambivalent statements in which the original connotation of the elements employed and the new signifying context in which they are inserted come into conflict."

l'altalena: Recalls the hammock of "Vento e bandiere" (1926).

rapidi voli obliqui: In contrast with the "voli senz'ali" of "Vento e bandiere"; Bonora (2, 32) sees "Bassa marea" as a kind of parodic reprise of that poem.

la discesa / di tutto: Cf. "Flussi"; descending motion is almost the primary action in Montale, whether as a figuration of entropy, as here, or as a symbolic action with Orphic undertones, as in the late poems of *Ossi di seppia*, "Di un natale metropolitano," etc.

un lugubre risucchio: Cf. "I morti."

negro vilucchio: The "morto / viluppo di memorie" of "In limine."

sul tunnel: Cf. the motet "Al primo chiaro. . . ."

Una mandria lunare: Recalls the "ultima greggia nella nebbia" of "Bagni di Lucca" and the "ciurma luminosa" of "Cave d'autunno"; Montale (Greco, 36): "The play of moon effects which pass across the earth and 'graze' it." Isella (2, 149) sees this as an echo of the Latin poem by Crashaw cited in reference to "Cave d'autunno."

Stanze / Stanzas (1927–29)

One of the most allusive and difficult poems of *Le occasioni*. "The topic is Clizia, her provenance, the miracle she is, her paradoxical presence-in-absence" (Cary, 298). The poem is a kind of surreal metaphysical rayogram, Lucretian in inspiration, according to Bonora (2, 28) —though Isella (2, 151) cites as sources the philosophical poetry of Leopardi, the "cosmic" Pascoli, and the scientific poetry of the minor nineteenth-century poet Giacomo Zanella; it is essential to the early elaboration of Clizia's quasi-angelic nature (albeit the poem, given its date of composition, belongs to the Arletta cycle [Forti 2, 57], and an autograph manuscript appears on the reverse of a copy of the early poem "Destino di Arletta" [tr. in *Oth*, 115ff.] [Isella 2, 150]). Unlike the other Arletta poems, however, according to Bonora (2, 28), "the inspirer of these lines is felt to be present, and the poet, in fixing his gaze on her, tries, though in vain, to travel in thought the long road which could lead beyond human history to the distant epoch of cosmic eruptions out of which her life had its beginning. The woman is unaware what complex of phenomena has made possible the portentous perfection of her body, in which the minute network of nerves seems to offer the picture of the very long journey taken by matter in its transformations. Only he who is able to see beyond appearances into the secret essence of things, he who is also convinced that the miracle is as evident as necessity, can penetrate this mystery: i.e., the poet himself."

Almansi (219), by contrast, reads this "abrasive and spiteful" poem in a much more nihilistic manner: " 'Stanze' originates from an easily surveyable background of Rimbaldian imagery . . . and dismantles it by demonstrating the ultimate inanity both of rational knowledge and irrational intuition. Nothing holds any longer: the poet's search is in vain, the woman's orbit moves 'beyond our human space' . . . the theme of 'Stanze' is our ignorance."

interminato / respingersi . . . oltre lo spazio: Cf. "interminati spazi" in Leopardi's "L'infinito."

putre / padule d'astro inabissato: Outstandingly harsh and disdainful Dantesque formula; *padule* is an inversion of *palude*.

un volo strepitoso di colombi: The insertion of a naturalistic image here is striking, achieving the very effect described by the image, itself repeated from the *osso* "Mia vita, a te non chiedo. . . ."

ignara: The presentation of "Clizia" here as unknowing, unaware, even passive is inconsistent with her later certainty and decisiveness; here she is more like the Arlettian proto-Clizia in "Il balcone," a "donna 'crepuscolare,' " as Montale himself called her.

una raggèra / di fili: Cary (299): "The beautiful third stanza evokes her *signs* as a play of correspondences with the unknown agency which sent her." Isella (2, 153): "Every single life is the point of convergence of a network of secret threads that bind it to the mysterious power of the universe."

una candida ala in fuga: The image of the wing as agency of death—and salvation— is widespread in Montale; cf., e.g., the "ala rude" of "Brina sui vetri . . ." or the "ali / di raccapriccio" at the end of "La primavera hitleriana."

vagabonde larve / . . . sciami: These lines "make explicit the poet's way of feeling, which is that of the man who sees the presence of death even in the manifestations of the happiest vitality" (Bonora 2, 30). The "larve" are those of "I morti"—they are also related to the "mandria lunare" of "Bassa marea," and reveal this and associated images as deathly. See also the "larve sulle golene" in "La primavera hitleriana."

corolla / di cenere: Cf. "la cenere degli astri" of "Arsenio." The image is entirely re-worked in "Nuove stanze," by which point the ashes have become associated with Clizia (cf. "cinerei i capelli" in "Il tuo volo"), perhaps as evidence of her having been singed by the divine light.

Voluta, / disvoluta è così la tua natura: Montale to Contini (*Eus*, 103): "*Voluta* and *disvoluta* from the verb *disvolere*" (to no longer desire what was desired before). Cf. Petrarch, CXIX, 42: "altro voler o disolver m'è tolto," which is echoed more directly in the "Violini" section of "Accordi": "volere non so più né disvolere" (tr. in *Oth*, 93). Bonora (2, 28) sees this as a psychological trait likening Arletta (/Clizia) to the restless Dora Markus, and indicative of a "controversial condition of will and acceptance" (2, 72).

Tocchi il segno . . . : Prefigures the action of the "festa di spari" at the climax of "Elegia di Pico Farnese"; Bonora (2, 28) says the lines imply Arletta's death and transfer to another realm. The close of the poem recalls Esterina's otherworldly dive at the end of "Falsetto," with the poet similarly left behind.

questa vaneggiante . . . su chi resta: Lonardi (92–93) notes that *questa/resta* is a typical Leopardian rhyme (found also at the close of "La casa dei doganieri," "Barche sulla Marna" [*questa/festa*], and elsewhere); *vaneggiante*, however, is Dantean (*Inferno* XVIII, 4–5).

Sotto la pioggia / In the Rain (1933)

One of the poems for Paola Nicoli (see note to the first motet), a Peruvian of Italian back-ground (hence the Spanish references).

'Por amor de la fiebre': Montale (*Op*, 919): "Words of Saint Teresa"—"for love of the fever," here evoked in a secular, erotic sense. The use of foreign terms "is one of the typical Eliotic practices with which Montale enriches his technique after 1930" (Isella 2, 156).

Sulla rampa materna: Montale (Greco, 37): "The house where her mother was born." Isella (2, 157): The stairs "of the hillside in Monterosso which lead to the house of his young friend's mother."

guscio d'uovo che va tra la fanghiglia: Contini (*Eus*, 29–30) calls this "one of the most secret and beautiful inventions in all of Italian lyric poetry!" For Marchese (3, 120), the *guscio d'uovo* is "a dead remain, the exact *pendant* of the 'guscio di cicala' " in the motet "Non recidere, forbice, quel volto"—and, by extension (see "Reading Montale," 422), a represen-tation of the writer's self. The image, which Contini sees as indicative of Montale's " 'mys-terious,' *associative*" non-methodic poetic practice which yields a poem "*after its entire evolution,*" offers a picture of the poet, here dancing with his interlocutor, as a will-o'-the-wisp at the mercy of events like the paper boats lost in the soapy slime of "Flussi."

la maschera: Montale (Greco, 37): Indicates the mask is "something like a defense." Isella (2, 158): "Even a life that is only apparent ('maschera') is something precious, *if* we *still* have the trigger ('sobbalzo') that suffices to tear us away from the void in which we're spinning ('mulinello') to find the path of lost time."

di là dal mulinello della sorte: The famous Argentine tango on the record is, as Arrow-smith (2, 156) says, a version of "the dance of life"; the "sobbalzo" is the skip of the record that will allow the poet to escape into his memory of her. Huffman (103): "Memory is a byproduct, a remnant, a scrap, a brief consolation 'left' by the 'eddy' [of fate]; it does not oppose fate but drives consciousness of it away, at least temporarily. . . . Thus, the poet can predict fate and both pray to it and seek to oppose it by praying for, as it were, an 'accident,' a temporary grace."

The image of the disk is elaborately developed in "L'orto."

strosci: Tuscan for *scrosci*; see *Inferno* XVII, 119.

Punta del Mesco (1933)

Montale (Greco, 37): "Between Levanto and Monterosso." The cape north and west of the Montale house at Fegina, hence an Arlettian locale. Arrowsmith (2, 157): "A promontory deeply pitted with huge marble quarries, where the marble barges and pile drivers are constantly at work and the seaside quiet is shattered by the sound of blasting."

Montale (Greco, 37): "The woman of Punta del Mesco is the same as in the first three motets. Thus the Spanish citation (from her language)." Greco (87) suggests that Montale here has confused "Punta del Mesco" with "Sotto la pioggia," but in any case, internal evidence implies that the poem belongs in the Arletta cycle; see below and Grignani (54–57).

Contini (1, 70) refers to this as one of the "rare shouts of triumph" in Montale's poetry, an exaltation of the recuperative powers of memory—cf. similar "occasions" in "Buffalo" and "Elegia di Pico Farnese."

all'alba: The beginning of the day, as Isella (2, 161) suggests, but also of life.

palabotto: Italianization of "pilot-boat."

il tuo passo sfiorava: Grignani (58) notes the "figurative style of Foscolo" here and in "lo scoglio / che ti portò prima sull'onde" of "Bassa marea," evocative of a kind of "aquatic semideity" (cf. "Falsetto").

Polene che risalgono: Montale (Greco, 37): Figureheads "that rise out of the sea where they are reflected."

qualche cosa di te: Recalls the "Nulla di te" of "Delta," also a poem for Arletta.

al davanzale: Cf. the "finestra che non s'illumina" of "Il balcone." Grignani (55) also mentions the window where the Nerina of Leopardi's "Le ricordanze"—"a sure typological model for Annetta [/Arletta]"—would appear while she was alive.

la tua infanzia dilaniata / dagli spari!: For Grignani (55–58), a reference to Montale's own traumatic experience of hunting as a child, alluded to in a number of late—and early, uncollected—poems, including "Lettera levantina" (tr. in *Oth*, 102–9), which link "Punta del Mesco" to Arletta (for a discussion of the theme, see note to "Il gallo cedrone").

Costa San Giorgio (1933; revised 1938)

Montale (*Op*, 921): "A pair walking on the well-known Florentine ramp [on the Oltrarno, just east of San Felice], and a bit higher [at one point, Irma Brandeis lived here (Contini 2, xii)]; it could in fact be called 'The Walk.' Maritornes is the one in *Don Quixote*, or one like her. It's known that *el dorado* was the myth of the *man* of gold, before becoming that of the *country* of gold. Here the poor fetish is now in the hands of men and has nothing to do with the 'mute enemy' who works below. . . . The poem was left half-finished: but maybe a development would be inconceivable."

Montale to Contini (December 11, 1935) (*Op*, 921): "Read this poetic effort of mine. . . . But think of the whole genuine background behind it. Do you know the *leyenda* to which it refers? It's the old (personal) form of that hallucination: here *doublée* with other meanings. Maybe too many. Still, it's a *carme* [song] of love (despairing)."

Montale told Rebay (2, 75) that the poem was written for the Peruvian Paola Nicoli, whom he "met in Florence in 1929–30."

El Dorado here, in this "inverse miracle" (Contini 1, 44), is "the God of the churches" (Cary, 305), an "idol" and hence blasphemous, whose "heavy presence" Montale decries—one of his many negative evocations of established religion in the later poems of *Le occasioni*. It is the Idol's influence that prevents Clizia/Maritornes ("an ugly servant girl [in Chapter XVI of Part I of *Don Quixote*] transformed by the demented imagination of Don Quixote into a beautiful damsel smitten with love for him" [Becker, 76]) from returning the poet's love; he is defeated, reduced to a mere "felled puppet." The title refers the reader back to the battle with evil evoked by "San Giorgio e il Drago" in the second motet, and the part it plays in the poet's relationship with his beloved.

Montale shows a tendency, starting from "Tempi di Bellosguardo," to work "di cultura," i.e., from cultural materials—perhaps in response to Eliot, as Isella (2, 156) suggests. Montale himself acknowledged this development in a 1933 letter to Contini (*Eus*, 3), adding, "but there has also grown in me a capacity for feeling that makes me less needful of material. I am disastrously growing younger." The "Peruvian legend of the man of gold . . . is the occasion for a desolate recognition of the end of values and the fall of idols, expressed in modes that become all the more demanding as a very 'old' personal 'hallucination' (we find its traces in 'Corno inglese' and also perhaps in 'Fine dell'infanzia') appears *doublée* with other meanings,' existential and historical. The discovery of evil following 'the end of childhood' (and now recorded in almost the same words as the poem of *Ossi di seppia* . . .) becomes here the heavy presence of a dethroned Idol, no longer with face or voice, who extends his exhausted and impotent arms over an infernal city now entirely remote from the sacred" (Luperini 1, 98–99).

Un fuoco fatuo . . . : Literally, an ignis fatuus, or will-o'-the-wisp, is a ghostlike light which sometimes appears over marshy ground or in cemeteries and is often attributable to the combustion of gas from decomposed organic matter (or bodies); here the labors of the gas man, who is lighting the streetlamps—(the "altra luce" is the next lamp, toward which he has quickly pedaled)—have produced a flame that reminds the poet of such an occurrence. Figuratively, the term refers to a deceptive goal or hope; *Fuochi fatui* was the title of a book of Sbarbaro's.

non s'apre il cerchio: Leopardian pessimism; cf. the image of the constricting circle in "La casa dei doganieri."

sui cammini . . . : The travels of the conquistadors.

fu lutto fra i tuoi padri: According to Isella (2, 168), a reference to Paola Nicoli's Peruvian origins.

lo stridere: Cf. "Cigola la carrucola del pozzo" and, by association with it, the image of the funicular—"Un cigolìo si sferra"—in the motet "Il fiore che ripete": all project a sense of the world as a mechanical (i.e., inhumane) contraption.

fantoccio: Isella (2, 170): "Synonym, in the Montalean system, of 'maschera' " (as in "Sotto la pioggia" and elsewhere); also "volto," "aspetto."

L'estate / Summer (1935)

Luperini (1, 102): "The incoherence and discontinuity of a reality reduced to a fragmentation of objects that are contiguous but unrelated, the senselessness of which is equaled only by the objective cruelty that brings them together and which condemns them to partiality and incompleteness, are rendered . . . by four images of incommunicability and reciprocal estrangement from their natural aspects . . . followed by four other images, also a 'catalogue,' of a spasmodic tendency to identity and completeness" (cf. the signs of evil and good in the *osso* "Spesso il male di vivere . . .").

L'ombra crociata del gheppio: Arrowsmith (2, 158): "A glancing ornithological omen of the predatory (Christian) shadow that blights life and requires such squandering surrender of individual existence, such needless extinction of vitality."

E la nube che vede?: An earlier version read "E la nube non vede?" (And the cloud doesn't see?).

Forse . . . : The first stanza, "which sanctions the division of the world" (Contini 1, 41), is followed, after a "profound hiatus," by the second movement "of a possible sign (the trout) and possible resurrection."

fanciulla morta / Aretusa: Arletta (note the assonance of the names), whose childhood self is here acknowledged as "dead" and transformed into a spring. Franco Fortini (quoted in Bonora 2, 38) sees the "polla schiusa" as a reference "to the spring of Syracuse" and, in the leap of the trout, "to the dolphins on Sicilian-Greek four-drachma pieces"—"an allusion to the idea of metamorphosis, indeed of reincarnation." (The image of the fish's glimmering will recur in "L'anguilla.")

non passerà la cruna: Cf. Matthew 19:24: "And again I say unto you, It is easier for a camel to go through the eye of a needle, than for a rich man to enter into the kingdom of God." Luperini (1, 103) sees "L'estate" as related to "Vasca," the "tropp'altro che / non passerà la cruna" recalling the "altro che striscia" which "lived and died and never had a name."

Occorrono troppe vite: Luperini (1, 103): "The absurd squandering of existence, in which the eventual realization of a life coincides with the failing of numerous others." Bonora (2, 225): "The subject himself is overcome amidst the diffused and cruel vitality of things in his attempt to emerge in a difficult and costly individuation." Cf. the fragmentation of the self described in "Ciò che di me sapeste."

Eastbourne (1933/35)
Montale (*Op*, 922): "In Sussex. The *August Bank Holiday* is the English *Ferragosto*"—a major Italian holiday, celebrating the Assumption of the Virgin, on and around August 15.

Montale (Greco, 38): "Bank holiday. The subject is *that Ferragosto*. The long, slow tide is *that* wave which comes in after low tide. Easy *sul pendìo* [on the slant—Montale is recalling an earlier draft] like my life, too, in those years, easy but threatened. My country is My fatherland, the hymn. The day is full of things and memories. The voice is the usual message of the absent-present one. The merrymaking's merciless because it doesn't erase the emptiness, the pain. In the sand, in *that* sunset. Evening is falling."

Rebay (3, 188–89) suggests that "Eastbourne" is part of an American diptych with "Verso Capua," both dealing with Clizia's American identity, that England is a screen for New England, and that "God Save the King" stands for "My Country 'Tis of Thee," which has the same melody (the words "mia patria!" [my country!] are quoted in the poem). It is equally plausible, however, that Montale is quoting another British patriotic anthem, "I Vow to Thee, My Country," by Sir Cecil Spring-Rice, which was set to music by Gustav Holst in *The Planets* and became a popular hymn (Bonora and Rebay hear an echo of a famous chorus from Verdi's *Nabucco*: "Oh, mia patria, sì bella e perduta").

Others, including Bonora, Forti, and Luperini, see the poem as part of the Arletta cycle, which seems more consistent with the ambiguous characteristics of this "lost" female figure, sign of a "previous, authentic life" (Contini 1, 43), who lacks the decision of the later Clizia and shares Arletta's shadowy tentativeness.

Franco Croce ("Le Occasioni," in *La Rassegna della Letteratura Italiana*, VII, 70, 2–3 [May-December 1966], 283, quoted in Isella 2, 175) suggests that the elaborate descriptive development of the poem embodies "the successive openings, closings, and seeking in the poet's mind"—a "first sketch" of the structure of "Palio," "Elegia di Pico Farnese," and "Notizie dall'Amiata."

Bank Holiday: Almansi and Merry (90) suggest that the term operates "in the same incantatory way as the name 'Buffalo.' "

Riporta l'onda lunga / della mia vita: Barile (2, 82) notes that the image of long, "gentle" waves recalls the beginning of Montale's 1926 poem "Dolci anni che di lunghe rifrazioni," sometimes called "Destino di Arletta" (Arletta's Destiny) or "Prima della primavera" (Before Spring) (tr. in *Oth*, 114–17). The association of "return" (here, the return of the waves) with the influx of memory goes back to "Crisalide" (Giorgio Cerboni Baiardi, quoted in Isella 2, 178); but see also "Carnevale di Gerti" and elsewhere.

sulla china: Cf., e.g., the "stupida discesa" of "Costa San Giorgio," the descent of the "cuna" in "Tempi di Bellosguardo."

voce di sangue: The association of blood with Arletta is confirmed in the 1972 poem "Annetta" (quoted in note to "Incontro"), in which Montale speaks of his feeling for her as "una punta che feriva / quasi a sangue" (a wound that hurt / till it almost bled). The blood, then, of the "voce di sangue"—and of the "labbro di sangue" of "Da una torre"—is, perhaps, also the poet's own.

m'agita un carosello: Cf. "Sotto la pioggia," where the poet is likewise sucked into a bewildering, if not threatening, vortex of unrestrained activity. See the related image of the spinning top in "Palio," where the eddy, however, metamorphoses into Clizia's flight, leaving a significant mark as well.

riconosco il tuo respiro: In "La casa dei doganieri" the poet could not hear the loved one breathing—an all-important sign of her spiritual as well as actual presence.

Anche tu lo sapevi, luce-in-tenebra: Isella (2, 180): "Beyond Love, Arletta is also knowledge of the evil that infects the world." Cf. John 1:4–5: "In him was life; and the life was the light of men. And the light shineth in darkness; and the darkness comprehended it not."

plaga: Dantesque.

l'acre tizzo: Isella (2, 181) notes the correspondence with the "favilla d'un tirso" at the end of MEDITERRANEO.

che già fu: Almansi and Merry (93): "Suggests that the remains of the Bank Holiday were once, but are now no longer, its essence and meaning for the poet. . . . This cancelling past remote tense [also] dominated 'Accelerato.' " See also the opening of "Dora Markus." The unusually strong verb further allies the poem with the Arletta texts.

Corrispondenze / Correspondences (1936)

The title is that of one of the most famous poems in *Les fleurs du mal*. The correspondences here are, according to Arrowsmith (2, 158), between the natural and man-made worlds; or else between the poet's reality and the "something else" which the "shepherdess without a flock" alone can read. Almansi, however (219), sees the poem, in its "anguished impact," as "almost a parody" of Baudelaire: "In Baudelaire everything holds together; in Montale nothing makes sense. To the tightly drawn structure of the rhymes—with ironic effect—corresponds an extremely loose structure of metaphors and analogies. In the optical illusion, the 'miraggio' of the poem, everything metaphorically points elsewhere . . . but the poet refuses to specify the location of this analogical alterity: hence the elsewhere becomes nowhere. The poet does not know . . . what the 'flockless shepherdess' reads in the forest of symbols, and his questions are in vain."

La mano . . . strame: The image recurs in "Nel parco," a poem which resonates with Arlettian themes; cf. also " 'Ezekiel saw the Wheel . . . ,' " "Cave d'autunno," and elsewhere.

Bassareo: One of the very few classical references in *Le occasioni*. Arrowsmith (2, 158): "Cult title of Dionysus, whose Maenads (or Bassarids [wearing fox skins—*bassara* in Greek = fox]), in a lost play by Aeschylus, tore Orpheus to pieces. Bassareus' 'chariot' has its modern counterpart in the distant train, just as the 'mirage of vapors' . . . is linked to the smoke of the train." (The undertones of Orphic sacrifice are consistent with the poet's portrayal of himself as erotic victim.)

Isella (2, 185): Dionysus' "chariot ('sonoro' because of the orgiastic dances that accompany it) is pulled by rams (animals sacred to him). Their woolly fleece, their 'crazy bleating,' are the mythic transfiguration of the clouds of heat that gather over the scorched earth in the dog days and of the dull rumbling of the thunder that accompanies them, without any rainstorm. Their source is the Latin verses of Crashaw already cited in reference to 'Cave d'autunno' (1931), and 'Bassa marea' (1932), where the first term of the equation ('rams' = 'clouds') is replaced, respectively, by 'swarm' and 'flock.' "

Barche sulla Marna / Boats on the Marne (1933/37)
Arrowsmith (2, 159): "In its lyrical *détente* and pastoral evocation of a gentler European civility [the title seems to echo that of Monet's *Barques sur la Seine à Auteuil*], the work is a tonal and thematic pendant to 'Bellosguardo Times.' . . . Each is set in . . . the uneasy temporal interim between an ominous future and a past to which one cannot return except in fantasy and nostalgia but which persists, in its evidence of human greatness and a humane order, as the measure by which the future must be assessed. This is the 'dream' against which the actual or breaking nightmare takes on a feeling of restless fatality."

For Lonardi (86ff.), the poem shares the dream's negation of reality with "Quasi una fantasia," here under the sign of Leopardian—but also Rimbaldian/symbolist—influence. Mengaldo (22): "Perhaps the most organic moment of Leopardianism in Montale."

Segui: Isella (2, 188): "Typical Montalean invitation" (cf. "Arsenio," the second movement of "Notizie dall'Amiata," and, in the negative, "Per un 'Omaggio a Rimbaud' ").

alberata: Montalean neologism, for *alberata*.

il sangue / del drago . . . : Montale to Contini (December 26, 1946) (*Eus*, 154): "The cinnabar-colored wall repeats or reflects or prolongs the 'dragon blood' of the row of trees, maples or others I couldn't say. They are two reds hard to translate into precise forms, as happens in painting."

ma dov'è . . . : The catalogue of questions recalls Leopardi's idyll "La sera del dì di festa" —as does the occasion of the poem evoked in its last lines (in parentheses, like the *senhal* of the motet "La speranza di pure rivederti")—but also the whole Western tradition of the *ubi sunt* epitomized by Villon's "Où sont les neiges d'antan?"

nel grido / concorde del meriggio: An idealized image of social unity (cf. the "unìsono vocale" of "L'ombra della magnolia . . ."), which conceals "the great ferment"—perhaps a veiled critique of Fascism (cf. the "urlo solo" of "Palio").

tra gli argini: Isella (2, 189): "Suggests an orderly flowing of life like the running of a solidly canalized river"; cf. the "acque . . . non più irose" of "Tempi di Bellosguardo."

bagliore: Montale (Angelini 2, 173): "The pale, pearly light of the failing day."

il domani velato che non fa orrore: Lonardi (89) sees this as a translation of "quel vago avvenir che avevi in mente" (that vague future you had in mind) from Leopardi's "A Silvia," revealing "the negative and tragic depths out of which the Leopardian idyll is born"; cf. also the "dubbia dimane" of "Falsetto."

Qui . . . : Isella (2, 190): "The breaking of the line marks the opposition of past [childhood] and present, dream and reality."

possiamo / scendere . . . : A slow-motion, adult-world reprise of the hectic Heraclitean descent of "Flussi," which this poem recalls in its bipartite structure, imagery, and thematics.

Elegia di Pico Farnese / Pico Farnese Elegy (1939)

Montale (*Op*, 932): "Pico Farnese: a village in the province of Frosinone" in southern Lazio, home of the writer Tommaso Landolfi (1908–79), where Montale visited him in March 1939. Isella (2, 195ff.) notes a number of correspondences with Landolfi's novel *La pietra lunare (The Moonstone)* (1939), the proofs of which Montale may have read while visiting his friend. It's likely the title alludes to Rilke's *Duino Elegies*, translated into Italian by Leone Traverso in 1937. The poem itself, like "La primavera hitleriana," also influenced by Rilke, is written in long lines, some of them the fourteen-syllable "versi martelliani," double *settenari* devised by P. I. Martello in the seventeenth century in imitation of the French alexandrine.

See Carpi (311–55) for a detailed analysis of the text, including Montale's revisions described in the letters to Bobi Bazlen quoted below.

Montale to Bazlen (April 29, 1939) (*Op*, 927): "Between the ingestion and the digestion of a plate of tortellini drowned in Chianti I very rapidly wrote the 'Pico Elegy,' which I enclose. Have Tom read it. . . . Write me immediately what you think."

Montale to Bazlen (May 1, 1939) (*Op*, 928): "Thanks; I feared worse. But usually, when one goes into details, the *objective* value of the means escapes me (especially with you). I don't know *up to what point* the different perception of certain nuances is due to my objective defects or to your physiologically diverse ear. Shall I explain myself? I don't know up to what point we hear in the same way the actual value of my verbal *impasto* [texture], I don't know to what degree you hear what's necessary and what's arbitrary in it. This apart from other difficulties in which the fault may be entirely mine, and of which I'll give you an example: in the two lines 'è l'Amore . . . messaggera imperiosa' [in an earlier draft] (which for me would be the center of the poem, the highest elevation of tone) there are elements which for me, subjectively, were extremely vital and not susceptible to neoclassical interpretation: the fringe that you saw earlier in the photograph of [Irma Brandeis], here the fringe of a wing, but in sum an anticipation of the incredible 'plumage' attributed to the forehead without error, i.e., the true fringe. 'Imperiosa' seems irreplaceable to me, 'messaggera' idem. Do you think that in eliminating the 'bossi spartiti' [divided box trees, again in the earlier draft] (which at Pico exist in Tom's garden) I would obtain a reduction of the deleterious effect you point out? Respond precisely on this point. I wanted here to be Blake-Rossetti, not Lipparini-Carducci. How much have I erred? Can it be enough to change the rhythm and leave the words?

"In the copy I'm sending I have marked the caesuras more clearly. Forgive me, I know you don't need them. . . . Mark the lines that are too prosaic or too classicist. Still, I have the impression that the first 12 lines are perfect and only apparently descriptive."

Montale to Bazlen (May 5, 1939) (*Op*, 929): "I've much revised the elegy, and not coolly. Now, I'd like to request your *exequatur*. Don't think of this or that line it could have gained or lost. The revisions have helped the whole poem. Earlier there was that series of ultimatums or categorical imperatives that ended with a shooting party . . . and various filler. Now the rhythm, too, develops more gradually from a static descriptive beginning to a narrative and lyric movement. Read without comparing point for point with the other copy and you'll agree. . . . As you'll see, 'prilla' is used also for 'brilla' [shines]. . . . The 'balena' and the 'cruccio' somehow come together with the 'incudine' and the 'calor bianco.' "

Montale to Bazlen (May 10, 1939) (*Op*, 930): " 'The childhood theater' is certainly ambiguous, it has both the meanings you uncovered. But only those who have been to Pico can be sure that the theater is a real theater where people perform; those who haven't been there will equally have the suspicion, the doubt, the suggestion of the real theater; because theater in the sense of *milieu* (the theater of the crime) would be very banal and difficult to attribute to Eusebius.

"So I'll leave the passage unchanged. It happens *often* to me (and often *voluntarily*) that I'm ambiguous in this way. For example, in the motet of the woman who's about to leave her cloud ["Perché tardi? . . ."]:

> A un soffio il pigro fumo . . . (?)
> *si difende nel punto che ti chiude*

it's clear that *nel punto* can have two meanings: at the *moment when* and in the *place where*, both of them legitimate. For Landolfi this uncertainty is horrendous, for me it's a richness. Certainly, in this case, the ambiguity is unconscious, spontaneous; in the case of the *theater* it's a bit planned. . . .

" 'Ma più discreto se . . .' It's effectively a suture, a transition. But one was called for, and this one is very discreet. To write 65 lines without a transition is almost impossible (for me). What about you?"

Montale to Bazlen (June 9, 1939) (*Op*, 931): "*Elegy*. If you force (or swell) the fruits of the persimmon etc. or destroy the old wives' tales (in the sense of tall tales) etc. your splendor is 'palese' [apparent]. The frigid vestibule *which was a theater* (in the two senses possible . . .) etc. The balconies *surrounded* by ivy etc. 'Se appare': 'and here *although* it seems your help cannot be heard there is nevertheless the skeet that shrills and is even so (if not precisely *your* help) a worthy key to the day, the only one worthy of you.' Key stands here for *grimaldello* [picklock] (you'll also find this word in the book [in "Tempi di Bellosguardo"], an instrument for opening; but maybe (I'm thinking of this now) it could also be a musical key (key of F, or G) in a related sense, and even *diapason* in the sense of the little instrument which allows harmonizing etc.; 'ignaro del mutamento'? perhaps ignorant of the celestial breeze that makes him, too, a participant in the miracle.

"As for the little stanzas it's impossible for me to render them in prose. They're extremely generic, though not obscure. I would have to rewrite the same words, arranging them as prose. Raise (you) the veil, count (you pilgrim) (or else you who watch) the veil [*sic*] (I don't know what it is, perhaps the veil of Maya [derived from Schopenhauer's *The World as Will and Representation*]). The vessels are ex-votos, the islands places in the naves [of the catacomb sanctuaries]. In the third are the sweets sold in the sacristies of sanctuaries, a reference to the mountain cleft like a vulva at Gaeta, references to candles etc. [Cf. the similar stanzas inserted in the closely linked poem "Palio"; Isella (2, 193) sees the two texts as "conceived as a diptych."]

"In the grottoes (of the islands mentioned above) there is the sign of the Fish which I believe to be one of the oldest Christian symbols; yet the doubt is expressed that Christian symbology (the green forest) depreciates life and that Christ needs to be continued perhaps in spite of himself. If you can, even changing everything, make a syncretist song where god and phallus seem to be equivocally mixed together; this is the meaning of all the south. A meaning, however, that the Poet (*sic*) doesn't approve without many reservations." Isella (2, 196) notes that Schopenhauer's text mentions both the fish as Christian symbol and the phallus "as symbol of the love lived on this side of the veil" of Maya, which is "drenched with an erotic vitality profoundly connected to death."

Le pellegrine: Le occasioni, as we have seen, is notable for its hostile investigations of organized religion (see also "Costa San Giorgio" and "Notizie dall'Amiata"), which is criticized for its irrational and subconscious motivations and is presented as exerting a malign psychic and social influence (cf. "L'estate"). At the same time, Montale was elaborating the terms of his own private religion, at this phase of which love—or Love—in the person of Clizia, as exemplified in "Elegia di Pico Farnese," mediates for the poet between the human and divine realms. Becker (61) notes that Montale's critique of the Church begins to acquire a political coloration toward the end of *Le occasioni*: "Beginning in the late '30s the poet's verse develops equations between totalitarianism's manipulation of the masses and organized religion's recruitment of the many."

Rebay (1, 36) notes that the hillside entrance to the Landolfi house in Pico opens onto a narrow street which runs into the church square, so that "a procession through the town to the church would pass directly under its windows."

alza . . . / numera . . . : Montale to Rebay (1, 50): "It could be the veil one has to raise in order to know the number of days and months we have left to live."

questo sepolcro verde: The green is the verdigris of the vaults above.

pigra illusione: Marchese (1, 111): "The assent to this primitive religiosity, passive and illusory . . . impregnated with physical eros" that is the "love of bearded women."

un vano farnetico: D'Annunzian (Mengaldo, 39).

scaccia: This verb becomes "distinctive of the aristocracy of Love" (Carpi, 325) in "Le processioni del 1949," a later recasting of the "Elegia."

Ben altro / è l'Amore: Carpi (335): "The religiosity of the 'bearded women' is drenched in eroticism: but not for this reason is it entirely rejected by the poet, in fact . . . it is only partially rejected, just as Christian symbology (which 'depreciates life' [or, literally, cuts it in half]) is only partially capable of responding to the needs of life in its entirety. Eroticism has to purify itself of sensual materiality and be sublimated into a metaphysical relationship, Christ has 'to be continued,' his work completed: the problem (the task of the poet) will be precisely this, to reach the high level of Love exorcizing the equivocal suggestions of the Fish" in order "to express a religiosity *not fetishistically irrational* but *spiritually cognitive*" (342). The lines of the second strophe "constitute the first document of the awareness with which Montale has already begun to organize the neostilnovistic-Christological ideology that will later be theorized in 'Iride' and developed in 'La primavera hitleriana' (and in general in the SILVAE); it should be added that the letter [of June 9, 1939, quoted above] that concerns these lines also offers the first formulation of that *malgré lui*, in reference to the continuation of Christ, which, variously elaborated, will be a constant in Montale, up to the extreme version of the uncrossable division between the original divine *fiat* and human history. Here in embryo, even, is the distant motivation of the future declaration of 'Nestorian' faith in a god-bearing Christ, progenitor of a privileged *gens* of 'incarnate creatures' who are bearers of divinity by association and not through hypostatic relationship, to which the Christ-bearing Clizia will belong: it is not by chance that it is here that she is first seen as a 'messenger' " (335–36).

Se urgi . . . i diòsperi: Montale to Rebay (1, 42–43): "If you swell the persimmons to their core, i.e., if you force—'urgi'—them to mature by virtue of this Panic power of Love which you represent or know how to arouse, or if you are reflected in the water, or if you destroy by the purity of your presence the fables of the bearded women, and protect your poet—one of the 'few,' over whose 'passing,' i.e., over whose life, Clizia watches—your splendor is apparent." Rebay says the *diòspero* is the Tuscan name for the persimmon—a fiery red fruit, according to Montale, who was thinking perhaps of the inaccurate Greek etymology "Diòs púr," "fire of Zeus," instead of the actual "grain of Zeus," and thus an instance of the elaboration of Clizia's fire imagery. The image is perhaps derived from Keats's "To Autumn": "To bend with apples the moss'd cottage-trees, / And fill all fruit with ripeness to the core; / To swell the gourd. . . ."

Macrì (2, 140–41) notes Clizia's "orgasmic-excitative 'urgency' " here, her "potent and divine fertilizing and fertilized nature," and notes the strong subliminal association (derived from Dante) of the word *urge* with *turge* (indicating tumescence). "With such sensual and naturalistic pregnancy Montale, like Dante and with the example of Dante, reinforces the allegory of divine love, with its perennial model, the Song of Songs" (348).

al trapasso dei pochi: Montale to Contini (October 31, 1945) (*Eus*, 115): "I fear that *trapasso* here was supposed to mean 'career,' death understood as the last stop." Bonora (2, 74): "Montale's aristocracy . . . is not mystical and esoteric, it's not first of all and specifically literary; rather, it has an ethical-political basis: it is the aristocracy of the few who haven't accepted the [Fascist Party] card, who, in order not to surrender to the mythology of the crowd and to resist the easy debasement of conscience, have stoically destroyed the very continuity of their selves when they could survive only at the cost of complicity, and they have reduced themselves and their work to an arid margin of objects or final means of resistance against the assault of mythology and the irrational."

uomini-capre: The *ciociari*, inhabitants of Ciociaria in Lazio, where the poem is set, traditionally wore goatskin leggings; but the image is consistent with Montale's disdain for "the horde" throughout *Le occasioni* and elsewhere.

il seme del girasole: Reference to the Ovidian Clytie, Clizia's ultimate mythological source (see note to "La primavera hitleriana"). Carpi (337): "The sunflower acts . . . as a metaphor for the light that breaks into the sepulchral obscurity of the 'grottoes' and brings back whole life: the sunflower names, and in fact carries in itself, a very different source of light than the Fish. [It] enters into the semantic field that will be that of the sun-Christ ('Altro-Lui') of 'La primavera hitleriana,' while the Fish represents the mummified and paganizing version of the originary Christ." (But see Macrì [2, 348] for further discussion of the erotic subtext of the image.)

dall'androne gelido: Rebay (1, 36): "The property of the ancient Landolfi family at Pico consists of a group of tall structures [the remains of an old castle], now unoccupied, overlooking a vast garden with fruit trees. The central building is distinguished from the others by a kind of large covered terrace, supported on the garden side by a semicircular arch. This is the 'frigid vestibule,' at one time used as a stage by the Landolfis for family theatrical performances."

un segno: Montale (Rebay 1, 48) indicates the sign is not the signal for the beginning of the shooting competition: "it's an imprecise sign of a metaphysical and transcendent value, not concrete and real."

prilla il piattello: As Montale notes in his May 5, 1939, letter to Bazlen, *prilla* (to whirl) also stands in for *brilla* (to gleam), an indication that the image is a Clizian *senhal*.

una chiave: Montale to Rebay (1, 49): "The one key of the day is Clizia's apparition, there is no other. In the shattering of the skeet there may perhaps be a reference to the particular violence that often accompanies her apparitions." The "Elegia," in fact, marks the point at which Clizia's angelic powers are first fully embodied.

Jacomuzzi (1, 127–45) makes a convincing argument for the efficacy of an allegorical, rather than metaphorical, reading of Montale's poetry, which is consistent with the stilnovistic methods of *Le occasioni*. "Reality and the sequence of events are treated in [Montale's poetry], from the outset, as 'ciphers' or 'signals' of the invisible; but the relationship between the two planes is not one of similarity or 'correspondence,' isn't recognizable in the structures of the sensible, and the movement and deciphering are accomplished through an agency that does not belong to the events themselves: by means of a key which the day *demands* and thus does not possess. The specific function of poetic language, in this perspective, can't be resolved in operations of substitution or in new modes of designation by analogy, as happens for him who locks himself in the prison of metaphors. It is focused in the capacity to establish together the possibility of a meaning and a supermeaning, to establish a relationship between the two planes that is not one of contiguity and resemblance but of change of meaning and meta-morphosis . . . on different levels of discourse, each endowed with its own autonomous sig-nifying coherence, according to the model of allegorical invention" (137–38).

l'umore dell'occhio: Jacomuzzi (1, 138): "We are in the presence of the allegorical theme of the eye as a mirror in which the external and phenomenal object is reflected, changed, and revealed: the same as the eyes of Beatrice (*Purgatorio* XXXI, 121–26) in which the double beast *raged*, and yet, staying *quiet* in itself, *was transformed into its idol* [i.e., its reflected image]."

lemure: Jacomuzzi (1, 139) says the word may mean "specter," an insubstantial, menacing nocturnal ghost, as well as a kind of monkey, also nocturnal: "The term designates the con-dition of the bearded women and goat-men, barbaric and primitive, almost prehuman, but also nocturnal, which now dissolves, at the break of day, the physical day that sees them depart and the day of Clizia who destroys them."

rifatto celeste: Jacomuzzi (1, 139): "That the boy is 'made' celestial ['again'; note the frequent use of the prefix *ri-* (*rifrange, rifatto, ricarica*) at the moment of ecstatic epiphany] defines above all the metamorphosis as a reconstitution and return to origins, out of time; and it's a substantial metamorphosis, as 'celestial,' which is a substantive here, a synonym for divinity, attests."

fanciulletto: Leopardian. The term implies the boy's ignorance, his obliviousness to the transfiguration occurring around him.

Anacleto: Angelini (2, 174): "This young boy was a valet at the home of the writer Tom-maso Landolfi, who had invited Montale to Pico Farnese. So much for the 'occasion' of the ending. But the name also includes a symbol, expressed in its double etymology. In part, it recalls the first popes in the person of one of the successors of Saint Peter and the Christianity evoked here in its most characteristic manifestations (pilgrimages, litanies, etched fish). But, on the other hand, *anaklētos* (from *anakalo*) = called to service, sobriquet for [Italy's] reviving militarism. In this word the entire political situation of 1939 is crystallized."

Jacomuzzi (1, 139), by contrast, sees Anacleto as a "precise case of allegorical personification in which the whole narrative of the 'Elegy' culminates"; he claims the first sense of the name (from *anakalèo*) is *"called on high* and even *called back"* (141), and "stands as analogous to 'rifatto celeste,' almost the contrary, secular and by litotes, of the Paraclete" ["the one called to help, the Intercessor," an epithet for the Holy Spirit]. Angelini's second sense, "radically different, alternative, and ironizing in respect to the first," is "that of warlike violence that is being mounted in a 'weather' that has just barely turned 'mild,' and for which the boy Anacleto is already actively working. . . . Anacleto is a positive figure of detachment from and victory over the 'dark forces of Ahriman,' the Zoroastrian all-destroying Satan or principle of evil [Montale, in "Augurio" (1944) (in *Auto*, 66; tr. in *Sec*, 10); he continues: "In us and for us is . . . realized a divinity, first terrestrial and later perhaps celestial ('celeste') and incomprehensible to our senses" (see "Visita a Fadin")], but also a negative figure of a new possible barbarism. Here surfaces the ideology, both teleological and civic, of the 'poor dismayed Nestorian' [of "Iride"], the rejection of the peaceful separation of human and divine, of transcendence and immanence. The divine appeal against 'empty raving' and 'dark wives' tales,' the 'celestial' condition as opposed to the 'lemur,' can always turn into their opposites; the celestial gods can always become the emblem of the new hordes of the 'pestilential Gods' of 'Il sogno del prigioniero' " (141–42).

Nuove stanze / New Stanzas (1939)

Montale to Contini (May 15, 1939) (*Op*, 933): "Having fallen into a state of *trance* (which happens to me rarely, because I usually write in conditions of cynical self-control), I've produced a sequel to the old Stanze that so pleased [Alfredo] Gargiulo.

"A sequel in a manner of speaking. These, which could be titled 'Love, chess, and wartime vigil,' but will instead bear a simple 2, are a little different. They're more Florentine, more inlaid, harder; but they seem good to me and I hope they will seem so to you, above all after a re-rereading. La Martinella, as you know, is the bell of Palazzo Vecchio; it only rings, according to [Aldo] Palazzeschi, to indicate 'disgrace.' Inter nos I've also heard it on certain occasions which you understand. . . ." (Isella [2, 202] maintains this is a reference to Hitler's 1938 visit to Florence, the subject of "La primavera hitleriana.")

Montale (Greco, 38): "*Altro stormo*, the war which is developing. Clizia's last days in Florence. *Le tue porte*, very generic. But she was Jewish. *Le fitte cortine*, that chance can hang so that the worst isn't seen. *Lo specchio ustorio*, the war, evil, etc."

Isella (2, 203): "In a letter to Bazlen of May 22, [1939,] Montale speaks of a certain *fantaisiste* tone in the first stanza, which rises to the 'classical' tone of the second. 'With the 3rd stanza the tone rises again; and in the 4th we're in a zone where the word classicism no longer makes sense. In this progression lies the secret of the *Stanze*.' "

The smoke of the Arlettian "Stanze" has metamorphosed into an allegorical attribute of Clizia's. For Marchese (1, 114), "the passage from Arletta-Annetta to Clizia couldn't be more clear" in the "surreal-metaphysical" atmosphere of the poem, while Bonora (quoted by Marchese, ibid.) emphasizes "the climate of enchantment and magic" evoked by the imagery of the first stanza.

Isella (2, 203): "The poem is born and develops in the gradual negating of the distinction between external and internal and between reality and symbol." The knights and bishops of the chess set transfer the chivalric, stilnovistic atmosphere (cf. Saint George and the Dragon in the MOTTETTI) that defines much of *Le occasioni* into a modern, bourgeois interior—albeit a hallucinatory one—only to resurface in a deeper key in the metaphor of the poet's vigil as "cavaliere servente" of Clizia.

degli scacchi: Luperini (1, 104): "The game of chess . . . is certainly 'a stylized image of war,' but it's also an allusion to the ways to keep it in check. It is an entirely intellectual symbol: chess is the game of intelligence and cool, which is played protected by the silence and intimacy of a closed and overstuffed ambience, in which, even so, the sacred rites of culture are celebrated."

La morgana: The fata morgana is a mirage in which an image appears suspended in the air—here of a city created by the smoke from Clizia's cigarette; cf. the "fuoco fatuo" of "Costa San Giorgio."

tregenda: The term recurs in "La primavera hitleriana."

incenso: Sacralizes Clizia's cigarette smoke.

Il mio dubbio . . . . : Most likely a reference back to "Stanze," in which the woman was "ignara" of her nature and her relationship to the world; the Clizia of "Nuove stanze," by contrast, is all-knowing, a "Sphinx," as Montale himself defined her in "Intentions" (*Sec*, 303).

nembo: Precursor of the "bufera" that will make its first appearances in "Tempi di Bellosguardo" and "Il ritorno."

si placa . . . domanda . . . : Marchese (1, 116): "Alludes respectively to the Christ-like sacrifice of Clizia and the holocaust of the Jews, and more generally to the victims of the war."

altri fuochi: Other fires, other forces, stronger than the judgmental flash of Clizia's gaze, according to Bonora (quoted in Marchese 1, 115–16); to Marchese, however, the fires are "true sacrifices, absurd rituals, non-metaphoric 'fires' "; or, perhaps, the fires ignited by the "burning mirror."

le fitte / cortine: Cf. the curtain in "La frangia dei capelli"; a development of the image of the screen that appears in "Quasi una fantasia" and "Forse un mattino andando. . . ." Cf. also the images that can't "hide the atrocious view" in "Iride."

una luce / . . . di nevaio: Cf. the "interno / di nivee maioliche" of "Dora Markus," favored site of female apparitions and transformations.

le pedine: The "automi" of the fifth motet; the "uomini-capre" of "Elegia di Pico Farnese." See note to "Elegia di Pico Farnese," and also Fortini, for an intelligent discussion of the sources of Montale's aristocratic or aristocratizing attitudes toward "others," particularly servants (see also note to "L'arca"). The chivalric mythos of *Le occasioni*, which is further elaborated in *La bufera*, is intimately linked with Montale's sense of himself, and above all his beloved, as separate from, more fully alive than, others, due to his clear vision and decisive rejection, shared with her, of the reality around them.

allo specchio ustorio: Cf. the image of the eye as mirror discussed in note to "Elegia di Pico Farnese."

occhi d'acciaio: Cf. the "sheer crystal gaze" of "L'orto." Cary (300): "The vigil's prize is surely one's authentic *mortal* soul. The *virtù* of resistance resides in *coscienza*, the persisting consciousness of good and evil. The guiding blazon is contemplative Clizia, keeper of the faith, she who says no, who realizes the divinity of man through her absolute commitment to human dignity, justice and the good. Clizia, as our lady of the chessboard, is the climactic sign of the *Occasioni* volume, while 'Nuove stanze' is the culmination of the thematic shift, under Amor, from suffering and negation to the idea of service and sacrifice first touched upon at the close of *Ossi di seppia* in 'Casa sul mare' and 'Crisalide' " (but see note to "Delta").

Il ritorno / The Return (1940)
Added to the second edition of 1940, along with "Alla maniera di Filippo De Pisis . . ." and the fifth and twelfth motets.

Montale (*Op*, 934): "Musical aria, in which Mozart's *Hellsnakes* alone would not justify the final squall."

Montale (in an early version of "Intentions" quoted in Angelini 2, 174): "We'll now see in a more extensive poem a whole landscape move and prepare itself, waiting for the hoped-for visit. It's the landscape of Bocca di Magra, at the border of Tuscany and Liguria [near the Cinque Terre], very resonant with the music of Debussy's saraband and the musical exercises of the Queen of the Night in Mozart's *The Magic Flute*: the hellsnakes. . . . Clearly the stormy petrel angel owned a good gramophone."

Contini (1, 150): Part of the "diary of 'return' situations composed of 'Bassa marea,' 'Sotto la pioggia,' 'Punta del Mesco,' 'L'estate,' and 'Il ritorno' itself." Grignani (59): "As the title suggests, a mental return to the locales of childhood grafted onto the present marine landscape of Bocca di Magra." Grignani argues persuasively that the poem belongs to the Arletta cycle, and that the "black / tarantula bite" is related to the "punta che feriva / quasi a sangue" of "Annetta" (1972) (quoted in note to "Incontro").

Like the Arlettian "Accelerato," which is also about a return and which this poem echoes in numerous ways, "Il ritorno" is one long sentence, punctuated by six repetitions of the adverb *ecco*. The poet Vittorio Sereni, who hears an unexpressed seventh in "eccomi" in front of the final words, "son pronto," writes (in "Il ritorno," *Letture montaliane, in occasione del 80° compleanno del poeta* [Genoa: Bozzi Editore, 1977]; quoted in Bonora 2, 97–98): "The signals, the percussion, the jolts of these *eccos* . . . prepare the screen on which will camp what once he would have called the 'miracle' and which now is rather thunderbolt, illumination, epiphany."

libeccio: Cf. "La casa dei doganieri," also an Arlettian poem.

lingueggiano: Isella (2, 210): "Appear and disappear quickly; are visible intermittently." Cf. "Casa sul mare": "Nulla disvela. . . ."

Duilio: According to Sereni, who vouches for the accuracy of Montale's description, Bocca di Magra was at the time reached only by ferryboat and "the very passage from one shore of the river to the other seemed to involve an important, meaningful decision; and even more, a ritual, a magic spell, as if it were a matter of moving from one world to another." Sereni attests as well that Duilio was a real character; nevertheless the Charon-like boatman (as in "Buffalo") lends a distinct "air of Acheron" to the scene. Bonora (2, 100): " 'Incerto lembo . . .' immediately translates into an emblem, that indefinable and perhaps nonexistent line of demarcation between life [Tuscany?] and death [Liguria, the world of the "dead" Arletta?]."

funghire velenoso d'ovuli: Literally, poisonous mushrooming of ovula. For Bonora (2, 108), with its suggestion of black magic (102), part of "a progressive approach to images from beyond the grave."

la veranda: Also the setting of "Due nel crepuscolo" (in which the "belvedere" was originally a "veranda"), whose subject, as Bettarini (1, 508) points out, is "questo tardo / ritorno."

scale / a chiocciola, slabbrate, . . . gelo policromo d'ogive: Montale ("La riviera di Ciceri [e la mia]," 1970, [*SM/A*, 1457]): "One of these towers, with multicolored windows and spiral stairs, rose from our villa, and I transferred it just as it was, in a poem, to Bocca di Magra." Cf. "Da una torre," where we find the "labbro"—"a sort of *senhal* of Annetta" (Isella 2, 211)—from which the metaphysical "slabbrate" here (literally, deprived of a lip; figuratively, chipped) derives.

Bonora (2, 109) suggests that the "multicolored ice of arches" "is the ice that the perception of death arouses with a physical horror: the very 'land of skeletons' that is filtered through the 'mullion flowers' of 'Da una torre.' "

nostre vecchie scale: Bonora (2, 109): "In the poem by now pervaded with a sense of horror of beyond the tomb, the old stairs are participating spectators in the event in which the poet, through the mediation of the beloved, sees the presentiments of dark magic that the landscape of Bocca di Magra has given him, resolved in the only form in which he can render them decipherable."

voce di sarabanda . . . Erinni fredde . . . una bufera . . . : See note to "Lindau" on this dance, evocative of social tension (it also recurs in "Dov'era il tennis . . ."). Sereni (Bonora 2, 110): "Atmosphere of 'tregenda' [cf. "Nuove stanze"] [which] arouses historical consciousness. However, we're now no longer at Bocca di Magra and even less in a time circumscribed by a date." The poem is swept up in "a whirlwind of displacement, of an unbelonging which nevertheless opens passageways to an arrival."

angui / d'inferno . . . : Quotation ("Gli angui d'inferno / sentomi nel petto" [I feel the snakes / of hell in my breast]) from the Queen of the Night's aria in the Italian version of Schikaneder's libretto for *The Magic Flute* (II, 8). An earlier draft of these lines read:

> o quando Erinni stridule nel cuore
> ventano angui d'inferno in una raffica
> di punte sulle rive; ed ecco il sole

(or when strident Furies in the heart / vent hellsnakes in a squall / of stinging on the riverbanks; and here's the sun).

una bufera: Recalls the "bufera infernal, che mai non resta" (infernal storm that never ceases) of *Inferno* V, 31. Bonora (2, 114): "A transposition, out of the infernal dark, of the crowd of 'miserable and nude' souls who crowd together on the sad shore of Acheron blaspheming God and their parents, the human race, the place and time of conception of their ancestors and themselves." Cf. the "bufera" in the third part of "Tempi di Bellosguardo."

il sole / che chiude la sua corsa: Bonora (2, 115) says that at Bocca di Magra the sun disappears suddenly, covered by Punta Bianco. "It disappears, it does not set." The image recalls the black sun of the Romantics, especially Nerval (see "El Desdichado").

il tuo morso / oscuro di tarantola: There are various critical theories as to the significance of the "tarantula's bite," which clearly seems related to the "punta che feriva / quasi a sangue" of "Annetta" (quoted in note to "Incontro"). One plausible reading is that the bite of memory (cf. "il pensiero che rimorde" in "Sotto la pioggia") recalls the poet to true feeling and renders him capable of enduring his past; or, as Arrowsmith (2, 163) puts it: "The bite also has the benefit of telling the poet he is still alive, not drowned or moldering in memory; hence his readiness." Cf. the late poem "Son pronto ripeto, ma pronto a che?" (I'm ready, I repeat, but ready for what?) in *D71/2*:

> Essere pronti non vuol dire scegliere
> tra due sventure o due venture
> oppure tra il tutto e il nulla. È dire io l'ho provato,
> ecco il Velo, se inganna non si lacera.

(Being ready doesn't mean choosing / between two misadventures or two fates / or between all and nothing. It means saying I've tried it, / here's the Veil, even if it deludes us it doesn't tear.)

Palio (1939)

Montale to Bobi Bazlen (May 25, 1939): "Take a look at this Palio written on the run: Simone Martini or rather Paolo Uccello & Calderonian underground & Eusebio etc." (Isella 2, 214).

The Palio is the renowned medieval horse race, still held twice each summer in the cobblestoned streets of Siena, the finish line of which is located in the concave main square, or *Campo*, of the city. The seventeen *contrade*, or wards, of Siena, each with its own colors and heraldic symbols displayed on banners carried proudly through the streets by young men in period costume, compete for the glory of winning the silk cloth that is the Palio (from Latin, *pallium*, mantle). The pageantry of the event is in key with the chivalric imagery that dominates *Le occasioni*; for Montale it suggests (Bonora 2, 71) "the thought of a new Middle Ages that could be the consequence of the obscuring of consciences" under the Fascist hegemony. The poem, says Isella (2, 214–15), is a *pendant*, a variation on the themes of "Elegia di Pico Farnese."

Montale and Irma Brandeis, accompanied by Elena Vivante and Camillo Sbarbaro, attended the Palio in 1938, as two poems in *Alt*, "Quartetto" and "Nel '38" (tr. in *Oth*), attest.

La tua fuga: Clizia's departure from Italy, in 1938, due to the promulgation of the Fascist racial laws. The first lines assert that she has not in fact vanished from the poet's life.

nella purpurea buca . . . : Cf. the hellish crowd scene of the bicycle race in "Buffalo." Crowds in Montale always carry infernal associations. The language here, patently Dantesque, prefigures (Isella 2, 216) the "fossa fuia" of "La bufera" and the "antro / incandescente" of "Giorno e notte."

di Liocorno e di Tartuca: Unicorn and Tortoise; like "Oca" [Goose] and "Giraffa" [Giraffe]: four of the seventeen *contrade* competing in the Palio. These seemingly giant animals contribute to the hallucinatory atmosphere of the poem.

troppa vampa . . . : Isella (2, 217): "The fire that is about to ingest the world (tragic fulfillment of the indications observed by your clairvoyance) is too lacerating a vision for you to be distracted." The past participle "consumati" agrees with "indizi."

odore di ragia e di tempesta / imminente . . . : Metaphoric references to the coming storm of war, as everywhere in the later poems of *Le occasioni*; but also "indications of that deeper life of things that a privileged creature can recognize, without accepting them passively, choosing for herself, differently from other men, 'a fate that escapes destiny itself.' . . . *Sorte* involves the idea of a choice, which is partly an act of will and partly personal privilege. This is why fate escapes destiny, which is the predetermination of events willed by an external force" (Bonora 2, 73–74).

un suono di bronzo: The ringing of "Sunto," the huge bell of the Torre di Mangia in the Campo of Siena. Isella (2, 217) notes the resonance with the ominous knelling of the Martinella in "Nuove stanze."

gloria di contrade: To glorify Clizia, "a privileged creature who is withdrawing from the common fate" (Marchese 1, 118).

la malcerta / mongolfiera di carta . . . orologio: Bonora (2, 75), who calls this description "metaphysical," speculates that Montale is thinking of the big mechanical clocks in which the movement of the figures can give the idea of "animated phantoms"—the phantoms in this case being the spectators; he sees the paper balloon as possibly "a sort of cloud of heat hanging over" the Campo, but admits that the description could be referring to "an actual occurrence." Isella (2, 218), on the other hand, suggests that the image may refer to the rising moon. An example, perhaps, of Montale's "excessive confidence in [his] material."

il sigillo imperioso: The seal, Clizia's ring, "sign of her celestial charisma" (Marchese 1, 118), which we learn later is set with a large ruby. Clizia's jewelry first appears in "Nuove stanze" as one of her salient attributes; it will gather significance in *La bufera*. Cf. "Gli orecchini": "Le tue pietre, i coralli, il forte imperio / che ti rapisce." Macrì (1, 77) notes the Dantean source, in *Paradiso* VII, 67–69: "Ciò che da lei sanza mezzo distilla / non ha poi fine, perché non si move / la sua imprenta quand'ella sigilla"; see also *Paradiso* XX, 76–78. Clizia was originally called "messagera imperiosa" in an early draft of "Elegia di Pico Farnese."

la luce di prima . . . : The light of "before" (like the "pergola di allora" of "Bassa marea"; "prima" was "allora" in an earlier draft) is the daylight, before it was darkened by "imminent storm." In Clizia's presence, in her honor, the "light of before" "falls on the heads of the spectators and spreads a lilylike brightness, which frees reality of its various and contradictory aspects and annuls and exalts them in a tragic brightness" (Bonora 2, 76); "sbianca" recurs in a similar context in "Il ventaglio." For the ambiguity of "dei," see Bonora (2, 77).

là: Seemingly not the otherworldly "là" below.

la preghiera: "The prisoner's song" (Marchese 1, 119), which prefigures "Il sogno del prigioniero" and echoes in form the prayer of "Elegia di Pico Farnese," written shortly before, is a kind of subliminal communication for Clizia from the poet (who cannot "escape [his] destiny" and is thus a prisoner, in several senses). Montale (Angelini 2, 175): "In 'Palio' appears the theme of the prisoner who, in 'The Prisoner's Dream,' is not *only* a political prisoner." Bonora (2, 78): "The voice whose echo comes back intervenes to allegorize the history of waiting and disappointment that summarize an entire existence." Bonora suggests Saba's "Sesta fuga" as a possible inspiration.

The first strophe originally read:

> non il re ma il tuo segno
> di filigrana dove
> con le dita o col passo
> senza traccia sfioravi.

(not the king but your sign / of filigree where / with your fingers or step / you passed without a trace.)

The later version unites prisoner and woman ("i nostri passi") in the freedom of the past, contrasted with the "sleep of stone" of "now"; the sign of the cross formed by the bars of the cell is ineffectual for the man who is lost in this prison, where death and life are identical. Montale (Angelini 2, 175): "At the time, I slept in a room on the ground floor [whose windows were] protected by cruciform bars." (It was in fact a room in the home of Matteo and Drusilla Marangoni, at via Benedetto Varchi, 6, in Florence [Marcenaro and Boragina, 125].)

prigione: Masculine; an archaic term for prisoner (cf. Michelangelo's "Prigioni" sculptures).

un'altra voce: Perhaps the one expressing the poem itself.

il ghirigoro d'aste . . . : For Bonora (2, 83), the Palio in Montale is a symbol of bygone values which repudiate the inauthentic imperialism of the Fascists: "In the ceremony of the Palio the poet recognizes a genuine vitality, which takes on the valor of a moral model. . . . His taste for the manners of aristocratic life . . . led him to recognize in the flight of the multicolored banners and in the roar of the crowd that just enthusiasm, that unrestrainable and lively concord of feeling, which had in fact become a farcical caricature in the political festivals of those years, with the 'oceanic' crowd, which had, on command, to demonstrate exultation and pride, responding in unison to the demands of the great chief." The ceremonials of Fascism are evoked in "La primavera hitleriana," in many respects a reprise and reconceiving of "Palio."

toto coelo *raggiunta*: Achieved everywhere (Latin: in all the world; totally), i.e., universal, pandemic: death as mankind's current general environment. "Raggiunta" suggests that this is not a necessary condition, but that it has been arrived at through human error (cf. "*il* giorno / dei viventi," below).

ergotante: From the French *ergoter*, based on the Latin *ergo*, "therefore," used frequently in medieval disputations.

C'era il *giorno / dei viventi*: Phrasing of Biblical intensity, in opposition with "morte toto coelo raggiunta": the one day of the living. It is the world evoked in the first strophe of the prisoner's prayer (cf. the parallelism with "c'era una volta . . . ," which emphasizes the legendary quality of "*the* day of the living"). (Cf. also the "grido / concorde del meriggio" of "the dream" in "Barche sulla Marna.") Bonora (in Marchese 1, 118) (perhaps too literally): "It signifies a time when political and moral values were not mystified, but appreciated and lived; and here we can recognize Montale's nostalgia for an era, not long distant, when men had been inspired by the principle of liberty and self-determination," which is to say "post-Risorgimento Italy, up to the years of Giolitti . . . the golden age of liberal democracy" (Bonora 2, 87).

il traguardo: The goal, not of the race but of life itself, the "oltrecielo" of "L'ombra della magnolia. . . ."

scampanìo: The pealing of the bells announcing the winning of the race; the thunder of the now-breaking celestial storm.

Così *alzati*: There are two possible readings here. "Alzati" can be a singular imperative, directed to Clizia, who is rising in flight, escaping "destiny itself"; or it can be a plural past participle, referring to the conjoined lovers (as in the first strophe of the prayer), aloft together. On this reading, here at the climax of *Le occasioni*, the poet's long vigil finally comes to an end; in the ecstatic close of "Palio" he achieves union, albeit sublimated, with his absent beloved, and their flight becomes one with the spinning of the top that is earthly existence; it will "blunt its point consuming itself, leaving nevertheless an etched groove, the sign (albeit modest) of a presence on earth that was not ephemeral" (Marchese 1, 120). (Cf. the ending of "Marezzo"—where the couple is likewise together, "Immobili così"; also "Barche sulla Marna.") Yet it is uncharacteristic for the poet to be capable of flight; more plausibly, it is Clizia alone who manages to escape destiny, leaving her "cavaliere servente" behind.

spunti: The word appears, though in a different sense, at the very beginning of the book, in "Il balcone."

il solco: See the same image in the last lines of "L'orto" and the related one in the last line of "Vecchi versi." The groove is a mark ("stampo") of human presence, and by extension a reference to the poet's work and to Clizia's (described in "L'orto"). Is "Poi, nient'altro" an explicit rejection of the notion of an afterlife? What matters here on earth is to "etch" a "groove," to live so as to leave an indication of significant existence.

Notizie dall'Amiata / News from Mount Amiata (1938–39)

Mount Amiata, an extinct volcano between Siena and Grosseto, is the largest land mass in southern Tuscany, in the way of the most direct route from Florence to Rome. It is now late autumn 1938; Clizia has returned to America.

Montale (Greco, 38): "More or less one of the three or four villages there [Isella (2, 225) suggests Abbazia San Salvatore or Arcidosso]. Villages with a Christian-Romanesque, not Renaissance, flavor. Therefore imagery from a bestiary (porcupine) or ancient religiosity (the icon). The floorboards, wooden beams. The cages, maybe empty, no certainly empty, but birdcages. *Che ti affabula*, that makes you material for fable. *Schiude la tua icona*, the icon is the subject.

"*Il borro*, little rivulet of water. *I libri d'ore*, symbols of old things. From the peak, effects of light, undetermined but almost artificial. The *rissa* of soul and body, the *rixa* about which there are writings in the popular literature. A more or less perpetual condition. (Amiata is the kingdom of David Lazzaretti; see the book of [G.] Barzellotti [*Monte Amiata e il suo profeta David Lazzaretti* (Milano, 1910)].)"

David Lazzaretti (1834–78), a native of Arcidosso, was the founder of a Christian "heresy" (Bonora 2, 65), the Jurisdavidians, who preached the advent of the age of the Holy Spirit. Hated by the political and religious authorities for his pauperistic and communitarian ideas (he considered himself Christ incarnate and aimed at replacing both King and Pope), he was killed in an encounter with public forces (Marchese 1, 124) during a procession of his "militia of the Holy Ghost," which numbered as many as 1,000. (See E. J. Hobsbawm, *Primitive Rebels: Studies in Archaic Forms of Social Movement in the 19th and 20th Centuries*, 2nd ed. [New York: Frederick A. Praeger, 1963], 65–73, for a rather more sociopolitical view of Lazzarettism.) Carpi (341) tells us that Barzellotti discusses Lazzaretti's "adventure as self-styled continuator of Christ, as authentic modern Christ-bearer; his *absences*, his going *far from his own* through divine will and in order to better fulfill his own work of salvation; his offering himself as 'a new Christ, as victim of the expiation of the sins of his fellows, and as mediator of a second alliance between humanity and heaven'; he also speaks throughout, as analogous to Lazzarettism, of the Guglielmite heresy according to which the new redeemer supposedly 'suffered in feminine form for our sins and saved Jews and pagans': a case of 'religious feminism,' of faith in 'Christ incarnate in female form,' " which "must have impressed [Montale] greatly in a moment in which he was in fact elaborating a poetics centered on a saving female religiosity destined to end in the celebration of the *Christian sacrifice of the absent one*."

Bonora (2, 71) says that "Notizie dall'Amiata" and "Elegia di Pico Farnese" make a pair of texts, both of which submit Christianity in its localized forms to highly critical scrutiny; in meteorological terms, in fact, the "Elegia" could be said to follow immediately after the "Notizie," in the calm following the storm.

As Arrowsmith (2, 168) notes, the final poems of *Le occasioni*, and particularly this one, "move simultaneously on . . . three levels . . . : personal, socio-historical, and universal (e.g., 'the honeycomb cell / of a globe launched in space'). The storm that figures so prominently in the first poem, 'Old Verses,' is by comparison a fairly simple though highly suggestive intuition of the apocalyptic *bufera* to come. The violent cosmic dimensions of the later storm are not fully comprehended in the earlier one, but, rather, hinted at in the child's anxiety over transience, death, and entry into the adult world. Or, in Montalean terms, the first poem functions as an anticipatory 'sign' of the last poem, in which the storm is transformed into a metaphysical nightmare, a life-asserting death wish. In much the same way, metaphorical motifs and details of the earlier poems have been fused in the last poem into a dramatic revelation of the light-in-darkness imagery of the *envoi*, 'The Balcony.' "

The first and third sections are largely hendecasyllabic, while the central section employs longer, more variable metrics.

murmure: Cf. the opening of "Sotto la pioggia."

elfi: Suggests the northern, mountainous character of the locale—and its magical nature.

i marroni esplodono: A forewarning of the coming explosion of Clizia's presence.

romperai: Montale to Bobi Bazlen (June 6, 1939) (quoted in Isella 3, 187): "For '*irromperai*' [enter forcibly], *farai breccia* [make a breach]. *Quadro* can easily be replaced by *scena* [scene]." Montale to Bazlen (June 18, 1939) (Isella 3, 187): "She does not break through in effect: she remains inside the niche or icon; but the wall breaks so the window can open. Your icon (subject) opens the window and reveals a luminous interior."

La vita / che t'affàbula . . . : Montale to Bazlen (June 18, 1939) (Isella 2, 227): "The life that portrays (*raffigura*) you is still (*yet*, even) too brief, if it contains you (it's understood that life '*before* seemed too long,' but it would be better not to say so . . .).'' Isella notes that *raffigurare* here also has the sense of *riconoscere*, to recognize, "a true key-word in Montalean gnoseology." Isella paraphrases the passage: "The life of your fabulator (too long in its habitual boredom) is in fact too brief if, when you appear, it falls to that life to be filled with the thought of you." (According to Antonella Francini, *affabula* was a term of Contini's which Montale adopted.)

contiene: Cf. "Verso Siena": "Ohimè che la memoria sulla vetta / non ha chi la trattenga!" and "Per album": "ero / già troppo ricco per contenerti viva."

Schiude la tua icona: Montale to Contini (January 11, 1945) (*Op*, 936): "I thought of it almost like the sudden opening of a counter window." Montale to Bazlen (June 6, 1939) (Isella 3, 200): "A *window opens* in the wall and reveals a luminous background, be it a niche or icon." The poet is invoking Clizia's magical angelic apparition, in the style of the traditional religion of this remote and unlikely place; her icon, her remembered image, casts sudden, incandescent light into the darkness surrounding him—an apocalyptic revisiting of the noted "bourgeois interiors" of "Vecchi versi" and "Dora Markus." Outside, however, in the larger world, the "maltempo" continues.

E tu seguissi: Optative subjunctive, indicating a desire contrary to fact; the vision has failed and Clizia cannot be present to explore the mysteries of his situation with the poet.

il pozzo profondissimo: Cf. "Cigola la carrucola del pozzo," with its "vision" separated from the poet by "a distance." Almansi and Merry (97): "The presence of the superlative can only be accounted for as an effort to reach the bottommost depth where the dead are supposed to live."

borro: Montale to Angelo Marchese (March 28, 1977) (Marchese 1, 323): ". . . in Tuscany any vein of water whatsoever that isn't torrential. Where the water is stillest it's possible to see the reflection of the moon or of stardust. Possible in theory, because I've never seen a *borro* at night." Isella (3, 202) notes that Irma Brandeis, in her translation of the "Notizie" (*Quarterly Review of Literature* XI, 4 [1962], 263–64), translates *borro* as "ravine."

allucciolìo: Pascolian neologism coined by Montale from *lucciolo*, firefly. The Galaxy, or Milky Way, is the "shroud of every torment" because it encloses the earth, locus of evil and suffering (Marchese 1, 123).

trapunti troppo sottili: Montale to Bazlen (June 6, 1939) (Isella 3, 202): "Designs, interweaving, *to weave, sottili*, or, if you will, impalpable, imperceptible, even febrile, if you like, *as you like it*."

fermo sulle due ore: Cf. the similarly static "giro / sicuro" of "Vecchi versi," and the fixity ("tutto è fisso") of "Crisalide" and elsewhere.

vento del nord: The violent *tramontana* (see "L'agave su lo scoglio"), according to Arrowsmith (2, 166) the wind that is the active principle in "Tempi di Bellosguardo" and several poems of *La bufera*. "Here the 'north wind' has been invoked: 1) personally, as scourging the passions (in this case, despairing of fulfillment); 2) culturally and politically, as an image of apparently inevitable historical forces, the freezing stormwind assaulting Italy from the Nazi north . . . and destroying all tradition and civilized values; and 3) cosmologically, as the apparition of a terrible fatality at the heart of things. . . . Paraphrased, the invocation to the north wind might go something like this: 'Come, fatal and destructive wind, seal me forever in my solitary cell! Make me despair, compel me to recognize the impossibility of ever escaping my condition! Give me oblivion and spare me the pain of ever remembering or hoping again!'" For Arrowsmith (2, 165), the passage invokes Beatrice's vision of the angelic cosmos in *Paradise* XXVIII, 79ff.

le antiche mani dell'arenaria: Marchese (1, 124): "Perhaps indicates cement of sand and quartz or the tenacious joining between blocks of stone . . . : more generically, the links of tradition." Cf. the "braccia di pietra" of "Nel Parco di Caserta." The "books of hours in the attic" recalls the aristocratic, antiquarian atmosphere of "Elegia di Pico Farnese"; that world, a world in which Clizia could become manifest, is being overwhelmed. Similarly, the painted image of an artificial and gay Vesuvius in the final motet [Luperini (1, 105) notes the like situations of the two poems: the poet writes in each] is countered here with the apocalyptic Amiata.

tutto sia lente tranquilla: Almansi and Merry (99) read "lente" as lens rather than pendulum: "Montale's 'lens' or 'filter' had never been 'tranquil.' He had always pointed it at an area which might have released a private mystery from an incarceration which matched our own. But [here] there is no mystery left, except time, which marks the passing of our life-imprisonment on earth."

rendi care / le catene . . . : Montale to Bazlen (June 18, 1939) (Isella 2, 229): "The wind makes the chains beloved because it validates (!) standing still, motionless, stasis instead of becoming; being instead of having to be."

le spore del possibile: Montale to Bazlen (ibid.): "The spores of possibility? . . . The germs of the hypothetical tomorrow, the seeds of a possible, plausible, unconcretized life, the sources of what could be and is not."

vampate di magnesio: Montale to Bazlen (June 6, 1939) (Isella 2, 229–30): "The flash of a kind of heat lightning that recalls the flash of photographs at official banquets, in short not lightning followed by thunder."

il lungo colloquio coi poveri morti: Cf. "I morti," and the "familial" poems in *La bufera*, which center on grieving memory. Bonora (2, 55–65) shows that an important source for the "Notizie" is Baudelaire's "La servante au grand coeur": "Les morts, les pauvres morts, ont de grandes douleurs." These lines also echo Pascoli's "Scalpitio" in the *Myricae*.

la cenere, il vento: Cf. "Arsenio" for these details and for the storm that is the occasion of both poems.

Questa rissa cristiana: See Montale's notes above. Isella (2, 224) paraphrases: "This unresolved and unresolvable conflict of mine between 'being' and 'having to be,' between soul and body." Montale wrote to Bazlen (January 17, 1939) (Isella 2, 224) about an earlier version: "A poor devil abandons himself to his fate near the gleaming furrow of a ditch (a little rivulet between cement banks), and has nowhere else to escape to. He stretches out, makes a cushion of a stone in the form of a wheel (a millwheel for pressing olives), and listens to a light rustling arising from the straw. It is the porcupines coming out to drink water (water as well as a trickle of pity)."

Luperini (1, 106–7): "The Christian-Romanesque past of the village seems to have here the same negative function as the pagan one of a Ciociarian town in 'Elegia di Pico Farnese': conduciveness to immobility, impeding of ascent . . . , reducing the cultural and ideal tension through the corporality indulged by the pilgrims and the goat-men." The impending war is presented in this context as an innate Christian struggle, the "more or less perpetual" battle between the instinctual (*uomini-capri*) and rational/spiritual values implicit in Christianity itself.

gora: Tuscan dialect, a likely borrowing, with the "cumulo di strame" four lines below, from Sbarbaro's *Resine*: "L'acqua della morta gora: / filtra nei porri della terra ognora / il fermento d'uno cumulo di strame" (Mengaldo, 78). Montale to Bazlen (June 6, 1939) (Isella 3, 187): "What has the millrace stolen from you? And who knows it? The little of me that (As little of me as) what is happening here can bring you, as little (or even less) of you as the millrace, the rivulet, the trickle that runs in its bed, its cement trough, can bring me (steal from you). *Tout se tient*, everything as is, but such 'correspondences' are little, given my hunger for identity. Except that the porcupines that are here, and which she dreams (*takes in*), are still in touch, etc."

Una ruota di mola, un vecchio tronco: A reprise of the details in part 1 (melon, cages, chestnuts on the hearth: the simplest and most evident of objects), which provided the setting for Clizia's apparition. By now, however, her presence has been internalized and sublimated in the *senhal* of the porcupines, whose emergence vindicates her anticipated apparition in part 1. Almansi and Merry (95), quoting G. De Robertis: "Objects become creature and symbol, but 'the creatures are impoverished while the symbols are grandiose.'"

la mia veglia: The "cavaliere servente"'s distant vigil is united with Clizia's deep sleep ("it's still night in America" [Marchese 1, 125]) through the Clizian *senhal* of the porcupines (cf. the jackals of the sixth motet). Contini (quoted in Almansi and Merry, 99): "The myth is reborn; and the emphasis falls on the religious connotation which permeates this whole crisis situation."

un filo di pietà: The "gora" above; a very small thing, but which carries truer knowledge of Clizia, has more to do with her than the great "Christian wrangle" does with the poet; the minimum that remains to imply resistance to and possible survival of the evil storm. Almansi and Merry (99) note that all three sections of the "Notizie" end with water imagery: "This liquid vision of human existence is the only lasting reality which Montale offers."

For Luperini (1, 108), the insistence on the old values has more than a little of the desperate to it: " 'Notizie dall'Amiata' is an allegory of intellectual conditions in the thirties. The act of writing, the call to Clizia—value, culture—, the 'vigil,' the attempt to bring forward the motives of 'the spirit,' conjoin the earthly measure to the cosmic, helping to redeem the first. The allegory seems, in sum, to want to resolve positively the crisis declared above all in Motet XX and in 'Tempi di Bellosguardo' (and, in more general terms, in 'Costa San Giorgio'). The ideology of poetry as privilege and salvation has found in the religious symbols of Christianity and in the literary ones of *stilnovismo* the necessary supports for its perpetuation. The siege of the 'goat-men' and the still more menacing one of the 'other swarm' of 'Nuove stanze' require a redoubling of vigilance, an overabundance of resistance, which end by flowing together into a representation of the literary function as such. And yet, this solution is only one among the possibilities: Montale insists on it with his usual 'decisiveness,' but he can't ignore its weakness. The doubts of 'Tempi di Bellosguardo' are temporarily removed, not erased: deep down, they continue to gnaw at the precarious certainties that the author pitches at the end of the book, as an extreme defense against an ineluctable and now overwhelming reality."

LA BUFERA E ALTRO / THE STORM, ETC.

Privately printed by Neri Pozza (Venice), 1956. Published by Mondadori (Milan), 1957.

A chapbook, FINISTERRE, issued in Lugano by the Collana di Lugano in 1943, became the first section of the larger collection; a second edition of FINISTERRE, published by Barbèra (Florence), in 1945, added "Due nel crepuscolo"; "Visita a Fadin" and "Dov'era il tennis . . . ," under the joint title "In Liguria"; the "Madrigali fiorentini"; and "Iride"—as well as facsimiles of autograph manuscripts, including Montale's uncompleted translation of Eliot's "Ash Wednesday."

Montale in "Intentions" (*Sec*, 303–4): "*Le occasioni* was an orange, or rather a lemon, that was missing a slice: not really that of pure poetry . . . , but of the pedal, of profound music and contemplation. My work to date ends with the poems of FINISTERRE, which represent, let us say, my 'Petrarchan' experiment. I've projected the Selvaggia or Mandetta or Delia [figures in the poetry of Cino da Pistoia, Cavalcanti, and Tibullus] (call her what you will) of the 'Motets' against the background of a war that is both cosmic and earthly, without an end and without a reason, and I've pledged myself to her, lady or shade, angel or petrel. The motif had already been contained and anticipated in 'Nuove stanze,' written before the war; it didn't take much then to be a prophet. It's a matter of a few poems, written in the incubus of 1940–1942, perhaps the freest I've ever written and I thought their relationship to the central theme of *Le occasioni* was evident. If I had orchestrated and watered down my theme I would have been better understood. But I don't go looking for poetry, I wait to be visited. I write little, with few revisions, when it seems to me I can't not do so. If even so I can't escape rhetoric then it means (at least for me) it's inevitable. . . .

"FINISTERRE, with its epigraph from d'Aubigné castigating the bloodthirsty princes, was unpublishable in Italy in 1943. Therefore I printed it in Switzerland and it appeared a few days before the 25th of July [the date of King Vittorio Emanuele II's dismissal of Mussolini as Prime Minister]. The recent reprinting contains a few unrelated poems."

By 1949, Montale was planning a new collection of poems, which he wanted to call *Romanzo* (Novel). He sent Giovanni Macchia, whom he had invited to write a preface to the book, the following table of contents:

> *Romanzo* (1940–1950). I: FINISTERRE (poems for Clizia)—La bufera—Lungomare—Serenata indiana—Il giglio rosso—Nel sonno—Su una lettera non scritta—Gli orecchini—Il ventaglio—La frangia dei capelli . . .—Finestra fiesolana—Giorno e notte—L'arca—*Personae separatae*—Il tuo volo—A mia madre—II: DOPO—Madrigali fiorentini (I and II)—Da una torre—Ballata scritta in una clinica—Iride—III: INTERMEZZO—Due nel crepuscolo—Dov'era il tennis . . .—Visita a Fadin—Nella serra—Nel parco—IV: COL ROVESCIO DEL BINOCOLO [WITH REVERSED BINOCULARS; later 'FLASHES' E DEDICHE]—Verso Siena—La trota nera—Lasciando un *Dove*—Di un Natale metropolitano—V: L'ANGELO E LA VOLPE [THE ANGEL AND THE VIXEN; later SILVAE]—Proda di Versilia—*Ezekiel saw the Wheel*—La primavera Hitleriana—Voce giunta con le folaghe—Ombra di magnolia—L'anguilla—Il gallo cedrone—*Nel segno del trifoglio* [*Under the sign of the clover*; later MADRIGALI PRIVATI]—So che un raggio . . . —Se t'hanno assomigliato . . .—Hai dato il mio nome . . .—Lampi d'afa sul punto . . . [later named "Le processioni del 1949"]—Mia volpe un giorno . . . [later "Anniversario"]—The End.
>
> P.S. There will be 7 to 10 poems added, in toto.

As Luperini (1, 176) points out, Montale's work as a translator, after he was relieved of his post at the Gabinetto Vieusseux in Florence, had offered him close exposure to the fiction of Melville, Hawthorne, Steinbeck, and others, and no doubt increased his interest, already evident in his view of the MOTTETTI, in the narrative dimension of his poetry (see Talbot also). Zambon (52–53) quotes a 1949 essay, "Mutazioni" (*Auto*, 86–89), in which Montale refers to the novel as the literary form "in which time, [and] the psychological sense that unites us to the past, are still perceptible," noting the relationship of the definition to this initial title for *La bufera*, which "revolves around the recuperation of the past and the sense of a duration or a continuity in his own 'history.' " (Montale also referred to Gozzano's poetry as a "short psychological novel" in 1951 [*Su*, 59].)

Lonardi (59) alludes to Mikhail Bakhtin's assertion that the novel, as the dominant literary form of the age, had influenced a tendency to "novelization" in other genres; Lonardi sees Dante's *Vita nuova* as the "model of a novel" for Montale (cf. Montale's comments below), citing the Gothic-medieval—and thus Dantesque—coloration of Montale's war imagery throughout *La bufera* as a contributory element. (He goes on to note, however, that Montale's "novel" lacks the soteriological and Christological "happy ending" of the *Vita nuova*; the dialectic between Clizia and Volpe, between transcendence and immanence, that forms the primary tension of the book remains unresolved, as represented in the double conclusion of "Piccolo testamento" and "Il sogno del prigioniero.")

The title that Montale finally chose for this, his greatest collection, and the one he himself preferred, his last work of "poetry-poetry" (Contini 2, xi), emphasizes its apocalyptic subject, the cosmic war against the Enemy which Clizia wins, only to be consumed in the process; but, as the additive *e altro* suggests, there is also " 'more' or 'something *else*' " (Arrowsmith 3, 165), i.e., the aftermath of the "uselessness and failure of the sacrifice" portrayed in *La bufera* (it can also be read as an indicator of the poet's allegorical intentions). Not only do Clizia and her saving message disappear, but her historical correlative, the war against universally recognized evil, is replaced by "the harder way" of a divided society uninformed by spiritual values. The poet's adventure in love continues in his "profane" experience with Volpe: if Clizia represented the goal of transcendence through sublimation, Volpe is the avatar of transcendence through immanence. But this new life is secondary, diminished, "a compensation or a surrogate," necessarily experienced in the light of the searing prior attempt at communion.

The drama of Clizia is expressed in religious terms, but her absorption into Christian allegory to which the poet does dutiful homage, in fact represents a defeat for him. Luperini (1, 111): "It's not a matter of a conversion to a revealed religion but of adherence to an inheritance of European culture and civilization of which Christianity is an integral part and of which the woman-angel is an allegorical manifestation. Christian symbology is adopted not so much for its doctrinal content as for its capacity to allude to an absolute value and to trace it back, through the figure of Christ, into historical humanity. . . . In the end, the failure of the religious hypothesis of incarnation is lived as the possible disappearance of value from the earthly horizon and thus from poetry."

Jacomuzzi (1, 53): "The religious appeal and its symbols . . . are evoked against meaninglessness as the only possibility of salvation, not so much as an object of faith as of hope; they are the 'objective correlative' of the unexhausted challenge of hope."

Luperini (1, 120–21): "*La bufera* is not at all Clizia's book, even if she securely appears in three sections . . . ; nor can it be read exclusively in a stilnovistic key. It is also the book of the revaluation of the *earthly*, of eros, of the instinctual. . . . And yet the story of *La bufera* is of hope and disappointments, of repeated attempts at salvation and corresponding failures, down to a final checkmate which nevertheless doesn't exclude either the pride of fidelity to itself or the 'wait' and the 'dream' of a different reality."

Montale's allegorical method condenses and intensifies in *La bufera*, once the engagement with Clizia has ended. For Jacomuzzi (1, 122–23), Montale rejects the pure poetics of the object, the "emblematic identification of object and situation . . . typical of *Le occasioni*," in favor of a more decisive, judgmental mode of figuration. "The subordination of metaphorical discourse to cognitive intention, the neutralization and definitive declassing of the repertory of things, images, and stylistic institutions to grade zero of value, and their significant survival only in the measure in which they are elements adopted by an ideological choice and by a will to judgment, are the fundamental aspects of the poetry of *La bufera*." The poet's most profoundly defining experience is over; what remains, essentially, is understanding and interpretation. Montale's stylistic decisions are guided now by "an idea of literature not as expression but as critical testimony and judgment, always essentially tried as a writing in a key, in a form of communication through allegories and enigmas" (123–24).

So the great amorous adventure of Montale's poetry comes to its ambiguous, open finale. In fact, as we know, the work does not end here; but the story is over, as the poet himself acknowledged. "My poetry is to be read together, as one single poem," he said in 1966 (*Tutte*, liii). "I don't want to make the comparison with the *Divina Commedia*, but I consider my three books as three canticles, three phases of a human life." And in 1977: "I've written one single book, of which I gave the *recto* first; now I'm giving the *verso*."

Montale considered the poems of FINISTERRE an appendix to *Le occasioni*, and at one point planned to add them to the sixth edition (*Op*, 937). "Finisterre" (Latin, *finis terrae*, end of the earth, or world's end) is both a cape in Brittany, Finistère, and a "wild cliff in Spain" (Pipa, 87), the westernmost point in Europe—or, as Angelini says (3, 167), "any other [location] suitable for this symbolic geography." Its meaning, as Montale implied in a letter to Contini (*Op*, 937), is "apocalyptic": the end of the world as he had known it brought on by the conflagration of the war. Montale (Greco, 48): "The title FINISTERRE is used in the broadest and most ambiguous sense (the war, actual and cosmic); the title of the Breton poem 'Verso Finistère,' on the other hand, has geographical significance."

The stilnovistic *trobar clus* of the earlier volume is intensified here, as Montale himself noted in an interview in *Quaderni della Radio* XI, 1951 (tr. in *Sec*, 312): "In my chapbook *Finisterre* (and the title alone is enough to prove it) the last great war in fact occupies the entire background, but only indirectly. . . . The opening epigraph alone would have been smoke in the eyes of the Fascist censors. . . . These are the lines of a man who well understood slaughter and struggle: Agrippa d'Aubigné [1552–1630; Huguenot poet and historian, author of *Les tragiques* (1577), from which Montale's epigraph to "La bufera" is derived, as was Baudelaire's to the first edition of *Les fleurs du mal*]. In short, Fascism and war gave my isolation the alibi that perhaps I needed. My poetry in those days had no choice but to become more closed, more concentrated (I don't say more obscure)."

What Montale meant by his " 'Petrarchan' experiment" is, according to Pipa (82–88), twofold. First there is the theme, borrowed from Petrarch, of the "sweet lady enemy" (*Canzoniere*, CCII), i.e., the strongly contrasting feelings, like Petrarch's love for the absent Laura and that of the stilnovistic poets for the angelic woman, that come to dominate Montale's presentation of Clizia in FINISTERRE. Petrarchan, too, is the emphasis on certain physical traits of Clizia's (bangs, jewelry—which Lonardi sees as derived from Foscolo, while Sanguineti finds sources in Gozzano and the *crepuscolari*), first developed in *Le occasioni* and here essential to Montale's figural mode. For Pipa, "Montale's love experience in FINISTERRE is both Petrarchan and Dantean . . . , mark[ing] a departure from Dante toward an earthlier conception of love"—a development central to the entire arc of *La bufera*. To Marchese (1, 134), Montale's "Petrarchism" "must be considered . . . an experience of suffering religiosity, closer—even linguistically—to stilnovism and to Dante, revisited with the entirely modern and existential anguish of someone far from the assurances of a theological fate, but who looks to love and through the woman for a secret meaning to the absurd and inhuman envelope enclosing history."

La bufera / The Storm (1941)

Montale (Greco, 45): "The war, in particular *that* war after *that* dictatorship (see epigraph); but it is also a cosmic war, forever and for everyone. . . . *I suoni di cristallo*: the hail. The place is undefinable, but far from me. *Marmo manna e distruzione* are the components of a character; if you explain them you kill the poem. *Più che l'amore* is NOT reductive. *Lo schianto*, etc.: images of war. *Come quando*: separation as for example in 'Nuove stanze.' *Sgombra la fronte*: a realistic memory. *Il buio* is many things: distance, separation, not even the certainty that she was still alive. The *tu* is for Clizia."

When it was published in *Tempo* (V, 89 [February 6–13, 1941]), an epigraph read: "Porque sabes que siempre te he querido . . ." (For you know I have always loved you . . .).

The poem, like many others, is one long period—not a sentence, actually, but a typical Montalean catalogue, in which objects pile up on each other in an allusive accretion of signifiers, a characteristic of the "objective poetics of *Le occasioni* that continues in *La bufera*, though the enumerations here are further complicated by a temporal dimension, in keeping with the historical orientation of the book" (Jacomuzzi 1, 11). Other examples of this trope in *La bufera* occur in "Di un natale metropolitano," "Argyll Tour," the second and last stanzas of "Proda di Versilia," and "Le processioni del 1949."

La bufera: See note to "Il ritorno" for discussion of the Dantean sources of this word, which appears twice in *Le occasioni*.

sgronda sulle foglie: Pascoli, "La canzone dell'Olifante," 25, 15: "Scorre tra l'erbe, sgronda dalle foglie, / bulica il sangue, come quando piove." (Note the other echoes in Montale's text.)

della magnolia: See "L'ombra della magnolia . . ." and elsewhere in *La bufera* ("L'arca," "Nel parco"), where the tree continually represents domestic integrity (it also appears in "Tempi di Bellosguardo").

marzolini: Ligurian dialect.

(*i suoni di cristallo . . .*): Perhaps a reference to Kristallnacht? Clizia, in her distant nest (the situation recalls that of "Dora Markus II"), is surprised by the sounds of war that the storm brings her; what she remembers are the emblems of an earlier, more humane life.

il lampo che candisce: Cf. the whiteness of the "luce di prima" in "Palio."

marmo manna / e distruzione: Despite what Montale says above: in part, references to Clizia's character (classical elegance, firmness, even hardness) and origin (she is Jewish and therefore partakes both of the manna of the Jews' covenant with God and of their destruction in the Holocaust). The conjunction of classical and Biblical imagery is characteristic of Montale's presentation of Clizia throughout *La bufera*.

strana sorella: Clizia has here become a "weird sister," a kind of witch, like the Sphinx of "Nuove stanze" or Gerti in "Carnevale di Gerti," as well as the poet's soul mate, more than an erotic object. The term indicates her absorption into the familial matrix (see the last paragraph of note to 'FLASHES' E DEDICHE).

i sistri . . . tamburelli: See Macrì (1, 85) for a discussion of the sources in Pascoli and elsewhere of Montale's dance-music imagery.

sulla fossa fuia: Dantesque borrowing, referring to the "bolgia" of the thieves (see *Inferno* XXIX, 49); Pipa (90): "the pit of thieves is . . . Italy fallen prey to 'that gang of thieves' [he is quoting from "Sulla spiaggia" in *Farf*] who were the fascists." The citation derives from D'Annunzio's drama *La nave*; Mengaldo (39): "it's probable that here Montale borrows the entire central, emblematic situation of the D'Annunzian tragedy linked to it (the 'sistra,' 'scalpicciare,' groping gestures), giving them new value as a 'correlative' exemplum of the war."

fandango . . . : Cf. the MOTTETTI and elsewhere for Montale's use of exotic (especially Spanish) dances to indicate social (and even cosmic) disorder. For the "gesto che annaspa," cf. the "squallide / mani, travolte" of "Gli orecchini."

dalla nube dei capelli: Another of Clizia's Petrarchan attributes, acknowledged by Montale as drawn from real life (see May 1, 1939, letter to Bobi Bazlen in note to "Elegia di Pico Farnese"); the phrase, however, also occurs in *La nave*.

mi salutasti . . . : Evokes the Orphic myth, in which Eurydice, forced to return to the underworld, leaves the poet behind. A recurrent situation in Montale (see, e.g., "Falsetto," "Stanze," "Di un natale metropolitano," "Se t'hanno assomigliato"). Cf. also the close of Leopardi's "A Silvia": "Tu, misera, cadesti: e con la mano / La fredda morte ed una tomba ignuda / Mostrava di lontano."

Lungomare / Promenade (1940)

Montale (Greco, 45): "Clizia is absent; it's all realistic, the balustrade and the rest. A small madrigal of secondary importance. *S'arriccia*: realistic detail."

il baleno . . . : Zambon (59) sees in the figure of Clizia's eyebrow the stilnovistic source for the rainbow imagery that dominates the great poems of the SILVAE below: "We observe how from the theme of the lashes arise the figures of the 'arco' [arc] and of the 'baleno' [lightning] destined to reconstitute themselves in the 'arcobaleno,' i.e., in fact in 'l'iride' [the rainbow] "

Su una lettera non scritta / On an Unwritten Letter (1940)

Montale (Greco, 45–46): "Poem of absence; of distance. I don't see obscurities in it. Many details are realistic. There is a background of war. . . . The 'tu' is far away, perhaps she doesn't exist and for this reason the letter is unwritten. Clizia is here but it's not necessary to give her that name. *Formicolìo* etc.: All real images of a life reduced to rare apparitions; here they don't have the value of a *senhal* like the two jackals."

A kind of negative sequel to "Notizie dall'Amiata." Rebay (2, 82) tells us that in 1939 Montale had been actively considering following Irma Brandeis to America; this unwritten letter reflects his indecisiveness on the subject and his inability, in part, to meet the challenge that Clizia represents. Finistère, as the westernmost point in Europe, sets him, in the poem, as near as possible to—though very, very far from—Clizia.

Sparir non so né riaffacciarmi: Luperini (1, 126) sees this as a reprise of a line from "Accordi" (1922) (tr. in *Oth*, 93). "Volere non so più né disvolere" (I no longer know desire or non-desire), "which involves not only the acceptance of mediocrity but also the possibility of some gratifying compensation (everyday life allowing greater association with concreteness and vitality; the theme of 'Accordi' returns again)." (The source in turn recalls the description —"Voluta, / disvoluta"—of the subject of "Stanze," and is ultimately derived from Petrarch CXIX, 42: "altro volere o disvoler m'è tolto.")

la bottiglia dal mare: Cf. "Style and Tradition" (*Sec*, 8): "If it has been said that genius is one long patience, we should like to add that it is also conscience and honesty. A work born with these characteristics does not need much more to reach to the most distant of ages, like Vigny's 'bouteille à la mer.' "

Nel sonno / In Sleep (1940)

Montale (Greco, 45): "Poem of war and memory. 'L'avversario' is the 'nemico muto' of 'Costa San Giorgio'; it may be evil or man's destiny. Various sounds and colors in the sleeper's memory."

giga crudele: Cf. *Paradiso* XIV, 118.

la celata: Continuation of the chivalric imagery of *Le occasioni* (see also "Il ventaglio").

sangue oltre la morte: Cf. the motet "Ecco il segno; s'innerva," in which Clizia's "passo" is "sangue tuo nelle mie vene," and the "sangue che ti nutre" of "Stanze"; but also the "voci / del sangue" of "Buffalo," the "voce di sangue" of "Eastbourne," and the "labbro / di sangue" of "Da una torre." Blood in *Le occasioni* is often associated with Arletta (see notes to "Eastbourne" and "Da una torre") and, more generally—as here—represents a denial of or opposition to death.

Serenata indiana / Indian Serenade (1940)

Montale (Greco, 46): "I'm afraid the title is Shelley's ['The Indian Serenade']. 'Il polipo' can be the whorls of the waves at sunset or the unknowable, the negative future. It's not for Clizia. Versilian landscape. It's not for the same character as 'Su una lettera non scritta.' "

Luperini sees the poem, despite Montale's denial, as partaking of the "demonization" or "shadowy transformation" (1, 125) that Clizia undergoes at this point in Montale's "experience of dark, destructive love" (Cambon, 196); cf. also the negative expostulation ("Oh ch'io non oda / nulla di te . . .") of "Su una lettera non scritta."

È pur nostro il disfarsi . . . : An earlier version read: "Come il nostro è il disfarsi delle sere" (The unraveling of the evenings is like ours). Characteristically, in revision Montale concretizes his expression.

Fosse tua vita: Wish contrary to fact; cf. "E tu seguissi . . ." in "Notizie dall'Amiata."

appartieni . . . : Note the hypermetric rhyme (appartie[ni]/te), which also occurs at the end of "Gli orecchini" (squalli[de]/coralli).

Gli orecchini / The Earrings (1940)

Montale (Greco, 46): "The 'elitre' are warplanes seen as deathly insects. 'Due vite,' yours and mine but also the fates of single individuals. 'Meduse,' shadows in the mirror, a realistic detail. The character is so absent as to seem almost dead. She emerges from the mirror still wearing her coral earrings. No allies to the north. 'Verrà di giù,' from the black of the unknowable. The 'volo' is hers. And whose could it be? 'La spugna,' symbol of what erases, but also realistic detail."

As we've seen, Montale's responses to Guarnieri on FINISTERRE emphasize uncertainty as to whether Clizia was alive; thus the possibility of her death is strongly present. As in the case of Anna degli Uberti, the inspiration for Arletta-Annetta, Clizia's withdrawal from the poet's life implies her demise, in effect. For Marchese, this plays a necessary role in the myth of Clizian salvation (2, 127): "In order for Clizia to be able to be the bearer of salvation and hope she must encounter death: it is there that her mission begins." The realistic/psychological basis for this sublimation, however, is also suggested in the poems. As Luperini (1, 129) puts it: "Already in FINISTERRE . . . we are in the presence of a contradiction: the relationship with Clizia begins to be described in its ambiguity, which alternates attraction and repulsion. Her 'ice' [cf. the source of her symbology in her name: "Brand/Eis"] can coincide with a death, which involves not only the female character . . . but also the subject." Montale's response to this, in part, is to begin to emphasize "the defense of life in its concreteness" (again Luperini, 1, 130).

Macrì (1, 85) underlines the historical antecedent for the poem, namely the Nazi murder of the Jews, and asserts that the earrings of the title "epitomize things of value stolen from graves after the massacres and ovens . . . hence the boldness and the evocative value of the exchange of real and symbolic in the gesture in which in an almost hieratic ceremony . . . her brothers readorn the familial remains with her 'corals.' . . . Her adornment as at the feast of Purim is a real and proper confirmatio ('fermano') of the rebel from her nation [because Clizia is Christian] and a lustratio [ritual cleansing] after the filthy sacrilege."

The poem's form is that of a Shakespearean sonnet. Montale published translations of several of Shakespeare's sonnets in the mid-forties, and drew from them not only formally but in the "expressive concentration" (Luperini 1, 176) which imitation of the English form demanded in translating the more extended English line. FINISTERRE includes seven sonnets, or "pseudosonnets" as Montale called them, of varying formality. Here, the rhyming, unlike in most of his work, is highly regular, emphasizing the artificiality of his enterprise.

il nerofumo / della spera: Cf. the "specchio annerito" of "Dora Markus," but Macrì (1, 76) insists on the deeper "infernal" "impressionism" and "Bergsonism" (as opposed to realism) of the image here (*spera* is Tuscan). *Nerofumo* is—says Avalle (25), in his exhaustive analysis of the structure and symbology of "Gli orecchini"—a stylistic borrowing from Mallarmé and, more generally, from the postsymbolists. The dark mirror reflects the "sooty black of the night" which seems to come from within the mirror. Note the similarity with the situation of "Cigola la carrucola del pozzo" and "Vasca," with the same "two movements, emergence and rising from the deep, which in Montale always underlie the thematics of memory" (Grignani, 186).

È passata la spugna . . . : Macrì (1, 89) reads the poem as a rewriting, in "a changed, but transitional, state of feeling," of "Dora Markus II" and other texts from *Le occasioni*: "The 'eraser' that couldn't cancel out the 'tale of . . . wandering' 'has passed' . . . , and means the complete absence of the earthly she from the 'oval'; 'the motors' throb' is succeeded by the droning of the 'elytra' and the 'insane funeral'; as is the 'written' 'legend' by the 'stamp' that will be reborn in the depths, in the love of parents and brothers in blood and spirit. The portraits in gold have been taken down from the neoclassical salon, and the great proud images of honor and inflexible love burn in the crucible, become starved, contorted hands . . . , which will place on the chosen one the 'corals' of another, future 'power.' The 'burning mirror' is an instrument of war!"

barlumi / indifesi: "Voli" and "barlumi," two characteristic attributes of Montale's feminine figures, converge here in a typical piling-up of associations, soon to be joined by the now-familiar "pietre" of Clizia's jewelry and by her "lampo." Lonardi (127) notes that the rhyme *traccia/scaccia* recalls a similar rhyme in Foscolo's "A Luigia Pallavicina caduta da cavallo," as does *fuggo/struggono*.

il forte imperio: Avalle (45): "In the hardness and the cold splendor of the jewels are recognized the attributes, the very destiny, of the absent one." The "imperio" of the beloved is the realm of her "spiritual superiority" (Marchese 1, 131); cf. the "sigillo imperioso" of "Palio"; Macrì (1, 84), however, sees it as the irrational and overwhelming dedication to madness represented by the war, which with a swipe of the sponge has eliminated the salvific, angelic feminine "phantom" from her heaven.

che ti rapisce: Marchese (1, 131): "The celestial *raptus* of the angel who is moving away from the poet on her salvific mission." But "rapisce," in its negative connotations, also suggests the poet's resentment at Clizia's absence against his will; cf. "Ghermito" in " 'Ezekiel saw the Wheel. . . .' "

fuggo / l'iddia che non s'incarna: Luperini (1, 126–27) sees a recurrence of the "rissa cristiana" of "Notizie dall'Amiata" in the "irreconcilability of the woman-angel, and her ethical hardness, with the base but also potentially rich and fascinating world of 'desires.' . . . The figure of Clizia presents herself then to Montale in a double and certainly contradictory way: as an incarnate divinity, herald of salvation, and thus as Christ-bearer (as she will be above all in 'Iride' and 'La primavera hitleriana'); or as 'goddess who won't become flesh,' an abstraction that must be irreconcilable with 'desires' and with earthly life. [In "Iride," Montale refers to himself as the "Nestorian," "the man who knows best the affinities that bind God to incarnate beings" (*Sec*, 304; see note to "Iride" on the Nestorian heresy).] In the second case an impulse of fear of a mysticism that will soon appear 'blind' (the adjective appears in 'L'orto' and 'La primavera hitleriana') and so cold that it can be compared to death prevails; so that in fact the 'desires' are preferable at least until they're 'burned' by the luminous evidence of an occasional epiphany. And it is wrong to look for positive or negative meanings in this term ["desires"] once and for all; with it the poet intends rather to connote an objective given, to acknowledge a real contradiction in his life."

struggono: Petrarchan (cf. CCXXI, 5–7, and CCLXIV, 77).

ronza il folle / mortorio: An amplification of the metaphor of the "elitre" onto a "cosmic," symbolic plane; Macrì (1, 84): "The totally irrational and overwhelming . . . madness . . . of the Enemy of man" (cf. the "follìa di morte" of "Nuove stanze").

le molli / meduse della sera: Avalle (63): "The slow sinking of night shadows in the mirror." But the misogynistic undertone of "Serenata indiana" and elsewhere is also present (cf. the "donne ilari e molli" of "Buffalo" and the "molle riverbero" in which the estranged woman appears in "Due nel crepuscolo"); Macrì (1, 77) points out that the feminine associations of "molli"—"the female essence fluidified" (82)—are here as well. Luperini (1, 127–28): "The return of the feminine ghost, transformed into a sort of funerary divinity by the act—almost a macabre coronation—with which the hands of the dead place the corals on her ears, takes on undeniably threatening aspects, also because of the undoubted 'isomorphism of medusas and feminine figures' [Greco, 128] and the parallelism between these viscous aquatic creatures and the octopus of 'Serenata indiana.'"

La tua impronta: The imprint of the "sigillo imperioso" of "Palio" (see note for the Dantean source of the image); another version of the "segno" (and "stampo") of the MOTTETTI (e.g., the "segni della morte" of "La speranza di pure rivederti"), though Marchese (1, 132) sees it as Clizia's "image"; Macrì (1, 77) calls it "the positive future of the negative present 'non è più traccia.'"

verrà di giù: Originally "di là" (from there) (cf. version published in *Prospettive*, 1940); "giù" renders more precise the infernal character of the locale; cf. "in giù" in " 'Ezekiel saw the Wheel. . . .' "

squallide / mani: One of the most discussed images in Montale's poetry. The hands recall the "mani scarni" of "Incontro" (see Avalle, 65–66). The poet wrote Avalle (66): "I deny that the hands were mine or those of the phantom. Perhaps they are hands that emerge from the tombs of people who were gassed or massacred (Jews like the phantom); but they can also be unidentifiable hands that rise from the void and fall back. The earrings were not pendants but clip-ons, of a kind that often require an extraneous hand." Re: the negative association of the earrings, Greco (128) notes "a change of sign depending on whether the woman wears [the corals] when she is alive or dead . . . and mentions "the well-known belief that coral loses its color when worn by someone running the risk of losing her life."

For Macrì (1, 84–85), the angel/phantom "rises in and from the tomb of her people with whom she has been reconciled. . . . The return of the 'molli meduse' is the embryonic condition of the new genesis, of reintegration into the community; the 'hands' that attach the 'corals' are the true protagonists and creators of a pact restructured under the seal of the patriarchs; if the 'coralli' (marine concretization of the 'molli meduse') are, as has been said, rendered essential in the 'forte imperio,' 'fermano i coralli' means to consolidate, confirm the sovereignty of reason and history."

travolte: Cf. "Ballata scritta in una clinica," in which the flight of the bull-god that has raped Europe enacts the same verb. Macrì (1, 89) notes that the word means, "Dantesquely, 'turned backwards,'" i.e., contorted. Cf. "sopra / qualche gesto che annaspa" in "La bufera."

La frangia dei capelli . . . / The bangs . . . (1941)

A second Elizabethan sonnet which elaborates Clizia's angelic myth, and which is based, as we know (see notes to "Elegia di Pico Farnese"), on a "realistic detail," Irma Brandeis's bangs, which become a Petrarchan-Baudelairean attribute of Clizia's, and which Montale transforms at will. The poem shares a great deal (as do certain aspects of "Il ventaglio") with Montale's translation of Shakespeare's Sonnet XXXIII (published in 1944):

> Spesso, a lusingar vette, vidi splendere
> sovranamente l'occhio del mattino,
> e baciar d'oro verdi prati, accendere
> pallidi rivi d'alchimìe divine.
> Poi vili fumi alzarsi, intorbidata
> d'un tratto quella celestiale fronte,
> e fuggendo a occidente il desolato
> mondo, l'astro celare il viso e l'onta.
> Anch'io sul far del giorno ebbi il mio sole
> e il suo trionfo mi brillò sul ciglio:
> ma, ahimè, poté restarvi un' ora sola,
> rapito dalle nubi in cui s'impiglia.
>   Pur non ne ho sdegno: bene può un terrestre
>   sole abbuiarsi, se è cosi il celeste.

(Literal translation: Often, to flatter heights, I saw the eye / of morning shine sovereignly, / and kiss the green meadows with gold, ignite / pale streams with divine alchemies. / Then [I saw] low mists arise, / that heavenly forehead clouded suddenly, / and fleeing west from the desolate / world, the star cover its face and shame. / I too at daybreak had my sun / and his triumph shone on my brow: / but, alas, he lasted only an hour, / seized by the clouds that snared him. / Still, I don't disdain it: well can an earthly / sun go dark, if the heavenly one is so.)

Montale (Greco, 46): "This time there's not absence but presence. No difficulties."

la fronte puerile: Macrì (1, 83): "Must be Mallarméan; Clizia's *imperiousness* likewise recalls the 'puerile triumph' and the 'child empress' of a feminine, solar myth."

gl'indulti: Juridical/theological term for concessions granted to persons or entities outside the law; emphasizes the angelic/"imperial" Clizia's "superego" function (and the poet's existence outside her sphere).

trasmigatrice Artemide ed illesa: Lonardi (128) notes that the reference to Artemis, or Diana, the chaste goddess of the hunt (another "iddia che non s'incarna"), is a classicizing borrowing from Foscolo (cf. a similar instance in "Falsetto"). The structure of the line, too, is Latinate. He also discerns (195) the influence of the saving but murderous sacred bird in Coleridge's "Rime of the Ancient Mariner." (See also Nerval's sonnet "Artemis" in *Chimères*.)

le guerre dei nati-morti: Cf. the "uomini-capre" of "Elegia di Pico Farnese," and other similar epithets for the great insensate majority of humanity.

marezzarlo: For Macrì (1, 82–83), the word (*marezzo* is derived from *marmo*, marble, because of the swirling pattern naturally found in the stone) is linked here with Clizia's stones and seal, rather than with the malign nature described in "Marezzo."

irrequieta: Cf. the "irrequietudine" of Dora Markus.

Finestra fiesolana / Fiesole Window (1941)
Montale (Greco, 46): "War landscape. At Fiesole [above Florence], where I was awaiting the 'liberating' troops."

Greco (130): "The opposition Clizia–war is . . . the fundamental motif of the poem: her light, the awaited flash of her look are counterposed to the unnaturalness of the present condition. And the ivy returns as in 'Tempi di Bellosguardo' as a symbol of fidelity."

The window setting recalls that of "Il balcone."

edere scarlatte: Montale (Angelini 3, 168): "Scarlet, because the war has begun." Cf. the "accesa edera" of "Flussi."

Il giglio rosso / The Red Lily (1942)
Montale (Angelini 3, 168): "A serenade"; (Greco, 46): "Symbol of Florence. Counterpoint between a youth spent in Florence and a maturity spent in the north (see 'Iride'). . . . Also cf. 'Nuove stanze' and 'La primavera hitleriana.' "

Greco (130): "From the first to the last line, the red lily follows the existential fortunes of Clizia." But the lily has been "sacrificed" by Clizia herself in favor of the "mistletoe," a symbol of Christmas and thus of her own salvific mission. Rebay (3, 186–87) notes that Clizia's scarf is the same as in "Verso Capua," i.e., the small white circles on her scarf here evoke the berries of the mistletoe, as they did the stars of the American flag there. The red of the lily (like the ivy of "Finestra fiesolana" and the corals of "Gli orecchini") is one of Clizia's fire attributes and, as Luperini argues (1, 128–29), here represents "the earth, 'desires,' " in contrast with the "incorruptible chill" (introduction of her ice attributes), which is "the chill of the inflexible moral and religious law that has forced Clizia to follow her God and leave Italy for her far-off country." And yet, at the moment of death, it will be the red lily, the humble, domestic ditchflower of Montale's god (cf. "Ballata scritta in una clinica": "the God who paints fire on / the lilies in the ditch"), "a God of dailiness and danger," that will be there in paradise, beyond the "rissa cristiana," to "make death a friend," thus "almost taking its revenge." (For the deep significance of the image of the "fosso," especially in FINISTERRE and the SILVAE, see note to "Il gallo cedrone.")

tempestano: In the sense, as Angelini (4, 392) points out, of thickly bejeweling, i.e., constellating—cf. the "bandiera stellata" of Clizia's scarf in "Verso Capua."

Il ventaglio / The Fan (1942)
Montale (Greco, 46): "Images of war seen or dreamed synthetically (the telescope) [cf. the part title, "Col rovescio del binocolo," in the plan for *Romanzo*, above]. The fan emerges out of the background, as the earrings did another time. He who has known you cannot really die; or rather, not even death has meaning for him who has known you."

Another highly allusive "pseudosonnet" (Montale to Contini, June 6, 1942) (*Op*, 943), its title drawn from the "éventails" of Mallarmé (Greco [142–43] finds parallels with Mallarmé's first "éventail" ["Avec comme pour langage"], which is also an Elizabethan sonnet). Its occasion is another "Petrarchan" attribute of Clizia's, drawn from her war chest of jewelry, "a holy relic in time of war" (Cary, 312). (According to Macrì [2, 11], the poem describes the disastrous rout of Italian forces at Caporetto in October 1917.) Cary's remarkable analysis continues (313–14):

"The poem is about the power residing in Clizia's fan which, since it is present (*là*), she has presumably left behind her—as it turns out, as a sign of her mission. 'Il ventaglio' is also a triumphant affirmation of her genuine and abiding presence—as contrasted with the sad images of her, lips, gazes, reduced and crystallized by memory.

"*Ut pictura* . . . : the sonnet starts with Horace's famous phrase from the epistle *Ad Pisones* ('Art of Poetry,' line 361: *Ut pictura poesis*—'As with painting, so with poetry'), which serves as a stage direction for what follows: the poem-image of the loveable past that the poet is occupied in trying to 'fix' on his absent lady's fan. The desperation informing this effort to take refuge in the past is indicated in the first clause of the second sentence with its references to military debacle and the heavy clouds of war and winter storm, while the second clause, with its startled *già* and shift into the present tense shows the miracle of the relic as it starts—not a return via memory but a resurrected presence in the replenished present. Thus 'already' through the mere contemplation of her fan the light begins to dawn, the storm begins to abate, while simultaneously the fan assumes . . . its coordinate roles as purveyor of winds (here a beneficent southern variety) and wing carrying back the angel of the storm. But no longer is she a mere 'refuge,' a fixed image or snapshot which the poet projects for the sake of his sanity. Here toward the poem's climax she is present, is directly addressed, and the miraculous possibility dawns that she is able to alter the balance of things. . . . The wing feathers that were her fan now bear light to the drowning visages of the 'victims' [cf. the "mani" of "Gli orecchini"], and also retributive justice to the fleeing hordes of Ahriman [see note to "Elegia di Pico Farnese"]. The extraordinary *mana* of her coming prompts the final question. What is the fate of those, like the Nestorian or the guilty ones, who must sustain her radiance face to face? The query, and its strenuous abruptness after the string of exclamations preceding it, sounds out the panting ecstasy with which, fanlike, the poem snaps shut.

". . . *Ut pictura* . . . suggests that this poem should be seen as a picture—which it is; indeed, it is a succession of them. The full passage in the epistle deals with the matter of perspective, how poems, like pictures, vary with distance, with conditions of light and shadow, with familiarity. But 'Il ventaglio' itself incorporates several perspectives and viewpoints— contrasting chiefly the tiny 'plane' of fixed memory with the immense living present that succeeds it. That is to say, the citation functions not only to place the action of the poem, but capsulize a major thematic concern of the poem itself."

Le labbra che confondono: Macrì (1, 91): "In the Dantesque and English sense of 'neutralizing an evil plan.'"

cannocchiale arrovesciato: Cf. the "lente" of "Marezzo."

giostra / . . . ordegni: Continues the medieval chivalric metaphors of *Le occasioni* (for "giostra" see *Inferno* XXII, 6, and *Purgatorio* XXII, 42). Lonardi (60) says *inostra* is "archaic-Carduccian," but Mengaldo (59) gives it as an example of Montale's "Dantism," possibly mediated through D'Annunzio, or "the biting experimentation," "particularly in the realm of metaphor," of Montale's friend the poet-priest Clemente Rebora (1885–1957); cf. also the "torri, / gonfaloni" of "Il giglio rosso."

sbiancano: As the "luce di prima" did to the heads of the spectators in "Palio."

sull'orde: Cf. "la lugubre attesa / dell'orda" in "La primavera hitleriana."

Muore chi ti riconosce?: Arrowsmith (3, 173) identifies this as an allusion to Exodus 33:20: "And he said, Thou canst not see my face: for there shall no man see me, and live"; while Lonardi (36) recalls the "crude destiny of Actaeon, who recognized Diana (and not by chance this pitiless, sporting, virginal goddess, so beloved of the 'Ligurian' Foscolo, is, among classical 'divas,' the one who returns most often in Montale)." He adds (199): "Truth-salvation can kill in the moment in which it is offered. This is because the eyes of the earth-bound man can't bear the lightning-flash, just as his feet can't support flight."

Personae separatae / Personae Separatae (1942)

Montale (Greco, 46–47): "Background of war. The scale is a falling star. 'Per lo sguardo d'un altro': seen objectively by one who looks at everything sub specie aeternitatis, we are barely an ephemeral, passing spark. 'Riano,' dialect expression for 'riale,' 'fosso,' 'botro' [ditch]. In Genoese, 'riàn' [see note to "Il gallo cedrone"]. Landscape of the Lunigiana, not better de-fined. The war background is not to be taken too literally, here and elsewhere. The war seen above all as metaphysical otherness, an almost permanent state of the dark forces that conspire against us. A state of fact almost ontological, in common parlance the forces of evil."

Here the focus is on separation from Clizia; her salvific powers are ineffectual where the poet is; they are only "separate characters" in a world where "two lives don't count" (cf. the pessimism of "Costa San Giorgio"). Greco (143) quotes a phrase from "Una 'Tragedia itali-ana' . . ." (Auto, 47), "two different masks, two personae separatae," which indicates the phrase's theatrical source (and which links the image to the "maschere" of "Due nel crepus-colo" and the related theme of the "volto" in Ossi di seppia).

Contini had written to Montale on November 19, 1942 (Eus, 77), on learning of the death of Montale's mother, mentioning a beloved student who had also recently died: "Now I'd like to pose . . . the subtle theological query whether in eternal life one can love certain individ-uated souls in particular, have questions asked and answered, and develop one's own rela-tionship with them historically. I'd like to understand souls as formae separatae (in this case the shell was a transparent screen behind which the emotions flowered too quickly)." The letter evidently influenced the composition of "Personae separatae," in which Contini (Eus, 83) declared himself "directly interested in part," and of "A mia madre" as well.

poca cosa . . . / poca cosa . . . : Recalls the anaphora in "Nuove stanze": "follìa di morte non si placa a poco / prezzo, se poco è il lampo del tuo sguardo"; see also the repetition of "troppo" below.

un perduto / senso: Cf. the "oscuro senso / reminiscente" of "Voce giunta con le folaghe."

le cave / ceppaie, nido alle formiche: Arrowsmith (3, 173–74) sees a reference to the myth of the Myrmidons, or ant-men, of Aegina (Metamorphoses VII, 523ff.; Inferno XXIX, 58ff.), who repopulated the island after a plague. Cf. Pascoli, "Romagna": "nido all ghiandaie."

Troppo / straziato . . . : The image of the human forest, related to the "human plant," etc., of Ossi di seppia (see note to "Arsenio"), is Dantesque in inspiration (cf. the "infernal hunt" in the wood of the suicides in Inferno XIII) and recalls the "sughereto / scotennato" of "Verso Capua" (its "furtivo / raggio" is what the poet is searching for here). Greco (133) sees the three "troppo" images as evoking the war on natural, historical, and metaphysical levels, adding, "The voice is the perennial voice of Evil, deaf to human destiny."

Lunigiana: Coastal Liguria, between Viareggio and La Spezia, with the high Apuan Alps in the near distance.

sospiro: For a discussion of the essential relationship between "form" and "breath" in Montale, see note to "Nella serra."

l'orror che fiotta: Macrì (1, 79) quotes *Inferno* XV, 5: "Temendo il fiotto che'nver lor s'avventa."

la luce . . . luce: Cf. Eliot, *Four Quartets* I, IV, 8–9: "After the kingfisher's wing has answered light to light"; and "A Song for Simeon" (translated by Montale in 1929): "light upon light."

L'arca / The Ark (1943)

Montale (Greco, 47): " 'Il vello d'oro' is any shroud which when it's lifted reveals memories. The magnolia is a simple tree and the 'latrato di fedeltà' ["baying loyalty"] is the dog's but also, naturally, the poet's. 'Calce e sangue,' images of the war seen as a permanent fact, almost an institution. Magnolia, dog, nursemaids, etc., all real memories."

La tempesta . . . : Cf. the storm of "La bufera," which is (also) the war, and which "breaks any false alliance with nature," and above all the "sameness of the interwoven hours," the "delirium of immobility" of "Arsenio" (Lonardi, 140).

il vello d'oro: The willow's umbrella becomes "the golden fleece" (cf. the "sudario" of "Elegia di Pico Farnese" and the "fascia di ogni tormento" of "Notizie dall'Amiata"). The shroud is the "schermo d'immagini," the Schopenhauerian "veil of Maya" that conceals reality, here the reality preserved in memory.

calce e sangue: Lime is used to cover and decompose dead bodies; "l'impronta [cf. "Gli orecchini"] / del piede umano" thus carries both life and death (cf. the "nati-morti" of "La frangia dei capelli . . ."), .

in cucina: The "focolare" of "A Liuba che parte" (and the "frigidaria" of "Tempi di Bellosguardo"), the very heart of family life (as in "Proda di Versilia" and elsewhere). "L'arca" is the first of the poems in *La bufera* in which Montale returns in a new, more nostalgic key to the territory of childhood and the family. Luperini (1, 130) notes that "A mia madre" and "L'arca" mark Montale's turning toward his past, chronologically coincidental with the death of his mother, who died in November 1942 (see note to "A mia madre").

la magnolia: In spite of Montale's assertion, the magnolia has symbolic resonance in *La bufera*, starting with "La bufera." Macrì (1, 108) calls it his "usual symbol of defense of the lares."

un latrato: Cf. the "ululo / del cane di legno" of "Ballata scritta in una clinica." Dogs in *La bufera* (cf. Piquillo in "Da una torre") are *senhals* of familial affection and faithfulness, often associated with death.

la mia arca: The ark is the same as Liuba's, which "will suffice to save" her (see "A Liuba che parte" and note, which quotes Montale's 1926 definition of the ark as "a few affections and memories that could follow me everywhere, unobscured"). Like that poem, "L'arca" draws on both classical and Jewish imagery; Luperini (1, 130–31): "The ark is the Biblical ark of the Pact between man and the divinity against the risk of their dissociation . . . and it carries to safety . . . the base and subterranean world of animality and the dead, of the 'desires' and of infancy. From this moment, the dead become the tutelary gods of a dimension of existence that cannot be represented by Clizia."

Giorno e notte / Day and Night (1943)

Montale to Glauco Cambon (October 16, 1961) (published in *Aut-Aut* 67 [January 1962], 44–45; in *Su*, 91–92): "In your very intelligent gloss on 'Giorno e notte,' published in *Aut-Aut* no. 65, you extracted from the poem what in musical terms would be the harmonics, the complementary sounds; and it doesn't matter if here it's a case of values that are more psychological than of sound or timbre. There is, however, the possibility of a down-to-earth explanation, which I'm proposing to you and which doesn't contradict yours. The poem is part of a cycle—FINISTERRE—which carries the dates 1940–42, published in Lugano in '43. The background of the whole cycle is the war, which I lived through in Florence (I've resided in Milan only since '48). It would be difficult to see poplars from a Milanese veranda; perhaps it's not possible in Florence, either. Still, in Florence nature invades the city the way it doesn't in Milan, where I couldn't imagine little piazzas with knife grinders and parrots. I submit that in the whole brief cycle the noise of the war (understood as a cosmic fact) is present, the wailing and shouts on the veranda become fully comprehensible as part of the 'basso continuo,' no less than the shot that reddens the throat of the perilous visitor. But who is she? Certainly, at the outset, a real woman; but here and elsewhere, in fact everywhere, *visiting angel*, hardly or not at all material. It's not necessary to attribute the floating feather to her, as if it had fallen in advance from her wings (if that weren't impossible). Feather, gleaming in the mirror, and other signs (in other poems) are nothing more than enigmatic presages of the event that is about to occur: the 'privileged' instant (Contini), often a visitation. And why does the visitor presage the dawn? Which dawn? Perhaps the dawn of a possible salvation which can be peace conceived as a metaphysical liberation. In and of herself, the visitor cannot return in the flesh, she has for a long time ceased to exist as such. Perhaps she has been dead a long time, perhaps she'll die elsewhere in that instant. Her task as unknowing Christ-bearer does not permit her any other triumph that is not failure here below: distance, suffering, insubstantial ghostly re-apparitions (see 'Iride' published in '43 [actually written in 1943–44 and published in '45] and included in the second edition of FINISTERRE, published by Barbèra), the bit of presence that is a memento, an admonition, for him who receives it. Her appearance is always angry, haughty, her exhaustion is mortal, her courage indomitable: if she is an angel, she preserves all her earthly attributes, she has not yet managed to disincarnate herself (cf. 'Voce giunta con le folaghe,' written several years later). Nevertheless, she is already *outside*, while we are *inside*. She, too, was *inside* (cf. 'Nuove stanze,' in *Le occasioni*), but then she left (cf. 'La primavera hitleriana') to complete her mission.

"If then one can see her as a nightingale—and why not a *robin*, who has a red breast and sings at dawn?—I have no trouble with this; what's important is that the translation from the true to the symbolic or vice versa always occurs unconsciously in me. I always begin with the real, I'm incapable of inventing anything; but when I start to write (rapidly and with few corrections), the poetic nucleus has had a long incubation in me: long and obscure. *Après coup*, afterwards, I know my intentions.

"The realistic given, however, is always present, always true. In the case of 'Giorno e notte,' barracks, hospitals, and trumpet sounds (reveille, the mess, furlough, etc.) belong to the picture of a militarized city. Nothing forbids seeing in this the profile of the perennial earthly inferno."

questa dura / fatica: The effort to sleep in the war-torn city, lacerated by noise: the daily life of the "incubi" ("nati-morti") who are not privileged with access to the transforming experience of Clizia's look. (It is worth noting that Montale was a lifelong insomniac.)

nell'antro / incandescente: A reference to the myth of the cave in Plato's *Republic*. Cf. the "androne gelido" of "Elegia di Pico Farnese."

perigliosa: Transference of the characteristics of the scene to Clizia; but she in herself is dangerous in that she demands to be followed in a way the poet finds impossible.

i chiostri e gli ospedali: Cf. the setting of "Ballata scritta in una clinica."

Il tuo volo / Your Flight (1943)

Montale (Greco, 47): "The two lights are perhaps those of the fire and the amulets. Landscape of human inferno visited by the usual harbinger-awakener. Here the details are not very realistic but symbolic (the 'girini umani'). A somewhat dreamlike poem but not incomprehensible. 'Vivagno' in the sense of edge (of the ditch)."

Macrì (1, 90) reads the poem in the light of "Gli orecchini": "The creature of love, purified in the underworld and reconciled with her mortal nation, re-emerges as protector and vindicates the secret pact between the poet and suffering, waiting humanity; the 'shadow' of absent flight . . . becomes 'your flight,' a title that is thus the emblem/reality of the poem."

ti stellano: Macrì (2, 245): "The bird Clizia (heliotropically facing eastward, toward Europe!) appears equipped with her feminine *amulets* (among them her 'scarf' [see "Verso Capua"]) transformed into *arms*, without losing their grace."

due luci . . . : The light of the fire of this infernal, i.e., Dantesque, scene contends with the light from Clizia's jewels (amulets in this case), which presumably reflect the light of the divine sun to which she is constantly looking. The "borro," here as elsewhere is, like the "fossa fuia" of "La bufera," an infernal Dantesque *bolgia*, which here represents a world of "human tadpoles."

rifavillano: As Arrowsmith (3, 175) points outs, a neologism, coined from *favilla*, spark.

cinerei i capelli: Arrowsmith (3, 176): The ashen color is "to indicate her affinity with those who had been physically incinerated by the war, gassed or massacred, and her own spiritual passage through Dante's purgatorial 'refining flame' ['il fuoco che gl'affina']." Ashes are a Clizian motif (cf. "Stanze" and "Nuove stanze"), no doubt originally derived from Clizia's "real" habit of smoking.

sulla ruga . . . : An elaborate baroque conceit; Clizia's furrowed brow is presented as an attribute of the heavens which she has appropriated in order to appear to mankind. The implication is that she no longer exists as an earthly creature. Cf. the "irrequieta . . . fronte" of "La frangia dei capelli. . . ."

la mano delle sete . . . : A reversal of the Orphic myth. Here it is Clizia, dressed in her symbolic raiment, who must try to lead the poet out of the world of the dead. But he fears that if she "breaks into the fire," if she engages more deeply in the infernal war-world in which he finds himself, she will be unable to return to save him.

A mia madre / To My Mother (1943)

Giuseppina Montale died in November 1942. The theological argument at the heart of the poem (it recurs in the poem about his father, "Voce giunta con le folaghe," as well) centers on the Nestorian heresy (see note to "Iride"), which posits Christ's essentially incarnate nature. Here, too, as in "Gli orecchini," Montale insists on "the *thisness* of human existence" (Cambon, 97), that earthly life is not a mere shadow of the heavenly—though he installs his mother, like his sister in the "Madrigali fiorentini" that follow, in the "crowded" memory that is the only afterlife he himself can subscribe to. Cambon (98): "Here a secularized Christian speaks who has lost all certainties but this and who, nevertheless, cannot bring himself to exclude a metaphysical dimension from life, since he is envisioning the possibility of a perfecting human individuality after death."

Macrì (1, 141): "The mystery of the sonnet, its sacredness, resides in the pure objectivity of the ghost who with the thread of her own faith weaves herself her own 'eliso,' the immortality of her family, by means of the singularity of her significant body parts. The son does not intervene with his own living memory (since she exists objectively, albeit in that very memory) nor does he *directly* exhort her not to abandon her remains (since *for him* she exists only in *his* memory); in effect, it would be absurd and monstrous if he wanted to break the circle of the faith with which she has constructed her 'eliso,' the same faith that leads the woman to abandon her body and allows her to believe in the certainty of another life. Such certainty is transformed in him into a 'question that you leave' 'in me,' whose answer he rejects, resolving this question, too, *in a gesture of his own* to preserve her happy in her heaven. Thus the conflict between otherworldly domestic life and its inherent dissolution in the suggestions and persuasions of her own faith ('it's not what *you believe*,' 'the question *you leave*') is resolved without impinging on the beloved person who remains immune in the freedom of her own destiny. This is an example, at its outer limits, of Montale's capacity to *poetare a parte objecti* [to poetize objectively], preserving his lyric subjectivity from pseudo-sentimental contamination, which taints similar domestic exercises."

la spoglia: Cf. Petrarch, CCCI, 14. "Gentile," too, is Petrarchan (Savoca, 68).

nell'eliso: Lonardi (52) points out this classicizing borrowing from Foscolo; but in Foscolo, "memory is the secular ark that it will be for Montale, but without doubts as to its sure, celestial navigation." Montale's "Proustian" sense of memory emphasizes its enormous responsibility coupled with its fragility, fallibility, and arbitrariness.

la domanda: Cf. the question asked in "Vento sulla Mezzaluna": "Do you know where God is?"

II. DOPO / AFTERWARDS

"After" the liberation of Florence by Allied troops in August 1944, but also after the "Petrarchan" experience of FINISTERRE. The poems of this brief section continue the focus on the dead that began in the late work of FINISTERRE, and in general on a world of aftermath. Stylistically, too, they are less artificial and symbolic, more derived from the data of dailiness, and thus predict the style—and form—of Montale's later poetry.

Madrigali fiorentini / Florentine Madrigals (1944)
An ironic reprise, perhaps, of the (Florentine) MOTTETTI; the musical motet (thirteenth century) is normally sung in Latin and has a sacred connotation, while the madrigal is "simple," "amorous," and "profane" (Zingarelli). The madrigal is the dominant musical form of the postwar poems of *La bufera*.

I. 11 settembre 1943
Montale (Angelini 3, 169): "The Germans and the partisans of the Republic of Salò (*repubblichini*) have reoccupied Florence; Mussolini has been freed." (Mussolini had been removed from office by the King and replaced by Marshal Pietro Badoglio on July 25; after the Italian armistice with the Allies on September 3, the Germans occupied the north of Italy, rescued Mussolini, and set him up in a puppet republic headquartered in the town of Salò.)

Montale (Greco, 47): "Herma was a model who was a friend of Vittorini's, an Austrian. 'Baffo buco' is Hitler with an allusion to pederasty [*Baffo*: mustache; *buco*: vulgar term for anus]."

Montale's note about the "Austrian" Herma is deliberately misleading. "Herma" is surely a *senhal* for Irma (Brandeis, i.e., Clizia), though she did indeed have Austrian (Jewish) ancestry (and may have been a friend of Vittorini). The "hope" that must now be wrapped up, sealed, and put away for the future has proven "vain," as Montale's note for his French translator makes clear, because of the Nazis' reassertion of control over northern Italy (see note to "Finestra fiesolana," a similar sort of song, defined by Montale as a "serenade"); it is the hope for universal liberation after the war expressed in "La primavera hitleriana," but also perhaps the "hope of even seeing you again" of the motets, which is also being sealed in the cold morning light.

Un vagabondo: Montale (Angelini 3, 169): "An airplane, naturally."

II. 11 agosto 1944

Montale (Angelini 3, 169): "Liberation of Florence."

Montale (*Op*, 948): "A Bedlington (terrier), thus a dog, not an airplane, as was thought, appeared on a stump of the bridge of Santissima Trinità [a Renaissance structure of great beauty by Bartolomeo Ammanati which had been mined by the Germans on August 4, 1944, during the British 8th Army's final advance on the city] in the dawn of one of those days. The gong echoes the one that told the family, 'Dinner is served.' (But the family is no more.)"

Montale (Greco, 47): "Paradise imagined as a hospital. My sister had died years earlier in a hospital and was religious."

One of the group of poems of family bereavement of this period, including "A mia madre," "L'arca," and "Da una torre," it parallels the larger losses of the war evoked in its paired poem with this expression of private grief.

Trinity Bridge: The quotation in English makes reference to the structure's fate as a British target during the taking of Florence.

Se s'infognano / come topi di chiavica . . . : Extremely brutal invective; cf. "Il sogno del prigioniero."

sorella mia: Cf. the "strana sorella" of "La bufera." Marianna Montale Vignolo, a deeply influential figure in Montale's early life (see *QuaG*), had died on October 15, 1938. Contini (2, vii) has noted that Marianna "prefigures all the women who watched over his life and are registered in his *canzoniere*." The familial bond is of the utmost importance here; the relation with Mosca in "Ballata scritta in una clinica," too, is primarily familial rather than erotic, for she and the poet, unlike Clizia, share the same god (see Baldissone).

Da una torre / From a Tower (1945)

Montale (Greco, 47): "Piquillo, name of an imaginary dog. I've had other dogs. The house was our house in Monterosso. Through the panes of the window panels seep the dead, more or less beloved and of the family."

Montale in *Il Politecnico* I, 6 (November 3, 1945) (in *Su*, 80–81): "A blackbird, and even a dog dead for many years, can perhaps return, because for us they count more as 'species' than as individuals. But it's difficult indeed to recover a destroyed village or to bring back 'a blood-red lip.' In Liguria, we call the bird that Giacomo Leopardi and the ornithologists name the 'passero solitario' [*monticola solitarius*, or solitary thrush] the 'merlo acquaiolo' [waterdipper]. Many professors, misled by the phrase 'te solingo augellin' ["you, lonely bird," in Leopardi's "Il passero solitario"], believe it to be a sparrow, that is, a creature very, very far from the solitude and the austerity of this melodious slate-colored bird. As to 'Perrito' [later Piquillo], which means little dog, his Spanish name and the mention of his long ears make us suppose he's a *Cocker Spaniel*. But who knows?"

Note in response by the editors of *Il Politecnico*: "The waterdipper flying away from the tower and the little dog who climbs its stairs remind him of those he once saw. It's thus as if they came back to life: this is why he says he *saw* the dog 'scattar dalla tomba.' But the last four lines speak of what can no longer return; from the mullioned windows of the tower, through the glass panes, the village is glimpsed, destroyed: 'un paese di scheletri.' And a person, a face, a mouth, a lip that was alive—'di sangue'!—and which is now even more lost and silent. Thus, in a harmonious simplicity (but only seemingly so: note the web of rhymes, *gruppetto/tetto, orgoglioso/festoso, tomba/tromba, conosciuto/orecchiuto/muto, colori/fiori*) . . . these twelve lines, which opened with the 'orgoglioso' flight of the bird, with his few notes (the 'gruppetto di flauto') and the joyous speed of the little dog, close with these two images of death and these two dark words (*scheletri/muto*)."

The tower, with its stained-glass windows, is the one moved to Bocca di Magra in "Il ritorno," where its "gelo" indicates its association with death, leading to the inference that the "labbro di sangue" is Arletta's (cf. the "voce di sangue" of "Eastbourne"). Her voice was already stilled, she was already effectively dead in the world of Montale's poetry; now, in the deathly after-battle atmosphere of the "paese di scheletri," she is doubly so ("più muto") (cf. "Annetta," in *D71/2*, quoted in note to "Incontro"). See Grignani (60–62) for a discussion of the "biographical-literary node" that conjoins Annetta-Arletta (who is also called "la capinera," the blackcap) with Leopardi's "passero solitario" and, hence, with his figures Silvia and Nerina.

Piquillo: Arrowsmith (3, 177) says the name is drawn from a comic opera of Dumas, but Lonardi (66) suggests the source may be a theatrical work of the same name by Nerval. Grignani (62–63) identifies the dog with the Galiffa of "Sul limite" and "L'angoscia" in *Farf*, also mentioned in a poem in *QuaQ*.

Ballata scritta in una clinica / Ballad Written in a Hospital (1945)
Originally titled "Ballata scritta in una clinica, per scaramanzia [for good luck]" (*Op*, 950). Montale to Contini (*Eus*, 111): "Perhaps it's not a *ballata*; you'll note the structure < >."

Montale (Angelini 3, 169): "In the month of August 1943 [*sic*; but he must mean 1944], we were in Florence, hidden in a cellar (the 'ventre della balena'), and were waiting to be liberated by the Allies, who had yet to enter the city, still partly occupied by the Germans, and who were bombing it, from Fiesole, blowing up the bridges and other mined structures [cf. "Madrigali fiorentini"].—'Nel cavo delle tue orbite': my wife was in a plaster cast and gravely ill. [Montale and Mosca were not in fact married until 1962, not long before her death.] A little bulldog made of wood was on the night table, with an alarm clock with luminous hands. The cross (below) was on the Red Cross flag on the [hospital] building. Thus in this Ballad two moments are brought together: first the allusion to our hiding, and later the hospital where they took my wife: both in these few days of battle and chaos."

Montale (Greco, 47): " 'Nel solco' . . . During and after the emergency. It was August. Mosca was in a hospital. The bull represents brute force, the war ["the Germans"—Montale (Angelini 3, 170)], Aries courage and salvation. At least, according to my astrological views in those days. The 'cane di legno' was on the night table in the room. 'L'altra Emergenza,' the beyond."

Macrì (1, 107) notes that "the sickly companion" is "primordial" in Montale—it goes back at least as far as the second and third motets—and also that it is "very Browning," and compares the situation of the "Ballata" with his "Confessions," as does Lonardi (131–32). Mengaldo (18) sees in the mirroring stanza structure (1-3-4-5-6-7-6-5-4-3-1) the perfect realization of a more loosely applied formal tendency that goes back as far as "I limoni" and "Egloga."

dell'emergenza: The state of emergency declared by the Germans under siege from the Allies, who are about to rout them out of Florence; also, however, the serious illness from which the poet's companion, Drusilla Tanzi Marangoni, known as La Mosca, was suffering. The poem marks her first appearance in Montale's poetry.

la folle cometa agostana: According to Marchese (1, 160), " 'insane' in that, traditionally, the [August] comet presaged disaster."

lo specchio: Mosca is the mirror in which the poet can recognize, know himself; cf. "il mio specchio" in "L'orto," and the mirror full of absence in "Gli orecchini," whose antecedents are the "pool" and "well" of *Ossi di seppia.*

Nel cavo delle tue orbite: Mosca's legendary myopia (see the XENIA in *Satura*), which is to be contrasted with Clizia's clairvoyance.

L'iddio taurino . . . : Jupiter, who in the form of a bull, carried out the rape of Europa. The same lowercase form of *dio,* with its pagan connotations, is used in "Gli orecchini." Avalle has noted the critique of blind instinctual vitalism the term implies. The Nazi god is countered by Aries, "astral talisman of spring and hoped-for liberation" (Greco, 139), drawn, according to Macrì (1, 103), from *Paradiso* XXVIII, 116–17ff.; or possibly a "figure of Christ and salvation" (Lonardi [36], who also notes the "Dantesque" collocation of classical and Biblical mythology). Cary (321): "The 'Ballata' is a veritable dance of esoteric apocrypha."

Montale associates Aries with the Florentine red lily of "Il giglio rosso"; he is an earthly ("del fosso") god of "dailiness and danger" (Luperini 1, 129), which, as we have seen earlier, Montale posits in contrast with Clizia's remote, absolute God, and which he shares, familially, with Mosca. Luperini (1, 133): "The choice of 'Il giglio rosso' (which contained . . . an implicit contrast between lily and mistletoe) is confirmed and strengthened: renunciation, too (very probably, the renunciation of Clizia is foreshadowed here), has its dignity, although such ethical reassurance [in Montale] normally requires feminine endorsement (in this case, that of Mosca)."

del ratto finale: The feared death of Mosca, but also the rape of Europe that is about to be carried out by the bull-god. Cf. "il forte imperio / che ti rapisce" of "Gli orecchini."

son pronto: An echo of Matthew 24:44: "Be ye also ready."

dell'altra Emergenza: "Emergenza" here also carries the connotation of "emergence," i.e., epiphany (Arrowsmith 3, 178), the sense of another reality painfully emerging into the poet's consciousness.

il bulldog di legno: Note the contrast of bull-god and bulldog, which in English is even starker. The dog, symbol here as elsewhere of homely loyalty, of a "revaluation of the 'vita di quaggiù' ['life down here'] in the presence of death" (Luperini 1, 134), is cousin to those of "L'arca" and "Da una torre," and its silent howl is, in effect, the "baying loyalty" of "L'arca." Luperini (1, 133–34) quotes a 1946 article, "Il mondo della noia" (*Auto,* 79–82): "In the life of those who have lived long enough there occur grave situations, real 'emergency' cases, in which everything seems to be destroyed and life seems to hang by a very thin thread. . . . [For man in these moments,] faced with nothing ["il nulla"] or with eternity, . . . only one sole possibility is thinkable, tangible, evident, infinitely dear the closer it is to disappearing: life down here, the same life we have seen, known and touched with our hands from the first years of childhood."

la porta stretta: Matthew 7:14: "Because strait is the gate, and narrow is the way, which leadeth unto life, and few there be that find it." Cf. also "la cruna" of "L'estate."

all'enorme / presenza dei morti: As in "Madrigali fiorentini," the historical situation and the poet's predicament are seen in parallel; here the casualties of the battle for Florence and the poet's own dead are linked.

III. INTERMEZZO

Luperini (1, 135): "The rediscovery of 'life down here' and the return to family grief come together in a . . . profound affective and ideological investment in the Ligurian world of childhood. . . . The urge to prose and the return to the land of childhood seem to coincide."

In the 1949 plan for *Romanzo*, this group, called IN LIGURIA, also included the paired poems "Nella serra" and "Nel parco," which, like the pieces in this group, revisit the landscape of *Ossi di seppia*.

Due nel crepuscolo / Two in Twilight (1926/1943)

Montale (*Op*, 954): "In the old notebook where, years ago, I found 'Dora Markus,' there were also these notes which bear the date September 5, 1926. I've retranscribed them, adding a title a little bit à la Browning ('Two in the Campagna') and inserting a few words where there were blanks or erasures. I also removed two useless lines. That is, I finished the work I should have done then, if I'd thought the sketch could interest me many years later."

What follows is a reconstruction from the ms. of the original version as presented in *Op* (951–54) (the material that was revised appears in italics):

> Fluisce fra te e me sul*la veranda*
> un chiarore *d'acquario, in queste sere*
> [*stremate*] *e luminose*, che deforma
> col profilo dei colli anche il tuo viso.
> Sta in un *mezzo* sfuggevole, reciso
> da te ogni gesto tuo: *taglia senz'orma*
> *od ombra questa zona* che ricolma
> ogni solco e *disfà prensile il* passo:
> con me tu qui dentro quest'aria *immobile*
> *che domanda*
> *l'esistenza del sasso.*
>   Ed io riverso
> nel potere che grava attorno, *sordo,*
> *questa miseria* di non riconoscere
> di me più nulla fuor di me: s'io levo
> *di poco* il braccio, mi si fa diverso
> l'atto *e* si spezza s'un*o schermo tremulo,*

dissolto e impallidito *in un ricordo*
del mio moto che più non m'appartiene;
se parlo ascolto *la mia* voce, attonito,
discesa all sua gamma più *rimota,*
spengersi all'aria che non la sostiene.

Così nell'aria che *si dora* all'ultimo
tripudiare del giorno
dura *un oscura*mento; *finché* un soffio
rissoleva *la vita,* in un frenetico
moto e deriva *da ogni più riposta*
pianta un tìnnulo suono che si *perde*
tra *i* fum*i della sera* e i primi lumi
punteggiano gli scali.

Nell'ora nuova le parole cadono
tra noi *leggiere, e passano.* Ti guardo
in un molle riverbero*: non so*
se ti conosco*: e* so che *più straniero*
non ti fui mai *che* in questo *nostro* tardo
ritorno . . . .
                    Nel silenzio passato
non era ombra di noi: *nostro è soltanto*
il viso che forzato *ora* s'incide
d'un sorriso.

(An *aquarian* brightness flows / between us on the *veranda, in these exhausted / and luminous evenings*, which distorts / your profile with the outline of the hills. / Each motion is cut off from you, stands against a fleeting *medium: / a slice* without a trace *or shadow, this zone /* that fills each furrow, *undoing your prehensile* step: / you here with me, inside this *immobile* air / *that wants / the existence of stone.* // And on my back / inside the power weighing down around, *deaf, / this misery* of not knowing / anything outside myself: / if I raise my arm *a bit,* the action / separates from me *and breaks up on a wavering screen, / dissolved and made* pale *in a* memory / *of my* motion *that no longer belongs to me;* / if I speak I hear *my* voice, *astonished,* / fallen to the bottom of its range, / *die* in the air that won't sustain it. // So *a darkening* lives on / in the *air that goes gold in the last / exultation of* the day; *until* a breeze / rouses *life,* in a frantic / *movement* and takes from *every most secluded / plant* a tinny sound that gets lost / *among the mists of the evening* and the first lights / *pricking out* the docks. // *In the new hour* words fall / lightly between us*, and pass.* I see you / through a watery wavering: I don't know / if I know you: *and* I know I was never / *stranger to* you *than here,* in this late / return . . . . *In the silence that has passed / there was no shadow of us: ours is only /* the face that, *forced, gets* etched / *with a* smile.)

Montale's revisions achieve concision, speed, contemporaneity (e.g., *remota* for *rimota*), concreteness; they also characteristically render the poem's action more impersonal. The ms. makes clear that "Due nel crepuscolo" is a poem for Arletta; the title, too, with its allusion to "the adolescent gloom of the crepuscolari" (Almansi and Merry, 15) and to the twilit cycle that Arletta's poems constitute, is a "late return" to the themes of the later *Ossi di seppia.*

The poem particularly bears comparison with "Vento e bandiere" (and with "Bassa marea" in *Le occasioni*) in setting and tone. Here, however, it is the poet who is "riverso" in the hammock on the veranda, and the poem in itself describes a reprise of a relationship that has already died. The imagery that conveys the poet's sense of disorientation and estrangement recalls very early poems (see the "Poesie disperse" in *Alt*, tr. in *Oth*) as well as the *osso* "Forse un mattino andando . . . ," which like this poem seems inspired by a passage in Tolstoy's "Youth" (see note), while the imagery of the masks evokes the discussions of *volto* and *aspetto* in "Là fuoresce il Tritone" and "Incontro" (see also "Personae separatae").

For the importance of Browning's influence on Montale here and elsewhere—he had been introduced to the Englishman's poetry by Ezra Pound, whom he met circa 1925 (though Lonardi [134] says Montale told him he did not read Browning before 1928)—see Barile (2, 130ff.) and Lonardi (passim). Far more than the title is derived from "Two in the Campagna," which ends: "Only I discern—/ Infinite passion, and the pain / Of finite hearts that yearn."

un fondo sfuggevole . . . : Cf. the "tremulo vetro" of "Vasca" and, more generally, the theme of the mirror (discussed in Avalle and elsewhere). Bettarini (1, 477) in this context evokes Baudelaire's "La mort des amants":

> Nos deux coeurs seront deux vastes flambeaux,
> Qui réfléchiront leurs doubles lumières
> Dans nos deux esprits, ces miroirs jumeaux.

(Our two hearts will be two huge torches, / Which will reflect their double lights / In our two spirits, these twin mirrors.) She adds: "To destroy, shatter, break ["si spezza su un cristallo"] is the verbal result of a life that looks into the mirror of the spirit"—and indicates a fragmentary conception of the self, as in "L'estate" and elsewhere. (Cf. similar imagery in "Elegia" [in *Alt*, tr. in *Oth*, 82].) Bettarini (1, 505) also notes the similarity of the dissociation of the self in Mallarmé's *Igitur*.

al sortilegio di non riconoscere . . . : Bettarini (1, 504–5): "The best approximation of the content of [this aspect of the poem] is given by Montale himself, in the same year, 1926, commenting on Saba's 'Il borgo' (in *Su*, 205): "The poet passes in the streets of the town where he dreamed, at twenty, of merging his life with that of all men, that incessant fever which alienates him from others finally pacified and defeated; and he remembers how in this 'descent' of his as a man among men he left a spy hole through which he might contemplate himself, and enjoy the bizarre spectacle of a self different from himself; and how the crack became a crevice, and soon the enchantment crumbled. A similar old bewilderment [*smarrimento*], which again assails the poet in the now-stilled streets of the town, is translated into high and stupefied words." See also the passage from Tolstoy's *Childhood, Boyhood, Youth* quoted in note to "Forse un mattino andando . . . ," which bears a strong resemblance to these lines, which also bear comparison with passages in "Incontro" and elsewhere in *Ossi di seppia*.

Dov'era il tennis . . . / Where the Tennis Court Was . . . (1943)
Montale (Greco, 47): "Sciacchetrà (schiaccia e tira 'spremi' [squash and draw 'squirts']) is the thick, sweet dessert wine made in the Cinque Terre. 'Il parente maniaco' was a cousin [see "Le piante grasse" in *Alt*, tr. in *Oth*]. The other characters are those in 'Donna Juanita' [a story in *Farf*, 20–25]."

le ville dei sudamericani: The allusions to South Americans, and in particular to the Peruvian city of Callao, evoke the young Peruvian of Italian extraction, Paola Nicoli, who was living in Genoa in the late twenties and to whom Montale addressed a number of poems in *Le occasioni* (see the first three motets and "Sotto la pioggia," with its Spanish citations); according to Macrì (2, 13), Montale's considerable familiarity with Spanish was due in part to his acquaintance with the Italian emigrants who had returned to the Cinque Terre from South America.

There is also a second quotation from the *Rimas* of the Spanish poet G. A. Bécquer, from whom Montale had taken the epigraph for the MOTTETTI. The entire poem reads as follows:

> *Del salón en el ángulo oscuro,*
> *de su dueño tal vez olvidada,*
> *silenciosa y cubierta de polvo*
> *veíase el arpa.*
>
> *¡Cuánta nota dormía en sus cuerdas*
> *como el pájaro duerme en las ramas,*
> *esperando la mano de nieve*
> *que sabe arrancarla!*
>
> *¡Ay! pensé; cuántas veces el genio*
> *así duerme en el fondo del alma*
> *y una voz como Lázaro espera*
> *que le diga "¡Levántate y anda!"*

(In the dark corner of the room, / perhaps forgotten by her master, / silent and covered with dust / the harp was seen. // What note slept in its strings / as the bird sleeps in the branches / waiting for the hand of snow / that knows how to pluck it! // Ah! think; how often genius / sleeps thus deep in the soul / and waits like Lazarus for a voice / to say, "Arise and walk!")

la sarabanda dei nuovi giunti: As elsewhere, the (usually ironic) invocation of a foreign dance indicates social upheaval. See note to "Il ritorno."

Liberty: Italian term denoting the extravagantly sinuous Art Nouveau style, derived from the work of the British designer Arthur Lazenby Liberty.

dell'inno tripolino: Martial anthem (1912) of the Italian conquest of Libya; it marks the end of the seemingly childlike innocence of the "circolo vitale" (see "Fine dell'infanzia").

nel circolo vitale: Luperini (1, 135): "The society of the present is contrasted with that of the past, destroyed by the advent of industrial civilization. A fracturing has occurred, a 'game' has been 'interrupted': everything—it's repeated in all three lyric prose pieces [the third being "Il lieve tintinnío del collarino," quoted below, which was published with "Dov'era il tennis . . . ," "Visita a Fadin," and part of "Verso Siena" in *Lettere d'Oggi* V, 3–4 (March-April 1943) but omitted from *La bufera* (see *Op*, 973–75)]—everything has changed. . . . The 'circle of life' of things, houses, and people . . . has been broken . . . and a 'cold' sense of an end, which [Montale's] own father was among the first and the few capable of noticing, . . . has taken its place. He now appears for the first time in Montale's work (he had died in 1931 . . .) as guardian of a well-determined world (and will be presented as such in 'Voce giunta con le folaghe.' . . . He represents 'the last story that counts,' the one lived by characters like

Fadin or Erasmus, who, in the piece left out of *La bufera*, lives in a 'house full of great shadows,' in which 'life was high, uncorrupted, without compromises.' We're at the very beginning of a polemic against mass, mechanized society . . . that will soon characterize the whole ideological horizon of the Montalean enterprise."

(Flavia Mercedes Gibelli, granddaughter of "Signora Paquita," has written a brief book, *Una domanda infinita: Ricordi intorno a Eugenio Montale* [Genoa: Marietti, 1989], which criticizes Montale for his unfeeling portrayal of her family but largely confirms the details of his sketch.)

Visita a Fadin / Visit to Fadin (1943)

Montale (*Op*, 956): "Sergio Fadin's *Elegie* [Elegies] (with a preface by Sergio Solmi) were posthumously published by Scheiwiller, Milan, 1943." A Venetian (born 1911), he died of an illness contracted during the Italian war in Africa, in the hospital at Chiavari, between Rapallo and Sestri Levante, on January 11, 1942.

Montale (Greco, 47): "Carlina was his wife; she later remarried and must have died recently. She played an instrument of Benozzo Gozzoli's angels, maybe the lute."

Il mare in basso . . . : The setting of the poem, with the villas of the "arricchiti"—and the values the poem celebrates in implied opposition to them—is the Ligurian world of "Dov'era il tennis . . ." and the entire INTERMEZZO section.

per la rampa . . . : Recalls "nella corsia / del paradiso" (Paradise imagined as a hospital) of the "Madrigali fiorentini."

sulla balconata degli incurabili: Cf. "Il balcone," from which Arletta, likewise marked by death, could see "la vita che dà barlumi." Fadin, too, with his "alone più profondo," partakes of otherworldly, even angelic, virtues.

un ordine diverso, per quanto quello . . . (. . . peggiore): This section, when it first appeared in *Lettere d'oggi* (see note to "Dov'era il tennis . . ."), read as follows: "un ordine diverso, per quanto quello in cui ci moviamo noi ritardatari sia certo il solo, così pazzesco com'è, in cui la divinità può svolgere i suoi attributi, recitare dinanzi a se stessa la sua parte. (Di tanto ha bisogno per esistere, l'infelice?)" ([And now to say you're no longer here is simply to say you've entered] another order, given that the one we move in, we stragglers, is certainly the only one, insane as it is, in which divinity can reveal its attributes, recite its part before itself. [Does it need all this to exist, unhappy thing?]).

The notion that divinity has need of mankind in order to express itself, which is fundamental to Montale's Nestorian immanentism (see note to "Iride") and which descends (Jacomuzzi 1, 119) from the Neoplatonic notion of another world behind the "world of appearances," is elaborated in the 1944 essay "Augurio" (tr. as "A Wish" in *Sec*, 9–11), in which Montale gives voice to his hopes for postwar Italian society, describing "the old battle of good and evil" as "the struggle of the divine forces fighting in us against the unchained forces of bestial man, the dark forces of Ahriman. Thus in us and through us a divinity is brought into being, earthly at first, and perhaps celestial and incomprehensible to our senses, which without us could not develop or become cognizant of itself."

Essere sempre tra i primi e sapere . . . : Cf. "the paralyzing awareness of one's fate" (Isella 2, 134) ("si muore / sapendo") of "Tempi di Bellosguardo." The notion of life as a "performance" echoes the trope of recitation of a part in the earlier draft quoted above. Cf. "Personae separatae."

La tua parola . . . : Cf. the last lines of Montale's tribute to Bobi Bazlen (*Sec*, 273–76):

"He paid dearly for his experience: certainly it was such that it could not be measured in the currency of this world."

IV. 'FLASHES' E DEDICHE / FLASHES AND INSCRIPTIONS

In early editions of *La bufera*, the part title of this section read "Lampi" instead of "Flashes"; Montale later opted to use "Flashes" throughout "because it's more restrictive than 'lampi' (in this case)" (*Op*, 957)—"a decision to emphasize the 'camera flash' of photographic memory (the 'jack-in-the-box' camera of 'Verso Siena')" (Arrowsmith 3, 181).

Montale (*Op*, 957): "The magnesium flashes and dedications . . . belong to the years 1948–1952."

Montale (Greco, 50): "All the flashes have a madrigalistic intonation, very different in this from the MOTTETTI and the OSSI."

Luperini (1, 136) notes that this group is inserted in the volume to "occupy a position analogous to that of the OSSI DI SEPPIA and the MOTTETTI in the first two books," though the "madrigalistic intonation, very different in this from the MOTTETTI and the OSSI" (Montale [Greco, 50]), and the variety of the settings of these snapshots from a "travel album" (Luperini 1, 137), many of them written in connection with the trips Montale made in these years as a special correspondent of *Il Corriere della Sera*, render them closer to echoes, in a lower key, of the brief *occasioni* in the first section of his second book.

In the 'FLASHES' E DEDICHE, Clizia "alternates" and contrasts with Volpe, a figure akin in some repects to the Dark Lady of Shakespeare's *Sonnets*, who offers sublunary carnal love, unattainable with Clizia, but which the poet, as one "of the race / who are earthbound" ("Falsetto"), must now content himself with.

Volpe's character becomes fully and definitively developed after the young poet Maria Luisa Spaziani (see note to "Da un lago svizzero") enters Montale's life in 1949, but a number of poems written for a woman identified only as G.B.H., "an employee of the Pier Bussetti travel agency ('Di un natale metropolitano')" (Montale [Greco, 48]), and perhaps for others, make up part of her cycle as well; like the Clizia of the MOTTETTI, Volpe's poetic character is derived from multiple sources, literary and cultural as well as personal and biographical. Montale (Greco, 51): "Too many events are mixed up in the Flashes for one to be able to read them autobiographically. The most one can say is that the character in the Madrigals is a counterfigure to Clizia in a profane key, but Clizia had died or disappeared forever."

In contrast to the love for Clizia, that for Volpe is "profane": openly erotic and unsublimated, particularly in the poems inspired by G.B.H., and this is reflected in the lower, more relaxed and ironic tone of the poetry. Luperini (1, 139): After "L'anguilla" of 1948 "the stilnovistic theme loses force, while the hypothesis of a Christ-bearing woman-angel, intermediary between man and divinity, also rapidly weakens." The poems, which now have a more prosaic, less elevated tone, reveal much ambivalence about these developments, not only in the "alternation" of the two figures but in Montale's self-deprecatory references to his own heavy "tomb" of a body (these disappear in the more metaphysical later Volpe poems), and in the clear associations of sexuality, both male and female, with decay and filth. One can see 'FLASHES' E DEDICHE as the threshing floor where the debate between these two conceptions of love, or rather the evolution from adherence to the spiritual-superego to a far-from-comfortable acceptance of the earthbound—qualified in the later, Neoplatonic poems by a kind of fusing of physical and metaphysical—is conducted. It appears that Montale is uncomfortable in a world without metaphysical bearings and that the brief phase of G.B.H. represents a passage from the Christological adventure with Clizia, which finds its apotheosis and catharsis in the SILVAE, to the Neoplatonic one with Volpe, where the profane soon becomes subsumed in Montale's construction of a secular religion of his own.

Lonardi (63–64): "Montale the reader of *La bufera* conceals the alliance and continuation of the domestic world"—the "closed circle" described in "Vecchi versi" of 1926—"the world controlled by the Mother, the world of the ark, with one of the two 'functions' (let's call it the Beatrice-function) that give life to its Beatrice-Antibeatrice narrative alternation. He conceals, in sum, the alliance of the Dead with the first of these two erotic figures. The Clizias, the Beatrices of an unattainable and unattained eros (according to Macrì, 'the metaphysical respect for the other, the non-demand to be loved, not to mention saved, is substantial') are in angelic extraneity because they are emanations of the maternal archetype, its figures. . . . Volpe constitutes the at least partial opposition to the domestic world of the Mother and Clizia, and Liuba is her most eloquent anticipation, Liuba who carries her lares with her, her hatbox her 'buoyant / ark.' . . . There is a conflict, in this the most conflictual of Montale's collections, of which the provisional critic Montale does not inform us, the conflict of Volpe with absolute fidelity to the Mother and her virginal figures (in Nerval, too, Artemis is oneirically *also* the Mother)."

Verso Siena / Near Siena (1943/1950)

Montale (Greco, 50): "The Ambretta has no water; perhaps we crossed it on foot: I don't think my god was present. He's a lowercase God."

The title evokes "Verso Capua" and "Verso Vienna" in *Le occasioni*. The second stanza was printed as a separate poem in *Lettere d'oggi* in 1943 with the dedication "a P.G., cartolina" (postcard); Montale had visited the writer Piero Gadda Conti at his farm not far from Siena in June 1942. Spaziani (321), however, claims the composition as a poem for Volpe. The poet's portrayal of himself as a "rebel" against God, an unwilling lover, recalls Clizian moments ("Su una lettera non scritta," "Serenata indiana") in FINISTERRE; and resonances with other texts —not to mention the date of composition, the setting, and the structure of the poem, with the central stanza in parentheses, reminiscent of the motet "La speranza di pure rivederti," "Barche sulla Marna," etc.—support the hypothesis that this "flash" memorializes the poet's obsession with memory (primarily an Arlettian-Clizian preoccupation) before the advent of Volpe. Still, the blasphemous reference to God—who is here as later equated with the poet's beloved, a construct associated as elsewhere in the 'FLASHES' E DEDICHE with consummated love—is a characteristic of the Volpe poems.

Ohimè: Recalls "Vento e bandiere," with its related apostrophe on the unrepeatable nature of experience: "Ahimè, non mai due volte configura / il tempo in egual modo i grani."

non ha chi la trattenga: Cf. "Potessi almeno costringere" in MEDITERRANEO.

sull'Ambretta: Stream in the environs of Siena; San Gusmé is a village fifteen miles east of the city.

sul punto: Recalls the willed ambiguity of "nel punto che ti chiude" in the motet "Perchè tardi? Nel pino lo scoiattolo" (1939) and in the contemporaneous "Elegia di Pico Farnese."

il mio Dio gittò la maschera . . . : "fulminò" is also reminiscent—a kind of lowercase reprise—of "se tu fólgore / lasci la nube" in the motet cited above. The God(dess) throws off her earthly guise (leaves her cloud), and reveals herself through her lightning flash ("lampo"); i.e., she takes a snapshot, the surviving keepsake—like the fan in "Il ventaglio"—which arouses "la memoria sulla vetta." For "ribelle," which rhymes with "porcelli," see Dante's "angeli ribelli" (*Inferno* III, 38) or, more suggestively, the blasphemous Capaneo in *Inferno* XIV, who was struck by lightning ("folgore aguta") (Macrì 1, 116).

Sulla Greve / On the Greve (1950)

Arrowsmith (3, 182) is right to call this poem "one of the most directly sensuous Montale ever wrote." The title refers the reader back to the epigram "Bibe a Ponte all'Asse" (see note), about a *trattoria* situated above the Greve River just south of Florence, suggesting this as the possible locale of the lovers' dinner/dance, symbolized here as a "carnal communion . . . a physical miracle of Cana," in which the watery whispering of the woman's velvet dress transubstantiates synesthetically with her breathing—always the most intimate of actions in Montale, richly symbolic of vitality (cf. "La casa dei doganieri" and elsewhere)—to become wine (i.e., sacred blood). This is a poem of physical consummation, of consumption, but the lovers' union is portrayed—as was true in certain Clizian poems, though this is clearly a poem for Volpe—in metaphors that have religious connotations.

ti sporgevi . . . : The opening lines evoke not only the scene but the very words of "Il balcone," as if in opposition; the past tense (in contrast with "ti sporgi") confirms a new dispensation. The interlocutor of "Il balcone," as we have seen, was marked by death; this is a poem about life. The characteristic catalogue of metaphors at the end of the first stanza evokes the woman's gradual coming into focus when "I barely could see you": at first she is perceived as an indistinct mass, then as the effect of a movement, then as motion itself, which dominates the poet's sensory world. In the second stanza (the world of "ora," the present), the woman's attributes achieve a metaphorical fusion that imitates the poet's (secular) communion with her. Cambon (162) notes the "far from accidental" rhyming of "mondo" with the woman's "profondo" "respiro" (see note to "Nella serra" on the essential significance of breathing imagery in Montale): "She rhymes with the universe, with the intact forces of it. Even the contiguousness of 'rondine' to 'mondo' in the arrangements adds to the spell, for 'rondine' almost rhymes with 'mondo,' therefore *becoming* the world of nature that its flight overarches. Animal emblem thus conspires with the overall sensuous imagery—an imagery proffered in the form of swift metaphoric identities or simple self-sufficient namings—to create a proper halo around the climactic feminine figure who does not have to be 'described' in order to assert her irresistible presence."

un solco / a imbuto. Cf. "the groove / that carves the wave and closes" in "Stanze." The furrow can be a symbol of effective action, of achieved significance (as at the end of "Palio" and elsewhere). A funnel-shaped furrow, however, suggests a draining hourglass, as in "Vento e bandiere," or the spinning of the top of "Palio"—images of eddying that echo throughout Montale's poetry.

una rondine: Cf. the swallow of "Lindau," which doesn't want "life to go." Volpe is also called "la mia rondine" in one of the MADRIGALI PRIVATI, "So che un raggio di sole. . . ."

glissato: Neologism, derived from the musical *glissando*, itself an " 'Italianate' term formed from the French *glisser*" (Arrowsmith 3, 182), along the lines of *vibrato* or *rubato*.

La trota nera / The Black Trout (1948)

The date and the references to the curls and the office suggest that, like "Di un natale metropolitano," this is a poem for G.B.H., a young Italian divorcée (see "Trascolorando" in *D71/2*) working for a travel agency, whom Montale had met in Florence in 1945 (*Tutte*, lxxiv).

Montale traveled to England at least twice that year, in March and June (also presumably in December).

Montale (in English, on ms.) (*Op*, 958): "Reading, 1948. Caversham Bridge. No trouts in this river! To Donald Gordon, this private poem of Eugenio Montale."

la trota annusa e va via . . . : The trout's motion recalls the surfacing of the desired image in "Cigola la carrucola del pozzo" or the "more than a streak" of "Vasca"; its carbuncle glare is a low-tone revisiting of the "silvery . . . / flash" of that earlier trout that recalled the "dead girlchild Arethusa" in "L'estate" and prefigures the action of the eel in "L'anguilla." ("Curvi sull'acqua serale" also recalls the "curvi uomini" fishing in an early draft of "Dora Markus II" and, by extension, the "assorto / pescatore d'anguille" in the motet "La gondola che scivola. . . .") Here again, however, as in "Sulla Greve," a previously metaphysical Clizian motif is reductively reactivated. This time the girlchild is alive, not at all "controcorrente"; her sign, her ringlet, is an index of pure sexuality. Rivers, which occur often in the 'FLASHES' E DEDICHE, also seem in themselves to connote sexuality.

Di un natale metropolitano / A Metropolitan Christmas (1948)
Another poem for G.B.H. Angelini (3, 171) points out that the title evokes both the metropolis of its setting and the underground system which frames the Orphic (or anti-Orphic) separation of the lovers at the end. Once again, the poem offers an ironic, reductive revaluation of Clizian themes. This Christmas could hardly be more profane: Clizia's mistletoe, "cluster of faith and frost," is here no more than a detail drawn from the intimacy of the woman's boudoir, a "bourgeois interior" in which no epiphany occurs; its mirror, unlike the one in "Gli orecchini," reveals only her "bergère curls" (defined by Littré as an "old-fashioned négligé coiffure" [Angelini 3, 171])—a recurrence of the "ricciolo" of the previous piece. But the poem takes a metaphysical turn at "a crossroads," as the appearance of "le anime" indicates, and the images allegorize the inability of the two "souls" to unite at their meeting point. "Bottles that wouldn't open" is a powerful metaphor for noncommunication and impotence, as is the "tardo frullo" of the pigeon/poet who cannot follow/save his Eurydice as she is borne helplessly down into her industrialized urban hell—"descent is the typical movement of this book" (Forti 1, 245) as throughout Montale—by the "automatic" stairs of the escalator.

Greco's (144–50) extensive analysis of the poem emphasizes the vivid reality of the woman's milieu, its occupation by things, but also the threat they represent, "subject[ing] her to their inhuman domination." Unlike Dora Markus, say, who was capable of resisting the forces of history, or, needless to mention, Clizia, the woman here has no way of countering "the automatic flux and the stairs that 'take' her [*slittano*—an unusual transitive use of a normally intransitive verb; cf. "il forte imperio / che ti rapsice" of "Gli orecchini"]. . . . The man is *incapable* of following her and she is a blind *prisoner* of her destiny . . . both [are] devoid (or deprived?) of will and determination: 'bottiglie che non seppero aprirsi.' " Luperini (1, 142) sees the poem, with its willfully prosaic (and ironic) tone and method, as the most significant antecedent of *Satura* and of Montale's late style in general.

Lasciando un 'Dove' / Leaving a Dove (1948)
Montale (*Op*, 958): "The *Dove* was a type of tourist airplane built in that era (1948)."

Presumably another poem inspired by G.B.H., this time set among the spires of the great Romanesque/Gothic (eleventh–fourteenth centuries) Cathedral of Ely in East Anglia, not far from Cambridge. As Arrowsmith (3, 183) says, the title is "also an allusion to the 'angelic' ash-

blond Clizia, who . . . is here abandoned by the poet for the brunette, the animal intensity
. . . and defiant vitality of the Vixen"—Montale's own Dark Lady, prefigured here in the
person of G.B.H. The downward revaluation of the 'FLASHES' E DEDICHE continues. The
cathedral is a sacred, and thus Clizian, locale, but the celestial light of the sun is rejected in
favor of Volpe's "smoldering fire." The poet's Arseniesque incapacity is further emphasized;
the "tardo frullo" of "Di un natale metropolitano" becomes a "tomba / che non vola" (in
apposition with the subject of the sentence, not with "il fuoco"; the poet's "tomb" contrasts
with the upward-thrusting spires of the cathedral). Arrowsmith rightly sees this as "an ironic
glance at the poet's torpid corpulence"; meanwhile Clizia's "eyes of steel" have been replaced
by the Dark Lady's derisive, sexually challenging stare.

Argyll Tour (1948)
Montale (Greco, 51): "A tourist trip [by boat] around Glasgow: it includes a visit to Fingal's
Cave" (on the Isle of Staffa, one of the Inner Hebrides, discovered by Sir Joseph Banks in
1772 and named after the hero of James Macpherson's eponymous "Ossianic" epic of 1762).

Presumably another G.B.H. poem. This seems to be a catalogue of images without great
symbolic weight, though after the metaphoric "chains loosening" (which works in a way similar
to the "intersection" of "Di un natale metropolitano"), the objects take on a more oneiric,
even hellish resonance which bears some resemblance to the atmosphere of "Il sogno del
prigioniero." (The "salti di tonno" recall the "delfini a coppie" of "Su una lettera non scritta.")
The only thing that can release the poet/slave from the obscenity of his base dream is the
apparition of his lady. A poem inspired, perhaps, by sexual guilt.

Vento sulla Mezzaluna / Wind on the Crescent (1948)
Montale (Op, 959): "Certain semicircular streets of Glasgow [sic] are called crescents or half-
moons."

Once again, the dedicatee of the poem is likely G.B.H. "Viaggiatore solitario," a 1946
piece written for Il Corriere della Sera and retitled "Sosta a Edimburgo" in Farf (217–19,
also collected in FdiC 17–18), is helpful in explicating the poem's imagery: "In Edinburgh, a
city where the principal squares have the shape and name of 'crescents,' or half-moons, rises
a church polygonal in form with an inscription inside it far longer than the many that decorated
the walls of our villages until two years ago. This interminable legend . . . celebrates no earthly
Capo nor any glory of this perishable world of ours. Proceeding by way of sage exclusions and
negations the winding spiral . . . tells the forgetful passerby where the Celestial Capo is not
to be found, where it is useless to look for Him . . . God is not where . . .—and the reader
must move a few steps and face another side of the polygon: God is not where . . .—and all
the places where life appears easy, pleasant, and humane, where God truly might be or might
be found, are listed in long series following this recurring reminder: God is not here, nor
here, nor here . . .

"One summer day I happened to trudge a long time inside this dense tangle, continually
retracing my steps and asking myself, with anguish in my heart and a dizzy head: But, in the
end, where is God, where is He?

"Maybe I actually asked my question out loud, for a distinguished gentleman crossing
the crescent . . . stopped near me and flatly denied that the solution to the problem could be
found on those Presbyterian walls, inside or out.

" 'God is not here, Sir,' he said with a seriously informed air; and taking a little Bible out of his pocket, he began to read some verses in a loud voice. Other people stopped and formed a circle around the reader . . . the crowd grew, one of the onlookers took another Bible out of his pocket and himself read, demonstrating his flat opposition to the first official's thesis. Soon there were three or four groups, each with a referee of the debate, an impromptu arbiter who granted or withdrew speaking privileges, summarized the pros and cons of the various arguments, tried to effect conciliations and mediations that may have been impossible. Strict Presbyterians or long-sleeved Arminians, Baptists, Methodists, lukewarm and indifferent Darbyists and Unitarians, men, women, and children, bourgeois and working men, employees and *rentiers*, all listened or spoke with a strange gleam in their eye. Bewildered at having excited this mystical hornets' nest, I moved away. . . . *God is not where* . . . Where was He? Had they found Him, then? I felt great anxiety and blamed myself for not having posed the question in precise terms for many years in my own country."

Il grande ponte . . . : The Forth Bridge, one of the longest and largest in the world. Marchese (1, 162) notes that the bridge in Montale carries associations with the metaphysical notion of "varco," which is opposed here by an imagined passage through the mire of the sewers (the negative associations with female sexuality are apparent); but the poet, who, echoing ("chiaviche") the "Madrigali fiorentini," now presents himself as a rat rather than the pigeon of "Di un natale metropolitano" in an equally negative phallic association (cf. also the "topo" of "Botta e risposta" in *Sat*), is not up to the challenge. Re: the significance of imagery of sewers, muck, etc., see note to "L'anguilla."

«*Sai dov'è Dio?*»: The poet's answer, for Marchese (1, 165), is a "bestemmia d'amore," an amorous blasphemy (a recurrent theme in Montale's poetry) which could well be: "God is in London, where my woman is" (cf. "il mio Dio" in "Verso Siena"). Marchese (1, 163) quotes L. Renzi (*Come leggere la poesia* [Bologna: Il Mulino, 1985], 88): "Both stanzas are about the woman, not one about the woman and one about God. Or rather: in both stanzas the poet speaks of the woman—and God." Macrì (1, 115), however, maintains that "the sense of the story remains in the poem: 'I knew and said' must be the ineffable negative, the *no saber* of Saint John of the Cross in contrast with the dogmatic positive certainty of the 'preacher' . . . , 'And what you do not know is the only thing you know' [Eliot, *Four Quartets*, "East Coker" III, 44]." Cf. the first of the *ossi*, "Non chiederci la parola. . . ."

sulla pece: The (filthy) darkened sky where God is not. This apocalyptic whirlwind is derisive, in key with the disillusioned tone of most of these poems.

Sulla colonna più alta / On the Highest Column (1948)
Montale (in "Sulla strada di Damasco," dated 1949 in *FdiC*, 70) describes the Great Mosque at Damascus (aspects of this piece are echoed in "Trascolorando"; see note to "Di un natale metropolitano"): "Taken up ["rapiti"] into another world we stay a long time contemplating the three minarets, atop one of which (the Eastern one), tradition affirms, Jesus will alight in person, to combat the Antichrist, shortly before the Last Judgment." Montale (Greco, 51): " 'I sette greti': there are many in Damascus, but little water."

Late return of the angelic Clizia, evoked not only by the sacred site in which the poem's occasion transpires, but by its Near Eastern location.

il Cristo giustiziere: Grignani (37) notes that the use of the determinative article *il* in Italian "transforms the name of Christ into an appellative, with a suspicion of dissociation with respect to belief."

capinere, / . . . girasoli: Grignani (69) sees in these emblematic references to both Arletta and Clizia a "farewell, the ceremony of sacrifice of sublimated or transcendent love in view of the earthly eros of the antibeatrice," i.e., Volpe (see note to the MADRIGALI PRIVATI). But the image can also suggest a private Peaceable Kingdom in which Montale's own lions and lambs will finally lie down together.

dell'Antilibano: The Anti-Lebanon is the range of mountains between Syria and Lebanon. A sign of Clizia's Near Eastern ancestry, like her epithet "Iri del Canaan" in "Iride"; in this respect and others—stilnovistic use of animals, *vischio/vischi, sterpi/fiori del deserto*—the parallels with that poem are notable. Rebay (3, 198) quotes a letter from Irma Brandeis which underscores the significance of such references: "My father and Louis D. Brandeis were second cousins. Both branches of the family were Austrian (for I do not know how many generations) before coming to the United States in mid-century. My grandfather married an English Jewess and my father married the daughter of a German Jewish family. I tell you this so you will avoid the mistake of reading Montale's references to Palestine or Canaan or the East as colorful background rather than as an awareness of a two-thousand-year-old blood heritage—and therewith a confraternity which deserves more thought than I think it has had."

vischio: Victory (albeit temporary) of Clizian-Christian mistletoe over the "black crowns of thorn" of the humble nettles with which the poet has crowned his Antichrist/Antibeatrice, symbolized here, perhaps, by the black crow (Volpe is associated with blackness/darkness throughout).

la Legge: The Jewish Law, i.e., the revelation of God set forth in the Old Testament.

per te: For this usage of the preposition (through, by means of), cf. "Siria": "ritrovai per te la voce"; also "Per te intendo" in "Sotto la pioggia" and elsewhere.

Verso Finistère/ Near Finistère (1950?)
First published in 1952, but the related Breton travel piece, "Il giorno del gran salvataggio," is printed in *FdiC* with the 1950 date. In any case, a poem for Volpe in the flesh.

Montale suggests (see note to FINISTERRE) that the name here has no apocalyptic significance; but the storm evoked in the poem is an ironic revisiting of the cosmic tempests of the wartime poems. Finistère is, in effect, a lowercase Finisterre.

piova: Dantesque, as is the rhyme with *prova* (*Purgatorio* XXX, 113/117): Macrì (1, 115).

l'arco del tuo ciglio: Macrì (1, 115) derives the image from the description in *Purgatorio* XXVIII, 64–65, of Matelda, "one of the Ladies to whom the poet compares his Clizia."

sull'intonaco albale . . . : Montale (Greco, 51): "There's an interior that mirrors what's outside."

prillano: See note to "Elegia di Pico Farnese" on Montale's use of this Pascolian (Macrì, 1, 115) word, which there stood also for "brilla." To Marchese (1, 176), the whirling movement recalls the spinning hotel door of "Eastbourne": "But the epiphany is not comforting in itself, as before; it is valid as a perplexed, precarious 'proof' of the existence of the divine or rather of the unavoidable mediation of the woman between the human and the Other, a theme reemphasized in 'Siria.' "

Forse non ho altra prova . . . : A restatement, less blasphemous than in "Vento sulla Mezzaluna," of Montale's "Nestorian" belief in the immanence of divinity within humans (see "Elegia di Pico Farnese," "A mia màdre," "Visita a Fadin," and discussion of the Nestorian heresy in note to "Iride"). The imagery of the beloved seeing through God's eyes is derived from *Paradiso* XXI, 49–50: "Per ch'ella, che vedea il tacer mio / nel veder di colui che tutto vede" (For she, who saw my silence / with the sight of him who sees everything), but the notion that the beloved sees *for* God is in keeping with the "blasphemy" expressed in "Visita a Fadin," that the attributes of divinity can only be revealed through the agency of humans.

Sul Llobregat / On the Llobregat (1954)
Once again, an alluvial locale, "the river one meets traveling from Barcelona to Montserrat" (Montale, *Op*, 959). Arrowsmith's analysis (3, 186) is witty and apt: "The poet—amateur ornithologist and professional music critic—is pedantically and professionally involved in *naming* his world, differentiating it; whereas the woman, at one with the world and nature, is all *being*; her abrupt gesture of stepping on the accelerator suggests both her capricious vitality and her impatience with her laggard and pedantic poet. We should note the antinomies— the 'poetic' camphor tree and the 'prosaic' accelerator—so characteristic of these poems." Arrowsmith adds that in Italian a *cucco* is a cuckold (as in English), while a *civetta* is a flirt.

Dal treno / From the Train (1951–52)
Montale (Greco, 51): "The yellow collar [necklace] of the doves is reminiscent by analogy of another necklace (maybe droplets) coming apart outside." (The image of the halo/necklace recurs in "Incantesimo" and in "Da un lago svizzero.") Montale also told Angelini (3, 172): "Astonished perhaps by the fire of her necklace, I couldn't see the color of the turtledoves, or any other color. There's a play on words here on the yellow ('solferino') of the turtledoves and the brilliant string of pearls *she* was wearing." As Macrì (1, 121) makes clear, however, the color in question must be blood-red, the color of religious (and thus also of profane) sacrifice.

   Sesto Calende is in the province of Varese, in Lombardy. The diaristic quality of the poem is typical of the later Montale.

   si sgranava: An allusion to the telling of the beads of the rosary: the "Petrarchan conceit" (Arrowsmith 3, 186) of Volpe's necklace as a vehicle of profane prayer.

   Per me solo / balenò: See the last lines of "Anniversario," and the close of "Se t'hanno assomigliato . . . ," both poems for Volpe. The private nature of their communion, which is so intense as to render the poet blind to the world beyond, stands in opposition to the universal salvation announced in the "baleno" of Clizia's stare. This contrast is a major theme of the late poems of *La bufera*. Macrì (1, 121) finds Dantean sources, both literal (*Inferno* III, 131– 34) and metaphorical (*Paradiso* XIV, 104/8), for "balenò."

Siria / Syria (1951–52)
Gratitude for the return of poetry inspired by his new relationship with Volpe. Arrowsmith (3, 186): In the last poems of 'FLASHES' E DEDICHE (roughly from "Verso Finistère" to "Incantesimo"), "the transcendental element in the poet's passion for the Vixen becomes more and more pronounced. So here where, thanks to the Vixen, the poet literally recovers his personal voice—that transcendental voice by which the lover moves up the Platonic ladder of Being, from the world of the senses to the same world transfigured in the life of the Spirit." This occurrence marks the reassertion of the metaphysical strain in Montale, in a fusion of Clizian mystical yearning with Volpean immanence.

   scala a Dio: The image is derived from Plotinus, perhaps via Hölderlin, whose influence is strongly felt in the last of the 'FLASHES' E DEDICHE.

   per te: See note to "Sulla colonna più alta."

i volti scarni . . . : At the Neoplatonic moment of epiphany, the world of appearances "dissolves and tends to nonbeing, the illusory order of nature breaks down ('il motore era guasto') and the signs of life ('il sangue') are tragically degraded to the anonymity of their function ('segnalava la via') . . . in sum, . . . 'the world fades out' ('Incantesimo')" (Jacomuzzi 1, 96). Cf. "le forme / della vita che si sgretola" of "Non rifugiarti nell'ombra" and "Svanire / è dunque la ventura delle venture" in "Portami il girasole. . . ."

Zambon (61) sees the "arrow of blood" as "the sign of an existential and poetic itinerary toward the divine (like that of the eel ['arrow of Love on earth'] in 'L'anguilla')."

Luce d'inverno / Winter Light (1951–52)
Like "Incantesimo," a poem written under the influence of the Neoplatonism of Hölderlin, seemingly a fresh enthusiasm of Montale's in this period. (Contini had published a translation of thirty-three poems, *Alcune poesie di Hölderlin* [Florence: Parenti] in 1941.) In the Neoplatonic context "*Helios* is constantly the image of the supreme divinity, mediator between the visible and intelligible worlds, distinct from the 'other' sun, with the same-named celestial body which is solely its physical copy; beyond the theological-philosophical schematism, the sun is imposed in the Montalean text as sign of a God absolutely transcendent of the world of the phenomenal and the multiplicitous" (Jacomuzzi 1, 117).

The poem can be read as an allegory of the poet's descent—as noted, the characteristic movement of the 'FLASHES' E DEDICHE—from the "high inhuman dawns" of his faith in Clizia to the terrifying new earthly love of Volpe. The appearance of her predatory attributes—her "scratch," her teeth marks—which recur in " 'Ezekiel saw the Wheel . . .' " and in the MADRIGALI PRIVATI, mark her full-fledged entry into the stilnovistic system of Montale's poetry and thus her new status as inheritor and supplanter of Clizia. Here, notably, it is the poet (rather than the Clizia of "Gli orecchini") who is "rapito" by the force of Volpe's personality. The contrasting images of the last stanza (pumice/jasper; sand/sun; mud/heavenly clay) are, says Jacomuzzi (1, 94), "signs of Hölderlin's 'tragic,' inasmuch as they embody the dialectical opposition of individual and universal, phenomenological-transitory and ontological-subsistent."

Jacomuzzi (1, 97): " 'Luce d'inverno' and 'Incantesimo' impose, against a Neoplatonic, Hölderlinian background which substantially negates the consistency and self-sufficiency of the world 'as seen,' a vigilant attention to the complex ambiguity of symbols which here tend to identify the invisible universe of intuition with poetry and the woman, visible and precarious companion in life." Each gives voice to the contrast between the Platonic sun/jewel/divine semantic camp of Clizia and Volpe's earthly, death-bound immanence.

Forti (1, 250): "A continual and perfectly articulated descent into Hell, marked by emotive nodes of anguish . . . the 'downward' movement analogous and opposite to the old lyric transcendence, in one who, digging in the now-subterranean sandstone of existence, finds there an indispensable beating of truth, perfectly formed, which has now become a metaphoric object."

cavagni / di polpi e di murene: Montale (Angelini 3, 172): "Evocation of a fish market in Syria"—though he told Guarnieri (Greco, 51) the Acropolis is that of Athens (Athens and Syria were the centers of Hellenistic Neoplatonic philosophy). The animals recall images (of contrasting nature) from "Serenata indiana" and "L'anguilla." The tooth marks of the "murene" also evoke the "tarantula bite" of "Il ritorno."

alla scintilla: Hölderlinian image for poetry "which is born from the tension and contact between" the individual/phenomenological and universal/ontological (Jacomuzzi 1, 94). Luperini (1, 142) notes the recurrence of the image of the spark of renewal out of ashes "from the contact/contrast between high and low" (Zambon, 75) (the spark is of course a metaphor for poetry itself) as well as the vocabulary ("scintilla," "fango," "nuovo / incenerito") of "L'anguilla" (1948).

Per un 'Omaggio a Rimbaud' / For an "Homage to Rimbaud" (June 30, 1950)
Montale (Greco, 51): "Refers to a woman who read and commented on Rimbaud from a lectern." (Maria Luisa Spaziani [see note to "Da un lago svizzero"] is, as well as a noted poet, a scholar and professor of French literature.) The poem was included in an anthology, *Omaggio a Rimbaud* (Milan: Scheiwiller, 1954), published for the centenary of the poet's birth.

Jacomuzzi's (1, 92–126) intensive structural analysis proceeds from the hypothesis that the poem is "the site of a declaration of poetics, [and] that such a declaration is the object of the text," and that it is placed between the Hölderlinian "Luce d'inverno" and "Incantesimo" to indicate a critique and negation of Rimbaud's symbolism. Jacomuzzi notes the opposition of the Volpean "farfalla," equated with the "farfalla di Dinard," of Montale's story, which he elucidates as a symbol of his poetry—here also representative of Volpe and hence of *her* poetry—with the partridge that represents Rimbaud. The judgmental nature of Montale's late poetry in *La bufera* moves the significance of description from the connotative to the denotative and thus away from the Orphic conventions of symbolism.

Tardi: Jacomuzzi (1, 103) discusses the frequency of the term and its increasing tendency to define "a programmatic will to difference and isolation" in the later Montale. The poetics of the "Omaggio" is also a declaration of cultural politics, of detachment and refusal to engage with the "red and black clerics" of postwar Italian culture. See note to "Il sogno del prigioniero" for further discussion.

l'esule di Charleville: In opposition with "Tardi uscita dal bozzolo": "there an exile and a wandering at the ends of the earth, here a liberation, the attainment of a perfection at the end of a process, a birth" (Jacomuzzi 1, 107). Rimbaud's exile is "diagrammed" in the "rapacious" flight of the partridge, dramatically and irregularly horizontal.

piume stroncate: Jacomuzzi (1, 105) notes the allegorical significance of the feathers as part of Montale's feminine sign system superimposed on the image of the butterfly. Cf. also the similar imagery in the depiction of the poet's attempt at flight in "Il gallo cedrone."

foglie di gardenia: The brightness of the leaves is opposed to the black asphalt ice of the street. Jacomuzzi (1, 105): "The procedure of superimposition and identification [which Montale practices here] is . . . one of the typical operations of Rimbaud's imagination and language, one of the elements of that poetics and that universe of images which Montale in the first part of this 'homage,' to make it a rare example of 'allusive art,' borrows and alienates in a context significant for its antithesis."

Jacomuzzi (1, 107): "At the end of the first part, then, the butterfly, woman-poetry, appears . . . as the sign of a poetry, of an idea of the poetic function, and, indivisibly, of a vision of the world over which she balances, symbol of liberation and rejection, bird, woman, butterfly, even 'angelic butterfly.' "

sul nero ghiaccio dell'asfalto!: Originally, "sull'asfalto di via [——́——]!" with a note below, "paroxytone name, trisyllabic, *ad libitum*." The revision, as with the dropping of "mia" from "mirabile / mia farfalla" of the opening, emphasizes the impersonality, the denotative as opposed to connotative, nature of Montale's language here. (The ice is perhaps a glancing reference to "Le transparent glacier des vols qui n'ont pas fui" of Mallarmé's sonnet about poetic impotence, "Le vierge, le vivace et le bel aujourd'hui.")

Il volo / tuo: Volpe's poetry, lifted on wings of silk and pollen, i.e., in stark contrast to the "volo / rapinoso" of Rimbaud.

terribile: Jacomuzzi (1, 121): "In [his] lyrics of Hölderlinian inspiration . . . (but also in all Montale's poetry), intellectual vision, the illumination that breaks out in the instant in which 'the world fades,' is always accompanied by the note of the terrible, emerges out of a tragic halo, the same one that accompanies the metamorphosis of the butterfly from servant to mistress [queen]."

nell'alone scarlatto: Cf. the scarlet ivies of "Finestra fiesolana" and the red lily of "Il giglio rosso" and "Ballata scritta in una clinica," in which the color red is associated with faith.

figlia del sole: Jacomuzzi (1, 116) notes how the sun, which is earlier generically symbolic in Montale, takes on more specific connotations in *La bufera*. Cf. here the "nuovo sole" of "Il giglio rosso," "the sign that presides over a second birth, which occurs not within time and the phenomenology of objects and history but in a *different and new* zone where *darkness* and *blindness* are surpassed in light and vision." On this sun is superimposed the Neoplatonic sun of Hölderlin, a central image in his poetry, which "indicates a point of view beyond history, feeds and illuminates a 'graft' [see "Il giglio rosso"] outside time, it is a name of the divine pronounced against a background of thought substantially negating the consistency of the phenomenal real, of the world of appearances" (118).

del suo primo / pensiero . . . . : "Nature, the sensible world, with all the weight of negativity that such names receive in [Montale]. . . . Servitude toward his first idea will thus be faith in the world of appearances, in reality" (Jacomuzzi 1, 119). Jacomuzzi quotes "Contrabasso" from the very early "Accordi" (tr. in *Oth*, 95–97), in which the interlocutor is his "imagination-poetry" already conceived as a "strayed voyager" taking flight in the "sumptuous realm of universal life" yet still confined to the "Dismal." "In the entire arc of Montale's poetry, in effect, there is no other 'servitude' than the passive faith in 'the deceivingness of the world'" (120). The escape from the cocoon is thus a metaphor for Volpe's escape from the "essential prison" of appearances. "Her 'padronanza,' then, will take place 'lassù,' beyond phenomenal certainty, in the refusal to be witness and imitation of time." The points of ellipsis typically indicate that the process is incomplete.

Incantesimo / Incantation (1948–54, most likely toward the end of this period)
Montale (Greco, 51): "Diotima is Clizia, the cicadas were in an Italian garden, but they help to prepare the evocation of Galilee."

The last of the Hölderlinian poems brings the 'FLASHES' E DEDICHE to a powerful erotic/spiritual climax. The title itself (and the figure of the "islands") is drawn from "Der Archipelagus," in which "the sun of the day, daughter (*prole*) of the Orient," symbol for Christ, "poetizing every morning," sends a "sweet incantation" to the waves of the sea. Diotima, "symbol [in Hölderlin] of love and of tragic-amorous poetry" (Jacomuzzi 1, 94) and here a figure for Clizia, who is referred to in the third person for the only time in *La bufera*, was the *senhal* of Hölderlin's own beloved, Susette Gontard. The name, which means "god-honored" or "god-honoring," is taken from the figure in the *Symposium* who "taught the transcendental dynamic that elevates lover and beloved, in a crisscrossing of mutual adoration and heightened expectation, toward the upper limits—that is, the potential divinity—of their human natures" (Arrowsmith 3, 188). Grignani (28): "The decisive swerve of the image is based on an exaltation of the secular rite: according to Hölderlin, the one experience of the divine permitted to poets. Basically, the one named is what the namer wants to be."

Montale (in "Lettera d'Albenga" [1963; *Auto*, 350]): "Hölderlin . . . believed in the existence of earthly divinities, living incognito among us. But it's not easy to meet one [the term is feminine]; only to poets is such a possibility granted. And this today is the only means of having a concrete experience of the divine."

nell'isole . . . : The inside is, according to the system elaborated by Jacomuzzi in his analysis of "Per un 'Omaggio a Rimbaud,' " the world of transcendental values beyond the deceiving "outside" "world of appearances," which fades in the lovers' elevating spiritual communion, here embodied as a "gentle flame."

l'amorosa cicala: An evident symbol of the poet's amorously roused inspiration (cf. the development of the same image in "L'ombra della magnolia . . ."), like Diotima of Platonic derivation. Cf. *Phaedrus* 259 b-c, where Socrates describes the legend of the cicada: "Once upon a time these cicadas were men—men of an age before there were any Muses—and . . . when the latter came into the world, and music made its appearance, some of the people of those days were so thrilled with pleasure that they went on singing, and quite forgot to eat and drink until they actually died without being aware of it. From them in due course sprang the race of the cicada, to which the Muses have granted the boon of needing no sustenance right from their birth, but of singing from the very first, without food or drink, until the day of their death." The cicada here vibrates more powerfully with the stronger, more profound Christ-bearing love of Clizia; but the beloved is herself "incandescent," and, as Cambon (163) notes, "just as Clizia took on some of the Vixen's earth-affirming attributes in 'L'anguilla,' the Vixen in turn can emulate her rival's Platonic drive toward sublimation." The flame congeals her experience into lava (cf. the last motet), a permanent residue, a "keepsake," the vehicle that will transmute her secular, "profane" love into one equal to Clizia's for Christ. The veil, the profane equivalent of the veronica of "Iride" (cf. also the veil of Maya in the hymn of "Elegia di Pico Farnese") is the veil of appearances that Volpe wore when she was affianced to her profane god (perhaps the poet himself—see "Anniversario"); the day will come when this veil will be raised and Volpe's God and Clizia's will conjoin. (The movement embodies the tendency in these later poems to fuse the two inspirational figures.)

fidanzata al tuo Dio: Macrì (1, 80–81) sees this and other Montalean imagery of "erotic-Christian mysticism" as derived from Coventry Patmore's *Religio Poetae*, quoted in Mario Praz's anthology *Poeti inglesi dell'Ottocento* (Bemporad, 1925).

V. SILVAE

In Italian, *selva*, apart from being a forest, can also be the notes which serve as the basis for a composition, "material for writing." This definition is derived from a Latin verse form, the *silva*; Arrowsmith (3, 189) quotes the Renaissance poet Poliziano, who wrote four long Latin *silvae*, on Statius' *Silvarum liber*: "*Selva* is the term employed by the philosophers for undifferentiated matter, which the Greeks call *hylen*. . . . From this it takes the name of that literary genre which Quintilian, in Book X of his *Institutes*, describes as follows: 'A different sort of defect is that possessed by those who want, as it were, to run through their subject with extreme rapidity and write extemporaneously, following the fire and impulse of inspiration. This genre they call *selva*. They then take up their work again and revise what they have thrown off; but their polishing is done in the words and the rhythm, while the subject matter remains, just as it was improvised, confusedly jumbled together.' "

In the 1949 plan for *Romanzo*, this section was to be called L'ANGELO E LA VOLPE (THE ANGEL AND THE VIXEN) continuing the "alternation" of the rival inspirations of the 'FLASHES' E DEDICHE. In *La bufera*, however, Montale begins the section with "Iride" (formerly in DOPO); he then adds "Nella serra" and "Nel parco," Arlettian poems moved from the Liguria-inspired INTERMEZZO section, and "L'orto," which is also at least partly Arlettian; he also reverses the ordering of "L'anguilla" and "Il gallo cedrone," and creates a separate section for the MADRIGALI PRIVATI. The section is thus transformed from a continuation of the dialectic of 'FLASHES' E DEDICHE into a reconsideration of familial bonds and childhood memories, which involve a new revaluing of the past.

Generally considered the apex of Montale's poetry, the SILVAE are written under the (weakening) sign of the vanished Clizia, who has now been virtually subsumed into her Christological, salvific function.

Iride / Iris (1943–44)

Montale (*Op*, 962): "The character is that of 'Il giglio rosso' and of the entire series of FINISTERRE. She returns in 'La primavera hitleriana,' in various SILVAE (also with the name of Clizia), and in the 'Piccolo testamento.' She had already been encountered in many poems of *Le occasioni*; for example, in the MOTTETTI and in 'Nuove stanze.' 'Iride' is a poem I dreamed and then translated from a nonexistent language: I am perhaps more its medium than its author. The figure in the 'Ballata scritta in una clinica' is someone else; different, too, is the one in 'FLASHES' E DEDICHE and the MADRIGALI."

Montale ("Intentions," *Sec*, 303–4): "But in key, terribly in key [with FINISTERRE], among the new additions is 'Iride,' in which the Sphinx of 'Nuove stanze,' who had left the east to illuminate the ice and mists of the north, returns to us as the continuation and symbol of the eternal Christian sacrifice. She pays for all, expiates all. And he who recognizes her is the Nestorian, the man who knows best the affinities that bind God to incarnate beings, not the silly spiritualist or the rigid and abstract Monophysite. I dreamed twice and rewrote this poem: how could I make it clearer, correcting and interpreting it arbitrarily myself? I feel it's the one poem which merits the charges of obscurity recently brought against me by Sinisgalli; but even so I don't think it should be discarded."

As Arrowsmith (3, 190) points out, there is no adequate translation for the polysemous term *iride*, but its denotations—rainbow, iris of the eye, iridescence, flower—all relate to the central notion of diffusion of light, which is very much "in key" with the elaboration of Clizia's imagery (cf. its reappearance in "L'anguilla"). Macchia (310) takes Montale's implication (above) that "Iride" represents "the memory of his past, the Florentine Iris, the Florentine lily" portrayed on the shield of the city (see "Il giglio rosso"). Macrì (1, 140–41) sees the poem as colored by "*maternal* 'light,'" and indeed it mixes references to both Clizia's family and religion and the poet's own (or, rather the religion—"rosario"—of his mother and sister). Though Montale emphasizes the "dreamlike" nature of the poem, it does not, in retrospect, seem terribly different in thematics or method from other work of the period; rather, it is, as Cambon (135) puts it, "an extreme formulation of values and embodiment of poetics." Macrì (1, 95): "The acme of plurality and coexistence is reached in 'Iride,' where the messenger from the Promised Land ('Iris of Canaan') lives in her pure disincarnate, transcendental autonomy in contrast with 'the poor dismayed Nestorian,' who in 'Gli orecchini' flees 'the goddess who won't be flesh.'"

San Martino: The Italian Indian summer; Saint Martin's Day is the first of November.

Arrowsmith (3, 190–91): "Montale's 'dream' begins with a 'seasonal sign,' the unexpectedly vivid, memory-stimulating, autumnal revival of the summer's apparently spent heat and passion."

Ontario: An allusion to Clizia's presence in America. To Marchese (1, 166) it is the reflection of the sunset on the lake that makes it appear like a furnace.

schiocchi di pigne . . . : The collocation of details recalls the beginning of "Notizie dall'Amiata," another autumnal "letter" to Clizia—as the sudden appearance of the veronica, to Cambon (122), parallels the emergence of Clizia's "icon." The "fumo d'un infuso di pa-paveri" is a clear echo of Keats's "To Autumn." Similarly, the *poco . . . poco* anaphora below echoes like constructions in "Nuove stanze" and "Personae separatae."

il Volto . . . : The veronica separates the poet from Clizia because she, unlike him, is Jewish (and because he, unlike her, is nonbelieving). Note the "audacious" (Marchese 1, 166) rhyme of *sudario* with *Ontario* and, later, *ossario* (and the assonance with *Nestoriano*).

zàffiri celesti . . . : Cf. *Purgatorio* I, 13: "Dolce color d'oriental zaffiro" ("Sweet color of the Oriental sapphire"—traditionally the finest kind). The sapphire, as well, symbolizes both Iride's Eastern provenance and her "celestial" nature (Dante's "zaffiro" is the Virgin). The gathered images of paradise, both celestial and earthly (the palm, too, has both Eastern and Christological significance [see the motet "Ecco il segno; s'innerva"]), do not prevent the Nestorian from perceiving the true charnel house that is life on earth during the war.

Nestoriano: Nestorius (381–451), Syrian patriarch of Constantinople, promoted a con-ception of the nature of Christ that earned him banishment in the desert, according to which the figure of Jesus contained two complete persons, divine and human, as opposed to the two natures united in one person of Catholic orthodoxy. Nestorius aimed above all to preserve the humanity of Christ, declaring that "Christ has two natures: one is that which clothes in flesh, another that which is clothed." The Monophysite, by contrast, believes only in Christ's divinity.

For Montale, Arrowsmith says (3, 191), "Christ was a man who 'carries God within him,' just as Clizia is a 'Christ-bearer' garbed in the vestments of God's angels."

dal naufragio . . . : Reference both to the bloodbath of the war and to the war against the Jews; the Biblical myth of the Flood is the controlling image here, and the ultimate source of the "rainbow" symbol; it also evokes other Montale poems in which the "ark" serves an essential symbolic function, namely "A Liuba che parte" and "L'arca."

un fuoco / di gelo: Collocation of Clizia/Irma Brandeis's opposing fire/ice *senhals* (as in the motet "Ti libero la fronte dai ghiaccioli"), inspired by the conjunction of summer and winter at San Martino, which suggests the extreme weather of Palestine.

il suolo / ch'è tuo . . . : Hers in that Clizia is Jewish, though never visited by her.

resina e . . . bacche: Cf. the "nimbo di vischi e pungitopi" below. The poet's rosary is made up of the berries of Clizia's Christian attributes, the holly and mistletoe.

Cuore d'altri . . . : As Cambon (126) points out, the first part of the poem is one complex sentence (a frequent occurrence, particularly in the later Montale). The recurrence of the veronica indicates that the second part "begins by rehearsing the introduction of Part One and consequently develops from the same thematic matrix to bring to fruition the chief ele-ments of that first part." Macrì (1, 95) suggests that the second part of the poem represents the vision of the Nestorian.

la lince . . . : Stilnovistic allegorical presentation, subject to various interpretations, of Montale's competing feminine spirits. Macrì (1, 95) sees the lynx as representative of "acute intellect and open struggle," while the "bel soriano" is "greedy and treacherous in ambush."

Rebay (3, 179): "The lynx, possibly mediated by the Dantesque 'lonza,' is fundamentally . . . nothing but a 'dream' image, and therefore a deformed one, of Mosca, whom the 'dream' represents 'inside-out' and not without cruelty (since Mosca was myopic) in the features of the feline with proverbially extremely acute eyesight. Mosca reappears immediately in the form of the little bird bearing her name, being stalked 'in the laurel'—thus within his private and even domestic territory—by a very different feline, the 'bel soriano,' i.e., the lovely Jewish woman here called 'Iride': 'soriano' ('Syrian') and, two lines later, 'sicomoro' are figures of metonymy generically designating the Judeo-Christian Near East." "Alloro" is likely also an ironic nod to Montale's vocation (see note to "Dora Markus"). Cf. the similar personal bestiary in "Sulla colonna più alta."

ma li credi tu eguali . . . : If Iris/Clizia steps beyond the shadow of the sycamore (like Zacchaeus, who climbed into a sycamore to see Christ [Luke 19:4]; see "Come Zaccheo" in *D71/2*), i.e., if she partakes of the Christian dispensation, then the two women become equal in Christ.

quella maschera . . . : The image of Christ's face on the veronica. It was "bloodied" before; here it has metamorphosed into royal "purple."

Iri del Canaan: Montale here melds the figure of Iris, messenger (*angelos*) of the Greek gods and annunciatrix of the dawn, with that of the visiting angel, come from Palestine (see the letter from Irma Brandeis in note to "Sulla colonna più alta")—with, as Marchese (1, 168) points out, a recollection of Clizia's actual name (Irma). The fusion of classical with Judeo-Christian motifs also occurs in "A Liuba che parte" and "L'arca." Orelli (70), however, quotes René Char's "Lettre amoureuse," in which he says that Iris is "a woman's proper name which poets use to designate a beloved woman and even some women whose names they wish to conceal."

Macrì (1, 98) cites *Paradiso* XXXIII, 118–19: "E l'un dall'altro come iri da iri / parea riflesso," describing the three circles of the Trinity; and Ezekiel 1:28: "As the appearance of the bow that is in the cloud in the day of rain, so was . . . the appearance of the likeness of the glory of the Lord."

quel nimbo di vischi e pugnitopi: The Christmas plants, here as elsewhere (cf. "Il giglio rosso") symbols of Clizia's Christian (and North American) mission, which takes her far from the desert flowers of her Palestine/Canaan heritage. The "nimbo" is the smoke from the "vampa" above. Macrì (1, 98): "Montale's 'nimbo' is the dissolving of the divine (immanent or transcendent) form in a halo of good."

tuoi germani: Macrì (1, 98): "He says not 'brothers' but 'germani,' i.e., 'brothers in the flesh, of the flesh.'"

all'imbarcadero / del nostro fiume . . . : Cambon (128) hypothesizes that "the apparition of Clizia-Iris in Montale's private Eden brings back to his memory a love tryst at a place in the Italian countryside, on a riverbank, that she and he know only too well; and the time of the tryst was obviously a St. Martin's day, retrospectively accounting for the initial reference." The imagery, meanwhile, seems to revisit that of "Il ritorno," where the sun also went quickly dark, and the landscape suggests the "edges of your beaches" of "La primavera hitleriana." Marchese (1, 168) posits that the "burchio" here represents the ship taking Clizia definitively to America, in contrast to the "bark of salvation" (with its "burchiello") in "Crisalide." For the image of the black sun, see note to "La primavera hitleriana."

Ma se ritorni . . . : To Cambon (128), the moment recalls the appearance of Beatrice to Dante in the earthly paradise atop Mount Purgatory in *Purgatorio* XXX.

la tua storia terrena: Clizia's earthly experience (i.e., with the poet) is over; the embers of the poet's memory, fanned by the Indian summer heat, go dark, like the sun. She is now entirely sublimated into her role as sacrificial representative of Christ and in fact, as the last lines suggest, is being subsumed in Him.

l'opera Sua . . . dev'esser continuata: Pauline language, a transposition of lines 29 and 30, perhaps a quotation (in italics) from Iris/Clizia. In his June 9, 1939, letter to Bobi Bazlen (*Op*, 931) (quoted in note to "Elegia di Pico Farnese"), Montale expresses "the doubt . . . that Christian symbology . . . depreciates life and that Christ needs to be continued perhaps in spite of himself," i.e., that Christ's salvific work needs to be carried on, in spite of the fact that he has been idolized, that institutionalized Christianity has been alienated from his essential teaching. Cambon (133–34): "Even the fact that the verb 'transform' replaces in the coda the noun 'form' of stanza 5 has semantic significance as an activation of meaning in the direction of transcendence. And if we cast a backward glance at the poem's formal itinerary, we shall realize that its binary structure . . . macroscopically mirrors the 'return' theme [as does the anaphora of the 'opera Sua/tua' transposition], which has to do with the magical transformations of memory."

Nella serra / In the Greenhouse (1945)

As we have seen above, "Nella serra" and its twin, "Nel parco," were originally intended as parts of the Ligurian "Intermezzo" section of the book, in which Montale returns to familial and childhood scenes, possibly with the aim of reinforcing values he sees as threatened in the postwar world. They are thus Arlettian in inspiration, and linked with the equally Ligurian "Da una torre." All three seem to Mengaldo (74) to be reminiscent of Pascoli, which is consistent with Montale's obsessive interest in the past in this phase: "The retrieval belongs to a returned 'impressionistic' tendency which Montale himself acknowledged (in a 1951 interview, 'Confessioni di scrittori [Interviste con se stessi],' [tr. in *Sec*, 310–15]): 'After the liberation I wrote poems of a more immediate inspiration that to some seem like a return to the impressionism of *Ossi di seppia*, but through the filter of a more careful stylistic control.' " The imagery of the poem—lemon house, children's drums, light globes, etc.—recalls moments from the first book: "I limoni," "Caffè a Rapallo," "Arsenio"; as Grignani (67) suggests, the dreamed fusion of the lovers in "Nella serra" is an inversion—and revindication—of the alienation memorialized in its presumptive counterpart, "Due nel crepuscolo."

un rosario . . . : Cf. the secular rosary of Volpe's necklace in "Dal treno" and the more sacral one of the preceding "Iride." The image here immediately opens the scene to transcendent experience, as does the "blazing" of the cochineal.

leggero: Only in a dream could the poet feel this; cf. the emphasis on his corporality in, e.g., "Lasciando un 'Dove.' "

la tua forma: To Grignani (67), this recalls the "forma che mi fu tolta" of the "momentary miracle of identification" in "Incontro." See Macrì (1, 79) for a discussion of the Dantean/Petrarchan derivation of this word, which he defines as "informative principle" and also "soul"; he sees the breath ("sospiro" in "Personae separatae," "respiro" here) also as a symbol of the soul. Here the two are literally interchangeable.

l'oscuro / pensiero di Dio: "oscuro" because unclear, mysterious; as elsewhere in *La bufera* (cf. "Vento sulla Mezzaluna," "Incantesimo," "Anniversario"). Cf. also the "first idea" of the Neoplatonic sun/god in "Per un 'Omaggio a Rimbaud.' " God is evoked for Montale in the fusion, here perhaps only dreamed, of the lovers.

sui pochi viventi: As elsewhere, the privileged few with access to the full experience of existence—which is touched with divinity.

Nel parco / In the Park (1946)

The companion piece/mirror image of "Nella serra": one the internal world of the dream, the other describing synesthetic fusion with the natural world. Grignani (67): " 'Nel parco' completes the experience of indistinction" between poet and beloved, this time reversing the imagery of "Due nel crepuscolo": "the 'disfarsi di se' [cf. also the "riso che non m'appartiene"] is positive, the opposite of the gesture that gets cut off and belongs to neither subject nor interlocutor." Grignani goes on to demonstrate the related rhymes (*intriso/viso* in "Nella serra"; *riso/viso* in "Nel parco"; *viso/reciso/diviso/sorriso* in "Due nel crepuscolo") that reveal the "mirroring" relationship of the poems. For her (68), "Nella serra" and "Nel parco" prepare the ground for the absorption of Arletta into Clizia in "L'orto": "If the woman with the 'hard crystal gaze' can transform the wholly interiorized heredity of infantile eros into a saving or prophetic message ('L'orto'), if her 'living shadow' arrives to exercise her own lucid rule even over the closed domestic circle ('Voce giunta con le folaghe'), this can occur through the force of the opposing tension that Clizia's solar stilnovistic definition creates in relation to the female 'tu' of an earlier season, who does not know projection into the future."

Nell'ombra della magnolia . . . : The "warped wheel" of "the magnolia's / ever-shrinking shade" is the poet's shrinking memory (cf. "nella memoria che si sfolla" of the motet "Non recidere, forbici . . ."). The magnolia here, as elsewhere (cf. "L'arca," other details of which also resonate with this poem), is the protector of the domestic realm.

la freccia: The imagery of wounding ("freccia," "punge le vene") recalls the description of Montale's memory of Arletta/Annetta in "Annetta" (quoted in note to "Incontro"): "non l'oblio ma una punta che feriva / quasi a sangue."

dal pioppo: Grignani (68) points out that the poplar figures in a number of Montale's stories about Monterosso ("La casa delle due palme," "Il bello viene dopo" in *Farf*), in which a primitive weapon like the "cerbottana" also appears.

L'orto / The Garden (1946)

The ecstatic and tragic ultimate vision of Clizia as Christ-bearer, elaborated in "Iride," in which the poet fantasizes a mystical union with a feminine other who recapitulates and subsumes all his (pre-Volpe) loves. As Bonora (quoted in Marchese 1, 173) says, "this is not the end of the myth of Clizia, but it . . . is the end of the truly religious moment of *La bufera*."

Io non so . . . : The extremely unusual, almost stuttering repetition of the phrase calls inescapable attention to the poet's uncertainty about the true meaning of his experience. As with "Iride," the first half of the poem is occupied by one sentence, in this case a willfully awkward series of hypotheses as to the messenger's nature and her relationship to the dominating ghosts of his past. Cf. Montale's comments about the nature of the "orto" in "La riviera del Ciceri (e la mia)" (1970; *SM/A*, 1459), which evoke "In limine," "Meriggiare pallido e assorto," and other poems from *Ossi di seppia*: "I'd be happy if some examples still survived of that miracle that few Italian regions possess: the kitchen garden ["orto"]; a few square meters not always protected by bits of broken bottle [atop a wall] in which a family found everything, I repeat everything, necessary for its sustenance. In these gardens, too, Pan poked out his head; but he had to make himself as small as a gnome, make himself domestic and useful, help the children draw water from the well. The Ligurian riviera was never halcyon or Panic in the torrential sense of the word [as we have seen, a critical passing reference to D'Annunzio's *Alcyone*]. It was rather, in its natural forms, anthropomorphic and exquisitely human, if lowercase."

prediletta / del mio Dio (del tuo forse): Though Jewish, and thus the creature of another God, Clizia has been chosen by Montale's own native God, "a god of universal love" (Marchese 1, 170)—an appropriation of the Jewish notion of the "chosen people." (Throughout *La bufera*, however, God, or god—for the poet and others—is a personal, not a communitarian, presence.)

nel chiuso . . . : The poet returns us to the site of the first poem of his first book, "In limine," i.e., to the domestic realm, the realm of his "ark," which has been expounded with increasing sympathy and insistence in *La bufera*. The imagery of the first of four 13-line stanzas (e.g., the "sail," reminiscent of the "bark of salvation" of "Crisalide" and the "celestial goshawk" of "Proda di Versilia," below) revisits the scenes of *Ossi di seppia*, but in a nostalgic and idealizing vein, as the poet brings together his early world, the world of Arletta and his familial ghosts, and his experience of Clizia, fusing them into one figure that represents the Other (the ultimate tendency of all of Montale's poetry; cf. his poem "Il tu" [*Sat*], where he says "in me i tanti son uno anche se appaiono / molteplicati dagli specchi" [in me the many are one, even if they seem / multiplied by mirrors]).

il tuo piede / attutito: A reprise of "Il passo che proviene / dalla serra sì lieve" in the motet "Ecco il segno; s'innerva," which also anticipates "il tuo passo che fa pulsar le vene," a few lines below, and hence an evocation of the beloved's former presence here in Monterosso (domain of the "serra"). Bettarini (1, 472) notes the resemblance to Valéry's "Les pas" in *Charmes*.

questo intrico: The garden, here pictured as a tangle of confused, multifarious memories. Cf. the "intrico dell'edera" in " 'Ezekiel saw the Wheel. . . .' "

quello che mi colse un'altra estate: The footstep of another summer, i.e., an earlier love from the period "before" the "folata" (cf. the same term in the Arlettian "Vento e bandiere"), the squall that broke the poet's mirror (an image of bad luck [Marchese 1, 171]; also of failed love [cf. "Ballata scritta in una clinica," where Mosca is described as "lo specchio / di me"]: the poet can only recognize himself in and through his beloved). The Edenic world invoked here is reminiscent of the "estremo angolo d'orto" of "Crisalide."

il picco irto del Mesco: Cf. "Punta del Mesco" (also an Arlettian poem). The Mesco is the mountain promontory jutting into the Tyrrhenian Sea just beyond Monterosso, the northwestern boundary of the "conca ospitale" of the Cinque Terre.

sulla celesta . . . : Recalls the *osso* for Paola Nicoli "Tentava la vostra mano la tastiera," with its scene of extraordinary sympathy that amounts to a spiritual fusion. The nest (i.e., bird) imagery (which refers to the "luì nidaci" above) is consistent with the presentation of Arletta elsewhere (e.g., as "la capinera").

un fólto ormai bruciato: Macrì (1, 113): "This word, like 'bronco,' 'sterpi,' and numerous others, carries us back to the wood of the suicides" in *Inferno* XIII; cf. "I morti."

L'ora della tortura . . . : The poem divides abruptly between the Edenic garden of the past and the hellish present, which Clizia has utterly understood (as in "Palio" and "Nuove stanze"; cf. her "eyes of steel" there with her "sheer crystal gaze" here). The language here is Dantesque (and Eliotic); see Macrì (1, 114).

l'opera di Vulcano . . . : Marchese (1, 172): "A powerful metaphor for the mystifications of Nazi-Fascist rhetoric that hid the preparation for the war." The disdainful personification

—with its elaborate amplification ("fuliggine," "caldana," etc.)—is typical of the later Montale (cf., e.g., "La primavera hitleriana" and "Botta e risposta," originally called "Le stalle d'Augià" [The Augean Stables], in *Sat*).

dì dell'Ira: The classical metaphor is superseded by a Christological reference to the story of Peter's betrayal of Christ. See Matthew, 26:33ff. As always in Montale, a fusion of historical reference (to the "forsworn" who betrayed European society to the Fascists) with, more broadly, the cosmic apocalypse that history has prefigured, "the day of Christ's death continued in the evil of history" (Marchese 1, 172).

non ti divise, anima indivisa: The totality, and hence the constancy, of Clizia's dedication to her mission, indeed of her spiritual reality. Cf. the similar structure of the Clizian epithet "tu / che il non mutato amor mutata serbi" of "La primavera hitleriana." Unlike the poet, who is "divided" from her by their separate faiths in "Iride," Clizia is in no way indistinct from her fate. Like her gaze, her very heart, which was once perhaps occupied by the image of the poet, has taken on the (inanimate) characteristics of one of her signal attributes, her light-refracting, indestructibly hard jewelry.

O labbri muti . . . : Macrì (1, 114): "Pseudo-Petrarchan invocation."

The two feminine figures are melded here, or rather Arletta is incorporated into Clizia, in a conjunction of their imagery. The lips recall the "muto" Arlettian "labbro di sangue" of "Da una torre" (lips have never been a Clizian attribute), here fused with Clizian flight imagery (as the Monterosso "path" [of "Punta del Mesco"] becomes a path of air). And the poet himself combines with Arletta/Clizia, in a figure—"o membra che distinguo / a stento dalle mie"—drawn from the conjoinings of "Nella serra" and "Nel parco," here activated on a sublimated plane. (The image of fusion perhaps also implies the "mirror" above.) Macrì (1, 81) derives certain of the beloved's attributes and epithets here, as in the Hölderlinian poems at the end of the 'FLASHES' E DEDICHE, from Coventry Patmore's *Religio Poetae* (see note to "Incantesimo").

o diti che . . . *i vivi infocano*: Cf. the "vampa" that invests Clizia's memory in "Iride."

o intento che hai creato . . . : As the poet conjoins with Clizia in this extraordinary moment of epiphany, Clizia becomes identified with the divine will, which created time beyond the limits of Clizia's human dimensions, and through which not only is her salvific influence diffused into the furthest reaches of the human domain (Nestorian divinity revealed in man, as in "Visita a Fadin"), but she is also rendered present in the terrible apparitions of the demonic and angelic (Thanatos and Eros [or Agape]) (Marchese 1, 174), each in its own way an intimation of the presence of the divine in the world.

angiole: Dantism; Macrì (1, 114) identifies the source as the *Vita nuova*.

il disco di già inciso . . . : A reprise of the pessimistic Schopenhauerian determinism of the early Montale, the "tutto è fisso, tutto è scritto" of "Crisalide." The "solco" is a mark of significant human presence, most powerfully prefigured in the "solco . . . inciso" at the end of "Palio" (but also reminiscent of the record in "Sotto la pioggia"). But the groove has already been etched, in a bitter revindication—with its ironic allusion to the technology of "mechanical man"—of the beneficent divine will so ecstatically apotheosized above, here acknowledged as a "wish contrary to fact." Clizia's destiny and the poet's, in spite of his ecstatic vision, are divided.

Macrì (1, 114): "The secret of the improbable single groove of the two destinies of the lovers lies in the exclamation 'O limbs that I can barely tell from mine,' which establishes an earthly/purgatorial condition for the incarnation of the divine ('I [still] flee the goddess who won't be flesh,' and it is a natural, fatal fleeing of the *self*). . . . The wish is lightning ('*surely your destiny conjoined with mine / would show a single groove*') in the dark hardness of the protasis ('If the power . . . were *another*'). But everywhere in *La bufera* temptation and provocation are the very *élan* of the poetry, in the tension between the two phantoms and the two realities of Woman and God."

(The image of history as an already printed record or tape is revisited, somewhat less pessimistically, in a 1962 essay, "L'uomo nel microsolco" [tr. in *Sec* 39–43].)

Proda di Versilia / Shore of Versilia (1946)

Written at Viareggio, not far from the Cinque Terre. Versilia is that part of the Tuscan coast, dominated by the Apuan Alps, which runs from Sestri Levante in the south to La Spezia in the north, and includes both Viareggio and the Cinque Terre. As in "L'orto," the scenes of Montale's childhood are nostalgically reviewed; they are the locus of prayer to his dead, already memorialized and sanctified in the poems of FINISTERRE, and now less and less present in the poet's failing memory—a recurrent theme since the MOTTETTI.

il compiersi: The same rejection of an afterlife as in "A mia madre," which involves the sanctification of earthly existence.

astore celestiale: The "bark of salvation" of "Crisalide," here superimposed over the Dantean image of the "celestial goshawk" (*Purgatorio* VIII, 104ff.) that chases away the threatening serpent. There is possibly also an echo of the albatross in Coleridge's "Rime of the Ancient Mariner." Arrowsmith (3, 194): "The effect . . . is to attenuate and darken, almost to deny, purgatorial hope."

Broli di zinnie . . . : Almost a rewriting of "Fine dell'infanzia," with borrowings from other poems near the close of *Ossi di seppia*, most notably "Crisalide." The "shadows" of the trees sacred to the poet's childhood (note also the references to nuns and monks, to religion in its familiar—though resisted—local form) soon metamorphose into the "loved shadows" of his "lost ones" (cf. "L'arca" and "Da una torre"). In his dream, the child manages what the adult never can, to pass beyond the "wall" that blocks him from experience (as in "In limine" and "Meriggiare pallido e assorto"), yet, in contrast to the high, almost ecstatic language of "L'orto," Montale's description here is precise, detailed, even prosaic: "humane."

le murene: Zambon (73–74) points out the moray eel's equivalence with the "anguilla," which here suffers the sacrificial passion that is central to Montale's understanding of "l'oscuro male universo," the dark universal ill of "Lettera levantina," quoted in the note to "Il gallo cedrone." See this note also for the significance of animal—and especially bird—sacrifice in Montale.

Anni di scogli . . . : The insistence on the "humanity" of Montale's early world, in contrast with "this boundless sea of muck and refuse," is in key with his postwar pessimism. After the disappearance of Clizia (and before the advent of Volpe) his only positive prospect is backward. Here the "respiro"—always an image of vitality (see note to "Nella serra")—is that of "sommersi," creatures that not only are underwater but have been drowned in the overwhelming sea of the present.

il pesce prete, il pesce rondine: According to Arrowsmith (3, 194), *pesce prete* is the Italian name for the stargazer; *pesce rondine* that for the flying gurnard.

Alice: Alice in Wonderland, who watched the Lobster Quadrille (see "Il condannato" in *Farf*)—a *senhal* of Arletta.

tempo che fu misurabile . . . : The secular, "knowable" "human time" in which Clizia moves in "L'orto," here opposed to an immeasurable and debased present. The sea of today, however, bears some resemblance to the hostile sea of MEDITERRANEO and other poems of *Ossi di seppia*; the present has been inimical in Montale from the outset.

'Ezekiel saw the Wheel . . .' (1946)
The title, originally an epigraph for the poem, is derived from the Negro spiritual "Ezekiel Saw de Wheel," the refrain of which goes as follows: "Ezekiel saw de wheel, / 'Way up in de middle ob de air, / Ezekiel saw de wheel, / 'Way up in de middle ob de air; / An' de little wheel run by faith, / An' de big wheel run by de grace ob God, / 'Tis a wheel in a wheel, / 'Way in de middle ob de air" (quoted in R. Nathaniel Dett, ed., *Religious Folk-Songs of the Negro as Sung at Hampton Institute* [Hampton, Va.: Hampton Institute Press, 1927], 60).

According to Arrowsmith (3, 194), Montale draws here not only from Ezekiel (1:15–21) and Revelation (4:6–9) but from Dante (*Purgatorio* XXIX, 100ff.) in creating "his own personal apocalyptic vision of Clizia." In fact, the dense accumulation of pregnant signs suggests that the poem, more than being "a concentrate of Arlettian themes" (Grignani, 64), addresses the fused Arletta/Clizia of "L'orto," i.e., a complex figuration of the poet's past, which he acknowledges he cannot leave behind in spite of his best attempts. The "tangle" takes the reader back to the "orto" of Monterosso, the locale of "Flussi," but the ivy recalls the Clizian symbol of faith in "Finestra fiesolana." The "pool," also in the Montale garden, evokes the site of the appearance of the "more than a streak" in "Vasca" and the recurrent image of the mirror as the locus of self-recognition (available only through the agency of a female counterpart, as we have seen), while the "icy" hand of the poet's persistent, gnawing memory combines two Clizian attributes. (Grignani [65] notes that "pallidi capelli" appeared in a first version of the Arlettian "Incontro.")

Macrì (2, 132–33) claims that "the principal source of Montale's Biblicism is English. . . . This personalized 'vision of Ezekiel' is in response to Eliot's 'A Song for Simeon,' translated [by Montale] in 1929, which is also a 'vision' of the 'salvation' of the 'Infant' or 'Word' inspired by one of the Christian psalms in the Gospel according to Saint Luke ('Nunc dimittis'), the pious Jew Simeon's canticle of praise and thanksgiving for having seen the prophesied Messiah, having held the Child in his arms in the temple. . . . What counts is the prophetic spirit that unites the two characters in the intimate nexus of prediction and reality between Old and New Testaments, which is the true meaning of Eliot's teaching."

a soffocar la tua voce: Cf. the "presenza soffocata" of "Delta" and the "voce prigioniera" of "Eastbourne." Likewise with "il breve / cerchio che tutto trasforma": Macrì (1, 83) notes as source the "gran cerchio d'ombra" of Dante's *rima* "Al poco giorno . . . ," and points out that "cerchio" is synonymous with the "fossa" of "Voce giunta con le folaghe" (see note) and with the "spera" of "Gli orecchini"; cf. also the atmosphere and imagery of "Il tuo volo."

in giù: Recalls "Delta" 's infernal "oscura regione ove scendevi," a drainlike image, symbol of the permanent loss of memory.

Most of the poem's echoes are linked with Arletta, as is the imagery of sand and burial, which recurs in a late Arlettian poem, "Il lago di Annecy" (in *D*71/2). But the "slipper prints" are Clizia's "felted" "step" in the eighth motet; and the "menacing Wheel," which opposes and supersedes (uppercase over lowercase) the "small circle," is the existential wheel of fate of "Eastbourne" and "Costa San Giorgio"—a generic Heraclitean symbol; it associates here with the emblems of Clizia's religion (it is derived from an Old Testament text, filtered through a Christian hymn), now as death-related and threatening as the Wheel itself, reflecting the poet's resentment of the "strong power" that has deprived him of Clizia. Yet the covenant with her ("in the shimmering dawn": cf. the hopeful dawn of "Il ventaglio," in which "maybe the day is saved") survives to defeat his attempt at suffocating it, the petals of the peach tree are infused with the "blood" of incarnate memory (as in "Eastbourne" and "Da una torre," etc.), and its pain survives vividly into the present. (The claw—Macrì [2, 134] sees Clizia portrayed "as an apocalyptic eagle out of John the Divine"—will become Volpe's.)

quando: Macrì (2, 133): "The temporal morpheme, explicit and implicit . . . marks the mystery of the Montalean occasion."

La primavera hitleriana / The Hitler Spring (1939–46)
Montale (*Op*, 966): "Hitler and Mussolini in Florence [their meeting took place on May 9, 1938]. Evening gala at the Teatro Comunale. Over the Arno, a snow of white butterflies."

The poem, patently unprintable during the war, ought to have been part of FINISTERRE. Clizia, thus, is vividly present in the poet's mind, as in the late poems of *Le occasioni*, including "Elegia di Pico Farnese" and "Palio," written at about the same time (they share the long line that Montale himself compared with Hopkins's "sprung rhythm"); but Clizia does not yet display the angelic attributes she will acquire as she becomes more remote. The controlling trope here is the opposition of her solarity, suggestive of her *senhal* name, with images of cold, activating the stilnovistic fire/ice contrast, evocative of the age-old erotic trope and embodied in the name Brandeis. The poem is organized around this opposition and others equally dynamic (summer/frost, fire/hail, spring/chill, seed/burned-dry, blind/sun); the oxymoron of the title suggests the image-structure that governs what follows.

Né quella ch'a veder lo sol si gira: The epigraph, to which Montale's attention was drawn —like the related one for the coeval "Alla maniera di Filippo De Pisis . . ."—by Contini's editing of Dante's *Rime*, is the inspiring source for Clizia's Ovidian name, here invoked for the first time (though the sunflower, "crazed with light," as in "Portami il girasole . . . ," is an image of long standing in Montale's poetry). To quote Contini's note (in Dante Alighieri, *Rime*, ed. Gianfranco Contini, 2nd ed. [Turin: Giuliano Einaudi Editore, 1970], 267): "Clizia, daughter of the Ocean and lover of the Sun . . . , having through her jealousy provoked the death of Leucothoe, was abandoned by the sun and changed into a heliotrope or sunflower; as the *Metamorphoses* (IV, 234–70) that suggested so much mythic material to Dante narrate. . . . The expression follows the final hexameter of the Ovidian episode: *Vertitur ad Solem mutataque servat amorem* [She turns toward the Sun and, transformed, harbors her love]."

The sonnet, of questionable attribution but supposedly written by Dante to a Venetian admirer and ally, reads as follows:

> Nulla mi parve mai piú crudel cosa
> di lei per cui servir la vita lago,
> ché'l suo desio nel congelato lago,
> ed in foco d'amore il mio si posa.
> Di cosí dispietata e disdegnosa
> la gran bellezza di veder m'appago;
> e tanto son del mio tormento vago
> ch'altro piacere a li occhi miei non osa.
>
> Né quella ch'a veder lo sol si gira
> e'l non mutato amor mutata serba,

ebbe quant'io già mai fortuna acerba.
Dunque, Giannin, quando questa superba
convegno amar fin che la vita spira,
alquanto per pietà con me sospira.

(Nothing ever seemed a crueler thing to me / than she whom I abandon life to serve, / since desire for her puts mine / in the frozen lake, and the fire of love. / Of one so cruel and disdainful / I content myself with seeing the great beauty; / and I am so desirous of my torment / that nothing else dares please my eyes. // Nor did she who turns to see the sun / and changed, preserves her unchanged love, / ever have as bitter a fate as I. / So, Giannino, when I have to love / this proud one for as long as my life has breath, / sigh with me a little out of pity.)

(Note the oxymoron "congelato lago" ["certainly of the heart, *Inferno* I, 20"—Contini]/ "foco d'amore," quite likely the inspiration for Clizia's "Brand/eis" *senhal*, which makes a rather tentative first appearance in Montale's poem.)

nelle cave segrete . . . : Recalls "Cave d'autunno," with its spring moon and its prediction of "the kindness of a hand." The poem is immediately pregnant with the dynamic of change, which counters the current "dead season." The setting, above the Arno, is reminiscent in some respects of "Tempi di Bellosguardo," or of "Carnevale di Gerti," though this time the view is from the north, at Fiesole (cf. "Finestra fiesolana"), where Montale spent part of the war.

Maiano: Village to the northeast of Florence, near Fiesole.

un messo infernale: The political agon that is the poem's occasion posited in cosmic terms. Hitler (cf. the "shadowy Lucifer" of "Piccolo testamento") is Clizia's demonic opponent.

alalà: Ancient Greek victory chant—"Eja, eja, alalà"—adopted by the Fascists.

un golfo mistico . . . : Theatrical term for the orchestra pit, derived, according to Mengaldo (20), from D'Annunzio, and used here to intensify the infernal scene (cf. "Buffalo") "with polemical distortion of meaning . . . and implicit judgment condemning an irrational and estheticizing culture which permitted or provoked" the current predicament.

la sagra dei miti carnefici: The holiday, declared in honor of Hitler's visit, of the butchers, i.e., of workingmen, political base of Fascism and supporters of its rampant militarism, but who are yet unaware of its fatal consequences.

trescone . . . : A lively country dance in which men and women continually change places. As throughout Montale (cf. "La bufera"), agitated movement to music is a metaphor for social disorder; here the dance suggests the moths' suicidal attraction to the "pale" lanterns, i.e., the fatal attractiveness of Fascism, in spite of its feebleness. Arrowsmith (3, 195–96) also sees a reference to "shattered angel wings"—the allusion to Clizia's wings, destroyed by her journey, as in the motet "Ti libero la fronte dai ghiaccoli" (1940), seems clear—and maintains the image is drawn from Plato's *Phaedrus* (248b), where the rational element can no longer control the chariot of the soul, with its horses going in different directions, "whereupon with their charioteers powerless, many are lamed, many have their wings all shattered, and for all their toiling they are balked, every one, of the full vision of Being, and departing therefore, they feed on the food of Seeming."

larve: The immature wingless forms of the moths, but also the ghostly apparitions of the dead.

le candele / romane, a San Giovanni . . . : The lovers' vows and farewells, "powerful as a religious obligation" (Marchese 1, 180), at the moment of Clizia's departure, set against the scene of fireworks in Hitler's honor in front of the Baptistry (cf. "definitive as baptism"), named for Saint John the Evangelist, patron saint of Florence. For the "horde," cf. the action of the crowd in "Palio."

ma una gemma rigò l'aria . . . : A symbolic metamorphosis of the arcing of one of the Roman candles of the night of San Giovanni (Gioanola, in Marchese 1, 180, defines it as a shooting star) into the gleam of Clizia's characteristic jewelry—perhaps the seal ring of "Palio"—a nocturnal negative of the arc of the rainbow, sign of the covenant with God and thus of hope for the future, its bands of color representing the seven guardian angels of Tobias (from the Apocryphal Book of Tobit, in which Raphael and six other angels "who carry on high the prayers of the saints" [Macchia, 312] protect Tobias "on his perilous journey to a faraway land, the consummation of a happy marriage, and a safe return trip" [Arrowsmith 3, 196]). Carpi (353) notes that the angel of Tobias and the "seed of the future" are derived from the second of Rilke's *Duino Elegies*, which had been translated into Italian by Leone Traverso in 1937, and adds that this angel, "apart from the Rilkean suggestion, fits well into the Montalean system: sponsor of the love between Tobit, the son of Tobias, and Sarah, creator of the miraculous return of sight for the blind Tobias, he is a classic angelic messenger of Love and light." (The abrupt eruption of the parenthetical apparition into the poem's catalogue of hopelessness, which then continues, imitates the apparition and disappearance of the saving sign.)

sinibbio: Tuscan; a cold north wind accompanied by snow. The association of Clizia with cold and with northern locales is established in the motet "Ti libero la fronte dai ghiaccioli," cited above. The north-south opposition will be underscored in the last line of the poem. The "fuoco/sinibbio" oxymoron, like the "congelato lago/foco" comparison in the *stil nuovo* sonnet, suggests Clizia's "Brand/eis" attributes.

se raggela / in morte questa morte: Note the emphatic use of the indicative, rather than the subjunctive, with "se."

Guarda ancora / in alto, Clizia . . . : Cary (304) compares this passage with "the first lines of *Paradiso* where the angelic Beatrice gazes eaglelike at the flaming sun (image of the omnipotent 'Other' ['Altrui'] or God) and the pilgrim Dante, gazing in turn upon her, feels himself to *trasumanar*, to be lifted up out of his heavy flesh towards what the poet calls 'the love that governs heaven.' The traditional figure for this spiritual transmutation—dramatized by Dante as a vital chain of amorous gazes—is the ladder of ascent whereby one mounts from the sensible world with its shadowplays of distorting *solarità* to the world of spirit, luminous with intellectual light." (In his notes Cary cites Irma Brandeis's book about Dante, *The Ladder of Vision* [see note to "Il ramarro, se scocca"], noting Montale's approving allusion to it in his lecture on Dante.)

il cieco sole: A translation of the terms of Clizia's "Brand/eis" *senhal* into the imagery of her solar *senhal*. The sun is blind because it is cold (cf. the "chilled sun" in the motet "Ti libero la fronte dai ghiaccioli"), as it must be to combat the infernal fire of the demons' war. But the sun of Clizia's "secret love" (Marchese 1, 180) may also be blind because Clizia herself, as a Jew, is unaware at this point ("inconsapevole" is Montale's word) of her Christ-bearing mission. By now, the poet's hostility to religion has been superseded by his acknowledgment of Christian altruism as a crucial component in the complex of values that must be called upon in combating the rapacious Enemy. The sun, blinded by the brilliance of the vision of the Other, recalls—by inversion—the "blinding" of the pawns by the "burning mirror" of the war in "Nuove stanze." The sunflower-sun of Clizia's love, which here has mystical/Dantesque as opposed to Neoplatonic origins, will be consumed in the overwhelming blaze of the divine heavenly body, an image, perhaps, of the final calling of the faithful to God at the Last Judgment.

nella sera / della loro tregenda: Cf. the "tregenda" of "Nuove stanze."

un'alba . . . bianca ma senz'ali / di raccapriccio: The dawn of a liberated future, unlike the vigil of San Giovanni, with its benighted religiosity (as in the "Elegia di Pico Farnese"). The poem, as Montale indicated in his introduction to a 1960 Swedish translation of his work (*Sec*, 319), implicitly rejects both political (here Fascist) and religious clerisies in favor of a new, unspecified freedom of which Clizia is here the harbinger. The uncharacteristically hopeful vision of universal salvation—bitterly disappointed in the later poems of *La bufera*—is reminiscent of the close of RIVIERE, which Montale himself later rejected as "too premature a synthesis and cure" (see "Anniversario" for a late "correction" of the poet's belied hopes). The wings of terror are those of the "insane" moths of the first line.

ai greti arsi del sud . . . : Southern Europe, "burned" and "sucked dry" by war, and awaiting salvation from Clizia's (and the Allies') north.

Voce giunta con le folaghe / Voice That Came with the Coots (1947)
Here, for the first and only time, Montale unites familial and erotic/religious themes in the most psychologically informed and parablelike of his poems, addressed directly to his father, dead since 1931. The title was originally "Una voce è giunta con le folaghe" (A Voice Arrived with the Coots); the final choice allows an ambiguity—the voice may be the poet's own, as Arrowsmith (3, 196) suggests, recovered through his confrontation with others (cf. the similar occurrence in "Siria"), or it may belong to the Clizian figure who speaks in the poem. To Cambon (98ff.), the poem is a representation of Montale's own "post-Christian Purgatory," deeply influenced by Dante; but, as he says, "the imaginative use of a congenial source portends freedom, not servitude."

Poiché la via percorsa . . . : The line, to Macrì (1, 120), recalls *Inferno* I, 24. The setting is the cemetery above Monterosso, where Montale's father is buried. The poet acknowledges that, at fifty, he is beyond the midpoint, the "mezzo del cammin," of his life. The line is a traditional hendecasyllable extended almost parodically by "è più lunga."

del sentiero da capre: Cf. "il sentiero delle capre" in Montale's 1929 translation of Eliot's "A Song for Simeon."

dove ci scioglieremo come cera: Dantesque image: " 'Wax' ('cera mortal,' *Paradiso* VIII, 128) is for Dante the raw material or 'mater' of mortal nature, before it is stamped or imprinted by the seal of Nature or emanations from the Divine Light" (Arrowsmith 3, 197).

vermene: The verbena, too, which, because of its little red flowers, the poet calls the "blood of cemeteries"—there is none other there—has a Dantean derivation (*Inferno* XIII, 100), as do the "giunchi," which symbolize humility in *Purgatorio* I, 95 (Macrì 1, 120).

senza scialle e berretto . . . : In the poet's vision, his father appears not familiarly, as he was portrayed in "Dov'era il tennis . . . ," but distanced, ghostly; the sound of mine explosions (as in "Punta del Mesco") provides an eerily naturalistic-phantasmagoric framework for the encounter.

L'ombra che mi accompagna . . . : The ghost of Clizia, clearly identifiable through her familiar attributes, which are characteristically both endearing ("childish bangs") and threatening ("severe brow"). Here, however, Clizia is not an angel but a quasi-Virgilian insubstantial shade, mediating between life and death (as Arrowsmith [3, 197] notes, the poem is ultimately not Dantesque but Virgilian in inspiration). Her association here with the figure of the poet's mother is patent.

posa sopra un'erma: An earlier version of "L'orto" began with a similar situation: "Io non so, prediletta / del mio Dio (del tuo forse) che ti posi / sui gradini scoscesi, se nel chiuso" (I don't know, favorite / of my God [and maybe yours] who sit / on the steep steps, if in the enclosure). Luperini (1, 154–55) notes that Clizia's assimilation with statuary emphasizes her hard, "marble," superego function.

il muto: Cf. the "più muto," i.e., dead "labbro / di sangue" of "Da una torre," also evoked by "the blood of cemeteries."

quella che scorporò l'interno fuoco: As Marchese (1, 182) notes, a beautiful Dantesque hendecasyllable.

(anni per me pesante): Originally, "anni per me pesanti" (heavy years for me); the more complex revision actively contrasts the predicaments of father and son, underscoring Montale's uncomfortable awareness (as in the G.B.H. poems of the 'FLASHES' E DEDICHE, written the following year) of his own massive corporality, which here separates him from his parent and Clizia, both of them gone from his world.

interito: Tuscan dialect: paralyzed or stiff, with a deathly undertone; a ghoulish pun. Marchese (1, 183): "The poet's encounter with his father recalls Aeneas' meeting with Anchises in the presence of the Sibyl or Dante's with his great-great-grandfather Cacciaguida in the presence of Beatrice. But the dialogue between living and dead doesn't take place here, nor does the son come to know the sense of his life, nor is he invested with any mission. From the dismay of the father, who fears he will be forgotten by his children, and from Clizia's harsh address, one can understand the meaning of this mysterious dialogue between the shades: the woman assumes the superego role that is proper to the father, condemning a useless and too-private memory."

In fact, Clizia's speech was originally delivered by the father; the "giunta" of line 41 was "giunto" (which explains the use of the Tuscan colloquialisms "interito" and "funghisce," intended to reflect the father's earthiness). To Almansi and Merry (103), Montale's "cavalier shift . . . shows that the most cherished messages of the poems emerge from formal rather than psychological preoccupations"; but the opposite interpretation seems more valid.

amor di Chi la mosse e non di sé: Cf. Beatrice to Virgil, *Inferno* II, 72: "Amor mi mosse, che mi fa parlare" (Love moved me and makes me speak). Note the use of "forse" above; the poet is not certain that Clizia will achieve the resurrection of the body, though in life she was inspired by the Unmoved Mover that is Christian *caritas* or *agape*.

al nuovo balzo: The new leap of faith which Clizia, in the next lines, exhorts the ghost of Montale's father to risk in divesting himself of his earthly attachments. Cambon (104) notes that the term recalls the "balze," or terraces, of Mount Purgatory, which "sometimes have to be conquered by some 'leap' with divine or angelic assistance. . . . What is involved here is a progress of the soul after death, an approximate equivalent of the purgation process on which *Purgatorio* so splendidly depends. . . . The 'jump' Montale's father is supposed to be taking before long corresponds in its way to the hard passage through the wall of flame in *Purgatorio* XXVII, which will lead to the harrowing but deeply yearned-for reunion with Beatrice. . . . It is possible to surmise that the outcome of the 'new jump' after the long period of 'unfleshing' or purification would be some kind of spiritual perfecting, the 'fulfillment of [individual] inexplicable life' that the Montalian persona invoked for his beloved dead ones and for himself in 'Proda di Versilia.' "

—*Ho pensato per te* . . . : Cf. Montale's comment in "Intentions" (*Sec*, 304) that Clizia "pays for all, expiates all." Cambon (106–7): "What [Clizia] figures forth . . . is the culmination of the entire purgatorial process for the father's reluctant soul, and implicitly for any other. . . . She urges him to transcend himself by leaving behind the part of his being that is definitely closed and unsusceptible to further development . . . just as Dante, once he has completed his purifying climb through Purgatory's terraces, and thereby shed his carnal weight, will take leave of Virgil and undergo a lustral immersion in Lethe [the river of forgetfulness] and Eunoe [the river of good memory] so that he can finally fly into Heaven under Beatrice's guidance." Is it not then plausible by extension that Montale is exhorting himself, attempting under Clizia's aegis, as he tried to do on his own in " 'Ezekiel saw the Wheel . . . ,' " to free himself of his memories of her, which are no longer fruitful? Cambon conducts a detailed analysis of the theme as developed in the story "Sul limite" in *Farf*, and quotes one character saying, "I wanted something in my life that was *finished*, do you understand me? something that would be eternal by dint of being finished." (See also "Sulla spiaggia" in *Farf* [Macrì 1, 144–45].)

abiezione / che funghisce su sé: Mengaldo (102) gives this as an example of the progressively abstract metaphorical reformulation of a term used more concretely, though also metaphorically, earlier on, in this case in "Il ritorno" ("funghire velenoso d'ovuli").

Il vento del giorno . . . : The closing lines break into Clizia's speech, much as the poet's ecstatic asseveration of victory interrupts the catalogue of dessication of "La primavera hitleriana," and the poet's vision fades, leaving his father unfulfilled. For Cambon (118), "the Montalian persona's hesitation to venture out into the wide open space (sea or sky) that is the locus of becoming, and his attendant nostalgia for the womblike enclosures (or for the safe terra firma), is at the center of his existential dilemma: To become or not to become? To be reborn or not to be reborn? Agoraphobia may even make him retreat into the sheltering womb of nonbeing." (Cf. the poet's similar indecisiveness in "Su una lettera non scritta" and elsewhere, here projected onto his father—another male incapable of flight.)

"Voce giunta con le folaghe" does not leave Montale's father in heaven, as his poems for his mother ("A mia madre") and sister ("Madrigali fiorentini," II) do, even if they are heavens of their own construction, but rather in an ongoing purgatorial limbo. Baldissone (52), a psychoanalytic interpreter who sees the shadow figure here as representing the poet's mother, suggests that the poem "tends to liberate him from his father forever, separating him from his children as if through the operation of a maternal choice." (Cf. in MEDITERRANEO "the rancor / that each son feels for his father.")

il vuoto inabitato . . . : Montale (Angelini 3, 174): "The uninhabited void created in us just before we exist or before we say yes to life: the void created in the clock just before the hour strikes." (The statement recalls the "whirring" that "spreads around me, / like clockworks when the hour's about to strike" in "Incontro"; cf. also the "sheer void" that is "the space that had opened for me" in "Il balcone.") To Arrowsmith (3, 199), the void is "the inexpressible X that precedes images or words, the X from which we come and into which we vanish. We remember it darkly only when we cease remembering; then, if at all, we *sense* it growing inside us, a fate that depends on us (as God depends on his believers, like Clizia) to confront and freely define. The ancient Greeks would have called that void Chaos . . . , not so much anarchic disorder as the matrix of the possible—the undifferentiated " 'ditch' of things." It is this "original generative 'Void'" [of the "Mothers" of "Nel Parco di Caserta"]" (Cambon, 116) that lies at the bottom of Montale's wells and pools, out of which the images of memory rise (see note to "Il gallo cedrone" for discussion of the source of the image in the ditch by the Montale house in Monterosso described in "Flussi," "Punta del Mesco," and elsewhere). (Cambon also compares the ending of the poem to the close of "Notizie dall'Amiata," with its "millrace . . . silting.")

What is being described here is a Proustian outburst of memory, the madeleine here being the cry of the coots, which somehow recalls his father to the poet. Such outbursts are the engendering "occasions" of Montale's poetry, often aroused by the smallest "signs": two jackals on a leash, a fan, the snapshot of "Verso Siena." Almansi and Merry (104): "Before these very lines could be written . . . the coots had to cry so that a voice could come across from another world. . . . The poem ends with a series of dots [as do "La primavera hitleriana," "Per un 'Omaggio a Rimband,'" and other Montale texts of this period, indicating uncompleted action] because other sounds and triggers, other small beasts and names and objects must exert the 'scatto del ricordo' before the poet can re-discover the world of his verse; before the world of his past can catch up with him, become his habitat again."

L'ombra della magnolia . . . / The Magnolia's Shadow (1947)
When it was published in *Le Tre Venezie* in late 1947, the poem had a subtitle in parentheses, "Altra lettera non scritta" (Another Unwritten Letter) (cf. "Su una lettera non scritta"). By now, the possibility of union with Clizia is long past, and the poet is faced with "the harder way" of life in the postwar "Big Freeze": "factional, often brutal ideologies, industrialization and industrialized values, mass culture" (Arrowsmith 3, 200). The protective shade of the magnolia, symbol of family life to which Montale returns again and again in *La bufera*, is diminishing as the poet's memory fades (as in "Nel parco"), and the cicada at its top (cf. "Incantesimo," with which this poem has other affinities) sings alone. Arrowsmith (3, 200): "The imagery is once again Platonic, intended to recall the paradisal summer setting of the *Phaedrus*, with its great plane tree filled with shrilling cicadas whom Socrates calls 'the mouthpieces of the Muses.'"

il tempo dell'unìsono vocale: The totalitarian unity of the "boundless power" of Fascism and, more generally, "the historically recurrent waves of mass irrationalism that may submerge the human polity at any age, not just the Fascist one" (Cambon, 147); but also the "easy" unity of a society joined in opposition to totalitarianism (cf. the equivocal "single roar" of "Palio" and "the harmonized / shout of noon" of "Barche sulla Marna"). The direct invocation of Clizia links the poem with "La primavera hitleriana," the only other place in *La bufera* where she is addressed by name. From the disillusioned perspective of 1947, the hopes for universal liberty given voice there now appear naive, another "premature synthesis" like RIVIERE. Cambon notes that the "unìsono vocale" is opposed by the "lone" voice of the poet/cicada.

rinsangua: Literally, replenishes with blood.

morire / al primo batter d'ale: Cf. the battles of "Il ventaglio."

un trastullo: Cf. the "facile giuoco" of "Il balcone."

la via più dura: Cf. Montale's 1944 essay "Augurio" (tr. in *Sec*, 9–11): "In the war which may be about to cease . . . it was relatively easy for us Italians to orient ourselves from the beginning. Even against our apparent interest, it was easy to intuit that the war would be lost *by those who were in the wrong*. . . . But imagine a war of the worlds for our children or grandchildren in which that kind of certainty was lacking: . . . a war which seemed like nothing more than a toss of the dice on the green table of history."

consunta / dal sole e radicata . . . : A catalogue of images of Clizia, first as earthbound sunflower and then as unfettered bird. Cf. the "spring drunk with the sun, / drunk by the sun" of RIVIERE. The "cold banks of your river" invoke the scenery of "Iride." Cambon (146) says that "the creeping cold has to do with the devitalizing climate of modern Western society," now congealing into the Cold War of "red cleric or black."

zenit nadir cancro / capricorno: A typically condensed late Montalean catalogue "with a quite Dantesque ring" (Cambon, 147).

tuo Sposo: Clizia's nunlike marriage to Christ is of another order than Volpe's to her God in "Incantesimo." Clizia's inflexibility in contrast with the omnipresent "rest," which parallels the poet's rejection of the "unìsono vocale," is otherworldly, while the exhausted poet ("the empty husk") describes himself in terrestrial, mortal terms. The "oltrecielo" (note the rhyme with *gelo*—the only one in this willfully antilyrical yet grandly rhetorical poem) by which she is being drawn is associated with death, but the poet hurls himself into it in a gesture, perhaps suicidal, that is ironically reminiscent of the "leap" of "Voce giunta con le folaghe," which his father could not make. (Cf. also the tormented question at the close of "Il ventaglio"—"Must he who sees you die?"—now despairingly answered here.) Cambon (148): "One cannot dwell in transcendence (unless one is the transfigured entity Clizia has become), one can only touch it and die." Yet the mullet's hurling prefigures the life-seeking thrust of "L'anguilla."

La lima che sottile / incide tacerà: Cf. "Clivo": "la lima che sega / assidua la catena che ci lega." Cambon sees this, like the "vuota scorza," below, as a reference to the poet's own voice. Arrowsmith (3, 200) cites Ecclesiastes 12:1–5: "Remember now thy Creator in the days of thy youth, while the evil days come not, nor the years draw nigh, when thou shalt say, I have no pleasure in them; . . . in the day when the keepers of the house shall tremble . . . and the grinders cease because they are few, and those that look out of the windows be darkened, . . . when the sound of the grinding is low, and he shall rise up at the voice of the bird, and all the daughters of music shall be brought low; also when they shall be afraid of that which is high, and fears shall be in the way, . . . and the grasshopper shall be a burden, and desire shall fail: because man goeth to his long home."

l'oltrecielo: Macrì (1, 108) calls this and similarly formed words—*oltretempo* in "Voce giunta con le folaghe," *oltrecosta* in "Nubi color magenta . . ."—hispanisms, and quotes Pietro Bigongiari, who says *oltrecielo* and *oltretempo* derive from Juan Ramón Jimenez's "Animal de fondo."

Addio: Farewell, but also literally, "to God," Clizia's destination, where the poet cannot follow.

Il gallo cedrone / The Capercaillie (1943)

In a letter of June 7, 1949 (*Op*, 967), Montale sent Contini an English translation (erroneously identified in *Op*, which prints it, as Montale's own; it has since been recognized [Barile 3, 53] as the work of Elemire Zolla). Montale dedicated the poem to his Florentine friend Guido Peyron, "painter and cook," who taught him how to paint.

Arrowsmith (3, 201): "The capercaillie (*kăp' erkāl'yē*) . . . (*Tetrao urogallus*) is the largest European grouse; the adult male reaches thirty-four inches in length and weighs as much as twelve pounds. . . . Generally gray, its breast is a brilliant metallic blue-green (hence its Italian name, *gallo cedrone*, or 'citron cock'). At mating time he perches on the topmost branch of a tree, challenging all rivals with 'a guttural retching cry' (R. T. Peterson), while the hens below await the results. Nests are laid on the ground and contain seven to nine marbled eggs. The bird's flight is brief and noisy, in short, the heavy, lumbering flight with which the heavyset Montale felt psychic and physical affinity."

For Lonardi (172), the poem is about "a regal animal, a Jove torn away from his domain—the domain of the air and the wind (and the woods)—and humiliated, forced to the naked earth, to the mud, to 'sink in this mire.' . . . The self identifies with this sacred animal, rendered divine . . . but dispossessed, condemned, the 'heavy flight' of the self who 'tries lumbering over a wall' in vain is not even truly reducible to a flight that is only metaphoric, only analogical, so much is it identified with the grouse's last attempt at life."

Much of the criticism of the poem, as above, focuses on the poet's identification with the wounded bird; but it would be uncharacteristic for his "tu" not to be somehow directed to another. Lonardi (180): "There is . . . a kind of double bridge, highly structured and, more than metaphoric, urgently and traumatically allegorical, that goes from the dying woodcock to the self, and from the self to the equally feathered, if exhaustingly vital, apparitions of the flying figures of the Feminine"—though here, of course, Montale's bird figure lacks the transcendence it achieves when associated with the female, especially Clizia. Zambon (27–43) offers a remarkable discussion of Montale's "obsessive" association of his principal feminine figures with the image of the wounded or sacrificed animal, usually a bird—an identification here also extended to the poet himself—and its sources in the poet's childhood experience.

In the late poem "Annetta" (D71/2), Montale writes:

> Altra volta salimmo fino alla torre
> dove sovente un passero solitario
> modulava il motivo che Massenet
> imprestò al suo Des Grieux.
> Più tardi ne uccisi uno fermo sull'asta
> della bandiera: il solo mio delitto
> che non so perdonarmi.

(Another time we climbed to the tower / where often a solitary thrush / modulated the theme that Massenet / lent his Des Grieux. / Later I killed one perched on the flagpole: / the only crime / I can't forgive myself.)

And in another late work, "Una malattia" ("A Malady" in *Oth*, 141), he reconfesses his crime: "I've killed only two robins / and a 'solitary thrush' half a century ago / and even if the judge turns a blind eye / I cannot do the same / afflicted as I am with the incurable / unpardonable malady / of pity."

As Zambon shows, the association of feminine figures with a sacrificially wounded bird goes back to Arletta/Annetta. The identification is clarified in the long 1923 "Lettera levantina," the first of the poet's letter-poems, addressed to Arletta, which remained unpublished until *Alt* (tr. in *Oth*, 103–9):

> Forse divago; ma perché il pensiero
> di me e il ricordo vostro mi ridestano
> visioni di bestiuole ferite;
> perché non penso mai le nostre vite
> disuguali

senza che il cuore evochi
sensi rudimentali
e immagini che stanno
avanti del difficile
vivere ch'ora è il nostro.
Ah intendo, e lo sentite
voi pure: più che il senso
che ci rende fratelli degli alberi e del vento;
più che la nostalgia del terso
cielo che noi serbammo nello sguardo;
questo ci ha uniti antico
nostro presentimento
d'essere entrambi feriti
dall'oscuro male universo.

(Perhaps I digress; but because / thinking of me and remembering you awakens / visions of little wounded animals; / because I never think of our / disparate lives / but my heart evokes / old rudimentary feelings / and images that stand out / in the difficult life / that is ours now. / Oh, I know it, and you feel it, too: / more than the feeling that makes us brothers to the trees and wind; / more than the nostalgia for the clean sky / that we held in our look; / this has united us, / our ancient sense / of having both been wounded / by the dark universal ill.)

The poet's identification with the wounded animal/bird is thus "rudimentary." But there is something more: the association of Arletta as well with a hurt, sacrificed bird, which expands to encompass all of Montale's heroines, seems to derive from a sense of unexpiated guilt on the poet's part. In the "Lettera levantina" he and Arletta are united in their understanding of the world, and the poet (as in "In limine" of 1924) conceives of his own role as oblatory, enabling the beloved to escape constricting necessity. By the time of "Incontro" (1926), however, Arletta is "drowned," and the poet is looking to be saved himself through the agency of an apparition, a phantom. The inference to be drawn is that the poet, for unstated reasons, feels a share of responsibility for her demise. Earlier in "Lettera levantina," Montale describes a childhood hunting expedition with a group of boys, one of whom shoots a bird (a 1947 story, "La busacca" [*Farf*, 32–36], gives a more lighthearted version of a similar event [the bird escapes]); he tells us, too, that Arletta's father was a hunter. The association of masculinity with the infliction of suffering thus underlies his conception of female victimhood. Zambon (41): "As a male, Montale shares responsibility for the sacrifice of the female; yet at the same time he identifies with the victim in whose sacrifice he is implicated." (Zambon notes a similar identification in "Il sogno del prigioniero": "I've become / the flight of the moth my sole / is turning into powder on the floor.") See note to "L'anguilla" for further discussion of the theme of the sacrificial animal.

Lonardi (173) notes "Il gallo cedrone"'s relationship in form (four four-line stanzas, structurally reminiscent of the *ossi brevi*) and in theme to Baudelaire's "L'Albatros" ("Le Poète est semblable au prince des nuées / . . . Exilé sur le sol au milieu des huées, / Ses ailes de géant l'empêchent de marcher" [The Poet is like the prince of the clouds / . . . Exiled on the ground in the midst of the shouting, / his great giant's wings prevent him from walking]). Montale, however, intensifies Baudelaire's poet/bird analogy into a total allegorical identification. For Lonardi, too, the image is linked to a childhood trauma associated with the shooting of a bird, a theme (see Grignani) that surfaces in Montale's late poetry. He also sees (183) signs of an oedipal struggle: "the infantile introjection of the Father as *vir*, as absolute power and kingliness; the agonizing death scene of the cock is at the same time also the scene of the death of a sacred and beloved part of the self and a sort of exorcism of salvation, exorcism insomuch as it involves that part, the infantile-omnipotent part, of the self."

la tua voce ribolle . . . : Cf. *Inferno* XIII, 42–43, where "words and blood" issue simultaneously from Pier della Vigne. Barile (3, 55) notes that the poem "oscillates continually between the two poles of painting and cooking."

rossonero / salmì: Barile (3, 55): "A coloristic-culinary notation . . . but also mystical, because the *salmì*, a method of cooking at a low flame until the ingredients amalgamate, at which Peyron was expert, is here an amalgam of 'sky and earth,' the colors of sky and earth mixed together (but why the sky? There's no blue in the red-black ragout, even if the wing refers by metonymy to flight and the sky), and in fact it is the nature of the bird, which belongs to the air and is now crusted over in the fire of cooking and the earth, and in the end its most profound mark, its emblem, the totemic nature of its being which unites in itself terrestrial nature with the divine—like the centaur of Maurice de Guérin—or Christ, or man."

nel fosso: Lonardi (176): "It's a word ready to be invested with memory and infantile suggestion; no more nor less than the muddy 'botro' in the adjacent 'L'anguilla.' . . . Both designate the ditch [*solco*], sometimes dry, sometimes mucky, that ran next to the house at Monterosso." Lonardi cites the 1950 story "Il bello viene dopo" in *Farf*: "The 'she' whom 'he' tells about his childhood, of garden warblers hunted and eels speared in the ditch, has already diagnosed a devotion to childhood as irrepressible as it is injurious in her companion: better that something carry away 'the memory of everything. Later—she says—you would be like a woman who has jumped over the *fosso*, who no longer fears anything. But you want to stay inside, in the *fosso*; to fish there for the eels of your past.' " Lonardi also cites other loci where the "fosso" represents the dwelling-place of memory—"Nel sonno," "Voce giunta con le folaghe"—but the image is woven into the very fabric of Montale's poetry, starting with naturalistic description in "I limoni" and "Fine dell'infanzia" (though it is invariably linked with the motion of descent), gathering metaphoric intensity in "Flussi" and the penultimate motet, and recurring almost obsessively in *La bufera* (see "La bufera," "Il giglio rosso," "Ballata scritta in una clinica," "L'anguilla"). Though the contexts change, the image is constant.

Era più dolce . . . : The construction parallels "Spendersi era più facile . . ." in "L'ombra della magnolia. . . ." The evocation of "living" here is congruent with Montale's nostalgia about the past, particularly the familial world of *Ossi di seppia*, which this poem recalls in its structure and in numerous references, and its association with cooking and thus with the kitchen, the heart of the home (in "Proda di Versilia" the poet tells us he slept next to the kitchen as a child). (Lonardi [177] notes affinities with "In limine" [cf. the key relation "vento-vita"; also the "muro," below], while the imagery of mud and roasting anticipates aspects of "Il sogno del prigioniero.") The opposition of a vital "then" with a degraded and destructive "now" is characteristic of this phase. Marchese (1, 186): "The opposition 'vento-limo' is evidently emblematic, as in Baudelaire's 'L'Albatros': it indicates not only the desacralization of poetry in the modern world, the fall of the crown, the exile of the artist among men like an uncrowned king; but it also alludes (if one takes as an explicit context 'L'ombra della magnolia . . .' [cf. "Spendersi era più facile . . ."]) to the post-resistance disillusionment of the poet, which will also involve the Clizian faith in salvation for all."

Sento nel petto . . . : Barile (3, 55): "Always, the throat and chest are the loci of the wound and illness" (cf. "Ballata scritta in una clinica").

il mio pesante volo . . . : As we've seen, in the 1948 poems for G.B.H. in the 'FLASHES' E DEDICHE and elsewhere, the poet refers frequently to his weight, and to his inability to fly. Here, in a kind of parody of Clizia's supernatural flight in the preceding poem (the reference to "frosted holly" certainly evokes her), the poet-bird is similarly earthbound, nontranscendent, and, as in "L'ombra della magnolia . . . ," "the attempt to breach [the distance between the poet and her means] condemning oneself to failure and death" (Luperini 1, 158). Marchese (1, 186): The "muro-volo" pair "repropose again the dualism necessity-freedom (miracle), prison-escape, in a context of renewed historical-existential pessimism, where one realizes the impotence of poetry to raise itself beyond the mediocre contingencies of a reality that is already 'mire,' 'mud,' and which will reveal itself . . . ever more degraded and rotten (hence Montale's comic-scatological language [in his late poetry])."

qualche piuma sull'ilice brinata: Cf. "Alla maniera di Filippo De Pisis . . . ," where the "cold balsam" has the same function as the "frosted holly" here. Also the "piume stroncate" in "Per un 'Omaggio a Rimbaud.' "

Zuffe di rostri . . . : An ecstatic reprise of "living," derived, Lonardi (185) suggests, from a 1942 poem by De Pisis, "Il fagiano bianco" (The White Pheasant): "(oh lotte nei boschi / taciturni e lontani! [oh struggles in the silent, / distant woods!])." As he (178) notes, "the evocative and gently optative developments occur in the even quatrains; while the uneven ones are more situational and in the present tense." Luperini (2, 177) sees a reference to Hopkins's "The Windhover": "Brute beauty and valour and act, oh air, pride, plume, here / Buckle!"

marmorate, divine!: The variegated eggs are a "sign of the divine, variegated being of things and nature" (Barile 3, 55). Cf. "La bellezza cangiante" (*QuaT*), Montale's own translation of Hopkins's "Pied Beauty." Barile (3, 57) suggests that the exclamation point derives from the last lines of Hopkins's "God's Grandeur": "Because the Holy Ghost over the bent / World broods with warm breast and with ah! bright wings." Montale copied Hopkins's poem into a 1943 notebook.

gemma: The word in Italian means both "jewel" and "bud." Macrì (1, 105) demonstrates that the "gemma" is the jewel of "La primavera hitleriana," whose "seed" has produced these "perennials": "The jewel belongs to Clizia, or is she herself."

luccica al buio: For Barile (3, 55), recalls the "Clizian" "luce-in-tenebra" of "Eastbourne." Cf. "lucore o buio" in "La bellezza cangiante."

Giove è sotterrato: Lonardi (184) identifies the allusion to Carducci's celebrated sonnet "Dante," the last line of which reads, "Muore Giove, e l'inno del poeta resta" (Jupiter dies, but the poet's hymn lives on)—a reference to Virgil, Dante's great type and predecessor, and the god he hymned, dead now like the god of Dante himself; what survives is his testament of faith, in the form of his poetry. Montale himself quotes the line, to negate it, in "L'èlan vital" in *D71/2*: "Muore Giove, Eccellenze, e l'inno del Poeta / NON resta." The assertiveness of the self-presentation, even given its intended irony, is remarkable, and indicative of the depth of the narcissistic injury the poet is expressing. Cf. his (putative) reference to himself as "Dio diviso / dagli uomini" in "Anniversario."

For Luperini (1, 157), the perennials' jewellike buds represent "the hope for survival"; for Lonardi (184), they are a symbol of potential renewal; the hymn, i.e., the poet's work, lives on in "Il gallo cedrone" in the "bruco," the larval form of the winged moth—an alle-gorical transmogrification of the chrysalis of Montale's early poetry, which glows in the dark —like the minimal glimmer of the "mother-of-pearl snail's trace" of "Piccolo testamento," the potential form of the "divine" marbled eggs that represent the poetic achievements of the past. "Jove" is underground, dead to the world, but not perhaps entirely extinct, as Arrowsmith (3, 203) suggests (after all, the gods are immortal); his poetry, at the very least, glows with the promise of a future.

L'anguilla / The Eel (1948)

Montale's best-known and most-loved poem, generally regarded as a high point of the modern Italian lyric. It is composed of one sentence (as are other poems and parts of poems, going back as far as "Corno inglese"); there are few end rhymes, but copious internal rhymes and assonance, particularly around the double *l* of *anguilla: capello, gorielli, ruscelli, scintilla, sep-pellito, brillare*, and, most resonantly in the last lines, the rhyming *gemella, quella*, and *sorella*.

Giorgio Orelli (Cima, 86) quotes Silvio Ramat's observation (*Montale* [Firenze: Vallecchi, 1965], 211) that the poem "is all one comparison: on the one hand, the negative aspects (cold seas, downstream flood, rock, mud, stagnant pools, dried-up brooks, drought, desolation, char-coal, buried stump, mire), on the other, the series of signs of life (siren, light, glimmering, torch, whiplash, arrow of Love, Edens of generation, life, spark, rainbow, shining; and 'from branch to branch' and 'from twig to twig' are also *positive*): the terms of the two series of oppositions are often located close together so that the animating force of the poem should quickly become apparent."

Arrowsmith (3, 204–5) emphasizes that the eel should not be read as essentially phallic, but that it incorporates both sexes, incarnating an "undifferentiated 'life force'" akin to Berg-son's *élan vital* (one possible source for the poem is Dylan Thomas's "The Force That Through the Green Fuse Drives the Flower," translated by Montale in 1946): "The eel's progress might be called a Bergsonian miracle performed in the teeth of necessity; both transcendence and immanence are in it. . . . Bergson's commonest metaphor for the movement of the spirit is a stream that carves its way through rock, but is inevitably shaped by the rock in turn. . . . In [his] words: 'Spirit borrows from matter the perceptions on which it feeds and returns them to matter in the form of movements which it has stamped with its own freedom.' . . . 'The Eel,' then, should be viewed as a cosmic love-poem, an account of the phylogeny of the human spirit as well as a dithyramb to the woman who inspired it," or, as Lonardi (101–2) puts it, "the anabasis of the Anima, in the Jungian sense, of its author" and "the maximum point of ascent in Montale's entire existential-poetic novel."

For Arrowsmith, Montale's inspiration is Clizia, though the eel also seems to encompass the chthonic, pagan attributes of Volpe; Montale told Ramat (Lonardi, 182–83): "Fu lei anche l'anguilla ma avrebbe potuto essere quell'altra" (She [Clizia] was the eel as well, but it could have been the other one [Volpe]). (Montale did not meet Maria Luisa Spaziani until 1949, but, as we have seen above, the counter-Clizian Volpe is already becoming flesh in the poems for G.B.H.) "L'anguilla" is the fruit, and, in its location at the end of the SILVAE, the culmination, of Montale's tendency to merge the feminine figures of the post-FINISTERRE poetry in a fusion of immanent and transcendent experience. Zambon (36) notes that the *gallo cedrone* and *anguilla* replicate the two dishes, the garden warbler and the eel (*capitone*), "on the mythical infantile menu" of "Il bello viene dopo" (see below), while Cambon (155–56) points out the long-standing contrapuntal relationship and "strange tension" in Montale between fish and bird images, representative of "water and air, silent amniotic enclosures and perilous open spaces": "two expressions of vitality, the subliminal and the sublimated, the whence and the whereto. They may conflict as in 'L'ombra della magnolia . . . ,' or they may coexist, as in 'Dora Markus' and 'Proda di Versilia'; in 'L'anguilla' the fish icon overpowers its rival . . . life affirmation versus transcendence." ("L'anguilla" was originally intended to precede "Il gallo cedrone.")

To Zambon (106), the poem "is, perhaps, without appearing so, the most achieved refiguration Montale has offered of his own poetry"—he notes (116) that "L'ANGUILLA is an anagram of LA LINGUA"—"it incarnates perfectly that ideal of the 'short long poem [*poema*]' . . . which Montale theorizes about especially in 'Let's Talk about Hermeticism' [*Sec*, 291–94] and which expresses the tendency toward an objectification without residues of sentiment, toward 'emotion which has become *thing*.' The creator of this poem, writes Montale, is 'the one who works his own poem like an object, instinctively accumulating meanings and metaphorical meanings, reconciling the irreconcilable within the poem so as to make it the strongest, surest, most unrepeatable correlative of his own internal experience.' " Zambon (112ff.) sees "L'anguilla" as "the perfect lyric synthesis" of Montale's early postwar views on poetry and its role in history, and compares it to the 1949 essay "Tornare nella strada" ("The Second Life of Art" in *Sec*): "This 'street' from which true art comes and to which it must return is nothing but a theoretical abstraction of the remote 'roads that lead to grassy / ditches [*fossi*] where boys scoop up a few / starved eels out of half-dry puddles' of 'I limoni.' . . . [The eel] represents precisely that 'life down here, the very life we have seen, known, and touched with our hands since the first years of childhood' ('Il mondo della noia' [1946] [*Auto*, 82])." Zambon (117) also quotes *QuaG* (17) (February 1917): "He who drags his feet in the mud and his eyes in the stars; he is the only hero; he alone is *alive*."

L'anguilla . . . : The eel as a figure in Montale's poetry goes all the way back, as we have seen, to "I limoni"; it appears also in the motet "La gondola che scivola. . . ." Typically, the image intensifies and becomes denser over time. Segre (137–38): "In *Farfalla di Dinard* the ditch of the eels becomes that of memory" (see Montale's remarks below). Luperini (1, 158): "In the eel the forces of instinct and the unconscious, always assimilated to the sea [in Montale], ally with those of stoic resistance, always assimilated to the earth. The eel is *anguis*, snake, a creature of the ground, mirebound and almost subterranean, but also pure marine energy, extreme inheritor of the vitality of Esterina [in 'Falsetto']. The attributes of ethicality and vitality unite in the sign of this fish-snake, an incarnate demon or, rather, a semi-pagan deity like the one adored by the bearded women of 'Elegia di Pico Farnese,' who in fact pray to a fish-god, encountering the disapprobation, then, of the poet, who contrasted them with the true ['Love'] of Clizia. . . . The situation, now, seems reversed, beginning with the use of the capital *L*, which in 'L'anguilla' denotes a profane love characterized by openly sexual symbols . . . : the eel is the arrow of Love on earth." And "the already-noted distancing of Clizia from God [and Christ], at least in his metaphysical dimension (which truly, for the poet, threatened to 'depreciate life'), is accompanied by a new quest for divinity. . . . The eel continues Christ *malgré lui*" (see note to "Elegia di Pico Farnese").

To Orelli's remark (Cima, 71) that Montale conflates characteristics of the salmon and the eel, the poet responds (Cima, 195–96): "It may very well be that I amplified the sphere of competence of the eel, but I was not aware of doing so. I know that eels make long journeys, but where they stop I truly can't say. Do they exist in the Baltic? Perhaps not; but there is the 'capitone,' which in Liguria is called 'grongo,' and is usually eaten sliced. . . . I don't know much about the salmon. On the other hand, I remember when, as boys, we fished for eels with a pitchfork, in a stream below the house. Several times we tried to light a fire to cook them; but they turned to charcoal."

The following passage from "Il bello viene dopo" (1950; *Farf*, 53–56), in which the eel, like the bird of "Il gallo cedrone," suffers a sacrificial death, is even more revealing (its imagery reminiscent of that of "Flussi," "Il ritorno," "Punta del Mesco," and other poems):

"The waiters went away and the man remained bent over the menu of dishes. 'Trout *au bleu*,' he said half-aloud. 'Sole *à la meunière*. Eel *alla livornese*.' Ah ah! No, it doesn't tempt me; but it reminds me of the muddy ditch that ran next to my house [see note to "Il gallo cedrone"]. Who knows if it's still there. It snaked, perhaps it still insinuates itself among rocks and canebrake and one can't get to the bank except at a few points. Whether or not it's true, if it has rained a lot, there are some pools of water, around which the washerwomen gather. But there are eels there, the best in the world. Rare, small, yellowish eels, difficult to see beneath the oily surface of the soap clouding the water. To catch one, you had to circle and edge one of those puddles with pieces of slate well stationed in the mud, then empty out the water in the palm of your hand and finally, before the water seeped in again, stand barefoot in the ditch and feel around among the pebbles and the decaying grass on the bottom. If the eel appeared and we had a pitchfork success was almost assured; a blow, and the eel, pierced and bleeding, was raised on high and then tossed on the bank, where it kept on writhing for a little while. Without a pitchfork, it was a serious matter; the eel slipped through our fingers, took refuge under a soap bubble, and disappeared. It took us half an hour of trouble to catch one twenty centimeters long, slimy, foul, half-gutted, inedible."

Zambon (60) also notes the phonic association *anguilla-angelo*, made use of by Montale himself in the 1969 poem "Sul lago d'Orta" (*QuaQ*) (in fact, "L'anguilla" as a whole could be seen as a tacit assertion of this analogy). Like Clizia in her incarnation as "donna-angelo," the eel "comes down from a north (both real and symbolic) covered with ice and mists . . . to a south devastated by war and evil [cf. the end of "La primavera hitleriana"] . . . a north-south itinerary which evidently corresponds to a descent from high to low, from heaven . . . to earth, with all the ethical and religious implications such a descent can assume." Zambon again (84–85): "If the eel then combines the angelic and celestial reverberations of Clizia with the earthly vitality of Volpe, if she condenses Beatrice and Antibeatrice, sacred and profane, transcendence and immanence, this provisional synthesis is achieved by means of the secret reapparition of a third figure, that of Arletta, who represents in a certain way also their common archetype or at least combines a knot of themes that tend to differentiate themselves in the two other principal female figures. . . . 'L'anguilla' thus marks, not only chronologically, the passage from Iride to Volpe, from the dream of a new 'dawn' of civilization for all to the desperate defense of a contingent and personal salvation, 'perdition and salvation' at one and the same time. But what makes possible this passage is the excavation of his own history to which Montale dedicates himself assiduously in the second half of the '40s and in particular the recuperation of the 'buried' figure of Arletta: 'L'anguilla' is the perfect success of this *repêchage*."

la sirena: Luperini (1, 160): "A pagan divinity, intermediary between men and gods, [who] lives like the eel both in the depths of the sea and on land, and holds the charm of song and of enchantment."

il Baltico: A glance in the direction of the cold north that is a constant association with Clizia.

gorielli: Versilian idiom (more usually *gorelli*) for rivulets; diminutive of *gora* (cf. "Notizie dall'Amiata," with its similar derivation of a message out of stagnation ["last ends of the earth"]); *botri*, too (cf. "Fine dell'infanzia"), is Tuscan, as are other similar words in the SILVAE, which represent, according to Luperini (1, 163), not only a return to the poet's "roots" but also Montale's recognition of "the need for a profound renewal of poetics as the one real alternative to the incumbent death of poetry."

il guizzo: Cf. "La trota nera"; here, however, the image has absorbed all the significance of Clizia's "flashes," as well as the "guizzo argenteo della trota / controcorrente" of "L'estate"; the eel thus also incorporates qualities of the "morta fanciulla Aretusa," i.e., Arletta. (See Orelli [87–89] for a discussion of the significance of the "guizzo" throughout Montale.)

torcia, frusta, / freccia d'Amore . . . : Marchese (1, 188) notes that these bisyllabic words allude to Cupid's attributes (arrows and torches) as well as describing the contorted, impulse-driven rising of the eel. "Amore," as we have seen, evokes "l'Amore," the poet's private amorous religion in "Elegia di Pico Farnese," only here it is the eel's sensual, earthbound love—"god and phallus . . . equivocally mixed together" (see Montale's June 9, 1939, letter in note to the "Elegia")—that is given pride of place. But Zambon (62) associates the figure of the arrow (and its arc), reinforced by the verb "scoccata," with the hunter Artemis/Diana, a figuration of Clizia (cf. "La frangia dei capelli . . .") and her precursors (e.g., Esterina).

morde l'arsura: Orelli (Cima, 76): "Among the most significant syntagms in Montale's poetry, almost the chiastic reversal of 'the death that lives' ('Notizie dall'Amiata'): alliterative syntagm, run through with Dantesque energy: 'morde,' as everyone senses, is 'morte' [death] with a simple relaxation of the dental; it hangs irresistibly back, toward 'acquamorta' [literally, dead water, ten lines above], . . . the most necessarily ambiguous conjunction of signs for the inevitable life-death relationship."

la scintilla . . . : Cf. similar imagery of rebirth out of ashes in "Luce d'inverno" and "Piccolo testamento." As Orelli notes (Cima, 77), this is the same moment of emergence as that of "life exploding from the drought" ("La farandola dei fanciulli sul greto"), the characteristic moment of epiphany in *Ossi di seppia*.

bronco seppellito: Cf. *Inferno* XIII, 26; also the "dry stalk" at the end of "Crisalide." Barile (3, 56) likens the spark to the "fresh firecoal chestnut-falls" (cf. also the allusion to the "castagni" above) of Hopkins's "The Windhover," noting that "sparks, coals, ashes [consistently associated in Montale with Clizia's religious function] . . . have a written tradition in English mystical and religious poetry, and particularly in Hopkins."

l'iride breve . . . : The "flash" of the eel evokes the rainbow, immemorial sign of man's compact with God, and also (cf. "Iride") its twin, Clizia's stilnovistic attribute, her flashing, jewellike eye (*incastonano* means, literally, "to set or mount"). Zambon (76) notes that the equivalence of the eel and the rainbow closes the arc of the SILVAE: "higher and lower arcs which reflect and alternate to 'continue' each other, which are inseparable as are 'immanence and transcendence' for Montale, but which can never be composed into . . . a totality."

nel tuo fango: Cf. the "limo," the "magma" of "Il gallo cedrone." The mud is "hers" because it is the "mire" of human existence in which Clizia finally becomes "endowed with flesh and blood" (Cambon, 159); she is "transmogrified into an earth goddess, more like Cybele or Venus than . . . Artemis," "a muddy Isis or Venus" (Sergio Solmi, *Scrittori negl'anni*, 307). (In the later Montale, mud becomes associated with meaning itself; in a 1969 poem, "Gli uomini che si voltano" [The Men Who Turn Back; an ironic nod to "Forse un mattino andando . . ."], the poet writes of Mosca, in a revisitation of "Iride": "Non apparirai più dal portello /

del aliscafo o da fondali d'alghe, / sommozzatrice di fangose rapide / per dare un senso al nulla" [You won't appear anymore at the door / of the hydrofoil or out of the depths of seaweed, / suscitator of rapid muddinesses / to give a meaning to nothingness]. And in "Dopo una fuga" [also 1969] he writes: "La poesia e la fogna, due problemi / mai disgiunti" [Poetry and the sewer, two problems / never unrelated].) Yet there is an echo here, too, of the fear of the female and her "muddy clutches" (Almansi and Merry, 109) that we find in the poems for G.B.H. in the 'FLASHES' E DEDICHE. Again, Almansi and Merry (110): "It is only the images of fish and mud seen *together* which can reveal the horror and mystery of this sexual union."

sorella: Luperini (1, 159): As the bearer of Love, and thus of value, the eel is Clizia's true "sister." "Her 'rainbow,' which survives even in the dryness of the desert (metaphor for the absence of values in contemporary society), alludes to the very fate of poetry, to its secret capacity for survival." Orelli (Cima, 87) notes that as "sister" to Clizia (who is herself referred to as the poet's own "strange sister" in "La bufera"), the eel is likened to the "desert flowers, your kin" of "Iride." (Contini [2, vii] has noted the importance of Montale's sister, Marianna, as the "precursor" of all the feminine figures in his poetry.) Sisterly, too, is the near-rhyme of *anguilla* and *sorella*, emphasizing the circularity of the underlying image of rebirth that animates the poem. Luperini (1, 161): "Instinctuality and vitality give a new meaning to death insomuch as they are born of the same root, in the Heraclitean circle which unites end and new beginning (a theme also central in Eliot's *Four Quartets*)."

Zambon (42–43) associates the eel with other sacrificial creatures (primarily birds) in Montale (see note to "Il gallo cedrone") and argues that it really symbolizes memory, that is, meaning: "That toward which 'L'anguilla' aims, though concealing it, is . . . its death, the culminating and ritual moment of sacrifice, described in ['Il bello viene dopo']." Lonardi (101–2): For the eel, "almost purified and sacralized in spite of herself by this mortal destiny, the long journey in water and mud becomes the metaphor for memory itself, for the obscure survival and mysterious return of the past; it is the very 'stigmata' of her passion that invest the eel with the profound message she carries: 'everything begins / when everything seems charcoal.'" At the climax of Montale's work, the eel and the wounded bird of "Il gallo cedrone" converge—as do the feminine figures Arletta, Clizia, and Volpe (see note on the "Madrigali privati")—to perform the action that is the central significance of Montale's poetry.

Zambon (14) notes that on first publication in *Botteghe Oscure* (July 1948), the poem was followed by a line of periods, "perhaps to suggest the possibility of a response," leading the way to the dialogic "Botte e risposte" of *Sat.*

VI. MADRIGALI PRIVATI / PRIVATE MADRIGALS

Montale (Greco, 48): "Here [in the MADRIGALI PRIVATI] the Antibeatrice appears, as in the *Vita Nuova*; like the 'donna gentile' [noble lady] whom Dante wanted to pass off as Philosophy [in the *Convivio*] though she supposedly was otherwise, since she aroused the jealousy of Beatrice."

Montale (Greco, 51): "The figure in the Madrigals is a counterfigure of Clizia in a profane key, but Clizia had died or disappeared forever." Montale (Cima, 194): "Clizia and Volpe are contrasted, one salvific, as one would say now, the other earthly . . . Dantesque, Dantesque."

As we have seen, the secular madrigal replaced the "rondels" of the *ossi* and the originally sacred motet as the lyric template for Montale's poetry after *Le occasioni* and FINISTERRE. The MADRIGALI PRIVATI represent the full flowering of this development; they are private because they evoke intimate experience intensely, and because the epiphanies and achievements they celebrate involve personal apotheosis, not the universal redemption promised by the "divine" love that inspired Clizia. For Almansi and Merry (113), the MADRIGALI are willfully noncommunicative, "folding themselves round in the most inscrutable protective barrier of autism. . . . They are insolent poems which do not want to be read at all and which oblige the reader to be insolent himself, to eavesdrop and bug the nostalgic mutterings of their author."

It is in the MADRIGALI that Volpe's figure acquires her essentially animal attributes; yet though innately "profane" in nature, as he puts it, as a Montalean icon she necessarily also offers transcendence; Arrowsmith (3, 207): "*Animal spirits* are her nature, yet she persistently displays signs of Clizia's spiritual power, while Clizia herself, in the closing lines of 'The Eel' is asked to recognize her affinity with her 'sister,' the incandescent eel."

As we have seen, Volpe, like Clizia, is a figure, a stilnovistic *senhal*, created out of various biographical and literary components, but primary among these is the poet Maria Luisa Spaziani. As a recent university graduate from Turin, the young writer (she was born in 1924) met Montale there on January 10, 1949 (Marcenaro and Boragina, 236), when he delivered a lecture, characteristically entitled "Poeta suo malgrado" (Poet in Spite of Himself). According to Spaziani (Spaziani, 323), the letters that Montale wrote her in the course of their relationship, which lasted until 1970, contain "many jokes, exercizes, acrostics, pastiches or various imitations of poets, both contemporary and from the past," often "studded with little drawings of 'volpi' [foxes] in flight and bears in pursuit ('Orso' was Montale's nickname in these letters)."

So che un raggio di sole (di Dio?) ancora / I know a ray of sun (of God?) can still (1949)
The first three madrigals, though published in *Botteghe Oscure* in 1949, were not included in the first edition of *La bufera*, though they were listed in the plan for *Romanzo* under the heading "Nel segno del trifoglio" (Under the Sign of the Clover).

The poem, finally added to *La bufera* in 1977 (a fact that underscores its private nature), is, as Cambon (167) calls it, "an anti-Motet of sorts, to celebrate presence and consummation," which resembles the contemporary "Sulla Greve" both in form and feeling. The ray of light here, rather than representing the absent beloved, becomes flesh itself, in another incidence of profane communion. These encounters always take place in "shadow," the realm of the carnal (cf. "Lasciando un 'Dove' "), and the transformations they involve are not sublimating but intensifying: the shadowy swallow's flight of "Sulla Greve" metamorphosing into the predatory attack of a hawk—a *senhal* of Volpe's elaborated in the poems that follow.

Hai dato il mio nome a un albero? Non è poco / You've named a tree for me? It isn't nothing (1949)
Also admitted to *La bufera* in 1977, this poem is, like the related "Per un 'Omaggio a Rimbaud' " (1950), a poem about poetics, celebrating (while also undermining) the naming function of poetry—an issue which goes all the way back to "Vasca" and "La farandola dei fanciulli. . . ." The poet rejects his beloved's attempts at characterizing him as an insensate object (a tree), and counters with a hectic catalogue, constantly metamorphosing because never adequate, of equivalents for her vitality—water, fire, breathing, etc.—each with a substantial heritage of its own in Montale's work. Yet it is Volpe's engendering presence (rather than her naming, i.e., poetizing, them?) that gives life to the things, i.e., to the world, that she labels:

the toad, flower, grass, and oak—which is also the poet himself—under whose protective shade (cf. "Nel parco," as well as "L'arca" and "Proda di Versilia") their amorous rites (represented in the clover's "fleshy petals" and the flaring fire) are enacted.

Se t'hanno assomigliato . . . / If they've compared you (1949)
Published with the first two madrigals in 1949, but added to the second Mondadori edition of *La bufera* in 1961. The poem expands the naming theme and its imagery ("the tree named after me") of the preceding poem into an ecstatic attempt at defining the "living oxymoron" (Cambon, 171–72) that is Volpe, "siren and redeemer in one"—as is the Clizia of "L'anguilla." (It is notable how often the poems for the poet Volpe revolve around issues of writing or expression.) The result is "the most dithyrambic effusion ever to issue from Montale's careful pen" (Cambon, 171).

For Almansi and Merry (114), who emphasize the hermetic qualities of the madrigals, the locales and details of the poem are unidentifiable and irrelevant (cf. the revisions to "Per un 'Omaggio a Rimbaud,' " where Montale first planned to insert a street name according to how it fit the meter of his line): "What use is it, for example, to know that the Cottolengo is a Turinese hostel for deformed children? The memories are personalized to such a degree that they do not admit of intrusion or intimacy. . . . The purpose is not to perform a self-analytic operation but rather to find an outlet for an overemotional passion, which explodes in the following lyric outbursts . . . a series of almost hysterical clusters of two or three lines, densely compact, sonorous, producing a total impression of unchecked lyric fulness. . . . In fact, none of these images are reasonable or justified. . . . The range of *signifiés* controlled by the solco-*signifiant* (lines 22–25) is a listing with abracadabra, incantatory qualities . . . hostile in practice to the carrying of any message except, when all is said and done, an exorcizing power." For Almansi and Merry, the "aesthetic force" of the "almonds" ("mandorle") of Volpe's eyes, as likewise with the "donnola/donna" pun, "is drawn from the audible rather than the visual qualities of the image," and thus, literally, is meaningless (cf. the similar pun, "l'amo/lamo," in "Per album"); the poem's "non-sense is a public fact, stated with astonishing emphasis" (115). Montale's imagery, however, has been "private" ever since the first poems of *Le occasioni*; if there is a difference here, it is one of degree. As the poet himself has emphasized, he always begins "with the real, [and is] incapable of inventing anything." Indubitably, the descriptive details of the poem are based on fact, and, as Almansi and Merry admit, "the poem accepts imports from other compositions: the fox, the bird's flight, the feathers, the fish, wings, embers, etc." As Cambon (176) puts it, "No matter how loose the connection between signifier and signified can occasionally turn out to be, the former never lets entirely go of the latter. . . . Semantic rarefaction is a far less typical occurrence than semantic condensation in Montale's poetical language. . . . Here indeed, after carefully testing the semantic possibilities of the term 'fox' vis-à-vis the very special woman that has elicited that analogical label from the limited wits of most people, the speaking persona impatiently discards the term as finally inadequate to the subtle task of denoting and connoting his nearly ineffable experience of the woman's identity."

Arrowsmith (3, 208–9), who sees the poem as "a good example of Montale's tradition-saturated (but not therefore intimidating or impenetrably erudite) allusive habits," describes it as "an antiphonal pendant to 'The Eel,' " which it equals in length and which, like it, consists of a single thirty-line "conditional sentence whose protasis ('If . . .') conveys the splendor and range of the Vixen's animal vitality, and whose apodosis . . . contains the poet's proclamation of her spiritual nature." Clearly, whether Montale wills it or not, the poem "reeks of meaning"; it would be impossible for him to divest the tools at his disposal of the signifying power they have acquired in a lifetime of poetic practice.

alla volpe: For the possible origin of the term, see note to "Da un lago svizzero."

felici, umidi e vinti: A revisiting of the first lines of "Crisalide," where the plants were "umide e liete."

lo strazio / di piume lacerate: For Grignani (69), the image suggests the earthbound Volpe's victory over her airborne competitors: "How not remember the hunting sacrifice of Arletta-the-blackcap or the more rarefied one of the 'perilous / harbinger of dawn' Clizia?"

all'immondo / pesce . . . : Arrowsmith (3, 209) sees the image as drawn from Plato's *Meno* (80a), where Meno compares Socrates to the stingray: "At this moment I feel you are exercising magic and witchcraft upon me and positively laying me under your spell until I am just a mass of helplessness. If I may be flippant, I think . . . you are exactly like the flat stingray that one meets in the sea. . . . My mind and lips are literally numb, and I have nothing to reply to you."

i ciechi: Recurrence of Montale's image of mankind at large as blind or otherwise insensate. His relation with Clizia, too, was that of a feeling, perceiving pair surrounded by "uomini-capri." Arrowsmith notes the reference to John (1:4–5): "In him was life; and the life was the light of men. And the light shineth in darkness; and the darkness comprehended it not."

le ali: Wings, to indicate Volpe's transcendent qualities (as in "Per un 'Omaggio a Rimbaud' "), thus ironically relating her to Clizia, as does the "incandescent forehead" below.

il solco: The furrow is, as noted elsewhere (cf. the last lines of "Palio" and of "L'orto"), a sign, a mark, of human presence—or, alternatively ("Il tuo volo," "Sulla Greve"), of the threatening mysteriousness of nature. Here Volpe's forehead is (Arrowsmith 3, 209) "marked with the 'signs' of her divinity . . . a veritable catalogue of the ambiguities of the poet's private religion of Love and the 'Stations of the Cross' it imposes upon him."

croce cresima . . . : Montale's most elaborate and ecstatic catalogue, matched only, perhaps, by that of "L'anguilla."

perdizione e salvezza: Cf. "marble / manna and destruction" in "La bufera"—a kind of similar condensed catalogue, in which Montale enumerates "the components of a character," that character being Clizia's. Here, as elsewhere, her attributes are being ironically absorbed into the figure of Volpe.

più che donnola o che donna: The pun implies that Volpe's animal *senhal* is meant to encompass her human nature, as the word *donnola* contains the word *donna*; but she is also "more," i.e., not only carnal but transcendent.

l'oro che porto . . . : The gold the poet carries is his potency, his vitality, his talent, his life-renewing offering to immortality, represented in the "ember" (cf. the ember of "L'anguilla" and the "gemma" of "Il gallo cedrone"). Cf. also "Lettera levantina" (1923) (tr. in *Oth*, 103–9): "Penso ai tempi passati / quando un cader di giorno o un rifarsi di luce / mi struggevano tanto / ch'io non sapevo con chi mai spartire / la mia dura richezza . . ." (I think of the past / when the end of a day or the return of light / hurt me so / that I never knew with whom to share / my hard wealth . . .). Also, the poet's riches evoked at the close of "Per album," below.

se, / lasciandomi, ti volgi dalle scale: The gesture rhymes with the closing image of "La bufera," in which Clizia, Eurydice-like, enters the dark; it also evokes the escalator of "Di un natale metropolitano," bearing the loved one inexorably down into the underground. Arrowsmith sees the stairs here as not Dantesque-purgatorial but, rather, an allusion to "the ladder or stairway that ascends from the love of beautiful bodies to the love of spiritual beauty itself" in Plato's *Phaedrus* (cf. the image of poetry as a stairway to God in "Siria"). "The Vixen's *semblable* is not Dante's transcendental Beatrice but the Platonic Diotima [cf. "Incantesimo"], for whom Eros and erotic transcendence are all rooted in the world, immanent, at least in their origin" (3, 209).

Le processioni del 1949 / The Parades of 1949 (June 7, 1949)
Montale to Contini (June 7, 1949) (*Op*, 969): "I've written a poem against the pilgrim madonna (recent Italian guise)." Several days later, the composition was sent to Contini with the title "Oltrepò" (Across the Po); according to Spaziani (322), it was meant to be part of a group of poems ironically labeled "Carmina Sacra" (Sacred Songs). In the Neri Pozza edition of *La bufera*, the poem was called "La primavera del '49" (Spring of '49), thus inviting comparison with "La primavera hitleriana." In that season, to mark the Catholic Church's consecration of Italy to the Virgin in preparation for the Holy Year of 1950 (Angelini 3, 175), and as part of its "anti-Communist crusade" (Luperini 1, 168), a weeping Madonna was carried in procession through northern Italy. The poem, which Montale, in a 1960 introduction to a Swedish translation of his poems, linked with "La primavera hitleriana," "Il sogno del prigioniero," and "Piccolo testamento" as "the testimony of a writer who has always rejected the clericalism that afflicts Italy today in its two opposing forms ('black' and 'red')" (*Sec*, 319), revisits the themes and concerns of the "Elegia di Pico Farnese" ten years later, once again disparaging the "love of bearded women," though the setting is now prosaic and suburban rather than feudal: a degraded, infernal landscape, redeemed only by the appearance of the loved one. Clizia is now Volpe, her apparitions actual rather than imagined; "il tuo istante / di sempre" recalls the "eternità d'istante" of "La bufera," but Volpe arises here, like the eel, out of the murky but generative canal (see note to "L'anguilla"), which recalls the "gora" of "Notizie dall'Amiata," the "gonfia peschiera" of "Il tuo volo," and other numerous representations of the omnipresent Montalean ditch; while the "soap bubble" evokes the "soapy slime" in the "ditch" of "Flussi." The "counter-Madonna" (Arrowsmith 3, 211), with the "furiously angelic" power of her animal vitality, dissipates the Holy Mother's pagan ("Cybele and her Corybants") rites.

   un rigurgito: Montale is decrying a return to the benighted religiosity so strongly critiqued in *Le occasioni*.

Nubi color magenta . . . / Magenta-colored clouds . . . (1950)
Originally titled "Il rosso e il nero" (the Stendhalian Red and Black). "Fingal's Cave" recalls the Scottish poems for G.B.H. (see "Argyll Tour"), while the anaphora at the beginning of the first and second stanzas anticipates the structure of "Luce d'inverno."

   pedala: Almansi and Merry (117–18): "The word is steeped in material immediacy, in the brute force of a heel pressing down on a bicycle pedal, yet at the same time it opens the gates of the fantastic, making way for dream flights, for the miraculous alternative, for the event which was not foredoomed. . . . Even a bicycle pedal, just like the pedal under a piano, can guide us to a greater profundity of music. . . . Montale's 'pedala, / angelo mio!' is a sentence from the poet's innermost resources, confirmed by a complete history of his lyric which has always strained toward this conclusion."

   angelo mio: Ironic reduction of the "angelic" to everyday erotic small talk—or vice versa.

dell'Agliena: "River near Siena" (Montale: Angelini 3, 175), with the erotic connotations characteristic of rivers in his work.

ala d'ebano: If Volpe is an angel, as she is described in the first stanza, she is revealed here as a dark one, in contradistinction to the brightness associated with Clizia (cf. the oppositions of "Lasciando un 'Dove' ").

Pafnuzio: Montale (Nascimbeni, 156): "[Volpe] was a young woman and from her came a character different from Clizia, a very earthly character. Confronted with the 'vixen,' I compared myself to Paphnuce, the monk who goes to convert Thaïs but is conquered by her. With her, I felt like an abstract man next to a concrete woman: she lived with all the pores of her skin. But I also received a feeling of freshness from her, the feeling above all of still being alive." Almansi and Merry assert (119–20) that Montale's source here is Anatole France's novel *Thaïs*, where, significantly enough, "the relationship between condemned savior and saved temptress is marked by the constant presence of a totem animal, the jackal . . . [which] is both a messenger of the devil and also a symbol of the woman, like the two jackals at Modena which conveyed a secret message" in the motet "La speranza di pure rivederti." For Almansi and Merry, France's novel attracted Montale because "it is all played out along an ambiguous line of demarcation between a metaphysical game and the parody of this game." They also see a reference to *Thaïs* in "Sulla colonna più alta," where Christ is supposed to stand on a pillar as the image-haunted Paphnuce does in the novel, becoming the first Stylite. They stress the ironic game-playing the poem involves, reminding us that neither France nor Montale "really believes in the erotic and metaphysical vortex which overwhelms their two protagonists."

un punto solo . . . : A favorite ambiguity (see note to "Elegia di Pico Farnese"). The image of union recalls the powerful evocation of breathing as spiritual communion in "Sulla Greve" and elsewhere.

della caverna: A reference to the "Fingal's Cave" of the first stanza, but also to both Plato's cave and "the cave of the instincts" (Angelini 3, 175). See also "Da un lago svizzero."

Per album / For an Album (1953)

Originally titled "Da un album ritrovato" (Out of a Found Album), the poem recapitulates the poet's life, from "daybreak" to "late" in terms of his search for his continually elusive "you." (Cambon [181] suggests that "Accelerato" is a precursor to the poem as "an essential narrative of the questioning persona's life from boyhood to maturity," which also "forecasts the mimetic pattern" of both "L'anguilla" and "Se t'hanno assomigliato . . . ," with their "drive of uninterrupted syntax to culminate in a question to the [unspecified] Thou.")

"Per album" is rich in allusions to the poetic history of Montale's relationship with Volpe. Remarkably, the beloved is described in terms that relate her both to the water-creature, the fish (the hook), and to the ethereal bird (the "piccionaia"; Montale also imagines himself as a pigeon in "Di un natale metropolitano"); she thus coalesces the characteristics of both poles of Montale's experience of the female (see note to "L'anguilla" on his fusion of the two figures in the late poems of *La bufera*).

l'amo: A fishhook, which in Ligurian dialect is *u lammu*, i.e., *il lamo*—a kind of baby talk, as it were. Likely a pun, as well, on "l'amo" (I love her).

guizzo di coda / . . . nei pozzi limosi: Clizia's sign in "L'anguilla."

dai colli monferrini: The hills of Monferrato, between Asti and Turin, Volpe's native ground.

larva . . . : Indicates Volpe's youthful, ephebic quality (cf. "Per un 'Omaggio a Rimbaud' "), while the "partridge" recalls "Il gallo cedrone." This fabulous "rosary"-list, descendant of the related chain in "L'anguilla," is the "fantastic nexus that binds childhood memories of the hunt, the world below, and the familial world of the kitchen, the 'bestiary' of memory and the 'bestiary' of love" (Zambon, 56–57). (Macrì [1, 124] compares the poem to "La busacca" in *Farf*, whose protagonist invents himself a zoo.)

gazzella zebù ocàpi: Rare, nearly otherworldly animals, heraldic *senhals* from the sacred bestiary of Montale's memory (see Zambon, 54ff.); cf. the jackals of the motets, the white ivory mouse of "Dora Markus," and elsewhere. In "Reliquie" (*Farf*, 156–60), the sick woman, a Mosca-like figure, says, "Our life is a bestiary, a seraglio even," and calls the okapi "that funny animal half ass and half zebra, whose memory you wanted to immortalize." (The okapi had been "discovered" by Julian Huxley, whom Montale knew in the late 1940s when Huxley was Secretary-General of UNESCO in Paris, and Montale was hoping to be appointed to the post of director of the organization's Section of Arts and Letters.) To the "him" in the story, however, it is "half ass, half zebra, half gazelle, half angel. An example unique in the world of a species believed to be extinct for centuries. . . . It trembles with terror if it sees humans: it's too delicate to exist among beasts like us." At the end of the story, a photograph of the okapi reveals "a curious beast with a wandering eye, a marvel that seemed to oscillate between a Bedlington terrier [see "Madrigali fiorentini"] and a badger, a pig and a roebuck, between a goat and the little ass of Pantelleria; maybe a mistake, a misprint that escaped from the Great Printer, but a paradise for the eyes, an ineffable hope for the heart."

il tuo volo: da una cucina: Zambon (57) sees a glancing evocation of the flight of the dove from the Ark after the flood. (See Zambon, 46–58, for an extended discussion of the importance of the kitchen as *"origin and center* of all human and poetic value" [as in "L'arca" (see note), "Dora Markus," "A Liuba che parte," "Elegia di Pico Farnese"].)

aperte per me solo: In the MADRIGALI PRIVATI, as their name implies, Montale recurrently emphasizes the personal, noncollective nature of his relationship with Volpe (see "Anniversario"). The flight of this dove brings not universal salvation but a message that has meaning for him alone.

tuo ciliegio: Volpe's cherry tree is analogous to the magnolia of the poet's childhood. The same tree reappears in "Incantesimo," written at about this time.

troppo ricco per contenerti viva: Isella (2, 227): "Already too full of the thought of you." Cf. "Notizie dall'Amiata": "La vita che t'affàbula è ancora troppo breve / se ti contiene!" and also "L'estate," with its reference to the "too much else" that "won't wriggle through the needle's eye," with its echo of Christ's prediction that it will be easier for a camel to pass through the eye of a needle than for a rich man to enter the kingdom of heaven. The formulation also recalls the "gold" the poet carries inside himself in "Se t'hanno assomigliato. . . ." Montale's line here fuses these images of abundance into a not-quite-rational image of emotional (and sensual) surfeit. Macrì (1, 122–23): "The flash of uncaught lightning remains in the mind (it couldn't be caught, but its light is necessary). Her absence 'alive' is compensated for, reclaimed and thus excluded, by her excessive presence in his memory."

Da un lago svizzero / From a Swiss Lake (1949)
Dated "September 1949" on first publication; republished with the additional explanation: "Ouchy [on Lake Geneva], September 1949." The first letter of each line forms an acrostic

on the letters of Maria Luisa Spaziani's name (see headnotes to the MADRIGALI PRIVATI). The poem, perhaps the most hermetic in Montale's work, conflates, Cambon (182) suggests, the poet's memory of World War I (cf. "Valmorbia, discorrevano il tuo fondo" and the motet "Brina sui vetri; uniti") with an erotically charged contemporary experience, perhaps a display of fireworks over Lake Geneva (Arrowsmith 3, 213), in the company of Volpe. The "ambiguous" (Cambon, 183) nature of the poem's imagery makes it difficult to decipher.

An earlier version, presumably from the papers of Maria Luisa Spaziani, was reproduced in *Il Giorno* (April 8, 1997, 18), and reads as follows:

Mia fucsia, mia volpe, anch'io fui il poeta
Assassinato che volle
Rompere il cielo sul folto
Intrico dove un tondo di zecchino
Accendeva il tuo viso, poi scendeva
Lentissimo fra porpora e zibetto.
Un punto solo che seguiva ansioso
Invocando la morte su quel tondo
Segno della tua vita aperta amara,
Atrocemente fragile e pur forte

Stasera in quella traccia
Pulsante in quella pista arroventata
Ancora reprecipita sul mio
Zero calamitato da un suo numero
In lui si perde e lo conserva.
Anitre nere a stormi con me cullano
Nell'alone lunare
Il mio dormiente idolo, fiore e volpe, fino all'alba.

(My fuchsia, my vixen, I too was the poète / Assassiné who wanted / To break open the sky above the tangled / Thicket where a sequined halo / Lit your face, then fell / Slowly among purple and civet. / A single point I followed anxiously / Calling out for death over that halo / Sign of your open bitter life / Abominably delicate yet strong. // Tonight in that pulsing / Track on that baking path / Again it falls back on my / Zero magnetized by one of its numbers / In which it's lost and saved. / Black ducks in flocks lull with me / In the halo of the moon / My sleeping idol, flower and vixen, until dawn.)

Mia volpe: Lonardi (66) suggests that Volpe's nickname may derive from René Char's *Feuillets d'Hypnos*, in which Char several times refers to "ma Renarde."

il 'poeta / assassinato': *Le poète assassiné* was the title of the last work of the French poet Guillaume Apollinaire, who died of a wound sustained in World War I. The reference, along with the warlike fire imagery, evokes Montale's own battle experience, but it also refers, no doubt, to the poet's condition as hopeless lover.

dove fa grotta: Cf. "Valmorbia, discorrevano il tuo fondo": "The bright nights were all a dawn, / and brought foxes ["volpi"] to my den." For the image of the cave as erotic locus, which it seems to suddenly become in line 4, cf. "Nubi color magenta. . . ."

un tondo di zecchino: Cambon (183) reports that Montale wrote him in 1980 that the image describes "a sunbeam filtered through the foliage"; cf. the fiery necklace in "Dal treno."

accendeva il tuo viso: The scene is reminiscent of the intense nearness of the beloved in "Nella serra" and "Nel parco."

toccare / un nimbo: Cf. the "last light crown of ashes" of "Stanze."

ove stemprarsi: The word rhymes with "bruciarsi" at the close of the poem, pairing the old "incendio" of the war and the new one of the poet's passion for Volpe—which here seems to threaten a kind of self-extinction.

invocavo la fine: Cf. "Ariete invocai" in "Ballata scritta in una clinica," likewise a poem with a wartime setting. Again imagery of battle blends into erotic blasphemy. The poet is in mortal danger, at the mercy of his merciless beloved.

atrocemente fragile e pur forte: A typical Volpean oxymoron; cf. her "strong, soft lip" in "Hai dato il mio nome. . . ."

quel solco: Cf. the use of this term in "Se t'hanno assomigliato. . . ."

ancora piombo: Recurrence of the poet's vision of himself as heavy flesh incapable of flight.

un'anitra / nera: Arrowsmith (3, 213): "Ducks, like coots, feed on the grasses in the lake bottoms. And it was commonly believed that a wounded duck or coot sought shelter by diving to the bottom and hiding in the weeds." The duck here is a *senhal* of Volpe (cf. the "black wing" of "Nubi color magenta . . ."); her flight—almost a suicide mission—which seems both to lead (inspire) and to threaten the poet, evokes that of the "gallo cedrone" which similarly "burns in the ditch."

Anniversario / Anniversary (for dating, see below)
Bettarini and Contini (*Op*, 971): "As it belongs to Volpe's group, the composition should not sensibly be distanced from 1949." Yet other "Volpe" poems, e.g., "Sul Llobregat" and "Incantesimo," are dated as late as 1954, and the title, with its implication of repetition of both the anniversary of Volpe's birthday and perhaps of the lovers' bond, implies a relationship of some standing; since Montale met Maria Luisa Spaziani in 1949, I suggest the earliest date for the poem would be 1950.

tua nascita: Here, as in several other poems for Volpe, her youth is emphasized (evoking "Crisalide," precursor in several respects of the Volpe poems). At the time Montale met Maria Luisa Spaziani, he was in his early fifties, more than twice her age.

sono in ginocchio . . . : Cambon (185) speaks of the "sacramental hyperbole of 'Anniversario,' which makes the Vixen a paramount cult object and a vehicle of deification." Yet the phrase "sono in ginocchio" is also part of the common language of love (it can be heard in the lyrics of popular songs), a surviving echo of the courtly love tradition. The poet's private religion, then, is "his religion of Eros" (Arrowsmith 3, 213), the terrestrial, unsublimated version of the religion of "l'Amore" in "Elegia di Pico Farnese"; yet this love has endowed him with a sense of well-being, of righteousness ("vinto il male," etc.) that is expressed in religious terms.

Arse . . . una vampa: Cf. "Stride la vampa," Azucena's aria in Act II of Verdi's "medieval" (Lonardi, 60) *Il Trovatore* (it is quoted from again in XENIA). But the image is found in many Montale texts, usually Clizian ones.

spiavo il tuo piumare: The second stanza describes the lovers' separate existences during the war, before they had actually met. Yet within the metaphoric terms of the composition the poet (again, as in "Crisalide") has "spied on," watched from the shadows, the development of his ephebe (cf. "Per un 'Omaggio a Rimbaud' ") since birth. Arrowsmith (3, 213): "*Spied because one does not, except by risking Actaeon's fate, look directly at divinity.*"

non per me ma per tutti: Cf. the hopes for universal freedom expressed in "La primavera hitleriana," which the poet feels have been betrayed (and which are linked with the fading from view of Clizia, who incarnated them). What he has found instead is private fulfillment, with its own transcendent import.

Dio diviso / dagli uomini . . . : The ambiguity of the phrase arouses various possibilities for interpretation. Is "Dio" in apposition with "me," in which case the poet—or, perhaps, the "Nestorian" of "Iride"—rendered "godlike through his feminine awaker's gift," here becomes identified with God himself, in "the hyperbole that surpasses all others in Montale's verse and universe" (Cambon, 186–87), even if he is only a "lowercase god"—Montale's words in reference to the phrase "il mio Dio" in "Verso Siena"? (Cambon asked Montale in 1977 if the phrase was vocative and was told it was not.) (Petrarch, too [Savoca, 68], was "diviso" from himself [CCXCCII, 3], from the world [CCCXXIII, 30], and from the "bel viso" of Laura [XXXVII, 29].) "Diviso" recalls "una distanza ci divide" in "Cigola la carrucola del pozzo," where the poet is held apart from the vision that rises from the depths of the will.

Throughout the Volpe poems, there are references to the lovers as divine, in the Hölderlinian tradition that the gods exist on earth in human form (see note to "Visita a Fadin"); but Cambon warns against taking such a statement too literally, adding that "to be 'God' at this juncture can only mean, for Montale, to have sustained spiritual fulfillment. . . ." "This is the still point" of convergence of the "intellectual plenitude" offered by "sublimating Clizia" with the "vital fulness" of Volpe's " 'animal' yet winged vitality." Yet the poet finds he is unable to share this epiphany generally: "It is bitter irony to have achieved godlike fulfillment . . . only to see its truth ignored or denied." According to this reading, the "clotted blood" may refer, as Arrowsmith suggests, to the poet-God's own ritual (Orphic) sacrifice, as in "Il gallo cedrone" (the image of blood on the trees is derived from " 'Ezekiel saw the Wheel . . .' "); for Macrì (1, 120) "the blood spattered or raised everywhere in *La bufera* is a simple . . . sign of the relationship between Christ and humanity," while Arrowsmith sees the poet, transported on high by his love, looking down on the battles of men (like Clizia/Artemis in "La frangia dei capelli . . .") and the trees bearing ripened fruit (cf. "su me, su te, sui limoni" in "Nella serra").

Cambon sees no possibility of ambiguity here; yet cannot "Dio diviso" also be read as an ablative absolute clause? In this case, the blood of human strife has corrupted the fruit of Eden (which the poet has enjoyed with Volpe), leaving God divided from mankind.

Regarding the paradox of collective as opposed to personal salvation, Arrowsmith rightly cites a passage from "Dominico" (1946) in *Farf* (91–92): "How far can the freedom of a single man, a freedom that isn't general but belongs to one man *against all*, interest us? I'm afraid . . . a man who lacks the religious sense of collective life also misses what's best in individual life, in man himself; a man is not a person if he doesn't take others into account, he's not fully a man if he doesn't accept others."

VII. CONCLUSIONI PROVVISORIE / PROVISIONAL CONCLUSIONS

For Almansi and Merry (122–23), the emphasis in the title "falls on the adjective"; the provisional nature of these closing, not concluding, "hypothetical gambits" is "not a sign of modesty or uncertainty, but rather a categorical imperative which calls for an overriding and permanent state of uncertainty." They are "poetic statements" which it is important not to endow "with an excessive political responsibility." Luperini (1, 170–71) sees the relaxation of metrical regularity and of formal closure as indicative of a loss of faith in poetry itself: "The decline of [Western] civilization, of its culture and its highest lyric tradition (of Orphic and romantic origin which becomes hermeticism) is lived, *tout court*, as the end of history and of poetry. Thus, as the crisis of that tradition becomes for him the crisis of the identity of poetry and of the very possibility of a survival, so the crisis of European civilization and its values becomes for him the loss of individual and social identity."

The binary nature of these nonconclusive conclusions implies that the fusion of Clizia and Volpe has not been total, though it is hard to say to which inspiring figure each of the poems is addressed, for each composition shows signs of the presence of both, as each recapitulates essential Montalean symbolic imagery (rainbow, ashes, flight). Both close, nevertheless, on a note of minimal hope, investing in the enduring "spark that says that everything begins" at the moment of greatest aridity. As in "Il gallo cedrone," a glow indicates the survival, in spite of everything, of a core of value in Montale's poetry itself; the dream is not over.

Piccolo testamento / Little Testament (1953)

Montale dated the poem "May 12, 1953." The title imitates the "testaments" of François Villon, the diminutive adjective characteristically undercutting the summary implication of the noun. The poem recapitulates major Montalean themes, in "a further tentative proposal to oppose the faint light of his own poetic discourse against those angelic or demoniacal irruptions which by now we know so well" (Almansi and Merry, 125). Like "L'anguilla" and "Se t'hanno assomigliato . . . ," the poem is thirty lines long.

calotta: The skullcap of the Catholic priesthood, here claiming for the poet a sacred or vatic role in contrast with the "red" (Communist: "factory") or "black" (Catholic/Christian Democrat: "church") clerisies whose mutual opposition dominated the Cold War politics of postwar Italy.

Solo quest'iride: A reprise of the imagery of "Iride," "L'anguilla," and other poems. The glimmer that goes all the way back in Montale's poetry, to "Il balcone" and even earlier, survives as the one faint but inextinguishable sign of enduring faith and hope.

la cipria: Like the "cenere" below, the ash of "L'anguilla," in which the spark of life is conserved (ash is a Clizian sign); what remains of the "spark from a beacon" of MEDITERRANEO.

nello specchietto . . . : Cf. the "amulet" which Dora Markus keeps with her makeup. As we have seen, the mirror is the essential locus of self-knowledge in Montale.

un ombroso Lucifero . . . : A Hitler (cf. "La primavera hitleriana") redivivus, this time in the great cities of the West (Britain, the United States, France); the implication is that postwar society, too, is potentially susceptible to demagoguery. The image is a pessimistic inversion of the "Messenger descending" of "L'orto," Lucifer's antagonist, Clizia, who was similarly exhausted by her salvific efforts (cf. "Ti libero la fronte dai ghiaccioli").

all'urto dei monsoni . . . : Cf. the storm in "L'arca," which attacks the poet's memories of childhood.

una storia: A story, a history; cf. the "histories" of "In limine," the "deeds" which will be unraveled in the "endgame of the future."

persistenza è solo l'estinzione: The pessimism of the statement is countered by the very act celebrated in the poem: the persistence of the faith and hope symbolized in the glimmer perceived "down there." To Almansi and Merry (125), the gravity of the phrase recalls the later Eliot, but Montale "avoids the intrusive grandeur of the *Four Quartets* and the solemnity implicit in any restoration of the metaphysical tradition, by transforming the ashes into face-powder and turning the rainbow of hope into a lucky charm."

l'orgoglio / non era fuga: The poet defends the "respectable keeping of distances" for which he was criticized in the postwar period, as he will in the famous 1971 polemic against Pasolini, "Lettera a Malvolio" (*D71/2*).

il tenue bagliore strofinato / laggiù: Like the "gemma" that is the poet's work in "Il gallo cedrone," the light is weak, almost buried, yet enduring.

Il sogno del prigioniero / The Prisoner's Dream (1954)
The figure of the prisoner derives from the stanzas of the prayer quoted in "Palio," and its imagery (bars, etc.) is revisited. The poet is portrayed again in terms of the chivalric metaphor of *Le occasioni*, where Clizia's faithful knight is cast into prison for his love; but the background now is the Cold War (cf. "polar air"), and the prisoner's dilemma in his times, in the sameness of a situation where dawns and nights are more or less identical, is, as Arrowsmith (3, 217) puts it, "the existential situation of a solitary man locked, like Dante's Ugolino, in the inward cell of the solipsistic ego, a spiritual darkness lit only by the 'glimmer' of the metaphorical lamp and the collective liberation of the troops of starlings outside his window." The poem uses slang borrowings from English and French to create a willfully dyspeptic, disillusioned, nonpoetic tone that will dominate Montale's future work. Yet the originary poetic impulse, the dream, remains the poem's controlling metaphor, as it is its driving force.

Il zigzag degli storni: The starlings are, as Arrowsmith (3, 217) points out, "Dante's crowd of carnal sinners, all driven by the blast of the hellish *bufera*" (*Inferno* V, 31); but they are also the poet's "only wings," though he identifies also with the flight of the helpless moth below, which, as Luperini (1, 174) points out, echoes (in a minor key) the flight of the "gallo cedrone." (See note for background to Montale's self-presentation here as both the moth and its torturer; similarly, below, he is unsure whether he is to be "stuffer or stuffing.")

battifredi: Pascolian.

focolare: The ultimate domestic site; see note to "L'arca."

La purga: Reference, among other things, to Stalin's purges, revealed and criticized after his death in 1953.

questo sterminio d'oche: Typical of the harsh, disdainful language, especially about politics, of the later Montale. The "oche" are second cousins of the "uomini-capre" of "Elegia di Pico Farnese."

obiurga: To Macrì (1, 126), an anglicism.

Tardo di mente: See note to "Per un 'Omaggio a Rimbaud' " concerning Montale's use of "tardo" to indicate an unwillingness to participate wholeheartedly in contemporary life. In "Slow," a 1953 story in *Farf* (138–41), the narrator, who says he "walks on foot" and possesses "neither a car nor a license," asks to join his city's branch of the Slow Club, which opposes "a decisively anachronistic . . . way of living . . . to the wear and tear of modern life."

il bruciaticcio / dei buccellati: "Buccellati" are Tuscan sweet biscuits; the reference to the ovens of the Holocaust is clear.

ho suscitato / iridi su orizzonti di ragnateli: West (91): "[The prisoner] is enclosed in an entirely inward, hermetic dream made up of self-generated illusions. The verb used to describe the creation of these final irises is *suscitare*, 'to conjure up' . . . ; it is a word that emphasizes the absolutely objective, internally generated status of the entire enterprise of dreaming and of elaborating poetic myths." Cf. the iridescence—it is notable that the "iríde" is an essential image in both "conclusions"—and the "spider's thread of memory" of "Piccolo testamento." (The "petali" evoke the peach petals of " 'Ezekiel saw the Wheel. . . .' ")

il mio sogno . . . : West (91): "In the final poem of the volume, at the moment of apparent summary and closure, Montale places one of the most open-ended of any of his lines: words that explicitly contradict the sense of an ending and instead point to the new elaboration in poems to come of the unfinished dream"—thus continuing the state of trance in which the poet's work first began.

Acknowledgments

Thanks are due, first of all, to Montale's principal publishers, Arnoldo Mondadori Editore, and in particular to Gian Arturo Ferrari and Claudia Scheu, for their cooperation and help over the years it has taken this project to come to fruition.

A fellowship from the John Simon Guggenheim Memorial Foundation in 1989 was the source of much-appreciated material support.

Many friends have generously read these translations and offered invaluable comments and suggestions, among them Frank Bidart, D. S. Carne-Ross, Annalisa Cima, Francesco Erspamer, Antonella Francini, Shirley Hazzard, Leila Javitch, Lawrence Joseph, Paul Muldoon, Frederick Seidel, Elisabeth Sifton, Rosanna Warren, Rebecca West, C. K. Williams, and Charles Wright. I am also grateful to the following for help of various kinds: Robertson and Paige Alford, Jonathan Burnham, Roberto Calasso, Esther Calvino, Andrea Canobbio, Giovanna Dalla Chiesa, Martin Gruber, Ned and Sue Hallowell, the late James Laughlin, Montale's first American publisher, and Gertrude Huston Laughlin, Christopher Maurer, Luciano Rebay, Vanni Scheiwiller. I want, too, to acknowledge the unfailingly cheerful forbearance and good will of Roger Straus and my other colleagues at Farrar, Straus & Giroux, especially my intrepid, eagle-eyed copy editor, Karla Reganold, who saved me from myself countless times, our peerless designer, Cynthia Krupat, and Anne Stringfield.

I have benefited greatly from the work of other translators of Montale, and have borrowed from them on more than one occasion. They include Patrice Angelini, Irma Brandeis, Alfredo de Palchi and Sonia Raiziss, Edith Farnsworth, Dana Gioia, George Kay, Robert Lowell, James Merrill, Edwin Morgan, Richard Pevear, Jeremy Reed, and Charles Wright. But my most significant such debt is to William Arrowsmith, my enduring interlocutor and, at times, antagonist during this long work. I was lucky enough to know Bill Arrowsmith during my early years studying Montale and regret that he did not live to bring to absolute fruition his own deep engagement with Montale's poetry, though the evidence of his attraction and devotion is available for all to read in the volumes of his translations published by W. W. Norton. Arrowsmith was a gifted scholar and teacher, and his lively commentary, which tends, in keeping with his own training, to emphasize classical and philosophic sources, has likewise represented a goad and a challenge. I have drawn from it freely in my own notes, while aiming to supply the reader with more of the context from which an Italian reader might approach the work. My way of hearing our poet's music, too, differs from Arrowsmith, who paid relatively little attention to form; occasionally, our readings of the text itself diverge as well. Nevertheless, I am cognizant of how much more difficult my own task would have been without his example, and I salute his vital contribution to the English reader's experience of Montale.

Last, and most important, I thank my daughters, Isabel and Beatrice, and, above all, my wife, Susan, for their abiding encouragement, inspiration, and love.

J.G.

Index of Titles and First Lines

[*Page numbers in roman refer to the text; those in italics, following poem titles, refer to the notes.*]

A Bedlington, blue lamb, pokes out, 301

A blooming belladonna smile, 97

A floating feather, too, can sketch your image, 293

A Liuba che parte, 176, *491*

A Metropolitan Christmas, 329, *564*

A mia madre, 296, *551*

A murmur; and your house gets blurred, 231

A sharp shot at the zig-, 185

A sound of trumpets comes, 107

A sweet inferno, gusting, funneled, 157

A vortice s'abbatte, 66, *462*

A white dove has landed me, 331

A will-o'-the-wisp dusts the street with powder, 235

Above the scribbled wall, 63, *461*

Accelerato, 188, *495*

Addii, fischi nel buio, cenni, tosse, 196, *498*

AFTERWARDS, 299, *552*

Aggotti, e già la barca si sbilancia, 120

Al primo chiaro, quando, 206, *505*

Alas, that memory at its height, 323

Albe e notti qui variano per pochi segni, 408

Alla maniera di Filippo De Pisis nell'inviargli questo libro, 184, *494*

Altri versi, 32, *451*

Altro effetto di luna, 166, *489*

Amid the blending, 163

An underwater brightness flows, 311

Anche una piuma che vola può disegnare, 292

Ancient one, I'm drunk with the voice, 67, *462*

And now the ripples of anxiety, 93

Anniversario, 402, *606*

Anniversary, 403, *606*

Another Moon Effect, 167, *489*

Antico, sono ubriacato dalla voce, 66, *462*

Argyll Tour, 332, 333, *565*

Arremba su la strinata proda, 60, *460*

Arsenio, 110, 111, *470*

Ascoltami, i poeti laureati, 8

At first light, when, 207, *505*

Autumn Quarries, 165, *489*

Avrei voluto sentirmi scabro ed essenziale, 74

Bagni di Lucca, 162, 163, 489

Ballad Written in a Hospital, 305, *554*

Ballata scritta in una clinica, 304, *554*

Barche sulla Marna, 244, *519*

Bassa marea, 224, *512*

Be happy if the wind inside the orchard, 5

Beyond Madonna dell'Orto . . . , 319

Bibe a Ponte all'Asse, 178, 179, *492*

Bibe, easy host, your brown-haired little Queen of Sheba, 179

Bibe, ospite lieve, la bruna tua reginetta di Saba, 178

Bliss of the cork abandoned to the current, 245

Boats on the Marne, 245, *519*

Brina sui vetri; uniti, 194, *497*

Bring me the sunflower, let me plant it, 47, *455*

Buffalo, 156, 157, *487*

But where to find the tomb, 29

Café at Rapallo, 21, *450*

Caffè a Rapallo, 20, *450*

Calm has returned, 95

Carnevale di Gerti, 170, *490*

Casa sul mare, 126, *475*

Cave d'autunno, 164, *489*

Christ the Judge, supposedly, 337

Christmas in the gleaming, 21

Chrysalis, 115, *472*

Cigola la carrucola del pozzo, 60, *459*

Ciò che di me sapeste, 48, *456*

Clamorous evenings, when the swing, 225

Clivo, 106, *469*

Cluster of faith and frost, the mistletoe, 329

Col bramire dei cervi nella piova, 338

Come la scaglia d'oro che si spicca, 288

CONCLUSIONI PROVVISORIE, 404, *607*

Corno inglese, 12, *447*

Correspondences, 243, *518*

Corrispondenze, 242, *518*

Costa San Giorgio, 234, 235, *515*

Crisalide, 114, *472*

Curvi sull'acqua serale, 326

CUTTLEFISH BONES, 37, *452*

Da un lago svizzero, 400, *604*

Da una torre, 302, *553*

Dal tempo della tua nascita, 402

Dal treno, 342, *568*

Dal verde immarcescibile della canfora, 340
Day and Night, 293, 549
Day is dawning, I can tell, 25
Debole sistro al vento, 58, 459
Delta, 134, 135, 476
Derelitte sul poggio, 214
Di un natale metropolitano, 328, 564
Dicevano gli antichi che la poesia, 344
'Dio salvi il Re' intonano le trombe, 238
Dissipa tu se lo vuoi, 78, 465
Dissolve if you will this frail, 79, 465
Distant, I was with you when your father, 195, 498
Don't ask us for the word to frame, 39, 453
Don't escape into the shade, 43, 454
DOPO, 298, 552
Dora Markus, 180, 181, 492
Dove il cigno crudele, 186
Dove se ne vanno le ricciute donzelle, 26
Dove t'abbatti dopo il breve sparo, 382
Dov'era il tennis . . . , 314, 558
Dov'era una volta il tennis . . . , 314
Dovrà posarsi lassù, 336
Due nel crepuscolo, 310, 556

È pur nostro il disfarsi delle sere, 276
E tu seguissi le fragili architetture, 260
Eastbourne, 238, 239, 517
Ecco bruma e libeccio sulle dune, 254
Ecco il segno; s'innerva, 198, 502
Eclogue, 99, 468
Ed ora sono spariti i circoli d'ansia, 92
Egloga, 98, 468
Elegia di Pico Farnese, 248, 520
Encounter, 137, 478
End of Childhood, 83, 466
English Horn, 13, 447
Epigram, 23, 450
Epigramma, 22, 450
Esterina, i vent'anni ti minacciano, 14
Esterina, twenty's out for you, 15
"Ezekiel saw the Wheel . . . ," 370, 371, 581

Falsetto, 14, 15, 448
Fanfan returns the victor; Molly's sold, 159
Fanfan ritorna vincitore; Molly, 158
Farewells, whistles in the dark, waves, coughs, 197, 498

Feeble sistrum in the wind, 59, 459
Felicità del sùghero abbandonato, 244
Felicità raggiunta, si cammina, 52, 457
Fiesole Window, 283, 546
Fine dell'infanzia, 82, 466
Finestra fiesolana, 282, 546
FINISTERRE, 266, 267, 539
FLASHES AND INSCRIPTIONS, 321, 561
'FLASHES' E DEDICHE, 320, 561
Florentine Madrigals, 301, 552
Fluisce fra te e me sul belvedere, 310
Flussi, 102, 469
Flux, 103, 469
Folta la nuvola bianca delle falene impazzite, 372
For an Album, 399, 603
For an "Homage to Rimbaud," 349, 570
Forlorn on the hill, 215
Forse un mattino andando in un'aria di vetro, 54, 458
Fra il tonfo dei marroni, 162
From a Swiss Lake, 401, 604
From a Tower, 303, 553
From the moment you were born, 403
From the Train, 343, 568
Frost on the windowpanes; the sick, 195, 497
Fu così, com'è il brivido, 188
Fu dove il ponte di legno, 180
Fuscello teso dal muro . . ., 34, 452

Gerti's Carnival, 171, 490
Ghermito m'hai dall'intrico, 370
Giorno e notte, 292, 549
Giunge a volte, repente, 72, 463
Gli orecchini, 278, 542
Gloria del disteso mezzogiorno, 52, 457
Glory of expanded noon, 53, 457
Godi se il vento ch'entra nel pomario, 4
Graduates in Economics, 327

Hai dato il mio nome a un albero? Non è poco, 390, 599
Happiness achieved, for you, 53, 457
Haul your paper ships on the seared, 61, 460
Heat-lightning at the outset, 395
Here few signs distinguish dawns from nights, 409
Here where the insidious cricket, 283
Here's mist and wild wind on the sandy, 255
Herma, seal with wax and string, 301

Ho cominciato anzi giorno, 398

Ho sostato talvolta nelle grotte, 70, 463

Ho visto il merlo acquaiolo, 302

Hoopoe, happy bird maligned, 63, 460

House by the Sea, 127, 475

I bimbi sotto il cedro, funghi o muffe, 332

I fanciulli con gli archetti, 102

I free your forehead of the ice, 203, 504

I know a ray of sun (of God?) can still, 389, 599

I know the moment when a raw grimace, 51, 456

I limoni, 8, 447

I miei morti che prego perché preghino, 366

I morti, 130, 476

I remember the moth that flew in, 153

I think back on your smile, and for me it's a clear pool, 45, 454

I turbini sollevano la polvere, 110

I would have liked to feel harsh and essential, 75

If at least I could force, 77, 464

If you were following, 261

If they've compared you . . . , 393, 600

If you appear in the fire, 295

If your wheel gets snared in tangled, 171

Il balcone, 148, 485

Il canneto rispunta i suoi cimelli, 54, 457

Il canto delle strigi, quando un'iride, 274

Il convento barocco, 168

Il fiore che ripete, 206, 505

Il fuoco che scoppietta, 28

Il fuoco d'artifizio del maltempo, 260

Il gallo cedrone, 382, 589

Il giglio rosso, 284, 546

Il giglio rosso, se un dí, 284

Il grande ponte non portava a te, 334

Il mare che si frange sull'opposta, 130

Il ramarro, se scocca, 200, 502

Il ritorno, 254, 527

Il rumore degli émbrici distrutti, 216

Il saliscendi bianco e nero dei, 198, 501

Il soffio cresce, il buio è rotto a squarci, 270

Il sogno del prigioniero, 408, 609

Il tuo volo, 294, 551

Il ventaglio, 286, 546

Il vento che stasera suona attento, 12

Il viaggio finisce qui, 126

I'm searching vainly for the point the blood, 227

In limine, 4, *445*

In Sleep, 275, *541*

In the Greenhouse, 359, *576*

In the magnolia's, 361

In the Park, 361, *577*

In the Park at Caserta, 187, *495*

In the Rain, 231, *514*

In the sky above the quarry, scored at dawn, 233

In the Style of Filippo De Pisis, on Sending Him This Book, 185, *494*

In the trough of the emergency, 305

Incantation, 351, *571*

Incantesimo, 350, *571*

Incontro, 136, *478*

Indian Serenade, 277, *542*

Infuria sale o grandine? Fa strage, 204, *505*

INTERMEZZO, 153, 154, *556*

Io non so, messaggera, 362

Iride, 354, *573*

Iris, 355, *573*

Is it for a swarm of dawns, for a few, 273

Is it salt that strafes or hail? It slays, 205, *505*

It seemed simple to make nothing from, 149

It was good getting lost, 99

It was like this, like the biting, 189

It was where the wooden bridge, 181

. . . its yellow floodtide cresting at the bend, 175

I've paused at times in the caves, 71, *463*

I've seen the waterdipper, 303

Keepsake, 158, 159, *488*

La bufera, 268, *539*

La bufera che sgronda sulle foglie, 268

La canna che dispiuma, 210, *507*

La casa dei doganieri, 222, *511*

La farandola dei fanciulli sul greto, 58, *459*

La folata che alzò l'amaro aroma, 32

La frangia dei capelli . . . , 280

La frangia dei capelli che ti vela, 280

Là fuoresce il Tritone, 50, *456*

La gondola che scivola in un forte, 204, *504*

La primavera hitleriana, 372, *582*

La rana, prima a ritentar la corda, 208, *506*

La rondine vi porta, 160

La speranza di pure rivederti, 196, *499*

La tempesta di primavera ha sconvolto, 290

La trama del carrubo che si profila, 166
La trota nera, 326, *563*
La tua fuga non s'è dunque perduta, 256
La vita che si rompe nei travasi, 134
L'agave su lo scoglio, 90, *466*
L'albero verdecupo, 114
Lampi d'afa sul punto del distacco, 394
L'anguilla, 384, *594*
L'anguilla, la sirena, 384
L'anima che dispensa, 202, *503*
L'arca, 290, *549*
Lasciando un 'Dove', 330, *564*
Late from your cocoon, miraculous, 349
Le pellegrine in sosta che hanno durato, 248
Le processioni del 1949, 394, *602*
Le tortore colore solferino, 342
Leaving a Dove, 331, *564*
L'estate, 236, *516*
Like a Fantasia, 25, *450*
Like the scale of gold that lifts off from, 289
Lindau, 160, 161, *488*
Listen to me, the poets laureate, 9
Little Testament, 407, *608*
Lo sai: debbo riperderti e non posso, 192, *497*
Local Train, 189, *495*
L'ombra crociata del gheppio pare ignota, 236
L'ombra della magnolia . . . , 380, *588*
L'ombra della magnolia giapponese, 380
Long before daybreak I started, 399
Lontano, ero con te quando tuo padre, 194, *498*
L'orto, 362, *577*
Low Tide, 225, *512*
Luce d'inverno, 346, *569*
Lungomare, 270, *541*

. . . ma così sia. Un suono di cornetta, 210, *508*
Ma dove cercare la tomba, 28
Madrigali fiorentini, 300, *552*
MADRIGALI PRIVATI, 386, *598*
Maestrale, 94, *467*
Magenta-colored clouds . . . , 397, *602*
Magenta-colored clouds were gathering, 397
Many years, and one still harder, 193, *497*
Marezzo, 120, *474*
Maybe one morning, walking in dry, glassy air, 55, *458*
MEDITERRANEAN, 65, *461*

MEDITERRANEO, 64, *461*

MERIGGI E OMBRE, 80, *465*

Meriggiare pallido e assorto, 40, *453*

Messenger descending, 363

Mia vita, a te non chiedo lineamenti, 44, *455*

Mia volpe, un giorno fui anch'io il 'poeta . . . ,' 400

Minstrels, 18, 19, *449*

Mistral, 95, *467*

Moiré, 121, *474*

Molti anni, e uno più duro sopra il lago, 192, *497*

MOTETS, 191, *496*

MOTTETTI, 190, *496*

MOVEMENTS, 7, *446*

MOVIMENTI, 6, *446*

My dead, to whom I pray so they may pray, 367

My life, I ask of you no stable, 45, *455*

My sadness, don't desert me, 137

*My vixen, I myself was once the "*poète . . . ,*"* 401

Natale nel tepidario, 20

Near Capua, 175, *491*

Near Finistère, 339, *567*

Near Siena, 323, *562*

Near Vienna, 169, *490*

Nel cielo della cava rigato, 232

Nel parco, 360, *577*

Nel Parco di Caserta, 186, *495*

Nel solco dell'emergenza, 304

Nel sonno, 274, *541*

Nella serra, 358, *576*

Nell'ombra della magnolia, 360

New Stanzas, 253, *525*

News from Mount Amiata, 261, *532*

Noi non sappiamo quale sortiremo, 72, *463*

Non chiederci la parola che squadri da ogni lato, 38, *453*

Non il grillo ma il gatto, 176

Non recidere, forbice, quel volto, 208, *506*

Non rifugiarti nell'ombra, 42, *454*

Non serba ombra di voli il nerofumo, 278

NOONS AND SHADOWS, 81, *465*

Not the cricket but the cat, 177

Notizie dall'Amiata, 260, *532*

Now and then, suddenly, 73, *463*

Now I feast not just my eyes, 325

Now in your Carinthia, 183

Now step, 27

Now that in the distance a mirage, 243
Now that the choir of rock partridges, 297
Now that with a flourish you've stubbed out, 253
Nubi color magenta . . . , 396, 602
Nubi color magenta s'addensavano, 396
Nuove stanze, 252, 525

O rabid sirocco, 91
O rabido ventare di scirocco, 90
Often I've encountered evil, 47, 456
Oh come là nella corusca, 214
Oh how there in the glittering, 215
Oh resta chiusa e libera nell'isole, 350
Oh stay locked and free, 351
Ohimè che la memoria sulla vetta, 322
Old Lines, 153, 486
On an Unwritten Letter, 273, 541
On the Greve, 325, 563
On the Highest Column, 337, 566
On the Llobregat, 341, 568
On the Threshold, 4, 445
Or che in fondo un miraggio, 242
Ora che il coro delle coturnici, 296
Ora non ceno solo con lo sguardo, 324
Ora sia il tuo passo, 26
Ormai nella tua Carinzia, 182
OSSI DI SEPPIA, 36, 452
Other Lines, 33, 451
Out of the incorruptible green of the camphor tree, 341

Palio, 256, 257, 529
Pareva facile giuoco, 148
Passata la Madonna dell'Orto . . . , 318
Passò sul tremulo vetro, 96
Per album, 398, 603
Per un formicolìo d'albe, per pochi, 272
Per un 'Omaggio a Rimbaud,' 348, 570
Perché tardi? Nel pino lo scoiattolo, 200, 503
Perdersi nel bigio ondoso, 98
Personae separatae, 288, 548
Personae Separatae, 289, 548
Piccolo testamento, 406, 608
Pico Farnese Elegy, 249, 520
Poems for Camillo Sbarbaro, 21, 449
Poesie per Camillo Sbarbaro, 20, 449
Poi che gli ultimi fili di tabacco, 252

Poiché la via percorsa, se mi volgo, è più lunga, 376
Pool, 97, 467
Portami il girasole ch'io lo trapianti, 46, 455
Potessi almeno costringere, 76, 464
PRIVATE MADRIGALS, 387, 598
Proda di Versilia, 366, 580
Promenade, 271, 541
PROVISIONAL CONCLUSIONS, 405, 607
Punta del Mesco, 232, 233, 515

Quando di colpo San Martino smotta, 354
Quando scesi dal cielo di Palmira, 346
Quasi una fantasia, 24
Questa rissa cristiana che non ha, 262
Questo che a notte balugina, 406
Qui dove il grillo insidioso buca, 282

Racketing catcalls spiral down, 67, 462
Raggiorna, lo presento, 24
Refrain, echoing, 19
Ricerco invano il punto onde si mosse, 226
Ricordo la farfalla ch'era entrata, 152
Ripenso il tuo sorriso, ed è per me un'acqua limpida, 44, 454
Ritornello, rimbalzi, 18
RIVIERE, 140, 482
Riviere, 142
Rombando s'ingolfava, 82
. . . rotto il colmo sull'ansa, con un salto, 174

Sarcofaghi, 26, 450
Sarcophagi, 27, 450
Sbarbaro, estroso fanciullo, piega versicolori, 22
Sbarbaro, whimsical boy, folds multicolored, 23
Scendendo qualche volta, 68, 462
Scirocco, 90, 466
Se appari al fuoco (pendono . . .), 294
Se la ruota s'impiglia nel groviglio, 170
S'è rifatta la calma, 94
Se t'hanno assomigliato . . . , 392, 600
SEACOASTS, 141, 482
Seacoasts, 143
See the sign; it flares, 199, 502
S'empì d'uno zampettìo, 358
Sere di gridi, quando l'altalena, 224
Serenata indiana, 276, 542
Shears, don't cut away that face, 209, 506

Shore of Versilia, 367, 580

SILVAE, 352, 353, 572

Since the road traveled, if I look back, is longer, 377

Siria, 344, 568

Sirocco, 91, 466

Sit the noon out, pale and lost in thought, 41, 453

Slope, 107, 469

Snatched me from the ivy's tangle, 371

. . . so be it. Blare of a cornet, 211, 508

So che un raggio di sole (di Dio?) ancora, 388, 599

So l'ora in cui la faccia più impassibile, 50, 456

Sometimes, coming down, 69, 462

Sotto la pioggia, 230, 514

Spesso il male di vivere ho incontrato, 46, 456

Stanzas, 227, 513

Stanze, 226, 513

su cui discende la primavera lunare, 164

Su una lettera non scritta, 272, 541

Suggella, Herma, con nastri e ceralacca, 300

Sul Llobregat, 340, 568

Sul muro grafito, 62, 461

Sulla colonna più alta, 336, 566

Sulla Greve, 324, 563

Summer, 237, 516

Syria, 345, 568

Tardi uscita dal bozzolo, mirabile, 348

Tempi di Bellosguardo, 214, 508

Tentava la vostra mano la tastiera, 56, 459

The Agave on the Reef, 91, 466

The ancients said that poetry, 345

The arc of your eyebrow ended, 339

The Ark, 291, 549

The Balcony, 149, 485

The bangs . . . , 281

The bangs that hide your childlike forehead—, 281

The baroque convent, 169

The Black Trout, 327, 563

The blood-red turtledoves, 343

The boys with snares, 103

The canebrake sends its little shoots, 55, 457

The Capercaillie, 383, 589

The carob's mare's-nest that stands stark, 167

The clatter of the rooftiles, shattered by, 217

The crossed shadow of the kestrel seems unknown, 237

The Dead, 131, 476

The deep-green tree, 115
The Earrings, 279, 542
The Eel, 385, 594
The eel, siren, 385
The Fan, 287, 546
The fire that spits, 29
The flower that repeats, 207, 505
The frog, first to strike his chord, 209, 506
The Garden, 363, 577
The gondola that glides, 205, 504
The great bridge didn't lead to you, 335
The green lizard, if it darts, 201, 502
The gust that lifted the bitter scent, 33
The Hitler Spring, 373, 582
The hope of even seeing you again, 197, 499
The House of the Customs Men, 223, 511
The intent wind that plays tonight, 13
The journey ends here, 127
The lampblack of the mirror shows, 279
The lemon-house was being over-, 359
The Lemons, 9, 442
The life that breaks apart, 135
The line of dancing children on the shore, 59, 459
The Magnolia's Shadow, 381, 588
The Parades of 1949, 395, 602
The pilgrims stopping over who have kept, 249
The Prisoner's Dream, 409, 609
The raveling of the evenings is ours, too, 277
The Red Lily, 285, 546
The red lily, if one day, 285
The reed that softly, 211, 507
The Return, 255, 527
The sea that founders on the other shore, 131
The shadow of the Japanese magnolia, 381
The song of the screech owls, when a rainbow, 275
The spirit that dispenses, 203, 503
The spring storm has upended, 291
The Storm, 269, 539
The storm that drums the hard, 269
The stormy weather's fireworks, 261
The swallow brings back blades of grass, 161
The thick white cloud of mad moths whirls, 373
The trumpets blare "God Save the King," 239
The well's pulley creaks, 61, 459
The white-and-black sine, 199, 501
The wind picks up, the dark is torn to shreds, 271

There the Tritone surges, 51, 456
This Christian wrangle that knows only, 263
This, which flickers at night, 407
Thundering, a throbbing sea, 83
Ti libero la fronte dai ghiaccioli, 202, 504
Times at Bellosguardo, 215, 508
To Liuba, Leaving, 177, 491
To My Mother, 297, 551
Toddlers under the cedar, mushrooms, 333
Tramontana, 92, 93, 467
Tu non m'abbandonare mia tristezza, 136
Tu non ricordi la casa dei doganieri, 222
Twig that juts from the wall . . . , 35, 452
Two in Twilight, 311, 556

Un Bedlington s'affaccia, pecorella, 300
Un dolce inferno a raffiche addensava, 156
Un fuoco fatuo impolvera la strada, 234
Un murmure; e la tua casa s'appanna, 230
Un vischio, fin dall'infanzia sospeso grappolo, 328
Una botta di stocco nel zig zag, 184
Una colomba bianca m'ha disceso, 330
Upupa, ilare uccello calunniato, 62, 460
Ut pictura . . . *Le labbra che confondono*, 286
Ut pictura . . . *The confounding lips*, 287

Valmorbia, discorrevano il tuo fondo, 56, 458
Valmorbia, flowering clouds of plants, 57, 458
Vasca, 96, 467
Vecchi versi, 152, 486
Vento e bandiere, 32, 451
Vento sulla Mezzaluna, 334, 565
Verso Capua, 174, 491
Verso Finistère, 338, 567
Verso Siena, 322, 562
Verso Vienna, 168, 490
Viene un suono di buccine, 106
Visit to Fadin, 319, 560
Visita a Fadin, 318, 560
Voce giunta con le folaghe, 376, 585
Voice That Came with the Coots, 377, 585

We don't know how we'll turn up, 73, 463
What you knew of me, 49, 456
When I came down from the sky above Palmyra, 347
When suddenly Saint Martin shunts his embers, 355

Where are they going, the girls with little curls, 27
Where the cruel swan, 187
where the moonlit spring descends, 165
Where the tennis court once was . . . , 315
Where the Tennis Court Was . . . , 315, 558
Where you fall after the sharp shot, 383
Whirligigs of wind stir up the dust, 111
Why wait? The squirrel beats his torch-tail, 201, 503
Wind and Flags, 33, *451*
Wind on the Crescent, 335, 565
Winter Light, 347, 569

You bail, already the boat lists, 121
You know: I'm going to lose you again, 193, 497
You won't recall the house of the customs men, 223
Your Flight, 295, *551*
Your flight, then, didn't fade out, 257
Your hand was trying the keyboard, 57, 459
You've named a tree for me? It isn't nothing, 391, 599